DHEW Publication No. (OE) 73–17002

STATEWIDE PLANNING IN HIGHER EDUCATION

by

D. KENT HALSTEAD

U.S. DEPARTMENT OF HEALTH, EDUCATION, AND WELFARE
Caspar W. Weinberger, *Secretary*
Charles B. Saunders, Jr., *Acting Assistant Secretary for Education*
OFFICE OF EDUCATION
John Ottina, *Commissioner*

Library of Congress Cataloging in Publication Data

HALSTEAD, D. KENT, date
    Statewide planning in higher education.

    Includes bibliographies.
    Supt. of Docs. no.: HE 5.6/2: ST 2.
    1. State universities and colleges—
Planning—United States. I. Title.
LB2329.5.H28   378.1′07′0973   73-20200

U.S. GOVERNMENT PRINTING OFFICE
WASHINGTON: 1974

FOREWORD

The nationwide trend to expand higher education enrollments, facilities, and resources—a phenomenon of the 1950's and 1960's—is veering in a different direction. Colleges and universities, instead of coping with problems linked to growth, will be faced in the coming years with such complexities as reducing expenditures and revising curriculums. They will also need to implement technological delivery systems now in nascent stages of development and use. Moreover, it will be essential that they concern themselves with extending postsecondary educational opportunities to adults of all ages. These so-called "new directions" in higher education will require as much, if not more, careful planning and coordination than were needed during the period of accelerated expansion.

This comprehensive handbook, which emphasizes major planning problems and their solutions, should enable administrators and others to enhance the professional skills they will need for the successful management and operation of statewide systems of higher learning.

Normally scholars research at their own pace, taking time to exhaust all sources of data and to ensure the validity of their findings. While Kent Halstead's book clearly reflects these characteristics of scholarship, unlike many other scholarly treatises it avoids the jargon of the discipline. The language chosen by the author will be easily understood by the working professional and the informed layman.

Statewide Planning in Higher Education contains so much useful information that it is destined to become the standard reference for all persons engaged in any phases of planning that affect the future of colleges and universities. Those of us who have conducted original research in this field will find an accurate delineation of our major contributions. Both practitioners and students of planning will discover that they have been provided with a carefully synthesized presentation of procedures and methodologies supported by exacting research.

No existing work contains this scope and depth in such a wide range of higher education planning topics. The fact that the content reflects the most recent and comprehensive thinking on the subject means that it has great potential for changing the outlook of practitioners: broadening their perspective, sharpening their technical expertise, making their planning effort more productive. The annotated bibliography further adds to the volume's definitiveness.

iii

Dr. Halstead comes close to exhausting the extant knowledge of higher education planning technology. If there are omissions or sketchiness of detail in certain areas, the reflection rests with the state of the technology itself rather than with the author. He has produced an exceptional work for which scholars, professionals, State officials, students, and interested citizens will be grateful for years to come.

Lyman A. Glenny, Director,
Center for Research and Development
   in Higher Education
University of California, Berkeley

PREFACE

Twenty-five years ago the first serious effort was made by a State to plan comprehensively a statewide system of postsecondary education. During the intervening years a considerable amount of useful planning experience and expertise has been acquired—initially by trial and error, more recently by organized and methodical research. Although many valuable works have been published on the subject, there is no single comprehensive study dealing with the theories, analyses, and procedures involved. This book has been written in an attempt to fill the gap.

There are three major reasons why a manual on statewide planning should be available: (1) An important undertaking in higher education, planning is of consequence to millions of students, teachers, and citizens. (2) As a continuing process, the subject is of concern to every State. (3) Since planning of this nature is a relatively new undertaking in many States, the considerable experience gained by previous practitioners can be of great benefit.

This volume is addressed primarily to State planning officers and technicians, college officials, teachers, and others responsible for higher education planning. To that end, the point of view and the special problems of State planning officers have been kept in mind. It is also hoped that the material may serve to some degree as a reference, particularly to those whose previous experience has not been extensive.

Although planners need to know something about a wide number and variety of topics, they often have little time to read indepth source material. Furthermore, the pace of State planning activities has been swift; the methodologies have often been obscured in final recommendations; and the relevance and contribution of each study have been difficult to assess. To be useful, information concerning the planning experience must be sifted and compressed, and an attempt has been made to collect and summarize in reasonably direct fashion the wealth of fact, experience, and opinion that currently exists on the subject. A high proportion of content in some areas is opinion, and includes that of the author. But the overall intent has always been to emphasize proven practices and verified knowledge.

No attempt has been made to provide answers to *all* the problems that may arise in State educational planning. There has been, on the other hand, a genuine effort to identify the major areas of concern and their component parts, to indicate the factors that should be taken into account,

v

and to suggest workable procedures that may be useful in arriving at solutions. While the content cannot be exhaustive at this stage, nor permanent at any stage (because of continual updating in planning), it does provide a basis for thinking about what can and cannot be accomplished in this specialized aspect of higher education.

In the preparation of this book, the approach has been eclectic; materials have been drawn from a wide variety of sources. In certain instances, where deficiencies were noted, the author's research supplements existing information. The data, while as up-to-date as possible, have been selected primarily to provide adjunct explanations, not statistical references. The bibliography, fully annotated, has been carefully selected to represent the major works of direct value to statewide planners.

A handbook such as this should be dedicated to the many individuals whose research and practice has formed the basis for much of the content. Their names are identified in footnotes throughout the text as well as in the chapter bibliographies. If their data and conclusions have been misinterpreted, the author assumes the responsibility. While many persons who have contributed in some way to this effort cannot be named here, there are a few whose contribution I should like particularly to acknowledge. These include Peter P. Muirhead, S. W. Herrell, and William C. Gescheider of the U.S. Office of Education, who created an environment within which it was possible to undertake the writing of this volume; Robert E. Jennings, Hartley Johnson, Eileen McGinnity, and Richard Levine, who served as research assistants; and Hope Chamberlin, the editor, who lent her considerable skill to bring more clarity and logic to the presentation.

I am especially indebted to a number of experts, each of whom read a chapter of the manuscript pertaining to his specialization within the statewide planning field: Harlan D. Bareither, James F. Blakesley, Roger E. Bolton, Joseph D. Boyd, Howard R. Bowen, Arthur D. Browne, Lanier Cox, André Danière, Abraham Frankel, Lyman A. Glenny, Tom Goins, Alan C. Green, Roger Hallenbeck, W. Lee Hansen, David S. Haviland, Bruce H. Jensen, T. R. McConnell, Stanley McElderry, Eugene P. McLoone, James L. Miller, Jr., Ben L. Morton, M. D. Orwig, Richard Ray, Ritchie Reed, Edward Sanders, J. Claude Scheuerman, Calvin F. Schmid, Charles Sherwood, Donovan Smith, Bill Somerville, Willard B. Spalding, William Wasserman, James Wattenbarger, Stanley J. Wenberg, and Jean Wirth. To all these colleagues I would like to express my appreciation, at the same time relieving them of any responsibility for conclusions and judgments that are my own.

D. Kent Halstead

CONTENTS

TABLES

Page

FIGURES

Chapter I

DESIGN FOR
STATEWIDE PLANNING

For over a decade U. S. colleges and universities have experienced unprecedented growth. This accelerated expansion stems from an increase in population and from the needs of citizens whose aspirations and goals have been rapidly advancing. The resultant problems for higher education are well known—financial stress, reduction in the quality of services, wasted resources, and student dissatisfaction. Less well known are the new approaches undertaken by higher education to meet these problems.

Two facts are clear: (1) Inevitable changes in society frequently create disproportionately complex problems on the campus, and (2) the only effective way to cope with these problems is to anticipate the changes that engender them and take appropriate action. It is now apparent that higher education has embraced planning as an activity inherent in its mission and essential to its well-being. That it must continue planning to meet problems of a magnitude nearly equal to that of the past is easily shown.

The 1960's decade is likely to have recorded higher education's greatest growth. Enrollment increased from 3.8 to 8.6 million students, annual expenditures rose from $7.7 to $27.1 billion, and the instructional staff grew from 292,000 to 592,000. *In this 10-year span higher education expenditures tripled and enrollments more than doubled while the college-age population expanded by only 50 percent.*

What can be said about the challenges for higher education in the decade ahead? The rate of expansion will be far less than that experienced during the sixties, yet, if current projections are accurate, colleges and universities will grow substantially in absolute terms. Increases of at least 2 million students and 70,000 teachers are anticipated; the 1980 budget could approach $50 billion, $23 billion over the 1970 level. (The difference between the 1960 and the 1970 annual budgets was $19 billion.)

If higher education is to respond effectively to this growth and critically attune itself to the diversity and adaptability society now requires, there can be no laxity in planning efforts. Education is not a commodity that can be designed and financed on short notice. It is a long-term investment requiring extended preparation and responsive leadership. The capacity of higher education to grow and to achieve vital goals during the years ahead will be greatly affected by the kind and quality of decisions planners make today. Thus planning cannot be considered as other than an immediate task of strategic importance.

1

PLANNING

To achieve educational objectives in a creative, orderly, and economically sound manner is a task demanding insight into not only the problems of the present but also those of the future, together with creative and intellectual pursuit of solutions and persuasive, persistent effort to implement programs. Planning is an all-encompassing activity that depends on participation at every level—institutional, State, regional, and national—and involves public and private and large and small institutions. If done well, the result could be a nation educated to a breadth, depth, and quality not previously envisioned. Therefore, planning is worthy of the higher education community's determination to summon and use all of its capabilities.

Planning Defined

One of man's most natural mental activities is deciding what to do and how to do it, an activity called *planning*. Although the term is seemingly a simple one, familiar to every educator, its meaning is not always accurately or fully understood.

Planning is not a process of speculating on probable events; rather, it is an attempt through foresight to generate action necessary to realize desired results. Fundamentally, planning is a process of deciding upon a course of action in order to make something happen which, without planning, might not happen. In more technical terms, planning determines the objectives of administrative effort and devises the means to achieve them.[1]

The principal value of planning is in the strategy it provides for reacting to probable and possible future events and changes. Perceptive planning will often identify potential problems before financial and emotional commitments make resolution of them difficult or impossible. By planning, events likely to take place are foreseen and a leisurely, scholarly anaylsis of "best" alternative actions is afforded. This minimizes the possibility of being unprepared to cope with a situation. Opportunity to identify and choose the best of available alternatives, consistent with established goals, adds the benefit of securing maximum returns with minimum costs. Finally, planning makes possible the control and direction of day-to-day operations.

Coordination and Planning

As commonly used, *coordination and planning* refers to the comprehensive functional breadth associated with the two terms as well as to the mutual

---

[1] Raymond E. Kitchell, "A Summary of Current Planning Concepts" (unpublished paper), Executive Office of the President, Bureau of the Budget, 1963.

support and strength conveyed by their use in combination. The terms, however, have distinctive meanings. *Planning* is the prearrangement of policy and methods to guide work toward given objectives. *Coordination*, on the other hand, is the securing of smooth, concerted action through effective interrelationships and recognition of common goals. Planning is *directional*: it establishes goals and guides action. Coordination is *operational*: it interrelates and unifies action to achieve predetermined goals.

Since planning is usually directed toward guiding more than one activity, and frequently more than one enterprise, coordination is an inherent and essential goal and a functional component of the planning process. Conversely, coordination of all but the simplest routine activities requires some planning—namely, deciding how to achieve the objectives of harmonious adjustment and interaction between parts. Thus, while coordination and planning are distinctive activities, from an operational standpoint they are inseparable. Coordination is generally included within the more encompassing concept of planning.

At a given level, coordination relates the parts of a system to the whole, interrelates parts within the system, and relates the parts and the system to external factors. Planning, at the same level, guides and directs the system as a whole, taking into account not only each of its parts but external factors as well. Throughout this text, the term *planning* will be used in its broadest meaning; in other words, it will include inherent coordinating activities.

Impetus Toward Planning

Current emphasis on the comprehensive planning role of the States should not obscure the fact that this function is a relatively recent[2] addition to long and extensive State involvement in higher education. Georgia, in 1785, was the first to charter a State university.[3] During the ensuing 40 years, State governments proceeded somewhat slowly in organizing State universities, even though the Northwest Ordinance, enacted in 1707, stipulated that new States admitted to the Union would be expected to support State universities through public land grants.

Early Federal encouragement, plus the added necessity in the 1830's of meeting a greatly expanded demand for teachers in response to a nationwide movement for free elementary education, provided real impetus to public higher education growth during the first half of the 19th century. Further encouragement came in 1862 with passage of the unprecedented Morrill Land-Grant College Act. Within 8 years, 37 States accepted the

---

[2] Beginning in 1912, with the first State surveys.

[3] The University of Georgia did not open until 1800, 15 years after being chartered. A second institution, the University of North Carolina, was chartered in 1789 and opened 6 years later, in 1795.

provisions, and ultimately 28 entirely new colleges of agriculture and mechanical arts were founded, all of which were to become in time full-fledged State universities.

The largest expansion has taken place in the 20th century. By the end of World War II, public higher education enrolled half the college students in the United States. Today, three out of four students attend public institutions. The spectacular growth in student population, in the 12 years since 1960, has resulted in a tripling of public enrollments.

Almost without exception the accommodation of this rapidly growing student body and the concern of State governments for the attending financial, organizational, and staffing problems have provided the principal impetus for State planning. Both State legislators and government agencies have recognized that efficient operation in a period of rapid expansion requires realistic and scientific budget requests, a sound rationale for establishing new institutions, and a division of responsibilities to eliminate wasteful duplication by competing institutions. The tie-in between coordination and planning has become quite apparent.

Second to the critical task of coping with problems arising from the growing magnitude of higher education was the recognition by State government officials of the need to formulate and implement a statewide approach to higher education. The movement for statewide planning and coordination is an effort by the State government to address itself to the whole of higher education—a scope decidely more complex and encompassing than the sum total of each individual institution's plan for the future. The following questions raised by Lyman Glenny point to the need for overall planning:

> How can the state provide a sufficient number of education places for new students? How can the state determine which colleges should become full-fledged universities and which should develop different roles and functions? What types and extent of research and public service activities are appropriate for each campus? Where should new colleges or new types of institutions be developed? What level of financing is really required for each campus to maintain a quality program?[4]

Faced with the necessity of answering such complex questions, legislatures and governors have turned to statewide planning as a basis for shaping sound public policy.

The Federal Government has also encouraged State planning. The Higher Education Facilities Act of 1963 fostered the establishment of 54 State facilities commissions. For many States, these commissions provided the first incentive for cooperation between public and nonpublic institu-

---

[4] Lyman A. Glenny, "Long-Range Planning for State Educational Needs," paper presented at a meeting of the Education Commissions of the States, Denver, Colo., May 7–9, 1967.

tions, albeit for the limited purpose of facility planning. An amendment to the 1963 act provided funds to the commissions for planning for construction needs. More recently, the 92d Congress passed new higher education legislation which provides Federal support, based on the development of appropriate statewide plans, for the expansion and improvement of post-secondary education programs in community colleges.

A third major impetus toward statewide planning stems from the almost universal demand by students, parents, and teachers for higher quality in education. State officials have had to face the fact that the drive for better higher education was prompted by some very real deficiencies in administration, faculty, curriculum, and facilities. Citizens have claimed, not without foundation, that "quality gaps" existed among the States, especially in such areas as accessibility, student aid, and instructional expertise. As States began to appreciate their individual shortcomings, they became committed to continual improvement of higher education and accepted statewide planning and coordination as vital instruments in achieving established goals.

Two other factors have stimulated the trend toward statewide planning. The first is the recent introduction and development of improved planning techniques. One example is the rapid, accurate handling of large volumes of complex data by computers and automatic data-processing equipment. Of greater importance, however, are the improved procedures being developed and published in special staff studies conducted in conjunction with master-plan development. The more sophisticated methodologies and analyses of these indepth studies, plus concurrent related research findings, have substantially improved the level of available resources and counsel.

DEVELOPMENT OF STATEWIDE PLANNING AND COORDINATING AGENCIES

The movement to establish institutionally governed, State-coordinated systems of higher education began less than 30 years ago. Real impetus for more centralized planning began in the late 1950's. The problems arising at that time from increasing demands for postsecondary education and ever-increasing enrollments were complex and difficult to solve. Furthermore, there was a lack of unity of purpose in higher education within States and little attempt to change established traditions and patterns to respond to the new and more diversified needs of State residents. What was clearly called for was a centralizing of both control and planning and the making of policy decisions at a higher level. The forming of State structures to provide centralized direction gives insight into the development of present-day planning practice and organization. This section, which contains some back-

ground on early history, traces developments through the 1950's and
1960's.[5]

The Pioneer Stage

For over 250 years, institutional autonomy was dominant in U. S. higher
education. It began with the founding of Harvard in 1636 and continued
until the turn of this century when the States began gradually to establish
governing boards. Autonomy persisted largely because of the simple nature
of the early American colleges. Statewide coordination was of little concern
and probably of little need to sparsely scattered institutions that offered
only a few programs to a small minority of the population. Geographical
distances, coupled with parochial viewpoints and professional jealousies,
provided little incentive for common effort. In the developing Nation,
rugged individualism prevailed: Each college pursued its own goals and
generally disregarded its counterparts, despite the fact that an almost
identical classical curriculum was offered.

By 1900, when the number of United States colleges and universities
had grown to nearly 1,000, their increasing diversity and complexity
augured well for coordination. The earliest attempts, however, amounted to
little more than informal "gentlemen's conferences," arranged annually
by the various State associations or councils in which most institutions held
membership. These 1- or 2-day sessions seldom resulted in more than an
exchange of information, and, since no research staff was available, little
or no attempt was made to prepare statewide studies or to adopt higher
education policies of significant impact.

In the first decade of the 1900's, a few States (Florida in 1905 and Iowa
in 1909) actually began to establish statewide coordination systems. Their
initial efforts consisted of consolidating the governing boards of individual
institutions into a single statewide governing board.[6] Since the resulting
"big board" had authority to determine matters of internal administration
of each institution, it also derived authority to coordinate overall policy
among member institutions.

---

[5] For the history of statewide coordinating agencies, see the following references in the
annotated bibliography: Robert O. Berdahl, *Statewide Coordination of Higher Education*;
M. M. Chambers, *Voluntary Statewide Coordination in Public Higher Education*; Lyman A.
Glenny, "State Systems and Plans for Higher Education" in *Emerging Patterns in American
Higher Education* (Logan Wilson, ed.); Lyman A. Glenny and Julie Hurst, "Current
Statewide Planning Structures and Powers" in *Statewide Planning for Postsecondary Educa-
tion: Issues and Design* (Lyman A. Glenny and George B. Weathersby, eds.), and Emogene
Pliner, *Coordination and Planning*.

[6] Several States approved a governing board for all State-supported institutions, while
many others (particularly in the 1920's) placed the normal schools and teachers colleges
under a single governing board, frequently the State board of education.

The statewide concept met with some resistance. By 1945 only 15 governing boards had been established. A major problem was the difficulty of securing political agreement to establish a single board and abolish all others in existence. Also, while a single board was a legal entity vested with the authority to coordinate and unify the system, in practice it did not always succeed. The main reason for failure was that member colleges looked with disfavor on any centralization which did not provide some degree of institutional autonomy.

None of the early efforts to effect coordination had made impact on what Glenny calls the "happy anarchy" (suggesting an absence of order rather than chaos or confusion). In fact, diversity and independence continued to dominate American higher education until after World War II.

Post-World War II and Current Status

The evolution of statewide coordinating agencies after World War II can be traced from the data in table I-1. What distinguishes the various types of agencies are (1) the make-up of the membership and (2) the degree of centralized authority granted by the State over public institutions. The typology is based on Robert O. Berdahl's summary of national trends in

Table I-1.—Number of coordinating agencies, by type classification: 1939-72

Type classification	1932	1949	1959	1964	1969	1972
No State agency	33	28	17	11	2	2
VOLUNTARY ASSOCIATION (high degree of institutional freedom)	0	3	7	4	2	1
COORDINATING BOARD (created by statute but does not supersede institutional governing boards)						
a. Majority of *institutional* representatives having essentially *advisory* powers	1	1	2	3	2	0
b. All or majority of *public* members having essentially *advisory* powers	0	0	3	8	11	8
c. All or majority of *public* members having *regulatory* powers in certain areas but not governing responsibility	1	2	5	7	14	18
CONSOLIDATED GOVERNING BOARD (charged with full responsibility for governing all institutions under its jurisdiction)	15	16	16	17	19	21

Source: Robert O. Berdahl, *Statewide Coordination of Higher Education,* American Council on Education, Washington, D.C., 1971, table 4, p. 35, and unpublished 1972 data gathered by Berdahl.

coordinating patterns, which, in turn, is a modification of an earlier version by James G. Paltridge.

The preferred agency to coordinate higher education during the post-World War II period was the statewide coordinating board. Under its aegis, overall coordination was provided by a superboard, yet institutional governing boards continued to operate. Such a system was popular because it was relatively easy to establish by statute and was more readily accepted by institutions reluctant to give up initiative and autonomy to a State governing board.

To Kentucky goes the distinction of being the first, in 1934, to adopt a coordinating board;[7] Oklahoma was the second, in 1941. In 1951 New Mexico adopted the coordinating form, over the next two decades 24 more States followed suit.

One initial advantage of the coordinating board over other types of agencies was its provision for a professional staff to conduct continuous planning and provide advisory services. A more basic and continuing advantage has been its ability to serve as an all-embracing forum in which a variety of other public and private institutions, commissions, and councils concerned with higher education can interact and respond to State coordination needs. A neutral agency, the coordinating board is able to serve objectively both the interests of the State and those of the educational community.[8]

Coordinating boards composed of a majority of institutional representatives have never been very popular. At one time or another only five States had such boards (California, Kentucky, Maryland, Minnesota, and Wisconsin); now all have switched to another type of agency. These boards had only advisory powers, and critics claim that the self-interest of institutional members restricted coordination efforts to those of immediate concern to the institutions represented. The membership preferred for coordinating boards is lay people, chosen ostensibly for impartiality and for their desire to protect the public interest.

Another form of coordination agency, the voluntary association, reached its peak (seven States) in the early 1950's, then declined. Currently only Nebraska uses this form. Voluntary agencies are composed of institutional officers whose chief interests encompass budget preparation and allocation

---

[7] New York established a Board of Regents in 1784, but it was not until 1961 that legislation was passed requiring that this board adopt procedures enabling it to exercise coordinating and planning powers.

[8] For a persuasive presentation of rationale in support of the coordinating board as opposed to a single governing board, see Lyman A. Glenny, Robert O. Berdahl, Ernest G. Palola, and James G. Paltridge, *Coordinating Higher Education for the 70's*, Center for Research and Development in Higher Education, University of California, Berkeley, 1971, pp. 1–12.

of legislative appropriations. As coordinating agencies, they accomplished little because of their inability to secure voluntary cooperation from competing institutional members.

Recent changes in coordinating patterns include a tendency on the part of coordinating boards to discontinue their advisory role in favor of regulatory powers. Somewhat unexpectedly, three States (Utah, West Virginia, and Maine) have recently replaced coordinating boards with a single statewide governing board. Some observers feel this was a response by political leaders to public demand for more accountability by higher education.[9] In support of the single board, it should be noted that States adopting it to effect coordination have retained it.

This brief history suggests that the emerging relations between higher education and State government coordination efforts create many issues and complexities. An idea of the attention being given to State coordinating boards is illustrated by the following topics delineated in published works: administrative procedures (Lyman A. Glenny, *Autonomy of Public Colleges*); impact on institutions of higher education (Ernest Palola, Timothy Lehmann, and William R. Blischke, *Higher Education By Design: The Sociology of Planning*); technical details about agency membership, staffing and powers (Emogene Pliner, *Coordination and Planning*); analysis of structures, functions, and relationships (Robert O. Berdahl, *Statewide Coordination of Higher Education*); impact of Federal higher education programs on statewide coordinating agencies (Lanier Cox and Lester E. Harrell, Jr., *The Impact of Federal Programs on State Planning and Coordination of Higher Education*); and guidelines for practice (Lyman A. Glenny, Robert O. Berdahl, Ernest G. Palola, and James G. Paltridge, *Coordinating Higher Education for the '70s*). Notes on these and other studies are given in the annotated bibliography.

Advent of the Master Plan

Paralleling more recent events in the development of State systems of coordination—and largely a product of resulting centralized planning—has been the steady growth and evolution of State studies in higher education. Extending over almost five decades, the State survey was the precursor of the modern State master plan.[10] The earliest surveys were conducted in 1912 by North Dakota, Pennsylvania, and Virginia. One of the most recent survey-type studies was prepared for Connecticut in 1964 by the U.S. Office of Education. No official count has been made of the number of

---

[9] Ibid., pp. 2–3.

[10] For a detailed history of higher education surveys through 1937, see Walter Crosby Eells, *Surveys of American Higher Education*, The Carnegie Foundation, New York, 1937, p. 538.

State surveys made during the interim 52 years, but the figure would be in the hundreds (51 surveys were recorded by 1936).[11]

The transition from State surveys to master plans was gradual; there was no sharp point of departure. Clearly, the monumental survey by the University of Chicago,[12] completed in 1933, contains content closely resembling that in present-day master plans. However, it was not until 1948 that a study was conducted which could truly be classified as a master plan. This study is the well-known "Strayer Report," which embraced the following:

1. Evaluation of the current and future needs of the State of California for education beyond the 12th grade.
2. Analysis of the needs of each area of the State for higher educational facilities, with special reference to emergency needs such as those in the Los Angeles and Sacramento areas.
3. Analysis of the needs of varying types of publicly supported higher education.
4. Consideration of desirable changes in the organization of publicly supported higher education.
5. Examination of the manner of support of public higher education in the State.[13]

The national attention received by this comprehensive report did much to dramatize the obsolescence of the State survey.

During the 1950's, master plans, or surveys closely resembling master plans, were developed in eight States. In 1954 California made a restudy of higher education. In 1956 A. J. Brumbaugh conducted studies in Florida and Louisiana, and in the same year, a governor's report, *Minnesota's Stake in the Future*, was issued. Plans were prepared in Tennessee and New Jersey in 1957, and the U. S. Office of Education conducted a survey for North Dakota in 1958. Also in 1958, John Dale Russell and John X. Jamrich directed an extensive survey of higher education in Michigan.

In the 1960's master plans came into their own. By 1969, 23 States had completed master plans; 8 others were in the process of completing master plans and an additional 7 expected to develop such a plan. Two additional States had no mandate for master plan development but were conducting overall planning as a continuous activity.[14] Of the 12 States without master plans in 1969, 2 had no State coordinating agency, 5 had consolidated governing boards (of the 5, 2 had only 1 public 4-year institution), 4 had

---

[11] Ibid., p. 13.

[12] University of Chicago, *The University of Chicago Survey*, Floyd W. Reeves, director, 12 volumes, The University Press, Chicago, 1933.

[13] University of California, *A Report of a Survey of the Needs of California in Higher Education*, submitted to the Liaison Committee of the Regents of the University of California and the State Department of Education by the Committee on the Conduct of the Study, George D. Strayer, chairman, 1948, p. 1.

[14] Louise Abrahams, *State Planning for Higher Education*, Academy for Educational Development, Inc., Washington, D. C., 1969, p. 8.

voluntary associations or had recently changed from this type of agency, and 1 had a coordinating board.

The distinction between a survey and a master plan is principally one of scope and emphasis. The survey focuses primarily on inspection and fact gathering, while the master plan, in addition to the foregoing, incorporates recommendations and a blueprint for action. Surveys are primarily descriptive; master plans are action oriented. Both types of studies include analysis and interpretation of facts, but an interpretation of trends and their application to future policies are matters usually associated only with master plans. The survey is usually limited in scope, whereas the master plan is comprehensive. Glenny identifies the characteristics which distinguish a master plan from a State survey as "the volume of data collected; the depth of analysis; the integration of programs, budgets, and building priorities to provide a unity of purpose; the full inclusion of the nonpublic institutions, and the means for step-by-step implementation of the plan, with simultaneous review and revision leading to fulfillment of major goals."[15]

CENTRAL CONTROL
VERSUS INSTITUTIONAL AUTONOMY

The debate regarding centralized versus decentralized authority in higher education has progressed beyond arguing the relative advantages and disadvantages of each. Discussion of the pros and cons of both central coordination and institutional autonomy has resulted in considerable agreement among educators about the relative merits of both practices.[16] The evidence also reveals—and herein lies the crux of the controversy—that a winning combination is a yet unidentified balance which would retain most of the advantages of central control with a minimal sacrifice of institutional sovereignty. What persists as a continuing and intriguing challenge—and an issue of no little disagreement—is the search for a compromise between central coordination and autonomy that would create an optimal balance. The balance sought is delicate, and equilibrium may exist only in theory. No effective planning agency can expect to fulfill all of the hopes and aspirations of each institution. No institution is likely to endorse all the co-

---

[15] Glenny, "Long-Range Planning for State Educational Needs," op. cit.

[16] For a listing of the pros and cons of coordination and a thorough discussion of autonomy and coordination, plus selected references on the subject, see Arthur D. Browne, "The Institution and the System: Autonomy and Coordination" in *Long-Range Planning in Higher Education* (Owen A. Knorr, ed.), Western Interstate Commission for Higher Education, Boulder, Colo., 1965, pp. 39–51.

ordination measures proposed by a central agency. Consequently, it is realistic to expect that some form of power struggle will always be inevitable. In fact, it should be welcomed as a healthy sign. But controversy should not be allowed to foster domination or isolation. Each State must avoid prolonged dissension by seeking workable measures to achieve independence and integration. It is likely that no two States will weigh the values of autonomy and coordination in exactly the same manner. Yet it is reasonable to suppose that a harmonious and dynamic interplay of independence and integration can be obtained if advocates on both sides will respect the recognized values inherent in autonomy and coordination and agree to work together toward common goals.

As provisional guides for establishing relations between institutions and the central system and for improving understanding of the basic concepts underlying the compromises involved, the following are suggested:

1. No panacea exists which can guarantee the advantages of system control and, at the same time, preserve complete institutional independence. By recognizing that an impasse cannot be circumvented, administrators can concentrate on securing a compromise which effectively balances both positions. The securing of this compromise will be a matter of debate and concession.

2. The great diversity among the States reduces the likelihood that a prototype organization or strategy for higher education can receive widespread acceptance unless it is substantially modified and adapted for local use. As pointed out by Browne, ". . . the complicity of relationships between a system and its institutions is somewhat personal; compatibility depends upon the participants involved. Coordinate relationships are indigenous to a particular set of circumstances, and thus, develop unique patterns."[17] In other words, each State must devise its own educational system, tailored to meet the unique circumstances in which it must operate.[18]

3. Extension of central planning and coordination authority should be considered by all participants as negotiable on the basis of mutual agreement between institutions and central staff. The burden of proof should remain with the coordinating agency. Institutions will accept coordination only on the basis of personal gain or if forced to comply. If the latter is to be avoided, the case for greater coordination must be presented by the central staff to the satisfaction of individual institutions. In practice, satisfaction gained in this manner tends to preserve and support institutional independence as the bulwark of a sound educational system.

-----

[17] Ibid., p. 45.

[18] For recommendations regarding possible means for strengthening relationships between institutions and the central organization, see section on "Commentary on Statewide Planning."

4. If colleges and universities are to remain viable, they must be permitted to operate in an atmosphere of freedom and independence. Only an appropriate measure of autonomy will protect academic freedom, preserve self-initiative for change and innovation, encourage healthy competition, and permit a responsible balance between institutional interests and those of society. If member colleges and universities are to survive as strong, independent participants and avoid coalescing into a mass lock-step system, the precious assets of self-direction, identity, and integrity must be maintained.[19]

5. Each campus should acknowledge that if impartially administered coordinating activities operate within a framework extending beyond that of institutional efforts, a realistic balance between complex and often conflicting forces and interests can be achieved. Then, too, a wider perspective can uncover unifying and motivating elements to stimulate concerted institutional action which best serves the common welfare, as well as the self-interests of each college and university. It follows that institutions should participate in coordination and central planning voluntarily, vigorously, and in depth, according to their inherent responsibility for progress and support of the public interest.

6. Any statewide system for coordinating higher education, to be complete and unfragmented, must include both public and private sectors, with special emphasis directed toward establishing rapport between all participants and encouraging mutual support.

PRINCIPLES OF ORGANIZING FOR STATEWIDE PLANNING

There is no common agreement regarding the type of organization that is most effective for statewide planning. Each State must discover its own, based on those experiences which determine the necessary functional arrangement. The singular characteristics of each State organization are generally the result of a unique historical development—one that reflects the traditions, values, and practices of not only the higher education com-

---

[19] It is possible, of course, that too much institutional independence could hurt diversity, e.g., each college might try to pattern itself after the leading university in the State. Proponents of strong central planning argue that some control is necessary to preserve diversity and protect institutional identity.

For further viewpoints on this topic, see James A. Perkins, "The New Conditions of Autonomy," and Logan Wilson, "Myths and Realities," in *Emerging Patterns in American Higher Education* (Logan Wilson, ed.), American Council on Education, Washington, D. C., 1965, pp. 8–28.

munity, but also the political process and the people. With rare exceptions, the organizational pattern and operations are molded by environmental factors and attitudes within the State. Since such factors and attitudes vary widely, the development of a planning and coordinating system equally acceptable and effective under different circumstances is extremely unlikely.

To guide and direct further development and/or modification of existing systems, certain generalizations or principles of organization have been identified through experience. A summary of the observations and assumptions of Fincher and Paltridge[20] regarding effective organizational models follows:

ORGANIZATION

1. *Planning should be conducted within a formal framework or structure.* The *functions* of the planning unit should be clearly delineated, and an adequate staff provided. The role of the planning specialist should be defined in nonambiguous terms. He should know and understand commitments that have already been made. A serious question of ethics confronts both public administrators and planning specialists when planning studies are requested to justify previous commitments or to delay administrative action.

2. *Emphasis should be given to systematic, long-range, continuing planning, as opposed to special or ad hoc planning.* While it will always be well for State commissions of public leaders to take periodic stock of their system of higher education, such commissions cannot remain in continuous session. Permanent centralized planning units or agencies, on the other hand, are capable of continuously collecting, evaluating, and interpreting data; furthermore, they are most effective if committed to systematic long-range planning.

3. *A higher education coordinating agency can deal more effectively with conflict between the institutions of education and the instrumentalities of State government if members representing the general public have a voting majority on the board.* Public-member coordinating agencies appear to have greater longevity and enjoy greater legislative support than boards composed of institutional members. A board with a majority of institutional representatives is likely to find it difficult to retain the continuing confidence of a legislature, especially if the legislature views the relationship as one of the "fox guarding the chicken

---

[20] Observations 1, 2, 4, 8, and 9, Cameron Fincher, "Planning in Higher Education" (unpublished monograph), Institute of Higher Education, University of Georgia, Athens, 1966, pp. 12–14. Tentative principles 3 and 5–7, James Gilbert Paltridge, *Conflict and Coordination in Higher Education*, Center for Research and Development in Higher Education, University of California, Berkeley, 1968, pp. 98–108.

For guidelines regarding board membership, board organization, and advisory committee operation, see Glenny et al., *Coordinating Higher Education for the '70s*, op. cit., pp. 13–24.

coop." It is also likely that such a board will have difficulty retaining the confidence of less powerful institutional members if major decisions are dictated in the interest of the largest and most prestigious university.

STAFFING

4. *Planning in higher education calls increasingly for specialized professional skills.* The collection of data needed, the identification of objectives and purposes, and the evaluation of data gathered require skills of analysis seldom present in State commissions composed of public leaders. On the other hand, it is well to recognize that higher education is unlikely to benefit from "a planning elite." The goals and objectives of higher education must be determined in "an open marketplace of ideas," not dictated by a clique of specialists. At the same time, planning specialists must be professional in the sense that they view society and the state in broad terms, yet do not permit themselves to be cast in the role of technicians who merely gather data but do not interpret it.

5. *The coordinating mechanism will function more effectively if its professional staff is independent of the staffs of the educational institutions, as well as of the staffs of State administrative agencies.* Arrangements whereby coordinating agencies depend on the administrative and fact-gathering offices of member institutions to supply staff for the coordinating board have two fundamental weaknesses: (1) Divided loyalties and shared hours usually do not permit sufficient time or continuity of personnel to allow preparation of studies and policy statements based on intensive research and long-term planning. (2) Staff member bias in favor of their own institution or the academic community vis-a-vis the legitimate fiscal or other concerns of the State administration or legislators may adversely affect decisive, objective proposals.

OPERATING PRINCIPLES

In general, a coordinating organization should attempt to create a viable equilibrium among such divisive forces as opposing goals, conflicting functions, or the competitive aspirations of various parties to coordination. A stable and reasonably equitable balance between the power of the participants and among external pressures can be encouraged by observing the following operating principles:

6. *A scheme of statutory coordination should be established to serve as a protector of the substantive autonomy of institutions.* By bringing order to competition, coordination can free institutions for productive innovation and the achievement of institutional distinctiveness. If a coordinating agency is strong enough to prevent usurpation or unnecessary duplication of institutional functions, it can prevent loss of autonomy. Conflicts usually ensue when framers of the rules allow their enthusiasm for order to restrict institutional functions that are properly and necessarily autonomous. Conflict can also

occur when institutional administrators or governing boards seek to extend the scope of their autonomy to the point at which even the slightest restriction impinges on their notion of institutional autonomy.

7. *A coordinating agency will function more effectively if the particular roles and distinguishing functions of the various institutions or institutional systems are clearly defined, if adherence to these definitions is enforceable, and if provision is made for future innovative change and modification of the definitions.* This proposition presupposes a comprehensive design for planning the State's total public higher education effort. Such a design would deter institutions from competing with each other in areas of inordinately high unit costs (medical education, for example), or of essential need but limited demand (e.g., schools of architecture). A prerequisite of such a plan is the sometimes long and tedious effort on the part of the coordinating agency to reach interinstitutional agreement on statements which will satisfy the legitimate goals and ambitions of the institutions involved. It is axiomatic that plans cannot be set in concrete for all time. So, if institutions are to be in a position to initiate new programs to meet new needs, it is necessary that plans which define institutional roles be open to amendment as well as enforceable.

8. Although frequently linked with administration, *the planning function should be clearly differentiated from executive duties* required for statewide administration of institutions and programs. Administrators at all levels must be involved in planning, but specialists whose principal responsibility is that of planning should avoid entangling institutional allegiances. In other words, the professional aspects of statewide planning should not extend beyond impartially identifying desirable goals and suggesting alternative practical means of attainment, including necessary coordinating measures. This function should not overlap the execution of policies which may or may not be derived from planning recommendations.

9. *A clear distinction is desirable between planning for a State system of higher education and planning for institutional development.* A centralized planning unit can materially aid individual institutions in setting institutional goals and making realistic plans for continued growth.[21] Responsibility for institutional planning, however, should remain in the hands of administrators and faculty members at a particular institution—with full recognition that detailed parts do not necessarily function as a unified whole. Knowledge of the State's total postsecondary educational scheme provides valuable perspective to administrators at individual institutions. Conversely, planning specialists should recognize the futility of trying to force any State system of higher education to implement a totally new "grand design."

---

[21] Within a system of higher education, institutional goals and plans usually must be formulated within general policies and differentiated functional assignments set forth in the master plan. Thus institutional planners have a vested interest in master plan development.

Fundamental changes are possible, but higher education planning must begin with what exists. The historical idcntity and traditions of existing institutions must always be considered in State planning.

PLANNING THEORY AND DIMENSIONS

The Planning Process

It is not particularly difficult to devise a procedure or method to be followed in a planning process. Numerous scholars and planning specialists have developed their own systems, none of which is without merit. Neither, however, is any one procedure or method particularly original or uniquely valuable. They all outline a process which is essentially one of diagnosis, design, and choice.

The particular planning strategy set forth here has no special merit other than possibly its synthesis of the essentials. The pattern involves six steps: (1) determining goals, (2) identifying problems, (3) diagnosing problems, (4) establishing premises, (5) searching for possible solutions, and (6) selecting a solution.[22]

While these steps have been separately identified, they are not necessarily distinctive, independent operations; moreover, it is not essential that they be followed in the sequence shown. The planning process inevitably consists of an interweaving of all actions; the various steps, if discernible, can be carried out concurrently or continuously, and with varying degrees of emphasis.

1. *Determining goals.* The beginning basis for sound planning is clear understanding of the ultimate ends or objectives. It is not possible to plan

---

[22] This planning strategy generally parallels the sequence presented by Kitchell, op. cit., pp. 8–14.

An example of an alternative planning strategy involves the following six sequential steps: (1) identification of problems, (2) diagnosis of the problem situation, (3) clarification of the diagnostic findings, (4) search for solutions, (5) mobilizing for change, and (6) making the actual change decisions. See Kenneth H. Hansen, "Planning for Changes in Education," in *Planning and Effecting Needed Changes in Education* (Edgar L. Morphet and Charles O. Ryan, eds.), Citation Press, New York, 1967, p. 25.

More recommended practice than theory are the model planning procedures proposed by Glenny and others, which deal specifically with State-level planning for higher education. Guidelines are presented for (1) establishing the planning focus, (2) planning for particular objectives on problems or issues, (3) coordinating and making the plan, (4) political coordination and action on the plan, and (5) creating a new planning base. See *Coordinating Higher Education for the '70s*, op. cit., pp. 34–39.

systematically for the unknown. Logical preparation requires a reasonably accurate understanding of what is to be accomplished, i.e., the mission or desired result.

Goals, initially defined and subsequently modified by the direction of an organization, cannot be established in a vacuum. They can be clearly stated only after a thorough analysis of the organization and its environment. For this reason, goal-setting and subsequent modification are continuing phases of planning, not merely the first step. Frequently, realistic goals cannot be specifically stated until *after* alternative solutions to existing problems have been determined.

2. *Identifying problems.* The basic reason for planning is to solve problems (questions proposed for solution) which impede or obstruct the achieving of a goal or goals. Problem areas can be identified by assessing the degree to which the organizational effort is or is not meeting its goals. More specific root problems can often be located and identified only through careful search and examination of operating procedures and environmental conditions. Sometimes, however, problems and their causes can be recognized only during a diagnosis of symptomatic conditions initially reported.

Problems arise from a myriad of causes. Within the educational community, the following have been cited as most common:[23]

a. Vague purposes.—When the goals, purposes, and policies of an organization are not clear or consistent, the result is lack of direction and emphasis in organizational efforts.
b. Operational procedures inconsistent with policies.—When policies are not supported by operational procedures, the resultant inconsistency suggests an internal and external conflict which encourages action in opposition to intent.
c. Complacency.—A problem exists when people within an organization see no possibility of operating differently or of doing things other than the way they are now being done.
d. Leaders' ignorance of how to effect change.—Another kind of problem exists when those in charge of an organization want to effect change but do not know how to go about it.

It should be pointed out that the sixth step in the planning process, "selecting a solution," is itself a basic type of problem, i.e., choosing among alternatives. When problems arise during a late stage in the planning process, it may be necessary to backtrack to identify causes, establish premises, and develop additional alternative choices.

3. *Diagnosing problems.* The third step in planning methodology— basically a research activity—is that of analysis and interpretation of

---

[23] Hansen, "Planning for Changes in Education," op. cit., p. 26.

statistical data and relevant information to clarify identified problems and discover their causes and ramifications. All problem situations must be fully understood before solutions can be attempted.

4. *Establishing premises.* Because all human activity is conducted under conditions of uncertainty, planning is necessary. Coping with the present and future requires constant anticipation and preparation according to expectations and needs. Anticipation of the future, then, is a necessary and crucial step in planning. And such anticipation should establish as clearly as possible the expected events upon which specific plans may be formulated.

Premises setting forth what is expected in the future may consist of statistical forecasts based on observed trends or recurring past events, or they may set forth policies and attitudes likely to govern future activities. While every effort should be made to concentrate on assumptions which have the highest possibility of eventual validation, assumptions of questionable validity—if not misleading—are useful for developing comprehensive plans because they take into account conceivable, although remote, possibilities and alternatives.

5. *Searching for possible solutions.* When preparatory planning steps have been completed, the more constructive phase of searching for possible solutions can begin. A most creative and challenging step, it is the heart of the planning process. Consequently, it should be conducted without any preconceived restrictions. At this stage, creativity is often stymied by premature attention to evaluation criteria, an activity which can prevent identification of valid but unlikely approaches. *Any* solution should be considered a legitimate possibility. At the very least, it should be recognized that even solutions which may eventually prove unsatisfactory can present certain advantages.

A simple and often adequate way of solving problems is to study the ways others have handled similar situations. Guidance from past experience is relatively easy to obtain, and it has the advantage of frequently providing practical, tested alternatives. Yet repetition and imitation of even the best of past practices do not always satisfactorily solve new and different problems. Creative alternatives, tailored to anticipated circumstances, are discovered only through research. And, although research alone is not planning, as a process for analyzing problems, developing alternative solutions, and providing clues to the most effective solution, it is an integral part of planning.

6. *Selecting a solution.* The final and often most difficult step in the planning process is that of comparing the alternatives being considered and deciding on the specific course of action which appears to be most appropriate to effect desired changes. Rational decisionmaking requires a careful

calculation of the advantages and disadvantages of each alternative, with emphasis on the crucial effectiveness and efficiency of each. (Is the task accomplished?) (At what relative cost?)

Other than performance over a period of time, there is no sure test to validate the correctness of a choice among alternatives. Nevertheless, at the time a decision is made there are a number of different ways to reduce the possibility of serious error. Some checks which can be made include (1) reviewing the planning process to expose weakness or errors in analysis, data inaccuracy, unexpected consequences, or even faulty premises; (2) conducting a pilot test to verify expected results; (3) hedging the decision, through implementation by stages, so that total commitment is not made until after initial results are known; (4) securing agreement from others to test accuracy by degree of acceptance.[24]

State Planning Functions

The following functions relevant to planning are deemed to be among those which constitute the province or proper business of State coordinating agencies.[25]

1. Delineating sharply and concretely the generally accepted broad educational objectives of the State and determining through analysis and assessment those objectives which should receive highest priority over a given period of time.

2. Preparing multiyear comprehensive plans designed to integrate the curriculum, research, and services of statewide higher education, to correct inadequacies, and to attain educational objectives.

3. Developing various program alternatives and, by systematic analysis and comparison, presenting for review specific recommendations.

4. Studying continuously and evaluating thoroughly existing State programs in order to determine their adequacy and compare benefits and costs.

5. Examining State and other sources of financial support in order to determine the potential for additional revenue, and developing legislative and other proposals which will take advantage of identified opportunities.

6. Collecting, interpreting, and managing descriptive and quantitative educational data in the State and Nation—data which relate to and have implications for educational planning—then applying such data to the development of plans.

---

[24] Kitchell, "A Summary of Current Planning Concepts," op. cit., p. 14.

[25] An adaptation and extension of functions listed by Jack Culbertson, "State Planning for Education," in *Planning and Effecting Needed Changes in Education*, op. cit., pp. 280–81.

7. Conducting and supporting research activities to determine cause-and-effect relationships, testing and analyzing the effectiveness of specific plans proposed and adopted, and developing assessment instruments and techniques.

8. Establishing coordinated working relationships and effective communication with all organizations and individuals directly concerned with planning.

It is important to recognize that, with the exception of certain assigned powers, the responsibilities of State coordinating agencies generally do not extend beyond providing leadership, advice, and recommendations. What powers the board is given generally relate to approval of new and existing degree programs and new campuses, preparation and presentation of a consolidated budget, and administration of State and Federal student grant and aid programs. In most other areas, final decisionmaking, mobilization for change, and implementation of adopted proposals are actions for which the colleges and universities, either individually or collectively, are responsible. In the public domain, these actions may be carried out through exercise of the executive and legislative power of the State government and its agencies. If plans are to be set in effective motion, circumstances will almost certainly require the coordinating agency to supervise the implementation of adopted proposals.

Master Plan Content

As the planning process is a continuous activity, so the master plan, regardless of its depth and comprehensiveness, is but a temporary guide, not a final solution. A master plan must be responsive to the needs of the State and its people, also to individual public and private institutions within the State. Since it is obvious that no one master plan will satisfy everyone, the plan itself must be constantly subject to review and revision. In essence, it must exist as a living document, subject to changes in State needs.

What clearly distinguishes a master plan from the usual State survey or special study is its unique combination of multiple elements, each functionally distinctive yet mutually supporting. The component features most often embodied in a master plan are:

1. Premises which form the basis for State educational objectives and which underlie the patterns of planning and coordination development

2. Immediate and long-range postsecondary educational goals of the State

3. Socioeconomic conditions of the State, and implications of these conditions for higher education (See chapter II.)

4. Analysis of a wide variety of topic areas

5. Supporting statistics and advisory studies
6. Integrated recommendations
7. Plans for implementation and simultaneous review of progress.

Within the foregoing general framework, State plans exhibit marked variation in content. Each master plan contains a unique selection and grouping of topics which reflect the individual pattern of the State—a pattern that distinguishes between subject matter requiring central decision-making (and thus suitable for inclusion in the master plan) and topics for which decisions at the institutional or campus level are more appropriate.

Under certain supporting circumstances, practically any component of higher education could be seriously considered a legitimate topic for master planning. Within the broad spectrum of master planning itself, two polar positions may be identified. At one end of the continuum are a few subjects demanding uniformity and coordination sufficiently universal in nature to make them inherently and ideally suited for central planning, even central control. At the other extreme, a great many activities are strictly the internal affairs of institutions, rightly falling within the province of each campus. Most matters regarding student affairs, faculty affairs, administrative appointments, planning of academic programs and courses, institutional budget preparation, and campus policing, for example, are *not* the proper business of a State coordinating agency. Such topics require local study and institutional governance—actions for which central planning and control cannot be a satisfactory substitute. Between these two positions are many topics which require the attention of both the campus and the central system, and for which the superiority of either institutional or central control cannot always be clearly demonstrated. It remains the task of the State planning agency, with the concurrence of various institutional members, to select from this intermediate group of subjects those suitable for statewide study which are also within the legal purview of agency operations.

There are no arbitrary rules to guide planners in distinguishing between topics suitable for inclusion within a total-system framework and those for which institutions are exclusively responsible. The previous discussion of control versus autonomy points out the inherent dangers of overcentralized planning. Certainly the burden of proof as to whether or not a topic warrants statewide study and planning falls on the central agency.

State master plans and institutional self-studies clearly differ in subject selection and emphasis, analytical procedures, and perspective. Some of these distinctions are noted by Browne:

Compared with the institutional plan, generally the system's plan discriminates more of its variables quantitatively than qualitatively; utilizes comprehensive data to measure the perimeters of the system; places emphasis on such matters as statewide educational opportunities, differential functions and programs, faculty demand and supply, relations with State government, procedures for equitable distribution of funds, etc.;

formulates policy controls and coordinative organization; displays more sensitivity to broad public sentiment and pressures, particularly those arising from taxpayers and legislatures, and less regard for local idiosyncrasies.

By contrast, the institutional plan devotes more attention to qualitative assessments of its elements; makes descriptive studies of institutional operations and programs; emphasizes such matters as student selection, curriculum revision, faculty recruitment and deployment, need for facilities, funding requirements, etc.; reviews the administrative organization as a means of facilitating programs and functions; and is sensitive to the idiosyncrasies and dynamics of institutional constituencies—students, faculty, administration, governing board, and alumni.[26]

To clarify further the distinction between system and institutional planning and the respective study areas of each, it is helpful to visualize the ultimate division of responsibility. The classification of entries in figure I-1, by expected echelon of principal decisionmaking, illustrates a possible final organization. Topics requiring central decisionmaking and warranting statewide planning and coordination have been entered above the horizontal line. Entries below the line include those basically within the jurisdiction of the institution or campus. This division of responsibilities is, at best, representative; what the figure depicts is only an illustration, not a recommended guide.

In a topic area, exclusive management by either the central organization or the individual institution is unlikely, even within a highly centralized system. The positioning of topics, therefore, indicates only those decisionmaking levels expected to be of major interest and responsibility. Intermediate echelons of control may be added, also regional or national divisions.

Planning Premises

The experience of many States suggests that certain guiding principles or premises may be identified to serve as a basis not only for establishing post-high school education objectives, but also for establishing desirable patterns of planning and coordination within a State system of higher education. The premises of major importance are, briefly, the following.[27]

1. Modern society's goals—whether economic, social, or political—can be achieved only through the development of human resources. Such

---

[26] Browne, op. cit., p. 41.

[27] Premises 1, 2, 3, and 5, with slight editing and rearrangement, are from *Education Beyond the High School: A Project for Oregon*, Post-High School Study Committee, a subcommittee appointed by the Educational Coordinating Council, Eugene, 1966, pp. 7–8. Premises 6–10, also edited, are from Michigan Staff Study No. 12, *Control and Coordination of Higher Education in Michigan*, by John Dale Russell, Lansing, 1958.

Figure I-1. — Illustrative worksheet for outlining the principal level of decisionmaking for selected component operations within a State system of higher education 1/

Decisionmaking level	1. Student entrance and passage through system	II. Higher education programs and service	III. State system and organizational structure	IV. Operating capabilities — A. Faculty	IV. Operating capabilities — B. Facilities	V. Financial support, allocation, and efficiency
Central decision	Equal and open opportunity Statewide student financial aid Application policy Nonresident policy Transfer policy Articulation between segments	Development of comprehensive program offerings Specialized programs Research centers Large research projects Estimation of trained manpower requirements	Institutional role and scope Criteria for establishment, expansion, and curtailment of programs and enrollment Geographic and institutional distribution of programs Planning and coordination Data collection & management Specialized libraries Academic calendar	Recommended salary scale Basic policy for appointment, tenure, and termination	Projection of space needs Project priority system for capital construction	Recommendations for State and local tax support Recommendations regarding tuition and fees Allocation of State funds between public and private sector and to individuals Allocation of State funds to institutions
Institutional or campus decision	Remedial work Counseling Institutional student financial aid program Admission criteria Student selection	Major academic fields Curriculum organization and development Instructional procedures Public service Innovative educational media Research organization and development	Institutional role and scope Institutional research and planning Cooperative arrangements Department and specialized program quotas	Academic freedom Recruitment Selection Appointment Rank and salary Promotion of research opportunities	Campus planning Design and construction of new facilities Utilization of physical plant	Allocation of funds within institution Research support and fiscal management

Control

Autonomy

1/ The concept for this type of chart was originally introduced by Provost Harry Porter, State University of New York Systems Office, Albany.

development is most effectively fostered when society makes available to its citizens the fullest opportunity for self-fulfillment, tempered by social needs. As a social endeavor, therefore, education is important to the individual and to society in general.

2. The increasing complexity of society requires human talents of a wide variety and achievement at many levels. Hence, the needs of society and the needs of individual self-fulfillment are both well served when a wide diversity of educational opportunities is made available in a manner that encourages their widespread use.

3. The "hand-minded"—simply because they are "hand-minded"— should not be treated as less important than the "book-minded." Since society has need for both, it has an educational obligation to both.

4. Opportunity for college study at all levels should be readily accessible to students throughout the State, and students should be able to choose colleges and programs on a basis other than cost.[28]

5. In a society as diverse as that in the United States, numerous types of institutions—some publicly supported, some privately supported—are necessary if the wide variety of post-high school educational opportunities the times demand is to be provided. Cooperation among these institutions in planning for post-high school educational needs is both desirable and essential.

6. The strength of a State program of higher education will depend on the quality of program and services offered by individual institutions. Therefore, the primary purpose of a State system of planning, coordination, and control should be to encourage all individual institutions within the system to attain optimum strength.

7. The presence of one or more well-performing institutions will not necessarily insure an effective State program of higher education. All institutions in the system must be sound.

8. Strength in an institution of higher education is closely associated with autonomy in the making of essential decisions affecting institutional operations. It is virtually impossible to build a strong institution unless the institution itself is given maximum self-determination in its operations.[29]

9. The coordinating function should be assigned to a single central agency that does not have responsibility for the operational control of any individual institution. By contrast, the control and management of the

---

[28] State-administered financial aid is generally based on individual student need and on overall expense. When institutional charges are high, part of the aid is usually in the form of loans. (See chapter IV for principles pertaining to administration of student financial aid.)

[29] Self-determination does not, ipso facto, insure quality; it is only a necessary prerequisite for building quality.

internal operations of a given institution should be left to an agency concerned only with that institution.[30]

10. Coordination functions can be carried on with what hopefully will be construed as minimal interference with essential institutional autonomy. Among the necessary functions of coordination are (a) devising plans for the orderly development of higher education in the State; (b) collecting and analyzing pertinent data concerning institutional programs, facilities, and finances; (c) giving advice and/or recommendations concerning the role and functions of institutions in the State system; (d) reviewing institutional requests for appropriations and making recommendations to the legislature regarding the financial needs of each institution; and (e) reviewing new programs, degree offerings, and physical facilities to ascertain their consonance with State plans.

Planning Topics

Within the complete scope of planning, the special subject areas are too numerous to list in detail. But on the basis of a careful survey of existing planning documents, the following constitute the core subject matter receiving greatest emphasis.

1. Components related to the goal of developing human resources to the maximum through encouragement and guidance of student entrance and passage through the higher education system; specifically,

a. A policy to provide equal and open educational opportunities beyond high school for all who seek and can benefit therefrom, with these opportunities continuing until each person's needs for economic and social self-sufficiency are met;

b. A program of high school and college counseling and remedial work to identify, conserve, and develop the talents of all citizens, and to encourage individuals to continue their education to the extent of their abilities and motivation;

c. Guidance for nonresident students with respect to admission standards, retention and transfer policies, and articulation among the segments;

d. A program of student financial support to enable each qualified individual, regardless of financial position, to attend an institution suitable to his needs, interests, and abilities; also, a related policy to deal with the proportion of financial aid to be borne by the student, his parents, and the government—State, local, and Federal.

---

[30] For a discussion of this topic and other requirements of planning and coordination, see A. J. Brumbaugh, *Statewide Planning and Coordination of Higher Education*, Southern Regional Education Board, Atlanta, Ga., 1963, pp. 35–41.

2. Components related to the goal of providing higher education programs and services to meet the diversified needs of the citizenry, as well as State needs for trained manpower and research requirements; specifically,

a. Means for providing comprehensive higher education programs to meet present and projected enrollments—baccalaureate, graduate, and professional; subbaccalaureate programs providing an opportunity for preparation in short-term specialized occupational areas and on the college level to ensure entry into semiprofessional, technical, or vocational fields, and adult education programs;

b. A plan for the development of higher education public service to the State—programs which will contribute to the social, cultural, and moral well-being of the citizenry;

c. A plan to promote and encourage research;

d. Recommendations for the continued improvement of instruction and curriculums, including experimentation with innovative educational media;

e. A program to provide the necessary training at recommended levels to meet carefully made estimates of trained manpower requirements;

f. A plan indicating how educational programs, by level and by type, will be distributed—by both economic-geographical region and institutions—so that cost factors and accessibility are fairly apportioned throughout the State.

3. Components related to the goal of providing a State system and organizational structure to achieve effective operation and orderly growth of higher education; specifically,

a. Designation of the immediate role or function of each institution within the State system, based on desired division of responsibilities, together with recommendations for future roles and coordination of efforts;

b. Establishing criteria for new 2-year colleges, 4-year colleges, and universities, as well as policy relative to institutional expansion and/or curtailment;

c. Provision for continuous planning, supportive research, data management, and coordination, with special attention to the private sector and to effective communication between State agencies and individual institutions;

d. A policy toward State or local governance of 2-year colleges;

e. Directions to guide and encourage institutions in making cooperative arrangements, especially the sharing of libraries, exchange of faculty, coordination of extension services, pooling of ETV network programing, joint use of research facilities, and scheduling of regional consortiums.

4. Components related to the goal of attracting and retaining a faculty of able and dedicated teachers, scholars, and researchers; specifically,

a. Conducting faculty supply and demand studies based on institutional education, research, and service obligations;

b. Establishing broad policies designed to secure and maintain a competent faculty: recruitment, salaries, staff benefits, teaching and service loads, research opportunities, tenure, and so on.

5. Components related to the goal of providing adequate and appropriate facilities and of securing efficiency in physical plant construction, utilization, and operation; specifically,

a. Projection of space needs and plans for the design and construction of new facilities, particularly as they relate to the campus master plan for expansion;

b. A system for the efficient utilization of physical plant facilities, on both daily and yearly basis;

c. A plan for financing capital construction and for determining priorities among institutions and campuses.

6. Components related to the goal of providing the fullest possible financial support for higher education, equitable distribution of funds, and efficient use of available resources to achieve the highest possible level of excellence; specifically,

a. Recommendations to guide and encourage State and local tax efforts to support higher education in order to maintain desired quantity and quality;

b. Recommendations regarding tuition and fees to be charged, consistent with student financial aid policies;

c. A policy for the support of research;

d. A policy for allocating State higher education funds among public, private, and other major sectors;

e. Procedures for determining the kind of financial recommendations needed to meet budgetary needs of individual institutions and assure fair distribution of money among the institutions.

COMMENTARY ON
STATEWIDE PLANNING

The more subtle and subjective aspects of the State planning operation defy rules, definitions, and formulas. They can be identified and examined only through perceptive observation and judgment of past experience. Therefore, the realistic circumstances of planning can perhaps best be understood through firsthand commentary by those currently engaged in the process. The following accounts provide insight into and information about some of the more important and often debatable dimensions. No prescription is intended. Few observations identify *all* of the realities. Furthermore, it is doubtful that each and every suggestion mentioned here would be advocated by all practitioners.

Planning principles. In summarizing the sessions of the 1965 Western Interstate Commission for Higher Education (WICHE) conference on long-range planning for higher education, Leland Medsker cited the following general principles as representative of thoughts expressed by the participants:

1. While a "master plan" is not sacred in the sense that every institution should have one, it is essential that each college develop some type of guideline in order to make certain decisions about the manner in which it will meet inevitable problems and pressures in each 5 (or more)-year period ahead.
2. There is probably an optimum time period for which planning should be done. The period cannot be so long as to preclude reasonable accuracy in projecting statistics and trends, nor can it be so short as to make planning meaningless.
3. Plans must be flexible enough to allow for change, yet rigid enough to encourage action. The dangers of overplanning may be as great as those of underplanning.
4. Planning should be deliberate, with provision for adequate time and money to be invested in it. It is not a weekend affair.
5. Planning at any level should be within the context of current and projected social and economic characteristics of the State and the Nation. This includes consideration of such factors as long-term occupational trends, advances in technology, and like matters.
6. Planning should also be done with a view to developing social and economic resources of the area served by the college.
7. Emerging tends in the patterns of college attendance are important factors in planning for higher education at either the institutional or State level.
8. The initiation of planning should be the responsibility of individual colleges and systems of higher institutions. The matter should not go by default to governmental agencies.

NOTE.—The need for individual colleges to perform their own institutional planning should be clearly distinguished and not confused with the fact that a central agency, representing either an education system or the State, is best suited to direct statewide planning activities.

9. Planning in regard to determining institutional purposes must be done from within, with outside help (if needed at all) limited to technical assistance.

NOTE.—While primarily set from within, the determination of institutional purposes needs the participation of other colleges affected by the functions and goals identified.

10. There must be consensus among those who make and those who implement plans. This argues for faculty and staff participation in institutional planning and for institutional participation in system planning.[31]

---

[31] Leland L. Medsker, "Resources for Planning: A Résumé," in *Long-Range Planning in Higher Education*, op. cit., pp. 119–24.

Advantages of statewide planning. In listing the principal advantages of statewide planning, Lyman Glenny suggests that the process:

1. Lessens or eliminates tensions and conflicts among institutions.
2. Focuses attention of the public on the whole system of higher education rather than on one or two of the larger institutions.
3. Helps to create among legislators and State executive officers a more favorable attitude toward educators and higher education.
4. Provides a relative increase in support for smaller colleges, which, thanks to the central agencies, are said to be financially better off than before coordination.
5. Affords, through assigning and enforcing differential functions, some protection of the traditional functions of the university and land-grant college against encroachment by teachers colleges and State colleges, and obtains for them financial support equivalent to, or greater than, that before coordination.
6. Provides, in a number of States, long-range capital-construction programs and schedules which, it is hoped, the legislature will agree to support.
7. Enriches program offerings throughout the public system by increasing support and preventing unnecessary overlap and duplication.[32]

Relationship between the system and institutions. Arthur D. Browne concludes his discussion of autonomy and coordination with some helpful suggestions for strengthening the relationship between institutions and the central organization. What follows are excerpts from his main points.

1. The relationships between the system and the institution should be viewed as complementary and mutually supportive. Institutions need to unite under a strong central leadership in order to achieve some of their purposes.
2. A clear-cut division of responsibility between the central office and local institutional staffs should be formulated.[33] Many systems . . . have formulated guidelines which describe the functions and responsibilities of each institution and the system as a whole . . . .

NOTE.—Glenny (1959) believes that coordinating agencies, like the Federal Government, should have enumerated powers, and that unenumerated powers should be reserved for institutional boards.

3. The central organization should seek to avoid intra-institutional administrative activities. Traditionally, the administration of colleges is the province of professionally trained personnel who grapple with these problems at the local level. External interference in administrative affairs undermines the morale of the professional staff and discourages local creativity and initiative.
4. Whatever types of controls are exercised by the central office should be devised specifically for fulfillment of its limited responsibilities. It is easy for controlling policies to proliferate. The governing board or coordinating council's leadership is demon-

---

[32] Lyman A. Glenny, *Autonomy of Public Colleges: The Challenge of Coordination*, McGraw-Hill Book Co., New York, 1959, pp. 204–05.

[33] Most observers, including Browne, recognize the impossibility of this task. The differences which arise between the central coordinating agency and the institutions encourage continual conflict not unlike that between the States and the Federal Government—conflict which, by its very nature, cannot always be resolved.

strated by its ability to govern well through general policies which keep certain controlling reins at the board level but which also protect local institutions from restrictive and picayunish regulations that may undermine their individual self-development.

5. Easily accessible lines of communication need to be established between the institutional units and the central agency. One of the hazards of a system is that the central governing power may become too far removed from the local units. It cannot remain on the local scene to keep a finger on the institution's pulse. Psychological and/or communication barriers may inhibit the central-local organization from functioning as a coordinated unit.

6. Competent fact-finding promotes better relations by alleviating distrust. The ability of a system to build a reservoir of factual information to describe current situations and project future conditions is an asset in improving system-institution relationships. True, data do not resolve controversies, but they shift negotiations to a more sophisticated plane.

7. The quality of leadership molds relationships. Difficulties arise in negotiations if either institutional or system officers consider the other to be less qualified and proficient.

8. The organization of a governing or coordinating board relates to its effectiveness. Organization is much less critical in creating effective relations than the personnel involved, but nevertheless it does play a significant role. The composition of the board or council is one key to its effectiveness. Ideally, board members should represent each institution but champion none. They need the knowledge of a specialist, coupled with the objectivity of a nonpartisan. Such a combination of virtues is nonexistent.[34]

New approaches to planning. Max Ways suggests that the following characteristics are typical of the "new style of private and public planning, problem solving, and choosing" being employed in planning-programing-budgeting-systems, operational research, systems analysis, and systems planning.

1. More open and deliberate attention to the selection of ends toward which planned action is directed and an effort to improve planning by sharpening the definition of ends;

2. More systematic advanced comparison of means by criteria derived from the ends selected;

3. More candid and effective assessment of results, usually including a system of keeping track of progress toward interim goals, as well as a "market-like" sensitivity to changing values and evolving ends;

4. An effort, often intellectually strenuous, to mobilize science and other specialized knowledge in a flexible framework of information and decision so that specific responsibilities can be assigned to the points of greatest competence;

5. An emphasis on information, prediction, and persuasion, rather than on coercive or authoritarian power, as the main agent of coordinating separate elements of an effort; and

6. An increased capability of predicting the combined effect of several kinds of simultaneous actions on one another, which can modify policy so as to reduce unwanted consequences or can generate other lines of action to correct or compensate for such predicted consequences.[35]

---

[34] Browne, op. cit., pp. 46–47.
[35] As quoted in Culbertson, "State Planning for Education," op. cit., p. 267.

Limitations of new planning techniques. Higher education throughout the country is increasing its use of such recently developed planning technologies as those associated with operations research (OR) and planning-programing-budgeting-systems (PPBS). Although agreeing that these new techniques hold substantial promise for more effective State education planning, Jack Culbertson points out[36] that there are certain limitations which must be recognized.

1. These techniques cannot make decisions nor can they replace judgment on the part of decisionmakers. Rather, the techniques can aid and support decisionmakers by providing pertinent data on alternative programs and courses of action. The decisionmaker, as a rule, will need to be responsive to values not encompassed by the new planning techniques.

2. The techniques to be employed require specific measures of output, yet it is a well-known fact that, in education, progress in achieving precise output measures is in its infancy. The main reasons are: (a) It is not easy to define educational goals with sufficient precision to make accurate measurements of output possible. (b) Even if goals are precisely defined, their number, variety, and nature are such that measurement is not easy.

3. Since the various techniques involve highly rational procedures, efficiency may tend to be the most influential factor in shaping choices. Due to the emphasis on precise measures of output, there is a tendency for planners, when using these techniques, to be overly influenced by economics, simply because measuring other values (e.g., human dignity) is extremely difficult.

4. The new planning techniques represent a special way of thinking and a rigorous approach to problem-solving. Since the roots of these techniques lie in such disciplines as economics and mathematics, the techniques themselves should not be viewed as simplistic procedures which will produce incontestable conclusions. They require highly disciplined thinking, coupled with the courage to examine assumptions and respect empirical data.

5. Educational planning based upon manpower requirements emphasizes the instrumental aspects of education. In other words, education is viewed as a means to achieve important economic and social goals, usually of a national character. In the manpower-requirements approach, full development of the unique talents of individuals, as an educational goal, would be considered only incidentally. Consequently, those fundamental educational goals not easily definable could be neglected by planners using this approach.

Tensions and paradox in planning. Despite the recent development of more rational, scientific, and systematized approaches to planning for educational

---

[36] Ibid., pp. 279–80.

change, some clearly unsolved problems remain. Four inherent tensions and paradoxes in planning, summarized here, have been identified by Kenneth Hansen.[37]

1. The individual and the group. While it is a generally accepted theory that the group process is a superior way to organize and conduct educational planning, involvement of all persons concerned with a given change may limit or delay action. The reason is obvious: The group process increases the likelihood of automatic rejection of new ideas by people who are involved but do not really identify with the change process. Involvement must be seen as valuable only insofar as it provides a necessary way to obtain as much insight, knowledge, and creativity as possible. When specified, detailed information needs to be sought out, ordered, analyzed, and reported; work must be done on a highly individual basis. At the point of specific decisionmaking, too, individual action may be more helpful than group effort.

2. Ends and means. Ends and means are inextricably interrelated, but they are not identical; therefore, one should not be mistaken for the other. In educational planning, confusion between desirable means and the desired end frequently results in too much emphasis being placed on the means, simply by permitting the means to become the end. Also important is insuring that ends and means are not too widely separated. Very rarely are means effective or valuable except in relation to ends. Still another precaution to be observed is against relying on the maxim that in American education everyone agrees on ends and disagrees only on means. A strong argument can be made that quite the opposite is true. There does not yet exist in any one State or group of States, or in the Nation as a whole, any fundamental agreement about the ends of education. There is, however, agreement on many of the means.

3. Research and philosophy. Both the research-oriented and the philosophy-oriented person, in gathering, analyzing, and interpreting data, and in determining educational and social goals, must move ahead one step at a time—on the basis of optimum information available—toward clearly defined goals. To wait for the ultimate in data can seriously impede planning for educational change.

4. The ultimate and the achievable. If any reasonable, defensible design is to be created to guarantee the ultimate in education for the future, it must be based on what is achievable. Full consideration must be given to consent, consensus, and compromise; in addition, multiple approaches must be tried and temporary plans sometimes put into effect.

Policy issues. In State planning for higher education, the arduous and critical task of policy formulation cannot be avoided. The issues involved are

---

[37] Hansen, "Planning for Changes in Education," op. cit., pp. 30–34.

often complex and controversial. The decisions usually require important value judgments, and the answers seldom please everyone. John D. Millett has raised some major policy-issue questions confronting higher education which State governments must resolve, in some way, for publicly sponsored and publicly supported institutions.

1. Should a State provide higher educational opportunity to out-of-State students? If so, how many should be admitted and how much should such students be charged?[38]
2. Should a State provide open admission to all high school graduates of the State or restrict college admission to a proportion of the high school graduates? Shall open admission be provided only at certain institutions of higher education or at all?
3. What should be the role of the State in providing public television, and should public television be provided through institutions of higher education?
4. To what extent should higher education be provided at institutions where students attend on a residential basis, and to what extent should higher education be provided at institutions where students attend on a commuting basis?
5. To what extent should the State seek to encourage research, and how should such encouragement be undertaken?
6. Should State governments assist private colleges and universities, and, if so, what manner of support would be most appropriate?
7. Should public higher education facilities and programs be expanded in major urban areas or should they be expanded on residential campuses in small communities?[39]

Questions related to the drafting of final recommendations. Although most master plans deal with a number of common topics, they vary greatly in scope and depth and in the extent of recommended change. Lyman Glenny has listed certain critical, perplexing questions which must be answered by State higher education planners before they can establish study parameters and policy essential to formulation and presentation of final recommendations:

1. How much change can be proposed in a statewide plan and be implemented successfully? Is it better to limit the plan to a few essentials or cover the waterfront? What are the practicable limits of achievable change?
2. How short- or long-range should the plan be? Should it extend to a 5-, 10-, 15-year period? What are the safe limits for projections? What are the motivating elements of a short-term verus long-range plan?
3. How much exposure should be given a drafted master plan before attempting final approval? To what extent should the plan be subjected to institutional negotiation, public hearings, and prior exposure to governmental officials, including legislators, in order to weed out the impractical, faulty, and unachievable proposals?
4. To what extent can a plan become a "package deal"? How do you prevent a sensitively balanced and finely adjusted plan from being dissected and mutilated in the political process of approval? Is it realistic to ask a legislature to accept all of a plan or none of it?

---

[38] A related question: How can States jointly provide educational opportunities to population centers divided by their respective borders?

[39] John D. Millett, an address before the Sixteenth Annual Legislative Work Conference, Southern Regional Education Board, White Sulphur Springs, W. Va., Aug. 27, 1967.

5. How much "reality" should be exposed in a plan? Should the bald financial facts, for example, which may frighten the governor and the legislature be given or should they be minimized in order not to jeopardize the plan? How much honesty is required, even though self-defeating.[40]

Implications of the planning movement. As educational planning develops and expands, it will affect a variety of organizations and agencies. Some of the implications for these groups and individuals arising from planning movements have been cited by Jack Culbertson.[41]

1. The important implication for universities and other organizations responsible for training educational administrators is the need to establish new short-term training arrangements to familiarize leaders in educational institutions and in education-related agencies with the nature and scope of new approaches to planning. In addition, resident indepth programs will be required to prepare substantial numbers of personnel actually to use the new planning methods in education.

2. The implication for State legislators and governors stemming from the new planning movement is the important responsibility they must assume to see that States achieve needed planning capabilities. In some cases, meeting this need will mean providing special financial support to strengthen existing planning agencies; in others, the creation of specially supported planning agencies. If planning is to be effective, a different kind of political behavior will be required—one based more on cost-benefit theory and public discussion than on traditional patterns of bargaining and private communications. Citizens will have more options to examine and more data on which to base their decisions.

3. To meet the increase in demand for planning data based upon some relationship between input and output measurements, professional organizations interested in education will have to change their approach to the collection and analysis of information by adopting systems-planning procedures.

4. Since systematic planning always involves a careful examination of existing practices and underlying assumptions, educational leaders and others intimately identified with education can, at times, expect to experience discomfort. For this reason, some defensiveness will inevitably be associated with national and State efforts to assess education. However, as the emergent planning and assessment movement develops, responsible educational personnel will undoubtedly adjust in a mature fashion.

5. New planning methods can provide citizens with more educational options to consider and more adequate data with which to examine these options.

---

[40] Lyman A. Glenny, "Long-Range Planning for State Educational Needs," op. cit.
[41] Culbertson, "State Planning for Education," op. cit., pp. 283–85.

BIBLIOGRAPHY

American Association of State Colleges and Universities, *Coordination and Governance of Higher Education*, Washington, D.C., 1971, 20 pp.

Three essays provide insight into the challenges of coordination in higher education. William K. Selden, in "Some Observations on the Coordination of Higher Education at the State Level," discusses basic issues and develops a set of principles as guidelines for effective coordination. Glenn S. Dumke explains why a democratic, consultative approach to academic governance has failed to cope successfully with the complexity of modern institutions, systemwide organization, and special-interest politics. "The days are over," he states, "when administrators can pass the buck to faculty committees or other groups of constituents for the actual enforcement of the regulations of the institution. There must be some unilateral decisions. There must be some taking of firm and prompt positions, and strangely enough, I do not think that faculties, in spite of all the talk to the contrary, really object to this method of administration." Dumke goes on to suggest that since every campus problem cannot be solved by rational argument, ". . . the administrator, in order to maintain his accountability, must welcome advice from many quarters but must not yield to demands for over-wide participation in the decisionmaking process." M. M. Chambers, author of the third essay, "Trends Among the States in Governance and Coordination of Higher Education," asserts that "The continued push for tighter and tighter centralization in State government, in the name of 'economy and efficiency' and of 'scientific management,' is in very large part a reach for political power." He suggests that the functions of a coordinating board may be properly limited to (1) gathering data, (2) making studies, (3) receiving information, and (4) making recommendations.

Berdahl, Robert O., *Statewide Coordination of Higher Education*, American Council on Education, Washington, D.C., 1971, 285 pp.

This study provides an indepth analysis of the structure. functions, and relationships of various types of State higher education coordinating agencies. The author attempts not only to narrow the differences in outlook held by higher education and State government, but to clarify the role of intermediary which State coordinating agencies perform between the States and colleges and universities. Considerable attention is given to the issues that distinguish academic freedom from university autonomy, to the responsibility of higher education to the public interest, and to the form and extent of coordination necessary to maintain autonomy and responsiveness. Other topics discussed include the relationship between the State and private higher education and between higher education and the public school system; also, the impact of Federal programs on State coordination. The influence of coordination on the nature and quality of decisionmaking in education is also examined, as are the decisionmaking procedures themselves, particularly those relating to planning, budget review, and program approval. Effective use is made of information and opinions gathered in an intensive field study of 19 State higher education systems. In the concluding chapter, the author presents some generalizations and recommendations to further understanding of the proper role of statewide coordinating agencies and to illustrate how the coordinating function may be most effectively performed.

Brumbaugh, A. J., *Statewide Planning and Coordination of Higher Education*, Southern Regional Education Board, Atlanta, Ga., 1963, 45 pp.

This work is a short summary of the ways in which 15 States have approached the problem of long-range planning for and coordination of higher education, with particular reference to the southern States. Of special value are the generalizations concerning requirements for effective statewide planning and coordination based on the experiences of existing agencies. Two introductory chapters discuss the "Why?" and "What?" of planning and coordination.

Carnegie Commission on Higher Education, *The Capital and the Campus: State Responsibility for Postsecondary Education*, McGraw-Hill Book Co., New York, 1971, 154 pp.

Like many Carnegie Commission reports, this is replete with detailed information. In the short, concisely written chapters, summary listings are often substituted for narrative text. The chapters cover the following: major themes; the goal and the issues; nature of State responsibility; the governor, the legislature, and higher education; coordination and planning; comparison of State effort; the State and the nonresident student; the State and private institutions; public and private tuition levels; public funds for private higher education; public accountability and institutional independence, and conclusions. Resident and migration data and State financing statistics are presented in appendixes. An exceptionally valuable book, it is "must" reading for members of State boards and commissions charged with responsibility for postsecondary education.

Carnegie Commission on Higher Education, *Governance of Higher Education*, McGraw-Hill Book Co., New York, 1973, 249 pp.

This report on governance studies six issues concerning the structures and the processes of decisionmaking in higher education: (1) adequate provision for institutional independence, (2) the role of the board of trustees and of the president, (3) collective bargaining by faculty members, (4) rules and practices governing tenure, (5) student influence on the campus, and (6) the handling of emergencies. It also offers some general observations about campus governance and identifies features of higher education governance in the United States that distinguish it from systems elsewhere.

Chambers, M. M., *Voluntary Statewide Coordination in Public Higher Education*, University of Michigan Press, Ann Arbor, 1961, 80 pp.

The author has assembled facts and opinions on the history, activities, successes, and failures of voluntary coordination in State higher education. Convincing argument is made that mandatory, coercive, and compulsory coordination leads to mass-produced higher education, with the best institutions being allowed to decline to a mediocre level. The author believes that excellence can best be maintained and advanced under conditions of voluntary liaison and cooperation. To support his position, he cites the trend away from coercion during the past 20 years. Separate chapters are devoted to an analysis of the systems of higher education in California, Colorado, Indiana, Ohio, and Michigan.

Coons, Arthur G., *Crises in California Higher Education*, Ward Ritchie Press, Los Angeles, 1968, 246 pp.

In the author's words, this volume presents "a story of California's problems of coordination, structure, major issues of governance, and relationships in higher education in the past decade and some conclusions therefrom based on the experiences and observations of the writer." A highly readable and informative study of the continuing and unresolved issues of higher education in California, the text is part autobiographical, part historical. The author draws upon his experiences as chairman of the California Master Plan Survey (1959–60) and as president of the Coordinating Council for Higher Education in California (1965–68).

Eulau, Heinz, and Harold Quinley, *State Officials and Higher Education: A Survey of the Opinions and Expectations of Policy Makers in Nine States*, Carnegie Commission on Higher Education, McGraw-Hill Book Co., New York, 1970, 209 pp.

This survey concerns the manner in which "legislators and certain State executive officials perceived the problems and issues of higher education, their attitudes toward various aspects of higher education, and their expectations of future development." The selected States include five with complex educational systems—California, Texas, Illinois, New York, and Pennsylvania—and four with less complex systems—Iowa, Kansas, Kentucky, and Louisiana. Those interviewed were legislators and staff members most intimately connected with legislation or appropriations for higher education, and also State executives. The respondents speak for themselves, with the authors giving only occasional appraisal and evaluation. What the respondents had on their minds is organized into nine topics: Prospects and Problems, Information Pressures, Control and Oversight in Higher Education, Financing Higher Education, Legislators and Academicians, The Junior College Phenomenon, Student Unrest: Causes and Cures, The University and Society, and Planning the Future.

Glenny, Lyman A., *Autonomy of Public Colleges: The Challenge of Coordination*, McGraw-Hill Book Co., New York, 1959, 325 pp.

This study is principally concerned with the question: "Which processes, which organizational pattern of state coordinating boards, and what kinds of relationships between these boards and institutions and other state agencies can secure the most effective diversification and improve the quality of higher education without unduly sacrificing the freedom, autonomy, and initiative of the affected colleges and universities?" The author, through an evaluation of the organization and operation of coordinating agencies in 12 States, draws many useful conclusions. His analysis is preceded by a comprehensive description of the development and existing patterns of coordination in higher education within the States prior to 1957. Four preparatory chapters are devoted to a detailed discussion of agency functions in planning and policymaking, program allocation, and budgeting.

Glenny, Lyman A., Robert O. Berdahl, Ernest G. Palola, and James G. Paltridge, *Coordinating Higher Education for the '70s*, Center for Research and Development in Higher Education, University of California, Berkeley, 1971, 96 pp.

This study presents workable guidelines, distilled from available research and existing practices, for postsecondary education planning by State coordinating agencies. The four authors have brought to the preparation of this report the benefits not only of their research in this field but of experience as coordinating executives and faculty board members. The recommendations, which deal primarily with the means for resolving problems in higher education, focus on procedure and process rather than on issues or substantive results to be achieved. The carefully reasoned recommendations cover coordinating board membership and organization, planning, program review, budgeting operations and capital, data bases for planning, administration of aid programs, and nonpublic higher education. The first chapter presents a persuasive rationale for statewide *coordinating* boards as opposed to *governing* boards.

Glenny, Lyman A., and George B. Weathersby, eds., *Statewide Planning for Postsecondary Education: Issues and Design*, National Center for Higher Education Management Systems at WICHE, Boulder, Colo., 1971, 123 pp.

As stated in the preface, the purposes of this publication are twofold: (1) to provide a state-of-the-art discussion of statewide planning for postsecondary education for the wide audience of the higher education community, and (2) to identify major areas amenable to future research and development of improved statewide planning and management systems. The text is concerned first with current issues, organizational structures, and trends in statewide planning for postsecondary education, then with alternative objectives and managerial procedures available to education leaders. Finally, papers are presented on the means to effect change in educational curriculums and the manner in which institutions can be expected to improve statewide planning.

Gott, Richard H., *Junior College Into Four-Year College: Rationale and Result in Two Institutions*, Center for Research and Development in Higher Education, University of California, Berkeley, 1968, 78 pp.

This study examines the rationale and implications of upward extension in two 4-year colleges which evolved from 2-year community colleges. The central question is whether it is possible for an institution to serve concomitantly and equitably both the original goals of the 2-year college and those superimposed by expansion to a 4-year college. Variables examined in providing an answer to this question include: formal intent of enabling legislation; goals and philosophy of the college; attitudes of administrators, faculty, and trustees; curriculum; costs to students; admission policy; and probation and retention policies. One of several of the author's important conclusions is the following: "It seems evident that there are several junctures at which the goals of the two different types of colleges conflict, and when this happens, the goals of the two-year college evidently tend to give way to those of the four-year college. Also, when the functions of the two-year college are compatible with or similar to those of the four-year college, they tend to be served better than those functions of the two-year college that are juxtaposed to or are in conflict with those of the four-year college."

Knorr, Owen, ed., *Long-Range Planning in Higher Education*, Western Interstate Commission for Higher Education, Boulder, Colo., 1965, 128 pp.

The diverse subjects in this collection of eight papers and discussions from the Sixth Annual Institute on College Self-Study for College and University Administrators (Berkeley, July 6–10, 1964) illustrate the many facets of higher education planning. Among the topics are general concepts and statewide system planning; also, the specifics of institutional planning for facilities and finance. A case study of institutional planning at Southern Methodist University in Dallas, Tex., and an introduction to systems-analysis planning are also included.

Martorana, S. V., and Ernest V. Hollis, *State Boards Responsible for Higher Education*, U.S. Department of Health, Education, and Welfare, Office of Education, U. S. Government Printing Office, Washington, D.C., 1960, 254 pp.

This book provides a benchmark study of the 1960 arrangements made by the States for governing and coordinating their higher education programs. It consists of three parts: an overview, analysis, and evaluation of State boards; a State-by-State description of the administrative organization of public higher education; and basic reference tables.

McConnell, T. R., *A General Pattern for American Public Higher Education*, McGraw-Hill Book Co., New York, 1962, 198 pp.

The author presents a comprehensive exploration of implications for future patterning of public institutions that he sees resulting from a lack of uniformity and rationality in American higher education and the great diversity in students, organization, control, and output. The text contains a discussion of the need for effective organization and strong coordination within the State if essential systematic development is to ensue. Many challenging questions are considered—questions arising from the assumptions on which planning must be based, the nature of future requirements, and problems of organization and institutional identity.

Minter, W. John, ed., *Campus and Capitol—Higher Education and the State*, Western Interstate Commission for Higher Education, Boulder, Colo., 1966, 192 pp.

This publication includes papers presented by Samuel B. Gould, Daniel G. Aldrich, Jr., Lyman A. Glenny, John F. Morse, Charles S. Benson, Fred Harvey Harrington, and T. R. McConnell at the Eighth Annual College Self-Study Institute. The authors explore various dimensions of the growing interdependence of government and higher education. Several papers delineate the problems of shaping effective patterns of statewide coordination and identifying State interest in higher education. Two authors assess the impact of Federal legislation on the university campus. Harrington introduces the interstate Compact for Education and discusses its present and future role. Excellent annotated bibliographies are included on each subject area.

Moos, Malcolm, and Francis E. Rourke, *The Campus and the State*, John Hopkins University Press, Baltimore, Md., 1959, 414 pp.

A noted study on the impact of State administrative controls on the management of State colleges and universities, this volume has as its central concern the threat which centralized administrative controls and actions impose on campus freedom—freedom that affects the vitality and effectiveness of institutional administration. Opinion as well as fact is presented—data from written and oral statements by hundreds of college and State officials. On the basis of the author's selection of materials, it appears that the trend toward administrative centralization has greatly restricted the initiative and imagination of institutional leaders and that there is valid argument for decentralization of authority in public administration.

Morphet, Edgar L., and Charles O. Ryan, eds., *Planning and Effecting Needed Changes in Education*, Citation Press, New York, 1967, 317 pp.

This volume contains papers by experts who examine strategies and procedures for implementing changes in individual schools, school systems, and State education agencies. The planning process and the establishment of priorities is carefully studied from many viewpoints, often in a highly technical manner. Because of its technical orientation and detailed and scholarly content, the book is particularly useful as a reference.

Palola, Ernest G., Timothy Lehmann, and William R. Blischke, *Higher Education by Design: The Sociology of Planning*, Center for Research and Development in Higher Education, University of California, Berkeley, 1970, 627 pp.

This study examines the nature of statewide planning in States with relatively long experience in this activity and analyzes the significance of planning in the operation and development of the different colleges and universities involved. Chapter I presents the conceptual framework for the study; viz., a systematic examination of statewide planning within the organizational context of statewide higher education networks. An individual network may be distinguished by (1) the degree to which provision is made for differentiation of functions, (2) the distribution of authority within the statewide educational hierarchy, and (3) the type of planning undertaken. Six factors are identified, which, when combined, form the basis for judging whether, in a given State, statewide planning is comprehensive or fragmented. These factors include the *scope* of planning activities, *priority* given to statewide goals, *research* as a continuous process, representative *participation*, strategy for *implementation*, and coverage of an adequate *timespan*.

Chapter II provides historical perspective. The ensuing four chapters present detailed information on the importance of planning to institutions in four States (California, Florida, Illinois, and New York). In the words of the authors, "Each case study is largely concerned with the critical decisions about educational goals and functional differentiation between institutions, integration and cooperation between various groups of colleges and universities, and especially cooperative arrangements between the public and private sectors, and the process and distribution of financial and human resources."

Chapters VII and VIII compare the impact of State planning on various types of public and private institutions of higher education. The last chapter presents a planning model for higher education applicable to statewide networks and identifies appropriate planning tasks for each of the three different levels within a given network.

Among the negative findings of the authors are that statewide planning "has been unable to define and eliminate unnecessary duplication of programs, nor has it been successful in discontinuing obsolete, inadequate, or expired programs; . . . has failed to integrate the private sector with the public sector in the orderly development of higher education; . . . has failed to promote cooperative efforts between institutions on a large scale; . . . . has given insufficient direct attention to the issues of quality, excellence, and substance in higher education, and . . . has been an *ad hoc* process."

Paltridge, James G., *California's Coordinating Council for Higher Education*, Center for Research and Development in Higher Education, University of California, Berkeley, 1966, 193 pp. plus appendixes.

This study analyzes the principal changes and developments in the organization and operating procedures of the California Coordinating Council for Higher Education since inception of the 1960 Master Plan. The reasons for these changes and the forces causing them are also discussed. The study focuses on three principal areas of change: (1) internal changes in organizational form and working procedures and the growth and development of new working mechanisms, (2) changes in the composition of membership, and (3) changes in organization and authority resulting from delegation to the council of administration and allocation of intrastate disbursements of funds under certain of the new Federal programs for higher education. Chapter II reviews the history of coordinating public higher education in California. Chapter III discusses the organizational structure of the present council, its prescribed functions, and its membership. The ensuing three chapters delineate the specific areas of change in the council as perceived by the author. He examines his findings in relation to basic assumptions regarding the growth, goals, and balance between authority and autonomy of coordinating agencies and also in relation to pertinent organizational theory. A concluding chapter offers a number of proposals suggested by the analysis.

Paltridge, James G., *Conflict and Coordination in Higher Education*, Center for Research and Development in Higher Education, University of California Press, Berkeley, 1968, 111 pp.

This study, which adds to the body of data on the characteristics and dynamics of State coordinating agencies for higher education, may prove useful in predicting the effectiveness, stability, and eventual success of such agencies. The Wisconsin Coordinating Committee for Higher Education, chosen as a case study, was examined to determine whether or not certain tentative assumptions about factors contributing to effective coordinating agencies are borne out in practice. While acknowledging that the Wisconsin experience is not a conclusive test, the author reviews the tentative assumptions in light of the findings, and also on the basis of similar experiences in a few other States.

Of particular interest to those concerned with the "conflict" aspect of coordinating higher education are descriptions of the Wisconsin experience in establishing committee authority versus institutional autonomy and in determining the jurisdictions and appropriate functions of the various institutions and institutional systems.

Pliner, Emogene, *Coordination and Planning*, Public Affairs Research Council of Louisiana, Inc., Baton Rouge, 1966, 149 pp.

The author presents a general discussion of the organization and operation of State higher education coordinating agencies. Included in six detailed tables and related text is information obtained from a 1965 Public Affairs Research questionnaire sent to all States: data on board composition and term of office of members, use of committees, size of budget, functions performed, and professional staffing. The latter two-thirds of the volume is devoted to a discussion of coordinating and planning in Louisiana.

Southern Regional Education Board, *New Directions in Statewide Higher Education Planning and Coordination*, Atlanta, Ga., 1970, 56 pp.

Included in this slim volume are papers reporting on the following: major issues in public higher education and expectations for statewide planning and coordination, requirements for effective statewide coordination of higher education, basic system elements for effective coordination, Federal programs and local planning for higher education, the Federal impact on statewide planning and coordination, implications and advantages for statewide planning and coordination of emerging systems, and relationships between public and private higher education.

Wattenbarger, James L., and others, *Coordination of Higher Education: An Annotated Bibliography*, Institute of Higher Education, University of Florida, Gainesville, 1970, 28 pp.

Williams, Robert L., *Legal Bases of Coordinating Boards of Higher Education in Thirty-Nine States*, The Council of State Governments, Chicago, 1967, 129 pp.

As of July 1967, 39 States, either by legislation or constitutional revision, had established (1) a single board of regents for all higher education or (2) a coordinating board—in addition to a board of trustees—for each institution in the State or for several groups of systems, such as a university system, a State college system, and a junior or community college system. This report sets forth the essential provisions of the legislative acts or constitutional amendments affecting the single, central, or coordinating board in these 39 States.

Wilson, Logan, ed., *Emerging Patterns in American Higher Education*, American Council on Education, Washington, D.C., 1965, 292 pp.

A collection of essays by well-known educational leaders and scholars, this book is directed primarily to the dynamics of growth in higher education and to the new forms developing in the relationships among colleges and universities and within institutions. It is organized into eight parts: the changing environment of higher education, institutional modifications, the emergence of State systems, voluntary arrangements, interinstitutional and interstate agreements, unified approaches to national problems, national associations in higher education, and national policy for higher education; problems and prospects.

Wright, Patricia S., ed., *Institutional Research and Communication in Higher Education*, Association for Institutional Research, Auburn, Ala., 1970, 280 pp.

Thanks to the broadest conceivable interpretation of communication, the 83 papers presented at the 10th Annual Forum on Institutional Research (and included in this volume) provide valuable insight into many aspects of planning. The nature and range of coverage are apparent in the following sample of contents: the role of higher education information systems in statewide planning, data requirements of a statewide board of higher education, communication between individual institutions and State agencies, institutional objectives and long-range planning, and criteria for establishing branch campuses.

This pamphlet lists 115 books and articles pertaining to State-level agency coordination of institutions of higher education and State-level planning.

Zwingle, J. L., and Mabel E. Rogers, *State Boards Responsible for Higher Education 1970*, U. S. Department of Health, Education, and Welfare, Office of Education, U. S. Government Printing Office, Washington, D. C., 1972, 197 pp.

This study consists of a factual description of arrangements made by the States for governing and coordinating their higher education programs in 1969 and 1970. On a State-by-State basis, the authors discuss statewide coordinating boards for higher education, State boards of education, and boards representing given types of institutions—e.g., universities, professional schools, land-grant colleges, and 4-year and 2-year colleges. The study includes organizational charts for each State, a basic reference table, and two appendixes relating to governing-coordinating functions.

Chapter II

SOCIOECONOMIC COMPARISONS AMONG STATES

Any serious planning for statewide higher education should begin with an assessment of socioeconomic conditions. The insight and perspective gained from such an assessment will not only give direction to initial planning efforts but also affect the value and soundness of final recommendations. In order to develop and implement a feasible master plan, it is necessary to take into account the basic character and climate of the State which the plan is intended to serve.

A first step in planning is to understand and interpret accurately State environment and needs. Information about the immediate environment must be gained from firsthand observation—from on-the-scene investigation. A wider perspective—knowledge beyond what local study can provide—may be obtained, in part, through interstate comparisons; in other words, by establishing one State's position relative to that in other States with similar characteristics. Provided certain precautions are observed, interstate comparisons may be used to aid in identifying existing deficiencies and determining realistic goals.

What is described in this chapter is a system for analyzing conditions within a State based on interstate comparisons. The system consists of State data and State rankings for 26 carefully selected measurements of educational accomplishment, underlying socioeconomic factors, and certain aspects of higher education organization and emphasis. The measurements are in the form of indexes which show the relation or ratio of one dimension to another. A procedure is presented for selecting State peer groups within which interstate comparisons are meaningful as indicators of true relative position because of near-common or similar existing circumstances.

The 26 measurements cover the following four areas:

1. Socioeconomic climate for support of education
2. Elementary-secondary school achievement
3. Financial support of higher education
4. Public higher education—organization, emphasis, and achievement.

45

CONCEPT OF COMPARABILITY

In making interstate comparisons, quantification of phenomena may be challenged on the basis that the emphasis placed on precise measurements tends to oversimplify relationships and block out common sense and judgment. The fact is that arithmetically precise measurements often have an uncertain and variable relationship to a phenomenon that is the real subject of interest. This inexactitude relegates such measurements to a supporting role, with experience, intuition, and common sense properly serving as principles in identifying realities.

Interstate comparisons must, nevertheless, be regarded as a useful research instrument, albeit a technique not likely to provide definitive answers. Central to the usefulness of interstate comparisons is the concept of comparability. Comparison is the process of examining relative values to discover characteristic qualities, whether similar or dissimilar. The objects to be compared must share some common identity which equates similarities or differences, i.e., an identity which places them side by side to reveal their true relative character. The common identity which States must share in order to be compared is usually similarity of socioeconomic characteristics and organization. In a strict sense, States should not only have similar potential for achievement and mode of operation but also similar objectives. When States closely resemble each other in these fundamental ways, they have a sufficiently common basic identity to permit values and achievements to be exchanged or transferred; i.e., the accomplishments of one State may be substituted for those of another. When such transferability is possible—when one State can view the accomplishments of another State as a realistic guide, benchmark, or goal applicable to its own efforts—then, and only then, does practical comparability exist.

The foregoing suggests the importance of comparability based on similarities. The myriad varying environmental conditions and operational arrangements naturally preclude the exact matching of circumstances in any two States. Yet, for comparative study, it is possible to group States by reason of similarity either in (1) basic socioeconomic strength to support education, (2) manner of organizing for education, or (3) emphasis on the various educational components. For example, although considerable variations in economic strength may exist among neighboring States, frequently States within the same geographic region exhibit similar socioeconomic conditions. Geographic location, however, is of little help in identifying States that have similar methods of organizing for higher education or which place similar emphasis on various segments and programs. Such factors can be better equated on the basis of relative rankings for such selected operating conditions as the public share of resident enrollment, the role of 2-year colleges, and the emphasis placed on graduate programs.

An explanation of how a trial State peer group may be chosen, together with the criteria to be employed, is presented in the next section. What should be remembered is that a suitable peer group can never be determined by formula alone; judgment is required. It follows, then, that it is the responsibility of each State to identify those other States which it feels offer the best guidance through comparison. Yet, however thoughtfully a peer group is selected, the effects of varying State circumstances on comparability are not eliminated altogether. Since each of the 50 States and the District of Columbia differs from the others in many basic ways, interstate comparisons must always be tempered by the strong likelihood that a number of unconsidered circumstances may contribute to and explain the differences noted.

PROCEDURE FOR MAKING INTERSTATE COMPARISONS

The recommended procedure for making interstate comparisons involves two preparatory steps: (1) study of the measurements to be compared, and (2) identification of peer States. Little real understanding can be gained from comparison of data unless the exact nature of the measurements involved and their limitations are known. To provide this information, a complete description of the 26 indexes selected for interstate comparisons follows, preceded by a brief listing of the criteria used for selecting the measurements. The tabular data are presented in tables II-1 (1970) and II-2 (1960)[1] (at the end of this chapter).

The importance of obtaining comparability when making interstate comparisons has been mentioned, as well as the fact that comparability can be improved by limiting comparisons to those peer States exhibiting similar conditions of potential, organization, and emphasis. Imposing such a restraint establishes a reasonably common base or reference level from which meaningful relative standings can be observed. Within a group of 5 to 10 peer States it is possible to identify challenging yet realistic goals and, at the same time, to gain a perspective concerning the home State's relative accomplishments.

The process of selecting the peer group is one of identifying States exhibiting those common conditions needed to secure comparability of data. The conditions for comparability depend on the type of data being considered. Consequently, separate peer groups must be identified for each of

---

[1] To become acquainted with the indexes and tabular format, the reader should at this point briefly study these tables.

the three topic areas in which interstate comparisons are to be made. The criteria by which peer groups are selected in each of the topic areas are as follows:

Elementary-Secondary School Achievement

•Composite socioeconomic climate (index 6)
•Personal income per capita (index 5)

Financial Support of Higher Education

•Capacity-burden ratio (index 13)

NOTE.—Because of possible economies of scale and differences in capacity to meet large fixed investments, comparisons between States that differ greatly in total population (table II-3, column A) should be avoided.

•Drawing power from high schools (index 22)

NOTE.—States which rely heavily on *local* government support of higher education must be given special attention.

Public Higher Education—Organization, Emphasis, and Achievement

•Peer group for financial support, excluding States not placing similar emphasis on 2-year colleges (index 24).

Using the State ranking data in table II-1, a trial peer group of 5 to 10 States can be identified in each of the three topic areas. There should be an approximately equal number ranking immediately above and below the home State position with respect to the aforementioned criteria. Experience and judgment can refine the selection. Neighboring States, for example, often exhibit similar socioeconomic conditions. Therefore, to insure some consistency with respect to the many intangible factors associated with different regions of the country, geographic proximity should be a consideration in peer-group selection. Similarly, discrepancies in population or land area should be avoided whenever possible.

As an illustration, using 1970 data (table II-1), consider Kansas the home State. To obtain comparability in elementary-secondary school achievement, peer States must be those which rank immediately above and immediately below Kansas in composite climate (index 6) and personal income (index 5). In both these indexes, the States are Washington, Minnesota, Arizona, New Hampshire, Oregon, Wyoming, and Virginia. The other States closely positioned to Kansas with respect to composite climate (index 6)—New Jersey, Nevada, Illinois, Vermont, New Mexico, and Utah—are excluded from the peer group because their personal income rank (index 5) relative to Kansas is either too high or too low.

To select the peer group for interstate comparisons of State government financial support of public higher education, the capacity-burden ratio (index 13) and the drawing power from high schools (index 22) are used. Thus, a reasonable peer group for Kansas might be the following four States: Michigan, Oregon, Nebraska, and Minnesota. Indiana, Georgia, Ohio, Virginia, New Mexico, Tennessee, Kentucky, Pennsylvania, and North Carolina have a capacity-burden ratio similar to that of Kansas but must be excluded from the peer group because the load on their public higher education sector is far lower than that of Kansas, where the drawing power from high schools (index 22) is a high 49 percent. Washington is excluded from the peer group because its drawing power from high schools (62 percent) far exceeds that of Kansas. It should be pointed out that within the peer group selected, Kansas and Oregon depend more than the other States on *local* government funding of higher education.

The third topic area for which a peer group must be selected is public higher education—organization, emphasis, and achievement. For this topic, States may be fairly compared only if they have similar financial strength to support education, enroll approximately the same share of residents in public in-State institutions (as opposed to private and out-of-State institutions), and are similarly organized for higher education—i.e., place the same emphasis on 2-year colleges, degree programs, and graduate education. As might be expected, no two States are even close to equivalency in all of these conditions. Therefore, to obtain some degree of comparability, the guideline should be the peer group for State government financial support, adjusted to exclude those States not placing similar emphasis on 2-year colleges. From the four-State Kansas peer group for financial support analysis, only Oregon and Minnesota are closely allied with Kansas in respect to the 2-year college share of public enrollment (index 24). If desired, the peer group may be further modified or enlarged by exercising judgment based on the emphasis placed on degree programs (index 25) and on graduate programs (index 26).

To illustrate the general form of an interstate comparison analysis, the following example—intended to be illustrative rather than complete—is offered.[2]

With Kansas as the home State, a brief summary of conditions over which Kansas has some control should be compiled. As a single source of comparison, consideration can be given to the accomplishments of Oregon, which, in many respects, is the closest peer of Kansas. Both States have approximately the same socioeconomic base and approximately equivalent elementary-secondary school achievements. In addition, they have about the same number of high school graduates per 1,000 population and a similar tax capacity to provide financial support. Furthermore, the public sector

---

[2] At this point, worksheet reproductions of table II-1 should be prepared. Colored-pencil tracings can be used to readily identify the peer-group States and the relative position of each.

in both States assumes a dominant role in educating citizens and places equivalent emphasis on the 2-year college role to accomplish this task. These common conditions suggest the realism which may be attached to any accomplishment level in Oregon that Kansas may choose as a goal (as of 1970)

Elementary-Secondary School Achievement

Peer group: Washington, Minnesota, Arizona, Kansas, New Hampshire, Oregon, Wyoming, and Virginia (selected on the basis of similar rankings in indexes 5 and 6)

Index	Rank of Kansas in eight-State peer group (1970)	Rank of Kansas nationally (1970)
Financial Support Achievement (#7)	6th	26th
Holding Power (#8)	3d	13th
Elementary-Secondary School Productivity (#2)	3d	11th
College-Entrance Rate (#9)	4th	12th
Composite Index (#10)	6th	18th

Commentary: In elementary-secondary education the achievements of Kansas are excellent from a national standpoint; moreover, they are average or above average within a peer group of high achievers. Kansas is within striking distance of top national ranking in holding power, productivity, and college-entrance rate. Additional expenditures per pupil, properly directed, might provide the boost necessary to reach these top levels. It should be noted that Kansas does not rank high (5th in peer group and 26th nationally) with respect to State tax capacity per capita (index 12) which, in part, explains the State's average national ranking in elementary-secondary financial support achievement.

Financial Support of Higher Education

Peer group: Michigan, Oregon, Nebraska, Kansas, and Minnesota (selected on the basis of similar rankings in indexes 13 and 22)

Index	Rank of Kansas in five-State peer group (1970)	Rank of Kansas nationally (1970)
Tax Effort (#14)	4th	41st
Allocation to Higher Education (#15)	3d	7th
Achievement Relative to Burden (#16)	2d	19th
Achievement Relative to Enrollment (#17)	5th	43d

Commentary: Kansas ranks low within its peer group and very low nationally in tax effort. While the amount of taxes collected relative to capacity is low, an exceptionally large proportion is allocated to higher education (18.51 percent). As a result, financial support achievement relative to the number of high school graduates is good. However, a large number of high school graduates enter public institutions within the State (49 percent); consequently, financial achievement relative to the college enrollment burden is very low. To remedy this situation Kansas must increase its tax effort.

Public Higher Education—Organization, Emphasis, and Achievement

Peer group: Oregon, Kansas, and Minnesota (selected on the basis of membership in the Kansas financial support peer group and similar rankings in index 24)

Index	Rank of Kansas in three-State peer group (1970)	Rank of Kansas nationally (1970)
Absolute Magnitude of Need (#18)	2d	27th
Student Tuition and Ability To Pay (#19)	1st	14th
Free-Access Education (#20)	2d	21st
Resources Available To Provide Quality (#21)	2d	25th
Drawing Power From High School (#22)	2d	9th
Public Share of Resident Student Enrollment (#23)	2d	14th
2 Year College Share of Enrollment (#24)	2d	19th
Emphasis on Degree Programs (#25)	1st	22d
Emphasis on Graduate Programs (#26)	2d	19th

Commentary: In public higher education organization, emphasis, and achievement, Kansas and Oregon are remarkably similar. Both States have a good elementary-secondary school system and enroll a higher percentage of high school graduates in the State's public higher education system. Most of the resident undergraduate students in Kansas and Oregon attend public institutions within their home State rather than attend out-of-State institutions. About 20 percent of the undergraduate public enrollment is in 2-year colleges. Both States spend about the same amount per student for instruction at 4-year institutions.

If comparisons with Oregon suggest any areas in which Kansas might improve, it would be in developing greater free-access education and in expanding graduate education programs.

CRITERIA FOR SELECTION
OF INDEXES

The 26 indexes presented in the ensuing section—with the exception of two composite ones—are not new. Most of the measurements are well known and frequently used in any study of the various aspects of higher education. A few measurements—the tax capacity index, for example—are less often employed and should receive greater attention.

In the preparation of this work, great care has been exercised in selecting the indexes. Over 100 State measurements relating to higher education were evaluated. A majority were rejected because their specialized content had little relevance to topics explored. One example is infant death rate. Although it has certain implications for higher education, none is sufficiently relevant or important to warrant inclusion. A substantial number of others were rejected because similar indexes, with minor variations, report essentially the same content.

It has not been possible to define all indexes to satisfy every selection criterion. In most instances those selected are deficient in a number of respects, yet they represent the best available single choice. In some cases, the unavailability of data has necessitated a compromise of certain criteria. What follows are the specific criteria considered:

For index specifications—

1. *The index should be defined in measurable terms.* This criterion requires that the index be measured by a physical count, which should minimize personal bias. Judgment and opinion should be reserved for interpreting and evaluating the prepared index.

2. *The index should be a relative measurement, reasonably independent of absolute size.* Indexes are generally ratios of a principal measurement to an appropriate base dimension, e.g., personal income per capita. Although this criterion encourages fair comparability by adjusting proportionally for State size, comparisons between States which differ greatly in size should be avoided. Large States generally have greater capacity to meet the heavy capital demands of physical plant expansion. Also, economies of scale may permit States with large systems of higher education to operate more efficiently at lower unit costs.

3. *The index should report the latest available data for the same year reported in other indexes.* This criterion, by encouraging the collection of most recent data, helps guarantee that the study will be relevant to current situations. For interrelated measurements and their analysis, consistency in reporting dates should be the rule. In trend analysis, a fixed datum point is also helpful. In this work, the availability of census data has determined, with a few exceptions, the 2 reporting years—1960 and 1970.

For index quality—

4. *The index should be a relevant measurement.* This criterion is particularly discriminative because it directs selection to only those indexes that are

important to matters at hand. To contribute substantially to understanding, the indexes selected should be clearly and decisively germane to the topic. Secondary considerations and "next-best" choices must be omitted if duplication and unnecessary complication are to be avoided.

Much of the confusion and disagreement surrounding interstate comparisons are due to the fact that a plethora of existing measurements has obscured key factors and detracted from central issues. Rigorous application of this criterion can help reduce both confusion and disagreement.

5. *The index should be valid; it should measure what it purports to measure.* The accuracy and value of any measurement is dependent upon judicious application of this criterion, in conjunction with the one pertaining to relevance. The validity of each index is defensible only on the basis of "face validity"—i.e., that the index appears to measure what the author and others have in mind (what they think they are measuring). In this work, considerable care has been exercised not only in selecting each index but also in identifying what it is believed to measure. Yet, since validity is relative, what each index actually does measure remains a matter for some personal interpretation.

The fidelity with which the indexes measure what they are intended to measure will vary with a particular State situation. For example, dollar amounts in different States do not measure comparable purchasing power unless geographical price differences are taken into account. Such price differences, and other special circumstances to be discussed later, cause index validity to vary among States and, consequently, to reduce comparability. When comparisons are limited to so-called peer groups, the presence of varying State conditions is reduced; consequently, uniformity in index validity is improved.

6. *The index should be discriminating.* This criterion rejects those indexes with a narrow range of reported values—indexes which do not distinguish the various State positions with sufficient clarity or difference to permit meaningful comparisons. The range between high and low values for selected indexes should be sufficiently large to allow recognition of a number of broad, yet reasonably distinct, ranking levels, e.g., high, low, and median groups. Small differences between closely ranked States have little, if any, significance.

7. *The index should be reliable.* This criterion encourages selection of dependable indexes that can be expected to measure with regularity the dimension sought. Since all selected indexes represent physical counts, any deficiencies in reliability are usually due to inconsistency in reporting and are, therefore, likely to be slight.

NOTE.—In any comparison of dollar amounts over time, the effects of inflation on purchasing power should be taken into consideration.

DESCRIPTION OF INDEXES

A responsible procedure for making interstate comparisons must necessarily begin with a thorough and accurate understanding of every measurement involved. This section provides a detailed description of each index and what it purports to measure, also certain applicable limitations. The source of data for each index is indicated in tables II-1, II-2, II-3 and in the sources for tables.

Caution Regarding All Dollar Amounts.—Dollar amounts used in this presentation are intended to reflect equivalent purchasing power among States. Since such equivalency does not in fact exist, adjustments may be necessary in some instances. Unfortunately, no adjustment factors are available to identify differences among the States regarding the purchasing power of dollars for goods and services in education.[3] A deficient (because it reports on a different "market-basket" of goods and services) but available substitute can be derived by noting urban-area differences in "comparable living costs." This index, published by the Bureau of Labor Statistics,[4] lists family budgets, at three levels, for an urban family of four in 40 U. S. metropolitan areas during the fall of 1971.

In 1971, comparative indexes of living costs based on an intermediate budget ($10,971) for a four-person family generally did not vary by more than plus or minus 15 percent of the U. S. average. High living costs were reported in Anchorage, Alaska (an index value of 136); Honolulu, Hawaii (119); Boston, Mass. (117); and in the New York-northeastern New Jersey area (115). Low living costs were noted in Austin, Tex. (86); Orlando, Fla. (88); and Atlanta, Ga. (89). In tables II-1 and II-2, dollar values for Alaska have been reduced 15 percent to equal a living-cost index value of 116.

Indexes not followed by an identifying asterisk indicate conditional factors over which the State has little, if any, control, and for which no quality level should be inferred from rank position. Since indexes identified with a triple asterisk (***) are to a large extent *controllable by the State, rank order suggests the general level of excellence.* A single asterisk (*) identifies indexes 22 through 26, all of

---

[3] Since teacher services constitute the major expenditure by schools and colleges, adjusting a State's educational expenditures by its relative teacher salary level is frequently advanced as a means of obtaining equivalent purchasing power. Such a method is acceptable if teacher services in the States being compared are of equal or at least similar quality.

[4] See U. S. Department of Labor, Bureau of Labor Statistics, Office of Information, "Autumn 1971 Urban Family Budgets and Geographical Comparative Indexes," *News,* Apr. 27, 1972.

which are largely *controllable by the State, yet the quality level associated with rank position in these indexes is largely a matter of interpretation based on intended emphasis.*

Socioeconomic Climate for Support of Education

The ensuing series of measurements consists of five socioeconomic characteristics that indicate some basic strengths and capabilities for State support of education. Overall climate and potential is suggested by the five measurements considered both separately and as a composite. The measurements are clearly interrelated, yet each is sufficiently distinctive and important to contribute independently to the total impression. Some measures may be considered more important than others (personal income per capita, for example); however, none should be regarded as individually decisive.

Index 1—*Educational Attainment* (median school years completed by persons age 25 and over)

NOTE.--The median school years completed represents the number that divides the distribution into two equal groups, one having completed school years above the median and the other having completed school years below the median.

This measurement indicates the formal educational attainment of a State's adult population. The educational level of a State suggests the degree to which the general population, by reason of formal educational experience, is likely to appreciate higher education and encourage and support its development.

Index 2—*Elementary-Secondary School Productivity* ***(public and nonpublic high school graduates as a percent of the 17-year-old population)

This productivity index measures a State's ability to produce individuals qualified for postsecondary education. A State in which a large proportion of the 17-year-old population graduates from high school generally has a strong elementary-secondary system with good holding power, as well as a State citizenry that encourages youth to attend school. Such factors are generally favorable for the support of higher education.

Index 3—*College Educated* (percent of persons age 25 and over with 4 or more years of college)

The college-educated population, by reason of its occupational status, political interest, and background knowledge, is apt to exert an influence on public affairs far exceeding its proportionate number. Thus, graduates who recognize the value of a college degree represent a State constituency likely to support and encourage the growth of higher education.

Index 4—*Professional Occupations* (percent of employed persons in professional, technical, and kindred occupations)

The professional component of a State's population is similar to the college educated in that it constitutes an element predisposed to strong support for higher education and can be counted on to encourage its development. The professional group consists of most college graduates (with the
notable exception of college-educated housewives), plus many other highly
trained individuals who, because of their professional stature, are likely to
be alert and responsive to the needs of higher education.

Index 5—*Personal Income* (personal income per capita)

Personal income per capita closely approximates consumer purchasing
power and reflects standard of living. Standard of living is a relative[5]
measure of the degree to which people are able to provide themselves with
the necessities and/or luxuries of life to which they are accustomed or aspire.
Important conditions of life which determine living standards include adequate food, clothing, shelter, employment, public services, health care,
education, transportation, and cultural and entertainment opportunities.
Poor people not only have fewer of all the aforementioned, but also less
ability to obtain them.

Personal income is also an indicator of the ability of citizens to pay taxes
from their immediate earnings. However, in this chapter more sophisticated
measures of fiscal capacity are used.

The income-producing component of the population generally consists
of residents between 18 and 64 years of age. The inclusion of dependent
children and the aged in the per capita denominator introduces a burden
factor. Per capita income reports the purchasing power or standard of living
of income-producing residents as well as an adjustment for the burden imposed by the State's dependent population. A State with a relatively large
dependent population has a proportionately lower per capita income and
standard of living.

Personal income is defined as the current income persons receive from
all sources (on a nationwide basis about two-thirds is from wages and
salaries). It includes transfers (payments not resulting from current production) from Government and business in the form of social security benefits,
military pensions, etc., but excludes transfers between persons. Although
most of the income is in monetary form, there are important nonmonetary
inclusions: chiefly, estimated net rental value to owner-occupants of homes,
the value of services furnished without payment by financial intermediaries,
and the worth of food consumed on farms.

---

[5] Standard-of-living comparison among States requires adjustment to obtain equivalent purchasing power.

Index 6—*Composite Climate Index* (average of rankings for measurements 1 through 5)

This index depicts the average rank of each State for measurements 1 through 5. As a composite measurement it is useful for the purpose of identifying peer States having similar socioeconomic environments to support education. To illustrate: At first glance Maine and South Dakota do not appear to have much in common, yet the five socioeconomic measurements and the 1970 composite index suggest great similarity in their overall climate for the support of education.

Although the composite index gives equal weight to each of the five measurements, personal income is probably the most important. Because of its importance, peer States selected on the basis of index 6 should be closely ranked with respect to personal income as reported in index 5. Wyoming, Virginia, Wisconsin, Iowa, and Nebraska are examples of peer States based on close rankings (in 1970) for both of these indexes.

Conversely, Michigan ranks too high in personal income and Montana ranks too low to be included within this socioeconomic peer group.

Elementary-Secondary School Achievement

Included in this section are four measurements of public elementary-secondary school excellence, plus a composite index. Overall excellence is best illustrated by considering the four measurements separately *and* as a composite.

Index 7—*Financial Support Achievement**** (estimated current expenditures for public elementary and secondary schools per pupil in average daily attendance)

This index reflects the *commitment* of State and local funds to support public elementary-secondary education at desired quantity and quality levels. Current expenditures include all amounts spent for administration, instructional services, plant operation and maintenance, fixed charges, and other school services. Caution should be exercised in interpreting this index as a measure of school quality, which, like most value considerations, defies definition and is essentially a matter of judgment. Attempts to measure quality have usually resulted in incorporating a number of criteria in a composite index of selected factors. Current expenditures, however, do represent a good *single* indicator of quality since they reflect many components of quality: student-teacher ratio, faculty salaries and related qualification requirements, and equipment and facilities. On the other hand, expenditures often do not properly account for many important but intangible factors that contribute to or detract from school quality. For example, the adverse effects of poor socioeconomic conditions on inner city schools often

reduce quality, while, at the same time, increase operating costs. Also, reporting simple dollar inputs does not account for differences among States
in the efficiency of their elementary-secondary school operations and the
resulting effects on quality.

NOTE.—As with all dollar amounts, greater comparability may be obtained by adjusting for regional variations in purchasing power.

Index 8—*Holding Power*** (public high school graduates as a percent of
9th-graders 3 years earlier)

The ability to hold students through graduation reflects not only the
general quality of education provided by the high school, but also, and perhaps equally important, the educational preparation of entering 9th-
graders.

Index 2—*Elementary-Secondary School Productivity*** (public and nonpublic
high school graduates as a percent of 17-year-old population)

The elementary-secondary school productivity index which reflects overall quality and retention ability is probably the single best measurement of
achievement at the elementary-secondary level (see explanation under
main entry for index 2).

Index 9—*College-Entrance Rate*** (State residents enrolled for the first
time in undergraduate degree-credit college programs anywhere, as a
percent of high school graduates of the State)

The ratio of first-time college students to high school graduates of the
previous year is an indicator of the percent of high school graduates entering
degree-credit programs in higher education. As such, it suggests the inclination of high school graduates to attend college, their academic qualifications, and the accessibility of postsecondary education. The desire and
ability of high school graduates to attend college is dependent on many
factors, the more important being the quality of the high school they attended, parental encouragement, the proximity of a college, and financial
resources.

Undoubtedly first-time college students (beginning freshmen with no
prior credits towards a bachelor's degree) are closely related to high school
graduates entering college in the fall following graduation, but, for a number of reasons, the two groups must not be considered homologous. First-
time figures include many individuals who, following a considerable time
lapse after high school graduation, enter college for the first time. In many
States such individuals account for at least 5 percent of the retention rate.
Such figures are offset somewhat by the fact that the first-time figures do
not include freshmen enrolled in extension centers or in terminal occupa-

tional and general studies programs not usually leading to a bachelor or a higher degree. Data for this index are available only for 1963 and 1968.

Index 10—*Composite Elementary-Secondary School Index**** (average of rankings for measurements 2, 7, 8, and 9)

This index reports the average rank held by each State for measurements 2, 7, 8, and 9. All four measurements are weighted equally. As a composite measurement, it is most useful in identifying States that appear to have made similar overall progress in elementary-secondary education.

Financial Support of Higher Education

This analysis is limited to *State* government support of higher education. Those who feel that both State and local governments constitute a more suitable tax base for support of higher education may wish to refer to the combined State-local government tax capacity and tax effort measures presented in chapter XIII. Justification for excluding local governments from the financing of public higher education is based on the fact that a majority of States do not rely on expenditures by local governments for such financing. In 34 States support of higher education by local governments is either minimal or nonexistent. In six States it represents only 5-to-7 percent of total State and local government expenditures for higher education operations, and in 10 States it is 10 percent or more of this total.[6] Because of their limited role, local governments are excluded from the fiscal analysis presented here—an analysis based exclusively on State government financial support of higher education.

Five aspects of financial support of higher education by State governments are reported in this section: burden, tax capacity, tax effort, allocation to higher education, and achievement. Because States have little control over burden and tax capacity, these may be considered independent variables. On the other hand, both the tax assessment rate and allocation of tax revenues to higher education can be controlled by the State; therefore, they are classified as dependent variables.

Explanations of each of the following indexes can be better understood if their interrelationship is known. The five aspects of State financial support

---

[6] In 1969–70, the following States relied most heavily on local government support of higher education (the percent of support provided by local government is indicated in parenthesis; all or most of the local government funding went to 2-year colleges except in New York): California (28), New York (24), Arizona (16), Illinois (15), Wisconsin (15), Wyoming (13), Mississippi (12), Kansas (10), Maryland (10), and Oregon (10). In 1959–60 only California provided most of its local funding to 2-year colleges; the percent from local government was as follows: New York (30), California (28), Mississippi (18), Ohio (14), Texas (11), Nebraska (9), Kentucky (9), and Kansas (8).

are related as follows:

$$\frac{\text{Tax Capacity } (\#12)}{\text{Burden } (\#11)} \times \text{Tax Effort } (\#14)$$

$$\times \text{ Allocation to Higher } = \text{Achievement Relative to}$$
$$\text{Education } (\#15) \qquad \text{Burden } (\#16)$$

Index 11—*Burden* (public and nonpublic high school graduates per 1,000 population)

The number of students graduating each year from high school is an appropriate measure of college enrollment *potential*. When expressed as a percent of total population, a relative measure of burden is obtained, i.e., the potential student load per State citizen.

Index 12—*Tax Capacity* (dollar amount of State tax capacity per capita)

State tax capacity measures the ability of State governments to obtain resources for public purposes through various kinds of State taxes. This capacity involves the financing capability of State *governments*, of which the wealth of local residents is only one contributing factor. Thus, per capita income is *not* equivalent to the measurement of tax capacity as it is discussed here.

Index 12 reports the tax capacity of States as measured by a "representative tax system" developed by the Advisory Commission on Intergovernmental Relations. In estimating the relative tax capacity of States by this means, a nationwide average "rate" for each tax is applied to the local tax base data. The tax base represents the extent of the activity in the State subject to the tax. For example, the tax base for the general sales tax is the dollar value of retail sales in the State; for motor fuel tax, it is the volume of highway fuel consumption. A State's tax capacity equals the aggregate potential-yield amount obtained from the various taxes if imposed at the aforementioned uniform nationwide rates.

Index 12 is based on the Advisory Commission's estimate of each State's 1966–67 per capita tax capacity expressed as a *percent* of the U.S. average. This relative measure (shown in the second column in index 12, tables II-1 and II-2) was multiplied by the *dollar amount* of State taxes collected per capita throughout the United States ($240 in 1970 and $102 in 1960) to equal the dollar amount of State tax capacity per capita for each State. Since relative tax capacity is fairly stable over time and no later or earlier comparable measurement of tax capacity is available, it was judged acceptable and also necessary to use the 1966–67 measurement for calculating 1960 and 1970 per capita dollar amounts. A complete discussion of State fiscal measures and support of higher education is presented in chapter XIII.

Index 13—*Capacity-Burden Ratio* (dollar amount of State tax capacity per high school graduate)

This index relates State government tax capacity to the higher education burden (as measured by the annual number of students graduating from high school). By relating taxing ability to need, the capacity-burden ratio places each State on much the same basis. This index, therefore, is useful in identifying peer States for interstate comparisons of fiscal effort and achievement.

Index 14—*Tax Effort**** (ratio of actual amount of State tax revenue collected to tax capacity)

State tax effort measures how much of the State tax capacity (index 12) is actually being used. The actual tax revenue collected by all States equals total tax capacity nationwide. Since the nationwide effort measure by definition is 100 percent, the effort measures for various States actually indicate how they compare in tax revenue performance with the national average.

Index 15—*Allocation to Higher Education**** (appropriation of State tax funds for higher education operating expenses as a percent of State tax revenue)

Because this ratio reports the degree to which State tax funds are used to finance higher education operating expenses, it suggests the relative importance of higher education in the allocation process.

State tax revenue equals State tax capacity (index 12) multiplied by State tax effort (index 14). Appropriations from State tax revenue for higher education operating expenses[7] include support not only for instructional programs (about 95 percent of total) but also for research, including agricultural and engineering experiment stations, and such other public services as general extension, adult education, and hospitals. Appropriations for operating expenses do not include either State support for buildings or reappropriated income that institutions receive from student fees and other nontax sources.

Index 16—*Achievement Relative to Burden**** (appropriation from State tax funds for higher education operating expenses per high school graduate)

This index reports State achievement in financially supporting higher education relative to *potential* enrollment burden. The relationship of index

---

[7] M. M. Chambers, *Appropriations of State Tax Funds for Operating Expenses in Higher Education, 1969–1970*, National Association of State Universities and Land-Grant Colleges, Washington, D.C., 1969.

16 to other indexes is as follows:

Capacity-Burden Ratio (#13) × Tax Effort (#14)

$$\times \text{ Allocation to Higher} = \text{Achievement Relative to}$$
$$\text{Education (#15)} \qquad \text{Burden (#16)}$$

The capacity-burden ratio (index 13) is a conditional factor that can be little altered to improve financial achievement. A low capacity-burden ratio limits achievement, even though a State may have a high tax effort (index 14) and allocate a large percentage of total State revenue to higher education (index 15). A State with a high capacity-burden ratio, on the other hand, has the potential for excellent financial support. Consequently, if a State with this potential shows poor achievement, it may need to consider a tax hike and/or enlargement of the higher education allotment.

Index 17—*Achievement Relative to Enrollment**** (appropriation from State tax funds for higher education operating expenses per full-time equivalent student in public institutions)

This achievement index is a per-student unit measure of State support of public higher education. It is calculated in the same manner as is index 16 except that the actual burden of student enrollment is substituted for the potential burden of high school graduates. This measurement reflects the commitment of State tax funds to higher education at appropriate quality levels to meet existing enrollment demand.

"Full-time equivalent enrollment" is computed by the formula used by the National Center for Educational Statistics, U. S. Office of Education; namely, full-time degree-credit enrollment (full-time students are those carrying at least 75 percent of a normal student-hour load or fulfilling other requirements, such as writing a thesis), plus .333 × part-time degree-credit enrollment, plus .568 × enrollment in occupational or general studies programs not generally creditable toward a bachelor's degree. All enrollment figures, recorded during the fall, include both resident and extension students.

"Full-time equivalent enrollment" is essentially a corrected headcount. Such a physical count does not truly measure actual student load since it does not take into account instructional cost differences between student levels (the cost of educating graduate students may be three times as high as that of undergraduates). Since States differ in the way they share responsibility for educating graduate and first-professional students (index 26), a more refined measure of student load can be obtained through adjustment of these variations.

Public Higher Education—Organization, Emphasis, and Achievement

The indexes in this section describe certain characteristics of the public higher education system. Because the roles played by component parts of State systems (2-year colleges, for example), vary so greatly from State to State, meaningful separate comparisons of the parts are not possible. Some States, for instance, have no public 2-year colleges; all undergraduates are enrolled in 4-year institutions.[8] In half the States, in which less than 15 percent of the total undergraduate enrollment is in 2-year colleges, the 4-year institutions shoulder most of the responsibility for educating freshmen and sophomores. In other States the opposite is true. In California, Florida, New York, Washington, and Illinois, which have more than 40 percent of the undergraduates enrolled in public 2-year colleges, these colleges take over much of the State educational responsibility at the lower division level, thereby allowing 4-year institutions, particularly State universities, to emphasize degree-credit programs and graduate and professional work.

Comparison of State universities is also not realistic since in many States their roles are substantially different due to the presence or absence of a 2-year college system. Similarly, little interstate comparability exists among 4-year State colleges, their role being dependent on the strengths and weaknesses of the State university and 2-year college programs.

Because of these and other organizational differences, the indexes in this section relate to the entire public higher education system in each State. Although such treatment tends to blur specific contrasts, it results in a more accurate overall appraisal. Thus, such indexes as "case of entrance" and "resources available to provide quality" reflect averages appraised collectively for *all* public institutions in the State. No inference should be drawn from these rankings regarding the relative standings of any individual component of a State higher education system.

Before introducing the indexes in question, an explanation concerning the merit that may be inferred from a "high" versus a "low" ranking is in order. Index 18 reports the absolute need for higher education as measured by high school graduates; consequently no value can be attached to a high ranking as opposed to a low one. Because index 19, "Student Tuition and Ability To Pay;" index 20, "Free-Access Education," and index 21, "Resources Available To Provide Quality," report factors which may be controlled by the State, a high ranking would be desirable. A triple asterisk (***), which identifies these indexes as controllable, indicates that the index values are ranked in descending order of excellence. Indexes 22 through

---

[8] In 1970, Alaska, Hawaii, Kentucky, Maine, and South Dakota had no public 2-year colleges.

26, which pertain to organization and emphasis in public higher education, are distinct from all previously presented measurements.

In considering these five indexes, whatever quality level is associated with rank position is a matter of interpretation by the individual State. A high rank is "better" or "worse" than a low rank only if the State organization of and emphasis on higher education is so oriented. For example, a State which historically has relied heavily on the private sector to provide residents a higher education may fully justify a low public enrollment share as measured by index 22. Similarly, a State, by virtue of its emphasis on 2-year associate degree programs and terminal occupational training, is entirely correct in assuming that a low ranking in degree-program emphasis (index 25) is consistent with its educational objectives. Thus, a high or low rank with respect to indexes 22 through 26 is significant only within the context of a peer group of States having similar educational goals, organizational patterns, and program emphasis. A single asterisk (*) identifies the five indexes as controllable but with *no quality level associated with rank position.*

Index 18—*Absolute Magnitude of Need* (public and nonpublic high school graduates)

Students graduating from high school represent the largest single source of potential college freshmen. It follows then that a yearly headcount of high school graduates within a State (including persons granted a high school equivalency certificate) represents a useful index of current college enrollment *potential*, exclusive of adults. For two reasons, the college-age population (youths 18 through 21 years old) has not been chosen to measure need. First, in States with many high school dropouts, the 18–21-year-old group would grossly inflate the real enrollment potential. Second, in States with a large number of nonresident college enrollees and/or a large number of military personnel on active duty the data would be distorted. (The reason: College students are counted where they attend college, rather than in their home State, and military personnel are counted at the military base where they are stationed.)

Index 19—*Student Tuition and Ability To Pay*** (average tuition at public universities and 4-year colleges per $1,000 personal income per capita)

The distinctive accessibility characteristics of public 2-year colleges— low tuition, non-selectivity, and reasonable commuting distance—are delineated in index 20. At the more selective public 4-year institutions, where less than one-fourth of the students commute, high tuition is likely not only to constitute a financial burden but also to be a critical factor governing ease of entrance. Only about one out of four students attending 4-year institutions relies on grants or loans as a major source of financial support. Most students receive family support to cover tuition and fees or earn the money through self-employment. The ability to make these payments is reflected in per capita personal income. The ratio of tuition charges to per capita personal income suggests the degree to which tuition and ability to pay encourage attendance at 4-year institutions.

Data are not available to adjust tuition and fees to account for the amount of institutional and State financial aid provided. Some States with relatively high tuition probably offer many scholarships and loans, whereas other States with low tuition may provide students comparatively little in the way of financial aid.

Index 20—*Free-Access Education**** (percent of population within commuting distance of a free-access college)

The criteria for free-access employed by Warren W. Willingham[9] in developing this index are twofold: 1) There must be an annual tuition charge of no more than $400, and 2) at least one-third of the freshman class must be composed of students graduated in the lower half of their high school class. Of the 642 public 2-year colleges studied, 92 percent met these criteria; 31 percent of the 433 public 4-year colleges also qualified, but only 1 percent of the 1,362 private colleges could be considered in the free-access category. This index is a basic description of the accessibility of postsecondary education. It suggests the degree to which a State has assumed its formal responsibility to provide educational opportunity to *all* residents at low cost and within a reasonable commuting distance. It should be kept in mind that since some colleges may be slightly more selective than the free-access criteria allows, they have been excluded from this classification even though they play a very significant role in making higher education available. Data for this index are available only for 1968.

Index 21— *Resources Available To Provide Quality**** (current expenditures for instruction and departmental research per degree-credit student at public universities and 4-year colleges)

A good single indicator of the potential for overall excellence of degree-credit instructional programs provided by 4-year institutions is the amount spent per student for instruction and departmental research. The expenditure level generally reflects a number of conditions usually associated with quality instruction: better faculty to the extent higher salaries are offered, smaller class size (resulting in higher unit costs), modern (and often expensive) laboratory facilities and instructional equipment, and a large

[9] See Warren W. Willingham, *Free Access Higher Education*, College Entrance Examination Board, New York 1970.

library. Dollar input, however, only represents the *potential* for instructional quality; actual quality performance depends on many intangible factors as well as on instructional efficiency and local prices.

Naturally, dollar expenditures cannot reflect the many nonpurchasable contributions to excellence. Furthermore, dollar amounts are governed by the ratio of expensive to less expensive educational programs—a ratio that is the result of organization and emphasis rather than a reflection of quality. States do not depend equally on 2-year colleges, with their lower unit costs, to educate undergraduates. States with a high proportion of undergraduate enrollment in 2-year colleges naturally spend less per student overall than States in which 4-year institutions dominate. For this reason, 2-year colleges have been excluded from the index 21 measurement.

States also do not share equally the burden of graduate education, a task considerably more expensive than undergraduate education. Since the proportion of graduate students to undergraduate students influences overall unit expenditures, without directly indicating the quality at either level, interstate comparisons of index 21 should be limited to peer States with similar emphasis on graduate education (index 26).

The "instructional and departmental research" category includes all current expenditures by instructional departments, colleges, and schools of the institution, including expenditures for research not separately budgeted or financed. Included, then, are office expenses and equipment; laboratory expenses and equipment; and salaries of department heads, professors and other instructional staff (including student assistants), technicians, secretaries, clerks, etc.

Index 22—*Drawing Power from High School** (State residents enrolled for the first time in degree-credit undergraduate programs at public institutions in their home State as a percent of high school graduates of the State)

The percent of high school graduates who enter public colleges and universities in their home State gives some indication of the capacity, attractiveness, and accessibility of public higher education in a given State. In addition, the drawing power ratio reflects conditions during the elementary-secondary education period that encourage youths to attend college. As mentioned in the discussion of index 9, first-time college students constitute a larger population group than do high school graduates entering college; the former include many who enter college for the first time after a considerable time lapse following high school graduation. The first-time figures, however, do not include freshmen enrolled in extension centers or those in terminal occupational and general studies programs not usually leading to a bachelor's or higher degree. Data for this index are available only for 1963 and 1968.

Index 23—*Public Share of Resident Enrollment** (undergraduate residents of a State attending public institutions in their home State as a percent of all undergraduate residents of the State attending anywhere) (Only students enrolled in degree-credit programs are reported.)

This ratio suggests the degree to which public institutions within a State educate State residents enrolled anywhere as undergraduate students. States ranked high by this index demonstrate that their public institutions possess greater attractiveness and holding power than do private and out-of-State institutions. This attractiveness and holding power may be due to proximity, financial feasibility, or quality—or to all three. Data for this index are available only for 1963 and 1968.

Index 24—*Two-Year College Share of Enrollment** (degree-credit enrollment in public 2-year institutions as a percent of undergraduate degree-credit enrollment in all public institutions)

Few statistics in this series exhibit as remarkable a range among States as do those for 2-year college enrollment. In 1969–70, seven States had no public 2-year colleges. At the same time, the seven States with the largest number of undergraduates in 2-year colleges enrolled 1,040,339 students, or 26 percent of the Nation's total public degree-credit undergraduate population (3,986,496 students).

Most 2-year colleges not only have open-door admission policies but also emphasize programs that meet the educational needs of the community. About three out of four resident students attending 2-year colleges are enrolled in lower division baccalaureate courses, the credit for which may be transferred to 4-year institutions. This proportion, of course, varies from State to State. Approximately one out of four resident students is enrolled in occupational training, adult education, or some other type of non-degree-credit program. States with extensive 2-year college systems that provide much of the lower division undergraduate education programs (as opposed to 4-year institutions) will rank high with respect to index 23. States that rank lower are those in which such functions may be performed by or shared with 4-year institutions.

Many philosophical and practical considerations enter into determining the role assigned 2-year colleges in a State system of public higher education. Some of these considerations will be discussed in chapter V. At this juncture, it is necessary only to recognize that meaningful comparisons may not be possible among States which differ greatly in 2-year college enrollment.

Index 25—*Emphasis on Degree Programs** (bachelor's degrees awarded as a percent of undergraduate degree-credit enrollment in all public institutions)

This index suggests the relative emphasis that State institutions place on 4-year degree programs as opposed to 2-year associate degree programs, adult education, and terminal occupation studies. States tend to rank low in this index if they emphasize 2-year associate degree programs, adult education, and terminal occupational training, all of which have a low potential for producing college graduates. Contributing to a high ranking are heavy reliance on 4-year institutions with selective admission requirements and relatively high tuition charges, both of which discourage marginal applicants.

Index 26—*Emphasis on Graduate Programs** (graduate and first-professional enrollment as a percent of bachelor degrees awarded by all public institutions)

A retention measurement, this index suggests the attractiveness and accessibility of graduate education as well as the inclinations and qualifications of students to pursue advanced studies.

TABLES OF RANKED STATE DATA

The working components of this chapter are table II-1 (1970 data) and table II-2 (1960 data). In these two tables State data and State rankings for 26 indexes are organized into four sections: socioeconomic climate for support of education; elementary-secondary school achievement; financial support of higher education; and, public higher education—organization, emphasis, and achievement.

All indexes, except index 19 are ranked in order of descending values. Indexes not marked by an identifying asterisk measure *conditional* factors over which the State has little control; therefore, rank position should not be interpreted as a level of State achievement. Indexes identified with a triple asterisk (***) to a large extent measure situations *controllable* by the State; therefore, rank order does represent level of excellence. A single asterisk (*) identifies indexes 22 through 26, all of which measure factors largely controllable by the State, for which the quality level associated with rank position is largely a matter of interpretation based on intended emphasis.

Table II-3 presents selected socioeconomic and basic higher education data used to compile many of the indexes in table II-1 and II-2. Identified by alphabetic letters, the heading descriptions of many indexes in table II-1 and II-2 refer to these letter designations; e.g., index 2 = column (C) ÷ column (B) in table II-3.

The District of Columbia, wholly urban and unique in most respects, does not lend itself to ready comparison with the States. The District is included in the tables, however, because its higher education needs are substantial (the number of D. C. high school graduates is larger than that in three States) and because it deserves the kind of identification, analysis, and planning appropriate to many of the States. The national totals shown in all tables include the District of Columbia.

Detailed credit information appears in the footnotes following each table. The source numbers refer to entries in the list of sources for tables.

Table II-1.—State and D.C. rankings for comparative analysis of higher education: 1970

SOCIOECONOMIC CLIMATE FOR SUPPORT OF EDUCATION

Educational Attainment			Elementary-Secondary School Productivity***			College Educated		
1. Median school years completed by persons age 25 and over[1]			2. Public and nonpublic high school graduates as a percent of 17-year-old population, 1969–70 (C÷B)			3. Percent of persons age 25 and over with 4 or more years of college[2]		
1.	Utah	12.5 103	1.	Vermont	94.3 124	1.	D.C.	17.8 166
2.	Alaska	12.4 102	2.	North Dakota	92.4 122	2.	Colorado	14.9 139
	California	12.4 102	3.	Maine	91.6 121	3.	Alaska	14.1 132
	Colorado	12.4 102	4.	Wisconsin	90.5 119	4.	Hawaii	14.0 131
	Nevada	12.4 102	5.	Iowa	89.8 118		Utah	14.0 131
	Washington	12.4 102	6.	Minnesota	88.8 117	6.	Maryland	13.9 130
	Wyoming	12.4 102	7.	South Dakota	88.1 116	7.	Connecticut	13.7 128
8.	Arizona	12.3 102	8.	New Hampshire	86.0 113	8.	California	13.4 125
	Hawaii	12.3 102	9.	Montana	85.4 113	9.	Delaware	13.1 122
	Idaho	12.3 102	10.	Nebraska	85.3 113	10.	New Mexico	12.7 119
	Kansas	12.3 102	11.	Kansas	84.5 111		Washington	12.7 119
	Montana	12.3 102	12.	Hawaii	84.2 111	12.	Arizona	12.6 118
	Oregon	12.3 102	13.	Pennsylvania	83.8 111		Massachusetts	12.6 118
14.	Connecticut	12.2 101	14.	Idaho	83.1 110	14.	Virginia	12.3 115
	D.C.	12.2 101	15.	Wyoming	81.2 107	15.	New York	11.9 111
	Iowa	12.2 101	16.	Massachusetts	80.8 107	16.	New Jersey	11.8 110
	Massachusetts	12.2 101	17.	Utah	80.7 106		Oregon	11.8 110
	Minnesota	12.2 101	18.	Oregon	80.2 106		Wyoming	11.8 110
	Nebraska	12.2 101	19.	Michigan	79.2 104	19.	Vermont	11.5 107
	New Hampshire	12.2 101		Ohio	79.2 104	20.	Kansas	11.4 107
	New Mexico	12.2 101		Washington	79.2 104	21.	Minnesota	11.1 104
	Vermont	12.2 101	22.	Connecticut	78.7 104	22.	Montana	11.0 103
23.	Delaware	12.1 100	23.	Colorado	78.4 103	23.	New Hampshire	10.9 102
	Florida	12.1 100		Delaware	78.4 103		Texas	10.9 102

State		
Illinois	12.1	100
Indiana	12.1	100
Maine	12.1	100
Maryland	12.1	100
Michigan	12.1	100
New Jersey	12.1	100
New York	12.1	100
Ohio	12.1	100
Oklahoma	12.1	100
South Dakota	12.1	100
Wisconsin	12.1	100
UNITED STATES	12.1	100
36. North Dakota	12.0	99
Pennsylvania	12.0	99
38. Missouri	11.8	98
39. Virginia	11.7	97
40. Texas	11.6	96
41. Rhode Island	11.5	95
42. Alabama	10.8	89
Georgia	10.8	89
Louisiana	10.8	89
45. Mississippi	10.7	88
46. N. Carolina	10.6	88
Tennessee	10.6	88
West Virginia	10.6	88
49. Arkansas	10.5	87
S. Carolina	10.5	87
51. Kentucky	9.9	82

State		
25. New Jersey	78.1	103
Rhode Island	78.1	103
27. New Mexico	77.9	103
28. Oklahoma	77.0	102
29. West Virginia	76.9	101
30. California	76.8	101
UNITED STATES	75.8	100
31. Indiana	75.2	99
32. Missouri	75.1	99
33. Illinois	74.8	99
34. Maryland	73.8	97
35. New York	73.4	97
36. Arkansas	73.0	96
37. Virginia	71.9	95
38. Tennessee	70.4	93
39. Nevada	70.3	93
40. N. Carolina	69.1	91
41. Arizona	68.4	90
42. Alabama	68.3	90
43. Kentucky	67.5	89
44. Louisiana	67.2	89
45. Georgia	67.0	88
46. Mississippi	66.6	88
47. Texas	66.3	87
48. Alaska	65.9	87
49. S. Carolina	64.6	85
50. Florida	63.8	84
51. D.C.	59.2	78

State		
25. Nevada	10.8	101
Rhode Island	10.7	100
UNITED STATES		
26. Florida	10.3	96
Illinois	10.3	96
28. Idaho	10.0	93
Oklahoma	10.0	93
30. Wisconsin	9.8	92
31. Nebraska	9.6	90
32. Michigan	9.4	88
Rhode Island	9.4	88
34. Ohio	9.3	87
35. Georgia	9.2	86
36. Iowa	9.1	85
37. Missouri	9.0	84
Louisiana	9.0	84
S. Carolina	9.0	84
40. Pennsylvania	8.7	81
41. South Dakota	8.6	80
42. N. Carolina	8.5	79
43. Maine	8.4	79
North Dakota	8.4	79
45. Indiana	8.3	78
46. Mississippi	8.1	76
47. Tennessee	7.9	74
48. Alabama	7.8	73
49. Kentucky	7.2	67
50. West Virginia	6.8	64
51. Arkansas	6.7	63

NOTE.—Second column equals percent of U.S. average.
*** Condition controllable by State. Rank suggests level of achievement.

[1] Source 7, table 140.
[2] Ibid, table 137.

Table II-1.—State and D.C. rankings for comparative analysis of higher education: 1970—Continued

SOCIOECONOMIC CLIMATE FOR SUPPORT OF EDUCATION—Continued

Professional Occupations		Personal Income		Composite Climate Index	
4. Percent of employed persons in professional, technical, and kindred occupations[3]		5. Personal income per capita (I÷A)		6. Average of rankings for measurements 1 through 5	
1. Alaska	19.5 132	1. D.C.	$5,401 138	1. D.C.	122
2. D.C.	19.1 129	2. Connecticut	4,865 124	2. California	115
3. New Mexico	19.0 128	3. New York	4,771 122	Connecticut	115
4. Maryland	18.9 128	4. Nevada	4,599 117	4. Colorado	113
5. Delaware	18.3 124	5. New Jersey	4,598 117	Hawaii	113
6. Colorado	18.0 122	6. Hawaii	4,521 115	Maryland	113
7. Connecticut	17.5 118	7. Illinois	4,501 115	7. Delaware	112
8. California	17.4 118	8. California	4,443 113	8. Alaska	111
Massachusetts	17.4 118	9. Massachusetts	4,361 111	Massachusetts	111
10. Utah	17.2 116	10. Delaware	4,332 110	10. New York	109
11. New York	16.7 113	11. Maryland	4,265 109	11. New Jersey	108
Washington	16.7 113	12. Michigan	4,058 104	Utah	108
13. Arizona	16.6 112	13. Washington	4,004 102	Washington	108
14. New Jersey	16.1 109	14. Ohio	3,965 101	14. New Mexico	106
15. Virginia	16.0 108	15. Pennsylvania	3,921 100	15. Minnesota	105
16. Hawaii	15.9 107	UNITED STATES	3,920 100	Vermont	105
Vermont	15.9 107	16. Alaska (4592)	3,903[4] 100	17. Arizona	103
18. Minnesota	15.7 106	17. Rhode Island	3,902 100	Kansas	103
19. Wyoming	15.2 103	18. Kansas	3,825 98	19. Nevada	102
20. New Hampshire	14.9 101	19. Minnesota	3,815 97	New Hampshire	102
UNITED STATES	14.8 100	20. Colorado	3,806 97	Oregon	102
21. Oregon	14.5 98	21. Indiana	3,779 96	Wyoming	102
				23. Illinois	101
				Virginia	101

Table A

Rank	State	Value	Percent
22.	Texas	14.4	97
23.	Kansas	14.3	97
	Montana	14.3	97
25.	Illinois	14.2	96
	Michigan	14.2	96
	Nevada	14.2	96
28.	Oklahoma	14.1	95
29.	Louisiana	13.9	94
30.	Florida	13.8	93
	Ohio	13.8	93
	Pennsylvania	13.8	93
	Rhode Island	13.8	93
34.	Wisconsin	13.7	93
35.	Missouri	13.6	92
36.	Idaho	13.5	91
37.	North Dakota	13.3	90
38.	Nebraska	12.9	87
39.	Iowa	12.7	86
	South Dakota	12.7	86
41.	West Virginia	12.5	84
42.	Alabama	12.4	84
43.	Indiana	12.3	83
	Maine	12.3	83
	Tennessee	12.3	83
46.	Mississippi	12.2	82
47.	Georgia	12.0	81
48.	Kentucky	11.8	80
49.	S. Carolina	11.5	78
50.	N. Carolina	11.0	74
51.	Arkansas	10.8	73

Table B

Rank	State	Percent
22.	Nebraska	95
23.	Oregon	94
24.	Missouri	94
25.	Wisconsin	94
26.	Iowa	94
27.	Florida	93
28.	Virginia	92
29.	New Hampshire	91
30.	Arizona	91
31.	Wyoming	90
32.	Texas	90
33.	Vermont	88
34.	Montana	86
35.	Georgia	85
36.	Oklahoma	84
37.	Maine	83
38.	Idaho	82
39.	N. Carolina	82
40.	Utah	82
41.	South Dakota	81
42.	New Mexico	80
43.	Tennessee	79
44.	Kentucky	78
45.	Louisiana	78
46.	West Virginia	77
47.	North Dakota	76
48.	S. Carolina	75
49.	Alabama	73
50.	Arkansas	71
51.	Mississippi	66

Table C

Rank	State	Value	Percent
25.	Montana	3,738	100
	Wisconsin	3,700	100
	UNITED STATES	3,697	100
27.	Michigan	3,688	98
28.	Iowa	3,681	97
	Nebraska	3,643	97
	Ohio	3,616	97
	Pennsylvania	3,585	97
32.	Idaho	3,581	97
	Rhode Island	3,535	96
34.	Oklahoma	3,525	96
35.	Texas	3,457	95
36.	Florida	3,370	94
	Maine	3,334	93
	Missouri	3,300	93
	North Dakota	3,251	93
	South Dakota	3,222	93
41.	Indiana	3,208	93
42.	Louisiana	3,195	91
43.	Georgia	3,165	87
44.	N. Carolina	3,128	86
	Tennessee	3,084	83
	West Virginia	3,071	83
47.	Alabama	3,054	83
	S. Carolina	3,012	83
49.	Mississippi[4]	2,990	82
50.	Kentucky	2,934	82
51.	Arkansas	2,849	80
	—	2,791	79
	—	2,575	78

NOTE.—Second column equals percent of U.S. average.

[3] Source 7, table 167.

[4] Reduced 15 percent to make the purchasing power comparable to that in other high-price areas in the United States.

Table II-1.—State and D.C. rankings for comparative analysis of higher education: 1970—Continued

ELEMENTARY-SECONDARY SCHOOL ACHIEVEMENT

Financial Support Achievement*

7. Estimated current expenditures for public elementary and secondary schools per pupil in average daily attendence, 1969–70[5]

Rank	State	Value	Index
1.	New York	$1,250	162
2.	New Jersey	993	128
3.	Connecticut	991	128
4.	D.C.	977	126
5.	Alaska (1,141)	970[7]	125
6.	Vermont	969	125
7.	Delaware	899	116
8.	Hawaii	891	115
9.	Maryland	882	114
10.	Oregon	881	114
	Wyoming	881	114
12.	Rhode Island	879	114
13.	Iowa	872	113
14.	Pennsylvania	871	113
15.	Wisconsin	869	112
16.	Illinois	853	110
17.	Michigan	842	109
18.	Minnesota	810	105
	Montana	810	105
20.	Washington	777	101
	UNITED STATES	773	100
21.	Arizona	768	99

Holding Power*

8. Public high school graduates in 1969–70 as a percent of public school 9th-graders in fall 1966[6]

Rank	State	Value	Index
1.	Minnesota	92.4	117
2.	Iowa	90.4	114
3.	California	90.0	114
4.	Hawaii	89.0	113
5.	Maine	88.1	111
6.	Vermont	87.8	111
7.	Washington	87.7	111
8.	Wisconsin	87.2	110
9.	North Dakota	87.1	110
10.	South Dakota	87.0	110
11.	Pennsylvania	86.2	109
12.	Nebraska	86.1	109
13.	Kansas	84.2	106
	Massachusetts	84.2	106
15.	Idaho	83.7	106
16.	Michigan	83.4	105
17.	Ohio	82.6	104
18.	Utah	82.5	104
19.	Colorado	82.3	104
20.	Rhode Island	81.8	103
21.	Connecticut	81.7	103
22.	Oregon	81.4	103
23.	Delaware	81.1	103
24.	Alaska	81.0	102

Productivity*

2. Public and nonpublic high school graduates as a percent of 17-year-old population, 1969–70 (C÷B)

Rank	State	Value	Index
1.	Vermont	94.3	124
2.	North Dakota	92.4	122
3.	Maine	91.6	121
4.	Wisconsin	90.5	119
5.	Iowa	89.8	118
6.	Minnesota	88.8	117
7.	South Dakota	88.1	116
8.	New Hampshire	86.0	113
9.	Montana	85.4	113
10.	Nebraska	85.3	113
11.	Kansas	84.5	111
12.	Hawaii	84.2	111
13.	Pennsylvania	83.8	111
14.	Idaho	83.1	110
15.	Wyoming	81.2	107
16.	Massachusetts	80.8	107
17.	Utah	80.7	106
18.	Oregon	80.2	106
19.	Michigan	79.2	104
	Ohio	79.2	104
	Washington	79.2	104
22.	Connecticut	78.7	104
23.	Colorado	78.4	103
	Delaware	78.4	103

Rank	State	Value	%
22.	Nevada	761	98
23.	California	744	96
24.	Florida	738	95
25.	Massachusetts	736	95
26.	Kansas	726	94
	Ohio	726	94
28.	Colorado	719	93
29.	Missouri	716	93
30.	New Hampshire	700	91
31.	Indiana	698	90
32.	Virginia	697	90
33.	Louisiana	690	89
34.	Nebraska	678	88
35.	Maine	677	88
36.	New Mexico	659	85
37.	South Dakota	656	85
38.	North Dakota	652	84
39.	West Virginia	640	83
40.	Kentucky	612	79
41.	Utah	609	79
42.	S. Carolina	594	77
43.	N. Carolina	584	75
44.	Idaho	573	74
45.	Georgia	572	74
46.	Oklahoma	565	73
	Tennessee	565	73
48.	Arkansas	548	71
49.	Texas	537	69
50.	Mississippi	503	65
51.	Alabama	461	60

Rank	State	Value	%
25.	Wyoming	81.0	102
26.	New Jersey	80.2	101
27.	Montana	79.9	101
28.	New Hampshire	79.7	101
29.	Illinois	79.6	101
30.	Indiana	79.5	100
	UNITED STATES	79.1	100
31.	Oklahoma	78.9	100
32.	Maryland	78.6	99
33.	D.C.	78.4	99
34.	Arizona	77.1	97
35.	Missouri	77.0	97
36.	New York	76.3	96
37.	Virginia	76.1	96
38.	New Mexico	74.9	95
39.	South Carolina	73.8	93
40.	Nevada	73.7	93
41.	West Virginia	72.4	92
42.	Arkansas	71.7	91
43.	Florida	70.8	90
	Tennessee	70.8	90
45.	Texas	69.3	88
46.	North Carolina	69.1	87
47.	Alabama	68.2	86
48.	Kentucky	67.9	86
49.	Louisiana	67.6	85
50.	Georgia	66.0	83
	Mississippi	66.0	83

Rank	State	Value	%
25.	New Jersey	78.1	103
	Rhode Island	78.1	103
27.	New Mexico	77.9	103
28.	Oklahoma	77.0	102
29.	West Virginia	76.9	101
30.	California	76.8	101
	UNITED STATES	75.8	100
31.	Indiana	75.2	99
32.	Missouri	75.1	99
33.	Illinois	74.8	99
34.	Maryland	73.8	97
35.	New York	73.4	97
36.	Arkansas	73.0	96
37.	Virginia	71.9	95
38.	Tennessee	70.4	93
39.	Nevada	70.3	93
40.	N. Carolina	69.1	91
41.	Arizona	68.4	90
42.	Alabama	68.3	90
43.	Kentucky	67.5	89
44.	Louisiana	67.2	89
45.	Georgia	67.0	88
46.	Mississippi	66.6	88
47.	Texas	66.3	87
48.	Alaska	65.9	87
49.	S. Carolina	64.6	85
50.	Florida	63.8	84
51.	D.C.	59.2	78

Note.—Second column equals percent of U.S. average.
*** Condition controllable by State. Rank suggests level of achievement.

[5] Source 3, p. 36.
[6] Source 14, p. 15 and 16, and source 15.
[7] Reduced 15 percent to make the purchasing power comparable to that in other high-price areas in the United States.

Table II-1.—State and D.C. rankings for comparative analysis of higher education: 1970—Continued

ELEMENTARY-SECONDARY SCHOOL ACHIEVEMENT—Continued

College-Entrance Rate***			Composite Elementary-Secondary School Index***	
9. State residents enrolled for first time in college anywhere as a percent of high school graduates of the State, 1968			10. Average of rankings for measurements 7, 8, 2, and 9	
1. Arizona	88	152	1. New York	119
2. D.C.	81	140	2. Connecticut	113
3. California	75	129	3. Hawaii	112
4. Washington	73	126	4. D.C.	111
5. New York	71	122	Washington	111
6. Wyoming	70	121	Wyoming	111
7. Illinois	68	117	7. Arizona	110
8. Connecticut	67	116	8. California	110
Rhode Island	67	116	9. Iowa	109
10. Massachusetts	66	114	New Jersey	109
11. Florida	65	112	Rhode Island	109
12. Hawaii	64	110	12. Oregon	108
Kansas	64	110	13. Illinois	107
Mississippi	64	110	Minnesota	107
Oregon	64	110	15. Massachusetts	106
16. Idaho	62	107	North Dakota	106
North Dakota	62	107	Wisconsin	106
Oklahoma	62	107	18. Kansas	105
19. Colorado	61	105	Montana	105
Texas	61	105	Vermont	105
21. Nebraska	59	102	21. Nebraska	103
New Jersey	59	102	22. Michigan	102
23. Montana	58	100	Pennsylvania	102
			South Dakota	102

UNITED STATES	58	100
24. Utah	57	98
25. Missouri	56	97
26. South Dakota	55	95
27. Arkansas	54	93
Nevada	54	93
29. Iowa	53	91
30. Maryland	52	90
Minnesota	52	90
32. Michigan	51	88
Ohio	51	88
34. Alaska	50	86
New Mexico	50	86
36. Kentucky	49	84
Louisiana	49	84
38. Delaware	48	83
Wisconsin	48	83
40. Alabama	47	81
Virginia	47	81
42. Indiana	46	79
Tennessee	46	79
44. New Hampshire	45	78
45. Pennsylvania	43	74
46. West Virginia	42	72
47. Georgia	41	71
N. Carolina	41	71
49. S. Carolina	39	67
50. Maine	34	59
Vermont	34	59

25. Colorado	101
Delaware	101
27. Alaska	100
Maryland	100
UNITED STATES	100
29. Idaho	99
30. Ohio	98
31. Missouri	97
Utah	97
33. New Hampshire	96
Oklahoma	96
Florida	95
Maine	95
37. Nevada	94
38. Indiana	92
New Mexico	92
40. Virginia	91
41. Arkansas	88
42. Louisiana	87
Mississippi	87
Texas	87
West Virginia	87
46. Kentucky	85
47. Tennessee	84
48. N. Carolina	81
S. Carolina	81
50. Alabama	79
Georgia	79

NOTE.—Second column equals percent of U.S. average.

*** Condition controllable by State. Rank suggests level of achievement.

8 Source 18.

Table II-1.—State and D.C. rankings for comparative analysis of higher education: 1970—Continued

FINANCIAL SUPPORT OF HIGHER EDUCATION

Burden			Tax Capacity			Capacity-Burden Ratio		
11. Public and nonpublic high school graduates per 1,000 population, 1960–70 (C÷A)			12. Dollar amount of State tax capacity per capita as measured by "representative tax system"[9]			13. State tax capacity per high school graduate (12÷11)		
1. North Dakota	19.98	140	1. Nevada	$449	187	1. Nevada	$38,180	227
2. South Dakota	18.85	132	2. Wyoming	353	147	2. D.C.	35,604	212
3. Montana	18.18	127	3. D.C.	324	135	3. Florida	22,581	134
4. Utah	17.75	124	4. Delaware	293	122	4. Wyoming	21,062	125
5. Wisconsin	17.71	124	5. California	283	118	5. Alaska	20,898	124
6. Idaho	17.67	124	6. Connecticut	281	117	6. Delaware	20,110	119
7. Minnesota	17.63	124	7. New Hampshire	271	113	7. California	20,085	119
8. Iowa	17.58	123	8. Illinois	269	112	8. Connecticut	19,972	119
9. Vermont	17.52	123	9. New Jersey	257	107	9. Illinois	19,664	117
10. Maine	17.21	121	10. Texas	254	106	10. Texas	19,614	117
11. Wyoming	16.76	117	Washington	254	106	11. New York	19,342	115
12. New Mexico	16.59	116	12. Colorado	252	105	12. New Jersey	18,463	110
13. Nebraska	16.36	115	Michigan	252	105	13. Louisiana	18,235	108
14. Oregon	16.23	114	Oregon	252	105	14. Maryland	18,148	108
15. Kansas	16.00	112	15. Louisiana	250	104	15. Missouri	17,526	104
16. Hawaii	15.98	112	16. Nebraska	247	103	16. Rhode Island	17,280	103
17. Michigan	15.63	110	New York	247	103	17. Arizona	17,234	102
18. Pennsylvania	15.61	109	18. Florida	245	102	18. Colorado	17,155	102
Washington	15.61	109	Indiana	245	102	19. Massachusetts	16,959	101
20. West Virginia	15.45	108	Maryland	245	102	20. Oklahoma	16,897	100
21. Ohio	15.17	106	Montana	245	102	21. New Hampshire	16,874	100
22. New Hampshire	15.06	106	New Mexico	245	102			
23. Colorado	14.69	103	Oklahoma	245	102			
24. Indiana	14.59	102	24. Alaska	242	101			
						UNITED STATES	16,819	100

Rank	State	Value	% of U.S. avg.
25.	Delaware	14.57	102
26.	Oklahoma	14.50	102
27.	Massachusetts	14.27	100
	UNITED STATES	14.27	100
28.	California	14.09	99
29.	Connecticut	14.07	99
30.	New Jersey	13.92	98
31.	Arkansas	13.86	97
32.	Mississippi	13.83	97
33.	S. Carolina	13.79	97
34.	N. Carolina	13.77	96
35.	Louisiana	13.71	96
36.	Illinois	13.68	96
37.	Alabama	13.67	96
38.	Missouri	13.58	95
39.	Maryland	13.50	95
40.	Virginia	13.44	94
41.	Rhode Island	13.31	93
42.	Arizona	13.23	93
43.	Kentucky	13.23	93
44.	Tennessee	13.18	92
45.	Texas	12.95	91
46.	Georgia	12.85	90
47.	New York	12.77	89
48.	Nevada	11.76	82
49.	Alaska	11.58	81
50.	Florida	10.85	76
51.	D.C.	9.10	64

Rank	State	Value	% of U.S. avg.
25.	Massachusetts	242	101
26.	Kansas	240	100
27.	Ohio	240	100
	UNITED STATES	240	100
28.	Minnesota	238	99
29.	Missouri	238	99
30.	Iowa	235	98
31.	Vermont	235	98
32.	Rhode Island	230	96
33.	Arizona	228	95
34.	Idaho	226	94
35.	Wisconsin	226	94
36.	Pennsylvania	223	93
37.	North Dakota	218	91
38.	Hawaii	214	89
39.	Maine	209	87
40.	South Dakota	206	86
41.	Utah	206	86
42.	Virginia	206	86
43.	Georgia	204	85
44.	Kentucky	194	81
45.	N. Carolina	194	81
46.	Tennessee	194	81
47.	Arkansas	187	78
48.	West Virginia	185	77
49.	S. Carolina	178	74
50.	Alabama	175	73
51.	Mississippi	161	67

Rank	State	Value	% of U.S. avg.
22.	Indiana	16,792	100
23.	Washington	16,272	97
24.	Michigan	16,123	96
25.	Georgia	15,876	94
26.	Ohio	15,821	94
27.	Oregon	15,527	92
28.	Virginia	15,327	91
29.	Nebraska	15,098	90
30.	Kansas	15,000	89
31.	New Mexico	14,768	88
32.	Tennessee	14,719	88
33.	Kentucky	14,664	87
34.	Pennsylvania	14,286	85
35.	N. Carolina	14,089	84
36.	Minnesota	13,500	80
37.	Arkansas	13,492	80
38.	Montana	13,476	80
39.	Vermont	13,413	80
40.	Hawaii	13,392	80
41.	Iowa	13,367	79
42.	S. Carolina	12,908	77
43.	Alabama	12,802	76
44.	Idaho	12,790	76
45.	Wisconsin	12,761	76
46.	Maine	12,144	72
47.	West Virginia	11,974	71
48.	Mississippi	11,641	69
49.	Utah	11,606	69
50.	South Dakota	10,928	65
51.	North Dakota	10,911	65

NOTE.—Second column equals percent of U.S. average.

[9] Source 1 (see text for computation).

Table II-1.—State and D.C. rankings for comparative analysis of higher education: 1970—Continued

FINANCIAL SUPPORT OF HIGHER EDUCATION—Continued

Tax Effort***		Allocation to Higher Education***			Achievement Relative to Burden***		
14. Ratio of tax revenue collected to tax capacity (J/A ÷ 12)		15. Appropriation of State tax funds for higher education operating expenses as a percent of State tax revenue, 1969–70 (K ÷ J)			16. Appropriation of State tax funds for higher education operating expenses per high school graduate, 1969–70 (K ÷ C)		
1. Hawaii	213	1. Montana	20.74	163	1. Washington	$3,587	169
2. D.C.	160	2. Oregon	20.36	160	2. Hawaii	3,395	160
3. Mississippi	140	3. Idaho	19.16	151	3. Alaska (3,396)	2,887[10]	136
4. New York	138	4. North Dakota	19.13	151	4. Arizona	2,799	132
5. Wisconsin	135	5. Washington	18.57	146	5. Florida	2,693	127
6. Vermont	131	6. Colorado	18.53	146	6. New York	2,692	127
7. N. Carolina	124	7. Nebraska	18.51	146	7. Colorado	2,687	127
8. Delaware	123	Kansas	18.51	146	8. California	2,664	126
9. West Virginia	122	9. Wyoming	17.38	137	9. Illinois	2,664	126
10. Alaska	121	10. Texas	17.22	136	10. Wyoming	2,637	125
S. Carolina	121	11. Iowa	16.17	127	11. Oregon	2,584	122
Washington	121	South Dakota	16.17	127	12. Nevada	2,571	121
13. Arizona	119	13. Utah	15.91	125	13. N. Carolina	2,514	119
14. Utah	115	14. Missouri	15.83	122	14. Idaho	2,371	112
15. Kentucky	114	15. Indiana	15.40	121	15. Texas	2,346	111
Maryland	114	16. N. Carolina	14.78	116	16. Rhode Island	2,288	108
Minnesota	114	17. West Virginia	14.29	113	17. D.C.	2,281	108
18. Illinois	110	18. Illinois	14.12	111	18. Kentucky	2,243	106
19. Ohio	109	19. Ohio	14.09	111	19. Kansas	2,215	105
20. Rhode Island	108	20. Florida	13.96	110	20. Michigan	2,202	104
21. Pennsylvania	107	21. Alaska	13.83	109	21. New Mexico	2,143	101
22. Michigan	106	Arizona	13.83	109	22. Utah	2,128	100
23. Georgia	103	23. California	13.63	107	23. Delaware	2,121	100
24. Massachusetts	102	24. Kentucky	13.58	107	24. Wisconsin	2,119	100

Rank & State	Value	% of U.S.
Virginia	102	
26. Maine	101	
UNITED STATES	100	
27. Arkansas	99	
California	99	
Idaho	99	
30. Illinois	97	
31. Iowa	96	
32. Louisiana	94	
33. Tennessee	92	
34. North Dakota	91	
35. Connecticut	88	
36. Florida	87	
37. Colorado	86	
38. Oregon	83	
South Dakota	83	
40. Oklahoma	82	
41. Kansas	81	
42. Indiana	80	
43. Montana	77	
44. Missouri	74	
45. New Jersey	73	
Wyoming	73	
47. Nebraska	72	
48. Delaware	69	
49. Nevada	68	
Texas	68	
50. Ohio		
51. New Hampshire	48	

Rank & State	Value	% of U.S.
25. Arkansas	13.56	107
26. New Mexico	13.21	104
27. Georgia	13.20	104
28. Michigan	13.02	103
UNITED STATES	12.70	100
29. Tennessee	12.69	100
30. Rhode Island	12.65	100
31. Minnesota	12.56	99
32. Maine	12.52	99
33. Wisconsin	12.44	98
34. Virginia	12.30	97
35. Hawaii	12.27	97
36. Oklahoma	11.86	93
37. Louisiana	11.84	93
38. New Hampshire	11.27	89
39. Alabama	11.03	87
40. Connecticut	10.81	85
41. New York	10.22	80
42. Vermont	10.01	79
43. Nevada	9.91	78
44. Mississippi	9.84	77
45. S. Carolina	9.81	77
46. New Jersey	9.48	75
47. Pennsylvania	9.00	71
48. Delaware	8.66	68
49. Maryland	8.51	67
50. Massachusetts	6.12	48
51. D.C.	4.01	32

Rank & State	Value	% of U.S.
UNITED STATES	2,118	100
25. Montana	2,117	100
26. Georgia	2,107	99
27. Iowa	2,046	97
28. West Virginia	2,042	96
29. Indiana	2,036	96
30. Missouri	2,007	95
31. Nebraska	1,993	94
32. Louisiana	1,989	94
33. Minnesota	1,912	90
34. North Dakota	1,883	89
35. Connecticut	1,882	89
Virginia	1,882	89
37. Arkansas	1,779	84
38. Maryland	1,740	82
39. Vermont	1,736	82
40. Tennessee	1,685	80
41. Oklahoma	1,605	76
42. Mississippi	1,560	74
43. Alabama	1,540	73
44. Maine	1,519	72
45. S. Carolina	1,492	70
46. Ohio	1,485	70
47. South Dakota	1,452	69
48. Pennsylvania	1,358	64
49. New Jersey	1,265	60
50. Massachusetts	1,051	50
51. New Hampshire	961	45

NOTE.—Second column equals percent of U.S. average of achievement. *** Condition controllable by State. Rank suggests level of achievement.

[10] Reduced 15 percent to make the purchasing power comparable to that in other high-price areas in the United States.

Table II-1.—State and D.C. rankings for comparative analysis of higher education: 1970—Continued

FINANCIAL SUPPORT OF HIGHER EDUCATION—Continued

	Achievement Relative to Enrollment***	
	17. Appropriation of State tax funds for higher education operating expenses per full-time-equivalent student in public institutions, 1969–70 (K ÷ D)	
1. Alaska (3,249)	$2,762[u]	204
2. New York	2,186	161
3. D.C.	2,058	152
4. N. Carolina	1,934	143
5. Illinois	1,893	139
6. Hawaii	1,797	132
7. Iowa	1,748	129
8. Connecticut	1,687	124
9. Rhode Island	1,684	124
10. Washington	1,682	124
11. Maine	1,606	118
12. Georgia	1,588	117
13. S. Carolina	1,558	115
14. Nevada	1,532	113
15. New Jersey	1,525	112
16. Kentucky	1,498	110
17. Idaho	1,497	110
18. Florida	1,493	110
19. Pennsylvania	1,479	109
20. Indiana	1,461	108
21. Virginia	1,437	106
22. Vermont	1,365	101
UNITED STATES	1,357	100

23.	West Virginia	1,315	97
24.	Texas	1,282	94
25.	Wisconsin	1,279	94
26.	Michigan	1,266	93
	Missouri	1,256	93
28.	Wyoming	1,243	92
29.	Delaware	1,236	91
30.	Minnesota	1,215	90
31.	Louisiana	1,211	89
32.	Arkansas	1,210	89
33.	New Mexico	1,189	88
34.	Nebraska	1,173	86
35.	Oregon	1,171	86
36.	Tennessee	1,140	84
37.	Maryland	1,138	84
	Montana	1,138	84
39.	Ohio	1,136	84
40.	Colorado	1,092	80
41.	Massachusetts	1,091	80
42.	California	1,087	80
43.	Kansas	1,068	79
44.	Alabama	1,045	77
45.	Utah	995	73
46.	Arizona	957	71
47.	North Dakota	913	67
48.	Mississippi	895	65
49.	New Hampshire	873	64
50.	South Dakota	872	64
51.	Oklahoma	777	57

NOTE.—Second column equals percent of U.S. average.

*** Condition controllable by State. Rank suggests level of achievement.

[11] Reduced 15 percent to make the purchasing power comparable to that in other high price-areas in the United States.

Table II-1.—State and D.C. rankings for comparative analysis of higher education: 1970—Continued

PUBLIC HIGHER EDUCATION—ORGANIZATION, EMPHASIS, AND ACHIEVEMENT

Absolute Magnitude of Need			Student Tuition and Ability To Pay***			Free-Access Education***		
18. Public and nonpublic high school graduates, 1969–70 (C)			19. Average tuition at public universities and 4-year colleges per $1,000 personal income per capita, 1960–70 (N÷5)			20. Percent of population within commuting distance of a free-access college, fall 1968[2]		
1. California	281,208	9.7	1. D.C.	18.1	19	1. Connecticut	87	207
2. New York	232,300	8.0	2. Hawaii	25.0	26	2. D.C.	82	195
3. Pennsylvania	184,100	6.3	3. Massachusetts	38.5	40	3. N. Carolina	68	162
4. Ohio	161,548	5.6	4. Texas	39.7	42	4. Mississippi	65	155
5. Illinois	152,064	5.2	5. West Virginia	48.1	51	5. Florida	64	152
6. Texas	144,946	5.0	6. Illinois	50.4	53	6. California	60	143
7. Michigan	138,700	4.8	7. Idaho	52.5	55	7. Maryland	57	136
8. New Jersey	99,798	3.4	8. California	57.4	60	8. Alabama	56	133
9. Massachusetts	81,165	2.8	9. Alaska	58.2	61	Illinois	56	133
10. Wisconsin	78,253	2.7	10. New York	58.3	61	S. Carolina	56	133
11. Indiana	75,784	2.6	11. Connecticut	60.2	63	11. West Virginia	54	129
12. Florida	73,678	2.5	12. Washington	60.4	63	12. Kentucky	52	124
13. N. Carolina	69,986	2.4	13. Nevada	73.9	78	Massachusetts	52	124
14. Minnesota	67,080	2.3	14. Kansas	76.6	80	14. Washington	51	121
15. Missouri	63,515	2.2	15. New Jersey	81.3	85	15. Virginia	50	119
16. Virginia	62,462	2.2	16. Louisiana	82.2	86	16. Oregon	49	117
17. Georgia	58,959	2.0	17. Montana	82.5	87	17. Hawaii	48	114
18. Washington	53,225	1.8	18. New Mexico	89.5	94	Louisiana	48	114
19. Maryland	52,962	1.8	19. Oklahoma	91.2	96	19. Wisconsin	47	112
20. Tennessee	51,700	1.8	Minnesota	91.2	96	20. New Hampshire	44	105
21. Louisiana	49,941	1.7	21. Missouri	93.6	98	21. Arkansas	43	102
22. Iowa	49,663	1.7	22. Rhode Island	95.1	99	Kansas	43	102
23. Alabama	47,086	1.6				Wyoming	43	102
24. Connecticut	42,655	1.5	UNITED STATES	95.2	100	24. Colorado	42	100

Rank	State	Value	%
25.	Kentucky	42,573	1.5
26.	Oklahoma	37,093	1.3
27.	Kansas	35,994	1.2
28.	S. Carolina	35,740	1.2
29.	Oregon	33,936	1.2
30.	Colorado	32,412	1.1
31.	Mississippi	30,653	1.1
32.	West Virginia	26,939	.9
33.	Arkansas	26,768	.9
34.	Nebraska	24,280	.8
35.	Arizona	23,440	.8
36.	Utah	18,795	.6
37.	Maine	17,103	.6
38.	New Mexico	16,860	.6
39.	Rhode Island	12,646	.4
40.	Montana	12,620	.4
41.	Idaho	12,596	.4
42.	South Dakota	12,557	.4
43.	North Dakota	12,350	.4
44.	Hawaii	12,307	.4
45.	New Hampshire	11,116	.4
46.	Delaware	7,985	.3
47.	Vermont	7,795	.3
48.	D.C.	6,880	.2
49.	Nevada	5,749	.2
50.	Wyoming	5,563	.2
51.	Alaska	3,497	.1
	UNITED STATES	2,899,025	100.0

Rank	State	Value	Index
23.	Oregon	95.7	101
24.	Maryland	100.4	105
25.	Delaware	101.3	106
26.	Nebraska	102.7	108
27.	Kentucky	107.1	112
28.	N. Carolina	112.8	118
29.	Florida	114.2	120
30.	Arizona	114.5	120
31.	Arkansas	119.0	125
32.	Tennessee	120.9	127
33.	Virginia	121.7	128
34.	Maine	123.0	129
35.	South Dakota	124.8	131
36.	Colorado	125.9	132
37.	S. Carolina	127.1	134
38.	Indiana	128.3	135
39.	Utah	129.9	136
40.	North Dakota	131.8	138
41.	Georgia	137.7	145
42.	Michigan	139.2	146
43.	Alabama	139.3	146
44.	Wisconsin	140.0	147
45.	Wyoming	147.4	155
46.	Pennsylvania	156.6	164
47.	Ohio	160.4	168
48.	Iowa	169.0	176
49.	Mississippi	195.0	205
50.	New Hampshire	221.8	233
51.	Vermont	230.0	242

Rank	State		
	UNITED STATES	42	100
25.	Missouri	41	98
	Rhode Island	41	98
	Tennessee	41	98
	Vermont	41	98
29.	Idaho	40	95
	Michigan	40	95
31.	Iowa	39	93
32.	Arizona	38	90
	New Jersey	38	90
	Texas	38	90
35.	New York	36	86
36.	Delaware	35	83
37.	Alaska	31	74
	Oklahoma	31	74
	Montana	31	74
40.	Georgia	30	71
	North Dakota	30	71
42.	Minnesota	29	69
43.	Pennsylvania	25	60
44.	New Mexico	22	52
45.	Utah	20	48
46.	Nebraska	16	38
47.	Ohio	12	29
	South Dakota	12	29
49.	Indiana	0	0
	Maine	0	0
	Nevada	0	0

NOTE.—Second column equals percent of U.S. average, except for subtable 18, where percent is of U.S. total.

*** Condition controllable by State. Rank suggests level of achievement.

[12] Source 22.

Table II-1.—State and D.C. rankings for comparative analysis of higher education: 1970—Continued

PUBLIC HIGHER EDUCATION—ORGANIZATION, EMPHASIS, AND ACHIEVEMENT—Continued

21. Resources Available To Provide Quality*** — Current expenditures for instruction per degree-credit student at public universities and 4-year colleges, 1969–70 (L÷M)

		Dollars	Index
1.	D.C.	$1,643	174
2.	Iowa	1,308	139
3.	Florida	1,265	134
4.	Wyoming	1,186	126
5.	S. Carolina	1,172	124
6.	Hawaii	1,163	123
7.	New York	1,123	119
8.	California	1,104	117
9.	Illinois	1,099	116
10.	Indiana	1,093	116
11.	Washington	1,079	114
12.	N. Carolina	1,062	112
13.	Vermont	1,052	111
14.	Michigan	1,039	110
15.	Pennsylvania	1,004	106
16.	Kentucky	971	103
17.	Georgia	965	102
18.	Ohio	962	102
19.	Wisconsin	960	102
20.	Colorado	954	101
	UNITED STATES	944	100
21.	Virginia	890	94

22. Drawing Power from High School* — State residents enrolled for first time in public institutions in their home State as a percent of high school graduates of the State, 1968[3]

		Percent	Index
1.	Arizona	79	198
2.	California	66	165
3.	Washington	62	155
4.	Wyoming	55	138
5.	Mississippi	52	130
	North Dakota	52	130
7.	Colorado	50	125
	Oregon	50	125
9.	Florida	49	123
	Kansas	49	123
	Oklahoma	49	123
	Texas	49	123
13.	Utah	45	113
14.	Montana	44	110
15.	Illinois	43	108
16.	Louisiana	42	105
	Nebraska	42	105
18.	Hawaii	41	103
	Michigan	41	103
	Missouri	41	103
	UNITED STATES	40	100
21.	Minnesota	39	98

23. Public Share of Resident Student Enrollment* — Undergraduate residents of State attending public institutions in their home State as a percent of all undergraduate residents of the State attending all colleges anywhere, 1968[a]

		Percent	Index
1.	Arizona	89	135
2.	California	87	132
3.	Louisiana	83	126
4.	Colorado	81	123
	North Dakota	81	123
	Washington	81	123
7.	Michigan	80	121
	Mississippi	80	121
	Oregon	80	121
	Utah	80	121
11.	New Mexico	79	120
12.	Oklahoma	78	118
	Texas	78	118
14.	Kansas	77	117
15.	Wisconsin	76	115
	Wyoming	76	115
17.	Alabama	75	114
	Montana	75	114
	West Virginia	75	114
20.	Minnesota	73	111
	Nebraska	73	111
22.	Florida	71	108
	Nevada	71	108
24.	Georgia	70	106

Rank	State	Value	%
22.	Montana	879	93
23.	Maryland	878	93
24.	Oregon	866	92
25.	Kansas	858	91
26.	Nebraska	850	90
27.	New Jersey	847	90
28.	Delaware	842	89
29.	Alabama	835	88
30.	Missouri	833	88
31.	Texas	817	87
32.	New Hampshire	799	85
33.	North Dakota	798	85
34.	Connecticut	794	84
35.	West Virginia	789	84
36.	New Mexico	772	82
37.	Minnesota	770	82
38.	Massachusetts	768	81
39.	Rhode Island	766	81
40.	Arizona	758	80
	Nevada	758	80
42.	Utah	750	79
43.	Mississippi	744	79
	Tennessee	744	79
45.	Maine	730	77
46.	Idaho	716	75
47.	Louisiana	682	72
48.	S. Dakota	677	72
49.	Arkansas	634	67
50.	Oklahoma	632	67
51.	Alaska (651)	553[14]	59

Rank	State		
	Nevada	39	98
	New York	39	98
25.	South Dakota	39	98
	Arkansas	38	95
	D.C.	38	95
	Idaho	38	95
	Wisconsin	37	93
29.	New Mexico	35	88
30.	Alabama	35	88
	Kentucky	35	88
	Ohio	32	80
33.	Indiana	32	80
	Maryland	31	78
35.	Tennessee	31	78
	West Virginia	30	75
37.	Iowa	30	75
	Rhode Island	27	68
39.	Georgia	26	65
40.	Connecticut	26	65
	Virginia	25	63
42.	N. Carolina	24	60
43.	Massachusetts	23	58
44.	Delaware	21	53
45.	New Hampshire	21	53
	New Jersey	21	53
	Pennsylvania	19	48
48.	Maine	18	45
49.	S. Carolina	17	43
50.	Alaska	16	40
51.	Vermont	15	38

Rank	State	Value	%
	Missouri	70	106
	Arkansas	69	105
26.	South Dakota	69	105
	Tennessee	69	105
29.	Indiana	67	102
	Kentucky	67	102
31.	Ohio	66	100
	UNITED STATES	66	100
32.	Hawaii	63	95
	N. Carolina	63	95
34.	Idaho	62	94
35.	Illinois	56	84
	Maryland	56	84
37.	Maine	55	83
38.	Virginia	54	82
39.	Iowa	52	79
	New York	52	79
41.	Vermont	51	77
42.	Delaware	50	76
43.	S. Carolina	48	73
44.	Pennsylvania	47	71
45.	New Hampshire	45	68
46.	Rhode Island	40	61
47.	Alaska	39	59
48.	Connecticut	37	56
49.	Massachusetts	34	52
50.	New Jersey	32	48
51.	D.C.	29	44

NOTE.—Second column equals percent of U.S. average.

* Condition controllable by State. Quality level associated with rank position is a matter of interpretation based on intended emphasis.

[13] Source 18.

[14] Reduced 15 percent to make the purchasing power comparable to that in other high-price areas in the United States.

Table II-1.—State and D.C. rankings for comparative analysis of higher education: 1970—Continued

PUBLIC HIGHER EDUCATION—ORGANIZATION, EMPHASIS, AND ACHIEVEMENT—Continued

24. 2-Year College Share of Enrollment*
Degree-credit enrollment in public 2-year colleges as a percent of undergraduate degree-credit enrollment in all public institutions, 1969–70 (E÷F)

	State	Value	Index
1.	California	62.7	207
2.	Florida	57.4	189
3.	New York	49.6	164
4.	Washington	46.7	154
5.	Illinois	42.4	140
6.	Wyoming	37.8	125
7.	Maryland	36.7	121
8.	D.C.	35.9	118
9.	Michigan	32.2	106
10.	Arizona	32.1	106
11.	Mississippi	30.7	101
	UNITED STATES	30.3	100
12.	Texas	29.6	98
13.	New Jersey	28.4	94
14.	Massachusetts	25.9	85
15.	Iowa	23.7	78
16.	Oregon	22.9	76
17.	Alabama	22.0	73
18.	Missouri	21.1	70
19.	Delaware	20.5	68
	Kansas	20.5	68
21.	Connecticut	20.3	67

25. Emphasis on Degree Programs*
Bachelor's degrees awarded as a percent of undergraduate degree-credit enrollment in all public institutions, 1969–70 (H÷F)

	State	Value	Index
1.	South Dakota	17.3	156
2.	S. Carolina	15.9	143
3.	N. Carolina	15.5	140
4.	West Virginia	15.4	139
5.	North Dakota	15.3	138
6.	Nebraska	15.2	137
7.	Arkansas	15.1	136
8.	Iowa	14.9	134
9.	New Hampshire	14.5	131
10.	Mississippi	14.4	130
11.	Alabama	14.3	129
	Maine	14.3	129
	Montana	14.3	129
14.	Kentucky	14.2	128
15.	Vermont	14.1	127
16.	Indiana	13.9	125
17.	Georgia	13.6	123
	Pennsylvania	13.6	123
19.	Louisiana	13.4	121
20.	Oklahoma	13.2	119
	Wisconsin	13.2	119
22.	Colorado	13.0	117
	Kansas	13.0	117
24.	Tennessee	12.9	116

26. Emphasis on Graduate Programs*
Ratio of graduate and first-professional enrollment in public institutions to bachelor's degrees awarded by public institutions, 1969–70 (G÷H)

	State	Value	Index
1.	Rhode Island	218.7	153
2.	Connecticut	209.4	147
3.	California	197.0	138
4.	New York	192.5	135
5.	Indiana	190.0	133
6.	Oregon	173.1	121
7.	Michigan	172.3	121
8.	New Jersey	169.6	119
9.	Maryland	166.2	117
10.	Arizona	163.5	115
11.	Iowa	160.0	112
12.	Illinois	159.3	112
13.	Virginia	155.4	109
14.	Nevada	149.6	105
15.	Pennsylvania	147.8	104
	UNITED STATES	142.6	100
16.	New Mexico	138.9	97
17.	Washington	133.0	93
18.	Massachusetts	132.9	93
19.	Kansas	130.6	92
20.	Kentucky	129.4	91
21.	Hawaii	128.2	90

Rank	State		
22.	Georgia	19.6	65
23.	Minnesota	15.6	51
24.	Pennsylvania	15.5	51
25.	Colorado	15.4	51
26.	Virginia	14.7	49
27.	Rhode Island	14.6	48
28.	N. Carolina	13.3	44
29.	Oklahoma	12.2	40
30.	Idaho	10.9	36
31.	North Dakota	9.2	30
32.	Ohio	7.7	25
33.	Nebraska	7.6	25
34.	Tennessee	6.9	23
35.	Utah	6.6	22
36.	Montana	6.2	20
37.	Wisconsin	4.9	16
38.	Arkansas	4.2	14
	New Mexico	4.2	14
40.	Louisiana	2.7	9
	Nevada	2.7	9
42.	Indiana	1.9	5
43.	West Virginia	1.5	5
44.	S. Carolina	1.0	3
45.	Alaska	0	0
	Hawaii	0	0
	Kentucky	0	0
	Maine	0	0
	New Hampshire	0	0
	South Dakota	0	0
	Vermont	0	0

Rank	State		
25.	Michigan	12.5	113
26.	Ohio	12.3	111
27.	Connecticut	12.2	110
	Utah	12.2	110
29.	Idaho	11.9	107
	Missouri	11.9	107
	Oregon	11.9	107
	Virginia	11.9	107
33.	Minnesota	11.6	105
	Wyoming	11.6	105
35.	Rhode Island	11.4	103
36.	New Mexico	11.3	102
37.	Massachusetts	11.1	100
	UNITED STATES	11.1	100
38.	Texas	11.0	99
39.	Illinois	10.4	94
40.	New Jersey	10.3	93
41.	Washington	10.2	92
42.	Arizona	10.0	90
43.	Hawaii	9.9	89
44.	Florida	9.7	87
45.	Maryland	9.3	84
46.	Delaware	9.0	81
	Nevada	9.0	81
48.	New York	8.2	74
49.	California	6.9	62
50.	Alaska	4.0	36
51.	D.C.	2.1	19

Rank	State		
22.	West Virginia	127.5	89
23.	Colorado	127.0	89
	Missouri	127.0	89
25.	Wyoming	125.4	88
26.	Delaware	121.7	85
27.	Wisconsin	120.2	84
28.	Florida	115.7	81
29.	Oklahoma	115.6	81
30.	Texas	114.9	81
31.	Ohio	114.2	80
32.	Utah	112.7	79
33.	N. Carolina	111.8	78
34.	Georgia	111.7	78
35.	Minnesota	110.1	77
36.	Tennessee	109.1	77
37.	Nebraska	96.7	68
38.	S. Carolina	94.7	66
39.	South Dakota	94.5	66
40.	D.C.	91.6	64
41.	Louisiana	89.1	62
42.	Alaska	84.2	59
43.	Alabama	77.3	54
44.	Maine	76.1	53
45.	Idaho	76.0	53
46.	Vermont	75.7	53
47.	Mississippi	67.6	47
48.	North Dakota	62.6	44
49.	Montana	57.9	41
50.	Arkansas	56.7	40
51.	New Hampshire	55.1	39

NOTE.—Second column equals percent of U.S. average.

* Condition controllable by State. Quality level associated with rank position is a matter of interpretation based on intended emphasis.

Table II-2.—State and D.C. rankings for comparative analysis of higher education: 1960

SOCIOECONOMIC CLIMATE FOR SUPPORT OF EDUCATION

Educational Attainment

1. Median school years completed by persons age 25 and over[1]

Rank	State		
1.	Utah	12.2	115
2.	Alaska	12.1	114
	California	12.1	114
	Colorado	12.1	114
	Nevada	12.1	114
	Washington	12.1	114
	Wyoming	12.1	114
8.	Idaho	11.8	111
	Oregon	11.8	111
10.	Kansas	11.7	110
	D.C.	11.7	110
12.	Massachusetts	11.6	109
	Montana	11.6	109
	Nebraska	11.6	109
15.	Arizona	11.3	107
	Hawaii	11.3	107
	Iowa	11.3	107
18.	New Mexico	11.2	106
19.	Delaware	11.1	105
20.	Connecticut	11.0	104
	Maine	11.0	104
22.	Florida	10.9	103
	New Hampshire	10.9	103
	Ohio	10.9	103

Elementary-Secondary School Productivity***

2. Public and nonpublic high school graduates as a percent of 17-year-old population, 1959–60 (C÷B)

Rank	State		
1.	Minnesota	79.3	122
2.	Iowa	77.1	119
3.	Nebraska	77.0	119
4.	Massachusetts	76.8	118
5.	Hawaii	76.6	118
6.	Oregon	76.2	117
7.	Wisconsin	75.6	116
8.	North Dakota	74.4	115
9.	South Dakota	73.6	113
	Utah	73.6	113
11.	Pennsylvania	73.0	112
12.	Washington	72.2	111
13.	Wyoming	71.9	111
14.	Oklahoma	70.7	109
15.	Connecticut	70.6	109
16.	Idaho	70.4	108
17.	Michigan	70.0	108
18.	Kansas	69.9	108
19.	California	69.7	107
20.	Ohio	69.1	106
21.	Montana	68.9	106
	New Hampshire	68.9	106
23.	New Jersey	68.2	105
24.	Indiana	67.8	104

College Educated

3. Percent of persons age 25 and over with 4 or more years of college[1]

Rank	State		
1.	D.C.	14.3	186
2.	Colorado	10.7	139
3.	Utah	10.2	132
4.	Delaware	10.1	131
5.	California	9.8	127
	N. Mexico	9.8	127
7.	Alaska	9.5	123
	Connecticut	9.5	123
9.	Maryland	9.3	121
	Washington	9.3	121
11.	Arizona	9.1	118
12.	Hawaii	9.0	117
13.	New York	8.9	116
14.	Massachusetts	8.8	114
15.	Wyoming	8.7	113
16.	Oregon	8.5	110
17.	New Jersey	8.4	109
	Virginia	8.4	109
19.	Nevada	8.3	108
20.	Kansas	8.2	106
21.	Texas	8.0	104
22.	Oklahoma	7.9	103
23.	Florida	7.8	101

Table 1

Rank	State	Value	% of U.S. avg.
	Vermont	10.9	103
26.	Indiana	10.8	102
	Michigan	10.8	102
	Minnesota	10.8	102
29.	New York	10.7	101
30.	New Jersey	10.6	100
	UNITED STATES	10.6	100
31.	Illinois	10.5	99
32.	Maryland	10.4	98
	Oklahoma	10.4	98
	South Dakota	10.4	98
	Texas	10.4	98
	Wisconsin	10.4	98
37.	Pennsylvania	10.2	96
38.	Rhode Island	10.0	94
39.	Virginia	9.9	93
40.	Missouri	9.6	91
41.	North Dakota	9.3	88
42.	Alabama	9.1	86
43.	Georgia	9.0	85
44.	Arkansas	9.0	84
45.	Mississippi	8.9	84
	N. Carolina	8.9	84
47.	Louisiana	8.8	83
	Tennessee	8.8	83
	West Virginia	8.8	83
50.	Kentucky	8.7	82
	S. Carolina	8.7	82

Table 2

Rank	State	Value	% of U.S. avg.
25.	New York	67.6	104
26.	Vermont	66.9	103
27.	Illinois	66.7	103
28.	Maine	66.0	102
29.	Colorado	65.7	101
30.	Missouri	65.6	101
31.	Delaware	65.5	101
	UNITED STATES	64.9	100
32.	West Virginia	64.3	99
33.	Rhode Island	62.7	97
34.	Nevada	60.7	94
35.	Arkansas	59.7	92
36.	D.C.	58.1	90
37.	Maryland	57.4	88
38.	New Mexico	56.7	87
39.	Florida	56.6	87
40.	Louisiana	55.7	86
41.	Tennessee	55.2	85
42.	Alabama	54.7	84
43.	Arizona	54.4	84
44.	N. Carolina	53.8	83
45.	Texas	52.8	81
46.	Kentucky	51.8	80
47.	Georgia	50.4	78
48.	Virginia	49.7	77
49.	Mississippi	49.2	76
50.	S. Carolina	46.3	71
51.	Alaska	41.9	65

Table 3

Rank	State	Value	% of U.S. avg.
	UNITED STATES	7.7	100
24.	Minnesota	7.5	97
	Montana	7.5	97
26.	Illinois	7.3	95
	Vermont	7.3	95
	Idaho	7.2	94
28.	New Hampshire	7.1	92
29.	Ohio	7.0	91
30.	S. Carolina	6.9	90
31.	Michigan	6.8	88
32.	Nebraska	6.8	88
	Louisiana	6.7	87
34.	Wisconsin	6.7	87
	Rhode Island	6.6	86
36.	Iowa	6.4	83
37.	Pennsylvania	6.4	83
	Indiana	6.3	82
39.	N. Carolina	6.3	82
	Georgia	6.2	81
41.	Missouri	6.2	81
	Alabama	5.7	74
43.	South Dakota	5.7	74
	Mississippi	5.6	73
45.	North Dakota	5.6	73
	Maine	5.5	71
47.	Tennessee	5.5	71
	West Virginia	5.2	68
49.	Kentucky	4.9	64
50.	Arkansas	4.8	62

Note.—Second column equals percent of U.S. average.
*** Condition controllable by State. Rank suggests level of achievement.

[1] Source 7.

Table II-2.—State and D.C. rankings for comparative analysis of higher education: 1960—Continued

SOCIOECONOMIC CLIMATE FOR SUPPORT OF EDUCATION—Continued

Professional Occupations

4. Percent of employed persons in professional, technical, and kindred occupations[2]

	State	%	Index
1.	Alaska	16.0	143
2.	D.C.	14.4	129
3.	New Mexico	14.2	127
4.	Delaware	14.0	125
5.	California	13.7	122
6.	Maryland	13.5	121
7.	Colorado	13.3	119
8.	Utah	13.0	116
	Washington	13.0	116
10.	Connecticut	12.9	115
11.	Massachusetts	12.8	114
12.	New York	12.5	112
13.	New Jersey	12.4	111
14.	Hawaii	12.1	108
	Wyoming	12.0	108
16.	Arizona	12.0	107
17.	Kansas	11.6	104
	Michigan	11.5	103
	Minnesota	11.5	103
	Virginia	11.5	103
21.	Oklahoma	11.4	102
22.	Montana	11.2	100
	UNITED STATES	11.2	100

Personal Income

5. Personal income per capita (I ÷ A)

	State	Income	Index
1.	D.C.	$3,017	136
2.	Nevada	2,856	129
3.	Connecticut	2,806	127
4.	Delaware	2,758	125
5.	New York	2,748	124
6.	California	2,709	122
7.	New Jersey	2,707	122
8.	Illinois	2,649	120
9.	Massachusetts	2,461	111
10.	Alaska (2,835)	2,410[3]	109
11.	Hawaii	2,380	107
12.	Washington	2,348	106
13.	Maryland	2,344	106
14.	Ohio	2,334	105
15.	Michigan	2,324	105
16.	Colorado	2,275	103
17.	Wyoming	2,261	102
18.	Pennsylvania	2,241	101
19.	Oregon	2,235	101
20.	Rhode Island	2,219	100
	UNITED STATES	2,215	100
21.	Indiana	2,188	99

Composite Climate Index

6. Average of rankings for measurements 1 through 5

	State	Index
1.	D.C.	130
2.	California	118
3.	Delaware	117
4.	Connecticut	116
5.	Colorado	115
6.	Washington	114
7.	Massachusetts	113
	Utah	113
9.	Alaska	111
	Hawaii	111
	New York	111
12.	Wyoming	110
13.	Nevada	109
	New Jersey	109
15.	Oregon	108
16.	Maryland	107
17.	New Mexico	106
18.	Kansas	105
19.	Minnesota	104
20.	Illinois	103
21.	Arizona	102
22.	Michigan	101
	Montana	101
24.	Nebraska	100

23. Oregon	11.1	99
Vermont	11.1	99
25. Nevada	11.0	98
26. Ohio	10.9	97
27. Texas	10.8	96
28. Illinois	10.7	96
Pennsylvania	10.7	96
30. Florida	10.3	92
Idaho	10.3	92
Louisiana	10.3	92
West Virginia	10.3	92
34. New Hampshire	10.2	91
35. Wisconsin	10.0	89
36. Nebraska	9.9	88
37. Indiana	9.8	88
Missouri	9.8	88
Rhode Island	9.8	88
40. Iowa	9.7	87
South Dakota	9.7	87
42. North Dakota	9.6	86
43. Maine	9.3	83
44. Tennessee	9.2	83
45. Alabama	9.0	80
46. Kentucky	8.9	79
47. Georgia	8.5	76
48. Arkansas	8.2	73
49. Mississippi	8.0	71
S. Carolina	8.0	71
51. N. Carolina	7.9	71

22. Wisconsin	2,176	98
23. Kansas	2,162	98
24. New Hampshire	2,144	97
25. Minnesota	2,115	95
26. Missouri	2,114	95
27. Nebraska	2,110	95
28. Montana	2,037	92
29. Arizona	2,032	92
30. Iowa	1,986	90
31. Utah	1,968	89
32. Florida	1,950	88
33. Texas	1,924	87
34. New Mexico	1,883	85
35. Oklahoma	1,861	84
36. Idaho	1,850	84
37. Maine	1,844	83
38. Vermont	1,842	83
39. Virginia	1,841	83
40. South Dakota	1,782	80
41. North Dakota	1,714	77
42. Louisiana	1,654	75
43. Georgia	1,639	74
44. West Virginia	1,594	72
45. Kentucky	1,575	71
46. N. Carolina	1,560	70
47. Tennessee	1,543	70
48. Alabama	1,488	67
49. S. Carolina	1,377	62
50. Arkansas	1,372	62
51. Mississippi	1,204	54

Ohio	100
UNITED STATES	100
26. Oklahoma	99
27. Idaho	98
New Hampshire	98
Pennsylvania	98
Wisconsin	98
31. Iowa	97
Vermont	97
33. Indiana	95
34. Florida	94
35. Rhode Island	93
Texas	93
Virginia	93
38. Missouri	93
39. South Dakota	91
40. Maine	90
41. North Dakota	89
42. Louisiana	88
43. West Virginia	85
44. Georgia	83
45. Alabama	79
North Carolina	78
Tennessee	78
48. Arkansas	75
Kentucky	75
S. Carolina	75
51. Mississippi	72

NOTE.—Second column equals percent of U.S. average.

² Source 7.

³ Reduced 15 percent to make the purchasing power comparable to that in other high-price areas in the United States.

Table II-2.—State and D.C. rankings for comparative analysis of higher education: 1960—Continued

ELEMENTARY-SECONDARY SCHOOL ACHIEVEMENT

Financial Support Achievement***			Holding Power***			Productivity***		
7. Estimated current expenditures for public elementary and secondary schools per pupil in average daily attendance, 1959-60[4]			8. Public high school graduates in 1959-60 as a percent of public school 9th-graders in fall 1956[5]			2. Public and nonpublic high school graduates as a percent of 17-year-old population, 1959-60 (C÷B)		
1. New York	$559	151	1. Wisconsin	81.7	119	1. Minnesota	79.3	122
2. New Jersey	497	135	2. California	79.5	116	2. Iowa	77.1	119
3. California	471	128	3. Minnesota	79.0	115	3. Nebraska	77.0	119
4. Delaware	460	125	4. Hawaii	78.6	114	4. Massachusetts	76.8	118
5. Alaska (530)	451[6]	122	5. North Dakota	78.6	114	5. Hawaii	76.6	118
6. Wyoming	450	122	6. Nebraska	77.5	113	6. Oregon	76.2	117
7. Oregon	441	120	7. Iowa	76.8	112	7. Wisconsin	75.6	116
8. Nevada	435	118	8. Wyoming	76.7	112	8. North Dakota	74.4	115
9. D.C.	433	117	9. Utah	76.2	111	9. South Dakota	73.6	113
10. Connecticut	430	117	10. South Dakota	75.8	110	Utah	73.6	113
11. Michigan	425	115	11. Oregon	75.3	110	11. Pennsylvania	73.0	112
12. Pennsylvania	404	109	12. Michigan	74.1	108	12. Washington	72.2	111
Minnesota	404	109	13. New Jersey	74.0	108	13. Wyoming	71.9	111
14. Illinois	402	109	14. Connecticut	73.2	107	14. Oklahoma	70.7	109
15. Montana	400	108	Massachusetts	73.2	107	15. Connecticut	70.6	109
New Mexico	400	108	16. Ohio	72.5	106	16. Idaho	70.4	108
17. Washington	393	107	17. Idaho	72.3	105	17. Michigan	70.0	108
18. Maryland	391	106	Montana	72.3	105	18. Kansas	69.9	108
19. Rhode Island	390	106	19. Washington	72.2	105	19. California	69.7	107
20. Wisconsin	385	104	20. Pennsylvania	72.1	105	20. Ohio	69.1	106
21. Colorado	382	103	21. Colorado	71.4	104	21. Montana	68.9	106
22. Louisiana	373	101	22. Rhode Island	69.8	102	New Hampshire	68.9	106
23. Arizona	370	100	23. Delaware	69.6	101	23. New Jersey	68.2	105
			24. Illinois	69.5	101	24. Indiana	67.8	104

	UNITED STATES	369	100
24.	Ohio	366	99
25.	Iowa	362	98
26.	Massachusetts	360	98
27.	Vermont	356	96
28.	Indiana	355	96
29.	New Hampshire	350	95
30.	Kansas	345	93
	South Dakota	345	93
	Utah	345	93
33.	North Dakota	335	91
34.	Missouri	331	90
35.	Texas	315	85
36.	Hawaii	313	85
37.	Florida	305	83
38.	Nebraska	300	81
39.	Oklahoma	292	79
40.	Maine	290	79
41.	Idaho	273	74
42.	Virginia	260	70
43.	Georgia	241	65
44.	West Virginia	240	65
45.	North Carolina	230	62
46.	Kentucky	217	59
47.	Tennessee	211	57
48.	Mississippi	209	57
49.	South Carolina	205	56
50.	Alabama	200	54
51.	Arkansas	191	52

25.	Kansas	69.1	101
	UNITED STATES	68.7	100
26.	New Hampshire	68.5	100
27.	Indiana	67.6	98
28.	Oklahoma	67.4	98
29.	Missouri	66.7	97
30.	Maine	66.5	97
31.	Vermont	66.4	97
32.	Florida	65.5	95
33.	New York	65.0	95
34.	Arizona	63.3	92
35.	Arkansas	63.3	92
36.	West Virginia	62.1	90
37.	Maryland	61.9	90
38.	Texas	61.0	89
39.	Alabama	60.7	88
40.	N. Carolina	60.1	87
41.	Mississippi	59.6	87
42.	Louisiana	59.3	86
43.	Nevada	59.1	86
	New Mexico	59.1	86
	S. Carolina	59.1	86
46.	Tennessee	58.8	86
47.	Kentucky	58.4	85
48.	Georgia	58.1	85
	Virginia	58.1	85
50.	Alaska	57.8	84
51.	D.C.	48.8	71

25.	New York	67.6	104
26.	Vermont	66.9	103
27.	Illinois	66.7	103
28.	Maine	66.0	102
29.	Colorado	65.7	101
30.	Missouri	65.6	101
31.	Delaware	65.5	101
	UNITED STATES	64.9	100
32.	West Virginia	64.3	99
33.	Rhode Island	62.7	97
34.	Nevada	60.7	94
35.	Arkansas	59.7	92
36.	D.C.	58.1	90
37.	Maryland	57.4	88
38.	New Mexico	56.7	87
39.	Florida	56.6	87
40.	Louisiana	55.7	86
41.	Tennessee	55.2	85
42.	Alabama	54.7	84
43.	Arizona	54.4	84
44.	N. Carolina	53.8	83
45.	Texas	52.8	81
46.	Kentucky	51.8	80
47.	Georgia	50.4	78
48.	Virginia	49.7	77
49.	Mississippi	49.2	76
50.	S. Carolina	46.3	71
51.	Alaska	41.9	65

NOTE.—Second column equals percent of U.S. average
*** Condition controllable by State. Rank suggests level of achievement.
[4] Source 4, p. 28.

[5] Sources 20; 21 (1959–60); and 22 (1956–57), p. 5.
[6] Reduced 15 percent to make the purchasing power comparable to that in other high-price areas in the United States.

Table II-2.—State and D.C. rankings for comparative analysis of higher education: 1960—Continued

ELEMENTARY-SECONDARY SCHOOL ACHIEVEMENT—Continued

College-Entrance Rate***			Composite Elementary-Secondary School Index***	
9. State residents enrolled for first time in college anywhere as a percent of high school graduates of the State, 1963?			10. Average of rankings for measurements 7, 8, 2, and 9	
1. California	80	157	1. California	127
2. Nevada	70	137	2. Wyoming	117
3. Illinois	63	124	3. New Jersey	113
4. Wyoming	63	124	Oregon	113
5. Idaho	62	122	5. Connecticut	111
6. D.C.	61	120	New York	111
7. Arizona	61	120	7. Illinois	109
8. Florida	61	120	Minnesota	109
9. Montana	59	116	Montana	109
10. Texas	57	112	Nevada	109
11. Washington	57	112	Washington	109
12. Connecticut	56	110	12. Massachusetts	108
13. Massachusetts	56	110	13. Utah	107
14. Utah	56	110	14. Iowa	105
15. Colorado	55	108	Michigan	105
16. Kansas	54	106	Nebraska	105
17. Nebraska	54	106	Wisconsin	105
18. Oklahoma	54	106	19. Colorado	104
19. Oregon	54	106	Delaware	104
20. New Jersey	53	104	South Dakota	104
21. Mississippi	52	102	22. Hawaii	103
22. Maryland	51	100	23. Idaho	102
23. North Dakota	51	100	Kansas	102
24. South Dakota	51	100	25. Pennsylvania	101

UNITED STATES	51	100
25. Missouri	50	98
26. Hawaii	48	94
27. Arkansas	47	92
28. Iowa	47	92
29. Kentucky	47	92
30. Alaska	47	92
31. New Mexico	47	92
32. New York	47	92
33. Louisiana	46	90
34. Rhode Island	46	90
35. Virginia	46	90
36. Delaware	45	88
37. Michigan	45	88
38. Minnesota	45	88
39. Ohio	45	88
40. Indiana	44	86
41. Tennessee	42	82
42. Wisconsin	41	80
43. New Hampshire	39	76
44. Pennsylvania	39	76
45. West Virginia	38	75
46. N. Carolina	36	71
47. Georgia	35	69
48. Vermont	35	69
49. S. Carolina	34	67
50. Alabama	32	63
51. Maine	31	61

26. D.C.	100
Ohio	100
UNITED STATES	100
28. Arizona	99
Rhode Island	99
30. Oklahoma	98
31. Missouri	97
32. Florida	96
Indiana	96
Maryland	96
35. New Hampshire	94
36. New Mexico	93
37. Texas	92
38. Alaska	91
Louisiana	91
Vermont	91
41. Maine	85
42. Arkansas	82
West Virginia	82
44. Mississippi	81
Virginia	81
46. Kentucky	79
47. N. Carolina	76
Tennessee	76
49. Georgia	74
50. Alabama	72
51. S. Carolina	70

NOTE.—Second column equals percent of U.S. average.
*** Condition controllable by State. Rank suggests level of achievement.

⁷ Source 19.

Table II-2.—State and D.C. rankings for comparative analysis of higher education: 1960—Continued

FINANCIAL SUPPORT OF HIGHER EDUCATION

Burden		Tax Capacity		Capacity-Burden Ratio	
11. Public and nonpublic high school graduates per 1,000 population, 1959–60 (C÷A)		12. Dollar amount of State tax capacity per capita as measured by "representative tax system"[28]		13. State tax capacity per high school graduate (12÷11)	
1. Utah	12.99 125	1. Nevada	$191 187	1. Nevada	$22,158 225
2. North Dakota	12.96 125	2. Wyoming	150 147	2. Alaska	20,236 206
3. Minnesota	12.79 123	3. D.C.	138 135	3. D.C.	19,799 201
4. Idaho	12.59 122	4. Delaware	124 122	4. Florida	13,016 132
5. Hawaii	12.42 120	5. California	120 118	5. Delaware	12,998 132
6. Iowa	12.22 118	6. Connecticut	119 117	6. Wyoming	12,931 131
West Virginia	12.22 118	7. New Hampshire	115 113	7. Texas	12,796 130
8. Oregon	12.14 117	8. Illinois	114 112	8. Maryland	11,620 118
9. Wisconsin	12.02 116	9. New Jersey	109 107	9. California	11,605 118
10. South Dakota	11.91 115	10. Texas	108 106	10. Louisiana	11,265 114
11. Massachusetts	11.83 114	Washington	108 106	11. New Mexico	11,195 114
12. Pennsylvania	11.78 114	12. Colorado	107 105	12. Illinois	11,166 113
13. Oklahoma	11.69 113	Michigan	107 105	13. Arizona	11,086 113
14. Wyoming	11.60 112	Oregon	107 105	14. Connecticut	10,917 111
15. Vermont	11.57 112	15. Louisiana	106 104	15. Colorado	10,797 110
16. Nebraska	11.50 111	16. Nebraska	105 103	16. New York	10,628 108
17. Montana	11.40 110	New York	105 103	17. Virginia	10,602 108
18. Michigan	11.28 109	18. Florida	104 102	18. New Hampshire	10,550 107
19. Washington	11.16 108	Indiana	104 102	19. New Jersey	10,511 107
20. Maine	10.92 105	Maryland	104 102	20. Rhode Island	10,166 103
21. Connecticut	10.90 105	Montana	104 102	21. Missouri	10,010 103
New Hampshire	10.90 105	New Mexico	104 102		
23. Arkansas	10.88 105	Oklahoma	104 102	UNITED STATES	9,846 100
24. Indiana	10.78 104	24. Alaska	103 101		

Rank	State	Value	%
22.	Washington	9,677	98
23.	Georgia	9,667	98
24.	Indiana	9,647	98
25.	Kansas	9,586	97
26.	Ohio	9,533	97
27.	Michigan	9,486	96
28.	Nebraska	9,130	93
29.	Montana	9,123	93
30.	Oklahoma	8,896	90
31.	Kentucky	8,868	90
32.	Oregon	8,814	90
33.	Massachusetts	8,707	88
34.	Vermont	8,643	88
35.	Tennessee	8,530	87
36.	N. Carolina	8,210	83
37.	Iowa	8,183	83
38.	Maine	8,150	83
39.	Pennsylvania	8,065	82
40.	Wisconsin	7,987	81
41.	Minnesota	7,897	80
42.	S. Carolina	7,772	79
43.	Idaho	7,625	77
44.	South Dakota	7,389	75
45.	Arkansas	7,353	75
46.	Alabama	7,334	74
47.	Hawaii	7,327	74
48.	Mississippi	7,320	74
49.	North Dakota	7,176	73
50.	Utah	6,774	69
51.	West Virginia	6,465	66

Rank	State	Value	%
25.	Massachusetts	103	101
26.	Kansas	102	100
27.	Ohio	102	100
	UNITED STATES	102	100
28.	Minnesota	101	99
29.	Missouri	101	99
30.	Iowa	100	98
	Vermont	100	98
32.	Rhode Island	98	96
33.	Arizona	97	95
34.	Idaho	96	94
	Wisconsin	96	94
36.	Pennsylvania	95	93
37.	North Dakota	93	91
38.	Hawaii	91	89
39.	Maine	89	87
40.	South Dakota	88	86
	Utah	88	86
	Virginia	88	86
43.	Georgia	87	85
44.	Kentucky	83	81
	N. Carolina	83	81
	Tennessee	83	81
47.	Arkansas	80	78
48.	West Virginia	79	77
49.	S. Carolina	75	74
50.	Alabama	74	73
51.	Mississippi	58	67

Rank	State	Value	%
25.	Ohio	10.70	103
26.	Kansas	10.64	103
27.	New Jersey	10.37	100
	UNITED STATES	10.36	100
28.	California	10.34	100
29.	Illinois	10.21	99
30.	N. Carolina	10.11	98
31.	Alabama	10.09	97
	Missouri	10.09	97
33.	Colorado	9.91	96
34.	New York	9.88	95
35.	Tennessee	9.73	94
36.	S Carolina	9.65	93
37.	Rhode Island	9.64	93
38.	Delaware	9.54	92
39.	Louisiana	9.41	91
40.	Kentucky	9.36	90
41.	Mississippi	9.29	90
	New Mexico	9.29	90
43.	Georgia	9.00	87
44.	Maryland	8.95	86
45.	Arizona	8.75	84
46.	Nevada	8.62	83
47.	Texas	8.44	81
48.	Virginia	8.30	80
49.	Florida	7.99	77
50.	D.C.	6.97	67
51.	Alaska	5.09	49

a Source 1 (see text for computation).

NOTE.—Second column equals percent of U.S. average.

Table II-2.—State and D.C. rankings for comparative analysis of higher education: 1960—Continued

FINANCIAL SUPPORT OF HIGHER EDUCATION—Continued

Tax Effort***		Allocation to Higher Education***			Achievement Relative to Burden***		
14. Ratio of tax revenue collected to tax capacity (J/A ÷ 12)		15. Appropriation of State tax funds for higher education operating expenses as a percent of State tax revenue, 1959–60 (K÷J)			16. Appropriation of State tax funds for higher education operating expenses per high school graduate, 1959–60 (K÷C)		
1. Hawaii	220	1. Montana	17.30	225	1. Alaska (1,836)	$1,561[9]	207
2. D.C.	157	2. Nebraska	16.70	217	2. Nevada	1,498	199
3. Washington	151	3. North Dakota	15.41	200	3. Washington	1,473	195
4. S. Carolina	133	4. South Dakota	15.34	199	4. Montana	1,466	194
Utah	133	5. Oregon	13.79	179	5. Oregon	1,338	177
6. Louisiana	132	6. Utah	13.09	170	6. Louisiana	1,307	173
Mississippi	132	7. Iowa	13.02	169	7. Wyoming	1,289	171
8. Arizona	131	8. Idaho	12.75	166	8. New Mexico	1,263	168
9. Delaware	129	9. Kansas	12.11	157	9. Arizona	1,233	164
10. New Mexico	126	10. Wyoming	11.89	154	10. California	1,161	154
11. West Virginia	123	11. Indiana	11.38	148	11. North Dakota	1,143	152
12. N. Carolina	122	12. Illinois	10.79	140	12. Utah	1,135	151
13. Alaska	117	13. Michigan	10.46	136	13. Michigan	1,083	144
14. Oklahoma	115	14. Minnesota	10.26	133	14. Kansas	1,080	143
15. Alabama	114	15. Washington	10.18	132	15. Idaho	1,048	139
California	114	16. Oklahoma	9.81	127	16. Iowa	1,027	136
17. Wisconsin	113	17. New Hampshire	9.50	123	17. Florida	1,021	135
18. New York	112	18. West Virginia	9.40	122	18. South Dakota	1,002	133
Vermont	112	19. New Mexico	9.06	118	19. Colorado	993	132
20. Arkansas	111	20. Colorado	8.97	116	Oklahoma	993	132
21. Michigan	110	21. Texas	8.96	116	21. Nebraska	938	124
Oregon	110	22. California	8.89	115	22. Indiana	905	120
23. Georgia	108	23. Wisconsin	8.88	115	23. Texas	879	117
Idaho	108	24. Louisiana	8.85	115	24. Illinois	878	116

Rank	State		
	Maryland	108	
26.	North Dakota	104	
	Rhode Island	104	
	Tennessee	104	
29.	Colorado	103	
	Florida	103	
	Minnesota	103	
32.	Maine	101	
	UNITED STATES	100	
33.	Iowa	97	
	Pennsylvania	97	
35.	Kansas	93	
	Massachusetts	93	
	Montana	93	
38.	Kentucky	92	
39.	South Dakota	89	
40.	Ohio	88	
41.	Virginia	85	
	Wyoming	85	
43.	Indiana	83	
44.	Nevada	81	
45.	Connecticut	80	
46.	Texas	76	
47.	Illinois	74	
48.	Missouri	72	
49.	Nebraska	62	
50.	New Hampshire	61	
51.	New Jersey	55	

Rank	State		
25.	Virginia	8.76	114
26.	Arkansas	8.57	111
27.	Arizona	8.51	111
28.	Nevada	8.20	106
29.	Missouri	7.90	103
30.	Alaska	7.79	101
31.	Alabama	7.78	101
	Mississippi	7.78	101
33.	Florida	7.74	101
	UNITED STATES	7.70	100
34.	Vermont	7.50	97
35.	Maryland	6.93	90
36.	Kentucky	6.54	85
37.	Georgia	6.52	85
38.	N. Carolina	6.19	80
39.	New Jersey	6.02	78
40.	Tennessee	5.59	73
41.	Delaware	5.27	68
42.	Rhode Island	5.21	68
43.	Connecticut	5.16	67
44.	S. Carolina	5.14	67
45.	Ohio	4.96	64
46.	Pennsylvania	4.21	55
47.	New York	4.01	52
48.	Hawaii	3.99	52
49.	Maine	3.87	50
50.	Massachusetts	2.48	32
51.	D.C.	.66	9

Rank	State		
25.	Delaware	877	116
26.	Maryland	858	114
27.	Minnesota	829	110
28.	Wisconsin	797	106
29.	Virginia	776	103
	UNITED STATES	754	100
30.	Mississippi	748	99
31.	West Virginia	744	99
32.	Vermont	724	96
33.	Arkansas	697	92
34.	Georgia	678	90
35.	Alabama	646	86
36.	Hawaii	630	84
37.	N. Carolina	617	82
38.	New Hampshire	601	80
39.	Missouri	568	75
40.	Rhode Island	540	72
41.	S. Carolina	527	70
42.	Kentucky	526	70
43.	Tennessee	490	65
44.	New York	474	63
45.	Connecticut	444	59
46.	Ohio	417	55
47.	New Jersey	349	46
48.	Pennsylvania	326	43
49.	Maine	317	42
50.	Massachusetts	200	27
51.	D.C.	21	3

NOTE.—Second column equals percent of U.S. average. Rank suggests level of achievement.

*** Condition controllable by State.

[9] Reduced 15 percent to make the purchasing power comparable to that in other high-price areas in the United States.

Table II-2.—State and D.C. rankings for comparative analysis of higher education: 1960—Continued

FINANCIAL SUPPORT OF HIGHER EDUCATION—Continued

Achievement Relative to Enrollment***

17. Appropriation of State tax funds for higher education operating expenses per degree-credit student in public institutions, 1959–60 (K÷D)

1. Iowa	$1,281	180
2. Pennsylvania	1,138	160
3. Montana	1,085	152
4. Illinois	1,059	149
5. Florida	1,038	146
6. Idaho	1,034	145
7. Louisiana	1,033	145
8. Nevada	993	139
9. Washington	990	139
10. Oregon	928	130
11. Indiana	871	122
12. D.C.	842	118
13. Maryland	821	115
14. Vermont	806	113
15. Arkansas	805	113
Michigan	805	113
17. South Dakota	789	111
18. Wisconsin	788	111
19. West Virginia	787	111
20. N. Carolina	772	108
21. Georgia	760	107
22. Wyoming	755	106
23. North Dakota	742	104
N. York	714	100

25. Virginia	712	100
UNITED STATES	712	100
26. Minnesota	711	100
27. New Mexico	709	100
28. Connecticut	682	96
S. Carolina	682	96
30. Missouri	678	95
31. Nebraska	675	95
32. Delaware	668	94
33. Utah	667	94
34. New Hampshire	659	93
35. Alaska (763)	649[10]	91
36. Alabama	635	89
37. Rhode Island	632	89
38. Oklahoma	625	88
39. Massachusetts	624	88
40. Kansas	615	86
41. New Jersey	572	80
42. Mississippi	567	80
43. California	564	79
44. Hawaii	563	79
45. Texas	546	77
46. Kentucky	541	76
47. Colorado	501	70
48. Ohio	483	68
49. Tennessee	480	67
50. Maine	457	64
51. Arizona	440	62

NOTE.—Second column equals percent of U.S. average.
*** Condition controllable by State. Rank suggests level of achievement.

[10] Reduced 15 percent to make the purchasing power comparable to that in other high-price areas in the United States.

Table II-2.—State and D.C. rankings for comparative analysis of higher education: 1960—Continued

PUBLIC HIGHER EDUCATION—ORGANIZATION, EMPHASIS, AND ACHIEVEMENT

Absolute Magnitude of Need		Student Tuition and Ability To Pay***			Free-Access Education***	
18. Public and nonpublic high school graduates, 1959–60 (C)		19. Average tuition at public universities and 4-year colleges per $1,000 personal income per capita, 1959–60 (N÷5)			20. Percent of population within commuting distance of a free-access college	
1. New York	165,736	8.9	1. D.C.	24.5	29	No data available for 1960.
2. California	162,515	8.7	2. Alaska	27.0	32	
3. Pennsylvania	133,353	7.2	3. Louisiana	33.3	39	
4. Ohio	103,864	5.6	4. Connecticut	33.5	39	
5. Illinois	102,891	5.5	5. New York	34.6	41	
6. Michigan	88,240	4.7	6. Illinois	50.6	59	
7. Texas	80,817	4.3	7. Washington	54.5	64	
8. New Jersey	62,911	3.4	8. Nevada	58.8	69	
9. Massachusetts	60,890	3.3	9. California	59.1	69	
10. Indiana	50,256	2.7	10. Idaho	59.5	70	
11. Wisconsin	47,485	2.6	11. S. Carolina	60.3	71	
12. N. Carolina	46,077	2.5	12. Florida	65.6	77	
13. Minnesota	43,654	2.3	13. Missouri	67.2	79	
14. Missouri	43,581	2.3	14. Massachusetts	67.9	80	
15. Florida	39,562	2.1	15. Oregon	72.0	84	
16. Georgia	35,490	1.9	16. Rhode Island	73.5	86	
17. Tennessee	34,721	1.9	17. Delaware	75.1	88	
18. Iowa	33,704	1.8	18. Montana	77.1	90	
19. Alabama	32,950	1.8	19. West Virginia	77.2	91	
20. Virginia	32,915	1.8	20. Kansas	79.1	93	
21. Washington	31,843	1.7	21. New Mexico	80.5	94	
22. Louisiana	30,641	1.6	22. Oklahoma	83.8	98	
23. Kentucky	28,435	1.5	23. Indiana	85.0	99	
24. Maryland	27,745	1.5				

Rank. State	%	Number
25. Connecticut	1.5	27,639
26. Oklahoma	1.5	27,216
27. Kansas	1.2	23,191
28. S. Carolina	1.2	22,988
29. West Virginia	1.2	22,737
30. Oregon	1.2	21,470
31. Mississippi	1.1	20,223
32. Arkansas	1.0	19,439
33. Colorado	.9	17,387
34. Nebraska	.9	16,227
35. Utah	.6	11,578
36. Arizona	.6	11,391
37. Maine	.6	10,589
38. New Mexico	.5	8,838
39. Idaho	.5	8,396
40. Rhode Island	.4	8,284
41. North Dakota	.4	8,193
42. South Dakota	.4	8,113
43. Hawaii	.4	7,864
44. Montana	.4	7,662
45. New Hampshire	.4	6,615
46. D.C.	.3	5,324
47. Vermont	.2	4,511
48. Delaware	.2	4,254
49. Wyoming	.2	3,829
50. Nevada	.1	2,458
51. Alaska	.1	1,150
UNITED STATES	100.0	1,858,023

Rank. State		
UNITED STATES	85.3	100
24. New Jersey	85.3	100
25. Texas	86.3	101
26. Hawaii	87.0	102
27. Maryland	87.5	103
28. Nebraska	89.6	105
29. Minnesota	94.6	111
30. North Dakota	96.3	113
31. Arizona	103.3	121
32. Michigan	104.1	122
33. Utah	107.2	126
34. Ohio	108.0	127
35. Wisconsin	108.5	127
36. Iowa	110.8	130
37. Colorado	113.4	133
38. Wyoming	115.9	136
39. Tennessee	119.2	138
40. Alabama	120.3	141
41. Kentucky	130.2	153
42. Arkansas	145.0	170
43. New Hampshire	150.7	177
44. South Dakota	155.4	182
45. Georgia	155.6	182
46. Maine	157.3	184
47. Virginia	162.4	190
48. N. Carolina	172.4	202
49. Mississippi	180.2	211
50. Pennsylvania	183.0	215
51. Vermont	330.1	387

NOTE.—Second column equals percent of U.S. average, except for subtable 18, where percent is of U.S. total.

*** Condition controllable by State. Rank suggests level of achievement.

Table II-2.—State and D.C. rankings for comparative analysis of higher education: 1960—Continued

PUBLIC HIGHER EDUCATION—ORGANIZATION, EMPHASIS, AND ACHIEVEMENT—Continued

Resources Available To Provide Quality***

21. Current expenditures for instruction per degree-credit student at public universities and 4-year colleges, 1959–60 (L÷M)

1. Vermont	$850	151
2. D.C.	848	150
3. Iowa	781	138
4. Michigan	743	132
5. Illinois	740	131
6. Montana	734	130
7. Wyoming	718	127
8. Idaho	700	124
9. Nevada	653	116
10. California	649	115
11. N. Carolina	638	113
12. South Dakota	629	112
13. Indiana	625	111
14. Ohio	618	110
15. Washington	611	108
16. Louisiana	607	108
17. Utah	597	106
18. Florida	596	106
19. New York	593	105
20. Arkansas	571	101
UNITED STATES	564	100
21. Kansas	550	98
22. Wisconsin	547	97

Drawing Power from High School*

22. State residents enrolled for first time in public institutions in their home State as a percent of high school graduates of the State, 1963[1]

1. California	71	229
2. Arizona	52	168
3. Nevada	49	158
4. Wyoming	46	148
5. Texas	42	135
Utah	42	135
Washington	42	135
8. Colorado	41	132
Florida	41	132
Oklahoma	41	132
11. Mississippi	40	129
Montana	40	129
North Dakota	40	129
14. Kansas	39	126
15. Louisiana	37	119
Nebraska	37	119
17. Idaho	36	116
18. Oregon	35	113
19. Illinois	34	110
20. Michigan	33	106
South Dakota	33	106
22. New Mexico	32	106
23. Missouri	31	100
UNITED STATES	31	100

Public Share of Resident Student Enrollment*

23. Undergraduate residents of State attending public institutions in their home State as a percent of all undergraduate residents of the State attending all colleges anywhere, 1963[1]

1. Arizona	88	152
2. California	85	147
3. Louisiana	78	134
4. North Dakota	77	133
5. Utah	76	131
Mississippi	76	131
7. Oklahoma	75	129
Texas	75	129
9. New Mexico	73	126
10. Kansas	72	124
Michigan	72	124
Nevada	72	124
13. Colorado	71	122
Washington	71	122
15. Wyoming	70	121
16. Montana	69	119
17. West Virginia	68	118
18. Minnesota	67	116
Nebraska	67	116
Wisconsin	67	116
Oregon	67	116
22. Florida	62	107
Arkansas	62	107
South Dakota	62	107
25. Alabama	60	104

Note.—Second column equals percent of U.S. average.

Rank	State		
23.	Pennsylvania	546	97
24.	Minnesota	544	96
	North Dakota	544	96
26.	Virginia	530	94
27.	Maine	513	91
28.	Georgia	512	91
29.	Colorado	495	88
30.	Maryland	493	87
31.	Hawaii	482	85
32.	New Hampshire	478	85
33.	Massachusetts	477	85
34.	Kentucky	472	84
35.	New Jersey	467	83
36.	Nebraska	466	83
37.	New Mexico	462	82
38.	Texas	460	82
39.	Connecticut	459	81
40.	Missouri	457	81
41.	Rhode Island	455	81
42.	Alabama	454	80
43.	Oregon	449	80
44.	Mississippi	442	78
45.	West Virginia	440	78
46.	Arizona	432	77
	Oklahoma	432	77
48.	S. Carolina	416	74
49.	Delaware	401	71
50.	Tennessee	393	70
51.	Alaska (399)	339[12]	61

Rank	State		
24.	Minnesota	30	97
	Wisconsin	30	97
26.	Arkansas	29	94
27.	Indiana	28	90
	Kentucky	28	90
29.	Maryland	27	87
	Hawaii	27	87
31.	West Virginia	26	84
32.	Ohio	23	74
	Tennessee	23	74
34.	Iowa	21	68
	Virginia	21	68
36.	Delaware	20	65
37.	Georgia	19	61
	N. Carolina	19	61
	Vermont	19	61
40.	Alabama	18	58
	New Hampshire	18	58
42.	Rhode Island	17	55
43.	Maine	16	52
	Massachusetts	16	52
	New York	15	48
46.	New Jersey	14	45
47.	Connecticut	14	45
	S. Carolina	13	42
49.	Alaska	12	39
50.	Pennsylvania		
51.	D.C.	8	26

Rank	State		
	Indiana	60	104
27.	Kentucky	59	102
	Georgia	59	102
	Hawaii	59	102
30.	Tennessee	58	100
	UNITED STATES	58	100
31.	Missouri	57	99
32.	Idaho	55	96
	N. Carolina	55	96
34.	Maine	54	93
	Ohio	54	93
36.	Vermont	49	85
	Virginia	49	85
38.	Illinois	46	80
	Maryland	46	80
40.	New Hampshire	45	77
41.	Iowa	44	75
	S. Carolina	44	75
43.	Delaware	43	75
44.	Rhode Island	39	68
45.	New York	37	64
46.	Alaska	34	59
47.	New Jersey	32	55
48.	Connecticut	30	53
49.	Pennsylvania	26	44
50.	Massachusetts	23	40
51.	D.C.	21	36

*** Condition controllable by State. Rank suggests level of achievement.

* Condition controllable by State. Quality level associated with rank position is a matter of interpretation based on intended emphasis.

[11] Source 19.

[12] Reduced 15 percent to make the purchasing power comparable to that in other high-price areas in the United States.

Table II-2.—State and D.C. rankings for comparative analysis of higher education: 1960—Continued

PUBLIC HIGHER EDUCATION—ORGANIZATION, EMPHASIS, AND ACHIEVEMENT—Continued

24. 2-Year College Share of Enrollment*			25. Emphasis on Degree Programs*			26. Emphasis on Graduate Programs*		
Degree-credit enrollment in public 2-year colleges as a percent of undergraduate degree-credit enrollment in all public institutions, 1959–60 (E÷F)			Bachelor's degrees awarded as a percent of undergraduate degree-credit enrollment in all public institutions, 1959–60 (H÷F)			Ratio of graduate and first-professional enrollment in public institutions to bachelor's degrees awarded by public institutions, 1959–60 (G÷H)		
1. California	61.2	309	1. South Dakota	18.4	163	1. Delaware	229.7	266
2. Wyoming	30.3	153	2. Pennsylvania	18.3	162	2. New Jersey	191.9	223
3. Florida	30.2	153	Vermont	18.3	162	3. New Mexico	165.4	192
4. Illinois	29.8	151	4. Arkansas	17.4	154	4. Indiana	164.2	190
5. Idaho	27.8	140	5. Iowa	16.9	150	5. Massachusetts	149.1	173
6. Mississippi	27.1	137	6. Montana	16.2	143	6. Connecticut	132.9	154
7. Washington	23.7	120	7. Massachusetts	15.8	140	7. Michigan	125.4	145
8. Texas	23.6	119	8. New Hampshire	15.6	138	8. Arizona	121.5	141
9. Arizona	20.6	104	9. N. Carolina	15.4	136	9. Maryland	120.8	140
			10. Kentucky	14.6	129	10. Iowa	116.9	136
UNITED STATES	19.8	100	11. Nebraska	14.5	128	11. Illinois	113.8	132
			North Dakota	14.5	128	12. New York	111.6	129
10. Michigan	17.7	89	13. Alabama	14.1	125	13. Ohio	110.0	128
11. Georgia	16.9	85	14. Connecticut	14.0	124	14. California	101.6	118
12. Missouri	15.8	80	Wisconsin	14.0	124	15. Washington	98.3	114
13. Maryland	15.2	77	16. Missouri	13.8	122	16. Minnesota	94.3	109
14. Utah	15.0	76	West Virginia	13.8	122	17. Kansas	86.5	100
15. Oklahoma	13.8	70	18. Mississippi	13.7	121			
16. Iowa	13.6	69	19. Oklahoma	13.5	119	UNITED STATES	86.2	100
17. Kansas	12.9	65	20. Minnesota	13.3	118			
18. Colorado	12.4	63	Utah	13.3	118	18. Wisconsin	83.3	97
19. North Dakota	9.5	48	22. S. Carolina	13.0	115	19. Florida	83.1	96
20. New York	6.2	31	23. Michigan	12.9	114	20. Kentucky	80.2	93
21. Nebraska	5.9	30	24. Kansas	12.6	112	21. S. Carolina	79.1	92

Rank	State	Value	Percent
22.	Wisconsin	5.6	28
23.	Minnesota	5.3	27
24.	N. Carolina	4.9	25
25.	Montana	4.7	24
26.	Massachusetts	4.3	22
27.	West Virginia	2.9	15
28.	Kentucky	2.4	12
29.	New Jersey	2.2	11
30.	New Mexico	2.1	11
31.	Maine	1.5	8
32.	Indiana	1.3	7
33.	Oregon	.6	3
34.	Pennsylvania	.6	3
35.	Alabama	0	0
	Alaska	0	0
	Arkansas	0	0
	Connecticut	0	0
	Delaware	0	0
	D.C.	0	0
	Hawaii	0	0
	Louisiana	0	0
	Nevada	0	0
	New Hampshire	0	0
	Ohio	0	0
	Rhode Island	0	0
	S. Carolina	0	0
	South Dakota	0	0
	Tennessee	0	0
	Vermont	0	0
	Virginia	0	0

Rank	State	Value	Percent
25.	Louisiana	12.6	112
26.	Colorado	12.4	110
27.	Oregon	12.3	109
28.	Tennessee	12.2	108
29.	Idaho	12.0	106
	Ohio	12.0	106
31.	Indiana	11.8	104
32.	Virginia	11.7	104
33.	New York	11.6	103
34.	Maryland	11.5	102
35.	Wyoming	11.3	100
	UNITED STATES	11.3	100
36.	Texas	10.7	95
37.	Hawaii	10.5	93
38.	Georgia	10.4	92
39.	New Jersey	10.2	90
40.	Rhode Island	10.1	89
41.	Delaware	10.0	89
42.	New Mexico	9.9	88
43.	Illinois	9.8	87
44.	Florida	9.6	85
45.	Nevada	9.5	84
46.	Washington	9.3	82
47.	Arizona	9.0	80
	D.C.	9.0	80
49.	California	5.8	51
50.	Maine	4.6	41
51.	Alaska	3.1	27

Rank	State	Value	Percent
22.	Tennessee	75.6	88
23.	Utah	75.0	87
24.	N. Carolina	73.4	85
25.	Oklahoma	71.0	82
26.	Nebraska	69.1	80
27.	Rhode Island	68.4	79
28.	Alaska	66.3	77
29.	Texas	65.9	76
30.	Colorado	61.0	71
31.	Maine	59.1	69
32.	Louisiana	53.0	61
33.	Oregon	52.2	61
34.	Virginia	50.0	58
35.	New Hampshire	47.8	55
36.	Missouri	46.2	54
37.	Alabama	43.7	51
38.	Pennsylvania	43.4	50
39.	West Virginia	42.2	49
40.	Wyoming	40.4	47
41.	North Dakota	38.7	45
42.	Vermont	38.5	45
43.	Arkansas	38.4	45
44.	Montana	37.5	44
45.	South Dakota	36.0	42
46.	Georgia	34.2	40
47.	Mississippi	31.3	36
48.	Kentucky	27.2	32
49.	Nevada	25.9	30
50.	Hawaii	23.9	28
51.	D.C.	0	0

NOTE.—Second column equals percent of U.S. average

* Condition controllable by State. Quality level associated with rank position is a matter of interpretation based on intended emphasis.

Table II-3.—State and D.C. socioeconomic data: 1960 and 1970

State or D.C.	TOTAL RESIDENT POPULATION (in thousands) A		17-YEAR-OLD POPULATION B	
	April 1, 1960[1]	April 1, 1970[1]	April 1, 1960[2]	April 1, 1970[2]
United States	179,323	208,185	2,862,005	3,825,343
Alabama	3,267	3,444	60,204	68,971
Alaska	226	302	2,746	5,303
Arizona	1,302	1,772	20,923	34,248
Arkansas	1,786	1,923	32,572	36,681
California	15,717	19,953	233,147	366,198
Colorado	1,754	2,207	26,458	42,199
Connecticut	2,535	3,032	39,135	54,213
Delaware	446	548	6,498	10,186
D.C.	764	756	9,166	11,629
Florida	4,952	6,789	69,923	115,522
Georgia	3,943	4,590	70,383	88,023
Hawaii	633	770	10,271	14,610
Idaho	667	713	11,920	15,164
Illinois	10,081	11,114	154,200	203,302
Indiana	4,662	5,194	74,098	100,765
Iowa	2,757	2,825	43,735	55,333
Kansas	2,179	2,249	33,174	42,573
Kentucky	3,038	3,219	54,922	63,046
Louisiana	3,257	3,643	54,985	74,364
Maine	969	994	16,056	18,678
Maryland	3,101	3,922	48,324	71,786
Massachusetts	5,149	5,689	79,314	100,503
Michigan	7,823	8,875	126,028	175,084
Minnesota	3,414	3,805	55,050	75,531
Mississippi	2,178	2,217	41,073	46,033
Missouri	4,320	4,677	66,424	84,596
Montana	672	694	11,123	14,772
Nebraska	1,411	1,484	21,079	28,477
Nevada	285	489	4,051	8,183
New Hampshire	607	738	9,598	12,931
New Jersey	6,067	7,168	92,205	127,811
New Mexico	951	1,016	15,578	21,638

Table II-3.—State and D.C. socioeconomic data: 1960 and 1970—Continued

State or D.C.	TOTAL RESIDENT POPULATION (in thousands) A		17-YEAR-OLD POPULATION B	
	April 1, 1960[1]	April 1, 1970[1]	April 1, 1960[2]	April 1, 1970[2]
New York	16,782	18,191	245,172	316,323
N. Carolina	4,556	5,082	85,698	101,352
North Dakota	632	618	11,012	13,368
Ohio	9,706	10,652	150,202	204,074
Oklahoma	2,328	2,559	38,491	48,197
Oregon	1,769	2,091	28,183	42,308
Pennsylvania	11,319	11,794	182,751	219,638
Rhode Island	859	950	13,219	16,193
S. Carolina	2,383	2,591	49,700	55,298
South Dakota	681	666	11,023	14,246
Tennessee	3,567	3,924	62,903	73,438
Texas	9,580	11,197	153,027	218,676
Utah	891	1,059	15,737	23,279
Vermont	390	445	6,735	8,262
Virginia	3,967	4,648	66,246	86,860
Washington	2,853	3,409	44,082	67,168
West Virginia	1,860	1,744	35,350	35,021
Wisconsin	3,952	4,418	62,787	86,437
Wyoming	330	332	5,324	6,852

[1] Source 8.
[2] Source 6.

Table II-3.—State and D.C. socioeconomic data: 1960 and 1970—Continued

State or D.C.	PUBLIC AND NONPUBLIC (EST.) HIGH SCHOOL GRADUATES C		FULL-TIME-EQUIVALENT ENROLLMENT IN PUBLIC INSTITUTIONS OF HIGHER EDUCATION D	
	1959–60[3]	1969–70[4]	1959–60[5]	1969–70[6]
United States	1,858,023	2,899,025	1,967,977	4,525,244
Alabama	32,950	47,086	33,541	69,409
Alaska	1,150	3,497	2,767	3,655
Arizona	11,391	23,440	31,893	68,565
Arkansas	19,439	26,768	16,829	39,352
California	162,515	281,208	334,567	689,160
Colorado	17,387	32,412	34,429	79,783
Connecticut	27,639	42,655	17,986	47,753
Delaware	4,254	7,985	5,586	13,701
D.C.	5,324	6,880	1,297	7,626
Florida	39,562	73,678	38,901	132,908
Georgia	35,490	58,959	31,621	78,239
Hawaii	7,864	12,307	8,798	23,261
Idaho	8,396	12,596	8,505	19,950
Illinois	102,891	152,064	85,187	214,032
Indiana	50,256	75,784	52,139	105,657
Iowa	33,704	49,663	27,017	58,114
Kansas	23,191	35,994	40,713	74,650
Kentucky	28,435	42,573	27,594	63,741
Louisiana	30,641	49,941	38,755	82,018
Maine	10,589	17,103	7,329	16,181
Maryland	27,745	52,962	28,980	80,936
Massachusetts	60,890	81,165	19,479	78,160
Michigan	88,240	138,700	118,679	241,323
Minnesota	43,654	67,080	50,831	105,601
Mississippi	20,223	30,653	26,635	53,426
Missouri	43,581	63,515	36,455	101,464
Montana	7,662	12,620	10,345	23,468
Nebraska	16,227	24,280	22,539	41,239
Nevada	2,458	5,749	3,708	9,647
New Hampshire	6,615	11,116	6,021	12,233
New Jersey	62,911	99,798	38,429	82,787
New Mexico	8,838	16,860	15,733	30,388

Table II-3.—State and D.C. socioeconomic data: 1960 and 1970—Continued

State or D.C.	PUBLIC AND NONPUBLIC (EST.) HIGH SCHOOL GRADUATES C		FULL-TIME-EQUIVALENT ENROLLMENT IN PUBLIC INSTITUTIONS OF HIGHER EDUCATION D	
	1959–60[3]	1969–70[4]	1959–60[5]	1969–70[6]
New York	165,736	232,300	109,944	286,021
N. Carolina	46,077	69,986	36,805	90,984
North Dakota	8,193	12,350	12,618	25,458
Ohio	103,864	161,548	89,569	211,108
Oklahoma	27,216	37,093	43,194	76,649
Oregon	21,470	33,936	30,947	74,882
Pennsylvania	133,353	184,100	38,178	169,039
Rhode Island	8,284	12,646	7,077	17,184
S. Carolina	22,988	35,740	17,753	34,220
South Dakota	8,113	12,557	10,299	20,903
Tennessee	34,721	51,700	35,435	76,411
Texas	80,817	144,946	129,886	265,193
Utah	11,578	18,795	19,703	40,205
Vermont	4,511	7,795	4,047	9,912
Virginia	32,915	62,462	35,871	81,838
Washington	31,843	53,225	47,355	113,494
West Virginia	22,737	26,939	21,479	41,831
Wisconsin	47,485	78,253	47,989	129,685
Wyoming	3,829	5,563	6,540	11,800

[3] Source 20, table R; source 21, table 23.
[4] Source 15.
[5] Source 17.
[6] Source 13, table 6.

Table II-3.—State and D.C. socioeconomic data: 1960 and 1970—Continued

State or D.C.	DEGREE-CREDIT ENROLLMENT IN PUBLIC 2-YEAR INSTITUTIONS E		DEGREE-CREDIT UNDER-GRADUATE ENROLLMENT IN ALL PUBLIC INSTITUTIONS F	
	Fall 1959[7]	Fall 1969[8]	Fall 1959[9]	Fall 1969[10]
United States	354,582	1,412,610	1,792,821	4,662,352
Alabama	—	15,553	31,594	70,783
Alaska	—	—	2,712	6,222
Arizona	5,929	23,180	28,758	72,277
Arkansas	—	1,661	15,774	39,368
California	193,410	491,221	316,092	783,707
Colorado	3,959	11,488	32,014	74,572
Connecticut	—	9,040	15,165	44,535
Delaware	—	3,491	4,550	17,001
D.C.	—	3,880	1,297	10,812
Florida	10,887	78,241	36,021	136,392
Georgia	5,177	15,365	30,624	78,273
Hawaii	—	—	8,583	23,383
Idaho	2,274	2,145	8,169	19,754
Illinois	22,837	93,825	76,629	221,319
Indiana	572	1,823	43,685	97,650
Iowa	3,076	11,674	22,567	49,174
Kansas	4,735	15,140	36,717	73,929
Kentucky	587	—	24,708	61,632
Louisiana	—	2,256	36,334	84,277
Maine	108	—	7,137	17,682
Maryland	3,866	32,423	25,437	88,362
Massachusetts	685	21,239	15,766	81,977
Michigan	18,088	74,097	102,205	230,324
Minnesota	2,381	17,537	45,164	112,384
Mississippi	6,968	15,718	25,678	51,268
Missouri	5,414	21,680	34,264	102,692
Montana	459	1,444	9,753	23,194
Nebraska	1,201	3,269	20,491	42,956
Nevada	—	303	3,619	11,179
New Hampshire	—	—	5,602	13,368
New Jersey	711	26,983	32,155	94,909
New Mexico	278	1,339	13,523	32,120

Table II-3.—State and D.C. socioeconomic data: 1960 and 1970—Continued

State or D.C.	DEGREE-CREDIT ENROLLMENT IN PUBLIC 2-YEAR INSTITUTIONS E		DEGREE-CREDIT UNDER-GRADUATE ENROLLMENT IN ALL PUBLIC INSTITUTIONS F	
	Fall 1959[7]	Fall 1969[8]	Fall 1959[9]	Fall 1969[10]
New York	6,022	169,440	97,381	341,306
N. Carolina	1,623	9,947	33,064	75,035
North Dakota	1,137	2,213	11,948	24,092
Ohio	—	16,869	79,097	219,307
Oklahoma	5,421	9,277	39,413	75,865
Oregon	167	15,356	29,077	67,140
Pennsylvania	206	26,010	35,369	168,124
Rhode Island	—	2,586	6,621	17,699
S. Carolina	—	275	16,102	28,200
South Dakota	—	—	9,660	20,341
Tennessee	—	5,453	32,445	78,962
Texas	28,568	81,986	121,297	277,220
Utah	2,690	2,645	17,918	40,328
Vermont	—	—	3,780	10,626
Virginia	—	12,202	33,886	82,904
Washington	10,271	51,529	43,369	110,229
West Virginia	597	604	20,295	40,462
Wisconsin	2,392	5,798	42,992	119,354
Wyoming	1,896	4,405	6,254	11,660

[7] Source 17.
[8] Source 13, table 6.
[9] (D-G)
[10] Source 13, tables 5 and 6.

Table II-3.—State and D.C. socioeconomic data: 1960 and 1970—Continued

State or D.C.	GRADUATE AND FIRST-PROFESSIONAL ENROLLMENT IN ALL PUBLIC INSTITUTIONS G		BACHELOR'S DEGREES AWARDED BY ALL PUBLIC INSTITUTIONS H	
	Fall 1959[11]	Fall 1969[12]	1959–1960[13]	1969–1970[14]
United States	175,156	736,754	203,279	516,723
Alabama	1,947	7,825	4,453	10,121
Alaska	55	208	83	247
Arizona	3,135	11,868	2,581	7,258
Arkansas	1,055	3,371	2,746	5,943
California	18,475	106,058	18,185	53,826
Colorado	2,415	12,350	3,960	9,728
Connecticut	2,821	11,352	2,123	5,420
Delaware	1,036	1,865	451	1,533
D.C.	0	207	117	226
Florida	2,880	15,360	3,465	13,271
Georgia	997	11,852	3,184	10,612
Hawaii	215	2,965	901	2,313
Idaho	336	1,791	983	2,358
Illinois	8,558	36,632	7,520	22,991
Indiana	8,454	25,868	5,150	13,612
Iowa	4,450	11,723	3,808	7,328
Kansas	3,996	12,558	4,622	9,614
Kentucky	2,886	11,300	3,598	8,731
Louisiana	2,421	10,068	4,569	11,298
Maine	192	1,920	325	2,524
Maryland	3,543	13,680	2,934	8,233
Massachusetts	3,713	12,115	2,491	9,115
Michigan	16,474	49,684	13,139	28,839
Minnesota	5,667	14,309	6,009	12,999
Mississippi	957	4,983	3,523	7,369
Missouri	2,191	15,451	4,738	12,170
Montana	592	1,917	1,578	3,312
Nebraska	2,048	6,323	2,965	6,536
Nevada	89	1,503	343	1,005
New Hampshire	419	1,068	876	1,938
New Jersey	6,274	16,641	3,270	9,811
New Mexico	2,210	5,057	1,336	3,641

Table II–3.—State and D.C. socioeconomic data: 1960 and 1970—Continued

State or D.C.	GRADUATE AND FIRST-PROFESSIONAL ENROLLMENT IN ALL PUBLIC INSTITUTIONS G		BACHELOR'S DEGREES AWARDED BY ALL PUBLIC INSTITUTIONS H	
	Fall 1959[11]	Fall 1969[12]	1959–1960[13]	1969–1970[14]
New York	12,563	53,781	11,260	27,931
N. Carolina	3,741	13,016	5,098	11,641
North Dakota	670	2,312	1,730	3,692
Ohio	10,472	30,823	9,523	26,999
Oklahoma	3,781	11,563	5,323	10,004
Oregon	1,870	13,877	3,579	8,019
Pennsylvania	2,809	33,735	6,467	22,828
Rhode Island	456	4,395	667	2,010
S. Carolina	1,651	4,236	2,088	4,475
South Dakota	639	3,332	1,775	3,526
Tennessee	2,990	11,160	3,955	10,225
Texas	8,589	35,162	13,036	30,598
Utah	1,785	5,537	2,381	4,913
Vermont	267	1,137	693	1,502
Virginia	1,985	15,289	3,971	9,841
Washington	3,986	14,904	4,055	11,207
West Virginia	1,184	7,940	2,806	6,226
Wisconsin	4,997	19,005	5,998	15,807
Wyoming	286	1,701	708	1,357

[11] Source 12, table 3. Adjusted to include first-professional enrollment.
[12] Source 13, table 6.
[13] Source 11. Adjusted to exclude first-professional degrees.
[14] Ibid., table 3A.

Table II–3.—State and D.C. socioeconomic data: 1960 and 1970—Continued

State or D.C.	PERSONAL INCOME (millions of dollars) I		STATE GOVERNMENT TAX REVENUE (millions of dollars) J	
	1960[15]	1970[16]	FY 1960[17]	FY 1970[18]
United States	$398,725	$798,949	$18,201.0	$48,352.9
Alabama	4,876	9,832	273.7	657.4
Alaska	649	1,400	27.1	85.9
Arizona	2,684	6,418	165.0	474.3
Arkansas	2,459	5,376	158.1	351.4
California	42,980	88,825	2,124.4	5,497.5
Colorado	4,022	8,468	192.5	470.1
Connecticut	7,138	14,786	238.1	741.8
Delaware	1,238	2,383	70.8	195.6
D.C.	2,311	4,067	165.1	390.9
Florida	9,746	24,938	521.7	1,421.1
Georgia	6,489	15,345	369.1	941.3
Hawaii	1,478	3,445	124.2	340.5
Idaho	1,241	2,310	69.0	155.9
Illinois	26,718	50,131	836.4	2,868.7
Indiana	10,225	19,679	399.4	1,002.4
Iowa	5,475	10,418	265.8	628.3
Kansas	4,712	8,598	206.6	431.0
Kentucky	4,792	9,901	228.5	703.0
Louisiana	5,399	11,130	452.7	838.8
Maine	1,796	3,235	86.9	207.6
Maryland	7,289	16,789	343.6	1,082.1
Massachusetts	12,680	24,851	491.1	1,393.7
Michigan	18,203	36,124	913.9	2,345.1
Minnesota	7,241	14,580	352.6	1,021.0
Mississippi	2,632	5,706	194.3	485.8
Missouri	9,149	17,350	312.9	820.9
Montana	1,383	2,349	64.9	128.8
Nebraska	2,990	5,570	91.1	261.3
Nevada	831	2,267	44.9	149.1
New Hampshire	1,305	2,660	41.8	94.8
New Jersey	16,528	33,085	365.2	1,332.3
New Mexico	1,801	3,185	123.2	273.5

Table II–3.—State and D.C. socioeconomic data: 1960 and 1970—Continued

State or D.C.	PERSONAL INCOME (millions of dollars) I		STATE GOVERNMENT TAX REVENUE (millions of dollars) J	
	1960[15]	1970[16]	FY 1960[17]	FY 1970[18]
New York	$46,281	$87,111	$1,961.0	$6,116.5
N. Carolina	7,143	16,331	459.4	1,190.2
North Dakota	1,087	1,848	60.8	121.6
Ohio	22,729	42,382	872.7	1,702.6
Oklahoma	4,350	8,488	275.4	502.1
Oregon	3,960	7,777	208.3	430.7
Pennsylvania	25,395	46,329	1,032.9	2,777.6
Rhode Island	1,897	3,711	86.1	228.7
S. Carolina	3,298	7,616	235.5	543.7
South Dakota	1,217	2,108	53.0	112.7
Tennessee	5,521	12,128	304.6	686.9
Texas	18,535	39,671	792.8	1,975.1
Utah	1,771	3,416	100.4	251.6
Vermont	716	1,545	43.5	135.2
Virginia	7,339	16,827	291.7	955.7
Washington	6,706	13,671	460.8	1,028.0
West Virginia	2,957	5,259	180.1	385.0
Wisconsin	8,615	16,351	426.2	1,332.8
Wyoming	749	1,181	41.5	84.5

[15] Source 5, August 1970, p. 34.
[16] Ibid., August 1971, p. 31.
[17] Source 9, table 21.
[18] Source 10, table 7.

Table II-3.—State and D.C. socioeconomic data: 1960 and 1970—Continued

State or D.C.	APPROPRIATIONS OF STATE TAX FUNDS FOR HIGHER EDUCATION OPERATING EXPENSES (thousands of dollars) K		CURRENT EXPENDITURES FOR INSTRUCTION IN PUBLIC UNIVERSITIES AND 4-YEAR COLLEGES (thousands of dollars) L	
	1959–60[19]	1969–70[19]	1959–60[20]	1969–70[21]
United States	$1,400,997	$6,138,777	$910,506	$3,764,132
Alabama	21,283	72,518	15,241	52,649
Alaska	2,111	11,876	1,104	4,186
Arizona	14,042	65,611	11,221	46,185
Arkansas	13,551	47,630	9,615	26,060
California	188,604	749,162	91,679	439,975
Colorado	17,271	87,094	15,019	71,950
Connecticut	12,273	80,270	8,257	37,177
Delaware	3,731	16,933	2,240	12,949
D.C.	1,093	15,693	1,100	11,728
Florida	40,392	198,438	16,696	92,965
Georgia	24,058	124,207	13,528	72,133
Hawaii	4,958	41,782	4,244	30,640
Idaho	8,799	29,862	4,361	13,882
Illinois	90,289	405,077	46,151	180,431
Indiana	45,463	154,313	32,224	133,059
Iowa	34,630	101,597	18,694	64,367
Kansas	25,036	79,721	19,782	61,242
Kentucky	14,954	95,478	12,750	70,845
Louisiana	40,062	99,352	23,533	62,793
Maine	3,356	25,984	3,706	14,314
Maryland	23,818	92,132	12,376	61,111
Massachusetts	12,167	85,278	8,961	55,949
Michigan	95,599	305,411	74,745	213,885
Minnesota	36,173	128,278	26,353	84,043
Mississippi	15,118	47,804	8,699	30,174
Missouri	24,744	127,487	14,181	80,377
Montana	11,230	26,715	7,253	20,796
Nebraska	15,217	48,386	9,934	39,100
Nevada	3,682	14,778	2,420	9,383
New Hampshire	3,973	10,685	2,877	11,531
New Jersey	21,982	126,250	17,607	71,641
New Mexico	11,165	36,126	7,136	27,666

Table II–3.—State and D.C. socioeconomic data: 1960 and 1970—Continued

State or D.C.	APPROPRIATIONS OF STATE TAX FUNDS FOR HIGHER EDUCATION OPERATING EXPENSES (thousands of dollars) K		CURRENT EXPENDITURES FOR INSTRUCTION IN PUBLIC UNIVERSITIES AND 4-YEAR COLLEGES (thousands of dollars) L	
	1959–60[19]	1969–70[19]	1959–60[21]	1969–70[21]
New York	$78,546	$625,341	$61,616	$253,310
N. Carolina	28,419	175,931	22,429	82,961
North Dakota	9,368	23,249	6,251	19,294
Ohio	43,331	239,891	55,343	224,293
Oklahoma	27,014	59,552	16,314	49,390
Oregon	28,719	87,683	13,820	56,883
Pennsylvania	43,471	250,000	20,721	176,488
Rhode Island	4,477	28,935	3,221	14,937
S. Carolina	12,113	53,316	7,384	37,684
South Dakota	8,128	18,227	6,479	16,026
Tennessee	17,022	87,137	13,930	62,956
Texas	71,021	340,046	46,577	188,317
Utah	13,139	40,000	10,156	32,423
Vermont	3,264	13,532	3,441	12,369
Virginia	25,544	117,578	19,009	76,507
Washington	46,909	190,903	22,645	79,457
West Virginia	16,919	55,005	9,191	37,704
Wisconsin	37,834	165,851	24,958	127,323
Wyoming	4,935	14,672	3,334	10,624

[19] Source 2, p. 3.
[20] Source 16, table II-E.
[21] Source: Unpublished OE data.

Table II-3.—State and D.C. socioeconomic data: 1960 and 1970—Continued

State or D.C.	DEGREE-CREDIT ENROLLMENT IN PUBLIC UNIVERSITIES AND 4-YEAR COLLEGES M		AVERAGE TUITION PAID AT PUBLIC UNIVERSITIES AND 4-YEAR COLLEGES N	
	Fall 1959[22]	Fall 1969[23]	1960[24]	1970[25]
United States	$1,613,395	$3,986,496	$189	$373
Alabama	33,541	63,055	179	397
Alaska	2,767	6,430	65	227
Arizona	25,964	60,965	210	410
Arkansas	16,829	41,078	199	332
California	141,157	398,544	160	255
Colorado	30,470	75,434	258	479
Connecticut	17,986	46,847	94	293
Delaware	5,586	15,375	207	439
D.C.	1,297	7,139	74	98
Florida	28,024	73,511	128	416
Georgia	26,444	74,760	255	459
Hawaii	8,798	26,348	207	113
Idaho	6,231	19,400	110	169
Illinois	62,350	164,126	134	227
Indiana	51,567	121,695	186	485
Iowa	23,941	49,223	220	622
Kansas	35,978	71,347	171	293
Kentucky	27,007	72,932	205	329
Louisiana	38,755	92,089	55	251
Maine	7,221	19,602	290	400
Maryland	25,114	69,619	205	428
Massachusetts	18,794	72,853	167	168
Michigan	100,591	205,911	242	565
Minnesota	48,450	109,156	200	348
Mississippi	19,667	40,533	217	502
Missouri	31,041	96,463	142	346
Montana	9,886	23,667	157	278
Nebraska	21,338	46,010	189	384
Nevada	3,708	12,379	168	340
New Hampshire	6,021	14,436	323	795
New Jersey	37,718	84,567	231	374
New Mexico	15,455	35,838	152	280

Table II-3.—State and D.C. socioeconomic data: 1960 and 1970—Continued

State or D.C.	DEGREE-CREDIT ENROLLMENT IN PUBLIC UNIVERSITIES AND 4-YEAR COLLEGES M		AVERAGE TUITION PAID AT PUBLIC UNIVERSITIES AND 4-YEAR COLLEGES N	
	Fall 1959[22]	Fall 1969[23]	1960[24]	1970[25]
New York	103,922	225,647	95	278
N. Carolina	35,182	78,104	269	362
North Dakota	11,481	24,191	165	394
Ohio	89,569	233,261	252	636
Oklahoma	37,773	78,151	156	301
Oregon	30,780	65,661	161	354
Pennsylvania	37,972	175,849	410	614
Rhode Island	7,077	19,508	163	371
S. Carolina	17,753	32,161	83	373
South Dakota	10,299	23,673	277	395
Tennessee	35,435	84,669	184	373
Texas	101,318	230,396	166	140
Utah	17,013	43,220	211	415
Vermont	4,047	11,763	608	795
Virginia	35,871	85,991	299	440
Washington	37,084	73,606	128	242
West Virginia	20,882	47,798	123	145
Wisconsin	45,597	132,561	236	516
Wyoming	4,644	8,956	262	521

[22] Source 17.
[23] Source 13, table 5.
[24] Source 16, table I-E (tuition); source 17 (enrollment).
[25] Source: Unpublished OE data (tuition); source 13, table 5 (enrollment).

SOURCES FOR TABLES

1. Advisory Commission on Intergovernmental Relations, *Measuring the Fiscal Capacity and Effort of State and Local Areas, Information Report*, U.S. Government Printing Office, Washington, D.C., 1971.
2. Chambers, M. M., *Appropriations of State Tax Funds for Operating Expenses in Higher Education, 1969–1970*, National Association of State Universities and Land-Grant Colleges, Washington, D.C., October 1969.
3. National Education Association, Research Division, *Estimates of School Statistics, 1970–71*, Research Report 1970-R15, Washington, D.C., 1970. Copyright, NEA.
4. ———, *Ranking of the States, 1960.* Copyright, NEA.
5. U.S. Bureau of Economic Analysis, *Survey of Current Business.*
6. U.S. Department of Commerce, Bureau of the Census, *1970 Census of Population, General Population Characteristics*, Final Report, PC(1)-B, U.S. Government Printing Office, Washington, D.C., 1971. Same citation for 1960 census.
7. ———, *1970 Census of Population, General Social and Economic Characteristics, United States Summary*, PC(1)-Cl. Same citation for 1960 Census.
8. ———, *1970 Census of Population, Number of Inhabitants*, Final Report, PC(1)-A, 1971. Same citation for 1960 Census.
9. ———, *Governmental Finances in 1960*, September 1961.
10. ———, *State Government Finances in 1970*, July 1971.
11. U.S. Department of Health, Education, and Welfare, Office of Education, *Earned Degrees Conferred 1969–70, Summary Data*, U.S. Government Printing Office, Washington, D.C., 1972. Same citation for 1959–60.
12. ———, *Enrollment for Advanced Degrees, Fall 1959*, 1961.
13. ———, *Fall Enrollment in Higher Education, 1969, Supplementary Information, Summary Data*, 1970.
14. ———, *Fall 1966 Statistics of Elementary and Secondary Day Schools*, 1967.
15. ———, *Fall 1970 Statistics of Public Schools*, 1971.
16. ———, *Financial Statistics of Institutions of Higher Education, 1959–60*, 1964.
17. ———, *Opening Fall Enrollment in Higher Education, 1959, Institutional Data*, Circular No. 606.
18. ———, *Residence and Migration of College Students: Fall 1968 Analytic Report*, 1970.
19. ———, *Residence and Migration of College Students, Fall 1963*, 1965.
20. ———, *Statistics of Nonpublic Secondary Schools, 1960–61*, 1963.
21. ———, *Statistics of State School Systems, 1959–60.* Same citation for 1956–57, Circular No. 572.
22. Willingham, Warren W., *Free-Access Higher Education*, College Entrance Examination Board, New York, 1970.

BIBLIOGRAPHY

American Council on Education, *A Fact Book on Higher Education*, Washington, D. C.

This series of pamphlets contains statistics on enrollment, faculty, students, and earned degrees, as well as information concerning the social and economic factors related to higher education. Data from a variety of government and private sources have been reproduced in charts and tables that review past developments, show projections, and emphasize the trends and relationships. A 50-page pamphlet is issued four times a year to update the charts and tables.

Folger, John K., and Charles B. Nam, *Education of the American Population*, U. S. Department of Commerce, Bureau of the Census, U. S. Government Printing Office, Washington, D. C., 1967, 290 pp.

This monograph not only reviews the educational status of the American population over time, as revealed in census data and other statistical materials, but also analyzes the relationship of school enrollment and educational attainment to social and economic characteristics of the population. In general, the study deals with the following questions: What has been the historical trend in extension of schooling in the United States? To what extent have different categories of the population shared in this educational achievement? How have social and economic forces affected the pace at which educational change has taken place? What have been some of the important consequences of educational improvement for American social institutions?

The monograph focuses on three major aspects of education: enrollment of students, characteristics of teachers, and educational attainments of the adult population. Both historical background and analyses of educational differences among important groups of the population are included. A summary chapter presents major findings and conclusions; the appendixes are concerned with the quality of census education data. The major contribution of this publication is that it calls attention to the valuable information and insights available from the decennial census.

Harris, Seymour E., *Higher Education: Resources and Finance*, McGraw-Hill Book Co., New York, 1962, 713 pp.

This major work on the economic aspects of higher education is fully annotated in the bibliography for chapter XII. Chapters 25, 26, and 27, which deal with differentials in higher education among the States based on interstate comparisons, contribute a complete analysis of selected aspects of higher education financing for 1957–58. Details concerning relative burden, efforts and capacity to finance, and achievements in higher education are included for all States except Alaska and Hawaii.

Harris, Seymour E., *A Statistical Portrait of Higher Education*, Carnegie Commission on Higher Education, McGraw-Hill Book Co., New York, 1972, 978 pp.

This statistical abstract concerning higher education contains roughly 700 tables with relevant commentary by the author. A lengthy introduction and a summary of the data available in each chapter provides a condensed interpretation of the findings. Part one, "Students," delineates undergraduate and graduate student characteristics, a profile of the college graduate, student expenses, and student aid. Part two, "Enrollment," contains chapters on population and educational attainment, degrees, institutions, enrollment in relation to population, international comparisons, and dropouts. Part three, "Faculty," deals with faculty characteristics, supply and demand, recruitment and mobility, pay, allocation of time, and scientific manpower. Part four, "Income and Expenditures," treats the nature and source of income, Government allocations, tuition, endowment income and investment policy, expenditures, physical plant, Federal funds for scientific activities, and the burden inherent in financing of education. Part five deals with productivity and the structure of higher education enrollment.

National Education Association, Research Division, *Rankings of the States, 1972*, Washington, D. C., 1972, 78 pp.

This annual report of 132 ranked lists of State data ". . . may be used in understanding, explaining, interpreting, and possibly evaluating various aspects of state school systems." The latest available statistics are drawn from 26 governmental and nongovernmental publications.

The tables are organized under 10 topics: population, enrollment and attendance, teachers, educational attainment, general financial resources, governmental revenue, school revenue, governmental expenditures and debt, school expenditures, and miscellaneous.

Simon, Kenneth A., and Martin M. Frankel, *Projections of Educational Statistics to 1981–82, 1972 Edition*, U. S. Department of Health, Education, and Welfare, Office of Education, U. S. Government Printing Office, Washington, D. C., 1973.

The authors assume in their projections that the 1961–62 trends in enrollment and retention rates, class sizes, and per-pupil expenditures will continue through 1981–82. Details of the methodology used in making the projections are set forth in the appendixes.

Simon, Kenneth A., and W. Vance Grant, *Digest of Educational Statistics, 1972 Edition*, U. S. Department of Health, Education, and Welfare, Office of Education, U. S. Government Printing Office, Washington, D. C., 1973.

The 11th in a series of annual publications, this 1972 edition offers an abstract of statistical information covering the broad field of American education from kindergarten through graduate school. Materials from numerous sources, including Office of Education statistical surveys and estimates, are utilized. The *Digest* is divided into five chapters: (1) all levels of education, (2) elementary and secondary education, (3) higher education, (4) Federal programs for education and related activities, and (5) selected statistics related to education in the United States. The higher education chapter contains information on a variety of subjects: enrollment, faculty and other professional staff, number and kinds of institutions, degrees, income, expenditures, property, and land-grant institutions. Recent additions to the *Digest* include summary data from a new survey of participants in adult education programs; Bureau of the Census data on the number of male college graduates in the population, by field of highest degree; information from the American Council on Education on the personal characteristics, professional backgrounds, and academic activities of college faculty members, and an up-to-date list of Federal funds available for education.

Chapter III

EXTENDING EDUCATIONAL OPPORTUNITY

Throughout the United States greater higher education opportunities than ever before exist; moreover, higher education itself is undergoing some radical changes—changes in pattern as well as direction. There are a number of reasons for this phenomenon: a heightened sense of widespread need for education beyond high school that has brought about the elimination of many barriers to college entrance; the dramatic growth of easily accessible 2-year colleges, with their concomitant contribution to the expansion of educational services to the community, and the broadening of the scope and extent of student financial-aid programs. These and other circumstances stem from the conviction that society's goals can best be achieved through the fullest development of human resources and that this development can be effectively fostered by providing equal and open higher educational opportunities for all qualified persons who seek them. While much progress has been made to extend educational opportunities, the need to establish a universal commitment to this goal, and to achieve it, requires continued effort.

The size of this task can be judged from an estimate of the number of qualified students who do not enter college following their graduation from high school. Several major studies have been conducted to ascertain this number.[1] Studies in succeeding years have generally shown higher attendance rates. Yet conclusions have also varied at any given point in

---

[1] In a 1959 study of 10,000 high school graduates, Medsker and Trent found that nearly 40 percent of those possessing college ability [graduates who were in the upper two-fifths of their high school graduating classes according to the Cooperative School and College Ability Test (SCAT)] did not enter college. See Leland L. Medsker and James W. Trent, *The Influence of Different Types of Public Higher Institutions on College Attendance From Varying Socioeconomic and Ability Levels*, Center for the Study of Higher Education, Berkeley, Calif., 1965, p. 28.

A Census Bureau followup of 1966 graduating high school seniors found that of those students with an average high school academic record of B— or better (53 percent of all high school graduates), 45 percent did not enter college either in the fall or in the winter of 1966. Of those with high ability scores (35 percent of all high school graduates), 19 percent did not enter college. Cited in Joseph Froomkin, *Aspirations, Enrollments, and Resources*, U. S. Department of Health, Education, and Welfare, Office of Education, U. S. Government Printing Office, Washington, D. C., 1970, p. 22.

time, mainly because those making the studies have not agreed on the levels of performance required of students considered "academically talented." A more appropriate term than "academically talented" might be "college-able." And the college-able talent loss may be defined as all high school graduates (and equivalents) who could qualify for postsecondary education by meeting existing admission requirements but do not matriculate because of such restraints as inability to pay, inadequate academic preparation, lack of motivation, social barriers, or because of the distance between home and an institution of higher learning. Within a group capable of college are many marginal students who probably would not complete all of their postsecondary training but who, if they wish to continue their education, deserve at least the opportunity to *begin* and accrue whatever gains may be had from limited exposure.

At the freshman level, a practical estimate of the redeemable national talent loss can be gained by examining the actual achievements in a few States that have very high college-entrance rates. States which in 1968 had the highest percent of resident high school graduates enrolled for the first time in degree-credit programs in college anywhere were as follows: Arizona, 88 percent; D.C., 81 percent; California, 75 percent; Washington, 73 percent; New York, 71 percent; and Wyoming, 70 percent.[2] These percentages would be even higher if first-time enrollments in non-degree-credit college programs were included. These statistics suggest that as high as 75 to 80 percent of the Nation's high school graduates have the ability and could reasonably be expected to *start* college if conditions were right. Such conditions, which would include open access for all to some form of postsecondary education, removal of financial barriers, a statewide 2-year college system, and a good elementary-secondary school system, are within the near-future capabilities of many States. If they existed nationwide today, it is reasonable to expect that the estimated (fall 1972) 60-65 percent college-entrance rate could be increased by 10 to 20 percent, or in roughly 300,000 to 500,000 more of the Nation's 2.9 million high school graduates entering postsecondary education. However hypothetical this illustration may appear, it suggests that a sizable number of capable students are lost following graduation from high school.[3]

---

[2] George H. Wade, *Residence and Migration of College Students, Fall 1968, Analytic Report,* U. S. Department of Health, Education, and Welfare, Office of Education, U. S. Government Printing Office, Washington, D. C., 1970.

[3] The failure of students to remain in college represents a second major loss of talent. It is estimated that, on the average, approximately half of those who enter college withdraw within 4 years. Many of the reasons for withdrawing, such as lack of ability or marriage, are understandable. Other contributing factors—family environment or early school experiences—that affect the will to persist may be beyond the province of higher education to correct. On the other hand, colleges can exert influence by discouraging and preventing students from dropping out due to financial difficulties and lack of guidance;

The reasons young people with college ability do not obtain a post-secondary education are numerous and well known. The major factors involved are:

(1) Restricted access because of social and economic class status, religion, race, or ethnic origin;
(2) Differences in motivation, values, and attitudes resulting from parental or peer-group influence and other socioeconomic circumstances;
(3) Inadequate academic preparation and/or in-school guidance;
(4) Unavailable or inadequate college programs—the deficiency may be in content, level, quality, or geographical accessibility; and
(5) Inability to meet expenses.

For the capable student wishing to attend college, these factors are becoming increasingly less of a handicap. Most U. S. colleges and universities welcome able students and are willing to support their attendance. A wide variety of high school projects are encouraging able but less motivated students to go to college, and once they are enrolled, more challenging work is being provided by early admission programs, advanced placement, and honors programs. For students in the upper ability ranges, these efforts have been highly successful. Thus the percentage of talented youths who do not enter college has been measurably reduced.

For less able youths and those whose talent is unidentified, the consequences of any obstacles are serious. Such is particularly true if they are of average ability, and are from socially disadvantaged backgrounds or minority groups or have had to delay college entrance. Affected most of all are marginal students from disadvantaged backgrounds who face the additional handicap imposed by ethnic and cultural caste status. Considerable effort and study has been focused on prospective students in these categories, but too often the recommended remedial programs have failed to materialize; consequently, success has been only modest.

To reduce waste of human resources and establish universal opportunity for higher education requires a national commitment and the combined efforts of private, State, and Federal sectors. Both Federal programs and those of private foundations have done much to improve the overall situation. Colleges and universities—working independently and strengthened by Federal support—have contributed greatly to meeting the educational needs of all citizens. But, since the basic responsibility lies with the individual States, it is obvious that if more massive and comprehensive effort is to be forthcoming, there must be greater State involvement. Only

---

also, to a lesser extent, through bringing about changes in student attitudes and values. See James W. Trent and Leland L. Medsker, *Beyond High School*, Center for Research & Development in Higher Education, University of California, Berkeley, 1967, ch. V, "Factors Related to Persistence in College."

at the State level can such critical areas as improved high school-college communication, better geographical accessibility, and expanded community-college and vocational-education programs be vigorously and effectively pursued. The fact is that the greatest success in extending educational opportunities has occured when a State system of higher education is actively involved and thoroughly committed to these objectives.

Many aspects of developing and supporting effective programs to extend educational opportunities require statewide planning. To construct a total program, such necessary tasks as organizing, coordinating, and providing leadership must be performed at the State level. And in the final analysis, the State is best qualified to determine the direction to take in extending educational opportunity.

The purpose of this chapter is to focus on direction—by describing some of the ways in which educational opportunities are being extended in a number of States, colleges, and universities. Although States appear to be uniformly committed to the goal of fully developing their human-talent resources, the great variation in actual success suggests that the more effective programs should be better explained and publicized. In some States only one out of three youths start college, while in others over 70 percent begin postsecondary training. Even in the more productive States, however, students from a deprived environmental background enter college with less frequency than do those from a higher socioeconomic climate.

Full and equal access to higher education is the *right* of every person capable of benefiting from some form of postsecondary education, including community colleges and technical or vocational schools. There are three basic, yet distinctive, approaches whereby educational opportunities may be extended to every qualified individual. The first, directed at maximizing the accessibility of postsecondary education, is to remove all existing social and economic barriers to entry. Central to this approach is the adoption of an equal, open-admission policy which, when coupled with provisions for student aid, will guarantee educational opportunity to all interested and qualified applicants, regardless of race, creed, national origin, or financial means. The second approach, student oriented, consists of "raising and fitting" student abilities and interests to the level of existing educational practices and available programs. Activities designed to accomplish this objective are usually described as "compensatory," in that they attempt to compensate for, or overcome, the effects of indifferent or even hostile backgrounds. Counseling and incentive programs also fall within this category. The third approach focuses on individual institutions and the State system. The task is to eliminate any roadblocks within the system—particularly those which prevent a smooth and effective transition from secondary school to college—and also to provide additional educational alternatives to meet the needs of a diversified student population. Curricular innovations, the creation of new kinds of colleges, and the expansion of occupational and adult training programs are examples of ways in which students can be provided with additional courses of study appropriate to their talents and interests.

In outline, the ways in which colleges and universities may extend educational opportunities are:

Through maximizing access to higher education

- •by adopting open-door admissions and observing equal rights
- •by assuring geographical proximity
- •by extending student financial aid on the basis of need

Through emphasizing incentive and compensatory programs

- •by encouraging a positive response to higher education
- •by sponsoring special plans to meet the needs of the disadvantaged
  —in recruiting and high-school counseling
  —in preadmission preparation
  —in remedial studies, tutoring, and personal attention
- •by modifying admission standards and introducing new criteria to estimate academic potential
- •by establishing special curriculums and extending 4-year programs

Through enhancing the educational environment

- •by improving articulation between high schools and colleges and between institutions within the higher education system
- •by creating new kinds of colleges
- •by introducing innovations in curriculum and programs.

ACCESS TO HIGHER EDUCATION

Mechanical obstacles to college entrance are the least difficult to remove and, for all practical purposes, they have been eliminated in many States. Accessibility exists when (1) an open-door admissions policy permits entrance to a suitable form of postsecondary education any high school graduate or other individual who appears to have a reasonable chance to succeed; (2) appropriate geographical proximity to higher education programs is provided; and (3) sound financial assistance is available to all needy students.

Open-Door Admission and Civil Rights

One of the most significant features of the community 2-year college concept is its open-door admissions policy. Such a policy guarantees every resident high school graduate (or equivalent)[4] admission to a suitable form of in-State postsecondary education and further guarantees those enrolled an equal opportunity to remain as long as they demonstrate academic potential and personal interest.

By 1970, public 2-year colleges had been established in 45 States.[5] Basic to the philosophy of the majority is that there is a place for every high school graduate who aspires to further education. This widespread commitment to higher education for all is in sharp contrast to the situation as late as 1960 when only 21 States reported utilizing an open-door policy.[6]

It is not surprising that so many States now place heavy emphasis on their responsibility to assist each individual to continue his education, and to do so without any restriction based on race, creed, or national origin. Educational theorists and social leaders are becoming more aware of the increasing responsibility of schools and colleges to develop all human potential and to serve as a major vehicle for integrating the individual with society. They agree that education has a humanistic role—namely, to develop in all youths the intellectuality, creativity, autonomy, and adaptability needed to cope with a changing, increasingly technocratic environment. To this role is added another: assisting the mass of the population in vocational development. The Nation has arrived at a period in human history when an automated society has little need for the talents of the uneducated, when even minimal survival skills require a trained mind and educated judgments. To meet the complex intellectual, vocational, and social demands of the latter half of the 20th century requires that *all* youths complete some form of postsecondary education.

The growing need for educational change brought about by the knowledge explosion in an age of technology has been paralleled by social pressure involving human rights. The dispossessed members in an affluent society are demanding total and meaningful integration in the mainstream in order to be able to share in the national wealth. More than any other single factor, equality of educational opportunity—and ultimately, of educational achievement—is viewed as crucial to this end.

---

[4] In many States, institutions are open to resident youths, 18 years of age or older, not possessing a high school diploma, who can present evidence of being able to pursue successfully a proposed course of study.

[5] Four additional States—Alaska, Hawaii, Kentucky, and Maine—have 2-year community colleges within a State university system.

[6] R. Grann Lloyd, "Admission Policy in State Supported Colleges and Universities," *School and Society*, vol. 88, Nov. 19, 1960, pp. 446–47.

Since the 1954 Supreme Court landmark decision ordering school desegregation, the majority of public colleges and universities—even those in the South—have adopted admission policies which, in theory at least, respect individual rights. Viewed in the perspective of time, greater accessibility through nondiscrimination is a fact. But it is also true that not all States place equal emphasis on nondiscrimination. In spite of major efforts since the late 1950's to increase opportunities for minority youths to attend college, limited progress has been made.

In 1971, only 8.4 percent of all college students were black and about one out of every three attended all-black colleges. This attendance rate contrasts sharply with the black proportion—12.5 percent—of the college-age population (18 through 21 years). Such a discrepancy is evidence that the task of equalizing educational opportunities for minority-group students involves much more than simply creating open accessibility.

The problem is not really one of combating overt discrimination; rather, it is one of improving educational opportunities for the black, Chicano, Indian, and other minority groups at every level and in proportion to need. In countless situations, providing equal opportunity and eliminating individual discrimination calls for particular awareness of the special needs of groups long segregated from the mainstream. Since most minority-group students are graduates of schools inferior in scope and substandard in quality, they seldom qualify for admission at most colleges, particularly those institutions that have raised their entrance standards and tuition. Genuine equal opportunity exists for minority groups only when they are equipped to compete fairly on the basis of potential rather than on initial performance. They cannot compete fairly when admission is based primarily on testing, when grants are awarded on the basis of demonstrated scholarship rather than on need, and when institutions are insensitive to the wide variety of special compensatory services required to offset the effects of deprivation. States which do not provide the necessary conditions for fair competition have not created realistic equal educational opportunity, even if they proclaim that their doors are open to all.

Geographical Proximity

The fact that the existence of a college in the immediate vicinity influences a student's decision to seek a higher education has been studied by Medsker and Trent[7] and more recently by Anderson, Bowman, and Tinto.[8]

---

[7] Medsker and Trent, op. cit., pp. 50–69.

[8] C. Arnold Anderson, Mary Jean Bowman, and Vincent Tinto, *Where Colleges Are and Who Attends*, McGraw-Hill Book Co., New York, 1972.

Both studies recognize that the main impact local accessibility exerts on attendance is the positive effects of a reduction in college expenses to the individual. If a college is conveniently located, a student can live at home and the financial burden is considerably lessened. As would be expected, both studies found that less able youths of humble or modest backgrounds would more often enter college if such an institution were located on their doorsteps. There is a clear contrast, however, between the findings of Anderson, Bowman, and Tinto and those of Medsker and Trent regarding the effect that presence of a local college has on the decision by more academically able and affluent high school graduates to attend college. Medsker and Trent found that a local college influenced the more able and affluent students to attend college as well as those students in the lower ability and status ranges. In the later Anderson-Bowman-Tinto study a local college appeared to have little if any effect on the college-going rate of able and/or affluent youths. Because conditions within higher education for the two studies differ substantially, a realistic comparison of data and findings is difficult. Between 1959 and 1966, the dates when the two investigations were conducted, there was a rise in the proportion of American youths who completed high school and also in the proportion of high school graduates who continued on to college. In the earlier Medsker-Trent study, youths with low-status backgrounds from noncollege communities displayed much lower rates of college attendance (especially at higher levels of ability) than did the respondents in the later Anderson-Bowman-Tinto study. This difference in noncollege community attendance rates partially explains the apparent support for the public junior college inferred from the Medsker-Trent data, as well as the pessimistic conclusions about the drawing power of 2-year colleges made by Anderson, Bowman, and Tinto, who state, "The much-desired expansion of attendance by able youth from low-status families cannot dependably be increased through the implanting of colleges closer at hand."[9]

The finding that attendance is determined mostly by ability and by family status means that the continued expansion of local colleges to extend educational opportunity can no longer be justified on the grounds that proximity contributes to equality for college-age youths. The fact that 4-year colleges and universities, as well as most private institutions, are becoming more selective may create a demand for more 2-year institutions. Also, there are still many communities that need to provide opportunities for adult education, remedial education programs, technical training, and the cultural and other community services that a local college could be expected to provide. Although it is time to reexamine the need for further expanding the network of 2-year institutions in this country, no one can yet

---

[9] Ibid., p. 283.

say there are too many, especially if the role of new institutions is revised to meet existing deficiencies in both geographical coverage and special program needs.

Financial Aid to Students

As reported at the beginning of this chapter, between 300,000 and 500,000 academically able high school graduates did not enter college in the fall of 1972. Of these, it is estimated that at least 1 in 10 were prevented from starting college because they could not afford the costs involved (see chapter IV). Thus, it can be estimated that as many as 50,000 high school graduates of college ability are currently being prevented from entering college for financial reasons.

Providing low-cost or "free" public higher education is only part of the answer. The absence of tuition charges reduces but does not eliminate the financial plight of many youths. They must have sufficient wherewithal to cover expenditures for tuition, room and board, books, travel, and personal incidentals. Still another financial consideration should be a separation allowance paid to families dependent on the earnings of a family member while said member attends college. Low-income students, often inadequately prepared and easily discouraged, can ill afford to divide their energies between the severe challenge of academic pursuits and job demands. The likelihood of success for such marginal students can, as a rule, be increased only if they are allowed to concentrate their attention on study and personal adjustment without the distraction and responsibility of outside work.

In establishing a statewide student financial aid program, the immediate questions facing planners and legislative bodies are: How many additional youths are likely to enroll in existing State public and private institutions if their financial needs are met? How much will it cost to provide this aid? Methodology for answering these questions, plus a guide to the basic principles for establishing a student aid program, are the subject of Chapter IV.

INCENTIVE AND COMPENSATORY PROGRAMS

Despite enormous progress in removing the economic barriers to education, social barriers stubbornly persist. Even open-door colleges are not attracting many youths—particularly those who seem unable to view college as a realistic possibility or who are so discouraged by their slow progress in achieving the college goal that they stop trying. Colleges and universities, particularly prestigious institutions, have long been accustomed to selecting a chosen few from many qualified applicants. Now, as they seek to capture the imagination and stimulate the ability of less academically capable youth, they are discovering that merely opening the doors wider is not enough. They must also find ways and means to encourage the disadvantaged to respond positively to higher education.

Encouraging a Positive Response to Higher Education

For those who want to attend college and believe they can, the way has been eased by removal of many of the economic barriers, and also by the national commitment that socioeconomic factors not be an obstacle to education at any level. However, for those who seem unable to find the will to attend, are discouraged by their progress in meeting requirements, or see no realistic possibility of attending, no parallel breakthrough has been achieved.

Of the 300,000 to 500,000 qualified high school graduates who fail to enter college, about one in seven discontinues his education for lack of motivation. Certainly the yearly loss of as many as 75,000 college entrants because of insufficient incentive and discouragement is a serious and embarrassing problem. While expansion of the opportunities for higher education is continued, a national effort must be made to focus attention on programs to encourage academic success among able young people who should go to college but who, for a variety of reasons, choose not to attend or quit trying.

A great deal is known about the differences in personal incentive and persistence toward higher education exhibited by various social groups. Research has repeatedly demonstrated that children from wealthy families seek higher education more frequently than do children from poorer families; that more white than nonwhite children go to college; that more boys than girls attend; that metropolitan youths go to college more often than do rural youths. Furthermore, it is known that prospective college students are more likely to be those with high-ability levels from the top ranks of a high school class. They believe that a college education is extremely important, make plans to attend, and receive encouragement from parents.[10]

Such information is both helpful and necessary to any understanding of personal incentive toward higher education. It also provides a clue regarding the ways to work effectively with individual students who should

---

[10] For a detailed study of the many factors affecting the immediate major pursuits of high school graduates, see Medsker and Trent, op. cit.

be encouraged to obtain a college education. If something is known about a given group to which an individual belongs, some prediction can be made about the probabilities of college attendance. Furthermore, through methods of partial correlation it is possible to observe certain differentials that appear decisive to college attendance. For instance, in a group of high-ability boys from homes of skilled laborers, the education of the mother was found to be an important differential in distinguishing those who planned to attend college from those having no such plans. With information of this detail, it is possible to identify certain groups that merit special attention and require some kind of incentive program—for example, youths of high ability from families of low economic status; also, children from certain racial groups, from certain religious groups, and from certain geographical areas.

Because so much emphasis is placed on group differences, it is necessary to point out what should be obvious. The fundamental characteristics that distinguish one group from another are subject to little if any change. The poor cannot quickly become rich or the dull, brilliant. There will always be minorities, rural youths, females, and urban whites. Since the groups themselves are subject to slow change, it is fortunate that their distinguishing characteristics *are not* the cause of motivational problems. Poverty does not destroy incentive, nor does race, age, ability, sex, or geographical location. The groups themselves do not discourage higher education. Certain attendant factors, however, do: absence of encouragement, isolation from cultural and academic experiences, and. parental and peer-group indifference. The point is well illustrated by this quotation:

> Children from low-income families do not fail to attend simply because they belong to this group but rather because a number of conditions are associated with low incomes—restricted educational cultural experiences in the family, association with others not attending college, occupational goals which do not involve college training, and similiar conditions. Girls do not fail to attend college simply because they are girls, but rather because of a number of conditions related to femininity—parental attitudes toward the education of women, the types of education provided for women by many coeducational institutions, attitudes of men toward the education of wives, and such.[11]

The fact that the group is not at fault, but rather related conditions affecting the individual within the group, explains why incentive and encouragement programs must attempt to gain an understanding of each individual. Regardless of how much is known about groups of students, it will always be necessary to have specific information about the individual— his needs, capacities, and values; also, about those circumstances in his

---

[11] Ralph F. Berdie, "Group Membership and Higher Education," *Higher Education Incentives and Obstacles* (Nicholas C. Brown, ed.), American Council on Education, Washington, D. C., 1959, p. 89.

life that have formed his attitudes toward education. Understanding an individual leads to a discovery of how that person's incentive and achievement for higher education can be enhanced.

What are the basic factors or conditions responsible for evoking and sustaining an individual's decision to continue or terminate his education? The following appear to be significant, and any one may be singularly decisive:

Personal Motivation and Achievement

1. Need or drive for self-fulfillment and achievement
2. Intrinsic pleasure and interest in learning
3. A pattern of successful achievement in academic and other related college-going activities

Social Encouragement and Practical Feasibility

4. Positive influence of family, teachers, peer-group, and community—all advocates of college as a desirable and achievable goal
5. Identification with parents, relatives, teachers, and others who have gone to college
6. Financial and other accessibility circumstances which make college a realistic possibility

Recognized Returns

7. Future financial benefits resulting from a college education
8. Expected satisfaction and enjoyment of the college experience and of other anticipated returns, such as finding a suitable marriage partner.

No miracle process has yet been devised to produce a positive response to higher education if none is present. Current incentive programs are attempting to use the foregoing factors to influence a student's attitude and disposition toward going to college. Introduction of high school students to college life through special summer programs, for example, may be expected to imbue less responsive students with an appreciation of the enjoyment of the college experience, and thereby enhance the possibility of their enrollment.

Incentive programs need not encourage self-fulfillment and achievement. Youths tend to possess such drives, and, in addition, are usually interested in learning as well. For most, the value of college is all-too-well understood. In most instances, what they lack is not the will to attend or an understanding of the importance, but rather success in achieving their own goals, which, in turn, supports continued effort and gives rise to higher goals. There are probably few students of ability who would not set college as a goal if they could view it as a realistic possibility. Too often, however, lack of support by unsympathetic parents and friends, together with discouraging progress in high school, combine to create an overwhelming belief in the impracticality of a college career. There is great difficulty in maintaining incentive toward a nearly invisible goal when one is faced with immediate failure and indifferent support. Incentive programs, therefore, should focus on clarifying the college-going goal in realistic terms, establishing patterns of achievement, and providing personal encouragement.

The cause-effect relationship between the multiple and unique circumstances of an individual's life and the development of incentive is extremely complex. Obviously, it cannot be explained by a list of contributive factors, but knowing what these factors are does provide some background for understanding the direction in which current incentive programs are moving. What follows are some of the interrelated methods being used to instill in able youths the desire to attend college, and to overcome discouragement among those who have given up hope of pursuing a post-secondary education.

1. By enhancing an individual's worth, *give each person an opportunity to gain insight and to develop a sense of his potential*. If a child is to change his image from that of being a mere struggler for survival to one which encompasses the likelihood of going to college, some change in parental attitudes must be effected. The expectation or at least the possibility of attending college must be developed early through intensive individual and group guidance and encouragement, cultural exposure, enrichment programs, etc., with as much parental involvement as possible.

2. Through early identification (in elementary school, if possible) of able children and a continuing program of counseling, *help the student know himself*. At an early age a child and his parents should be informed of his academic potential, interests, and abilities. Then a plan should be instituted to direct family vision toward appropriate programs of self-realization.

3. *Interpret the college concept* to youths and their parents in an effort to turn ignorance and indifference into viable interest. Through personal guidance and extensive use of all mass communication media, inform students, teachers, counselors, parents, and interested organizations of the advantages of a college education. Also, publicize all available post-secondary opportunities, including academic programs, admission standards, financial aid, compensatory practices, preparatory course requirements, and the like.

4. *Establish patterns of academic success, and, at the same time, make schoolwork more interesting and rewarding*. Enlightened teachers, small classes, enrichment programs, and intensive guidance all contribute to better achievement and increased aspiration. Teachers should express their high expectations and encourage academic confidence through success in the classroom. Subject matter should be made interesting and relevant so that students see the need to study, learn to enjoy it, and seek to continue learning. A stimulating environment minimizes the chances of intellectual stagnation.

5. *Reduce effects of personal problems and emotional handicaps* resulting from such factors as social isolation, conflict in the home, juvenile delinquency, and others associated with deprived or maladjusted children.

6. *Through counseling and guidance, identify the educational needs of students.* Teachers and counselors should help students find attainable goals to which they can legitimately aspire.

Assisting the Disadvantaged

In a recently published scientific work, Edmund Gordon and Doxey Wilkerson[12] challenge the idea that compensatory education is the most appropriate way to meet the problems of the disadvantaged. Remunerative programs attempt to compensate for, or to overcome, the effects of hostile, different, or indifferent backgrounds by raising children to a level at which they can be reached by *existing* programs. Gordon and Wilkerson argue that it is the school which must make concessions; that it must accept children as they are and find educational techniques best suited to their needs. They point out that the primary requisite is to strengthen the teacher-learning process. Teachers, they suggest, should better understand the nature and cause of a disadvantaged child's low achievement, then devise learning situations to enable him to acquire the knowledge many other children are already assimilating. Although relatively little is known about the specific kinds of educational experiences disadvantaged children need, teacher behavior and attitude appear to be critical to effective learner-environment interaction—far more important, for example, than pedagogical or curricular innovation.

In view of the fact that compensatory education is emphasized disproportionately vis-a-vis education appropriate to developmental need, what is the proper role of compensatory programs in higher education? Since it is axiomatic that some able individuals will continue to emerge from the educational system frustrated, embittered, demoralized, and uneducated, colleges must, insofar as possible, prevent such from happening. The problems of the disadvantaged, of course, begin long before college—in grammar school and even kindergarten. Consequently, those who have passed through the lower system and can benefit from college must be provided with the kind of formal education from which they can gain a sense of both personal success and commitment to learning, as well as the necessary educational tools to continue their education.

It is essential that colleges and universities suffer no delusions with respect to who can benefit from compensatory efforts and what realistic returns can

---

[12] Edmond W. Gordon and Doxey A. Wilkerson, *Compensatory Education for the Dis advantaged—Programs and Practices: Preschool Through College*, College Entrance Examination Board, New York, 1966.

ɔe expected. Higher education compensatory programs should seek to nfluence motivation, values, learning opportunities, and other environmentally conditioned habits, and thereby improve the academic *performance* ɔf *able* youths who, mainly because of social, economic, and educational leprivation and discrimination, have not been able to fully develop their ɩbilities. Critical to success is the need to match compensatory efforts and tudent selection with the academic program. Students must be brought ɔ a point where they can successfully compete. Institutions which offer an nclusive, diverse, and pertinent curriculum designed to accommodate a ɩeterogeneous student population may be successful in compensating for the vide range of student abilities. On the other hand, college compensatory ɛfforts that do not provide special curriculums at suitable levels of difficulty nust be directed toward students who give high evidence of readiness to ucceed. If no fundamental changes are provided at the curriculum level, ɽouths who give evidence of not having the necessary intelligence or notivation to compete successfully and persist are poor choices for comɔensatory efforts. No amount of tutoring and remedial help at the college ɛvel will markedly influence intelligence per se. While there is considerable lisagreement on the issue, Arthur R. Jensen[13] and others give strong ɛvidence of the heritability of intelligence and of its unsusceptibility to mprovement by environmental changes. If this theory is valid, it seems ikely that compensatory programs designed to produce individuals who ːan successfully compete in college must be directed to youths who give ɛvidence of scholastic aptitude *appropriate to the institution and curriculum.* ͡urthermore, if substantial advances in ability cannot be realistically ɛxpected, compensatory programs should be directed toward, and evalɩated by, improvement in scholastic performance, basic skills acquired, ɽalues learned, etc.

Present college and university compensatory programs are designed ɔoth to help disadvantaged students enter college and, following admission, ɩelp them succeed. Practices to help disadvantaged students enter college ɩnclude recruiting procedures, modified admissions, preparatory courses, ɩnd financial aid. Practices designed to help disadvantaged students after their admission include counseling, credit and noncredit remedial courses, ɩnstruction in how to study, tutoring, special curriculums, and time extensions for completion of degree requirements. Details concerning these practices, their extent and distribution, are described extensively in recent studies (see bibliography). What follows is a brief delineation of current practices at the University of California.

The Berkeley Special Opportunity Scholarship (SOS) program is an ɛxcellent example of present-day compensatory techniques being used to

---

[13] Arthur R. Jensen, "How Much Can We Boost IQ and Scholastic Achievement?" *Harvard Education Review*, vol. 39, no. 1, Winter 1969, pp. 1–123.

prepare economically disadvantaged high school students for college and to assist them during their freshman and sophomore years. The purpose of the high school phase (a component of Upward Bound) is to make higher education a real and compelling choice for able but disadvantaged youngsters. To accomplish this objective, such youngsters are offered 4 successive years of summer school experiences in combination with year-round tutoring, guidance, and various other activities designed to kindle educational aspirations. The purpose of the summer program is to strengthen basic skills and widen and deepen student vision and imagination. Followup activities during the academic year, centered in the public schools, are designed to further academic success and involve students with college-going experiences.

Those features of the Special Opportunity Scholarship-Upward Bound project at Berkeley which seem to contribute to its effectiveness can serve as useful guidelines:[14]

1. *Recruiting students at the 9th-grade level* takes advantage of the extensive knowledge that junior high school counselors have of their students, thereby making a careful selection possible. Even more important is early identification and provision of special help before these students begin to suffer failure, frustration, or alienation in senior high school.

2. *Promise of ultimate grant assistance* to the extent of real need through the first 2 years of college for deserving students who continue in the program, qualify for college entrance, and have made a reasonable effort and shown reasonable achievement. This grant reward encourages effort and commitment.

3. *A strong academic emphasis*, with provision of two solid academic courses each summer for all students, one of which must be English. Since students earn high school credit for these two basic academic courses, their marks can contribute to grade averages calculated from high school transcripts.

4. *Early integration into college life*. The natural and orderly use by Upward Bound students of university educational, cultural, and recreational facilities on an equal footing with regular university students encourages them to identify with college life and, in all probability, to assume and expect a college career for themselves.

5. *Intimate student participation in decisionmaking* through student government, committees, and instructional teams. Emphasis is less on discipline and control than on improving the work environment and promoting human relationships, mutual understanding, and respect. Many channels of communication encourage students to express their views and concerns and, in so doing, to find satisfaction for their needs.

---

[14] Owen Chamberlain and Mark Rosensweig, "Special Opportunity Scholarships," *The Weekly Magazine*, vol. 3, no. 2, May 9, 1968, p. 14.

6. *Continuity and heterogeneity of staff* connote stability and provide young people with varied models of well-integrated and adequate personality types of contrasting age, sex, ethnic background, and experience. Most instruction is carried on by teams that include public school teachers, chosen for their experience with disadvantaged youths and demonstrated effectiveness; university instructors; university graduate students with very strong academic backgrounds, and who, by interest, experience, and commitment, are especially qualified to work with disadvantaged youths; and some carefully chosen senior university students.

7. *Formal and informal intercourse between students from all secondary grades.* Interest groups, recreation, and student government bring together students from all 4 high school years. Older college students, who serve as assistant teachers in the program, are given a legitimate and natural role in guiding and helping younger students. Elective courses draw upper grade students together. All of these practices make for stability and thereby facilitate the adjustment of younger pupils to the program and its opportunities.

8. *Comprehensive health examination and generous health services.* Students have the benefit of regular university health services, including a comprehensive physical examination, which may reveal serious health deficiencies.

The merits of all of the various compensatory practices are beyond the scope of this book. A review of the literature, however, leads to the following general observations:

• College education has become one of the normal expectations of nearly all middle-class and well-to-do youth in American society. Postsecondary education should also be a realistic choice of racial and ethnic minorities and the poor. Yet few predominantly white colleges and universities seem to realize how seriously inadequate and unequal an opportunity they offer these "different" students. And since only a small number of institutions have more than minimal compensatory programs, the number of minority-group and low-income students being served is small. Colleges doing little to aid the disadvantaged, in defense of their position, point to lack of funds, enrollment pressures, fear of lowering academic standards, etc. But in terms of social responsibility and justice to all individuals, it is clear that higher education can and must increase its efforts to help the disadvantaged solve their problems.

• Identification of scholastic potential, having recently undergone substantial redirection, is now more realistic, especially as it applies to culturally different and deprived students. Some years ago it was thought that recruiting disadvantaged youngsters merely required identifying academically talented pupils by testing for obviously superior psychological traits. Almost immediately the efficacy of these tests became suspect. Some tests of intelligence, aptitude, and achievement central to the effort were found to be culturally loaded and misleading when applied to certain disadvantaged students. Furthermore, the intellectual abilities of some individuals were likely to be masked by widely held preconceptions concerning the groups to which they belonged.

As a result of these observations, new guidelines for talent identification have emerged. Nevertheless, in view of present curriculum design, scores on the various scholastic aptitude tests, augmented by high school grades, are still the best evidence of an individual's readiness to succeed in college and cannot be ignored without the serious risk of academic failure. Furthermore, these criteria apply almost as equally to blacks and other minority groups as to whites.[15] On the other hand, ability is not always matched by performance. For this reason, it is now recommended that, in addition to test scores and high school grades, other evaluations be made—in as many areas as possible—to more accurately identify students appearing to have the attributes necessary for success in college. Another recommendation is that all criteria should be applied to the individual student with less rigidity than previously; moreover, that general information concerning the characteristics of disadvantaged pupils, particularly their character and motivation, be incorporated in the final assessment. A *complete* profile of test scores, school record, family background, academic progress, special skills and aptitudes, scholastic strengths and weaknesses, and any number of other observations deemed relevant will minimize the risk of excluding students because of too-narrow testing or too-strict standards.

In adopting this approach to talent identification, the University of California at Berkeley, under the Educational Opportunity Program (EOP) for minority and low-income students, has revised its admissions criteria. Among the significant questions asked are these:

1. Does the applicant have the necessary high school preparation for his intended major? Minority groups were found to be almost universally deficient in physical science and mathematics. Applicants interested in majoring in these fields were accepted if they were ready for college calculus; otherwise, they were given financial aid for junior college preparatory work.

2. Does the applicant's high school grade record show improvement? While 60 percent of the applicants did not have a "B" average in university-required courses (the UCB entrance requirement), those who had improved their marks were deemed "promising" and were, therefore, accepted.

---

[15] J. C. Stanley and A. C. Porter, "Correlation of Scholastic Aptitude Test Score with College Grade for Negroes Versus Whites," *Journal of Educational Measurement*, vol. 4, Winter 1967, pp. 199–218.

3. Does the applicant's pattern of course selection indicate increasing interest in college preparatory work? Evidence of some preparation for college had to have been demonstrated in high school.

4. Do letters of recommendation suggest the applicant's ability to do college work? Each applicant was asked to secure three to five letters from counselors and teachers in a position to speak about his academic ability.

5. Does the applicant's self-assessment statement indicate an ability to overcome or circumvent his problems? Applicants most likely to succeed gave evidence of being able to resolve their problems. On the other hand, students preoccupied with their problems were not considered as promising as those who were resolving their difficulties.[16]

•Are remedial studies the answer to scholastic deficiencies? The answer is both "yes" and "no." While formal remedial noncredit courses in 4-year colleges and universities have not been as effective as had been hoped, precollege summer preparatory programs are enjoying greater success than had been anticipated. For example, since 1966 the USOE/Office of Economic Opportunity's Upward Bound program has provided intensive tutorial and counseling services to more than 32,000 high school students. Of these, more than 70 percent entered some form of postsecondary education. The lack of motivation and involvement on the part of students, often cited by teachers of formal incollege remedial programs, may be more a symptom than a cause of unimproved academic performance; poor quality and planning of such programs is more likely to be the reason for the failure of these programs. On the other hand, precollege activity involving imaginative and flexible teachers, close student-teacher contact, and the effective use of college and university students as tutor-counselors appears to be the most dramatic compensatory development in higher education during recent years.

•As first-level remedies—financial assistance, modified admission policies, talent searching, and remedial course work—are increasingly employed to improve opportunities for high-risk students, greater attention must be devoted to second-level problems if disadvantaged students are to make the college adjustment. Toward this end, Gordon and Wilkerson recommend that serious work begin now on such problems as (1) modification of the mental postures and learning patterns in inefficient young adult learners;

---

[16] The initiator and director of the Educational Opportunities Program, Bill Somerville, found that over a 2-year period, during which these criteria were applied, the dropout rate of students selected for the Educational Opportunity Program was 17 percent. In comparison, the freshman dropout rate for the University as a whole was 23 to 25 percent (the freshman class represented the top 12 percent of high school graduates in California). The high retention rate among EOP participants can, of course, be attributed to the personal attention each student received.

(2) devising of alternate input systems for the acquisition of knowledge banks for the student who suffers from major deficits in information as well as from underdeveloped skills for acquiring such knowledge; (3) relationship of the availability of social or cultural reference groups to persistence and attrition rates among minority-group college students; and (4) the differential interaction between aspiration, motivation, opportunity, resource mobilization, and achievement.[17]

•Julian C. Stanley of John Hopkins University argues the basic principle, applicable across socioeconomic levels and races, that students best achieve their academic goals at institutions where they are not too poorly (or well) prepared to compete academically.

Students would not seem to be served best academically by being admitted to those major universities and selective colleges for which they lack even marginal readiness. The same 3,000 colleges in this country provide enough variability in academic difficulty to accommodate almost every high school graduate who wishes to be a college student. Some of the relatively few selective institutions of higher education will feel it their duty and privilege to change their entrance standards considerably and provide special curricula on a small-to-moderate scale for children of the poor. Their planners need to keep firmly in mind that principles of learning in school and predictiveness of tests apply at least as fully to the disadvantaged as to the advantaged. Therefore, really fundamental changes at the curricular level will be necessary before students hitherto academically underqualified for the college are admitted.[18]

•In a study for the Southern Education Foundation, John Egerton[19] found that viewpoints differed as to whether high-risk students should be accorded special attention or treated in the same manner as all other students. Some institutions, of the opinion that the disadvantaged student has enough problems to overcome without the stigma of being identified as a risk, made every effort to conceal students' academic and economic handicaps. Others, believing that the special support activities required—lighter class loads, special courses, extensive tutoring, and the like—are essential to a student's success, made no overt attempt to hide them. The risk students themselves had mixed feelings about the question, at times expressing both resentment and appreciation for either approach.

---

[17] Gordon and Wilkerson, op. cit., p. 173.

[18] Julian C. Stanley, "Achievement by the Disadvantaged" (letter), *Science*, vol. 163 no. 3866, Feb. 14, 1969, p. 622.

[19] John Egerton, *Higher Education for "High Risk" Students*, Southern Education Foundation, Atlanta, Ga., p. 14.

•Many educators, recognizing that handicaps affecting disadvantaged youngsters are probably deeply rooted by the time they reach high school, contend that any remedial effort in college is too late and cannot make up for previous educational deficiencies. Evidence supports the idea that special efforts to help the disadvantaged child should be initiated in the early grades. Yet the responsibilities of society to the youngster who reaches college age without such assistance cannot be ignored. The question still to be answered is: To what degree can the progressive effects of discrimination and cultural differences be overcome in young adults?

THE EDUCATIONAL ENVIRONMENT

Educational opportunities could be greatly expanded if roadblocks to progress were removed and the number of alternatives open to youngsters increased. Not only should all high school graduates be able to continue their education at a suitable postsecondary institution but the required transition should be made as easy as possible. And once a student has embarked on a program of higher education, progress should be based on aptitude and accomplishments. Students beginning their postsecondary education at any institution, including 2-year colleges and technical institutes, should be able—if they so desire and are qualified—to transfer to 4-year colleges to earn a baccalaureate degree, and, if qualified, to enter a graduate or professional school.

Throughout a student's learning career, a succession of educational alternatives should be available from which he may select a course of study most appropriate to his talents and interests. The opportunity to choose among different institutions, curriculums, and student-faculty associations should exist at every educational level. For those who are undecided about the career they wish to pursue or who have made the wrong choice, colleges and universities should provide alternatives either by offering a progressively more demanding general education or through organizational flexibility. Not enough is yet known about career preparation and requirements or about college characteristics and environment to permit, with any degree of precision, the pairing of student, institution, and curriculum. Until such relationships are better understood, many students will make false starts and find it necessary to change direction. For these young people, the system must be flexible; it must be willing and ready with attractive alternatives.[20]

---

[20] For a detailed discussion of this topic, see T. R. McConnell, *A General Pattern for American Public Higher Education*, ch. 9, "The Individual Student and the System," McGraw-Hill Co., New York, 1962.

Articulation

The transition from secondary to higher education is a responsibility left almost entirely to the individual student. Any interactions are principally between the student and his prospective college, between the student and his high school counselor and teachers, and between the student and his parents and friends—with the student always the connecting link. Very few efforts have been made by the two systems involved—the high school and the college—to act together to make the student's education an organic whole. In a majority of cases, there are no lines of communication between the school and the college other than those established by the student in his back-and-forth contacts. As a result, many of those admitted to college are not properly located and insufficiently prepared.

Such imperfect articulation is somewhat surprising in view of the fact that the alleged concern of both high school and college is to place the "right" student in the "right" institution. Ostensibly, the school seeks to prepare and guide its college-bound students so that they can enter and succeed in those colleges perceived as "right" for them, while the college seeks to enroll a given number of students of the kind desired. Unfortunately, the two educational systems involved have not been interested in seeking a smooth and effective transition to the degree that they would attempt to secure enough information about the total arrangement to make it work effectively. Clearly, both systems view the problem of articulation less seriously than do the students.

Establishing meaningful communications is immensely complicated if for no other reason than the sheer magnitude of the information flow. There are about 22,000 public and private high schools in the United States and over 2,500 institutions of higher education. Eighty percent of the high school graduating classes total less than 100 students. Assuming a median graduating class of 50, approximately half the students will pursue some form of postsecondary education. If these 25 college-bound students collectively contact as few as 30 different colleges and universities, a total of 660,000 school-college interchanges would be established.

To ensure that a student's transition from high school to college is smooth and effective, a variety of approaches are needed. At least five require joint effort by schools and colleges:

(1) Since an individual student's ability to decide wisely in selecting a college is central to an effective transition, the finest possible counsel in helping him make a choice should be available. Students often do not have very accurate perceptions about the colleges they choose, and the persons on whom they depend for information are usually not able to provide it. Parents and friends, although not necessarily the best informed, may exert more influence than either teachers or counselors. Since a considerable degree of irrationality characterizes the entire process of choosing, the

process itself could be vastly improved if prospective college students were not only acquainted with a logical and systematic procedure for selecting the "right" college but also taught to appreciate the controlling factors and relevant considerations. Guidance, particularly in choosing an institution within a State system of higher education, should be made available to every prospective enrollee through written instructions and orientation lectures.

(2) The entire relationship between high school and college curriculums requires greater understanding and alignment. What courses are appropriate for college preparation and how essential are they to a student's success? A surprising fact is that approximately 25 percent of students entering college have not been enrolled in a college-preparatory program.[21] Another startling fact is that the number of years a student studies a particular subject in high school appears to have no significant effect on the grade he makes in that subject in college.[22] The curriculum area obviously deserves further research; in the meantime, immediate improvements could be effected if schools and colleges would join in closer consultation and mutual study of the problem.

(3) Greater flexibility should be provided between college preparatory programs and college entrance requirements. Preparatory programs should be so designed that they will be reasonably suitable no matter what college a student attends. Individual colleges should not prescribe entrance requirements in the expectation that students will prepare exclusively for their program. Overall, requirements should be broadly defined, not limited to certain courses for certain colleges.

(4) Adequate information should not only flow between college and high school but should also be effectively transmitted. The value and interpretation of printed material now available to students and schools about colleges—including commercially published guides—should be investigated. Special orientation catalogs containing postsecondary educational opportunities within the State should be available to resident high school seniors. Channels of communication should be expanded and made more efficient. It may be feasible, for example, to lease telephone lines to permit prospective students to contact distant colleges at reduced rates.

(5) Students should be given as much guidance as possible—concerning themselves, possible career choices, and institutions they might attend. With computers, it is possible to match individual profiles rapidly with institutional and occupational characteristics. Once such data are in hand, the student can identify not only those colleges that attract persons most

---

[21] Natalie Rogoff Ramsey, "College Recruitment and High School Curricula," *Sociology of Education*, vol. 38, Summer 1965, pp. 297–309.

[22] Bert L. Sharp, "College Achievement: Its Relationship to High School Achievement Experiences and Test Scores," *Personnel Guidance Journal*, vol. 41, no. 3, 1962, pp. 247–50.

like himself but also the probabilities of success he can expect in various institutions and occupations. A great deal more research is necessary to determine the relationship between aspiration, ability, education, and goal attainment. And since it will be many years before computer guidance systems are common, greatly improved counseling procedures are needed now to cope with the increasing complexities of career decisions—particularly those related to the disadvantaged student—and appropriate preparation.

Curricular and Program Innovations

As has previously been pointed out, lost educational opportunity in American colleges and universities today stems, in large measure, from the fact that outmoded curriculums and teaching techniques fail to meet the needs of students and of society in general. The central assignment of institutions of higher education has long been to prepare individuals for definite roles in industry, finance, government, and the established professions. The person whose motivation parallels these career categories has little reason to question a prescribed curriculum. But the simple fact is that a constantly growing proportion of students requires and demands the kind of education not molded in the traditional fashion or along established lines of professional or business success. The most dissatisfied—often the best students—complain of the irrelevance of the curriculum to their energies and interests. Equally dissatisfied, although usually less vocal, are the large numbers of marginal students and adults who, having been given equal access to higher education, require an education oriented to the real world. One indicator of the magnitude of boredom and discouragement resulting from obsolete curriculums and ineffective teaching is the high number of college dropouts (about one-half of those who enter college do not graduate).

There are several reasons why so many students are dissatisfied with the present-day formal curriculum offered by American colleges and universities. Young people growing up in the affluent economy of the 1960's and 1970's have felt less pressure to become a job holder immediately. In addition, they have been inspired to pursue goals other than attaining good grades or being admitted to graduate school. In contrast, most colleges are still primarily engaged in preparing young people solely for job security.

Another source of student discontent is the fact that colleges have neglected the nurturing functions while maintaining strict controls and penalties. Faculty withdrawal into areas of their professional concerns, meaningless work assignments, pressure on grades, and similar old-line tactics confront the student with demands and restrictions not being offset by sincere concern for the individual. Not inappropriately, students are demanding of colleges the right to some special care and attention.

Today's undergraduates are also more sophisticated. They are better prepared in high school, often have studied or traveled abroad, served in the Peace Corps, or participated in domestic social action. Such students enter college with a critical, often cynical, attitude toward the educational system. Consequently, they are impatient with perfunctory teaching and textbook generalizations.

Student dissatisfaction plus new conceptions about higher education, and developments in industry, commerce, and technology that have created new job demands and career opportunities, contribute to a situation calling for curriculum innovation and reform. A variety of approaches are being taken, seven of which are cited here.

•Some of the educational ideas guiding faculty and administrators in planning college programs are illustrated by the following principles regarded as basic by Beloit College in establishing a new undergraduate curriculum in 1964:[23]

1. Education should be improved in both breadth and depth. The interrelatedness of knowledge should become an ever more important part of the curriculum. Overall goals of education should be measured in terms of acquisition of knowledge rather than in terms of earning passing marks. Area examinations in broad subject-matter divisions and comprehensive examinations in the major field of study should be instituted as aids to measuring acquisition of knowledge.

2. A truly significant effort should be made to develop the self-generating student who will continue his education on his own after graduation. Students should spend a smaller proportion of their time in class than formerly and a greater proportion doing independent reading and research.

3. All students should share a common academic experience, preferably a course or a group of courses, both at the beginning and near the termination of their undergraduate careers. An important component of this shared experience should be a meaningful convocation program, closely related—at least in part—to the academic program of the college.

4. The student's experience in his field of specialization or major should be so arranged that he may embark upon it early in his academic career.

5. The student should be as free as possible from the strait jacket of required courses and should be allowed freer and earlier access to a meaningful elective program.

6. The academic lockstep should be broken. Variety of many kinds should be possible—variety in types of experiences and in the ways such

[23] Sumner Hayward, "The Beloit Plan," *Liberal Education*, vol. 50, pp. 335–48, October 1964. The Beloit Plan comprises 29 principles, 16 of which have been selected and combined in this presentation.

experiences are worked into the life of the undergraduate. Every attempt should be made to give the student a truly meaningful offcampus experience for at least one term. It is hoped that the relationship between his oncampus academic experience, both in depth and breadth, and his offcampus experience will help him achieve perspective and maturity. Students should, when appropriate, be given the opportunity to sample the educational fare of other first-class educational institutions, both in the United States and abroad, and to receive credit for successful completion of such work.

7. English composition, both oral and written, should be taught in a meaningful subject-matter context. That is, in addition to the gaining of proficiency in expression, the student should be exposed to significant ideas with which to express himself, and in turn these ideas should be a part of his entire education.

8. The development of significant skills in mathematics, in foreign languages, and in physical education should be part of each undergraduate's experience.

9. The program of the college should be of such a nature that the student, if he so chooses, may be involved with it during all 4 years as an undergraduate—even during his "vacation" term. Better student use of such "vacation" terms should be made by enabling him to involve himself, if he so desires, in activities which have real academic relevance or relevance to his future life work.

10. To prevent a student's efforts from being unduly fragmented, a single academic course should require about one-fourth of his study time.

•Educator Nevitt Sanford[34] suggests that colleges and universities can promote new trends and desirable advances in certain potentially fertile areas by rewarding neglected forms of excellence. Among the fields receiving little attention and which could be made fruitful through awards for excellence are such disciplines as the social sciences, poetry, and art; interdisciplinary work; the master teacher; educational achievement not measured by grades; and significant group activity.

•Curricular and extracurricular activities, faculty-student relationships, and faculty interaction programs should all be designed on a sufficiently limited scale so that communities of people can be drawn together by common involvement, shared interests, and friendship. Relatively small groups working on matters of real significance seem to be the key to developing coherent communities.

•Student subcultural groups require activities and outlets for the educational values they seek. A college at which student subcultures exist should

[24] Nevitt Sanford, *Where Colleges Fail*, Jossey-Bass, San Francisco, Calif., 1968, pp. 21-9.

recognize the special needs of these groups and provide opportunities for them to harmonize with and enrich the institutional community.

•The overall appropriateness of contemporary education to the disadvantaged pupil should be investigated. In order to accommodate the special learning problems of developmentally handicapped persons, substantial modifications must be made in curriculum material, content, and methods. Equally important to redesigning formal curriculum is the need to make adjustments in the social, psychological, and physical environments in which learning occurs.

•Institutions of higher education should seek to provide conditions which create a spirit in which leisure is enjoyed and respected. ". . . the university should accept leisure as an essential in the lives of men and should provide ways for its creative use. . . . It should seek to have its students and faculty select wisely from the many leisure-time activities and enjoy them as complete and worthwhile experiences."[25] So that work can be properly balanced with recreation and cultural pursuits, a wide range of easily accessible leisure-time activities should be available to students and faculty.

•The extremely wide range of heterogeneous abilities among students attending community 2-year colleges—particularly those with large enrollments located in urban areas—requires curriculum developments in four major areas: (1) a quality lower division curriculum broad in scope and challenging for the student who will eventually transfer to a 4-year program; (2) a curriculum involving new teaching methods and new approaches for underachieving and culturally deprived students; (3) a program of technical and vocational education for students seeking employment after 1 or 2 years of college; and (4) a varied, rich curriculum for adults.

BIBLIOGRAPHY

Anderson, C. Arnold, Mary Jean Bowman, and Vincent Tinto, *Where Colleges Are and Who Attends*, McGraw-Hill Book Co., New York, 1972, 303 pp.

   The authors have made a detailed analysis of the relationship between college accessibility and college attendance in several States. They conclude that for most youths nearness to one or more colleges has little effect on the likelihood of an individual's going to college—regardless of the type of institution. Attendance is determined mostly by ability and by family status, not by proximity to a college. Geographical proximity alone does

---

[25] Lewis B. Mayhew, "Institutional Factors and the Learning Environment," in *The College and the Student* (Lawrence E. Dennis and Joseph F. Kauffman, eds.), American Council on Education, Washington, D. C., 1966, p. 227.

not encourage youths from families of low socioeconomic status and youths who have had poor primary and secondary school experiences to attend college. For those in these categories, costs must be low, admission requirements minimal, and remedial programs available. And even if these conditions are met, proximity is still of minor importance.

The authors recognize that if a local college is also an open-door or free-access institution, the costs of attending college will be lower—a factor of special importance to less able youths from poor families. It is among the latter that the largest net differentials are found in the overall college attendance rate between local free-access colleges and noncollege communities. The cost advantage of a local college was found to be of negligible importance to college attendance by youths from high-status, affluent families.

Astin, Helen S., Alexander W. Astin, Ann S. Bisconti, and Hyman H. Frankel, *Higher Education and the Disadvantaged Student*, Human Service Press, Washington, D. C., 1972, 359 pp.

This research study seeks to determine whether or not compensatory programs improve the chances that the disadvantaged will pursue a college education successfully. Answers to the following questions are sought: To what extent do higher educational programs for the disadvantaged serve their clients? What types of programs or program components show the greatest promise? Which of the various college environments and experiences facilitate the educational and personal growth of disadvantaged students? The study also attempts to determine to what extent the educational needs of disadvantaged students differ from those of the more advantaged and whether success and failure are associated with the same factors in both instances. The last two chapters provide preliminary answers based on an analysis of data from longitudinal studies of student development during the college years as well as on a study of special programs at selected institutions.

Baskin, Samuel, ed., *Higher Education—Some Newer Developments*, McGraw-Hill Book Co., New York, 1965, 342 pp.

This volume is concerned with the compendium of new ways of teaching and learning and new program ideas that are being instituted in today's colleges and universities. Developments discussed by the authors include new colleges; new programs at already established institutions; college curriculum organization; new programs and procedures used in independent study; study abroad; programs for the superior or honor student; use of new media and technology; use and design of college buildings and facilities, particularly as they affect teaching and learning; the community as a resource for learning; programs for the improvement of college teaching and administration; year-round education; programs of interinstitutional cooperation; and financing of college and university programs.

Brown, Nicholas C., ed., *Higher Education Incentives and Obstacles*, American Council on Education, Washington, D. C., 1959, 165 pp.

In this volume is a conference report of 16 papers identifying the forces that tend to stifle personal incentive among talented but disadvantaged youths toward obtaining higher education, and the means whereby such forces can be counteracted. Three major topics are examined: (1) the present status of research on the subject of personal incentive; (2) decisions of youth concerning higher education (obtained by means of State and regional surveys); and (3) methods of encouraging various social groups to seek a higher education.

California Coordinating Council for Higher Education, *Increasing Opportunities in Higher Education for Disadvantaged Students*, Sacramento, Calif., 1966, 75 pp.

This study describes the steps taken by one State to improve its educational program in such a way as to increase higher education opportunities for disadvantaged students. Specific topics covered include the status of existing recruitment efforts, special counseling and tutorial programs designed to increase motivation toward higher education, extent of participation in work-study programs, kinds of financial aid available, requirements for special courses or curriculums, and the role of the 2- and 4-year colleges and the university in increasing opportunities for disadvantaged students. Recommendations are expressed in terms of removing the financial, geographical, motivational, and academic barriers to increased opportunity.

Carnegie Commission on Higher Education, *A Chance To Learn: An Action Agenda for Equal Opportunity in Higher Education*, McGraw-Hill Book Co., New York, 1970, 31 pp.

A Chance To Learn concentrates on the goals, agenda, and policies concerned with access to and success within higher education institutions for an increasingly diverse student population. Specific short- and long-term equal opportunity goals are spelled out, together with step-by-step recommendations for achieving these goals. By 1976, the Carnegie Commission predicts, all financial barriers to higher education should be removed and all forms of racial discrimination on campuses eliminated. Suggestions for improving educational opportunity cover such aspects of the problem as elimination of segregation, teacher education, educational opportunity centers, recruiting, use of the campus as a summer camp, and verbal skills training. To indicate the scope of institutional change required if educational opportunity is to be enhanced, the commission has compiled, from its research and from observations on campuses across the country, an equal-opportunity checklist for the academic community. At the national level, the commission recommends that a unit be created within the U. S. Office of Education to "study, recommend upon, and monitor policy and strategy; to devise measures of progress and issue annual evaluation reports; to serve as a clearinghouse for materials and consultation; to propose further means to articulate the efforts at all educational levels; and to coordinate and oversee the activities within each regional area."

Coleman, James S., and others, *Equality of Educational Opportunity*, U. S. Department of Health, Education, and Welfare, Office of Education, U. S. Government Printing Office, Washington, D. C., 1966, 737 pp.

The extraordinary findings of the "Coleman Report" are that no significant inequality exists in school facilities for children of minority groups, and that the small differences which do exist have little or no discernible relationship to student-achievement level. Also of significance is the close tie found between academic achievement and the classroom social environment. The social environment, measured by social-class origins of students, appears most critical in the later grades, and is also somewhat more important for black than for white children. There is no question that the survey has some faults, many of which the authors themselves have conceded, but, despite these flaws, the effect of the Coleman Report has been to present a massive challenge to the simplistic notion that educational dollars, or what these dollars buy, are an adequate measure of the equality of educational opportunity. Henry Dyer, in the *Harvard Educational Review* (Winter 1968) states that "the Coleman results have the unfortunate, though perhaps inadvertent, effect of giving school systems the false impression that there is not much they can do to improve the achievement of their pupils." Critics argue that the Coleman Report understates the effectiveness of devoting more resources to the education of black children. Yet few believe that equality of resources alone can achieve equality of educational opportunity. Samuel Bowles, in the same issue of the *Harvard Review*, says that equality of educational opportunity can only be brought about through major changes in society at large, including changes in the distribution of political power between races and among social classes.

Dennis, Lawrence E., and Joseph F. Kauffman, eds., *The College and the Student*, American Council on Education, Washington, D. C., 1966, 390 pp.

The 46 essays in this volume constitute both a broad and a searching look at the present-day college student, the intellectual climate of mass education in which he has been raised, and the campus environment in which he finds himself. Who are today's youths and why do they go to college? What do they believe and where are they heading? How can higher education serve their needs and help them toward worthwhile goals? In answering these questions, the authors identify and assess the relationships between youths and the undergraduate college, together with the responsibilities each has toward the other. Many points of view are presented: those of college administrators, faculty members, public officials, and the students themselves.

Egerton, John, *Higher Education for "High Risk" Students*, Southern Education Foundation, Atlanta, Ga., 1968, 59 pp.

Presented in this work is the report of a study whose basic purpose was "to discover what some of the predominately white, four-year colleges and universities are doing to make higher education available to low-income and minority-group students who lack the credentials—but not the qualities—to succeed in college." An outline of general observations summarizes some of the incidental but valuable findings of the survey. The best "high-risk" programs of several public and private colleges are reviewed in some detail.

Gordon, Edmund W., and Doxey A. Wilkerson, *Compensatory Education for the Disadvantaged*, College Entrance Examination Board, New York, 1966, 299 pp.

This book contains a digest, analysis, and critical evaluation of nationwide preschool-through-college programs of compensatory education for the disadvantaged. In addition to identifying the disadvantaged and describing the programs, the authors discuss such vital subjects as the reasons for compensatory education; teacher recruitment, preparation, and inservice training; curriculum innovation; the role of parents and the community; the inadequacies of existing thought and action on overall approaches to education for the disadvantaged; and challenges for the future. Chapter 6 contains an extended discussion of compensatory practices in colleges and universities.

McConnell, T. R., *A General Pattern for American Public High Education*, McGraw-Hill Book Co., New York, 1962, 198 pp.

This study proposes a public-institution pattern through which a State can provide a system of education adequate to satisfy not only the demands of its heterogeneous student population but also those of the diverse adult sector. The author discusses problems involved in the statewide organization of public higher education and analyzes methods by which it can be more efficiently organized. He also proposes ways of maintaining the primacy of major State universities.

U. S. Department of Health, Education, and Welfare, Office of Education, *Trends in Postsecondary Education*, U. S. Government Printing Office, Washington, D. C., 1970, 261 pp.

The papers in this collection that deal either directly or indirectly with capabilities for expanding educational opportunity are as follows: "The Decision to Go to College An Accumulative Multivariate Process," James W. Trent; "An Examination of Financial Barriers to College Attendance," W. Lee Hansen; "An Examination of State Efforts to Remove Financial Barriers to Postsecondary Education," Joseph D. Boyd; "The Role of the Junior College in Providing Postsecondary Education For All," P. K. Patricia

Cross; "Public Postsecondary Occupational Education in the United States," Charles V. Mercer; and "Private Vocational Schools: Their Emerging Role in Postsecondary Education," A. Harvey Belitsky.

Willingham, Warren W., *Free-Access Higher Education*, College Entrance Examination Board, New York, 1970, 240 pp.

State planners seeking to extend educational opportunities by making educational resources more widely available should find this book useful. The factors on which the author bases his definitions of free-access are tuition and selectivity. His criteria for free access are that the annual tuition not exceed $400 and that at least one-third of the freshman class be composed of high school graduates from the lower half of their class. To identify those populations within a 45-minute commuting distance of a free-access college, the author presents State-by-State profiles, using demographic tables, maps, and an analysis of the characteristics of each State. The percentage of the population within commuting distance of a free-access college ranges from the low of zero in Maine, Indiana, and Nevada to a high of 87 percent in Connecticut, 68 percent in North Carolina, and 65 percent in Mississippi. Free access to higher education nationally is graphically illustrated by means of a map of the United States showing areas served by free-access institutions and by tables showing countrywide comparative levels of accessibility, population, and estimates of additional colleges required.

A related study by Richard I. Ferrin, *A Decade of Change in Free-Access Higher Education*, also published by the College Entrance Examination board, compares free-access data for 1958 and 1968 to determine the extent of change that has taken place over the past decade. During this period the number of free-access colleges—almost all public— increased from 538 to 789. In those areas in which 30 percent of the population lived within commuting distance of a free-access college in 1958, the percentage increased to 42 in 1968.

Chapter IV

FINANCIAL AID
TO STUDENTS

The social and economic well-being of any nation is determined in large measure by the level of education its citizenry achieves. It follows, then, that if as many people as possible are to be educated to their highest potential, financial aid to needy students must be a primary consideration.

Higher education planners have long agreed that student financial assistance is a legitimate and important part of their responsibilities. As a result of this consensus, there is widespread acceptance of the premise that no able student should be denied access to education beyond high school solely because of his inability to pay.

This chapter presents in detail (1) State procedures to assess financial needs of the student population, and (2) State actions to eliminate cost as a barrier to college attendance.

In undertaking studies for the purpose of recommending sound co-ordinated financial aid programs, State planners are primarily concerned with two major factors:

(1) Establishing principles and assumptions to serve as the basis for analysis and recommendations, and

(2) Determining the number of students requiring financial assistance and the overall cost of an aid program.

GUIDING PRINCIPLES
AND ASSUMPTIONS

Financial assistance programs in most States are beset with a number of problems worthy of planners' attention. Some of these are minor but others are not—they involve issues and goals bearing directly on program effectiveness.

When a State assesses its student aid program, it might well begin by considering the various purposes to which such a program should be directed. Some of the more important policy questions related to establishing financial aid goals are the following:[1]

—To what extent should student choice of institutions be broadened?

—How much should private education be encouraged to increase enrollment in order to reduce the expansion burden placed on public institutions?

—How vigorous an attack should be launched against dropout and stretchout problems?

—What priority should be given to using financial aid money to move less affluent students from deprived areas to an oncampus environment, versus using such funds to establish new 2-year colleges to which these same students could commute?

—Which institutions should adopt a nonselective admission policy designed to give all college-age youths, regardless of their secondary-school records, a chance to go to college?

—With respect to grants versus loans, what should be the proportion awarded to the less bright and less talented students and to those who are stronger intellectually?

Serious, indepth consideration of these and similar types of questions leads to formulation of sound policy and to development of a broad concept of the purposes to which student aid should be directed. Some assistance in laying the groundwork can be gained by reviewing the guiding principles or conclusions recommended in various State studies.[2] The following premises and principles, when justified by the State and modified as required by local circumstances, may serve as basic guides to effect an orderly, efficient, and sound system of student financial aid.

BASIC PREMISES:

1. Because many qualified young people either do not enroll in colleges and universities or drop out before completing degree or certificate programs, society suffers a substantial loss.

2. The opportunity to enroll in institutions of higher education should be available to all young people who may reasonably be expected to benefit from such study.

3. Able students who are, for financial reasons, prevented from attending institutions of higher learning should have the opportunity to qualify for financial assistance, either from institutions, the State, or the Nation.

---

[1] Developed in consultation with Edward Sanders, then (1968) vice president of the College Entrance Examination Board.

[2] Many of these recommendations are adapted from studies by the Illinois Board of Higher Education and the Maryland Advisory Council for Higher Education. See *Scholarship and Financial Aids* (a report to the Illinois Board of Higher Education), Report of Master Plan Committee P, Springfield, 1966, pp. 7–8; *Statewide Planning*, Report of the State of Maryland Advisory Council for Higher Education, Baltimore, 1967, ch 8, pp. 3–4.

4. It is desirable that students be permitted free choice among the various institutions—large or small, public or private—insofar as such freedom does not interfere with admission policies or effective use of State resources. (Aid programs should not differ so radically among institutions within a State as to inhibit or prevent a student from attending a college of his choice.)

SPECIFIC PRINCIPLES:

1. Qualifications of Recipients

a. Awards should be limited to residents of the State.

b. To be eligible for financial aid, a student must be admitted to, and continue in, a recognized nonprofit postsecondary educational institution in the State. (A State attempting to calculate the cost of making postsecondary education available to all must consider the effect such changes in admission eligibility will have on overall aid funding requirements.)

c. If funds for student financial assistance are limited, necessitating differential treatment of applicants, first consideration should be granted to those needy students who give evidence of having the greatest potential for successfully continuing their education. If limited funding necessitates further restrictions, preference should be given to full-time, as opposed to part-time, students, and to undergraduates in preference to graduate and professional students.

2. Utilization of Awards

Awards should be valid at all public and private nonprofit postsecondary educational institutions within the State, regardless of a student's vocational or education objectives.

3. Amount of Awards

a. The amount of the award (grant plus loan total) should be based on financial need[3]—need determined by the difference between actual resident or commuter student expenses and the amount parents and/or students can contribute without being subjected to excessive financial strain. An additional allowance should be provided to poor families deprived of the earnings of offspring enrolled in college.

---

[3] To encourage and reward scholastic excellence, States may elect to give recognition to those applicants who elect to take a qualifying examination. The top 5 to 10 percent (scholastically), for example, might be designated as State scholars. Such recognition awards are generally assigned without regard to financial need.

Established *student expenses* may be defined as legitimate expenses incurred while attending college.[4] These include tuition and fees, textbooks and equipment, commutation, room and board, and reasonable personal expenditures.

How much a student and his parents can reasonably be expected to contribute should be based on the degree to which the total financial strength of the family exceeds the amount needed to meet essential family living expenses. Evaluation of a family's ability to pay should be based on a need-analysis system subject to adjustment to account for particular circumstances.

b. Participating students should be encouraged to meet a portion of their educational expenses through employment.[5] The opportunity to participate in a planned work-study program can provide reinforcement for learning, valuable job experience, and a sense of personal contribution to self-development.

c. The amount of financial aid should be adjusted to take into account all grants and scholarships a student receives from other sources—private and public. To encourage a student to seek alternative grantors and to encourage the latter to continue to aid education, there should be some net gain to the student for obtaining outside aid; consequently, State aid should not be cut by the exact amount awarded by other sources.

d. The award should be limited to the normal time span required to complete the degree program for which the student is enrolled (usually a maximum of 5 years for undergraduate training).

4. Overall Funding and Grant/Loan Allocation

a. The goal should be an optimum financial assistance program sufficiently funded to provide adequate awards to *all* qualified students. No one should be denied educational opportunity because financial assistance is unavailable.

b. The amount of an award should always equal the student's need. If institutional resources are limited, loans should receive first consideration (up to the amount each student can repay without suffering undue financial hardship). To supplement a loan, additional aid may be supplied through a

---

[4] If a State must operate on a limited aid budget, it may, with justification, amend this definition to include "maximum-level tuition." Whenever such is the case, it is axiomatic that needy students will be forced to base their choice of institution not on preference but on cost. Consequently, the more expensive private institutions will be placed at a competitive disadvantage.

[5] Part-time students with a relatively high earning potential are expected to contribute more than full-time students; their financial need, while usually less than that of full-time students, should nevertheless be given equal priority.

grant—in an amount not to exceed a predetermined maximum.[6] If a student requires more help than that provided by the loan/grant combination, he should be prepared to choose a less expensive institution.

5. Program Administration

a. State programs of financial assistance should receive continuing review and evaluation.

b. Awards should be announced to high school seniors as early in the academic year as possible.

c. Administration under a central agency is essential in order to improve efficiency of operation and to assure communication and extension of opportunity to the persons whom the program is intended to serve.

d. The central agency administering a State financial aid program should publicize the program in such a manner that, insofar as possible, every high school student within the State needing financial help will be made aware not only of the availability of financial assistance for postsecondary education but also of the application procedures.

CRITERIA FOR DETERMINING PARENTS' CONTRIBUTION

The question of who should pay for higher education is determined to a large extent by society's assessment of the dividends it receives from colleges and universities.

Most States have indicated they are ready and willing to assume a proportionate share of the cost of higher education. And at the top of their financial priority list is an all-important objective—to make sure that economic barriers do not prevent a single high school graduate from participating in the kind of postsecondary education for which he meets the entrance requirements and in which he remains in good standing.[7] However, since State resources are limited, it is obvious that to achieve this goal, costs of higher education must be shared between the taxpaying public and students and/or their parents.

---

[6] Grants may be limited, for example, to amounts not exceeding a reasonable student budget—or a portion thereof—at a typical public institution.

[7] Although States are not adverse to insisting on high academic records as a prerequisite for admission to any institution of higher learning—public or private—the majority will not accept financial need as a barrier to entrance.

Therefore, in establishing a State financial aid program, among the first questions to be answered is: "What proportion of expenses can either the student or his family reasonably be expected to pay *during the college-enrollment period?*"[8] Most students can enter and remain in college only if the expenses involved can be borne with relative ease. Consequently, the key to expense-sharing is the amount that constitutes the tolerable financial burden a student and/or his family can assume.

The best way to estimate the amount of financial support parents can contribute toward college expenses is by detailed computation. Currently a number of systems are in common use. Of 636 representative colleges and universities surveyed in 1968,[9] 58 percent utilized the College Scholarship Service need-analysis system of the College Entrance Examination Board;[10] 23 percent used the income tax method devised by the U. S. Office of Education;[11] 14 percent relied on their own institutional or State system; and 5 percent employed the American College Testing Program.[12] Basic to each of these systems is a standardized method of determining a family's ability to pay—a method that takes into account the fact there are certain family peculiarities which financial aid officers will need to consider individually. An understanding of the working of these systems and their rationale is a definite prerequisite to establishing any sound method of need-analysis.

In order to understand need-analysis systems, a brief summary of the general theory involved is necessary. To simplify the presentation, such complicating factors as the parents' contribution potential from non-income-producing assets and the student's contribution will be omitted. The discussion will concentrate on the principal source of the *family's* contribution: revenue from income alone—specifically from wages or salaries, rents, return on investments, or, in the case of the self-employed, net earnings.

At the risk of oversimplification, it can be said that most approaches to assessing family ability to pay involve the design of a computation system consisting of five basic parameters. The controlling variables, plus the total

---

[8] Part of the financial burden that must be assumed by a student while enrolled is the monetary value of all loans (plus interest) that must eventually be repaid.

[9] Thomas McKay, M. D. Orwig, and Walter Kunz, unpublished data from the U. S. Office of Education: "Survey of Need-Analysis Methods Used in Institutions of Higher Education," Spring 1968.

[10] College Scholarship Service, *Manual for Financial Aid Officers, 1972 Revision*, College Entrance Examination Board, Princeton, N.J., 1972.

[11] U. S. Department of Health, Education, and Welfare, Office of Education, *Determining Awards Under Federal Student Aid Programs* (2d revised edition), Washington, D. C., March 1968.

[12] The American College Testing Program, *Handbook for Financial Aid Administrators 1972–1973*, Iowa City, Iowa, 1972.

Figure IV-1. — Model of expected contribution toward educational expenses based on parents' income

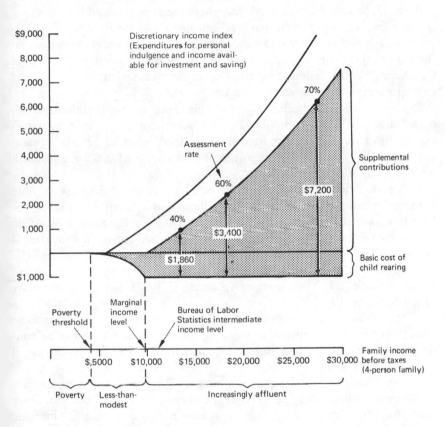

concept of the model, are discussed on the pages which follow and are graphically illustrated in figure IV-1.

Most systems are based on the concept of three income ranges: *a poverty range*, limited to families not expected to contribute to educational expenses; *a less-than-modest income range*, limited to families who can afford to contribute toward board and incidentals; and *an increasing affluent range*, limited to families able to pay for student expenses beyond those of basic maintenance. Specific and indepth criteria for determining these parameters are the following:

1. Identification of the poverty-threshold income level at which families are considered to be just emerging and therefore able to contribute only a

token amount (less than $100, for example) to the student's educational expenses. Below this income level no contribution is expected. Immediately above this level, the near-poor family can be expected to make increasing contributions toward the *essentials* of board and other student maintenance costs. The 1971 poverty threshold for a nonfarm family of four was $4,137. This index, prepared by the U. S. Bureau of the Census, provides a range of poverty income cutoffs adjusted by such factors as family size and composition, sex and age of the family head, and farm-nonfarm residence. At the core of this definition of poverty is a nutritionally adequate food plan ("economy" plan) designed by the Department of Agriculture for "emergency or temporary use when funds are low."[13]

2. Identification of the basic cost of child rearing that families of moderate means normally provide. For families with a moderate income, expenditures for such basic necessities as food, clothing, medical care, etc.—exclusive of housing—amount to approximately $1,000 for a 9-month period (the academic year).[14]

3. Identification of the marginal income level at which families are able to meet the basic cost of child rearing without undue hardship. It is reasonable to expect that parents with less than a marginal income will *not* be able to contribute the entire basic cost of child rearing toward educational expenses. The marginal income level, though substantially above the poverty threshold, is probably below what is labeled by the Bureau of Labor Statistics as "intermediate income" ($10,971 for a four-member urban family in 1971).[15]

4. Identification of an index of discretionary (easily reallocated) income which may be used to indicate the more affluent family's ability to contribute an amount toward student expenses in excess of the basic cost of child maintenance.

As family income increases, greater amounts[16] are spent on such personal-indulgence items as tobacco, alcoholic beverages, recreation, contributions, and gifts. More importantly, higher income means a substantial increase

---

[13] For more information on the poverty threshold, see U. S. Department of Commerce, Bureau of the Census, *Current Population Reports*, Series P-23, no. 28, and Series P-60, nos. 81 and 82.

[14] Based on a weighted average budget change, the College Scholarship Service of the College Entrance Examination Board estimates that this amount in 1971 was approximately $1,050 for a 9-month period. See James L. Bowman, *Some Thoughts and Reflection Regarding Parental Ability To Pay for Higher Education*, CSS position paper, Princeton, N.J. revised April 1971.

[15] U. S. Department of Labor, Bureau of Labor Statistics, *Three Standards of Living for an Urban Family of Four Persons* (spring 1967), BLS Bulletin 1570–5; updated by BLS in "Autumn 1971 Urban Family Budgets and Geographical Comparative Indexes," Apr. 27, 1972, Washington, D. C.

[16] At all income levels, expenditures for personal indulgence remain a relatively constant 11 to 12 percent of income before taxes (see table IV-1).

in the amount of money available for discretionary investment and savings (excluding mortgage and life-insurance payments). Since money spent on personal-indulgence items and for investments and/or savings can be diverted to other channels without seriously lowering the family's standard of living, it represents money parents can reallocate for educational expenses.

What a family contributes toward educational expenses would not, of course, be derived exclusively from the aforementioned categories. To meet college expenses, families elect to change their spending patterns in many different ways. However, personal-indulgence expenditures and investments and savings can be well defined and clearly modified; therefore they constitute a measurable and reasonably valid indicator of the overall potential of parents to reallocate income.

In table IV-1 (based on income before taxes of a family of four) the expenditures for personal indulgence and the amount available for investment and savings are depicted for a wide range of income levels. It should be noted that income for investment and savings below the marginal

Table IV-1.—Relationship of discretionary income to family income before taxes, urban families of four persons

Monetary income before taxes	Expenditures for personal indulgence[1]	Income for investment and savings[2]	Discretionary income index: personal indulgence and income for investment and savings col. (2) + col. (3)	Ratio col. (4) to col. (1)
(1)	(2)	(3)	(4)	(5)
1,589	180	(626)	(446)	—
2,622	320	(1,088)	(768)	—
3,694	449	(998)	(549)	—
4,857	596	(712)	(116)	—
5,999	571	(606)	65	1%
7,451	881	(424)	457	6.1%
9,773	1,132	76	1,208	12.3%
13,770	1,637	507	2,144	15.6%
27,451	2,686	6,181	8,867	32.3%

NOTE.—Negative values appear within ( ).

[1] Included are expenditures for current consumption of tobacco, alcoholic beverages, gifts and contributions, recreation, and one-half of food consumed away from home.

[2] Income available for investment and savings is monetary income after taxes, less disbursements for insurance, gifts, and contributions, and all current consumption expenditures. Said income is available to increase assets and reduce liabilities, make equity payments for real estate, and for savings. At low-income levels, a negative amount generally reflects prior use of savings, an increase in debt, or business losses.

Source: U.S. Department of Labor, Bureau of Labor Statistics, Consumer Expenditures and Income, Supplement 2, Part A, to BLS Report 237–38, Government Printing Office, Washington, D.C., 1968, p. 7. BLS will update findings following a consumer expenditure study for 1972–73.

income level is negative, an indication that savings have had to be used for current consumption, that there has been an increase in indebtedness, or that business losses have been incurred.

5. Identification of a progressive rate of assessment to be applied to discretionary income for the purpose of calculating parents' supplemental contribution for student expenses.

Supplemental support (above basic cost of child rearing), which begins at the marginal income level, rises in proportion to the discretionary income index. The exact amount that can readily be reallocated for student expenses is a matter of judgment. If the "total parents' contributions" suggested by the College Scholarship Service are used as a guide, approximately 70 percent of the discretionary income index for a family of four can be reallocated at the $27,500 income level; 60 percent at the $18,500 level; and 40 percent at the $13,750 level.

This brief discussion of the theory[17] of evaluating family ability to pay is intended to serve as an introduction to the complexities of need evaluation. Because of the growing complexity and wide variation in nationwide living standards, each State—if it is to derive the greatest possible benefit from available financial aid—will need to give further careful study to the overall problem, especially to the parent-contribution aspects as they relate to higher education.

A MODEL FOR NEED-ANALYSIS

Recommendations to increase State financial aid to students can be justified, in part, by two economic facts of life—namely, the large number of youths with academic potential who cannot afford to go to college and the significant number who, though enrolled, must constantly fight for economic survival.

As a means of calculating student financial aid needs, a mathematica. model may be used—one which encompasses, at least in theory, a majority of the variables and assumptions required for a realistic solution. Such a model, explained in this section, requires State data input as well as adjust

---

[17] The theory itself, developed in 1969, represents a joint effort on the part of the author and Thomas McKay and M. D. Orwig of the Division of Student Financial Aid, Burea of Higher Education, USOE, both of whom contributed many useful ideas and informa tion.

ment to local constraints. For illustrative purposes, theoretical national data have been used, and program operations have been assumed which are consistent with the objectives of student financial aid programs in many States.

The function of the model is twofold: (1) to determine the number of high school graduates in a State who, though motivated to attend college, are denied higher educational opportunities because they lack the money and are unable to earn it, and (2) to determine the cost of a State financial aid grant program (to be supplemented by loans) that will provide appropriate assistance to such youths. The model is designed to identify the financial needs of eligible youths who *are not now* attending college. No attempt has been made to determine whether or not existing programs are adequate to meet the financial needs of students currently enrolled.

Theory

This model is based on a theory originally advanced by André Danière, research professor at Boston College.[18] Danière's theory is that the potential college entrance rate of poor youths, if given financial assistance, can be gauged by the existing entrance rate of youths with similar college aptitude from high-income families. What this means is that if 80 percent of high school graduates with good scholastic aptitude, from families with incomes in excess of $10,000, enter college, then the 60 percent of poor youths who presently enter college, with the *same* aptitude, from families with incomes of less than $5,000, could be expected to rise to near the 80 percent level *if* financial barriers to college entrance were removed and *if* adequate motivation were provided.

For many qualified youths from deprived backgrounds, low motivation, limited aspirations, and indifferent parents are strong deterrents to college entrance. So powerful are these factors that often they cannot be overcome simply by providing financial assistance. No recent studies have been conducted that determine, with assurance, the relative importance of motivation vis-a-vis financial need to nonattendance among college-able youths. In the model, estimates are used to indicate the proportion of potential enrollees for whom lack of motivation is solely decisive in preventing college entrance. The fact that no authoritative figures are available reflects a serious deficiency in current data, and the use of estimates naturally places the validity of the model outputs in a questionable light.

---

[18] See André Danière, "The Benefits and Costs of Alternative Federal Programs of Financial Aid to College Students," in Joint Economic Committee, Congress of the United States, *The Economics and Financing of Higher Education in the United States*, U. S. Government Printing Office, Washington, D. C., 1969.

Data Requirements

Model operation requires the State to collect input data identifying the relative influence of socioeconomic status and college aptitude on attendance rates at successive academic levels of a randomly selected group of State high school seniors. Because of known differences between males and females in their propensity to pursue higher education and in the influence of socioeconomic status and scholastic aptitude on their educational attainments, separate tabulations should be made by sex. (To simplify this presentation, such a procedure was not followed.)

The two variables are:

(1) College aptitude measured by those tests that estimate promise of performance. The distribution should be divided into quartile categories.

(2) Family income before taxes. Since family income is correlated with most indicators of socioeconomic status, it is used in the model as a reasonable substitute for a composite index of social class in order to facilitate computations. The distribution should be divided into five approximately equal groups.

The desired relationships are:

(1) For the group (cohort) component graduating from high school, a cross-classified distribution of college aptitude and family income.

(2) For the group component beginning in-State postsecondary education; i.e., college freshmen, (a) a cross-classified distribution of college aptitude and family income, and (b) a cross-classified distribution of family income and control-type of institution; i.e., public or private university, 4-year or 2-year college.

In addition to the preceding information, the following normative data for institutions of higher education in the State, by type and control, are required: (1) student charges (room, board, tuition), (2) undergraduate class-to-class retention rates, and (3) ratio of dormitory residents to commuter students.

In the following discussion of model operation, theoretical example data (actually estimated national norms for 1966) are used to illustrate the computational procedures involved and suggest the general relative values of input variables and model outputs. The bivariate relationship between family income and college aptitude for the selected group, which is strictly theoretical, has been derived by adjusting the data of Sewell and Shah[19] to conform to national parameters. In general, all known distributions of a single variable have been maintained by adjusting the cross-classified cellular data in each bivariate table to produce the given parameters. All

---

[19] William H. Sewell and Vimal P. Shah, "Socioeconomic Status, Intelligence, and the Attainment of Higher Education," *Sociology of Education*, vol. 40, no. 1, Winter 1967, pp. 1–23.

original sources are cited, but in no instance should the originators be held accountable for any of the estimated data presented.

Model Operation

Operation of the model involves 10 steps. These are first listed in outline form then explained in the ensuing text.

Restraints

STEP 1. Determining restraints under which model will operate, consistent with State policy.

Enrollment

STEP 2. Measuring the distribution of high school graduates, by family income and college aptitude.

STEP 3. Measuring the distribution of high school graduates entering college the following fall, by family income and college aptitude.

STEP 4. Computing the percent of high school graduates entering college in the fall following graduation, by family income and college aptitude.

STEP 5. Estimating the increase in college entrance rates of high school graduates as a result of removal of all economic barriers. Calculating the expected increase in high school graduates entering college.

Pricing

STEP 6. Measuring the attendance pattern of entering freshmen, by family income and by type and control of institution. Calculating the attendance distribution of those additional high school graduates expected to enter college as a result of removal of all economic barriers.

STEP 7. Determining typical undergraduate student budgets, by type and control of institution.

STEP 8. Computing the expected contribution by parents and student toward college expenses.

STEP 9. Computing the amount of student financial aid required, by family income and by type and control of institution.

STEP 10. Calculating the average financial aid requirement per additional high school graduate entering college as a result of removal of all economic barriers. Calculating total program costs.

Restraints

STEP 1. Determining restraints under which model will operate, consistent with State policy.

Various parameters and restraints control operation of the model. They define participant eligibility, utilization, amount and form of awards, and overall funding level of the program. In determining these limits, existing State goals and policy must serve as a guide. For purposes of demonstrating model operation, the following restraints are assumed:

Participant eligibility:

    a. High school graduate or equivalent
    b. State resident
    c. Accepted for admission or matriculated as an undergraduate—under existing admission requirements—at a recognized nonprofit postsecondary educational institution within the State
    d. Demonstrated financial need

Utilization of awards:

    a. Nonspecified in terms of vocational choice and geographical location within the State
    b. Valid at all recognized nonprofit postsecondary educational institutions in the State

Amount of awards:

Limited to the difference between established resident or commuter student costs and the amount parents and students can reasonably be expected to contribute without being subjected to undue financial hardship; adjusted to take into account all nonrepayable grants and scholarships received by students from other sources.

Overall funding level of program and type of awards:

Proportion of grants to loans must be such that the financial needs of all qualifying students are met; a grant maximum must be established.

Table IV-2.—High school graduates, by family income and college aptitude[1]

| Average family income quintile[3] | College aptitude quartile[2] | | | | Total |
	Low 4th	3d	2d	High 1st	
Low 5th	250	210	190	150	800
4th	230	200	190	180	800
3d	210	210	200	180	800
2d	180	200	210	210	800
High 1st	130	180	210	280	800
Total	1,000	1,000	1,000	1,000	4,000

NOTE.—Total cohort of high school graduates equals 4,000.

[1] Theoretical example.
[2] Aptitude quartile divisions for total cohort, based on Army General Classification Test scores of 98.5 110 (mean), and 121.5.
[3] Quintile divisions for total cohort, based on family incomes of $5,300, $7,600, $10,000, and $13,000.

Enrollment

STEP 2. Measuring the distribution of high school graduates, by family income and college aptitude.

Because circumstances vary, each State must conduct its own survey to determine the existing association between economic status and college aptitude of high school graduates. A randomly selected appropriately sized group of State high school seniors will provide the required data. Once obtained, the data can be assembled in a bivariate table similar to table IV-2, which depicts an estimated aptitude-income matrix for the United States.

As part of a statewide testing program,[20] any number of acceptable group-administered tests can be used to predict general overall levels of future academic performance. Because the number of youths who graduate from high school fluctuates, the mean and quartile scores for any given test will vary from State to State. No particular significance need be attached

---

[20] Many group tests have proved to be useful in predicting future scholastic achievement. Among those suitable for use at the adolescent and adult levels are the College Entrance Examination Board Scholastic Aptitude Test (SAT), the American College Testing Program Examination (ACT), the College Qualification Test (CQT), and the Cooperative School and College Ability Test (SCAT). These and other tests can be used to predict, with acceptable validity, the likelihood of a student achieving success in college academic work. For detailed reviews, see Oscar Krisen Buros, ed., *Mental Measurements Yearbook* (6th ed.), The Gryphon Press, Highland Park, N. J., 1965.

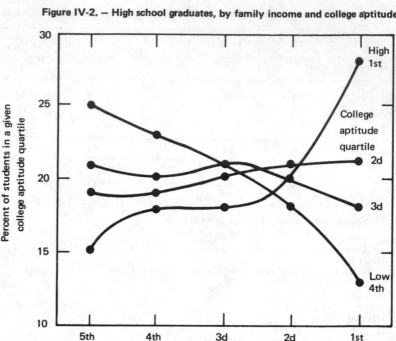

Figure IV-2. — High school graduates, by family income and college aptitude —1/

1/Theoretical example.

to the exact values involved. As a matter of interest, however, the quartile
divisions for high school graduates based on the Army General Classification Test (AGCT)[21] occur generally at scores 97-98, 110 (mean), and
120-121.[22] Quartile scores may be significantly higher in States with
selective elementary-secondary systems and slightly lower in States in which
most youths graduate from high school.

National data giving the distribution of family income for high school
graduates are not readily available. A reasonable substitute is the distribution of total monetary income of families in which the age of the head
of-household is 35 to 54 (the general age range for most parents of high

----

[21] The Army General Classification Test may be used to measure general mental ability and scholastic aptitude. To support justification of the many uses claimed, however,
complete set of new validity and reliability studies are needed. AGCT scores are used i
this study because they include the required national data for *all* high school graduate:

[22] Information is based on 1949 data. The IQ scale resembles that of the AGCT
the average score for the *total* population is 100 on both; the spread of scores is approx
mately the same.

Table IV-3.—**High school graduates entering college the following fall, by family income and college aptitude**[1]

Average family income quintile[3]	College aptitude quartile[2]				Total	Percent distribution
	Low 4th	3d	2d	High 1st		
Low 5th	62	71	80	90	303	13.8
4th	81	96	105	133	415	18.9
3d	78	101	120	140	439	20.0
2d	68	98	128	168	462	21.1
High 1st	74	111	149	241	575	26.2
Total	363	477	582	772	2,194	100.0
Percent distribution	16.6	21.8	26.5	35.1	100.0	

NOTE.—Total cohort of high school graduates equals 4,000.

[1] Theoretical example.
[2] Aptitude quartile divisions for total cohort, based on AGCT scores of 98.5, 110 (mean), and 121.5.
[3] Quintile divisions for total cohort, based on family incomes of $5,300, $7,600, $10,000, and $13,000.

school seniors). For U. S. families in this category in 1966, the quintile divisions occurred at incomes of $5,227, $7,595, $9,926, and $12,961.[23]

The relationship between family income and college aptitude of high school graduates delineated in table IV-2 is graphically illustrated in figure IV-2. What the latter shows is that family income is distributed normally only for high school graduates in the two middle-aptitude quartiles; i.e., approximately 20 percent of all students fall within each family-income quintile. High school graduates in the lowest aptitude quartile are from proportionately more families of lower income. Proportionately fewer students with low aptitude come from high-income families. The reverse is true for students with the highest measured aptitude: a greater proportion from high-income families, fewer from low-income families. This theoretical distribution is based on the general findings of Sewell and Shah.[24]

STEP 3.   Measuring the distribution of high school graduates entering college the following fall, by family income and college aptitude.

The purpose of this step is to ascertain the association between the economic status and college aptitude of those high school graduates from

---

[23] U. S. Department of Commerce, Bureau of Census, "Consumer Income," *Current Population Reports*, Series P-60, no. 53, U. S. Government Printing Office, Washington, D. C., 1968.
[24] Sewell and Shah, op. cit.

Figure IV-3. — Illustrative distribution of Army General Classification Test scores for high school graduates and students entering college

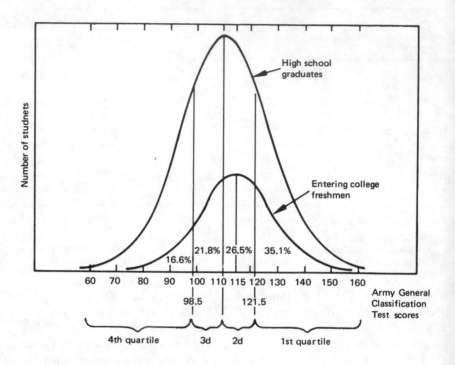

Source: Dael Wolfe, ed., America's Resources of Specialized Talent, Harper and Brothers, New York, 1954.

the cohort (constituting a subgroup) who enter college in the fall following graduation. The values of family income at the quintile divisions and the scores of college aptitude at the quartile divisions are those previously cited—i.e., for the total cohort. Estimated national data of the type required appear in table IV-3.

The distribution of entering freshmen classified by the cohort college-aptitude quartiles has been equated with the result of a shift in the aptitude-distribution curve—from a mean score of 110 for the high school graduate cohort to 115 for the subgroup who enter college. On the AGCT scale, students who matriculate average about five points higher than do all students who graduate from high school.[25] This shift reflects the more

---

[25] Dael Wolfe, ed., *America's Resources of Specialized Talent*, Harper and Brothers, New York, 1954, p. 146.

Table IV-4.—Percentage of high school graduates entering college in the following fall, by family income and college aptitude[1]

Average family income quintile[3]	College aptitude quartile[2]				
	Low 4th	3d	2d	High 1st	Total
Low 5th	25	34	42	60	38
4th	35	46	55	74	52
3d	37	48	60	78	55
2d	38	49	61	80	58
High 1st	57	62	71	86	72
Total	36	48	58	77	55

NOTE.—Total cohort of high school graduates equals 4,000.

[1] Theoretical example.
[2] Aptitude quartile divisions for total cohort, based on AGCT scores of 98.5, 110 (mean), and 121.5.
[3] Quintile divisions for total cohort, based on family incomes of $5,300, $7,600, $10,000, and $13,000.

rigorous intellectual selection which takes place as students move up the educational ladder.

STEP 4.   Computing the percent of high school graduates entering college the following fall, by family income and college aptitude.

The family income and college aptitude of high school graduates who enter college the following fall may be determined by dividing the number of entering freshmen in each cell of table IV-3 by the corresponding number of high school graduates in table IV-2. The resulting attendance ratios, based on estimated national data, are shown in table IV-4. In the lowest socioeconomic and lowest aptitude group there is only a 25 percent probability that an individual will enter college; in the highest socioeconomic and aptitude group, an 86 percent probability. For the total cohort of 4,000 high school graduates, 2,194 entered college—an overall entrance rate of 55 percent.

To assist in visualizing the relationship between aptitude test scores, family income, and college-entrance rate, the data in table IV-4 are graphically illustrated in figure IV-4. It is well known that the probability of entering college rises with an increase in either aptitude test scores or family income. Of the two factors, college aptitude facilitates college

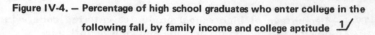

Figure IV-4. — Percentage of high school graduates who enter college in the following fall, by family income and college aptitude 1/

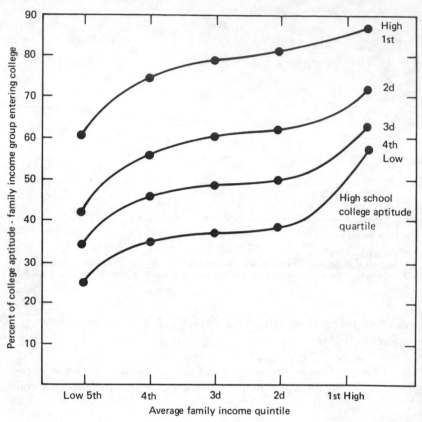

1/ Theoretical example.

entrance to a considerably greater degree than does socioeconomic level. However, very high and very low economic conditions have an extremely pronounced effect on attendance. Furthermore, the probability of enrolling in college lessens more sharply for youths with low aptitude as the family income decreases than it does for youths with high aptitude.[26] The greater influence that family income and its associated socioeconomic status exert on attendance rates of youths with low aptitude versus those with high academic potential is shown in figure IV-4.

As figure IV-4 indicates, socioeconomic factors have a negative effect on college attendance. What is particularly disturbing is that, despite the

_____

[26] Ibid., p. 163 and Sewell and Shah, op. cit., p. 13.

emphasis placed on directing financial aid to those needy students who are *most able*, the number of talented youths who do not enter college increases sharply as the family income decreases.

Undoubtedly economic barriers play a role in preventing high school graduates from below-average income levels from attending college; however, most studies contain evidence that, unless a person really *wants* to go to college, not even the existence of such a necessary adjunct as financial aid is likely to cause him to enroll. It is equally important to recognize that even when family capability to pay student expenses increases, motivation continues to be an increasingly important determinant in matriculation.

In view of the foregoing, further increases in enrollment resulting from an expansion of already substantial aid programs are likely to be modest, the reasons being lack of interest and inadequate school preparation, two powerful deterrents to college entrance.

> STEP 5.   Estimating the increase in college entrance rates of high school graduates as a result of removal of all economic barriers. Calculating the expected increase in number of high school graduates entering college.

While economic barriers prevent many capable students from going to college, the exact number dissuaded primarily because of inadequate finances can only be estimated. In 1965 only about 1 high school senior in 10 mentioned finances as the chief deterrent to college attendance. The remainder cited such reasons as learning a trade (23 percent), taking a job (20 percent), no desire (15 percent), marriage (8 percent), and (poor) scholarship (7 percent) for not continuing their education. However, one out of seven students from low-income families mentioned financial deterrents as contrasted with 1 out of 12 among children whose family income exceeded $5,000.[27] With more youths entering college and with increased financial aid being made available, the importance of finances as a deterrent to college attendance will obviously decline.

New attendance-rate curves can perhaps best be projected by revising existing curves upward, while at the same time preserving their general contour. If this procedure is followed, one illustration of what might happen to freshmen enrollments on a national level as a result of removing economics as a barrier to college entrance can be seen in figure IV-5. The dash-lines represent the expected higher entrance rates resulting from establishing

---

[27] Unpublished tabulation by A. J. Jaffee and Walter Adams from a special survey conducted by the U. S. Bureau of the Census. Reported in Joseph Froomkin, *Aspiration, Enrollments, and Resources*, U. S. Department of Health, Education, and Welfare, Office of Education, U. S. Government Printing Office, Washington, D. C., 1970, p. 21.

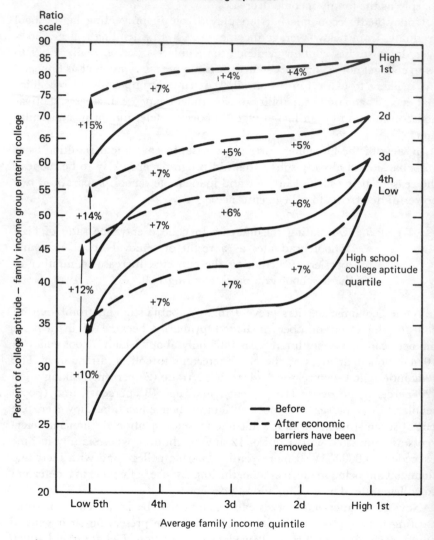

Figure IV-5. — Expected improvement in college entrance rates of high school graduates as a result of removal of all economic barriers, by family income and college aptitude [1/]

[1/] Theoretical example.

NOTE — The vertical axis is expressed on a ratio, or logarithmic scale -- i.e., equal vertical distances reflect equal proportional (as distinguished from absolute) changes.

an open-door admission policy designed to satisfy the financial needs of all youths who meet existing entrance standards. The estimates reflect a relatively stable situation reached after a 3-to-5-year adjustment period. For each ability level, the expected new entrance rates have been patterned after the curves of previous rates (solid lines), the old and new rates intersecting at the highest income level ($13,000), a point at which improved financial aid is not expected to increase attendance. In families with incomes above $13,000, most parents—especially those with only one child in college—are financially able to pay most student expenses, with the possible exception of some charges at the most expensive institutions.

From the data in this figure it can be seen that the group which will benefit the most from a comprehensive student financial aid program are youths in the lowest socioeconomic strata. Among students in this group scoring low in college aptitude, the college entrance rate is expected to rise from 25 to 35 percent (+10 percent). Those with high college aptitude from low-income families may have a 72 percent probability of entering college versus the current 57 percent (+15 percent). For all youths of high aptitude, the probability of attending college will be fairly uniform, ranging from 86 percent at the highest income level to 72 percent at the lowest.

The additional number of freshmen who can be expected to enroll may be calculated by applying the changes in entrance rates from figure IV-5 to the distribution of high school graduates in table IV-2. Calculations are shown in table IV-5. From the high school graduate cohort of 4,000 students, an additional 245, or 6.1 percent, could be expected to enter college if an all-encompassing program of student financial aid were instituted. Projecting this calculation nationally, 160,000 more freshmen would enroll. States that already have substantial aid programs could expect the percentage of additional enrollees to be smaller. However, in areas where aid programs are now minimal, as many as 15 to 20 percent more youths would enter college if financial aid were increased.

Pricing

The financial aid required by an individual student equals the difference between the educational expenses at a given institution and the contribution which can reasonably be expected from the student and his parents. The cost of a comprehensive student aid program for a known number of new participants can be estimated by computing the amount which new individuals in each family-income group will need. For computation purposes, it will be necessary to anticipate the pattern of attendance at various public and private institutions within the State, classified by level of student tuition charges and room and board expenses.

Table IV-5.—High school graduates and the additional percent and number of graduates expected to enter college in the following fall as a result of removing all economic barriers, by family income and college aptitude[1]

| Average family income quintile[3] | College aptitude quartile[2] | | | | Total |
	Low 4th	3d	2d	High 1st	
Low 5th	250	210	190	150	800
	10%	12%	14%	15%	12.5%
	+25	+25	+27	+23	+100
4th	230	200	190	180	800
	7%	7%	7%	7%	7%
	+16	+14	+13	+13	+56
3d	210	210	200	180	800
	7%	6%	5%	4%	5.6%
	+15	+13	+10	+7	+45
2d	180	200	210	210	800
	7%	6%	5%	4%	5.5%
	+13	+12	+11	+8	+44
High 1st	130	180	210	280	800
	0%	0%	0%	0%	0%
	+0	+0	+0	+0	+0
	1,000	1,000	1,000	1,000	4,000
Total	6.9%	6.4%	6.1%	5.1%	6.1%
	+69	+64	+61	+51	+245

NOTE.—Total cohort of high school graduates equals 4,000—see table IV-2.

[1] Theoretical example.
[2] Aptitude quartile division for total cohort, based on AGCT scores of 98.5, 110 (mean), and 121.5.
[3] Quintile divisions for total cohort, based on family incomes of $5,300, $7,600, $10,000, and $13,000.

STEP 6.   Measuring the attendance pattern of entering freshmen by family income and type and control of institution. Calculating the attendance distribution of the additional number of high school graduates expected to enter college in the fall following graduation as a result of removal of all economic barriers.

In pricing, the first step is to determine the attendance patterns of resident freshmen with different family incomes; in other words, the number enrolled at each of the public and private higher educational institutions in the State. An important factor to keep in mind is that, since improved student aid is likely to encourage more low-income students to attend more expensive institutions, a shift in enrollment patterns can be expected.

Because no supporting data regarding enrollment shifts are available, for purposes of this presentation the pattern of new entrants has been assumed to be similar to that of current resident freshmen. In table IV-6 is an illustration of an estimated national distribution of entering freshmen, classified by their attendance at public and private institutions and at 4-year and 2-year colleges. As will be noted, this table shows that as family income increases, a greater proportion of youths enroll in either universities or private 4-year colleges. Students from lower income families tend to enroll, initially at least, in 2-year colleges and public 4-year colleges.

In the parentheses in table IV-6 is the numerical distribution of the 245 additional high school graduates expected to enter college as a result of removal of all economic barriers. This distribution is obtained by mul-

Table IV-6.—Percent distribution of high school graduates entering college in the following fall, by family income and by type and control of institution[1]

| | Average family income quintile[2] | | | | | All family income |
	Low 5th	4th	3d	2d	High 1st	
All institutions	13.8	18.9	20.0	21.1	26.2	100.0
Public						
Universities	16.4	20.6	22.0	22.7	22.7	21.0
	(16.4)	(11.5)	(9.9)	(10.0)	(0)	(48.7)
4-year colleges	27.1	23.8	22.0	18.0	18.1	19.4
	(27.1)	(13.3)	(9.9)	(7.9)	(0)	(58.2)
2-year colleges	34.4	34.4	33.1	30.9	30.9	30.3
	(34.4)	(19.3)	(14.9)	(13.6)	(0)	(82.2)
Private						
Universities	3.3	4.1	5.0	6.4	6.4	6.4
	(3.3)	(2.3)	(2.3)	(2.8)	(0)	(10.7)
4-year colleges	13.9	12.4	13.4	17.5	17.5	18.4
	(13.9)	(7.0)	(6.0)	(7.7)	(0)	(34.6)
2-year colleges	4.9	4.7	4.5	4.5	4.4	4.5
	(4.9)	(2.6)	(2.0)	(2.0)	(0)	(11.5)
Total	100.0	100.0	100.0	100.0	100.0	100.0
	(100)	(56)	(45)	(44)	(0)	[3](245)

[1] Theoretical example.

[2] Quintile divisions based on family incomes of $5,300, $7,600, $10,000, and $13,000.

[3] Distribution of the 245 additional high school graduates (from table IV-5, total cohort equals 4,000) expected to enter college in the fall following graduation as a result of removal of all economic barriers is shown in parentheses. For example, in the 4th family-income quintile, which shows 56 additional high school graduates, 20.6 percent, or 11.5 students, are expected to attend public universities.

tiplying the number of additional high school graduates in each family-income quintile (from table IV-5) by the related attendance pattern. To illustrate: in the 3d family-income quintile, which shows 45 additional entrants, 22.0 percent, or 9.9 students, are likely to enter public universities.

STEP 7. Determining typical undergraduate student budgets by type and control of institution.

The annual budget of an undergraduate student attending college must adequately reflect both educational expenses and living costs. Educational expenses include tuition and fees, textbooks, and other study materials; living costs, on the other hand, encompass room, board, commutation, and personal expenses. Many institutions consider $150 for books and supplies and $400 for personal expenses to be average. The student-in-residence must add board-and-room charges, while the commuter must add an amount which will reflect the cost of room and board at home, as well as the cost of meals consumed away from home. It is estimated that the average annual at-home board-and-room expense is $500.

Table IV-7 illustrates—on a nationwide basis—typical student budgets for institutions of different types and control. The amounts are estimated to be sufficiently adequate for maintenance, thus permitting a student to pursue his studies without undue financial pressure. Room-and-board charges represent weighted averages for both commuters and resident students.

STEP 8. Computing the expected contribution by parents and student toward college expenses.

The purpose of this step is to determine for each family-income group the amount that the student and his parents can reasonably be expected to contribute toward college expenses. The mean family income for each of five socioeconomic groups should be used as the financial-status level to determine the corresponding parental contribution. Whatever computation system is used should equitably assess the parents' ability to pay.

National data illustrated in table IV-8 include the mean incomes for five groups, the corresponding parental contributions, and student contributions from summer earnings.

STEP 9. Computing the amount of student financial aid required, by family income and by type and control of institution.

Financial need is the difference between the amount of money the student and his parents can reasonably be expected to contribute toward college expenses and the amount required to attend a particular institution.

Table IV-7.—Typical academic-year budgets for undergraduate students, by type and control of institution attended[1]

Type and control	Tuition[2]	Room and board[2] (R) = Resident (C) = Commuter		Books and supplies	Personal expenses	Transportation	Total
Public							
Universities	$ 283	(R) $740×55% (C) $500×45%	$632	$150	$400	$200	$1,665
4-year colleges	195	(R) $610×60% (C) $500×40%	566	150	400	200	1,511
2-year colleges	103	(R) $550×5% (C) $500×95%	502	150	400	100	1,255
Private							
Universities	1,316	(R) $980×70% (C) $500×30%	836	150	400	200	2,902
4-year colleges	885	(R) $805×75% (C) $500×25%	729	150	400	200	2,364
2-year colleges	754	(R) $759%30% (C) $500×70%	577	150	400	100	1,981

[1] Theoretical example.
[2] Dollar amounts and percentages estimated from unpublished data, Office of Education, U.S. Department of Health, Education, and Welfare.

Table IV-8.—Expected contribution from parents and students toward college expenses, by family income[1]

Average family income quintile[2]	Mean family income	Parents' contribution[3]	Average student contribution[4]	Total
Low 5th	$ 4,350	$ 100	$300	$ 400
4th	6,500	500	300	800
3d	8,700	900	300	1,200
2d	11,300	1,350	300	1,650
High 1st	17,800	2,600	300	2,900

[1] Theoretical example.

[2] Quintile divisions based on family incomes of $5,300, $7,600, $10,000, and $13,000.

[3] Amounts from income which parents with 2.5 dependent children could be expected to contribute annually toward college expenses of a child, provided the family claims the standard Federal income tax deduction.

[4] Based on average yearly earnings of $430 for both male and female undergraduate students. It is assumed that from these earnings the typical undergraduate could save $300 to contribute toward college education expenses.

For the five family-income categories, this difference can be determined by subtracting total family contributions in table IV-8 from student budget requirements for each type of public and private institution in table IV-7. For example, when the $400 contribution by families in the lowest income quintile is subtracted from the $1,665 student budget at a public university, it is evident that $1,265 in financial aid will be required by a student from this family-income category who attends a public university. Individual student financial aid requirements by family income and by institutional type and control are illustrated in table IV-9.

> STEP 10. Calculating the average financial aid requirement per additional high school graduate entering college as a result of removal of all economic barriers. Calculating total program costs.

Using illustrative national data, it is estimated that college entrance rates would increase 6.1 percent (245 additional college entrants out of a cohort of 4,000 high school graduates) if a comprehensive program of student financial aid were instituted. The distribution of these 245 additional entering freshmen by family income and by type of public or private institution they would likely enter is depicted in table IV-6. Table IV-9 identifies the student's financial aid requirements by family-income group and by type and control of institution. By combining the data from these two tables, it is possible to calculate the average unit cost of financial aid for the entering freshmen, and also total program costs.

Table IV-10 illustrates the calculation by which a unit cost of $822 per additional entering student is determined. Program costs for each cell in the family-income and institution-type-control matrix are determined by multiplying the respective student financial aid requirements in table IV-9 by the corresponding number of additional entering freshmen in table IV-6. The resultant cost for 245 additional entrants is $201,290, or $822 per student.

The theoretical example data involve 2,638,000 students graduating from U. S. public and private high schools, with about 55 percent, or 1,450,000 graduates, entering college the following fall. Data from the model suggest that this entrance rate could be increased by an additional 6.1 percent if all financial barriers to entrance were removed. It is estimated that the 160,000 additional entering freshmen would require, on the average, financial aid amounting to $822 per student; total 1st-year program costs would be $132,000,000. Assuming a conservative 2.5 multiplier persistence factor—that the undergraduate enrollment of recent high school graduates equals freshmen entering college from high school multiplied by 2.5—the 4-year enrollment increase would be approximately 400,000. Finally, if the $822 financial aid requirement per freshmen student were extended to the sophomore and upper division levels, 4-year program costs would total approximately $330 million.

Table IV-9.—Student financial aid requirements, by family income and by type and control of institution[1]

Type and control	Student budget	Average family income quintile[2]				
		Low 5th	4th	3d	2d	High 1st
		Total family contribution				
		$400	$800	$1,200	$1,650	$2,900
Public						
University	$1,665	$1,265	$ 865	$ 465	$ 5	$ 0
4-year college	1,511	1,111	711	311	0	0
2-year college	1,255	855	455	55	0	0
Private						
University	2,902	2,502	2,102	1,702	1,252	[3]225
4-year college	2,364	1,964	1,564	1,164	714	[3]50
2-year college	1,981	1,581	1,181	781	331	0

[1] Theoretical example.
[2] Quintile divisions based on family incomes of $5,300, $7,600, $10,000, and $13,000.
[3] Accounts for students at nadir of income group.

Table IV-10.—Calculation of financial aid program costs, by family income
and by type and control of institution[1]

Type and control	Average family income quintile[2]					
	Low 5th	4th	3d	2d	High 1st	Total cost
Public						
University	$ 1,265	$ 865	$ 465	$ 5	0	
	×16.4	×11.5	×9.9	×10.0	0	
	$ 20,746	$ 9,948	$ 4,604	$ 50		$35,348
4-year college	1,111	711	311	0	0	
	×27.1	×13.3	×9.9	×7.9	0	
	30,108	9,456	3,079	0		42,643
2-year college	855	455	55	0	0	
	×34.4	×19.3	×14.9	×13.6	0	
	29,412	8,782	820	0		39,014
Private						
University	2,502	2,102	1,702	1,252	225	
	×3.3	×2.3	×2.3	×2.8	0	
	8,257	4,835	3,915	3,506		20,513
4-year college	1,964	1,564	1,164	714	50	
	×13.9	×7.0	×6.0	×7.7	0	
	27,300	10,948	6,984	5,498		50,730
2-year college	1,581	1,181	781	331	0	
	×4.9	×2.6	×2.0	×2.0	0	
	7,747	3,071	1,562	662		13,042
Total cost	$123,570	$47,040	$20,964	$9,716	0	$201,290 for 245 students, or $822 per student

NOTE.—Total cohort of high school graduates equals 4,000; number of additional entering students equals 245.
For each cell, program costs equal student financial aid requirements in table IV-9, multiplied by the number
of additional entering freshmen from cohort, table IV-6.

[1] Theoretical example.
[2] Quintile divisions for total cohort based on family incomes of $5,300, $7,600, $10,000, and $13,000.

BIBLIOGRAPHY

American College Testing Program, *Handbook for Financial Aid Administrators*, Iowa City, Iowa, 1972, 141 pp.

As stated in the foreword, this handbook has three objectives: (1) to provide a framework and perspective for the student financial aid profession which will be particularly helpful to the novice aid administrator; (2) to offer constructive suggestions for the administration and management of an aid office; and (3) to assist the aid administrator in understanding and using the ACT Student Need Analysis Service.

College Scholarship Service, *Manual for Financial Aid Officers*, 1971 revision, College Entrance Examination Board, New York, 1971.

This manual constitutes a major reference source. It is organized in five parts: the financial aid officer, student self-help, techniques in financial aid administration, the widening scope of financial aid, and need-analysis. The 26 subtopics include college financial aid principles, student employment, the place of loans in financial aid, research, talent searching, the expanding role of State scholarship programs, and the theory of need-analysis. In the appendixes are charts and tables for need-analysis computation. The bibliography includes 156 entries.

Hansen, W. Lee, "An Examination of Barriers to College Attendance," In U. S. Department of Health, Education, and Welfare, Office of Education, *Trends in Postsecondary Education*, U. S. Government Printing Office, Washington, D. C., 1970.

The author presents a comprehensive picture of the impact of financial barriers on college attendance patterns based upon 1966–67 data. The study reviews the impact of financial barriers and ways to offset them and considers enrollment patterns and family income, the financial costs of college and how people pay for them, and financial aid resources and their distribution. This information is then applied to several broad classes of institutions in order to bring out the interrelationships among financial need, college costs, and financial aid.

Mertins, Paul F., *Financial Statistics of Institutions of Higher Education, Student Financial Aid*, U. S. Department of Health, Education, and Welfare, Office of Education, U. S. Government Printing Office, Washington, D. C., 1968, 66 pp.

The author presents statistical tables of student financial aid funds disbursed by institutions of higher education in fiscal year 1965–66. The data are classified by type of program, type of aid, sponsorship of funds, and academic level of recipients. Summaries are presented on a national, regional, and State basis; also by control and level of institution. Data in this detail have not been collected by the U. S. Office of Education since 1965–66.

Sanders, Edward, and Hans Paler, *The Financial Barrier to Higher Education in California*, California State Scholarship Commission, Claremont, 1965, 295 pp.

This book is concerned with an analysis of the financial assistance needed by California college students. The following specific points are covered: the number and dollar-amount of undergraduate scholarships required; present and future student loan needs of disadvantaged students; the need for a program of graduate scholarships; and provisions for additional assistance to students from unduly deprived backgrounds. The authors also describe the effect on student financial needs of tuition charges of varying levels in institutions of public higher education within the State. And, finally, they consider the degree to which finances influence personal and or family opinions regarding higher education, together with the extent to which institutional policy changes can eliminate financial barriers. An excellent bibliography is included.

West, Elmer D., *Background for a National Scholarship Policy*, American Council on Education, Washington, D. C., 1956, 160 pp.

Compiled from a review of literature covering the entire field of scholarships, this report presents and correlates the data basic to formulation of a national scholarship policy for higher education. Extensive quotations from hundreds of studies and reports are used effectively to develop four main topic areas: the problem, sources of funds, motivational factors relating to college attendance, and the administration of scholarship programs. Required studies are suggested. Bibliography of 347 entries is included.

Chapter V

DIFFERENTIAL FUNCTIONS
OF COLLEGES AND UNIVERSITIES

The principle of differential functions as applied to higher education is as follows: *Institutions should play distinctive roles in developing a diversified educational program in order to meet, with efficiency and economy, the varied needs of the youth and citizenry of the State.* This principle serves as an important basis for organizing and coordinating the purposes and programs of public higher education. Its application results in a spectrum of functions, grouped to meet student need for accessibility and program blend, that strengthen institutional coherence and independence.

The first two sections of this chapter describe the need to establish differential functions as a positive basis for developing a diversified program of higher education and the specialized responsibilities of 2-year colleges, 4-year colleges, and universities in meeting this need. What follows in the third section is a brief statistical description of the consequences which the application of differential functions to public higher education has had on the college environment and on students and faculty. The fourth section consists of a review of the forms of governance used by State higher education systems.

There are many areas in which distinctions between 2-year colleges, 4-year colleges, and universities may be observed. The use of admission, retention, and transfer policies to maintain quality and assist in placing students, for example, is uniquely interpreted by each of the three types of institutions and often by individual institutions in each of the categories. Other distinctions—the articulation problem, for example—have common solutions applicable at every level. These two topics are discussed in a special section of this chapter.

Still other areas in which distinctions are found are discussed in chapter VI: resolution of the problem of size, recruitment and retention of faculty, doctoral-level graduate programs, and sponsored research. There are of course many other areas in which the effects of establishing differential functions are manifest, most notably in library operations (chapter IX), financial operations (chapter XII), and budgeting (chapter XIV).

THE NEED FOR
DIFFERENTIAL FUNCTIONS

A substantial (although possibly declining) degree of specialization cha-racterizes U.S. institutions of higher education.[1] The three main segments can be readily identified: the 2-year community or junior college with its service and transfer functions; the 4-year senior college, which is the prin-cipal instrument for degree-oriented undergraduate education; and the university, which serves as a citadel of scholarship, research, and graduate and professional training. The clarity with which this trichotomy can be distinguished does not, unfortunately, necessarily extend to the ways and means whereby specialization, as an organizational tool, can most effec-tively be employed.

A policy of providing for differential functions in higher education means that certain academic programs are allocated among institutions accord-ing to levels of instruction and emphasis, and that certain other functions (e.g., research, extension, and public services) may also be distinctively as-signed to individual institutions. In support of this policy, these arguments are advanced:

1. *Establishing differential functions promotes the development of high-level spe-cialized skills and the supporting resources essential to the achievement of excellence.*

A basic reason for establishing differential functions among institutions of higher education was cited by Adam Smith when he wrote in 1776 ". . . the division of labor, by reducing every man's business to some one simple operation, and by making this operation the sole employment of his life, necessarily increases very much the dexterity of the workman. . . ." He also cited the fact that time is saved if one does not move from one sort of work to another and that concentration of attention on a simple opera-tion encourages more inventive use of machinery.[2]

Nothing in higher education is precisely analogous to the increases in worker productivity resulting from a division of labor, but similar effi-ciencies and expertise can be developed by college faculty and administrators willing to concentrate on well-defined programs and functions. Some higher

---

[1] In studying changes in higher education over the past decade, Harold L. Hodgkinson concludes that diversity, while still a fact, is declining. His findings suggest that institu-tions of higher education are more similar than they were in the past. However, institu-tional size continues to establish substantial differences in institutional life. See Harold L. Hodgkinson, *Institutions in Transition—A Study of Change in Higher Education*, Carnegie Commission on Higher Education, Berkeley, Calif., 1970.

[2] Adam Smith, "The Advantages of the Division of Labour," *An Inquiry Into the Nature and Causes of the Wealth of Nations*, Modern Library edition, Random House, New York pp. 7–11.

education programs that require the assembly of human talents and the nurturing provided by specialization at the institutional level include liberal education, graduate and professional training, research, and programs for disadvantaged students.

2. *Differential offerings are an effective means of supplying educational programs consistent with a wide range of enrollment demand and student needs.*

Providing education services proportional to enrollment demand and student needs is the least controversial justification for establishing differential functions. If the demand for an educational product is small, economy dictates that the service be provided only in the amount required. (Nonparticipating institutions are automatically specialized to the extent that their course offerings do not include the limited service.) This principle, when applied to sparsely populated areas with limited support capabilities, encourages the concentration of certain educational services in a single, centrally located, and usually first-class facility. Any fragmentation of effort, which normally results in a number of small competing marginal facilities, is to be avoided. In practice, application of this principle ranges from the thousands of consolidated elementary and secondary schools serving rural counties across the country to a few tristate medical schools meeting the professional needs of large regions.

Except for certain imperfections in the market, the demand and supply of college program offerings are governed by student preferences and entrance restraints. If there is little demand, enrollment capacity should be correspondingly small. However, for most educationl programs there is a minimum enrollment necessary to support the curriculum and permit efficient instruction. To meet minimum enrollment requirements when student demand is small and scattered, educational programs must be concentrated in a few institutions. Nowhere is this better illustrated than in the exclusion of graduate and most professional training from all but a few highly qualified institutions. Allocating these functions almost exclusively to universities creates their unique role in higher education. Such a practice is justified because of the need to concentrate both rare students and rare faculty to form a critical mass conducive to advanced training and scholarly inquiry. Paralleling this differential function of universities is the special assignment given to 2-year colleges; namely, bringing together exceptional teachers and counselors and disadvantaged youth, both scarce commodities. Whenever student demand for an educational service is limited and/or educational resources are scarce, full utilization and conservation require that functional responsibilities be distinctively and restrictively allocated.

Whereas the allocation of graduate and professional training to certain universities is dictated by limited demand, the allocation of much of lower division undergraduate education to 2-year colleges is dictated by widespread demand. Higher education enrollment naturally pyramids from a broad supporting base of lower division undergraduates to a narrow apex of graduate and professional students. A lessening of demand and the increasingly rigid standards at higher levels are the basic causes of attrition; losses are also attributable to a variety of economic and motivational factors.

On a national scale the proportional enrollments in lower division, upper division, and graduate and professional levels at all institutions in 1971 was roughly 10:4.4:2.3. At universities these proportions were 10:7.8:5.7, and at 4-year colleges, 10:7.7:2.7 (see figure V-1). At a majority of universities and degree-oriented 4-year colleges, the desired balance of enrollment levels to provide a consistent yet progressive community of students from freshmen through seniors does *not* include a massive lower division component. At the extreme, quite the opposite is true: nearly equal upper and lower division enrollments are favored by faculty seeking to emphasize upper division level programs and reduce lower division teaching chores.[3] Such a close balance is in fact achieved at some institutions by the use of highly selective admissions that strictly limit the number of entering freshmen and eliminate possible poor risks. These restrictive practices by 4-year colleges and universities, considered legitimate in order to preserve student quality and enrollment balance, have forced the development of alternative *separate* means to accommodate the increasingly large number of youths seeking at least 2 years' postsecondary training. By enrolling the largest share of these students[4] through open-door admission policies, 2-year colleges not only have permitted 4-year colleges and universities to strengthen their traditional degree-oriented mission but also have added new dimensions to higher education programs and services.

3. *Area and accessibility requirements for postsecondary education are most economically met if new 2-year colleges are established with strict observance of their specialized mission.*

In meeting community needs, junior and community 2-year colleges serve small areas and thereby encourage local student attendance and per-

---

[3] Some institutions concentrate most of their energy on upper division and graduate education. The University of California, for example, enrolls twice as many juniors and seniors as freshmen and sophomores. In Florida, Illinois, New York, and several other States, some new State universities do not admit *any* freshmen or sophomores, only community college transfers.

[4] On a national basis 2-year colleges enroll 43 percent of lower division students; 4-year colleges, 32 percent; and universities, 25 percent. Two States where 2-year colleges enroll a higher percentage of lower division students are California (75 percent) and Florida (66 percent). Source: George H. Wade, *Fall Enrollment in Higher Education 1970: Supplementary Information Summary Data*, Department of Health, Education, and Welfare, Office of Education, U.S. Government Printing Office, Washington, D.C., 1971

Figure V-1. – Distribution of student enrollments by instructional level and type of institution: 1971

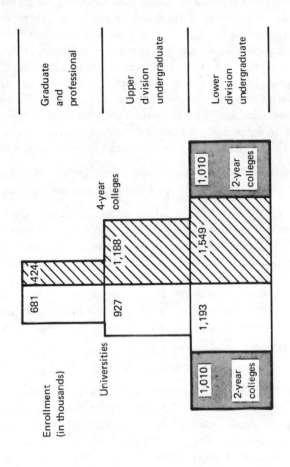

Enrollment
(in thousands)

Graduate
and
professional

Upper
division
undergraduate

Lower
division
undergraduate

Universities
4-year
colleges
2-year
colleges

681   424
927   1,188
1,193   1,549   1,010
1,010   2-year
colleges
2-year
colleges

Resident enrollment including full- and part-time degree- and non-degree-credit students.

Source: George H. Wade, Fall Enrollment in Higher Education, 1971, 1971, U.S. Department of Health, Education, and Welfare, Office of Education, U.S. Government Printing Office, Washington, D.C., 1973.

mit commuter attendance. Construction of 2-year colleges accessible to every community with a reasonable potential enrollment is a costly endeavor. From the standpoint of economy, 2-year college offerings should therefore be limited to those community-oriented programs which require accessibility; e.g., lower division undergraduate degree work, technical-vocational training, and continuing education. States are not usually in a financial position to support the more costly upper division programs at the community level nor does student demand warrant such support. Furthermore, there is strong evidence to suggest that the accessibility requirements for upper division programs are substantially less than they are for lower division; i.e., proximity of educational opportunities is less important in influencing junior and senior students to *remain* in college than it is in encouraging high school graduates to enter college.[5]

4. *Providing differential entrance requirements and retention standards establishes patterns of student characteristics consistent with program requirements.*

The application of differential functions in higher education extends to specialized institutional policies for the admission and retention of students. These policies range from open-door admissions at 2-year colleges to highly selective entrance requirements for university graduate programs. All such policies account for differences in the quality requirements of the different curriculums and instructional levels. Since such policies also help direct students to programs consistent with their abilities and interests, student energy and finances are minimized and educational efforts maximized.

5. *Establishing differential functions results in more effective use of limited resources and sometimes in a reduction in unit costs.*

The effective use and preservation of scarce resources is always an objective of productive effort. The two rarest elements in higher education that need to be used effectively and preserved are the human talents of teachers and scholars and the financial and leadership support they receive. These crucial ingredients are sufficiently scarce to demand great attention. Establishing differential functions provides unique environments that promote effective resource use. Nowhere is this better demonstrated

---

[5] Medsker and Trent, in their study of the influence of different types of public higher education institutions on college attendance, found that community junior colleges are the most effective in stimulating high school graduates to go on to college. The "low cost and closeness to home" was given as one of the most important reasons. In contrast, students who listed the major State universities as their first choice cited "good academic reputation" as the leading reason. It can be assumed that upper division students attending 4-year colleges and universities would also be less concerned about geographical proximity. See Leland L. Medsker and James W. Trent, *The Influence of Different Types of Public Higher Institutions on College Attendance From Varying Socioeconomic and Ability Levels.* Center for the Study of Higher Education, Berkeley, Calif., 1965.

than in the specialized role universities play in supporting research. A sensible division of functions assigns to the university, with its related graduate and professional programs, the primary responsibility for research. By and large the most compelling reason for this allocation is the costly nature of research—in faculty time, facilities, and library resources. The high cost requires that it be concentrated on those campuses most capable of effective and efficient research performance. Another reason that research is linked to universities is that contractors rely heavily on first-rate institutions whose demonstrated accomplishments engender confidence. But more than economics is involved. Since the number of scholars capable of productive research is limited, those available gravitate to the universities where they constitute the critical mass necessary for joint interdisciplinary approaches to difficult and complex research problems.

Although sponsored research is *primarily* conducted by universities, the research efforts of individual faculty members should be encouraged at other institutions. It is unfortunate, in the opinion of this observer, that sponsored research has been so highly concentrated at a few institutions, and that, as a consequence, smaller colleges have been deprived of the support necessary to stimulate creative effort. For example, only one-tenth of State-funded research is allocated to 4-year colleges and none goes to 2-year colleges.

Some evidence suggests that unit costs for lower division education are less at 2-year colleges than at 4-year colleges or universities. This has been chiefly attributed to the fact that lower faculty salaries are paid at 2-year colleges. In the public sector, however, average faculty salaries at 2-year colleges are currently competitive with those in other types of institutions at all academic ranks. The single exception is that of full professors; they are paid more by universities.[6]

Unit costs of instruction are, of course, proportional to the level of faculty salaries. But cost studies in which the salary level and class size do not remain reasonably constant do not provide valid comparisons. When an effort is made to achieve constant instructional quality, careful examination suggests that variations in unit costs are usually due chiefly to the extent to which such adjuncts as administration, research, supplies and equipment, public service, and student activities are added to classroom and instructional costs.

The most immediate measure of unit instructional costs is teaching salaries per student credit hour (SCH) or per annual full-time equivalent

---

[6] American Association of University Professors, *At the Brink—Preliminary Report of the Economic Status of the Profession, 1970–71*, AAUP, Washington, D.C., 1971, p. 40. The nearly equivalent salary level for the three types of institutions is largely a result of the fact that the high 2-year college faculty salaries in California and New York substantially raise the national average.

(FTE) student. Teaching salary is defined as that portion of the instructor's total salary paid for actual classroom teaching and class preparation; other aspects of a faculty member's time are excluded. This measure of productivity is increased either by lowering teaching salaries or by increasing the student-faculty ratio by enlarging class sizes or by increasing faculty teaching loads.

Because these three factors—teacher salaries, class size, and faculty teaching load—influence instructional quality, they should *not* be subject to differential rules that distinguish between 2-year colleges, 4-year colleges, and universities. Instruction should be of comparable quality for all three segments or institutional types. An illustration of this point is the situation in California shown in table V-1. Teaching salaries per student credit hour and per full-time-equivalent student (columns 4 and 5) are very nearly equal for all three segments. The lower student-teacher ratio at the university (column 2) is due in part to the extensive use of teaching assistants; their use also explains the university's lower average faculty salary (column 3) at the lower division level. Thus in terms of the most immediate costs of instruction, unit costs for lower division education in California are the same for all three higher education segments. Insofar as this balance of financial support promotes equal instructional quality, it is to be recommended.

If such other expenses as clerical salaries, student wages, and supplies and equipment directly related to classroom work and preparation are considered, clear distinctions between the three segments appear. In terms of "teaching expense" (columns 6 and 7), the lower division at California junior colleges is about 20 percent less costly than it is at the university ($12.15 per SCH compared to $15.28 per SCH); lower division at the State colleges falls between the two. In terms of the very broadly interpreted "instructional expense" (columns 8 and 9), which include the teaching expense plus the cost of departmental and institutional administration public and professional services, student activities and counseling, and for the university, departmental (unsponsored) research, even greater differences are evident. When these more comprehensive costs are considered, the lower division in California junior colleges is about 40 percent less costly than it is at the university ($14.69 per SCH compared to $23.6 per SCH).

Thus it appears that the higher costs of lower division instruction at the university and the senior college vis-a-vis the junior college are the result (at least in California) of more extensive and costly teaching adjuncts and of broader functions in the area of research and public service.[7] The Ca

---

[7] For a more detailed discussion of this topic and the source of these conclusions, se John M. Smart, *Feasibility and Desirability of Eliminating Lower Division Programs at Selecte Campuses of the University of California and the California State Colleges*, Coordinating Counc for Higher Education, Sacramento, January 1967, pp. 122–27.

Table V-1.—Unit costs of lower division instruction and other related factors for public higher education in California: 1963–64

| | Mean class size | Student-teacher ratio[1] | Teaching salary[2] per FTE staff | Teaching salary[2] | | Teaching expense[3] | | Instructional expense[4] | |
				per SCH	per annual FTE student	per SCH	per annual FTE student	per SCH	per annual FTE student
	(1)	(2)	(3)	(4)	(5)	(6)	(7)	(8)	(9)
Junior colleges	28	27.33:1	$3,965	$ 9.68	$145	$12.15	$364	$14.69	$441
State senior colleges (LD)	28	27.47:1	4,194	10.19	154	13.66	410	19.27	578
University of Calif. (LD)	30	21.13:1	3,029	9.56	144	15.28	458	23.63	709

NOTE.—SCH = student credit hour; FTE = full-time-equivalent; LD = lower division.

[1] Student-teacher ratio equals full-time-equivalent (FTE) students per FTE teaching staff.

[2] Teaching salary is that portion of the salary paid to the instructor for actual classroom teaching and class preparation (other aspects of a faculty member's time excluded).

[3] Teaching expense includes the teaching salary and all clerical salaries, student wages, and supplies and equipment directly related to classroom work and preparation.

[4] Instructional expense includes the teaching expense plus the cost of departmental and instructional administration, public and professional services, student activities and counseling, and, at the university, departmental (unsponsored) research.

Source: John M. Smart, *Feasibility and Desirability of Eliminating Lower Division Programs at Selected Campuses of the University of California and the California State Colleges,* Coordinating Council for Higher Education, Sacramento, January 1967, tables 11, 12, 18, and 19.

ifornia data appear to bear out the contention that a junior college may indeed be able to offer the lower division at substantially less *overall* cost than can a university or a 4-year college. These savings, of benefit to taxpayers and parents, are generally passed on to junior college students in the form of lower tuition and expenses. The establishment of differential functions is the principal reason such savings are possible.

6. *A comprehensive and balanced program of higher education requires that certain specialized low-demand offerings be differentially assigned to designated institutions.*

In addition to a reasonable division of the usual responsibilities in higher education, certain specialized curriculums essential to a comprehensive program of offerings should be allocated to selected institutions. Most often these specialized programs are within the purview of the university's multiple education, research, and service functions. Special curriculums and programs that may be allocated to single institutions on a one-of-a-kind basis include educational programs for the handicapped (e.g., a speech correction institute), agriculture stations, material-testing laboratories, educational testing centers, a State historical library-archives and related study program, a natural history museum, continuing education, and special culture enrichment programs (e.g., film classics, music appreciation, etc.).

7. *Certain institutional specialization should be encouraged to promote the advantages to be derived from campus location, existing commitments, and historical precedent.*

The intent of differential functions is often viewed narrowly. Granted that a division of responsibilities does impose major restrictions, such restriction are nevertheless mission oriented and directional rather than detailed Within the general anticipated pattern, great latitude for original and crea tive interpretation should be encouraged to provide the diversity and stim ulus necessary for healthy competition. While the allocation of function does not normally extend to details, in no instance should such an allocatio be interpreted as restricting such natural and derived advantages as ar afforded an institution by its location, faculty, history, campus, and com munity relationship. If such distinctions are recognized, they should b encouraged by positive supporting assignments.

8. *As a controlling device, the assignment of differential functions provides for o derly expansion without either lessening responsibilities or proliferating them exce sively.*

Some degree of restraint is required in the allocation of programs amon State institutions if the basic mission of each type of institution is to be pr served and unnecessary duplication avoided. Control is needed, for e ample, to limit the expansion of graduate work in institutions ill-suited and unprepared to undertake such work. On the other hand, such work should be encouraged in certain other institutions. A danger to the integrity of the basic functions of colleges exists, however, if they are allowed to over-extend the scope of their services. This would be the case, for example, if the community service and continuing education roles of a 2-year college were gradually preempted by ever-increasing responsibilities for upper division education. In this regard some States have gone so far as to prohibit 2-year colleges from becoming 4-year institutions. Such an extreme measure has been criticized, as have allocation plans which tend toward standardization and rigidity.

Any scheme for allocating functions and programs must be flexible enough to permit excellence to rise and surface where it will. Institutions of any given type need only conform to an overall pattern; individual units need not nor should not be expected to be exact duplicates. Whenever latitude results in growth and development, the mission of the institution should be reappraised. Providing for such reappraisal recognizes, according to the Illinois Planning Commission, that ". . . excellence often arises out of a fortuitous combination of faculty members and resources with little or no planning." Admittedly, this is an area in which pros and cons exist on both sides of every decision. As a practical matter, each case must be judged on its own merits, with control being exercised and rules interpreted, as the circumstances suggest, in the best interests of the State.

FUNCTIONS AND RESPONSIBILITIES OF THE SEVERAL TYPES OF HIGHER EDUCATION INSTITUTIONS

The present pattern of U.S. higher education is characterized by a tripartite system of institutions identified as 2-year junior or community colleges, 4-year senior colleges, and universities. Together they form an interlocking structure to provide collegiate and graduate education for young persons and adults and also to conduct significant public service and research. By assignment of differential missions, each of the three higher education divisions or segments performs these multiple functions with varying emphasis. Furthermore, because of differing requirements, the enrollment load assumed by each segment varies significantly among the States (table V-2).

Before discussing the effects which have resulted from differentiating the educational programs of 2-year colleges, 4-year colleges, and universities, it is important to mention that overlapping in purposes and programs does

Table V-2.—Proportional degree-credit enrollments, by institutional type and control relative to total public enrollment, by State: Fall 1972

	PUBLIC				PRIVATE		
	All institutions	Universities	4-year colleges	2-year colleges	Universities	4-year colleges	2-year colleges
United States	100	37	35	28	12	21	2
Alabama	100	33	46	21	0	16	1
Alaska	100	100	0	0	0	16	0
Arizona	100	54	8	38	0	19	1
Arkansas	100	52	46	2	0	18	2
California	100	13	33	54	5	10	1
Colorado	100	50	38	12	9	6	0
Connecticut	100	26	41	33	13	51	3
Delaware	100	81	10	9	0	5	14
Dist. of Columbia	100	0	67	33	400	17	7
Florida	100	27	24	49	8	15	1
Georgia	100	21	61	18	3	15	3
Hawaii	100	75	0	25	0	9	0
Idaho	100	33	58	9	0	8	21
Illinois	100	41	21	38	18	25	3
Indiana	100	99	0	1	9	27	0
Iowa	100	67	15	18	12	45	5
Kansas	100	54	25	21	0	12	2
Kentucky	100	48	52	0	0	20	2
Louisiana	100	36	61	3	12	5	0
Maine	100	100	0	0	0	38	0
Maryland	100	45	74	31	8	18	0
Massachusetts	100	26	51	23	90	55	9
Michigan	100	40	33	27	3	13	1
Minnesota	100	50	32	18	0	24	0

Mississippi	100	31	43	27	0	11	3
Missouri	100	39	38	23	16	21	2
Montana	100	68	24	8	0	12	0
Nebraska	100	72	22	6	8	18	0
Nevada	100	50	43	7	0	0	0
New Hampshire	100	64	36	0	0	93	0
New Jersey	100	24	48	28	9	30	4
New Mexico	100	72	26	2	0	9	0
New York	100	7	51	42	33	32	1
North Carolina	100	31	53	16	11	26	7
North Dakota	100	63	22	15	0	4	0
Ohio	100	77	16	7	3	32	0
Oklahoma	100	45	38	17	6	10	3
Oregon	100	41	35	24	3	14	0
Pennsylvania	100	52	34	14	19	59	2
Rhode Island	100	62	30	8	0	77	0
South Carolina	100	58	29	13	0	35	7
South Dakota	100	64	36	0	0	27	0
Tennessee	100	39	51	10	7	25	3
Texas	100	36	35	29	8	13	1
Utah	100	70	25	5	66	2	0
Vermont	100	77	23	0	0	77	15
Virginia	100	41	39	20	0	20	2
Washington	100	37	22	41	0	17	0
West Virginia	100	36	54	10	0	18	2
Wisconsin	100	26	65	9	7	14	2
Wyoming	100	67	0	33	0	0	0

NOTE.—All enrollments, both public and private, are relative to *total public* enrollment equal to 100. It should be pointed out that in a few States (Alaska and Kentucky, for example) public 2-year college enrollments are reported as part of the university system.

Source: U.S. Department of Health, Education, and Welfare, Office of Education, "Opening Fall Enrollment in Higher Education" (prepublication release, preliminary data), December 1972.

exist and cannot be avoided. Usually there are distinct differences in emphasis and level of instruction among the three types of institutions. In such areas as objectives, curriculum, and instructional methods, however, the distinctions are not necessarily clear-cut. The educational system as a whole should be viewed as one continuum, with the parts hardly distinguishable at their interfaces.

Some of the numerous effects that differentiating education programs have had on 2-year colleges, 4-year colleges, and universities are discussed in this chapter and in chapters VI, VII, IX, XII, and XIV. Since some of the discussions are problem oriented rather than descriptive, pointed reference to distinctions among the three types of higher institutions may not appear. A few topics are, by their nature, of special interest only to one type of institution (sponsored research and doctoral programs, for example). A reading of all sections should provide a reasonably clear picture of the characteristics which distinguish the 2-year college, the 4-year college, and the university.

The University

Two quotations eloquently describe the role of the university and its central responsibility. The noted educator, Robert Maynard Hutchins, recognizes that the university must be more than a conglomerate if it is to meet societal needs for training, information, and service:

> A university has to be an intellectual community because nothing can be understood in isolation. The university's aim is to draw the circle of knowledge. Its great role is to tame the excesses of the experts by forcing them to consider their disciplines in the light of the others.[8]

The intellectual and spiritual functions of the university are described by the distinguished columnist, Walter Lippman, as follows:

> The community of professors is, in the modern world, the best available source of guidance and authority in the field of knowledge. There is no other court to which men can turn and find what they once found in tradition and in custom, in ecclesiastical and civil authority. Because modern man in his search for truth has turned away from kings, priests, commissars and bureaucrats, he is left, for better or worse, with the professors.
>
> . . . The universities, therefore, are not only the depositories of wisdom. They are also laboratories where alchemists work, whose function it is to transmute knowledge into human wisdom. If the scholars do this, insofar as they do this, they transcend

---

[8] Robert Maynard Hutchins, "The University and the Multiversity," *The New Republic*, Apr. 1, 1967, p. 17.

the sterile controversies about the two cultures, the scientific and the humanistic, and they learn to transcend the intellectual puzzle about specialism and generalism. For knowledge transmuted into wisdom places the sciences and the humanities within one universe of discourse.[9]

Programs and activities emphasized by universities include the following:

1. *Comprehensive offerings.* Ideally, the university is the only institution capable of offering a comprehensive range of subjects. The complete university is not only comprehensive in the range of disciplines it offers; it also provides study at every instructional level, from 1st-year undergraduate study through the doctoral degree level, and offers opportunities for post-doctoral scholarship.

2. *Graduate education.* At the heart of the university are its scholars, special facilities, research activities, and graduate programs. This rare and costly environment is so difficult to create and maintain that progression from a 4-year senior college to a university cannot even be attempted without a clear demonstration of unusual potential. Aside from high cost and the scarcity of scholars, most graduate programs are confined to universities because study of high quality cannot be successfully carried on in isolation. Interrelation among fields of knowledge and their mutual interdependence make it difficult to provide high-level work in one subject without providing similar work in related or cognate disciplines.

3. *Professional education.* The university generally has exclusive jurisdiction over training in certain professions.[10] These include dentistry, law, medicine, veterinary medicine, theology, and graduate architecture.

4. *Sponsored research and technical services.* The university is the primary agency for conducting sponsored (organized) research. The scarcity of qualified researchers, the need for multidisciplinary approaches to problem-solving, and the costly equipment and facilities required explain in part the need to concentrate research at the university level. So endowed, the university must share its special talents. Most universities normally provide reasonable access to their libraries, computer centers, research facilities, and other special facilities, admitting qualified citizens, agencies, and members of the faculties of other higher education institutions.

5. *Public service.* Clearly, a traditional function of the university is to provide a wide range of public service. Visible evidences of such service are the allocation of faculty time to community betterment, the existence of university extension programs, and other efforts designed to disseminate knowledge developed within the university. Because a university has the intel-

---

[9] Walter Lippman, "The University," *The New Republic*, May 28, 1966, pp. 18, 20.

[10] Whatever distinction can be made between professional training and graduate study ...ies in the didactic occupational orientation given professional students as opposed to the ...equential approach to graduate study.

lectual freedom to pursue truth, it serves society as both critic and designer of the future.[11]

The 4-year College

Senior 4-year colleges perform functions that are distinct from those of 2-year colleges on the one hand and from those of universities on the other. Among all three types of institutions some degree of overlapping is, of course, inevitable and desirable. However, the fact that the 4-year college shares its programs and purposes with its counterparts does add to its problem of creating a separate identity. Much of the distinctiveness of 4-year colleges is due more to cultivated differences among them than to any overall unique entity. The genius of the 4-year college lies not so much in the uniqueness of its role but in the excitement, creativity, and excellence with which it approaches its mission. The 4-year college remains a most effective means of serving the widely varied needs of a particular geographical area and the equally diverse needs of students.[12]

Programs and activities emphasized by 4-year senior colleges include the following:

1. *Baccalaureate programs.* The independence of the 4-year college fosters a conscious and deliberate effort to provide high-quality undergraduate programs leading to the baccalaureate degree. With the exception of a few prestigious undergraduate-oriented universities, this emphasis is the unique province of the 4-year college. All 4-year colleges have as their core curriculum baccalaureate programs in such traditional areas as liberal arts and science. In addition, many of these colleges offer professional programs that may be undertaken at the undergraduate level: teacher training and business administration, and (to a lesser extent) agriculture, engineering, and nursing.

In the wake of shifting lower division students to 2-year colleges, 4-year colleges and universities began to place increased emphasis on upper division and graduate programs. A few 4-year colleges have eliminated the lower division program entirely. Such action has been criticized as educationally and administratively unsound, yet there appears to be no absolut need for an integrated undergraduate curriculum. A lower division genera education bloc and an upper division specialized bloc constitute a norma pattern. The requirement that a student pursue a 4-year program at on location and under one administration, while probably desirable, is nc

---

[11] Malcolm Moos and Francis E. Rourke, *The Campus and the State*, Johns Hopki Press, Baltimore, Md., 1959, pp. 317–18.

[12] For a broad examination of 279 4-year State colleges, see the study by E. Alde Dunham, *Colleges of the Forgotten Americans*, described in the bibliography.

imperative. Such a requirement cannot in fact be fulfilled by substantial numbers of students who transfer from one 4-year institution to another or from a 2-year to a 4-year college. Excluding the lower division may be appropriate for those 4-year colleges that wish to emphasize 3-year master's degree programs (junior, senior, and graduate years). However, when innovations of this nature are attempted, the possibility of problems arising in articulation and in enrollment must be recognized. Before an institution takes such a step it should examine the results achieved by other institutions that have departed from conventional collegiate curriculum patterns (all aspects of restructuring undergraduate programs can be reviewed in a study prepared by John M. Smart for the California Coordinating Council for Higher Education.)[13]

2. *Master's programs.* An expanding role of 4-year colleges is that of providing a 5th year of study leading to a master's degree. These graduate programs generally should be confined to those few fields in which the quality of work at the senior level has demonstrated the department's competence to support education at the master's level. The addition of many master's programs at 4-year institutions and the upgrading of junior and senior year work is gradually bringing about an improved educational structure between the 5th (master's degree) year and those beyond. The few 4-year public college programs leading to the doctorate are almost always offered in association with the State university.[14]

3. *Community oriented programs.* In many communities the only institution of higher education able to provide high-level community services is the 4-year college. In addition to the cultural influence afforded by its library and specialized staff, a 4-year college offers adult education programs, conferences on a variety of subjects, continuing education programs and consulting and advisory services.

4. *Research.* While the primary responsibility for organized or sponsored research lies with universities, the upgrading and adding of master's-level work at 4-year colleges has motivated them to establish the research base required for quality programs. Most research in publicly supported 4-year colleges is designed to benefit students and the State. In most instances, this research is not sponsored by grant or contract but performed by faculty members as part of their regular instructional and departmental service. Only an estimated 11.8 percent of all sponsored research conducted by institutions of higher education is performed at the 4-year college level (see table VI-6).

---

[13] Smart, op. cit.

[14] In a few States 4-year colleges have "emerged" as universities by expanding their doctoral programs. In view of statistics that indicate an "overproduction" of doctorates, such expansion is open to question.

The 2-year College

The 2-year community or junior college has emerged as an answer to education beyond the high school for an ever-increasing number of Americans. These colleges share certain characteristics which make them a distinctive segment of the higher education structure. With the majority, the chief characteristic is their accessibility. A local college is a potent factor in motivating youths to continue their education. One reason is the relatively low cost: tuition is either free or minimal, and dormitory fees are non-existent for students living at home. Furthermore, since almost all 2-year colleges are "nonselective" or "open door," the opportunity to pursue an education beyond the high school is available to many more students than would otherwise be the case. Traditionally, community and junior colleges are rooted in their locality, governed by local citizens, and supported by local and State taxes. A final and important shared characteristic is that teachers at 2-year colleges concentrate on their teaching responsibilities perhaps to a greater extent than do faculty at other types of institutions. The special emphasis is not on research but on teaching excellence.

There is some inconsistency in the terms used to identify 2-year institutions. They are variously referred to as junior colleges, community colleges, community-junior colleges, or simply as colleges. In those States in which 2-year institutions stress lower division degree-credit programs, the term junior colleges is used. The community college title is reserved for institutions emphasizing 2-year occupational programs and community service. While such a distinction could be helpful, it is not commonly observed. Furthermore, since all 2-year colleges share many common characteristics and since each reflects the special needs of its own community, any title differentiation is a matter of degree rather than of absolute distinction. In this text, the term 2-year college applies to both community and junior colleges, without regard to program emphasis.

Programs and activities emphasized by the 2-year college include the following:

1. *Occupational education.* The 2-year college is primarily responsible for technical and semiprofessional training designed to provide enrollees with occupational competence in a wide variety of fields within a 2-year period or less.[15]

---

[15] Occupations that typically require at least 2 years of college-level *technical* training include engineering technician; architectural and structural draftsman; medical, dental, and scientific technician; business specialist (of many kinds), etc. *Semitechnical* or advanced skills usually requiring 1 or 2 years of post-high-school training include those of mechanics and repairmen who service office machines, computers, machinery, transportation equipment, radio and television sets; also, structural metal workers; operators and maintainers of heavy machinery and equipment; automotive specialists; and general administrative assistants.

2. *General education,* The 2-year college is responsible for undergraduate general education. Satisfactory completion of 2 years' work in this program is generally recognized by the awarding of the associate of arts degree. Credits earned are as a rule transferable to a 4-year college or university; in some cases they can be applied toward degrees in such professional fields as teaching, engineering, medicine, nursing, and architecture.

3. *Guidance services and remedial education.* Junior and community colleges are not only expected to provide strong guidance programs to help each student choose an occupation consistent with his interests, aptitudes, and abilities, but also to assume a greater responsibility than either 4-year colleges or universities for providing compensatory education programs for students whose previous education has been limited or inadequate.

4. *Community services and continuing education.* Two-year colleges are responsive to the desires, needs, and ambitions of the residents of a given geographical area. These colleges serve individual communities by educating young people as they progress toward maturity by (a) making available such resources as faculty, students, equipment, and facilities; (b) providing citizen guidance and counseling; and (c) improving the community through research and planning. Two-year colleges are also dedicated to providing educational opportunities for adults through refresher courses, occupational training, and cultural and recreational activities.

Institutional Descriptive Data

The establishing of differential functions among the segments of higher education should in no way discourage institutions from seeking to maintain individuality within the broad functional responsibilities assigned. Toward this end it is important that objective information about a given institution be available regarding admission policy, campus size, curriculum, staffing, etc. Furthermore, since a college or university is a *competitive* enterprise with respect to other colleges or universities, it is particularly important that institutional data of a *comparative* nature identify areas of relative strength and weakness.

The well-recognized heterogeneity of American higher education has been the subject of studies[16] that have documented differences in the quality and character of college environments, including differences in students, administrative practices, faculty, intellectual and social climate, and other factors. A primary example is Astin's 1968 landmark study, *Who Goes Where*

---

[16] See Alexander W. Astin, J. L. Holland, T. R. McConnell, Paul Heist, C. Robert Pace, and others. Recommended for initial reading is Alexander Astin, *The College Environment,* American Council on Education, Washington, D.C., 1968.

to College?.[17] Because it considers key student and environmental characteristics of individual 4-year institutions, it is a useful tool for colleges and
universities that are seeking self-identification. Also of value are the reports
of the American Council on Education which provide timely national normative data useful in identifying differentials and assessing changes among
the major types of public and private higher educational institutions.

Who Goes Where to College? presented for the first time comprehensive information about the students, curriculum, and environment of 1,015 4-year
U.S. colleges and universities. Each institution was described in terms of
five characteristics pertaining to such factors as the entering student body,
selectivity, size, and the proportions of baccalaureate degrees awarded in
six broad fields of study. When plotted, the factor scores establish an institution's "profile," which in turn can be interpreted through visual comparative analysis. A type of comparison especially helpful in identifying the
unique characteristics of a given institution involves comparison of that institution's profile with an average profile of a selected group of similar institutions; e.g., institutions of a particular type, control, and location (public 4-year colleges in the Midwest, for example). Several outstanding characteristics of the group as well as of the individual institution in question
may be revealed by plots of this nature.

Following Astin's initial study, the American Council on Education, in
response to the continuing need for comparative information on college
environments, developed an Inventory of College Activities. This inventory
consists of various dimensions of student behavior and subjective impres-
sions based on statistically weighted summaries of student responses to
selected questions. The dimensions deal with several key areas of undergraduate life: the peer environment—interpersonal behavior; the peer
environment—noninterpersonal behavior; the classroom environment; the
administrative environment; and the college environment. Norms for these
dimensions have been reported for the 1966–67 freshmen class, as measured
in August 1967 and again in 1971.[18] Percentage normative data are presented by sex and for both sexes combined, and are subdivided by the basic
type of institution in which the students initially enrolled for their first
college term—2-year colleges, 4-year colleges, universities—plus the total
for all institutions combined. These data permit participating institutions
to compare their percentage position for the various dimensions with the
average scores of similar schools. The measurement techniques developed

---

[17] Alexander W. Astin, *Who Goes Where to College?*, Science Research Associates, Inc.,
Chicago, 1965. (See bibliography.)

[18] Alan E. Bayer, David Drew, Alexander Astin, Robert Boruch, and John Creager,
The First Year of College: A Follow-up Normative Report, American Council on Education,
Washington, D.C., 1970; and Alan E. Bayer, Jeannie T. Royer, and Richard M.
Weff, *Four Years After College*, American Council on Education, Washington, D.C.,
1973.

and the inventory findings should be useful to administrators seeking a better understanding of their institutional environment.

In addition to the data provided by the Inventory of College Activities, the American Council on Education routinely publishes various normative data and longitudinal studies helpful in identifying the college environment. Some examples of the various initial normative data for freshman students that help distinguish the different nature of the three types of higher education institutions are presented in table V-3. Table V-4 delineates student-related institutional characteristics, while table V-5 consists of indicators of the professional background and academic activity of college faculty.

Although the foregoing brief introduction to the ACE data bank merely indicates the comprehensiveness and detail of the total file, it also suggest the research potential available and should encourage State and institutional researchers to explore with the council their special interests.

ENVIRONMENT AND
STUDENT DEVELOPMENT

The impact that different college environments exert on a student's development is of vital concern to State planning agencies intent on establishing appropriate differential functions among the segments of higher education. To obtain different educational outcomes, the segments must be designed with an understanding of how student behavior relevant to the goals of a given institution is affected by the dynamic influences that characterize the college. Knowledge of the interactions between students and their college environments is also of value in matching the college-bound student with an appropriate institution.

Because of the complexities of analysis in the aforementioned areas and the extensive longitudinal research required to assess student development, most States have not conducted such studies. Moreover, the problems of defining the criteria of student development, identifying relevant and measurable observations of student behavior, and designing research methodology are largely unsolved. A principal difficulty is that some of the ways in which college students change are certainly unrelated to college experiences; that is, they would take place even if the individuals did not attend college. In the words of Mervin B. Freedman,[19] "Unequivocal empirical

---

[19] Mervin B. Freedman, "Impact of College," in *New Dimensions in Higher Education*, no. 4, U.S. Department of Health, Education, and Welfare, Office of Education, U.S. Government Printing Office, Washington, D.C., 1960, p. 7.

Table V-3.—Norms for freshmen, by type of institution: Fall 1972

	All institutions	All 2-year colleges	All 4-year colleges	All universities
Rank in high school class				
Top quarter	43.5	21.2	52.1	65.5
Second quarter	33.5	38.7	32.8	26.3
Third quarter	20.3	35.0	13.6	7.4
Lowest quarter	2.7	5.1	1.6	.7
Average grade in high school				
A or A+	6.7	2.3	7.7	12.2
A−	10.6	4.9	12.8	16.7
B+	18.8	12.5	21.9	24.3
B	25.8	25.5	26.9	24.6
B−	14.4	16.8	13.6	11.7
C+	14.3	21.6	11.1	7.2
C	9.0	15.5	5.8	3.2
D	.5	.9	.3	.1
Distance from home to college				
5 miles or less	12.8	21.6	7.9	6.0
6–10 miles	13.6	21.2	9.2	8.0
11–50 miles	24.9	31.9	23.5	15.6
51–100 miles	13.8	10.1	15.2	17.9
101–500 miles	26.0	11.7	31.5	41.2
More than 500 miles	8.8	3.5	12.7	11.4

	All institutions	All 2-year colleges	All 4-year colleges	Al. universities
Reasons noted as very important in selecting this college				
Relatives wanted me to go	9.9	10.9	9.8	8.3
Wanted to live away from home	17.9	8.4	21.5	27.1
Has a good academic reputation	48.4	33.1	55.6	60.9
Has a good athletic program	10.5	8.5	12.6	10.1
Offered financial assistance	17.5	14.0	22.1	15.7
Most friends going here	3.9	5.8	2.7	2.8
Low tuition	19.6	25.5	15.3	17.1
Advice of someone who attended	17.1	17.1	17.7	16.1
Special educ. program offered	27.0	26.8	27.5	26.7
Not accepted anywhere else	3.4	4.6	2.8	2.4
Advice of guidance counselor	6.9	8.9	6.6	4.4
Wanted to live at home	12.6	20.1	9.2	6.0
Estimated parental income				
Less than $3,000	4.5	6.6	4.0	1.8
$3,000–$3,999	3.5	5.0	3.0	1.6
$4,000–$5,999	6.1	8.1	5.7	3.7
$6,000–$7,999	8.2	10.0	7.8	5.6
$8,000–$9,999	10.4	12.1	10.0	8.3
$10,000–$12,499	16.8	18.2	16.0	15.8

Number of college applications				
This college only	47.2	60.5	36.9	41.8
One other	18.7	16.3	20.4	19.9
Two others	14.8	10.9	17.9	16.3
Three others	6.0	5.8	11.5	10.2
Four others	4.7	2.7	6.2	5.7
Five others	2.9	2.0	3.7	3.1
More than five others	2.6	1.8	3.3	3.0
Number of college acceptances				
This college only	40.3	53.3	32.7	35.7
One other	27.2	26.0	28.1	27.2
Two others	18.0	13.1	21.3	19.4
Three others	8.7	5.1	10.9	10.1
Four others	3.4	1.6	4.2	4.4
Five others	1.3	.6	1.7	1.7
More than five others	1.0	.4	1.2	1.4
Highest degree planned anywhere				
None	3.4	6.8	1.6	1.1
Associate (or equivalent)	8.1	19.9	1.6	1.1
Bachelor's (B.A., B.S.)	37.3	36.5	37.5	38.4
Master's (M.A., M.S.)	27.4	20.7	33.4	27.7
PH.D. or ED.D.	8.9	4.6	11.2	11.5
M.D., D.O., D.D.S., or D.V.M.	7.2	3.7	7.3	12.3
LL.B. or J.D. (law)	4.5	2.1	5.3	6.7
B.D. or M.DIV. (divinity)	.4	.4	.5	.2
Other	2.8	5.3	1.6	1.0
$12,500–$14,999	13.5	13.3	13.4	13.7
$15,000–$19,999	14.8	12.6	15.7	17.0
$20,000–$24,999	8.9	6.3	9.5	12.2
$25,000–$29,999	4.3	2.7	4.8	6.4
$30,000–$34,999	2.9	1.8	3.2	4.2
$35,000–$39,999	1.8	1.1	2.0	2.6
$40,000–$49,999	1.7	.9	1.9	2.6
$50,000 or more	2.7	1.4	3.0	4.5
Major sources of support				
Part-time or summer work	33.3	35.8	30.5	33.6
Savings from full-time work	10.2	12.4	8.8	8.9
Spouse's employment	2.1	3.3	1.5	1.1
Parental or family aid or gifts	53.6	43.5	55.9	67.1
Parent's military service	2.1	2.6	1.8	2.0
Personal military service	2.0	3.3	1.4	.7
Scholarships and grants	21.8	15.6	28.1	21.7
Loans-NDEA, Gov't insured, college	16.1	12.7	20.0	15.5
Other repayable loans	5.9	5.2	7.0	5.3
Concern about financing college				
No concern	35.6	38.1	33.6	34.6
Some concern	49.4	47.6	50.1	51.3
Major concern	15.0	14.3	16.3	14.1

Source: American Council on Education, Office of Research, The American Freshman: National Norms for Fall 1972, ACE Research Reports, vol. 7, no. 5, Washington, D.C., December 1972.

Table V-4.—Student-related characteristics of institutions, for 2-year colleges, 4-year colleges, and universities: 1967

Characteristics of institutions	2-year colleges	4-year colleges	Univ.
Ability requirement for admissions			
SAT[1]	18	60	52
CEEB	4	27	24
ACT	31	28	21
B-Average in high school	69	84	70
Median scores on SAT			
Less than 800	7	6	0
800–832	3	1	0
833–865	66	23	42
866–897	6	6	0
898–930	9	11	4
931–962	2	6	1
963–995	3	10	7
996–1026	1	9	11
1027–1060	2	9	7
1061–1190	1	13	16
Greater than 1190	0	6	11

	2-year colleges	4-year colleges	Univ.
Median scores on ACT			
Less than 18	15	11	2
19	66	24	41
20–21	11	15	5
22–23	5	23	22
24–26	2	19	18
Greater than 26	1	7	12
Distribution of revenues from student aid funds (per student)			
$ 0–25	47	16	7
$ 26–50	11	13	8
$ 51–75	27	13	7
$ 76–100	1	24	10
$101–200	3	23	53
$201–300	11	7	9
Greater than $300	0	4	5

Percentage of full-time students awarded scholarships

0	37	21	38
1–9	44	21	28
10–19	13	23	24
20–29	2	18	8
30–100	2	17	2

Percentage of full-time students given aid through jobs

0	55	23	44
1–9	25	15	27
10–19	12	27	19
20–29	3	17	6
30–100	5	17	3

Percentage of full-time students given loans

0	55	22	41
1–9	32	20	28
10–19	8	31	22
20–29	3	16	7
30–100	2	11	3

Percentage of full-time students given financial aid

0	44	22	45
1–9	16	3	3
10–19	17	10	17
20–29	11	15	17
30–39	5	20	10
40–100	8	30	7

[1] SAT = Verbal plus quantitative standard scores.

Source: John A. Creager and Charles L. Sell, *The Institutional Domain of Higher Education: A Characteristics File*, ACE Research Reports, vol. 4, no. 6, American Council on Education, Washington, D.C., 1969.

Table V-5.—Professional background and academic activity of American college faculty: 1969
(percentage distribution)

	2-year colleges	4-year colleges	Universities
Highest degree held			
Bachelor's or less	17.1	6.2	4.5
Master's (except professional)	64.2	40.2	22.9
Professional (except medical)	11.2	9.9	7.4
Medical degree	0.8	0.9	8.8
Ph.D. or Ed.D.	5.1	38.6	52.7
Other doctorate	1.6	4.2	3.6
Percentage checking that during graduate school			
Was a teaching assistant	28.6	50.2	61.2
Was a research assistant	11.2	28.3	45.0
Was awarded fellowship over $1,000	25.2	46.4	55.2
Had faculty "sponsor" for job	19.3	30.8	44.1
Major field of postgraduate degree			
Business, commerce, and management	5.4	4.0	3.3
Education (incl. phys. ed.)	17.0	11.9	8.5
Biological sciences (incl. agriculture)	4.1	4.7	10.8
Physical sciences (incl. mathematics)	8.3	12.1	11.2
Engineering (incl. architecture)	2.4	5.0	8.2
Social sciences (incl. psych. and geog.)	6.9	11.7	12.1
Fine arts	6.5	8.0	5.1
Humanities	16.3	20.6	13.3

	2-year colleges	4-year colleges	Universities
Percentage using teaching methods in most/ some courses			
Term papers	56.0	63.9	45.2
Frequent quizzes	84.7	68.4	48.6
Teaching assistants	2.2	12.2	30.5
Closed-circuit television	7.7	8.4	6.0
Machine-aided instruction	27.2	15.3	11.3
Number class hours per week			
None	3.5	4.4	11.5
1–4	7.2	10.8	21.0
5–8	8.8	20.6	32.6
9–12	17.6	42.1	22.8
13 or more	62.7	22.2	12.1
Total students in classes			
None (incl. no answer)	3.4	3.8	8.8
Under 25	12.7	15.8	24.0
25–49	16.7	23.1	22.5
50–99	29.5	33.7	24.6
100–249	33.3	21.6	16.5
250 or more	4.4	2.0	3.5
Percentage reporting influence opportunities (great deal or quite a bit) on			
Departmental policies	68.0	61.1	55.1
Institutional policies	24.1	18.7	11.1

Health fields	1.8	1.3	9.0
Other professions (incl. social work, law, journalism, library science)	1.9	2.8	3.8
All other fields (incl. home ec., industrial arts)	1.6	1.4	2.1
None, no postgraduate degree (incl. no answer)	27.8	16.4	12.6
Present rank			
Professor	6.2	19.6	27.2
Associate professor	10.9	21.9	22.5
Assistant professor	15.7	31.0	29.6
Instructor	40.5	19.0	15.1
Lecturer	0.9	5.5	2.9
No ranks designated	20.9	1.4	0.3
Other	4.9	1.7	2.5
Basic salary for academic year			
Below $7,000	12.4	8.7	7.0
$ 7,000–$ 9,999	40.2	34.3	17.0
$10,000–$11,999	20.4	22.2	18.3
$12,000–$13,999	16.4	14.3	17.1
$14,000–$16,999	8.9	10.9	16.9
$17,000–$19,999	0.9	5.3	11.3
$20,000–$24,999	0.3	3.0	8.2
$25,000 and over	0.3	1.2	4.2
Teaching responsibilities			
Entirely undergraduate	96.0	69.3	27.8
Some undergraduate, some graduate	0.9	23.2	47.0
Entirely graduate	0.0	4.6	19.2
Not teaching this year	3.0	3.0	6.0

Teaching-research interest			
Heavily in research	0.7	2.2	6.3
Both, lean toward research	3.7	12.9	28.9
Both, lean toward teaching	19.3	36.0	37.2
Heavily in teaching	76.2	48.8	27.5
Number of professional articles published			
None (incl. no answer)	76.3	51.1	29.5
1–4	20.5	32.2	29.7
5–10	2.1	8.5	14.1
11–20	0.6	4.3	10.3
21 or more	0.4	3.9	16.3
Personal career rating			
Very successful	26.4	21.0	26.3
Fairly successful	68.0	71.6	67.8
Fairly or very unsuccessful	5.5	7.3	5.9
Percentage rating of institution as excellent or good on			
Intellectual environment	45.2	44.5	58.8
Faculty salary	47.9	45.5	47.1
Teaching load	40.8	46.5	57.8
Student/faculty ratio	51.0	56.9	50.2
Administration	54.0	50.5	50.8
Effectiveness of campus senate	43.7	37.8	37.2
Research resources	34.7	30.2	601.
Availability of research funds	11.6	15.7	44.6
Cultural resources	30.0	37.0	53.6

Source: Alan E. Bayer, *College and University Faculty: A Statistical Description,* ACE Research Reports, vol. 5, no. 5, American Council on Education, Washington, D.C., June 1970.

determination of the differential effects of college experience [is] impossible to attain. Required for such a study would be two groups of high school students alike in every way except that one goes on to college, while one does not. The very fact that students choose not to go to college makes them a somewhat inadequate control group." The author goes on to point out, however, that comparing high school graduates who do not go to college with those who do and comparing the similarities and differences among students in many different kinds of colleges can reveal much about the special nature of college influence.

One influence which colleges undoubtedly exert on students is to increase or enhance their knowledge of subject matter. According to Dr. C. Robert Pace of Syracuse University, "On the basic objective which we might call the transmission of significant knowledge, the colleges are in fact successful. With almost no exception across the country where *achievement* testing has been applied, the average scores of seniors, juniors, and sophomores are *significantly* higher than the average scores of freshmen—whether tested cross-sectionally or longitudinally."[20] It has also been clearly demonstrated[21] that individuals do better when grouped with good students. Students attending colleges at which the average ability was high performed significantly better on comprehensive achievement tests than did students with the same initial ability enrolled in colleges at which the average ability was low.

Other kinds of student changes are more difficult to measure. Dr. Freedman again: "Evaluation of how students' personalities or characters change, understanding of the factors which influence them little or a good deal during the student years, or estimation of the extent to which a life pattern has been altered by attendance at college are complex issues. A study which sheds light on matters like this very likely requires much ingenuity and effort."[22]

Adding to the problems of criteria and measurement is the recognition that there is a significant relationship between the outlook of college students and the spirit of the times. To appreciate this fact, one need only contrast the involved and often militant youth of the 1970's with the "gloriously contented"[23] college generation in the 1950's.

In an attempt to shed light on the effect of college environment on student development, the American Council on Education has instituted a large-scale program of longitudinal research. The major objectives of this

---

[20] C. Robert Pace and G. G. Stern, "An Approach to the Measurement of Psychological Characteristics of College Environments," *Journal of Education Psychology*, vol. 49, 1958, pp. 269-77.

[21] William S. Learned and Ben D. Wood, *The Student and His Knowledge*, Carnegie Foundation for the Advancement of Teaching, New York, 1938.

[22] Freedman, op. cit., p. 2.

[23] Philip E. Jacob, *Changing Values in College*, Harper, New York, 1957.

program ". . . are to assess the impact that different college environments have on the student's development and to provide a source of current, readily available descriptive information about the population of college students."

This ACE research program is designed to obtain information about the inputs, outputs, and environments in higher education institutions. Outputs are the operational manifestations of educational objectives—those student skills, attitudes, and behavior patterns that an institution either influences or attempts to influence. Inputs are the talents, skills, aspirations, and other potentials for growth and learning that the student brings with him to the institution. Environments include those aspects of an institution (student characteristics, teaching practices, peer associations, curriculum, facilities, etc.) capable of affecting the overall development of a student. The principal objective of the research program is to determine how these environmental variables affect student performance.[24]

Some early results of ACE's efforts have been presented by Alexander Astin, director of research.[25] The nature of the findings deserves review here, for it appears that a major breakthrough in assessing the *comparative* impact which different types of institutions have on students is imminent. The general plan of the program is to gather data from freshmen when they first enter college and to collect longitudinal followup data at periodic intervals thereafter. In the comparative analysis a total of 48 dependent variables were studied, including 28 items concerning a student's observable behavior during his freshman year, 15 items reflecting his attitudes on various issues, his degree of satisfaction with the freshman year, his freshman-year grade average, and the dropout rate following the 1st year of college.

In order to assess the impact of different types of institutions on each of the 48 dependent variables, an "expected" performance rate, based on characteristics of a student's background, was computed for each variable. A stepwise regression analysis was employed. The expected performances of each background characteristic for all students attending each of nine types of institutions were then averaged separately. The mean expected freshman performance rates for each variable were then compared with the mean actual occurrence rates of students during their freshman year. The results of this comparative analysis of college impact are presented in Table V-6.)

---

[24] Important work in this area is also being performed by Pace. See C. Robert Pace, *The Influence of Academic and Student Subcultures in College and University Environments*, U.S. Department of Health, Education, and Welfare, Office of Education, Cooperative Research Project no. 1083, University of California, Los Angeles, 1964.

[25] Alexander W. Astin, "College Impact on Student Attitudes and Behavior," paper given before the American Educational Research Association, New York, Feb. 6, 1971.

Table V-6.—Effects of six types of institutions on student attitudes and behavior: 1968

Dependent variable	2-year colleges	Technological institutions	Roman Catholic 4-year colleges	Protestant 4-year colleges	Public universities	Private universities
Behaviors						
Overslept and missed a class or appointment	−	−	−		+	+
Typed a homework assignment			+		−	+
Participated in organized demonstrations	+	−		−	−	−
Failed to complete a homework assignment on time		−			+	
Was a guest in a teacher's home		+	−	++	−	−
Rode on a motorcycle		−	−			
Slept or dozed in class					−	
Studied with other students			++	−	−	
Did extra (unassigned) reading for a course				+	+	
Tutored another student				−	−	−
Saw a foreign movie						
Took a tranquilizing pill		−		+	+	+
Discussed religion			+			
Took vitamins					−	
Visited an art gallery or museum				+	+	+
Took a trip more than 500 miles					+	
Got a traffic ticket						
Missed school because of illness						
Smoked cigarettes	+	−	−	−	−	
Discussed politics					+	
Played tennis				+	+	−
Drank beer	−		+	+	−	
Discussed sports		−			+	
Asked a teacher for advice after class		−			−	

Attitudes

College faculty are more competent than students to specify the curriculum

Parents should be discouraged from having large families

Colleges would be improved if organized sports were de-emphasized

Scientists should publish their findings regardless of possible consequences

Realistically, an individual person can do little to bring about changes in society

The chief benefit of a college education is that it increases one's earning power

My beliefs and attitudes are similar to those of most other college students

Faculty promotions should be based, in part, on student evaluations

Student publications should be cleared by college officials

College officials have the right to ban persons with extreme views from speaking on campus

Students from disadvantaged social backgrounds should be given preferential treatment in college admissions

Most college officials have been too lax in dealing with student protests on campus

Returned for a 2d year

Freshman grade average

Satisfied with college

Note.—A plus sign (+) indicates that the mean actual score was significantly ($p < .05$) higher than the mean expected score; a minus (−) sign indicates that the mean actual score was significantly lower than the mean expected; a blank indicates that the two scores were not significantly different.

Source: Alexander W. Astin, "College Impact on Student Attitudes and Behavior," paper given before the American Educational Research Association, New York, Feb. 6, 1971.

Since the findings at public and private 2-year colleges were very similar, they are reported as one set of results. Because public and private nonsectarian 4-year colleges significantly affected only a few of the outcomes, the the results for these institutions are not reported. What is indicated in the column below a particular type of college is the particular pattern of effect that the college exerted on the various dependent variables. Two-year colleges, for example, had a negative impact on student drinking and smoking and a positive impact on relatively conservative student attitudes. The row adjacent to one of the items reveals how student performance on that item was affected by different types of colleges. The frequency with which students failed to complete a homework assignment on time, for example, is positively related to attendance at 2-year colleges, technological institutions, and Protestant 4-year colleges, yet negatively related to attendance at Roman Catholic 4-year colleges.

The American Council on Education is continuing to collect data to determine the comparative effects on students of different colleges. Astin points out that the crude typology of the institutions used in this initial investigation probably conceals many important differential effects of institutions. Such will not be the case when several additional analyses of institutional impact, currently in progress at ACE, are completed.[26]   These will include the effects of such institutional variables as size, selectivity, academic competitiveness, peer group interaction, and other environmental features.

GOVERNING STRUCTURE

The means by which institutions of higher education within a State can be appropriately governed depend partly on historical tradition, partly on political strength and compromise, and partly on sound principles of organization. The multiplicity of institutions related to the various aspects of public and private higher education clearly indicates the complexity of the problem. Furthermore, the varied circumstances inherent in the many State systems preclude the developing of any standardized governance pattern equally viable for all States. However, the emergence in many States of a tripartite system of public higher education together with the

---

[26] For findings from more recent studies, see Alexander W. Astin, "The Measured Effects of Higher Education," *The Annals of the American Academy of Political and Social Science*, vol. 404, November 1972, pp. 1–20.

introduction of some basic consistencies among State governing arrangements suggest that certain principles and practices can be used as guidelines.

One principle of the U.S. democratic process widely applied in the governance of institutions of higher education is that the public interest is best served if control is vested in a deliberative body of citizens who are not members of the operational agency. With the exception of a few proprietary institutions, all public and nonprofit private institutions of higher education are governed either directly or indirectly by nonsalaried boards or commissions whose members are charged with representing the public interest. Such institutional governing boards select the chief administrative officers and are responsible for the policy, development, and planning necessary to guide the institution toward its stated objectives. The president of the college and other appropriate institutional officers are ordinarily given broad executive power to act in accordance with overall board policies, to conduct detailed planning, and to present proposals for consideration and make periodic reports to the board.

There also seems to be general agreement on the part of both the public and private higher education sectors that a central coordinating agency is essential to effective statewide planning, coordination, and review. Such an agency is expected to discharge its obligations in a fashion consistent not only with the needs of the citizens and other individual institutions but, also with those of the education system as a whole. (The principles under which State coordinating agencies are established are described in chapter I.)

The relationship between the two aforementioned principles is based on a third commonly accepted principle—namely, that a proper concern of the statewide coordinating agency is policy and planning, not executive decision. The latter is the appropriate function of the boards of governance at the various institutions and of their administrative officers. Although coordinating boards as a rule have no direct control over institutional governance, the various ways in which this concept is interpreted often lead to difficulty in establishing sound methods for institutional governance and for statewide planning and coordination. The challenge is to obtain through organizational structure and assignment of responsibilities a desired balance between the aims of coordination and local governance.

Evaluation Criteria

If governance arrangements are to be effectively evaluated and if alternatives are to be compared, criteria for these purposes are essential. Six assumptions and related criteria for evaluating governance proposals, developed by Leland Medsker, follow in slightly condensed and modified form.[27]

Assumption 1. Basic to any discussion of control is a consideration of values. Educational institutions, like other organizations, are rationally structured and goal directed. Perhaps the most important set of values is what Phillp Selznick calls "the evolving character of the organization as a whole."[28] If institutional character is to evolve, desirable and realistic goals are essential. Therefore, the question is how organizations are to be governed so as to coordinate their human and material resources and thereby realize these goals. In the evolvement of institutional character, types of colleges as well as individual institutions must establish goals which they constantly seek to achieve.

A criterion: The control pattern must be one which recognizes an institution as an entity with a character that must be achieved through the pursuit of goals. In other words, an institution is a personality which, like a human being, has—or should have—hopes and ambitions to be fulfilled. If they remain unfulfilled, an institution, like a human being, can be expected to become nonproductive.

Assumption 2. Despite the close relationship between financial support and control, there are philosophical and pragmatic reasons why the two elements, for planning purposes, should be considered separately as well as jointly. Admittedly, the importance of adequate financial support and of financial control cannot be underestimated, nor can the ways in which financial control affects the college program be minimized. There would appear to be a danger, however, in assuming that the control pattern must parallel the financial pattern. Mort and Reusser have touched on this point in their book, *Public School Finance:* "The support system must be built up on terms of the problems of taxation, both the economic and the practical, and the control system should be built up in terms of what in the long run promises the best results in the educational enterprise and in the satisfaction of the citizens."[29]

---

[27] Originally devised for evaluating community college governance proposals, these criteria have been modified here for general application. See Coordinating Council for Higher Education (California), *A Consideration of Issues Affecting California Public Junior Colleges*, Sacramento, April 1965, pp. 46–47.

[28] Philip Selznick, *Leadership in Administration*, Row, Peterson, and Co., New York, 1957, p. 38.

[29] Paul R. Mort and Walter C. Reusser, *Public School Finance*, McGraw-Hill Book Co., New York, 1951, p. 41.

A criterion: The legal entity that directs the college need not necessarily procure all or even most of the tax money supporting the college. College planning should be done within the framework of all higher education, and if major State funds are the means of support, the stewardship of these funds, with proper reporting procedures, can be vested in control bodies that may be more effective than the State. Note that this principle does not stipulate that support and control must be vested in separate bodies, only that they *may* be.

Assumption 3. A relationship exists between control effectiveness and the proximity of the controlling agency to the institution it controls. The authors of *Public Administration* distinguish between control-executive or administrative control and democratic control. They state that the democratic principle requires that the exercise of control over policy or action be placed as close to the people as is feasible, all other principles considered.[30]

A criterion: A college control body should be as close as possible to the people the college serves. In other words, there should be local control within a State system. When feasible, the majority of the people served by a college should have the right to participate in the selection of the governing board. This in turn implies that the boundaries of the college should correspond closely to the area from which the college draws most of its students.

Assumption 4. The governing board of any educational institution is charged with a serious and time-consuming responsibility. According to the Middle States Association (in a publication prepared for faculties, trustees, and others interested in improving or establishing 2-year institutions), "Good trustees undertake their office with a sense of responsibility and a readiness to take enough time to study and understand educational problems and practices and to become acquainted with their own institution in more than a superficial way. Lack of time, failure to take enough time for the work is often the reason why a trustee proves inadequate."[31] Although this statement was directed to individual trustees, it applies as well to governing boards.

A criterion: Members of college governing agencies must not assume so many additional responsibilities that the time and energy available to the college are curtailed.

---

[30] M. E. Dimock and G. O. Dimock, *Public Administration*, Rinehart and Co., New York, 1953, p. 86.

[31] Middle States Association of Colleges and Secondary Schools, *Junior Colleges and Community Colleges*, Document No. 4, December 1958, p. 60.

Assumption 5. Those in whom the control of a college is vested must believe in the institution. The Middle States Association again: "Good trustees believe in the institution they control. They are its disinterested and impartial governors and at the same time its loyal interpreters and aggressive supporters."[32] Sometimes it seems logical for one board to have jurisdiction over two or more agencies but if it does, one institution may be deprived of what Selznick calls "institutional integrity." He believes that "The fallacy of combining agencies on the basis of logical association of functions is a characteristic result of the failure to take account of institutional integrity."[33] Such an opinion should serve as a warning.

A criterion: As far as the controlling agency of a college is concerned, no conflict of interest can exist between the college and any other institution for which it is responsible. Its dedication to the unique characteristics of the college must be total.

Assumption 6. Colleges cannot operate in a vacuum. Close coordination must exist between individual institutions and groups of colleges, as well as between all other segments of education. Such coordination need not, however, mean control. For example, in those States where each college is under the jurisdiction of its own board, coordination at the State level should only insure the proper functioning of these institutions in regard to the State's educational needs and resources. In discussing the fine line between coordination and control, Mort and Reusser have stated: "Most legislative action should be structured in nature. It should be concerned with setting up a framework within which the local administrative bodies can operate effectively."[34] Where to draw the fine line or how to establish the framework for coordination and yet preserve local autonomy is a matter which needs further discussion.

A criterion: Any State plan for colleges should be just that: a State plan. Each institution should have its own individuality. If governed by a local board, it should be autonomous, subject only to minimum standards imposed and enforced by the State. Yet each college and group of colleges is not exempt from the responsibility to coordinate with other segments of higher education. An appropriate State agency should be assigned this coordination function and instructed to observe requirements essential to preserve institutional autonomy. The State agency should set policy and assist in the maintenance of it; moreover, its effectiveness should be subject to evaluation.

---

[32] Ibid., p. 61.
[33] Selznick, op. cit., p. 63.
[34] Mort and Reusser, op. cit., p. 46.

Models

In attempting to establish a structural organization that promotes both coordination and governance functions, the many State systems of higher education have developed a wide variety of organizational patterns. Yet two trends are discernible. In most States some form of multilevel pattern exists—one which reduces the number of basic units that a single board must govern or coordinate. The special needs of the various "types" of institutions are frequently recognized by creating semiautonomous subdivisions within the total system. Within such subdivisions separate boards are able to give undivided attention to a particular group of like institutions.

Even though similarity in types of programs and services may have considerable relevance in determining which institutions are to be assigned to the jurisdiction of a common governing or coordinating board, it is not the exclusive determining factor. Equally important, and of greater importance to an integrated university, is the unification of an expanding institution whose various components (campuses) must be interrelated in order to carry out common goals. Institutional typology as a primary means of distinguishing families of institutions for common governance or coordination should not be interpreted as binding member institutions (or campuses) within the system to a particular type of educational program; neither should it define their destinies in advance. Diversity of program within the system should be encouraged and, in the case of universities, must be developed.

For whatever purposes of unification institutions are grouped, a number of different governing-coordinating organizations are possible—differing primarily in the degree of centralized control desired. Three commonly employed are illustrated in figure V-2. They are only suggestions. Each State must approach its governance problems from the point of view of its own philosophical orientation, the strengths and weaknesses of its educational structure, and the directions and goals it intends to pursue.

Type "A"—Single governing board and president, separate campus provosts. This type of organization is usually employed to govern the component campuses of a large, complex, yet integrated multipurpose university at which *unity* of action toward agreed-upon goals or policies is essential. Institutions employing this type of pattern include, among others, the Universities of California, Illinois, Missouri, North Carolina, and Wisconsin. The president or chancellor, who is the chief administrative officer of the university as a whole, is responsible for executing the policies of the governing board, for coordinating the component basic units, and for overall planning of intercampus responsibilities. Day-by-day operations and administration of the separate campuses are usually delegated to provosts. The functions of the governing board, legislative and judicial in nature, include

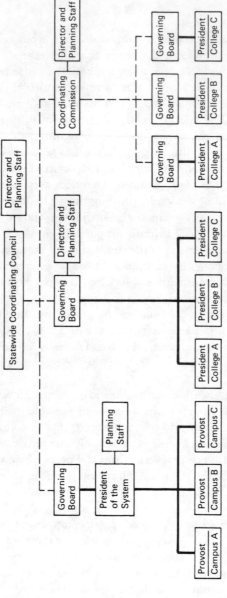

Figure V-2. — Types of governing structures in public higher education

Type "A" – Single governing board and president, separate campus provosts.

　Suitable for a large integrated university with multiple campuses requiring unified control.

Type "B" – Single governing board, separate college presidents.

　Suitable for 4-year colleges that form a system requiring central control for systematic development.

Type "C" – Single coordinating commission, separate college governing boards and presidents.

　Suitable for 4-year or 2-year colleges where interests are best served by local independent governance that provides for intermediate coordination of member institutions.

– – – coordination
——— governance

policy formation, delegation responsibilities, study of long-range problems and tasks, and selection of the chief administrative officer.

As the university grows and becomes increasingly complex, the widening span of control and associated reduction in centralized managerial effectiveness, together with the increasing need for autonomy and self-governance by the separate campuses as they mature and seek their own identity, require that this form of organization be periodically reappraised and that modifications be introduced as required. However, when and if there is wide diversification of the parts, a greater dependence on the system as a whole is needed, and the task becomes one of "integrative regulation." The key to university integrity is a situation in which "... each campus enjoys and benefits from the advantages of specific autonomies, while deriving equally important values from the complex integrated unit."[35]

Type "B"—Single board, separate college presidents. In this type of organization, a number of similar institutions, usually 4-year senior colleges, are placed under a single board for the purpose of central governance. Each college has its own president who is responsible to the central board. In planning college development, each president has considerable influence over policies and decisions reached by the central board. The board exercises general supervision over the colleges and, subject to certain approval action by the statewide coordination board, has broad responsibilities for policy planning and budgetary matters affecting all member institutions. The scope and complexity of the work generally requires strong leadership by a single officer (director), appointed to serve continuously as an agent for governance, coordination, and, most importantly, for planning and development. Such organization, while not commonly employed, may be appropriate when relatively strong central control is desired to develop systematically a cohesive family of mutually supporting institutions.

Type "C"—Single coordinating commission, separate college governing boards and presidents. Suitable for strong independent institutions or colleges requiring local governance, this type of organization is concerned solely with centralized coordination and planning activities. It may be employed by large, mature public 4-year colleges as well as by independent private institutions that seek some alignment with the State system. It meets the special local governance needs of 2-year community colleges and at the same time provides the overall coordination necessary to develop a coherent statewide community college system.

---

[35] For a perceptive and informative commentary on university integrity and related topics, see David D. Henry, "University's Official Response to Board of Higher Education Study on Governance," *Faculty Letter*, no. 207, University of Illinois, Urbana, Nov. , 1970.

Since each college has its own president and governing board, it can develop its own individuality. In the case of the community college, governance is established at the local level where it properly belongs. (The needs of the local community are best served when the college board is completely separate, not combined with the administration of a high school or other educational unit.)

The responsibilities of a coordinating commission are much the same as those of a statewide coordinating council, except that they are limited to a particular group of institutions and in some instances are subject to final approval by the council. The usual responsibilities include the following: establishing general policies and planning and conducting studies; reviewing and offering advice on curriculum proposals; giving recommendations for the establishment of new institutions; performing assigned coordination responsibilities; maintaining an information and accounting system; administering State and Federal student aid and support programs; and reviewing annually budget requests. In areas in which greater central control may be deemed desirable, e.g., approval of tuition and fee changes, determination of boundaries for area education districts, distribution of State and Federal construction aid, and certain budgetary matters, the coordinating commission may be granted authority to establish more directive policies.

In a variation of this organization, the intermediate coordinating commission is eliminated, and each self-governing institution in a group reports directly to the statewide coordinating council. The council itself then becomes the only State agency with a complete and comprehensive picture of the growth and development of a group of institutions as a whole. If large numbers of institutions are involved, it is possible that a massive bureaucratic structure could develop. But in small States with few institutions requiring minimal interaction, this approach should be considered because it encourages institutional independence, creativity, experimentation, and change. Whatever central coordination is required, a single agency can accomplish it. Advocates of this approach suggest that since a layer of organizational structure is removed, each institution is provided easier access to decisionmaking at the State level, and the ability of each college president to direct his institution is thereby strengthened.

ADMISSION, RETENTION, AND TRANSFER POLICIES

State coordinating councils generally are responsibile for developing policies that determine admission and retention standards at institutions comprising a State system of higher education. In view of the differenti-

functions of 2-year colleges, 4-year colleges, and universities, policies for the admission of students cannot be expected to be uniform at all institutions within a single system. Yet diversification does not necessarily warrant unique policies for each individual campus. The pattern emerging in some States is that of distinctive (yet partially overlapping) selection standards for each segment or group of institutions having like functions. Within a segment the standards are fairly uniform. Establishing such an admissions pattern is being recognized more and more as within the realm of State-level policy. Statewide coordination of admission to public colleges and universities is necessary in order to consider deliberately and structure, within a total system context, distribution of student enrollments, allocation of programs among institutions, and guidelines for student transfers.

Controversy over admission and retention policies has generated complex and persistent problems for which no universal answers have appeared. The task of identifying, from among the many who seek further educational development, the few "qualified" to receive it clearly presents philosophical issues of concern to society as well as to individuals. Such issues are not easily resolved, yet a number of ideas are emerging that have fundamentally influenced admission and retention policies.

None has been of greater consequence than the concept of "universality" of college opportunity. Nearly all public 2-year colleges require only a high school diploma for admission, and there are signs that even this single criterion will be eliminated. The trend is to admit 18-year-old applicants capable of benefiting from the instruction offered. In States that have an adequate number of 2-year institutions the open door policy has for all practical purposes eliminated entrance selectivity for resident high school graduates willing to begin their college education at a community or junior college.

Even as entrance standards have been extended to provide equal educational opportunity, the need for selectivity has been reduced by the diversity of 2-year college offerings: vocational-technical, continuing, and general or liberal arts. This wide range of career alternatives can accommodate an equally wide range of student interests and abilities. Improved "pervasive counseling," which encourages less able students to choose non-degree programs within their capabilities, has also made it possible for 2-year colleges to maintain relatively unrestricted admission standards without a corresponding increase in the number of student dropouts.

As a result of extending educational opportunity at the 2-year college level, the problem of selectivity has been shifted to 4-year institutions. They in turn have begun to stiffen their entrance requirements, knowing that such action does not close the college door to capable but less qualified freshmen. The continued use of less-than-perfect methods of predicting college achievement now results in less waste of unrecognized talent and fewer injustices to students capable of continuing their education but denied access to selective 4-year institutions. Those denied admission can always start at a 2-year college. This alternative has greatly reduced the unrealistic yet understandable pressure under which selective institutions have operated in an attempt to prejudge accurately and fairly the performance of all applicants—an impossible task.

Still another concept influencing admission and retention policies is the argument against *prior* judgment of who can and who cannot profit from further education. It is expressed by those who recognize only *current* academic failure as a conclusive measure of inability and/or lack of interest. In practice, 2-year colleges admit students through an open-door policy (little or no attention is paid to high school credentials) and allow them to continue until low grades or failure clearly demonstrate they do not deserve to be retained. While admittedly there is some waste of time and effort when an individual fails college work, as well as some related loss to the institution and to the taxpayer, such an experience is not totally without benefit to the student. He gains more realistic career goals. Moreover, the fact that many academic "risk" and marginal students do earn baccalaureate degrees demonstrates that there is as yet no magic "cut-off" point above which all students will succeed and below which all will fail. For the public sector responsible for providing equal educational opportunity to all State citizens, this is a convincing argument in selecting and retaining students for placing greater emphasis on college performance than on admission qualifications. It is an especially important mandate for 2-year colleges.

Selectivity (Reasons for and Interpretation of)

The right of public higher education to select and sort its students has been repeatedly recognized. In 1962 T. R. McConnell stated that "a democratic system of higher education need not accord all students the privilege of attending the same kinds of institutions, any more than it need permit all to pursue the same curricula."[36]   More recently the Carnegie Commission reiterated this principle, declaring that each State should provide universal access to its *total* system, but not necessarily to each of its institutions.[37]

Public policies regarding admission and retention of college students must be in accord with the philosophic, economic, and social setting of the individual State. The many dissimilarities in such areas as number and type of educational institutions within the State, amount of financial support, number and quality of high school graduates, and history and tradition of col

---

[36] T. R. McConnell, *A General Pattern for American Public Higher Education*, McGraw-Hill Book Co., New York, 1962, p. 83.
[37] Carnegie Commission on Higher Education, *A Chance To Learn: An Action Agenda for Equal Opportunity in Higher Education*, Berkeley, Calif., Mar. 2, 1970.

lege attendance require that admission and retention policies conform to local circumstances and needs. Certain policies which are good for one State may or may not be good for another State. On the other hand, admission and retention policies should be attuned to the times insofar as current trends are consistent with State objectives. They should also be based on sound principles that reflect desired outcomes.

While innumerable lists of pros and cons for selective admission and retention have been proposed, the following should not be overlooked:

1. Selectivity is necessary to achieve desired student ability levels. The goals and purposes of an institution are best served by selection and retention of those students whose interests and abilities make for a constructive association. While this principle applies to all disciplines and academic layers—lower division, upper division, and graduate—there is considerable difference in emphasis. A wide range of student aptitudes is required for successful completion of the various academic programs and curriculums of colleges and universities, and as higher academic levels are reached, greater ability is required. Therefore, to achieve desired aptitude and ability grouping in higher education, selectivity must be both *differential*—accounting for differences in curriculum requirements—and *progressive*—increasingly more discriminating at higher academic levels. The consequences of applying both differential and progressive selectivity policies to three segments of public higher education that differ both in curriculum and in level of emphasis are evident.

The trend in restrictive admission policies thus far adopted can be described as follows: (1) "open admissions," used by most community or junior colleges, whereby all State residents who meet simple minimum requirements, usually the acquisition of a high school diploma, are admitted; (2) "selective admissions," used by 4-year senior colleges, whereby those students with abilities and interests judged not compatible with successful pursuit of a baccalaureate program are eliminated; and (3) "competitive admissions," used by universities, whereby the best qualified students are selected from among a large number of applicants.

Public 2-year colleges are generally required by law to accept all resident high school graduates. These institutions are not required, however, to readmit students who the institution believes—usually because they have a record of failing marks—lack either the ability or interest to continue. For students electing to transfer to 4-year institutions with advanced standing, the junior college experience serves as a proving ground and screens out candidates for upper division work. Junior and community colleges also serve an exploratory or guidance function in that they provide students in search of programs consistent with their interests and abilities the opportunity to transfer from one curriculum to another. After a trial period in a 2-year college, many students may properly be advised to withdraw. For all of the aforementioned reasons. the rate of student turnover[38] in 2-year colleges can be expected to be high. A high turnover per se does not necessarily indicate that the institution has not fulfilled its purpose.

Both the university and 4-year college, particulary those emphasizing upper division work, generally attempt to be much more exacting in selecting students than the 2-year college. Effort is directed toward restricting entrance to those whose high school performance[39] is usually well above average and who give indication of successful college performance[40] in their chosen field. The function of the public 4-year college is not to educate an intellectual elite but to prepare graduates for leadership and service in a wide variety of vocations for which 4 or 5 years of college study are desirable. The purpose of admission standards in the 4-year college, then, is to restrict selection of students capable of completing a curriculum that leads to these goals.

Because of the diversity of curriculums and related student aptitude requirements among public 4-year colleges, even within the same State, uniform standards of admission are not recommended. Differences in admission and retention policies among colleges should be permitted if it can be demonstrated that such differences are required by the program and type of student. Furthermore, it is probable that a particular college, while holding to a recommended minimum standard for admission to most curriculums, may be justified in setting higher standards for certain others.

The university's traditional emphasis on high scholarship leading to professional and graduate level education requires that top students be attracted. Accordingly, most admission policies are designed to appeal to the most promising high school graduates. While there are some alternative means by which students may gain admission to State universities, most institutions require high school grades of A and B in certain "subject patterns."[41] For those deficient in scholarship, the university may grant admis-

---

[38] The dropout rate among students who left during their freshman year for voluntary reasons was 16 percent at 2-year colleges, 8.9 percent at 4-year colleges, and 8.3 percent at universities (1966–67). At the three types of institutions, the dropout rate due to unsatisfactory academic work or for disciplinary reasons was similar: 4.1 percent, 3.9 percent, and 3.6 percent, respectively. Bayer and others, *The First Year of College: A Follow-up Normative Report*, op. cit.

[39] Approximately 52 percent of the freshmen entering 4-year colleges and 65 percent of the freshmen entering universities in the fall of 1972 had been in the top quarter of their high school class, whereas only 21 percent of those who enrolled in 2-year college had ranked as high (see table V-3).

[40] The 1st-year retention rate for entering freshmen in 1966–67 was 81 percent at 2 year colleges, 87.2 percent at 4-year colleges, and 88.1 percent at universities. Baye and others, *The First Year of College: A Follow-up Normative Report*, op. cit.

[41] In the fall of 1972 the percentage of freshmen entering college with high school grade averages of C+ or lower was 38.0 percent at 2-year colleges, 17.2 percent at 4 year colleges, and 10.5 percent at universities. American Council on Education, Offic of Research, *The American Freshman: National Norms for Fall 1972*, Washington, D.C. 1972, p. 36.

sion by examination. In some cases, students are accepted if they rank in a high percentile of their graduating class.

2. *Selectivity is necessary if resources limit the capacity of institutions to serve all educational needs.* Although great strides have been made toward providing higher educational opportunities for all youths, particularly at the lower division level, resources remain limited. Especially for such costly programs as graduate and professional studies, limited finances will continue to necessitate highly selective admission and retention practices

3. *Selectivity is necessary to help place students in the right programs and to redirect the efforts of misplaced and unqualified students into more constructive channels.* Selectivity as practiced in a program of "persuasive counseling" is desirable to encourage students to pursue careers consistent with their abilities and interests. While a few high school graduates may not be capable of college work, the vast majority, if properly placed, will benefit from some form of postsecondary education. Once admitted, however, only those who maintain a reasonably satisfactory standard of accomplishment should be allowed to continue.

Selective and competitive admissions based on a combination measurements provide a much more accurate basis for predicting college performance than does reliance on any single factor. Factors most frequently used by colleges and universities to select students for admission include the following:

a. *Academic performance in high school.* There is sufficient consistency in human behavior to expect that academic performance in high school will bear a reasonable relationship to academic performance at the college level. In general, this proposition has been confirmed by numerous studies that have revealed that high school performance is the single best predictor of college performance. All other measurement factors add only small weight to the accuracy of the prediction derived from this measurement.[42] Of course the validity of predicting probable college success on the basis of high school grades, or in the case of a transfer student, on those earned at another college, will not hold up if a disproportionate number of high or low grades have been awarded. The lack of uniformity in marking systems with-

---

[42] Literally thousands of studies have been conducted, based on different combinations of various cognitive measures, to predict academic success at the college level. Data reported for the Yale class of 1966 illustrate the predicative value of various measures and indexes. Scholastic Aptitude Test (SAT) scores alone had a predictive validity coefficient of .30 with freshman grade average; when combined with SAT-Mathematical and Achievement Test scores, the coefficient increased to .38. The secondary school record alone had a predictive validity coefficient of .46; in combination with a predictive index and Scholastic Aptitude Test (SAT) scores, the coefficient increased to .52. This study and others are reviewed by Paul S. Burnham, "Prediction and Performance," in *From High School to College—Readings for Counselors*, College Entrance Examination Board, New York, 1965, pp. 65–71.

in secondary schools can be partially overcome by judging students on the basis of their relative standing in their respective graduating classes.

b. *Scores on standardized aptitude and/or achievement tests.* Test scores are not a substitute for grades in predicting a student's ability to do successful college work, but they are factors that should be combined with grades in selecting students for retention, particularly at the higher academic levels.

c. *Subjective factors.* Subjective judgment of such performance indicators as recommendations of high school officials, student interviews, and participation in high school extracurricular activities is difficult, time-consuming, and far from conclusive. However, colleges that seek students who can benefit most from their program may find that students who have earned high grades in high school are sometimes too well prepared to benefit greatly from certain lower level college training. Students want to be challenged, even to risk failure; colleges, on the other hand, by seeking only the most able students, appear to want only success, to fear failure. By assigning proportionately more weight to an applicant's maturity, motivation, and other subjective factors, and by correspondingly decreasing the emphasis on academic performance, colleges may enhance their knowledge of who can benefit most from what they have to offer.

Establishing and Validating Standards

Institutions generally establish their admission, retention, and transfer standards by a process of trial and error. No recommendations can be made as to what grade average, percentile rank, or examination score requirements will produce a desired student enrollment. These values must be discovered by experience and continually revised to meet changing conditions. Norms that are too high result in too few students and in an overall average ability level that exceeds academic requirements. Norms set too low result in an excess of students, many of whom cannot meet academic requirements.

Admission standards are valid if they restrict admission to those applicants whose educational needs can be properly met by the college and whose abilities indicate probable scholastic success. Indicators of valid admission and retention standards include (1) low dropout rates among freshmen during the first semester or year, (2) high retention and graduation rates, (3) low rates of dismissal for poor scholarship, and (4) follow-up studies of rejected applicants which reveal that the rejection appears to have been fair and justified.

When capacity is limited, admission standards must also perform an allocation function—namely, diverting applicants from one institution to another and from one segment to another to avoid overcrowding and to balance enrollments. Among the better criteria for choosing, among qualified applicants, those to be admitted to a particular institution (when all cannot be accommodated) are the following:

1. The best (qualified) students should be granted their first choice.

2. Continuing students or those being readmitted should be given preference over new students.

3. Applicants who live within commuting range could be given preference over those who will require dormitory accommodations.

4. The more advanced student could be favored over the less advanced.[43] To this list may be added a fifth criterion:

5. Preference could be given to students who seek admittance to special programs in which vacancies exist; whose admission would contribute to student balance or desired mix; or who wish to prepare for occupations in which there is a scarcity of employees.

A Selectivity Measure

The number of able students who want to enroll at a college divided by the number of freshmen admitted is a good single indicator of how "selective" an institution can be. The relative standings in an array of such indexes provide perspective and some insight into the relative selectivity potential open to a given college. Such an array of data for public universities is presented in table V-7. (A similar table for public 4-year senior colleges can easily be constructed from source date.[44])

Specifically, the index reports the number of male and female National Merit Scholarship Qualifying Test (NMSQT) participants with scores above 113 (the top 31 percent) indicating the college as their first choice, divided by the number of first-time freshman students enrolled in fall 1964. This ratio has been variously referred to as an index of "popularity" or measure of "estimated selectivity."[45] While the index is a fairly precise measure of the average ability level of the entering class, it is not an exact measure for two reasons. First, the student may not apply for admission to the college he indicates as his first choice. Second, the institution may select its students on some basis other than academic ability. The index, therefore, most nearly measures the likely *potential* or probable opportunity that an institution has to select its students from many applicants of high academic ability.

---

[43] From Arthur G. Coons, chairman, The Master Plan Survey Team, *A Master Plan for Higher Education in California, 1960–75*, California State Department of Education, Sacramento, 1960, p. 80.

[44] Robert C. Nichols, *College Preferences of Eleventh Grade Students*, Research Reports, vol. 2, no. 9, National Merit Scholarship Corporation, Evanston, Ill., 1966.

[45] Ibid., p. 4, and Astin, *Who Goes Where to College?* op. cit., p. 55.

Table V-7.—Public university rankings in selectivity potential, based on popularity with high-ability students relative to size: 1965

Rank	University	Index[1]	Rank	University	Index[1]
1.	University of Michigan	101	45.	University of Connecticut	22
2.	University of Calif. (Berkeley)	74	46.	University of Wyoming	22
3.	University of Calif. (L.A.)	59	47.	Mississippi State University	21
4.	University of Texas	58	48.	University of Delaware	21
5.	Iowa St. Univ. of Sci. & Tech.	49	49.	University of Idaho	21
6.	University of Iowa	48	50.	Oklahoma St. Univ. Agr. & Sci.	20
7.	Univ. of Calif. (Santa Barbara)	46	51.	Texas Technological College	20
8.	University of Wisconsin	45	52.	University of Georgia	20
9.	Univ. of N.C. (Chapel Hill)	42	53.	University of North Dakota	20
10.	SUNY at Albany	41	54.	Bowling Green State Univ. (Ohio)	19
11.	University of Kansas	41	55.	University of Maryland	19
12.	University of Massachusetts	41	56.	Colorado State College	18
13.	University of Calif. (Davis)	40	57.	Indiana University	18
14.	University of Calif. (Riverside)	38	58.	Northern Illinois University	18
15.	University of Florida	38	59.	University of Arizona	18
16.	Penn State University	37	60.	University of Louisville	18
17.	SUNY at Buffalo	35	61.	University of Missouri	17
18.	University of N.C. (Raleigh)	35	62.	University of New Mexico	17
19.	University of Maine	33	63.	University of Utah	17
20.	Washington State University	33	64.	North Dakota State University	16
21.	University of Nebraska	32	65.	University of Cincinnati	16
22.	Univ. of Vermont & St. Agr. Col.	32	66.	University of South Dakota	16
23.	Auburn University (Alabama)	31	67.	University of Kentucky	16
24.	University of Colorado	31	68.	Clemson University (S.C.)	15
25.	Miami University	30	69.	Rutgers, The State University (N.J.)	15
26.	Purdue University	30	70.	University of Toledo	15

27.	University of Illinois	30
28.	University of New Hampshire	30
29.	University of Oregon	30
30.	Virginia Polytechnic Institute	30
31.	Florida State University	29
32.	University of Minnesota	28
33.	University of Mississippi	26
34.	University of Hawaii	25
35.	Montana State University	24
36.	Ohio State University	24
37.	Texas A & M University	24
38.	West Virginia University	24
39.	Michigan State University	23
40.	University of Alabama	23
41.	University of Arkansas	23
42.	University of Oklahoma	23
43.	CUNY City College	22
44.	Kansas State Univ. Agr. & App. Sci.	22
71.	University of Virginia	15
72.	Louisiana St. University & A & M	14
73.	South Dakota State University	13
74.	University of South Carolina	13
75.	University of Tennessee	13
76.	Wichita State University (Kans.)	13
77.	Arizona State University	12
78.	Ohio University	12
79.	Southern Illinois University	12
80.	Kent State University (Ohio)	11
81.	Northern Texas State University	9
82.	University of Alaska	9
83.	University of Rhode Island	9
84.	New Mexico State University	8
85.	University of Nevada	7
86.	Utah State University	6
87.	Florida A & M University	1

[1] The index of selectivity potential is the number of high-ability students (National Merit Scholarship Qualifying Test Scores greater than 113) of both sexes indicating a preference for the college as a percentage of the number of freshman admitted the previous year.

Source: Robert C. Nichols, *College Preferences of Eleventh Grade Students,* Research Reports, vol. 2, no. 9, National Merit Scholarship Corporation, Evanston, Ill., 1966.

ARTICULATION BETWEEN
2-YEAR AND 4-YEAR COLLEGES

It is estimated that each year as many as 150,000 to 200,000 of the million students enrolled in institutions of higher education face the prob lem of transferring from 2-year to 4-year colleges.[46] As community college continue to develop their potential, the number of transfer students wi increase and thereby place an even greater burden on articulation mach nery. The problem of numbers will be further complicated by the increase diversity in programs offered by 4-year colleges. To cope with the situ ation it will be necessary for State higher education systems to develo appropriate policies and guidelines covering transfer students. Uniformit of programs should not be expected nor is it desirable. Yet the difference that exist in such areas as the structure and content of general educatio programs, course prerequisites, and methods of instruction and gradin create common transfer problems, the solution to which can be sought onl in a context of interdependence and shared responsibility.

To meet new developments and to improve a not-too-satisfactory recor in performing the transfer function, State planning agencies need to re examine those policies, practices, and programs of their member institu tions which might affect the mobility of 2-year college students and thei performance after they leave the 2-year college. Of invaluable help in thi connection are the important findings of Knoell and Medsker based on large-scale national investigation of students who transferred from 2-yea to 4-year colleges and universities. Their second study, *Articulation Betwee Two-Year and Four-Year Colleges*,[47] published in 1964, contains many data o significance both to institutions and State coordinating agencies, as we as valuable suggestions for improving the admission, orientation, and coun seling of students from 2-year colleges. What follows is an abstract of th more important findings and conclusions as reported by the authors. Th complete text is, of course, recommended to every education planner.[48]

---

[46] While the average ability-level of 2-year college freshmen is less than that of the counterparts in 4-year institutions (21 percent of 2-year college freshmen rank in the to quarter of their high school class compared to 52 percent for freshmen enrolled in 4-yea colleges), one out of five 2-year college students plan to earn a bachelor's or higher de gree. See American Council on Education, *The American Freshman: National Norms fo Fall 1972*, Washington, D. C., 1972, pp. 36, 37.

[47] Dorothy M. Knoell and Leland L. Medsker, *Articulation Between Two-Year and Fou Year Colleges*, Center for the Study of Higher Education, University of California, Berke ley, 1964. A summary of the results, *From Junior to Senior College: A National Study of th Transfer Student*, has been published by the American Council on Education. (See bibliog raphy.)

[48] Also recommended: Joint Committee on Junior and Senior Colleges of the America Association of Junior Colleges, American Association of Collegiate Registrars and Ac

The primary study group consisted of 7,243 junior college students in 10 selected States who transferred in the fall of 1960. Three calendar years following their transfer, 62 percent had obtained their baccalaureate degrees from institutions to which they were admitted. An additional 9 percent, still enrolled, were expected to graduate during the 4th year after transfer; thus, the probable graduation rate was about 71 percent. An indeterminate number of the dropouts transferred to other colleges. When augmented by the number of these dropouts who succeeded elsewhere, the ultimate rate of graduation for the 1960 transfer group was estimated, perhaps conservatively, at between 75 and 80 percent. At the other extreme, the number of students whose grades were so poor following transfer that they could not continue their education was very small.

Variation in Performance

A major objective of the Knoell and Medsker study was to determine those individual and institutional factors which might account for the observation that students in some 4-year colleges were much more successful than students in other colleges. A principal finding was that all or most junior college students could successfully earn a degree following transfer *if* they would select 4-year institutions and major fields appropriate to their ability and prior achievement. The proper matching of transfer students and institutions at the upper division level was deemed just as important, if not more important, as the matching of high school graduates, and institutions at the freshman level.

No single meaningful conclusion can be drawn about the quality of transfer student performance because of the vast differences among the 4-year institutions that participated in the study. Transfer students from the same junior college, with very similar grades often in the same major field, achieved quite different degrees of success in different 4-year institutions. Such was the case not only in terms of their progress toward earning a degree but in terms of their upper division grades.

Despite the effects of diversity, certain persistent factors affecting the differential performance of transfer students were observed that suggest ways in which both institutions and statewide coordinating agencies can improve articulation.

—In some States, 2-year college transfer students had a much better chance of success than they did in others. The success factor appeared to be related to the following differences: higher standards for admission to

missions Officers, and the Association of American Colleges, *Guidelines for Improving Articulation Between Junior and Senior Colleges*, American Council on Education, Washington, D. C., 1966.

2-year colleges and for transfer to 4-year institutions, greater diversification of curricular offerings among various types of 4-year colleges, and better articulation and guidance programs.

—When selective admission standards at the freshman level were not extended to students being admitted with advanced standing, the competition problem was intensified by virtue of the fact that transfer students had to compete for grades with nontransfer students whose ability had been more carefully screened.

—The success of students who transferred after 2 years in junior college was remarkably greater than that of students who transferred after only 1 year (or less than 2). The two probable reasons are (1) junior colleges may actually do a better job of preparing transfer students in 2 years than in 1, and (2) less able students may be discouraged from transferring during the sophomore year. The increased maturity of students as a result of 2 years of junior college is also a likely factor in their better performance since the the personal adjustment they must make at the 4-year institutions is often a difficult one.

—In terms of persistence in completing degree programs, the record of part-time students in 4-year colleges was not as good as that of full-time students. Many students who combined full-time employment with part-time study withdrew from the college whenever the pressure of time or other matters became great.

—Transfer students had about the same probability of eventual success in the various academic majors. This finding suggests that 2-year colleges can offer lower division programs that prepare students satisfactorily for transfer in most major fields—if the 2-year institutions establish good articulation with 4-year colleges.

Difficulties Experienced by Transfer Students

The Knoell-Medsker study revealed that about one-third of the graduates who transferred as full-time students with junior standing needed more than 2 years to complete their programs in the 4-year colleges. The primary reason that they required more time was not poor grades: only 19 percent had grade-point averages that would have prevented them from graduating, even if they had satisfied all other requirements. The findings suggest that in most major fields the large majority of transfer students who did not graduate in 4 years simply lacked the required credits. Subsequent to transferring, they did not, in the ensuing 2 years, attempt to meet credit and course requirements for graduation. Among the factors responsible were: temporary withdrawal; decision to change major field; selection of a rather specialized major for which the 2-year college had not offered adequate lower division preparation; and other specific curriculum problems arising from lack of articulation between the programs of the 2- and 4-year colleges. The time factor probably could be reduced if junior and community colleges would study the detailed performance of their transfer students to determine which course and articulation problems could be rectified.

As previously noted, a sizable reduction in attrition could be effected if a method were devised whereby each transfer student was placed in an institution at which he would have a better-than-even chance of success. In reviewing the Knoell and Medsker study, T. R. McConnell commented on the overall problem as follows:

> The transfer student's academic record in the four-year college or university is the outcome of subtle accommodation between his attributes and the characteristics of the institution he enters or the particular part of the institution in which he studies. That is to say, the student's success will depend on going to one institution rather than another, or choosing the "right" major among various possibilities. The probability of academic success, therefore, is in part a function of the range of alternatives open to a junior college graduate when he chooses a four-year institution. Some states offer, through their public and private colleges and universities, a much wider range of opportunities than others. For example, in certain states a student may be able to choose among institutions whose student bodies differ greatly in average scholastic aptitude. He may have open to him, too, a much wider range of specializations than he would have in other states or regions. He may, in fact, reside in a state which will have some institution in which each junior college graduate conceivably could find a program in which he could succeed . . . Whether the junior college transfer succeeds or not will depend on a fortunate conjunction of the student's abilities, aptitudes, aspirations and intellectual dispositions with the characteristics of the institution he attends.[49]

In a more recent paper,[50] McConnell suggests that although the problem the transfer student faces in choosing an appropriate institution and program is a formidable one, certain tools are now available to provide assistance. One that he mentions is the Omnibus Personality Inventory.[51] It was designed to reveal students' intellectual dispositions (such as interest in ideas), whether for their intrinsic value or pragmatic use, their degree of personal autonomy and intellectual independence, their relative constraint or freedom of impulse and expression, or their general emotional stability. Also available are the Pace College and University Environment Scales[52]

---

49 Dorthy M. Knoell and Leland L. Medsker, *Factors Affecting Performance of Transfer Students from Two- to Four-Year Colleges*, Center for the Study of Higher Education, University of California, Berkeley, 1964, p. iv.

50 T. R. McConnell, "The Context of the Articulation Problem," paper given at State University of New York, Buffalo, Mar. 23, 1970.

51 Paul Heist and G. Yonge, *Omnibus Personality Inventory Manual*, The Psychological Corporation, New York, 1968.

52 C. Robert Pace, *Analyses of a National Sample of College Environments*, University of California, Los Angeles, 1967.

that identify institutional stress in such areas as practicality, community awareness, propriety, and scholarship. Pace has also devised methods of describing subcultures and of characterizing such institutional features as administrative, curricular, instructional, and extracurricular structures and activities. These instruments provide the student and his counselor with a profile of educationally relevant characteristics for mutual assistance in the process of determining the best available educational option.

Another area in which transfer students experience difficulty is in securing financial aid. To rectify this situation, a critical examination of the current philosophy of financial aid and the nature of existing programs as they affect transfer students is needed. Most students who begin their degree programs in 2-year colleges are not regarded as scholarship contenders. On the other hand, they are encouraged to embark upon a two-plus-two program with at least a tacit assumption that, if they do satisfactory work, some form of aid will be available to them at the time of transfer. The cost of attending a 4-year college is considerably higher than the cost of attending a junior or community college, yet many students must transfer with little or no family backing, very limited savings, and no monetary resources to finance their education beyond the first semester or 1st year at a 4-year college. Those 2-year college students who take jobs in order to earn money to pay expenses after transfer often neglect their studies. All of these financial problems identify what is probably the most ignored individual in the student aid picture—the transfer student. In the interests of both society and the individual, attention should be given by States to reserving funds for deserving transfer students at the junior level, as well as for entering freshmen.

Knoell and Medsker found that students with unsatisfactory grades encountered a number of specific problems. Most of those experiencing academic difficulty who took an English proficiency examination at the junior level did not pass it—at least not the first time. While failure to pass resulted in no dismissals and only occasionally in a delay in completing graduation requirements, it appeared to be symptomatic of other academic problems. Students who had not completed general education requirements before transfer were also more prone to failure. At some 4-year colleges the rate was higher in prescribed general education courses than in first-level elective courses. It was in the humanities and natural science, however, that the largest number of students experienced difficulty. Since 2-year students could have completed nearly all general education requirements before transferring, it appeared that either negligence or poor counseling prevented them from doing so. The implication of these findings is that transfer students should remain in a junior or community college until they have completed all general education courses, proficiency requirements, and sequence courses.

Both the delayed graduation and failure of transfer students could be reduced by improved counseling at all levels—high school, 2-year college, and 4-year college. Counselors must become aware of the interdependence of the various levels and segments of education and of the need for long-range planning by students. Both counselors and teachers tend to be familiar with the colleges in which they received their own training, yet uninformed about the many other institutions to which their students apply for admission. This is particularly true at the newer community colleges.

The transfer students' need for both counseling and academic advice is often acute during the 1st year following transfer—the time when many are still unsure of themselves or uncertain about their decisions and choices. Four-year institutions may find it advantageous to employ advisers who have a philosophical commitment to the 2-year college and are willing to become well acquainted with all aspects of the junior and entire community college network.

Many 4-year institutions overlook transfer students when planning orientation programs, offering counseling services, extending invitations to participate in social and extracurricular activities, and above all, when arranging for guidance during initial registration. The entering freshman continues to be the preferred client of 4-year institutions, particularly in their student-service programs; the transfer student is usually forced to adjust to his new situation as best he can.

In addition to improvements needed in the area of counseling, it seems desirable that cautious but deliberate attempts should be made to intensify the instruction of university-bound students during their 2d year in junior or community college. Since the number who transfer to universities is usually quite large, it should be possible to introduce them to some special work during their 2d year, including perhaps additional library and written assignments, various types of testing, seminars, etc. Such innovations would make it possible for the 2-year college to narrow the gap between the high school and the university and provide substantial benefits to students who intend to transfer.

Test Results and Grades

There is so much overlap in academic ability among those transfer students who graduate and those who drop out that aptitude test scores do not distinguish very effectively between those who succeed and those who fail. If 2-year college grades are applied scientifically to screen, counsel, and/or select transfer students, there should be little need to introduce test results as further evidence of student capacity to do satisfactory work in the upper division. In other words, if a student's junior or community college grades are good and his occupational goals reasonable, test results probably should not be a criterion to deny admission to transfer students.

A large number of high school graduates with considerably less ability than the average university freshman are succeeding in 2-year colleges and graduating from 4-year institutions with baccalaureate degrees in many different fields. On the other hand, some students with more than average ability do poor work in high school, earn barely satisfactory grades in junior college, and are poor candidates for upper division standing—at least in the major universities. Thus many 4-year institutions must be capable of accommodating transfer students with a wide range of ability and motivation.

The average ability level of graduates who begin their highest education at major universities is above that of their counterparts who begin baccalaureate degree programs at 2-year colleges. There is, however, considerable overlap. This difference in average ability, reflected in university grades, is compounded by the often difficult academic and personal adjustment that transfer students must make when they enter the university as upperclassmen. When groups of students of comparable ability compete for grades in the upper division, the chances are good that transfer students will earn grades as high as those of nontransfer students. Following transfer, few junior college students with high ability and good grades are handicapped in competing with nontransfer students for admission to graduate school.

What is needed is a sound rationale for setting grading standards in 2-year colleges and the establishment of a proper relationship to standards in 4-year colleges. Different grading practices now in use are in many instances unfair to students, particularly to those who transfer. Within a given State a particular junior or community college will probably have a near-zero grade-point differential with some institutions and a fairly sizable one with others. Before a 2-year college evaluates and/or changes its grading standards, it is recommended that it annually examine its grade-point differentials with *each* 4-year college to which a sizable number of its students transfer. Because of the status factor involved in grading, a 2-year college may be tempted to try to reduce the differential with the major State university to near zero while ignoring differentials with the other 4-year colleges. It should be noted that any arbitrary lowering of grades in an attempt to close the gap with the major universities may unfairly handicap students seeking to transfer to other 4-year colleges.

BIBLIOGRAPHY

Altman, Robert A., *The Upper Division College*, Jossey-Bass, San Francisco, 1970, 202 pp.
    This book is an excellent history of the development of U. S. upper division colleges that admit only students who have completed a minimum of 2 years of collegiate study

Although the number of these colleges is small (perhaps no more than 15), the concept of modifying the traditional 4-year baccalaureate degree structure to more sharply distinguish between general or preparatory education and professional or research-oriented junior- and senior-year work is extremely significant. The contention that the true university does not exist until it ceases to offer the preparatory or nonuniversity courses that constitute the bulk of freshman and sophomore offerings has seldom been implemented in this country. Although some institutions have chosen to concentrate on the 3d, 4th, and postgraduate years, few have eliminated freshman and sophomore courses. On the other hand, the emergence of 2-year colleges is a direct outgrowth of the theory that the baccalaureate degree program should be divided into lower and upper levels.

The author describes some of the operational difficulties that upper division institutions have encountered. Low enrollment explains in part the reluctance of many to eliminate the first 2 years. Yet, to meet mounting enrollments, establishing upper division institutions may serve as a viable alternative either to the conversion of existing 2-year colleges to 4-year colleges or to the creation of new 4-year institutions.

American Council on Education, *ACE Research Reports*, Washington, D. C.

Research Reports, published on a continuing basis by the ACE Office of Research, provide statistical descriptions of the differential functions and characteristics of 2-year colleges, 4-year colleges, and universities. A major project of the council is a large-scale program of longitudinal research on student development in higher education. The major objectives of this program are ". . . to assess the impact that different college environments have on the student's development and to provide a source of current, readily available descriptive information about the population of college students." In addition to student data, comprehensive information concerning college environments, staff, and administrative policies is furnished. For example, a recent and most informative report is *College and University Faculty: A Statistical Description* by Alan E. Bayer. All reports have acquired a reputation for detail, systematic organization of data, timeliness, and—most important—content value.

Astin, Alexander W., and Calvin B. T. Lee, *The Invisible Colleges: A Profile of Small Private Colleges with Limited Resources*, Carnegie Commission on Higher Education, McGraw-Hill Book Co., New York, 1972, 146 pp.

Invisible colleges, according to the authors, are those with a small, nonselective enrollment. Privately administered, they total nearly 500. This study examines their history and administrative characteristics, as well as the makeup of the student body, the campus environment, and the impact of environment on enrollees. Comparisons are made with their polar opposite, the elite private colleges, and with their chief competition, the 4-year public colleges. In addition, three key questions are answered: (1) What is the specific plight of the invisible colleges? (2) In what ways, if any, do they justify their existence? and (3) What can be done to strengthen them? To keep invisible colleges solvent, the authors recommend that outside aid be furnished. They also suggest that each State make a thorough inventory of its educational needs to determine whether or not invisible colleges may help fill one or more of those needs and that colleges with fewer than 1,000 students increase their enrollment by "several hundred."

Astin, Alexander W., *Who Goes Where to College?*, Science Research Associates, Chicago, 1965, 125 pp.

This report is based on a study of the freshman classes that entered 248 colleges and universities in the fall of 1961. From the data provided by the 127,212 students who answered a brief questionnaire, plus certain other information available about them, 52 measures of student characteristics were obtained. By statistical procedures, these 52 measures were reduced to a set of six "freshman input factors"—intellectualism, aestheticism, status, leadership, pragmatism, and masculinity. It was found that reasonably accurate estimates of five of these six characteristics could be obtained from data known about all institutions. (Only the leadership factor could not be estimated with satisfactory accuracy.) Thus it was possible to compute estimates of the five freshman input factors for 1,015 U.S. 4-year colleges and universities. These estimated freshman input scores are listed for each institution, together with scores on the eight scales of the Environmental Assessment Techniques: selectivity, size, and six personal orientations based on the number of baccalaureate degrees awarded in various fields of study.

Blocker, Clyde E., Robert H. Plummer, and Richard C. Richardson, Jr., *The Two-Year College: A Social Synthesis*, Prentice-Hall, Englewood Cliffs, N.J., 1965, 298 pp.

The writers of this volume address themselves to two major points: (1) the relationship between the 2-year college as an institution and the society that it was created to serve, and (2) the controversial issues of various aspects of 2-year colleges. The authors begin with an analysis of the primary groups that mold and shape the 2-year college as an institution—the general social milieu, the informal and legally organized groups outside the college, the students, and the faculty. From this base the study considers the three major adaptive responses of the college as an organization: administration, curriculum and instruction, and student-personnel services. In conclusion, the authors summarize their observations within three general categories: (1) educational roles, (2) organization and control (internal and external), and (3) financial support.

Brick, Michael, and Earl J. McGrath, *Innovation in Liberal Arts Colleges*, Teachers College Press, Columbia University, New York, 1969, 173 pp.

This study ascertains some of the trends and thrusts of innovative practices on U. S. liberal arts college campuses. The authors describe novel and creative practices in curriculum design, instructional methods, student involvement, and college structure and organization. A few of the most innovative institutions are described fully. A questionnaire sent to 1,209 liberal arts colleges was used to collect data on innovative practices.

Brooking, Walter J., *Criteria for Technician Education: A Suggested Guide*, U. S. Department of Health, Education, and Welfare, Office of Education, U. S. Government Printing Office, Washington, D. C., 1968, 84 pp.

Based on the accumulated experience of successful programs and the consensus of more than 100 administrators and experts in the field, this publication presents guidelines for establishing quality programs for technicians at the postsecondary level. Beginning with a description of who technicians are and what they do, the guide describes special problems in defining, initiating, and operating programs; the essential physical facilities; the library; the faculty; student selection and services; and the curriculum.

Brown, J. Douglas, *The Liberal University: An Institutional Analysis*, McGraw-Hill Book Co., New York, 1969, 263 pp.

This book, by the dean emeritus of the faculty and former Princeton University provost, was written, in the author's words:

. . . to analyze the purposes, organization, policies, and the processes of a particular type of university; that is, the "liberal university" as later defined. In this analysis, the aim has been to keep constantly in mind the interrelations, tensions, and interactions normally present in the operation of an institution which must be responsible to many categories of constituents. The emphasis is, therefore, upon *how* these various elements and interest can be brought into moving equilibrium in advancing the mission of the institution.

As viewed by the author, key attributes of a liberal university include such characteristics as being man centered, not knowledge centered; value centered rather than neutral or aloof from values; being concerned with fundamental knowledge and its integration; given to emphasizing independent study and individualized instruction; and seeking to encourage individual freedom and to promote individual responsibility. From this description the author proceeds to discuss the constituent elements, functioning, and problems of a liberal university in this sequence: organization, the presidency, the faculty, the administration, the trustees, the students, and the alumni. Attention is directed principally toward policies and administrative arrangements that can form a consistent whole. Some of the most rewarding chapters (in latter sections of the book) deal with issues concerning academic policy, questions of economy and control, and problems of external relations.

The author draws on his 21 years of experience as dean and provost and his earlier specialization in the study of industrial relations and organization to provide a wealth of observation and analysis. Among the topics he covers are academic freedom and tenure, the relation of teaching and research, the role of the university press, the optimal size of enrollment, the control of subject coverage and specialization, the control of sponsored research, and faculty salary policies and procedures.

Carnegie Commission on Higher Education, *New Students and New Places*, McGraw-Hill Book Co., New York, 1971, 158 pp.

In this report the Carnegie Commission projects enrollment in higher education to the year 2000 and estimates the ways in which this projection would be affected by implementation of commission recommendations. Also included are enrollment data and projections based on the commission's classification of institutions of higher learning. The report presents policy recommendations relating to (1) the growth of institutions, (2) the importance of continuing innovation and variety in higher education, (3) the need for new institutions, and (4) more flexible patterns of student participation in higher education. In suggesting optimum sizes for different kinds of institutions, the commission recommends that further consideration be given to the development of consortia and federations of colleges in order to counteract the undesirable effects of institutional gigantism. It also urges that more options for educational experiences be provided both on and off the campus and makes a strong plea for continued diversity in American higher education, especially through adequate support of the Nation's private colleges.

Carnegie Commission on Higher Education, *The Open-Door Colleges: Policies for Community Colleges*, McGraw-Hill Book Co., New York, 1970, 74 pp.

The descriptive chapters in this report—those dealing with the role and goals of the community college, its growth and development, size, governance, and accreditation, are noteworthy for their clarity, brevity, and content—three characteristics rare in much of today's educational rhetoric. The major contribution of this volume, however, is that it looks to the future; it considers new enrollment projections, the need for additional community colleges, and some expectations, proposals, and recommendations. The enrollment projections for 2-year institutions are on a State-by-State basis to 1980 and on a nationwide basis to the year 2000.

Corson, John J., *Governance of Colleges and Universities*, McGraw-Hill Book Co., New York, 1960, 209 pp.

This book deals with college and university governance as appraised by a professional management consultant and educator. The study is based on a limited observation of the governing processes in a number of institutions and on the results of conversations and correspondence concerning the administration of higher education with college and university trustees, presidents, deans, and teachers. The author's objective was to determine what characteristics of the academic enterprise will dictate the kinds of governance required in the future.

The first chapters present the characteristics which distinguish the college or university as a social organization and identify which ones must be accommodated in whatever system of governance is established.

The basic yet subtle dissimilarities that exist between the roles of the trustees, the president, the deans, the department heads, and the faculty, compared with the roles of their counterparts in business and industry, are discussed in chapters 3 to 5. Chapter 6 endeavors to answer the following questions: Are the processes by which a president gets things done through a faculty and the attendant staff of a college or university different from those by which the chief executive of a corporation stimulates the productivity of his staffs? And if the processes do differ, why? Chapter 7 explores the nature and weight of the influence exercised by such external groups as alumni, government, accrediting associations, foundations, and donors on decisionmakers within an institution.

Dunham, E. Alden, *Colleges of the Forgotten Americans: A Profile of State Colleges and Regional Universities*, second in a series of profiles sponsored by the Carnegie Commission on Higher Education, McGraw-Hill Book Co., New York, 1969, 206 pp.

This book is probably the most thorough, comprehensive, and up-to-date description of the 279 U. S. institutions generally known as 4-year State colleges and regional universities. The significance of these institutions is indicated by the author's contention that their enrollment share of 1 in 5 college students today ". . . will be 1 in 4 tomorrow and 1 in 3 the day after tomorrow." The rapid change in function and growth that these institutions have experienced is illustrated in the first chapter by brief descriptions of three institutions: Kansas State Teachers College (building upstream); State University of New York College at Brockport (moving rapidly); and Western Michigan University (well on its way).

The history and number of State colleges is traced in chapter 2. Alden delineates their role change from post-high-school academies to normal or teachers colleges to 4-year liberal arts colleges (with emphasis on teacher education, industrial arts, and home economics), and finally, to multipurpose State colleges. Subsequent chapter headings include the following: Educational Pressures (internal and external); The Financing of State Colleges; One End of the Log—Students, and Other End—Faculty; What Shall be Taught?; The Urban Crisis; and Seven Years Later—Alumni. The last chapter concludes with a recommendation that ". . . state colleges and regional universities take the lead in establishing a new and different doctoral degree specifically focusing on the preparation of undergraduate teachers, with special concern for lower division teaching, whether in two- or four-year institutions." David Riesman provides a perceptive commentary.

Fields, Ralph R., *The Community College Movement*, McGraw-Hill Book Co., New York 1962, 360 pp.

A detailed and comprehensive study, this book depicts not only the historical and the contemporary (1962) picture of the community college but also the probable course o its future development. Part I traces the community college idea from its inception to the community-serving concept. Part II contains accounts of the struggle by five community colleges to design programs to meet identified needs. Special attention is focused on two critical problems facing community colleges: (1) whom they should serve, and (2) what vocational education they should offer.

In examining the future of community colleges, the writer chooses three topics that appear to be of the greatest importance: (1) the problems of breadth of program, (2 how teaching can be improved, and (3) the cost to be borne by enrollees.

Gaff, Jerry G., and Associates, *The Cluster College*, Jossey-Bass, San Francisco, 1970, 249 pp.

By offering a research base for and a tentative early assessment of the cluster college, this book provides valuable insight into and definite knowledge about this new form of educational organization.

In part 1 Gaff describes the cluster college concept and organizational plan, the advantages of the pattern per se, areas of cooperation and sharing among the colleges, and the various routes by which such a federation can be established. The second chapter, which surveys the internal structure of cluster colleges, focuses on the many innovations incorporated within programs. Part 2, a collection of previously unpublished empirical studies, attempts to determine how well the structures adopted by cluster colleges realize stated educational purposes.

The following questions are among those figuring in the research: Have cluster colleges created a greater sense of community and fostered a more personal approach to the education of undergraduates than more monolithically structured schools? Do colleges on the same campus have different educational climates that in fact create structured diversity? Have the internal innovations produced vital intellectual communities? Has the experimentation extended into other parts of the university? At what personal and economic price have the advantages of cluster colleges been purchased? To what extent do students and faculty utilize the services and facilities of other schools in the union?

Gross, Edward, and Paul V. Grambsch, *University Goals and Academic Power*, American Council on Education, Washington, D.C., 1968, 164 pp.

This study examines the differences between the actual goals of universities, as perceived by administrators and faculty members, and the preferences of those responsible for goal definition and achievement. The research instrument was a direct-mail questionnaire. It included, among other items, a list of 47 goals: those manifested in a product of some kind and those end objectives of persons responsible for maintenance activities. The findings are based solely on statements of intended goals. Respondents were asked to state whether they thought a given goal *was* important—that is, whether it was strongly emphasized at their institution, and whether they thought it *should be* important.

A large variety of intriguing relationships were determined from the data gathered: the relationship between university goals and university location (urban versus rural); type and control of the university; productivity (measured by the number of doctorates awarded); university prestige; and graduate emphasis. Probably most significant are the measurements of congruence between perceived and preferred goals, and the implications inferred by the authors. Chapters are devoted to the power structure and perceived goals and to the conflict between administrators and faculty over goals.

These findings should not only enlighten academic leaders but also encourage them to reassess their own institutional goals.

Harris, Seymour E., ed., *Challenge and Change in American Education*, McCutcham Publishing Corp., Berkeley, Calif., 1965, 346 pp.

This collection of 32 papers and commentary features contributions by a remarkable group of participants at a seminar with the same title held in 1961 at the Harvard University Graduate School of Public Administration. All of the papers are thoughtful and informative, and many have the depth and precision commonly found in scholarly journal articles. The content is extensively reviewed and summarized in the editor's introduction. Able commentaries by Kenneth Deitch conclude each of 16 major topics. Some subjects of special interest to planners are State versus Federal power in education, Federal Government and university research, State and local investment in education, and the role of the liberal arts college.

Hodgkinson, Harold L., *Institutions in Transition: A Profile of Change in Higher Education*, The Carnegie Commission on Higher Education, McGraw-Hill Book Co., New York, 1971, 295 pp.

This comprehensive study deals with changes that have been made in higher education—specifically, with who has initiated change and who has supported or resisted it, how the campus community has interacted under the stress of change, and what the major consequences of change have been. Three primary data sources were used: From the first, the U. S. Office of Education, a "statistical history" of changes in higher education over the past two decades has been compiled; from the second, a questionnaire answered by 1,230 college presidents, an assessment of specific changes on each campus has been drawn; and from the third, case studies of five institutions that had undergone what were considered major changes, some or all of the changes other institutions might experience in the future have been described.

One of the more interesting findings is that *size* is a more significant factor in sorting out institutional differences than either control (e.g., public, private, sectarian, or nonsectarian) or the highest degree awarded. As a campus grows, the faculty turnover increases, as does student unrest; in addition, there is less significant contact between the administration and either the faculty or the students. On the other hand, a large campus means a more select student body, more Federal support, and more prestige. Such benefits, however, may not always outweigh the disadvantages resulting from increased size.

Some of the specific types of changes studied include those affecting students, faculty, and administration; institutional characteristics (e.g., control, composition of student body, vertical extension); and institutional movement (e.g., small to large, 2-year to 4-year). The most significant changes are ranked, and the way they were achieved is described. Separate chapters are devoted to an analysis of student protests and to the academic preparation and mobility of presidents.

Hodgkinson, Harold L., and L. Richard Meeth, eds., *Power and Authority*, Jossey-Bass, San Francisco, 1971, 215 pp.

In this volume the points of view on campus governance of 12 professional educators is presented. Walter Schenkel opens with an historical background of those institutional changes in universities specifically related to changes in the governance configuration. Rodney Hartness discusses definitions of power and authority and compares American and British systems of trusteeships. Richard Meeth, who focuses on the dysfunctional elements generated by administrative-faculty relationships, concludes that administrators should relinquish some of their power. Kingman Brewster encourages the development of more avenues for student participation in governance but is skeptical of either participatory or representative democracy as a way of arriving at final university decisions. He strongly advocates administrative accountability as the answer to legitimate student demands that they be protected from an incompetent and unresponsive administration. Robert Powell identifies student power as a fundamental, not political, educational principle and offers some practical guidelines for creating a democratic university.

Robert Johnston explains that faculty and administrators must revise the new and uncertain values and social priorities being fashioned by students rather than repeatedly defend old values and decisions. T. R. McConnell follows his discussion of governance conflicts between the administration and the faculty with various means whereby tension can be reduced. Ray Howe discusses faculty roles and outlines the adjustments that will be needed if collective bargaining is to succeed.

Harold Hodgkinson suggests that if social institutions are to cope better with the larger populations with which they must work, selective decentralization is the key to redesigning the internal government structure. Daniel Bell advances the thesis that the controlling problem of the governance of universities in the 1970's will be the resolution of a crisis in legitimacy—the authority that justifies use of power by virtue of position. Ralph Huitt delineates the problems that public universities will encounter during the 1970's with State and Federal Governments, faculty unions, and dissident students; his aim is to lighten the administrative load. Earl McGrath advocates changing the composition of boards of trustees to include a representative selection of lay citizens, faculty ,and students. In a final chapter, Hodgkinson reviews the content and suggests that some difficult concepts will require further study.

Keeton, Morris T., *Models and Mavericks: A Profile of Private Liberal Arts Colleges*, Carnegie Commission on Higher Education, McGraw-Hill Book Co., Inc., New York, 1971, 191 pp.

An informative study of private liberal arts colleges, this volume gives attention both to their problems and to solutions. Private 4-year liberal arts colleges have not only enriched the academic world by their diversity but have been a source of much creative thinking and innovation. As models of institutional autonomy, however, they have set standards that have become of concern to individual students. Keeton believes that if these institutions receive adequate public support they can continue to make significant contributions. Such support is justified, he says, on the basis that higher education is a joint investment by individual students and the general public. Legislators, he contends, should base appropriations on estimates of the equitable sharing of costs for the educational services provided by both public and private institutions. Keeton's proposals for public support are outlined within the general context that private colleges should accept more students whenever doing so would be advantageous to taxpayers and to State governments. He also believes that private colleges should undertake and sustain ventures in qualitative achievement for which they are particularly well suited. Some of these undertakings will naturally be rooted in a philosophical or religious perspective; an approach inappropriate or illegal for a State-supported college.

Other ventures will be uniquely appropriate to a particular private college because of its resources in people, tradition, control, revenue, etc. Keeton further recommends that the internal government and management of private colleges be substantially changed to ". . . reflect a climate enhancing, on one hand, the freedom of constituent groups within a college to pursue their objectives and, on the other hand, mutuality in the support which each group accords to others and to the college as a whole."

Kerr, Clark, *The Uses of the University*, Harvard University Press, Cambridge, Mass., 1963, 140 pp.

As former president of the University of California, Clark Kerr is eminently qualified to diagnose and evaluate the nature and qualities of the university as it is being reshaped by the reality that new knowledge is the most important factor in economic and social growth. The "idea of a multiversity" is discussed in a stimulating first chapter that traces the development of the modern American university. What emerges is a nonconfining "city of intellect" in which individuals—both students and faculty—identify less with the total community and more with its subgroups. Kerr justifies this modern fractionalized conglomerate with the statement that ". . . it has few peers in the preservation and dissemination and examination of the eternal truths; no living peers in the search for new knowledge; and no peers in all history among institutions of higher learning in serving so many of the segments of an advancing civilization."

Two forces—the land-grant movement and Federal support of scientific research—that beyond all others have molded the modern American university system are discussed at considerable length in the second chapter, which also includes eight suggestions for more effective Federal involvement.

As to the future of the university, Kerr devotes most of the last chapter to the consequences of talent concentration and university clustering, the concerns of alumni with "things past" and of faculty with outside responsibilities and loss of unity, and the new faces of change: growth, shifting academic emphasis, and involvement in the life of society.

Knoell, Dorothy M., and Leland L. Medsker, *From Junior to Senior College: A National Study of the Transfer Student*, American Council on Education, Washington, D.C., 1965, 102 pp.

This summary contains the results of a nationwide study of the performance of transfer students and the problem of articulation between 2-year and 4-year colleges that was conducted by the authors at the Center for Study of Higher Education in Berkeley.

As explained in the foreword, predicting the success of transfer students is a relatively complicated problem:

His academic performance in the four-year college or university was the outcome of a subtle accommodation between his attributes and the characteristics of the institution he entered or the particular part of the institution in which he concentrated his studies. The success of the transfer student was a function of his characteristics, the range of alternatives open to him when he chose a senior institution, the academic standards and the total climate of the senior college to which he transferred, and the interaction between the characteristics of the student and the institution.

In an all-important concluding chapter, the authors point out the significant implications their study can be expected to have on the assessment of individual characteristics; the definition and dissemination of the attributes of 4-year institutions; counseling, admission, and academic placement of students; and finally, the articulation and coordination between particular institutions.

Kruytbosch, Carlos E., and Sheldon L. Messinger, eds., *The State of the University*, Sage Publications, Beverly Hills, Calif., 1970, 379 pp.

Subtitled "Authority and Change," these 16 collected papers share "a concern with the problem of authority in the university—its changing bases, uses, emergent forms, and prospects." The editors state that the papers do not add up to a "model" of the contemporary university; rather, they represent a set of field notes, mainly empirically based, that capture important aspects of "what is happening" within the university. The list of contributors is impressive, and their presentations (dealing mostly with the Berkeley scene) provide sorely needed insight into the strain and tension within the university that relate to the capacity of an institution to govern itself.

Sample chapters and their authors include: "Conceptions of the University: The Case of Berkeley" by Martin Trow; "Predicaments in the Career of the College President" by David Riesman; "Faculty Participation in University Governance" by Kenneth Mortimer and T. R. McConnell; "Ruling out Paternalism—Students and Administrators at Berkeley" by Michael Otten; and "Bell, Book and Berkeley" by Martin Trow.

Ladd, Seight R., *Change in Educational Policy: Self-Studies in Selected Colleges and Universities*, a general report prepared for the Carnegie Commission on Higher Education, McGraw Hill Book Co., New York, 1970, 231 pp.

These 11 case studies concern institutions that submitted themselves to self-examination in such matters as the improvement of teaching, the relationship of teaching to research the function of the grading system, the adequacy of advising techniques, the optimum size of classes, and the scope and organization of the curriculum. A few studies examine such sensitive areas as institutional governance and opportunities for students to participate in policymaking.

The whole fascinating stream of events at each institution is revealed: the circumstances that give rise to the appointment of committees, the selection of members, the organization of investigations, the conduct of the studies, the findings and recommendations, and finally, the results and achievements. As Katharine E. McBride states in her commentary, "this study of studies cries for a reappraisal in five or ten years as to what will eventually happen as a result of these studies."

Lee, Eugene, C., and Frank M. Bowen, *The Multicampus University*, The Carnegie Commission on Higher Education, McGraw-Hill Book Co., New York, 1971, 481 pp.

This book describes the multicampus university—specifically the system of governance at the Universities of California, Illinois, Missouri, North Carolina, Texas, and Wisconsin; the State and City Universities of New York; and the California State colleges. The authors, who examine the distribution of authority within and surrounding the multicampus university, give primary attention to the authority of the systemwide administration of the multicampus university and to the impact of this authority on other elements of university governance.

The study is divided into three parts. Part 1, which considers the environment of multicampus university governance, emphasizes both external factors in academic governance (primarily the impact of State government and the overall statewide organization of higher education) and internal factors (the organization and history of each of the nine multicampus systems). Part 2 is concerned with multicampus governing structures. Separate chapters consider governing boards, the central administration, a systemwide faculty, and student organizations. Part 3 focuses on the processes that make up academic governance in the multicampus setting. The six chapters in this section are devoted to academic plans, budget administration, admissions, faculty and administrative personnel, public and governmental relations, and business affairs. In each of these chapters attention is concentrated on the particular role the multicampus administration plays in university governance. The authors' overall conclusions emphasize three "dimensions" of the multicampus university: its origins, its organization, and its size. The authors evaluate the strengths and shortcomings of this type of university as they appeared in 1968–69. In the final chapter the authors list some of the critical issues facing higher education in the 1970's and ways by which the multicampus university can contribute to their resolution.

Medsker, Leland L., and Dale Tillery, *Breaking the Access Barriers: A Profile of Two-Year Colleges*, sponsored by the Carnegie Commission on Higher Education, McGraw-Hill Book Co., New York, 1971, 183 pp.

In this report the authors consider the problems, issues, concerns, and proclaimed attributes of junior colleges as they assume a greater role in the evolving pattern of higher education. The report, in addition to presenting a statistical portrait of U.S. junior colleges, deals with such aspects as clientele, functions, program control, staffing, financing, and planning. A separate chapter is devoted to the special problems of private 2-year colleges.

The volume is packed with informative statistics, thoughtfully interpreted, and includes a summary, with issues and recommendations, that deserves special attention. As Joseph Cosand writes in his commentary, "Certainly, the authors have provided a great service to both educators and lay citizens by bringing together in one publication facts, figures, and pro and con discussion concerning the role of the community college—yesterday, today, and as projected for tomorrow."

Medsker, Leland L., and George W. Clark, *State Level Governance of California Junior Colleges*, California Coordinating Council for Higher Education, Sacramento, 1966, 100 pp.

Through questionnaires, interviews, and documentary research, the advisability of establishing a separate State board for California junior colleges is examined. The findings, interpreted by the staff of the Center for Research and Development in Higher Education (Berkeley), were that a separate board would be advisable based on: (1) certain advantages of visibility and identification with junior college affairs, (2) overwhelming approval on the part of the parties most affected, (3) likelihood of a strong contribution to junior college development in the State, (4) facilitation of articulation, (5) benefits to local institutions, and (6) general practicality from a legal point of view. All aspects of each issue and problem are presented, and related procedures in other States are examined. The result is an impressive marshalling of facts and opinions that should be of considerable value to officials debating the nature of a coordinating agency for junior colleges at the State level.

Millett, John D., *The Academic Community: An Essay on Organization*, McGraw-Hill Book Co., New York, 1962, 265 pp.

It is fortunate that Dr. Millett has adopted the essay form, for it enables him to examine a host of topics with absolute candor. The author explores the internal structure and process of higher education as a unique institution, and for which ". . . ideas drawn from business and public administration have only a very limited applicability." His commentary is broadly organized under the major headings of organization, higher education as an institution, faculty, students, alumni, and administration. In the concluding chapter he considers the struggle for power within the academic realm, and emphasizes the importance of consensus among constituent elements of the academic community which ". . . abhors absolute power."

The breadth of coverage of the subject makes the book essential reading for every college administrator.

National Academy of Sciences, *The Invisible University*, Washington, D.C., 1969, 310 pp.

This report presents national data on a heretofore seldom-examined subject: postdoctoral study. The bulk of information was gathered from five questionnaires: (1) a census of all U.S. citizen postdoctorals in the United States and abroad to elicit information on the background of the postdoctoral, the nature of his appointment, and his subsequent plans; (2) a departmental questionnaire to determine the nature of the environment in which most postdoctorals find themselves and where they are likely to be employed after their postdoctoral study appointment; (3) a faculty questionnaire to determine the relationship of the postdoctoral to research activities; (4) a questionnaire to determine the value of postdoctoral experience to the individual and to compare careers of postdoctorals with those who have earned a doctoral degree but have not yet engaged in postdoctoral study; and (5) an open-end questionnaire (to be answered by each institutional coordinator) to determine institutional attitudes toward postdoctoral education.

The first chapter contains a review of the history of postdoctoral education. Succeeding chapters cover the composition of the postdoctoral population; the significance of postdoctoral education for the individual, for the department, and for the institution with which he is temporarily associated; the character of postdoctoral education in different fields of study; and the manner in which postdoctoral studies are supported and their cost. The report concludes with recommendations based on the findings.

Rarig, Emory W., *The Community Junior College: An Annotated Bibliography*, Teachers College, Columbia University, New York, 1966, 114 pp.

This book, although not up to date, represents the first detailed, annotated compilation of books, articles, and reports on the history, growth, and problems of the community junior college. The approximately 400 entries are organized into eight major areas of study: history, functions and purposes, organization and administration, students, programs, personnel, facilities, and research.

Rauh, Morton A., *The Trusteeship of Colleges and Universities*, McGraw-Hill Book Co., New York, 1969, 206 pp.

Writing in the first person, the author makes this scholarly study of trustees and trusteeship a thoroughly enjoyable reading experience. The book embodies the views of many people who have written on this topic or whose ideas were obtained by the author in some 110 interviews. Further, the results of a survey of 5,200 trustees from 536 colleges have been used throughout. The book's special merit, however, lies in the warm, personal style of the author and in the breadth of his 20 years of uninterrupted experience as a practitioner in higher education.

Some of the many topics covered are: The Characteristics of Trusteeship; The Basic Responsibilities of Trustees; The Relationships of Board and President; Faculty, Trustees, and the Educational Program; Development of a Board and the Mechanics of Board Organization; and The Special Nature of Trusteeship at the Public University, the Junior College, and the Catholic College.

Sanford, Nevitt, *Where Colleges Fail: A Study of the Student as a Person*, Jossey-Bass, San Francisco, 1968, 229 pp.

The ensuing paragraph from the foreword expresses the intent and content of this stimulating book: "My aim in *Where Colleges Fail* is to help restore the student to his rightful place at the center of the college's activities. I state the case for individual development as the primary aim of education, present a theory of how students actually develop, and then apply it to various aspects of the student's development and the college's educational procedures. Finally, I suggest ways in which colleges might take advantage of outside pressures instead of merely submitting to or ignoring them."

In what really amounts to a series of essays, Professor Sanford begins by arguing that colleges *fail* whenever they treat the student as less than a person; that learning depends on recognition of the whole personality, not on abstract intelligence alone, and that colleges will improve only as they are guided by a theory of how students actually develop. Within the context of these theories, the author examines such aspects of development as social responsibility, academic achievement, creativity, and the integration of sex in the personality. He also describes how education is helped or hobbled by student peer culture, by various styles of teaching, and by the size and coherence of the institution itself.

Shulman, Carol, *Governance*, number 1 of a compendium series of research programs and proposals, ERIC Clearinghouse in Higher Education, George Washington University, Washington, D.C., May 1970, 23 pp.

This slim volume is a compendium of ongoing or recently completed research studies and programs pertaining to the governance of colleges and universities. Following an introductory essay are brief descriptions of 61 studies, a few of which have relevance to statewide governance problems. None of the studies, however, deals specifically with statewide governance.

Smart, John M., *Feasibility and Desirability of Eliminating Lower Division Programs at Selected Campuses of the University of California and the California State Colleges*, Coordinating Council for Higher Education, Sacramento, Calif., 1967, 157 pp. plus appendixes.

To this reviewer's knowledge, this single study is the only indepth attempt that has been made to investigate the desirability and feasibility of eliminating lower division programs at 4-year institutions. Two aspects for study are set forth in the introduction: (1) a concern for the quality of lower division instruction and (2) the cost of that instruction at both large graduate-oriented institutions and smaller undergraduate institutions. Consideration is given to the role played by public junior colleges and other institutions in providing lower division training; also, to their possible role in situations wherein lower divisions might be eliminated.

The study is organized in three parts. Part I considers the rationale for an undergraduate curriculum pattern and modifications of traditional patterns. Part II, an examination of the lower division of the California system of higher education, includes a description of the system and its constituent subsystems, a study of the movement of students within the system, and a review of a number of other matters relevant in any policy determination to curtail lower division programs. Part III, a recapitulation of the findings made in the first two sections, discusses conclusions in terms of policy objectives and recommendations.

Smith, Robert M., George F. Aker, and J. R. Kidd, eds., *Handbook of Adult Education*, Adult Education Association, The Macmillan Co., New York, 1970, 594 pp.

This fifth edition follows the central purpose set forth in the first edition: "To correlate in convenient reference form data relating to the many activities that have come to term themselves adult education enterprises." While the entire volume is of value to higher education planners, chapters of special interest deal with the role that community colleges, 4-year colleges, and universities play in adult education, in vocational-technical education, in continuing professional education, and in program development and evaluation. A recommended reading list supplements each chapter.

Stuckman, Jeffrey A., *Statewide Coordination of Community Junior Colleges*, Institute of Higher Education, University of Florida, Gainesville, 1969, 45 pp.

This study analyzes the junior college organizational structure in Florida and Illinois, States which have adopted a system wherein each college is under the operational control of a local board but is coordinated by a State-level junior college board. After reviewing the necessity for statewide coordination, the author develops guidelines for coordinating function-implementation practices related to authority placement, institutional autonomy, institutional-agency cooperation, and institutional-agency conflict. Six recommended function-implementation practices are offered for consideration.

There are two other companion volumes in this series: *The State Director for Community Junior Colleges* (James L. Wattenbarger, William A. Gager, and Jeffrey A. Stuckman) and *State Level Staffs for Coordination and/or Control of Community Junior Colleges* (by the same authors plus Melvyn Sakaguchi).

U. S. Department of Health, Education, and Welfare, Office of Education, *Suggested 2-Year Post High School Curriculums*, a series, U. S. Government Printing Office, Washington, D. C.

This series suggests 2-year post-high school curriculums for such technological fields as mechanical repair, data processing, chemistry, instrumentation, civil government, forestry, water, metallurgy, food processing, architecture and building, child care and guidance, diesel servicing, recreation program leadership, ornamental horticulture, and many others. The text includes, as a rule, a suggested detailed curriculum plan; course outlines with examples of texts and references; sequence of educational procedures; laboratory layouts, equipment, and costs; a discussion of the library and its use; faculty and student services; and a selected list of scientific, trade, and technical societies concerned with the type of training involved.

Willingham, Warren W., *The No. 2 Access Problem: Transfer to the Upper Division*, Access Research Office, College Entrance Examination Board, Palo Alto, Calif., 1972, 85 pp.

Smooth student transfer from 2- to 4-year institutions, a basic requirement of the hierarchical model of higher education now being developed by many States, is a task that is becoming increasingly important as community college enrollment grows and the transfer movement expands. This study examines specific problems that arise from the unique circumstances of students transferring from one institution to another after 2 years of study; e.g., the need to maintain the following: articulated curriculums between two institutions, junior college guidance and senior college orientation, appropriate admissions procedures and academic standards, and proper recognition of credit previously earned. The bibliography features 116 entries.

Chapter VI

THE SEARCH FOR EXCELLENCE— SELECTED RESPONSIBILITIES

Most State higher education agencies have accepted, in considerably differing degree, the responsibility for providing leadership to improve the quality of higher education. The reluctance by some to assume this responsibility is due, in part, to the fact that they perceive the search for excellence as principally an institutional function, particularly the domain of the faculty. Excellence has been and will continue to be most closely associated with individual institutions, yet the need for quality in State systems of higher education is increasingly being recognized and examined. Much of the totality of excellence at this level stems from the influence of those State planning boards and coordinating agencies that have been able to provide the professional wisdom and broad perspective not usually available within an individual institution.

It should be assumed that a strong State higher education agency can be a powerful agent for developing institutional quality. Once regulatory and supervisory functions become routine, such an agency can, for example, allocate high priorities to leadership activities. Of overriding importance is the selection of institutional officers whose posture or intellectual stance is innovative, creative, and demanding of excellence. Conservative leaders with a granite-like resistance to change cannot be expected to provide expert assistance and creative service to institutions. Since many States cannot afford large professional staffs to give counsel on all educational problems, the search for quality must be a joint effort between the State, the colleges and universities, and the community. The cooperative search for improved quality may be achieved through regional or statewide conferences, demonstration centers, and/or the use of task forces to evaluate programs and make recommendations. It may also be desirable to establish within the State planning agency a special division, which, however modestly staffed, can concentrate on raising the quality of education through design, evaluation, and dissemination of new ideas and practices.

Ewald Nyquist has suggested that an emergent function of a State planning agency is "to act more like a combined management consultant firm and philanthropic foundation, able to provide consultative services on a wide variety of problems and to make available money to bring about correction and change on the basis of formulated plans judged by adopted

261

state criteria."[1] There can be no doubt that State planning agencies are accountable for the quality level achieved through funds expended under their aegis. As public demands for accountability grow, State agencies can be expected more and more to use their yet relatively untapped fiscal powers to encourage improvements by critical program budgeting and other evaluative means.

To identify and assess areas requiring improvement in quality, State higher education agencies have a number of direct approaches at their disposal. Examples include:[2]

—developing regional and statewide plans that incorporate proposals for improved quality

—providing State plans for the administration of federally aided programs.

—developing statewide studies that support institutional efforts to examine areas of deficiency

—developing and promulgating guides and information to assist institutions in developing excellence in selected areas

—conducting State and regional leadership conferences on a variety of pioneering developments in education

—encouraging collegiate-sponsored inservice training programs in substandard areas

—encouraging institutions receiving State aid 'to correct critical areas of weakness in the quality and opportunity of education

—encouraging the systematic development of such programs as educational television, computer-assisted instruction, interlibrary cooperation, and electronic data processing, all of which require State-level coordination and master planning

—encouraging institutional research, experimentation, and innovation through the establishment of State aid programs for these specific purposes.

The search for excellence at any administrative level too often is more effective in identifying and articulating problems than in providing the means for their solution. Effective solutions, if they are to be found at all, usually evolve in three stages: (1) the acquisition of knowledge and skills, (2) deliberate and perceptive application of this knowledge and these skills to the study and analysis of the problem, and (3) a creative endeavor to find a solution. Fittingly, the easiest of the three—at least the component formally taught—is the first: the acquisition of knowledge and skills. With competent people, a State planning agency can do much to promote professionalism and expertise within its own organization by assembling a reference library of planning philosophy and technology. (In this regard, the bibliography in this publication and in others can be of assistance.)

---

[1] Ewald B. Nyquist, "Some Strategies and Procedures in Effecting Changes," in *Designing Education for the Future: Planning and Effecting Needed Changes in Education*, Edgar L Morphet and Charles O. Ryan, eds., Citation Press, New York, 1967, p. 313.

[2] Ibid., p. 312.

As statewide higher education planning agencies prove their competence, the research community will be increasingly impressed by the evolving procedures and technology. Few educational activities appear to have had so weighty an impact yet so little recorded observation and study as statewide planning. The addition of recent studies to some earlier investigations is beginning to remedy this situation.[3]

This chapter delineates the four topics which deserve—and are receiving—greater attention by State planners who seek excellence in specialized areas. The first topic concerns institutional size. Earlier pressures to expand enrollments seem to have inundated campuses with more students than either space or program justifies. The second topic, the recruitment and retention of faculty, while not a problem at the present time, is, nevertheless, an area in which institutions must maintain a competitive position in order to bargain for the exceptional scholar and to cope with possible future shortages. The third and fourth topics, doctoral-level graduate programs and sponsored research, deserve more State-level study at a time when growing institutions, rightly or wrongly, are gradually assuming responsibilities previously considered the special purview of a few elite universities. Because a discussion of these topics cannot be more than introductory in this context, only material which appears most relevant to the needs of State-level planners seeking initial guidance is included. References giving indepth coverage of the subjects are listed in he bibliography.

INSTITUTIONAL SIZE

In higher education, as in other social systems increasing in size, it is necessary to preserve the best of the educational community and its goals while keeping pace with the complex demands for growth. Too often in the past, expanding colleges and universities have permitted complexity to

---

[3] For a short inventory of research concerning higher education planning, see Robert O. Berdahl, *Statewide Coordination of Higher Education*, American Council on Education, Washington, D.C., 1971, pp. 39, 40; also, Dale M. Heckman and Warren Bryan Martin, *Inventory of Current Research on Higher Education 1968*, McGraw-Hill Book Co., New York, 1968.

Other recent studies include Lyman A. Glenny, Robert O. Berdahl, Ernest G. Palola, and James G. Paltridge, *Coordinating Higher Education for the '70s*, Center for Research and Development in Higher Education, University of California, Berkeley, 1971; and Lyman A. Glenny and George B. Weathersby, eds., *Statewide Planning for Postsecondary Education: Issues and Design*, National Center for Higher Education Management Systems, WICHE, Boulder, Colo., 1971.

interfere with achieving an integrated whole. Concerning this situation, Nevitt Sanford offers the following view:

> . . . [the] traditional means of holding the university together are breaking down: as higher education becomes financially available to a wider socioeconomic range, the student body becomes less homogeneous; and as dormitory capacity is exceeded, a declining proportion of college students are living on campus. Teacher-student contacts are diminishing—partly as a result of the very differentiating forces which, ironically, we would hope such contacts could mitigate. Leisure has all but vanished under the pressure of demands for excellence, even though free time is essential for making friends and for sorting through the confusing diversity of college life. In the midst of such academic incoherence, we need to strengthen the forces of integration.[4]

Although a few institutions are resisting the trend toward bigness, the question for most is not whether to grow but how—according to what pattern. Bigness itself is not the root of the problem, nor is complexity or growth. The problem is for the institution, large or small, to discover what style of development is proper if it is to preserve its identity and internal consistency.

Coherency, the Central Issue

The consequences of increasing size and complexity have often led colleges and universities to be concerned with what Sanford calls the preservation of *coherency*;[5] i.e., preserving a cohesion and congruity of part arising from a common relationship and an interconnection of thought. While a variety of organizational components may establish community coherence, grouping *students* into distinctive, semi-autonomous units is critical to achieving a desired balance between bigness and smallness. Emphasis on the student group as the basic community is the result of an observed decline in the intellectual interchange between students and between students and faculty as educational institutions have grown. Newcomb[6] has referred to the fact that on large campuses, student peer groups are divorcing themselves from intellectual concerns as a kind of "academic anonymity." The large institution with a heterogeneous student body appears least able to provide an environment for students that encourages the personal contacts and close associations required for mutual

---

[4] Nevitt Sanford, *Where Colleges Fail—A Study of the Student as a Person*, Jossey-Bass, San Francisco, 1967, pp. 177–78.

[5] The concept of a learning community's coherence and its relationship to the size, leadership, internal structure, and educational style of the college has been carefully studied and reported by Nevitt Sanford, ibid., pp. 175–182.

[6] Theodore M. Newcomb, "Student Peer-Group Influence," in Nevitt Sanford, ed, *The American College*, John Wiley and Sons, New York, 1962, pp. 469–88.

intellectual concern. The observations of McKeachie detail the problem:

> In a large college the statistical chances that another student in the same class will
> be in the same living group are smaller than in a small college. Students in a larger
> college with many courses, and even many sections of the same course, have few com-
> mon intellectual experiences. Consequently it is difficult for them to communicate
> about intellectual problems outside of class, and the common concerns which become
> the basis of social communication are football, the student newspaper, dating, and the
> dormitory food. With such barriers to interstudent education, the professor misses the
> good feeling one experiences when he finds that his teaching has provided an intellec-
> tual stimulus reaching far beyond his classroom.[7]

In an effort to minimize the drawbacks created by massive size, particularly those affecting students, large institutions are experimenting with
various kinds of subdivisions. Designed to establish genuine student and
student-faculty communities, the subdivisions employ various unifying
forces: a common curriculum, a shared living-learning environment, an
isolated geographical location, a special educational style, a common
commuter status, etc. In the case of a large multipurpose university, such
communities may be many in number but distinctive from each other even
though on the same campus. If the campus is large, it is likely to include
more than one community; if small and closely knit, there may be only a
single community encompassing the entire student enrollment and faculty.

The best-known approach to the grouping of students is the "cluster
college" concept. Initiated in 1925 in Claremont, Calif., it has since been
adopted and developed by perhaps as many as 50 institutions.[8] By definition,
the cluster idea refers to the dividing of a central institution into small
satellite colleges, each usually having its own president and dean. Such
co-adjacent colleges are sheltered by the economic strength of the parent
institution, which also provides some measure of overall program and
student diversification. The individual units make possible enrichment of
instruction; more important, their small size and separate identities preserve
the *community* as an active ingredient of teaching and learning. An example
is Santa Cruz, a "campus core" of the University of California, which
encompasses a graduate school, central library, and certain other common
facilities requiring elaborate paraphernalia.

Another approach to student grouping is Michigan State University's

---

[7] W. J. McKeachie, "Procedures and Techniques of Teaching: A Survey of Experimental Studies," in Nevitt Sanford, ed., *The American College*, op. cit., p. 355.

[8] Recommended studies of the cluster college include: Jerry G. Gaff and Associates,
The Cluster College, Jossey-Bass, San Francisco, 1970; Louis T. Benezet, "College Groups
and the Claremont Example," in *Emerging Patterns in American Higher Education*, Logan
Wilson, ed., American Council on Education, Washington, D.C., 1965, pp. 199–203;
"The Conference on the Cluster College Concept," *The Journal of Higher Education*, vol.
38, no. 7, October 1967.

"living-learning" program, wherein "colleges" within residence halls provide intimate student-faculty involvement. Such an arrangement not only establishes a learning environment in the student's resident life and provides convenient opportunities for students to meet and talk with their teachers but also relates the learning experience and the living experience in such a way that one reinforces the other.[9] What this approach and the cluster and similar concepts prove is that institutions of mammoth size can be organized into coherent subdivisions providing breadth of offerings and diversity, while at the same time preserving small, semi-autonomous communities.

Guidelines

Except in the case of the small college that seeks to create of all faculty and students a single community, it would serve no relevant purpose to define optimal *overall* institutional size. For large colleges and universities what is important is the size of the communities within each institution. Even if overall size were meaningful, no recommendations could be made because of the multiplicity of factors, distinctive for each institution, upon which such recommendations must be based: (1) the diversity of educational programs and the kind of interrelationships desired, (2) the variety of students admitted and the degree of heterogeneity desired, (3) the educational style and the importance attached to the community concept, (4) the ability to maintain and improve program quality, (5) the ability to operate economically and provide necessary supporting services, (6) the ability to recruit and retain qualified faculty, and (7) the commuter-versus-resident enrollment status and whether the location is urban or rural.

In view of the existence of such highly variable factors (none of which can be accurately measured), it is not surprising that optimum overall size is variously interpreted by colleges and universities or ignored altogether. The incredible range of enrollment figures among various types of higher institutions is shown in table VI-1. The extremes are startling: a junior college with more than 30,000 students, a university with fewer than 3,000 students, a university with over 50,000 students on a *single* campus, and hundreds of colleges with an enrollment under 200. Certainly it is apparent that the median size increases according to the type of institution: 4-year senior colleges are larger than community colleges, and universities are the largest of all. Other than this reality, however, there is no evidence that institutions have agreed upon an optimum size. Contributing to the size variance, of course, is the fact that the newer institutions have not yet reached their optimum size. On the other hand, the gigantic size of some

---

[9] John A. Hannah, "The University as a Matrix," *The Journal of Higher Education*, vol. 38, no. 7, October 1967, p. 382.

Table VI-1.—Number of institutions of higher education, by size of enrollment and by type and control of institution: 1971

Control and type of institution	Size of enrollment								
	Less than 200	200 to 499	500 to 999	1,000 to 2,499	2,500 to 4,999	5,000 to 9,999	10,000 to 19,999	20,000 to 29,999	30,000 or more
Public universities	—	—	—	—	1	13	32	24	24
Private universities	—	—	—	1	10	30	16	7	1
Public 4-year	2	7	20	72	85	97	50	10	3
Private 4-year	176	202	336	348	81	20	3	1	—
Public 2-year	6	54	133	233	135	81	49	4	2
Private 2-year	71	90	49	22	4	1	—	—	—

Source: U.S. Department of Health, Education, and Welfare, Office of Education, *Digest of Educational Statistics, 1972*, U.S. Government Printing Office, Washington, D.C., 1973.

mature institutions appears to be due to the fact that, for all practical purposes, size as a restraint has been ignored. At those multipurpose universities that have established cluster colleges and other student groupings, total institutional enrollment is of little significance since the subdivisions reflect the actual working size.

If standards for overall enrollment at colleges and universities cannot be established, what characteristics are legitimate topics for recommendations as to size? Useful guidelines have been developed in five areas: (1) the minimum initial enrollment essential to new colleges if they are to develop successfully, (2) desirable growth rates, (3) the size required if a liberal arts curriculum is desired, (4) the size of a genuine community of students and faculty, and (5) desirable sizes based on possible economies of scale. Recommendations in these areas serve as useful points of departure in the examination of individual cases.

Minimum Initial Enrollment

The success of a newly established college depends on many factors, the main ones being evidence of need, financial support, community interest, student accessibility, proximity to other institutions, and leadership. All are important, but perhaps none more so than evidence of real need, most often identified by estimated initial enrollment and potential future enrollment. A college which remains very small will tend to become ineffective, inadequate, and uneconomical to operate. What, then, should the size criterion be? The most detailed investigation of this question, conducted by Morrison and Martorana, pertains to junior colleges only.[10] The authors' findings, based on both an opinion sample and a review of regulatory criteria, reveal that the 200–400 student enrollment range for a beginning junior college is acceptable, the upper total being preferred, especially if the college plans to offer a comprehensive program. The authors also conclude that a potential enrollment of 400 full-time students at the end of 5 years appears to be necessary in order to provide adequate breadth of program.[11] Some States, on the other hand, have set a higher figure. California law, for example, stipulates that no junior college district may be formed if the estimated potential average daily attendance of the district is less than 900 full-time students.[12]

The initial enrollment necessary to support on an economically sound

---

[10] D. G. Morrison and S. V. Martorana, *Criteria for the Establishment of 2-Year Colleges*, U. S. Department of Health, Education, and Welfare, Office of Education, U. S. Government Printing Office, Washington, D. C., 1961.

[11] Ibid., p. 61.

[12] California Coordinating Council for Higher Education, *California's Needs for Additional Centers of Public Higher Education*, CCHE, Sacramento, 1964, p. 13.

basis a basic complement of courses at a 4-year college is less clear. Very little data are available. It is reasonable to believe, however, that if positive growth factors are present, a 4-year college with a limited curriculum could be established and survive its 1st year with as few as 400 students, the same number as recommended for a junior college. But in order to attract a qualified faculty and justify an adequate library, laboratories, and related facilities required by a 4-year institution, an enrollment of 750 or more must be reached quickly. This number is necessary if the full complement of courses expected of a liberal arts college awarding the baccalaureate degree is eventually to be offered.

Growth Rates

To meet the educational needs of the State, most public institutions must expand to accommodate a continuous increase in applicants. The rate of growth will necessarily vary according to enrollment pressures, the size of the college, and the pattern of organization. A new college located in an area of high potential enrollment might properly double in size for a year or two until local demand is met. On the other hand, an old, prestigious 4-year college catering to high-ability students throughout the State may grow at a very modest rate (proportional to the number of in-State high school graduates).

The Illinois Board of Higher Education, has recommended growth rates as follows:[13]

Institutional size	Rate of growth per year
2,500 students	20 percent
5,000 students	15–20 percent
10,000 students	10–7 percent
More than 15,000 students	7–5 percent

It has declared that too rapid growth tends to make it difficult if not impossible to assimilate new faculty members. Board members have also stipulated that a shortage of qualified instructors could result in a considerable turnover of personnel and the hiring of some persons with limited qualifications. Excessive growth rates may also tend to increase the number of conflicting situations, shortages, and similar problems likely to annoy and alienate students. Finally, too rapid growth may adversely affect relations between the college and the citizens of the community, particularly if it

[13] Master Plan Committee L, *Institutional Size and Capacity*, Illinois Board of Higher Education, Springfield, 1966, p. 4.

precipitates awkward handling of land acquisition, increased traffic flow, area sprawl, student rebellion, etc.

Enrollment and Curriculum

How large should an institution be to provide a sufficiently diverse liberal arts curriculum? Authorities suggest that 60 faculty members are sufficient to teach most educational disciplines in a liberal arts college.[14] If the student-faculty ratio is 15 to 1, the student body would total approximately 900. It should be noted that 60 full-time faculty members could not be expected to teach a full complement of major courses in the traditional fields unless they had adequate junior staff support. If the faculty is limited to 60, most special-interest courses could be offered only on a periodic basis—e.g., once every 4 years. Probably 100 full-time faculty members is a more reasonable minimum.

Whether or not one agrees with any of the aforementioned guidelines, identifying optimal size by first determining curriculum, faculty, and student-faculty ratio is both simple and eminently practical. How better can college size be gauged than on the basis of these three crucial factors?

Definition of a Genuine Community

Perhaps the most quoted commentary concerning the size best suited to the development of a genuine community of faculty and students is that of Gilbert White. While president of Haverford College in 1954, he discussed the desirability of an institution remaining small in the face of an impending increase in the number of college and university applicants:

> In the light of that prospect, we may re-examine the reasoning behind our decision to avoid further expansion. The primary consideration was a size which would permit the development of a genuine community of faculty and students. Experience with enrollments ranging from 100 to 600 had convinced the Haverford faculty that somewhere between 400 and 500 the college passed the point at which every member of the student body might hope to know the others, and at which faculty members might expect to know all the students by sight. At present all members of each class do know each other. It does not follow that all persons in the College who might expect such acquaintance in fact achieve it, but so long as the possibility and expectancy exist, many are likely to strive for it, and some may arrive at it. A larger enrollment makes such a relationship impossible.

---

[14] Robert S. Babcock, "The Creation of Three Swarthmores," *The American Oxonian* vol. 55, no. 4, October 1968, p. 234. For a slightly different and more complicated approach (including a course list, optimal section size, and student course-selection pattern), see Robert W. McEwin and Kalixt S. Synakowski, "Planning College Enrollment for Academic Efficiency," *Journal of Higher Education*, vol. 25, no. 6, June 1954, pp. 301-06.

From it may come, with proper cultivation, a number of benefits in the educational process. Students may develop personal acquaintance with a substantial proportion of the faculty. Students are obliged to live, outside as well as within the classroom, with others having quite different vocational interests, skills and family backgrounds: the group is too small to permit large and lasting cliques of students having special interests. Heavy responsibility for management of student government and the honor system can be placed upon a student body in which each member has a clear identity for the others. There can be a regular period of common worship and meditation. Intellectual discussion of problems of broad interests, such as those posed in Collection, as well as the classes, can be widely shared. In the whole atmosphere of the College there can be, given the right people; a joining of respect for each individual's development with a sense of common aims and responsibility.[15]

The experiences in 1954 that led Haverford to arrive at a size which provided the environment it sought may no longer be relevant in the 1970's. The need in this decade is for practical guidelines by which students at a large institution may be grouped in meaningful communities, whether by internal organization, the addition of a new campus section, limiting the size of individual departments, or simply by establishing some form of partial isolation, autonomy, and distinctiveness to give identity to each individual.

Economies of Scale

One argument favoring expansion of enrollment assumes that there are economies of scale which can be exploited to obtain lower unit costs without altering function or quality. Because almost all college programs have some fixed and/or one-time costs that do not increase in proportion to enrollment growth, virtually all aspects of college operations appear to be subject to decreasing unit or average costs per student as the scale of operation (enrollment) increases. The relationship between unit costs of capital construction and enrollment levels is also indicative of economies of scale, and should receive consideration in determining whether students in a given area are to be served by one or several college campuses.

Economies of scale in college operations are derived from certain essentially indivisible functions—general administration, library, student services, and plant maintenance—that do not increase proportionately as enrollment increases.[16] For example, regardless of enrollment, a college

---

[15] *Haverford College Bulletin* (Report of the President), vol. 53, no. 2, October 1954, p. 7–8.

[16] For an outline of approaches to realizing various economies of scale in different areas of university operation, see Ferdinand K. Levy, "Sources of Economies of Scale in Universities," in *The Economies and Financing of Higher Education in the United States*, Joint Economic Committee, Congress of the United States, U. S. Government Printing Office, Washington, D. C., 1969, pp. 295–302.

normally employs only one president, one chief librarian, one dean of students, and so on. Because facility space requirements also tend to decline in proportion to student enrollment as the institution grows, related expenditures for plant operation and maintenance may likewise be reduced on a unit-cost basis. Expenditures for countless other activities are related only partially to enrollment.

Although operating costs and facility requirements tend to decline in proportion to enrollment growth, there may be a size at which average unit or per student costs reach a minimum and cease to decline. Since any increase in enrollment beyond this size will require duplication of certain administrative and supporting units if quality operations are to be maintained, unit costs will begin to rise (diseconomies of scale). Studies to date suggest that unit costs tend to decline over a wide range of enrollments and approach a nearly constant value at higher enrollment levels without any indication of when diseconomies of scale may begin.

Empirical proof of theoretical cost-saving possibilities is rather difficult to accumulate, for in order to determine valid decreasing unit costs it is essential that all variously sized colleges be comparable. In other words, the quality and diversity of programs offered must be equivalent, or nearly so, in terms of the type and method of instruction, teacher excellence, class size, curriculum offerings, and so on. Yet institutions of different sizes are seldom equal in these respects. When comparing capital expenditures, unit costs depend on the quality of architectural design and materials used. Since these may vary greatly from institution to institution, comparative analysis is seldom possible. In a few instances, however, reasonable comparisons of educational activity and related facility costs can be made between groups of like institutions within a single State system. A State-coordinated group of junior colleges, for example, is likely to have common functions and goals, curriculum offerings, salary schedules, staffing patterns, architecture, etc., which, in economic terms, suggest that these institutions differ principally in their scale of operation.

In determining whether or not decreases in unit costs are valid, the quality and diversity of instruction offered at those colleges being examined must be generally equivalent, regardless of the enrollment figures. In California, for example, the smaller junior colleges do not appear to offer the same diversity or range of courses as do the larger junior colleges.[17] Such is probably the case, though to a lesser degree, in many small 4-year senior colleges, which, if they are to operate economically, must somewhat curtail their curriculum. If larger colleges offer a greater range of courses than do smaller institutions by spending more per student, then the case

---

[17] California Coordinating Council for Higher Education, *Meeting the Enrollment Demand for Public Higher Education in California Through 1977—the Need for Additional College and University Campuses*, CCHE, Sacramento, 1969, p. F2-1.

for economies of scale would be ambiguous. But the data indicate that large colleges simultaneously offer a more extensive curriculum and operate at generally lower unit costs than do the small colleges. Thus, as long as larger colleges maintain a superiority in diversity and range of courses, the added cost of such programs only reduces the savings accruing from larger-scale operations—the economies of scale are still present. Also as a general rule, as institutions grow they are more likely to offer higher faculty salaries and provide added support personnel and facilities. Since such functional improvements tend to increase rather than reduce unit costs at larger institutions, any savings secured through economies of scale are further reduced.

One variation in instructional practice that unquestionably prevents comparability for purposes of determining economies of scale is the distortion introduced by differences in the student-faculty ratio. Since faculty salaries and proportionately funded supporting expenditures constitute a major component of total operating outlays, this ratio is of major importance in any comparison of operating costs. The student-faculty ratio (explained in greater detail in chapter XIV) varies not only according to the average class size and faculty teaching load but also according to the amount of course work each student takes. The number of course units which a student takes is generally similar in all colleges and also invariant with respect to college size. Faculty teaching workload, normally a matter of institutional policy, is not related in any logical way to campus size. On the other hand, at some groups of institutions the most important factor governing the student-faculty ratio—class size—is positively and significantly related to institutional enrollment. A facilities inventory-utilization study conducted in Indiana indicates, for example, that a direct relationship exists between average class size and campus enrollment. Class sizes in the study ranged from an average of about 21 students at colleges with an enrollment of less than 500 to more than 32 at institutions with more than 5,000 students.[18] The study also revealed that the average classroom capacity is also directly and positively related to campus size. If such a relationship is true generally, larger colleges can be expected to have high student-faculty ratios and lower instructional costs per student. To interpret the lower unit costs resulting from this difference in institutional methodology as an economy of scale, however, would be erroneous and misleading. Class size, insofar as it is a pedagogical matter of choice, is not a factor contributing to economies of scale. However, where small classes and high unit costs are the unavoidable consequence of an institution's small size, economies of scale are clearly involved.

---

[18] James F. Blakesley and others, *Indiana Facilities Utilization Survey for Colleges and Universities, Fall 1967*, Indiana Advisory Commission on Academic Facilities, Bloomington, 1968, pp. 141, 142.

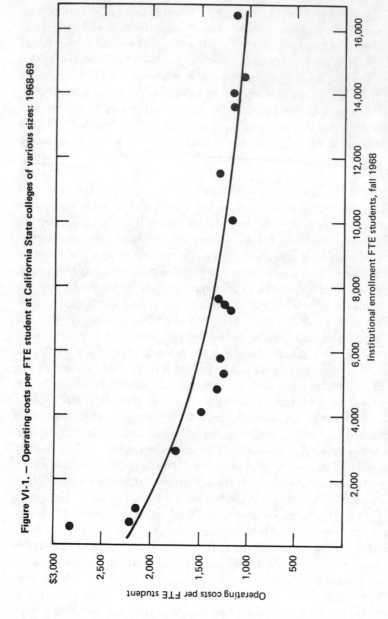

Figure VI-1. — Operating costs per FTE student at California State colleges of various sizes: 1968-69

Source: California Coordinating Council for Higher Education, Meeting the Enrollment Demand for Public Higher Education in California Through 1977, Sacramento, 1969, appendix D.

A recent empirical study in California illustrates the magnitude of economies of scale that may be present in college operations.[19] The data for 18 State colleges (plotted in figure VI-1) show that operating costs per full-time-equivalent (FTE) student in 1968–69 decreased from approximately $2,100 per year at State colleges with fewer than 1,000 students to approximately $1,100 at institutions with an enrollment of 14,000 or more. . In the absence of reported evidence to the contrary, it may be assumed for comparability that these institutions followed similar course and sectional policies resulting in roughly equivalent average class sizes, also that their functions and programs were generally similar.

As the California study illustrates, economies of scale in college operations can be demonstrated within a State system of higher education. However, if large numbers of more heterogeneous institutions were to be chosen for study, comparability would not be feasible. This fact is plainly demonstrated by the startling variance in per student expenditures for administrative and general expense by the groups of institutions shown in table VI-2. Among 227 private liberal arts colleges, for example, administrative expenditures in 1961–62 ranged from $100 per student to seven times that amount. For each type-control group, between 90 and 95 percent of the institutions were within the indicated per student expenditure range. Examination of related scatter diagrams for each group of institutions shows no logical relationship between unit costs and institutional size. Thus it is evident that an empirical demonstration of economies of scale demands that only institutions substantially similar in every respect other than size be examined.

As previously noted, economies of scale can be applied to capital costs as well as to operational costs. Certain physical facilities have basic capacities that serve a wide range of student enrollments. The size of the gymnasium, theater, auditorium, student center, and the corporate yard that usually exist in some form on every campus is only partially related to total enrollment. In many instances, the percent of the student body which the library can seat is inversely related to campus size; moreover, because a core collection serves the basic curriculum, regardless of the size of the student body, the relative amount of space required for housing the collection may decline as the institution grows.

The Indiana facilities utilization survey (1967) revealed that space per FTE student for classrooms, teaching laboratories, library, and general-use facilities was inversely related to campus enrollment size. Space for offices and medical care was relatively uniform for institutions of different sizes, while large institutions allocated a greater amount of space per student for

---

[19] California Coordinating Council for Higher Education, *Meeting the Enrollment Demand for Public Higher Education in California Through 1977*, op. cit., appendix D.

Table VI-2.—Administrative and general expenditures per student, by type and control of institution: 1961–62

Institution type and control	Enrollment	Administrative and general expenditures per student, 1961–62	
		Range[1]	Median value
77 public universities	under 30,000	$100–$250	$166
57 private universities	under 15,000	67– 575	220
77 public liberal arts colleges	under 6,000	60– 270	125
227 private liberal arts colleges	250 to 2,500	100– 700	330
263 public junior colleges	under 1,600	17– 175	75

[1] Range includes 90–95 percent of institutions.

Source: Unpublished U.S. Office of Education data.

research laboratories and for support and other miscellaneous facilities. Overall, nonresidential space declined from 173.6 square feet per FTE student on campuses with 500 or fewer students to 124 square feet per student on campuses with an enrollment over 5,000.[20]

To illustrate the magnitude of economies of scale in capital construction, the California study of 16 senior colleges is exemplary.[21] The data show the total cumulative amount expended for capital construction by each institution from its initial establishment through 1966–67. Total expenditures range from a low of $3,949 per FTE student to a high of $15,454 per FTE student. The data plot (see figure VI-2) reveals a nonlinear regression. The curve suggests that economies of scale are more likely to reduce total investment in physical plant per student during the early stages of institutional growth. The initial one-time expenditures essential to campus planning, land acquisition, site development, and basic utilities required to establish a new campus are largely responsible for the exceedingly high capital investment by small new campuses.

As the California State college study indicates, it is nearly three times as expensive to construct facilities for each additional FTE student at a small college than at a college with an enrollment of around 12,000. A campus of 2,000 students requires unit capital expenditures of $10,100 per FTE student, or a total investment of $20.2 million. For a campus of 4,000 students, the cost would be $8,600 per student or $34.4 million overall. Thus, an expansion of from 2,000 to 4,000 students would involve an additional expenditure of $14.2 million. Yet an increase of 2,000 students

---

[20] Blakesley and others, op. cit., p. 57.

[21] California Coordinating Council for Higher Education, *Meeting the Enrollment Demand for Public Higher Education in California Through 1977*, op. cit., appendix D.

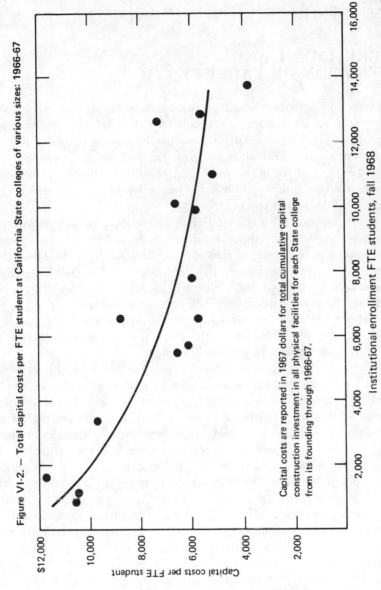

Figure VI-2. — Total capital costs per FTE student at California State colleges of various sizes: 1966-67

Capital costs are reported in 1967 dollars for total cumulative capital construction investment in all physical facilities for each State college from its founding through 1966-67.

Source: California Coordinating Council for Higher Education, Meeting the Enrollment Demand for Public Higher Education in California Through 1977. Sacramento, 1969, appendix D.

at an institution with 12,000 enrollment would cost only $5 million (14,000 students × $4,900 per student less 12,000 students × $5,300 per student).

RECRUITMENT AND RETENTION OF FACULTY

This section deals briefly with a fundamental concern of every institution: how to attract and retain a qualified and competent faculty. During the past decade, as the need for new faculty members nearly doubled, recruitment assumed critical importance. Even with a surplus of applicants in the 1970's, high turnover rates and continued efforts by colleges to upgrade their faculties combine to create strong competition for the exceptional scholar and teacher.

Colleges respond to this challenge in many ways. Too often, however, an institution considers its competitive position limited by factors beyond its control—prestige and campus size and location, for example. Since many of the more important factors that appear to influence candidates in choosing faculty positions are subject to change, such an outlook is overly pessimistic. By offering desirable teaching assignments, reasonable teaching loads, and a responsive administration, institutions unable to match the dollars, stature, and visibility of the more prestigious colleges and universities can attract and retain qualified and competent faculty.

When jobs go begging, a college must make adjustments. Either it must plan less ambitiously, utilize its available staff more fully, offer more attractive jobs, or, if such actions fail, lower its job qualification standards. To cope with faculty shortages, most institutions probably will have to adopt one or more of these strategies from time to time. But as a continuing policy, making faculty jobs as attractive as possible is the best solution.

To attract qualified faculty involves three major activities: (1) periodic study to determine what factors influence a prospective candidate to select or reject a given faculty position, (2) a continuing program of upgrading those factors identified as the most influential in decisionmaking, and (3) interviews with each applicant to discover which motivations influencing his or her choice may warrant special attention on the part of the institution.

The importance of each of the determinant factors in an applicant's decision to choose a faculty position has been studied with sufficient thoroughness to serve most institutional needs.[22] The most recent definitive

---

[22] Much excellent work on this subject has been done by Ruth Eckert and associates. A principal study, which contains a list of additional references, is Ruth E. Eckert and John E. Stecklein, *Job Motivations and Satisfactions of College Teachers*, Cooperative Research Monograph No. 7, U.S. Department of Health, Education, and Welfare, Office of Education, U.S. Government Printing Office, Washington, D.C., 1961.

Table VI-3.—Determinants of faculty job choice between top two alternatives

Choice variable JOB-RELATED FACTORS *Compensation factors* Environmental factors	Choice index[1]	Primary control of choice variable			
		Policy and management	Financial strength and budgeting	Long-term development	Unalterable or externally controlled
COURSES TAUGHT	3.7	X			
TEACHING LOAD	3.4	X			
RESEARCH FACILITIES AND OPPORTUNITIES	3.3		X		
COMPETENCY OF COLLEAGUES	3.3			X	
Salary	3.2		X		
Future salary prospects	3.2		X		
REPUTATION OF SCHOOL	3.1			X	
QUALITY OF STUDENTS ·	3.1			X	
ADMINISTRATION AND ADMINISTRATORS	3.0	X			
Cultural opportunities	2.9				X
Congeniality of colleagues	2.9	X			
Academic rank	2.8	X			
Fringe benefits	2.4		X		
Nearness to graduate school	2.4				X
Climate	2.1				X
Nearness to friends and relatives	2.1				X
Moonlighting opportunities	1.8				X

[1] In response to the question "How important were each of these factors in your decision to choose your current job instead of your next best alternative?" three options were given: "very important," "important," and "not important." For each of the 17 factors, five times the number of "very important" responses, three times the number of "important" responses, and one time the number of "not important" responses were added. The "choice index" was obtained by dividing the added products by the total number of responses.

Source: David G. Brown, *The Mobile Professors*, American Council on Education, Washington, D.C., 1967, p. 150.

study of job choice factors is the 1964 survey of 7,600 newly appointed faculty members conducted by David G. Brown and reported in *The Mobile Professors*.[23] In order of importance, the 17 factors that influenced faculty applicants to choose their current job instead of the next best alternative are shown in table VI-3. Each factor is classified as job related, compensa-

[23] David G. Brown, *The Mobile Professors*, American Council on Education, Washington, D.C., 1967.

tion, or environmental, and for purposes of this presentation further identified according to the general nature of its control—i.e., policy and management, financial strength and budgeting, gradual long-term development, and unalterable or outside institutional control.

Some words of caution before proceeding: Rarely are the factors influencing job choice given the same weight by different professors. Because the average rankings are for a hypothetical "typical" professor, the substantial differences among individuals cannot be ascertained. Brown, however, identifies some important differences in choice variable rankings among selected faculty groups.[24] For example, of special concern to professors who spend more time researching than teaching is the availability of adequate research facilities. To Ph.D. scholars, authors, academic scientists, and professors at large, prestigious institutions, the availability of research facilities is more important than any other single factor. Research facilities are of much less significance to teaching-oriented faculty (ranked 4th) and nonpublishing faculty (ranked 5th) at small institutions (ranked 7th) and at low-prestige institutions (ranked 7th). The competency of colleagues is of special concern to young professors (ranked 4th) and far more important to faculty choosing large institutions (ranked 3d) than to those choosing small institutions (ranked 8th). Professors attracted to small colleges are more conscious of the quality of the student body than those attracted to large institutions (ranked 3d versus 11th).

Knowledge of these types of differentials can be of considerable assistance to institutions hiring faculty members who fall predominately within one or more of the classification groups. Since 2-year institutions, for example, usually attract few research-oriented people, the pattern of ranking among job choice variables is substantially different than that of 4-year institutions.

Brown cautions that the validity of the "choice index" measure is subject to at least two sources of error. It is possible that those questioned may not know why they chose the job they did, or if they know, they may be unwilling to admit that they did not follow a rational or an "acceptable" pattern. In the case of some considerations, such as salary, the fact that small differences exist among institutions means that these factors will be less influential than might be the case if greater differences existed. It is also true that there are minimum characteristics for certain factors below which the job is unacceptable. In such cases, the factor in question becomes critical, in a negative sense, to the initial acception or rejection. For example, Brown points out that professors will not give a second thought to a job if they view the administrators as incompetent, misdirected, or improperly constrained.[25] At the beginning stages of the decisionmaking

---

[24] Ibid., table 66, pp. 153–55.
[25] Ibid., pp. 159, 162.

process, the primary determinant of job choice is the option for independence of action and academic freedom. If these minimal conditions are not met, the attitude and ability of administrators becomes the most important factor in job choice. Once job options are narrowed to the *two best*, the decision to accept one and reject the other is usually based on the variables in the order of importance shown in table VI-3.

Of the top nine variables upon which the typical professor bases his decision, the emerging pattern indicates that seven are job related and not associated with compensation or environmental factors. In addition, five of the top six determinants are subject to relatively immediate institutional improvement through either better management or budgeting. Except for cultural opportunities, the five variables that are generally unalterable or primarily outside of institutional control are the least important determinants. It is encouraging to note that, overall, the evidence indicates the importance of those job related and compensation factors that *can be strengthened* by the institution and that lesser importance is placed on those choice variables over which the institution can exert little if any control.

Choice variables subject to institutional policy and management. It is fortunate for institutions that the two strongest influences on professors choosing a job—courses to be taught and required teaching load—are the ones to which an institution can most readily respond. Because professors seek teaching responsibilities consistent with their professional interests and abilities, it follows that their preference will be in three areas: (1) graduate level courses, (2) courses within individual areas of interest, and (3) assignments that are neither dissimilar nor unrelated. Such preferences are most easily accommodated by universities with large and diversified curriculums; small colleges usually find it difficult to expand course offerings solely to attract the faculty they want.

Professors also want "reasonable" teaching loads so as to have substantial time for discretionary use. The range in teaching loads varies greatly. In 1963 a national survey of faculty members showed that 11 percent of persons engaged primarily in teaching taught 5 or less credit hours; 36 percent taught 6 to 10 hours; 43 percent taught 11 to 15 hours; and 8 percent taught 16 to 20 hours.[26] These statistics suggest that institutions requiring a teaching load of more than 15 credit hours are in poor position to attract faculty.

Three other variables subject to improvement through policy and management are administration, congeniality of colleagues, and academic

---

[26] Ralph E. Dunham, Patricia S. Wright, and Marjorie O. Chandler, *Teaching Faculty in Universities and Four-Year Colleges, Spring 1963*, U. S. Department of Health, Education, and Welfare, Office of Education, U.S. Government Printing Office, Washington, D.C., 1966, p. 115.

rank—ranked 9th, 11th, and 12th, respectively. These determinants are, if considered collectively (in one academic department, for example), likely to create an attraction or cause a repellent greater than if considered individually. For a young person considering a professional career, the integrity and competence of the administration and the friendship and support of coworkers are especially important. Equally inviting would be an initial offer of an assistant professorship rather than the lower rank of instructor. The best universities can, of course, maintain strict standards in awarding academic rank, but less prestigious colleges, to be competitive, may have to resort on occasion to offering senior rank to applicants less than fully qualified.

Choice variables subject to financial strength and budgeting. Research facilities, salary, salary prospects, and fringe benefits are all primarily dependent on the wealth of the institution and on the priority given to each in the budget. Except for research facilities—essential to the dedicated scholar, author, and scientist—these factors are not the most important elements in job choice. Overall, salary, salary prospects, and fringe benefits rank 5th, 6th, and 13th, respectively. Evidence gathered by Brown[27] and others supports the theory that salary is an important factor up to a point, beyond which the increment changes in net advantage tend to be relatively small. Salary differentials of the magnitude typical in the current market rarely influence job choice decisions.

Conversely, certain financial considerations that can be arranged may add the precise inducement necessary to attract a hard-to-recruit faculty member who seeks something special. One fringe benefit that contributes significantly to the satisfaction of faculty members is the research leave or sabbatical. Another is free tuition for faculty children. Still others include the option of renting a university-owned house, reimbursement for moving expenses, quality teaching-research assistance, special secretarial help, a family medical and hospital insurance plan, use of campus athletic and recreational facilities, reserved oncampus parking, a retirement plan, a travel expense account, and a well-appointed faculty club. While fringe benefits are unlikely by themselves to secure faculty, as reinforcing agents they may strengthen the overall attractiveness of the job.

Choice variables requiring long-term development. The three variables requiring long-term development—competency of colleagues, reputation of school, and quality of students—are closely related; whether considered separately or in concert, they appear to serve as a strong magnet in attracting faculty. There is little an institution can do to "manage" these factors other than to foster their gradual improvement. A single department can be strength-

---

[27] Brown, op. cit., p. 157.

ened somewhat more rapidly by implementing a more selective admission policy, establishing endowed chairs, hiring illustrious "names," obtaining large research contracts, etc.

Unalterable or externally controlled factors. Those variables over which an institution can exert the least control rarely are the determinant factors in job choice. Such factors as climate and proximity to friends and relatives are clearly unalterable, as are, to a large extent, cultural and graduate school opportunities outside the institution. With the exception of cultural opportunities, these variables, together with moonlighting opportunities, crowd the bottom of the list. However, if job seekers view all environmental aspects as a single composite factor, the aggregate influence of location will be more significant in job choice than otherwise indicated.

DOCTORAL-LEVEL GRADUATE PROGRAMS

Part of the gigantic growth pattern of higher education today is not only that more youths begin college but that they stay longer. For more than a decade the rate of growth in graduate enrollment has exceeded that of undergraduate enrollment (9.4 percent annually compared to 8 percent during 1962–1972). While overall growth is expected to decline, graduate enrollments will continue to grow at a faster rate than undergraduate enrollments. Further, there has been a decided shift in enrollment to the public education sector. In 1956 slightly more than one-half of all graduate students were enrolled in private institutions. A decade later this percentage had fallen to 40 percent; 60 percent were enrolled in public institutions. By 1976 it is expected that nearly 75 percent of all graduate students will attend public colleges and universities. Thus graduate enrollment in the public sector increased 300 percent during the 1956–67 decade (from 133,000 students in 1956 to 411,000 in 1966) and is expected to increase another 240 percent (to 986,000) by 1976. The corresponding growth of undergraduates in both public and private institutions from 1966 to 1976 is expected to be 180 percent.[28]

The number of master's degrees awarded outnumbers doctorates (excluding first-professional degree) approximately 8 to 1. Still, the most distinctive element in graduate education is doctoral-level work. Part of its distinction is that it primarily involves research. In addition, it brings to a

---

[28] *Source*: Kenneth A. Simon and Martin M. Frankel, *Projections of Educational Statistics 1980–81*, U.S. Department of Health, Education, and Welfare, Office of Education, U.S. Government Printing Office, Washington, D.C., 1972, pp. 36–37.

campus a community of outstanding scholars, thereby enhancing the intellectual atmosphere of the entire institution. For these reasons and because of a general need to restrict doctoral-granting authority to a relatively few institutions of recognized high quality, the focus in this section will be on doctoral-level graduate education.[29]

Although the expansion of graduate enrollment is almost universal, the geographical distribution is far from even; moreover, serious deficiencies in graduate education opportunities exist in some States. According to statistics on doctoral productivity in each State (see table VI-4), 26 States produce fewer than the national average of 10.2 doctor's degrees granted by public institutions per 100,000 population and fewer than the 15.8 granted by all institutions. Six States plus the District of Columbia are deficient in the number of doctoral degrees awarded by public institutions but meet or surpass the overall national average because of the presence of highly productive private institutions. For this group, the deficiencies in the public sector may be a truer measure of State graduate needs than is indicated by the combination of both sectors, since private institutions often serve the Nation as much as they do the State in which they are located. Although the private sector in another group of three States (Nebraska, Delaware, and Montana) is below average, the public institutions are not; they produce more doctorates per resident population than the national average. The 15 States in Group A are in the most advantageous position: the productivity at both the public institutions and at all institutions exceeds the national averages.

In view of the rapid growth in graduate enrollments, the recent evidence of a national overproduction of doctorates, and the lack of graduate opportunities in some States, there is clearly a need for more effective State planning and control. Without some control or a master plan, unrestricted multiplication of doctoral programs can lead to overproduction and to an eroding of competition that lessens the quality of both faculty and students. To avoid such consequences, most States carefully appraise the qualifications of institutions seeking approval to grant doctorates and evaluate such requests on the basis of the ongoing overall program of graduate education within the State.

Such a policy was responsible, in part, for the fact that only 40 institutions were added to the 142 permitted to grant the doctoral degree between 1958 and 1968. Despite this modest increase, the accelerated rate at which doctoral programs are being expanded at these institutions and at smaller ones has increased their share of the total U.S. doctoral production. Between 1961 and 1970, small institutions (annually awarding fewer than 100

---

[29] Excluded are doctoral programs in such professional schools as seminaries and medical and law schools.

Table VI-4.—Doctoral productivity, by State and by control of institution: 1970–71

State	Doctor's degrees per 100,000 population		Public institutions surplus (+) or deficit (−) in doctor's degrees conferred compared to national average	Doctor's degrees conferred		
	Public institutions	All institutions		Public institutions	Private institutions	All institutions
United States	10.2	15.8	—	20,788	11,319	32,107

A. States in which doctoral productivity at public institutions and at all institutions is greater than the national average:

State	Public institutions	All institutions	Surplus/deficit	Public institutions	Private institutions	All institutions
Michigan	20.0	20.2	+870	1,777	16	1,793
Indiana	23.1	26.1	+668	1,199	156	1,355
Wisconsin	20.7	21.7	+463	915	45	960
Iowa	24.8	24.9	+411	700	2	702
Colorado	25.2	29.7	+331	557	99	656
Oregon	22.3	23.6	+253	467	27	494
Washington	16.8	16.8	+225	574	—	574
Minnesota	16.1	16.1	+224	613	—	613
Arizona	22.0	22.0	+215	396	—	396
Utah	29.9	37.2	+209	317	77	394
Oklahoma	17.2	18.3	+180	442	25	467
Kansas	17.2	17.2	+151	387	—	387
New Mexico	17.9	17.9	+78	182	—	182
North Dakota	19.1	19.1	+55	118	—	118
Wyoming	26.5	26.5	+54	88	—	88

Table VI-4.—Doctoral productivity, by State and by control of institution: 1970–71—Continued

State	Doctor's degrees per 100,000 population		Public institutions surplus (+) or deficit (−) in doctor's degrees conferred compared to national average	Doctor's degrees conferred		
	Public institutions	All institutions		Public institutions	Private institutions	All institutions
B. States in which doctoral productivity at public institutions is greater than the national average, but at all institutions is below the national average:						
Nebraska	14.9	15.0	+70	222	1	223
Delaware	13.7	13.7	+19	75	—	75
Montana	11.0	11.0	+5	76	—	76
C. States in which doctoral productivity at public institutions is below the national average, but for all institutions is greater than the national average:						
Rhode Island	4.8	21.9	−52	45	162	207
Illinois	9.7	18.8	−58	1,079	1,007	2,086
District of Columbia	—	76.1	−77	—	576	576
California	9.7	16.8	−114	1,927	1,422	3,349
Connecticut	5.2	17.1	−152	158	361	519
Massachusetts	4.6	31.5	−319	263	1,528	1,791
New York	2.8	18.5	−1,353	512	2,858	3,370
D. States in which doctoral productivity at public institutions and all institutions is below the national average:						
Hawaii	9.9	9.9	−1	78	—	78
Mississippi	10.1	10.1	−1	225	—	225
Ohio	10.2	13.3	−4	1,085	334	1,419
South Dakota	7.8	7.8	−16	52	—	52
Idaho	8.0	8.0	−16	57	—	57

Alaska	4.0	4.0	−19	12	—	12
Vermont	5.4	6.3	−21	24	4	28
Nevada	3.9	3.9	−31	19	—	19
New Hampshire	4.1	7.3	−45	30	24	52
Maryland	8.6	14.1	−62	339	213	552
Maine	2.5	2.5	−76	25	—	25
West Virginia	5.8	5.8	−76	102	—	102
Florida	9.1	10.3	−77	618	84	702
Arkansas	6.0	6.0	−81	116	—	116
Texas	9.5	12.1	−82	1,063	295	1,358
Alabama	7.7	7.7	−87	265	—	265
Tennessee	7.8	12.3	−96	305	179	484
Georgia	8.0	9.9	−101	369	87	456
Virginia	7.9	8.0	−108	367	5	372
Missouri	7.7	13.8	−117	361	284	645
Louisiana	6.5	10.7	−134	238	153	391
South Carolina	4.7	4.8	−142	123	2	125
Kentucky	5.0	5.9	−169	160	30	190
North Carolina	9.8	14.2	−253	499	224	723
Pennsylvania	7.7	13.9	−298	908	728	1,636
New Jersey	3.3	7.7	−493	240	311	551

Source: Mary E. Hooper, Earned Degrees Conferred, 1970–71, U.S. Department of Health, Education, and Welfare, Office of Education, U.S. Government Printing Office, Washington, D.C., 1973.

Table VI-5.—Ten-year trend in doctoral productivity, by institutional capacity: 1960–70

Institutional capacity[1]	Number of institutions	Doctoral degrees conferred		Percent of all degrees conferred	
		1960–61	1969–70	1960–61	1969–70
200 or more	25	6,502	14,266	61.5%	47.8%
100–199	32	2,296	7,554	21.7	25.3
50–99	34	1,084	4,299	10.3	14.4
20–49	32	393	2,147	3.7	7.2
19 or less	150	297	1,607	2.8	5.4
Total	273	10,572	29,873	100.0	100.0

[1] Average annual number of doctoral degrees conferred during 10-year period.

Source: John L. Chase, *Doctor's Degrees Conferred by All U.S. Institutions: By State, Academic Field, Sex, and Institution, 1960–61 Through 1969–70*, U.S. Department of Health, Education, and Welfare, Office of Education, Washington, D.C., 1972. Such professional schools as seminaries and medical and law schools are excluded.

doctoral degrees) more than quadrupled their doctoral degree output (from 1,774 to 8,053), and their share of total doctoral production increased from 16.8 to 23 percent (see table VI-5).

Among the factors normally considered in appraising the qualifications of an institution seeking approval to grant doctorates are the following:[30]

1. The proposed program must be consistent with and in support of the objectives of the institution. In turn, the proposed program must be supported by the institution—by insuring quality at the undergraduate and master's level of instruction and by providing other doctoral programs in complementary fields of study.

2. The relationship of the proposed program to existing programs in other State institutions should be assessed. Unnecessary duplication must be avoided.

3. The need for a doctoral program in a particular field should be established in terms of society's need for persons with the qualifications represented by graduates of any proposed program.

4. No doctoral program should be initiated without strong prospects for growth and future excellence. The personnel at any institution beginning doctoral training not only should understand the long tradition of excellence associated with the degree but also should be aware of the responsibilities inherent in instruction at this level.

5. The institution should be prepared to provide and improve the

---

[30] A composite of the guidelines recommended in the State plans of Ohio and Oregon.

resources required for quality graduate programs. Of highest importance is a graduate faculty of scholars. The institution must be prepared to meet such graduate faculty needs as salaries, instructional load, research opportunities, sabbatical leave, etc. The institution should have, or be able to acquire within a reasonable length of time, the library, research facilities, and other necessary physical facilities and equipment required by a graduate program.

6. The institution should have adequate resources in the form of fellowship awards, assistantships, and loan funds to support graduate students.

The quantitative challenges which a State or region may face in graduate education can be easily measured. Less visible, although no less exacting, are the demands for quality that graduate programs impose on an institution. No other component of higher education requires greater leadership, organization, and resources than does graduate education. However real these elements are, an exact prescription of what constitutes the necessary ingredients for a quality graduate program has yet to be delineated. Of some assistance is an examination of the characteristics of institutions with quality graduate programs as opposed to those without quality programs. A profile of institutional characteristics producing high-quality graduate programs has been prepared by the National Science Board. Efforts to improve the quality of graduate education or to establish new graduate programs can be guided by NSB conclusions as to what constitutes high quality in graduate education.[31]

1. Quality is an attribute of the total institution, including the graduate division—not merely of one or more of its parts.

2. Although size will not insure high quality, high-quality graduate institutions are for the most part large institutions, high-quality academic departments are large departments, and high-quality graduate programs tend to be characterized by relatively large student-faculty ratios. Factors supporting the emphasis on size are the following: (a) high-quality graduate institutions have generally made a significant commitment to graduate education in terms of size relative to the undergraduate divisions; (b) high-quality graduate institutions have large funding resources for faculty, libraries, and research facilities; and (c) well-qualified students tend to seek admission to the highest quality institutions, thereby contributing to their quality and, at the same time, generating pressure for expansion.

3. The most critical resource of a graduate institution is its faculty, and within the faculty, the position of full professor is an important correlate of institutional quality. Not only do full professors numerically constitute

---

[31] National Science Board, *Graduate Education Parameters for Public Policy*, NSB, National Science Foundation, U.S. Government Printing Office, Washington, D.C., 1969, pp. 165–66.

the largest faculty rank in the highest quality institutions, but their financial compensation, in national competition, is a decisive factor in establishing and maintaining the quality of the institution.

SPONSORED RESEARCH

Research and development (R. & D.) in the United States is very big business. It is primarily sponsored and conducted by the Federal Government and private industry. Of the estimated $28 billion spent for R. & D. in 1972, 54.3 percent was funded by the Federal Government and 40.4 percent by industry. Industry, supported by its own and by Federal funds, performed 68.5 percent of all basic research, applied research, and development. The share performed by other sectors was as follows: Federal Government, 14.3 percent; colleges and universities, 10.9 percent; federally funded R. & D. centers associated with universities and colleges, 2.8 percent; and other nonprofit institutions, 3.5 percent.[32]

The Federal Government is also the primary source of funds for basic and applied research at U. S. colleges and universities.[33] Federal funds accounted for 79.2 percent of total R. & D. support in fiscal year 1971; the remainder was provided by State and local governments (6.3 percent) and nongovernment organizations (14.5 percent) (see table VI-6).

In 1971 the amount spent on research by colleges and universities was estimated at $1,865 million, which was slightly over $700,000 per institution, or $2,600 for every faculty member. R. & D. activity was not, however, evenly distributed. In fact, with the possible exception of endowment holdings, no aspect of higher education is more concentrated in a few very prestigious institutions than is sponsored research. The real heavyweights in college and university research are the handful of major institutions with unexcelled faculties and facilities—institutions at which research is an integral part of the academic program, inseparable from

---

[32] U. S. Department of Commerce, Bureau of the Census, *Statistical Abstract of the United States: 1972*, U. S. Government Printing Office, Washington, D. C., 1972, p. 521.

[33] Of the total of $3,480 million in Federal support to institutions of higher education for all purposes in fiscal year 1971, $1,544 million or 45 percent was used for research and development. The Federal agency sources of this R. & D. support were as follows: National Institutes of Health, HEW, 37.0 percent; Department of Defense, 15.6 percent; National Science Foundation, 14.0 percent; Department of Health, Education, and Welfare (exclusive of the National Institutes of Health), 8.1 percent; National Aeronautics and Space Administration, 8.3 percent; Atomic Energy Commission, 5.8 percent; Department of Agriculture, 5.3 percent; all other sources, 5.9 percent.

Source: National Science Foundation, *Federal Support to Universities, Colleges, and Selected Nonprofit Institutions, Fiscal Year 1971*, U.S. Government Printing Office, Washington, D.C., 1973, p. 47.

Table VI-6.—Revenues for sponsored research[1] at institutions of higher education, by type of institution: Fiscal year 1971

(Amounts in thousands of dollars)

Source	Universities	Other 4-Year	2-Year	Total
Federal Government	$1,313,344 (70.4%)	$161,501 (8.7%)	$1,662 (.1%)	$1,476,507 (79.2%)
State & local government	97,647 (5.2%)	20,351 (1.1%)	275 —	118,274 (6.3%)
Nongovernment	232,654 (12.5%)	37,447 (2.0%)	551 —	270,652 (14.5%)
Total	$1,643,645 (88.1%)	$219,299 (11.8%)	$2,489 (.1%)	$1,865,433 (100.0%)

[1] Exclusive of revenue for Federal Contract Research Centers and other service programs ($831,324,000) and other separately budgeted research ($161,345,000) for research bureaus, research institutes, agriculture and engineering experiment stations, etc.

Source: Paul F. Mertins and Norman J. Brandt, *Financial Statistics of Institutions of Higher Education: Current Funds Revenue and Expenditures 1970–71*, U.S. Department of Health, Education and Welfare, Office of Education, U.S. Government Printing Office, Washington, D.C., 1973.

scholarship. Twenty-six of these institutions in fiscal year 1971 received at least 1 percent of the $1,544 million in Federal funds allocated to colleges and universities for research and development. Collectively, these 26 universities accounted for 49 percent of all R. & D. Federal funding. The 100 top-ranking institutions received 86 percent of all R. & D. Federal funds and the top 200 received 98 percent.[34] Thus 200 institutions, 8 percent of the total of 2,606, received nearly all of the Federal dollars allocated to colleges and universities for research and development.

It is not difficult to recognize the circumstances that are responsible for and to a large extent justify the concentration of research at a few institutions. At present the number of persons qualified to carry on this highly specialized activity is limited. Such individuals naturally gravitate to institutions conducting outstanding research. Another reason is the fact that much Government-sponsored research requires the use of costly and not infrequently rare equipment and material. Atomic reactors, particle accelerators, and the like are some of the more expensive research tools which only a few large universities can afford to buy and operate. Finally, the repeated demonstration of research competence by large universities establishes their reputation and builds confidence among supporting agencies that perpetuate funding patterns.

Although the dominance of federally supported research at a few universities is widely recognized, State responsibility toward research should not be overlooked. Thirty-five States are represented by at least one public university on the list of the top 100 institutions receiving Federal research funds in 1971. Moreover, much research in the social sciences, humanities, and arts is performed, albeit on modest budgets, by many institutions in all States. The State's role should be to provide financial support that will extend research activities to a broader spectrum of institutions and also to encourage independent research and scholarship in areas serving State interests. In addition, the States should assist their principal public and private universities to obtain Federal support proportional to their research capabilities.

While there is no yardstick for measuring an institution's true capacity to perform research, the most obvious factor is personnel. The persons involved must be not only well qualified in their fields but also creative and industrious. A source of faculty *quality* ratings (to be used as an indicator of institutional capacity to perform research effectively) is Allan Cartter's *An Assessment of Quality in Graduate Education*, published in 1966 by the American Council on Education.[35] Cartter conducted a subjective survey among academic scholars as to the quality of the graduate faculty at 106 universi-

---

[34] Ibid., p. 60.

[35] An updated companion report by Roose and Andersen, *A Rating of Graduate Programs*, was published by the American Council on Education in 1970. (See bibliography at end of chapter.)

ties. Universities which averaged 10 doctorates a year during 1953–62 were included. One hundred or more judgments were obtained for most of the 29 fields of study surveyed. Departmental chairmen and senior and junior scholars were asked to describe the quality of the graduate faculty in their respective fields in the following subjective terms: "distinguished," "strong," "good," "adequate," "marginal," "not sufficient to provide acceptable doctoral training," and "insufficient information." While serious questions may be raised as to the validity of an opinion survey on faculty quality, the professional qualifications and knowledge possessed by the judges, their high degree of consensus, and the agreement between survey results and other indicators of institutional quality support the reliability of the findings.

The fields of study which received the largest amount of Federal research support are the life sciences (48 percent of total Federal R. & D. support), physical sciences (17 percent), and engineering (10 percent). In 1971 support in these three fields amounted to 82 percent of the total research funding for colleges and universities provided by the Department of Defense; 86 percent of that provided by the Department of Health, Education, and Welfare; 58 percent of the funds provided by the National Science Foundation; and 76 percent of the funds provided by the National Aeronautics and Space Administration.[36]

Cartter's study evaluated the graduate faculty of 17 academic disciplines in the biological and physical sciences and in engineering. From these ratings an index was computed to report the *average* score for the graduate faculty in 17 disciplines at 82 universities. If an institution had no department in a given discipline, a "marginal" rating of 1.50 was assigned, indicating a minimal capability to perform sponsored research. The relationship between this index and the average amount of Federal funds received for research and development during the 1964–66 period is shown in figure VI-3.

While the plot obviously indicates a positive correlation between the quality and number of graduate departments in the disciplines examined and the amount of Federal support received for research, a wide variance exists. The most heavily funded institutions received twice as much Federal support as the least funded institutions having the same index ratings. Thus, most institutions with an index score of 1.50 to 2 received Federal research funding ranging from $3 to $6 million; those scoring from 2 to 2.50 generally received from $6 to $13 million, and institutions scoring 2.70 and above received, in most instances, between $12 and $35 million.

This quality and number index of graduate departments provides only an *estimate* of each institution's *potential* for performing research in the disciplines involved. Even if this potential were precisely known, there are

---

[36] National Science Foundation, op. cit., p. 66.

Figure VI-3. — Relationship between the quality and number of science and engineering graduate departments at major universities and the amount of Federal support received for research and development: 1964-66

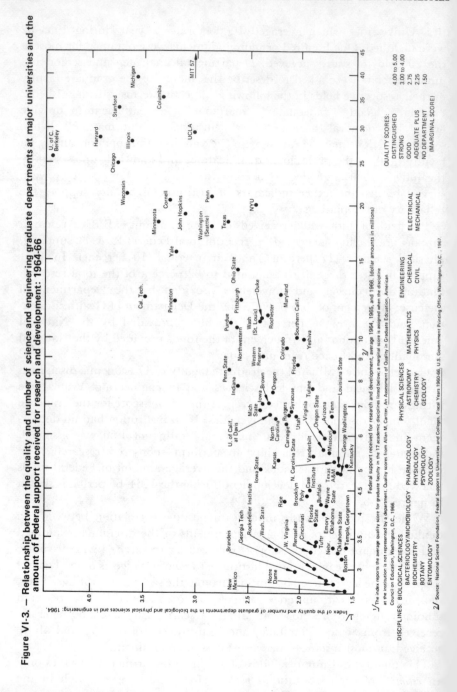

1/ The index reports the average quality score for graduate faculty in the 17 academic disciplines listed below; a marginal score is assigned when the discipline at the institution is not represented by a department. Quality scores from Allan M. Cartter, An Assessment of Quality in Graduate Education, American Council on Education, Washington, D.C., 1966.

Federal support received for research and development, average 1964, 1965, and 1966, (dollar amounts in millions)

DISCIPLINES:	BIOLOGICAL SCIENCES	PHYSICAL SCIENCES	ENGINEERING
	BACTERIOLOGY/MICROBIOLOGY	ASTRONOMY	ELECTRICIAL
	BIOCHEMISTRY	CHEMISTRY	MECHANICAL
	BOTANY	GEOLOGY	CHEMICAL
	ENTOMOLOGY	MATHEMATICS	CIVIL
	PHARMACOLOGY	PHYSICS	
	PHYSIOLOGY		
	PSYCHOLOGY		
	ZOOLOGY		

QUALITY SCORES:
DISTINGUISHED   4.00 to 5.00
STRONG   3.00 to 4.00
GOOD   2.75
ADEQUATE PLUS   2.25
NO DEPARTMENT   1.50
(MARGINAL SCORE)

Index of the quality and number of graduate departments in the biological and physical sciences and in engineering: 1964.

2/ Source: National Science Foundation, Federal Support to Universities and Colleges, Fiscal Years 1960-66, U.S. Government Printing Office, Washington, D.C., 1967.

a great many other factors which establish and govern the ability of an institution to effectively conduct sponsored research. Some universities are by choice less research oriented and more student or community oriented. If the faculty has a decided preference for basic research and independent study, for example, the institution may turn down restrictive service or development contracts even though they are well funded. Some institutions become entangled in long-term contractual commitments that extend their research activities beyond that initially visualized or desired. The geographical location of an institution often may have a strong bearing on its suitability as a research center or an institution may maintain and operate highly specialized equipment—factors which have little to do with the quality of the faculty. Finally, the index estimates research potential only in the biological and natural sciences and in engineering; research capabilities in the social sciences and humanities are not reported. It is also clear that research funding often is not proportional to the talent required. The merit of a project and the possible significance or impact of its outcome may prompt overly generous support. Staffing in both quantity and quality may exceed actual needs. Sums allotted for equipment and its operation, expendable supplies, administration, travel, and other overhead expenses may also result in total funding disproportionate to the talent required.

For comparison purposes, the influence of the aforementioned factors, to a degree, can be partially neutralized by careful selection of peer institutions. For example, if two large midwestern public universities with similar institutional purposes and goals receive disproportionate research funding in comparison with the relative quality and number of their respective graduate departments, such a discrepancy may warrant further investigation if for no other reason than to determine and perhaps justify the disparity. Determining the causes of discrepancies should be useful to those institutions that wish to attract more research funding.

By way of summary, sponsored research in higher education, while certainly big business, is not evenly distributed throughout the American higher education system. The top 200 institutions received a disproportionate 98 percent of the total $1,544 million in Federal funds allocated for R. &. D. in 1971; only $33 million went to the other 377 institutions receiving such funds. The remaining 2,029 colleges received no Federal money for research. Similarly, only about one-fourth of all college and university faculty members engage in separately budgeted research.[37] The

---

[37] Dunham, Wright, and Chandler, op. cit., p. 37.

According to 1969 ACE data, the teaching-research interests of faculty are as follows: .1 percent heavily interested in research; 19.8 percent interested in both teaching and research but more inclined toward research; 34.4 percent interested in both teaching and research but more inclined toward teaching; and 41.8 percent heavily interested in teaching. See Alan E. Bayer, *College and University Faculty: A Statistical Description*, ACE Research Reports, vol. 5, no. 5, American Council on Education, Washington, D. C., 1970, p. 15.

reasons for the concentration of money and talent are threefold: (1) the buyer's demand for research excellence—a relatively rare commodity; (2) the large proportion of research funds allotted to the natural sciences and engineering; and (3) the fact that only a few institutions can afford the unique and costly equipment required for the research. Whatever the reasons, the consequences of denying smaller institutions the stimulus provided by research are far reaching. The need to involve more institutions in funded research is clearly evident. State planning agencies are in an excellent position to assert a strong influence in this regard.

BIBLIOGRAPHY

Berelson, Bernard, *Graduate Education in the United States*, McGraw-Hill Book Co., New York, 1960, 346 pp.

Although some of the information in this first comprehensive study of graduate education in the United States is out of date, the book remains a basic beginning text. The report is organized into three sections: (1) past, (2) present and near future, and (3) conclusions, commentary, and recommendations. All aspects of graduate education are explored: institutions, organization, administration, programs, faculty, and students. The strength of the book lies in the author's clear perception of central issues and in his perceptive commentary. A full range of discerning questions are discussed: the balance between graduate education programs and other competing functions, the quality of students, the capacity of institutions to meet future enrollment demands, the academic quality of institutions, the problem of professionalization, the length of doctoral study, evaluation of graduate work, etc.

Brown, David G., *The Mobile Professors*, American Council on Education, Washington, D.C., 1967, 212 pp.

A principal reference on all aspects of the academic labor market, this book is based on information supplied by college presidents and on data collected from a nationwide sample of more than 13,000 college teachers in their 1st year with a new employer. Dr. Brown identifies, describes, and evaluates the current procedures by which college teaching jobs are found and filled. Important to both the college administrator and college teacher is the author's detailed discussion of the many decisionmaking factors involved in searching for and finding a job. Such factors as size, type, prestige, and location of the institution; economic and environmental aspects of the job itself; discrimination based on sex, religion, and race; and balkanization by submarket are all examined. Present job-search methods are explained and a wage-employment theory suggested. Dr. Brown makes 25 recommendations for more effective utilization of the academic labor market, including establishing both a journal listing academic vacancies and an academic register of available personnel.

Creager, John A., *The American Graduate Student: A Normative Description*, Office of Research, American Council on Education, Washington, D. C., 1971, 190 pp.

This study provides a wide variety of information on graduate students: their backgrounds, their current status and experiences, and their future expectations. The data are based on responses to 76 questionnaire items by 33,119 graduate students from 153 institutions. The survey information was weighted in order to obtain a normative description of the American graduate student according to sex, type and control of institution attending, department of graduate study, and five categories of the highest degree that the student expects to earn.

Heiss, Ann M., *Challenges to Graduate Schools*, Jossey-Bass, San Francisco, 1970, 328 pp.

This volume is the latest and most definitive examination of a multitude of issues that graduate schools face if they are to reform and revitalize their critical role in higher education. The author, in studying the strengths and weaknesses of the doctoral programs of some of the most outstanding graduate institutions, provides insight into the following basic problem areas (among others): purpose and nature of graduate study and its value to the individual and to society; goals and purposes of students who pursue graduate studies; organizational forms of graduate education; balance (or lack of it) in preparing teachers and in preparing researchers; doctoral program requirements; faculty characteristics; and cost of graduate education. While not all of the 29 recommendations in the final chapter are new, they are convincingly stated and ably supported by the author's investigation. It is a book of exceptional value to the graduate community.

Mayhew, Lewis B., *Graduate and Professional Education, 1980*, McGraw-Hill Book Co., New York, 1970, 38 pp.

This essay, written for the Carnegie Commission on Higher Education, is an impressionistic projection of graduate and professional education to the year 1980. Quantitative data of various sorts support the author's interpretation. According to the introduction, "What emerges is a picture of graduate and professional education in which enrollments, programs, costs, and hoped-for significance are expanding rapidly, but for the most part in orthodox ways and in response to pressures long operative in the American milieu."

National Science Foundation, *Federal Support to Universities, Colleges, and Selected Nonprofit Institutions, Fiscal Year 1971*, U.S. Government Printing Office, Washington, D.C., 1973, 122 pp.

This annual report includes current levels and trends in Federal funding of research, development, and other activities performed by universities and colleges. The information, given by geographic locality and institutions, is related to such other indicators as the distribution of science degrees awarded. Frequently cited in studies of research funding are this report's tables listing the 100 universities and colleges receiving the largest amount of Federal funds for research and development and for science-related activities. A special section deals with federally funded research and development centers administered by universities and colleges. Detailed tables in the appendixes list, by institution, total Federal support, funds for research and development, and obligations for R. & D. plant. Additional tables include geographic division, State, and funding agency.

Roose, Kenneth D. and Charles J. Andersen, *A Rating of Graduate Programs*, American Council on Education, Washington, D.C., 1970, 115 pp.

This companion volume to an earlier study by Allan Cartter, *An Assessment of Quality in Graduate Education* (1966), is an appraisal of graduate faculties and programs as reflected by the views of informed observers regarding their reputations. Thirty-six disciplines are considered. The peer groups making the judgments are scholars and departmental chairmen who were asked to evaluate their respective disciplines at 130 institutions that awarded 100 or more doctorates in the 1958–1967 decade. Ratings were requested based on (a) the quality of the graduate faculty, (b) the effectiveness of the doctoral program, and (c) an estimate of recent changes in the quality of graduate education. The quality of the faculty was rated in seven categories: distinguished, strong, good, adequate, marginal, not sufficient for doctoral training, and insufficient information. Numerical scores were assigned to each rating term, with the resulting average scores being used to determine rank and to classify institutions.

Chapter VII

MEETING AREA EDUCATIONAL PROGRAM AND CAPACITY NEEDS

Reduced to its simplest terms, the fundamental purpose of higher educa-tion planning at the State level is to provide information and recommenda-tions for the development of a total statewide system of postsecondary education that residents expect and society requires. This system and its programs are not generally viewed as complete until (1) institutions can enroll all persons able and willing to pursue college-level work, and (2) societal needs for trained workers are met.[1]

Some of the qualitative aspects of developing such a system—providing more educational opportunities, defining the differential functions of in-stitutions, and establishing guidelines for excellence—are discussed in pre-vious chapters. A model to assist in identifying the total reservoir of human talent that a system of higher education must eventually accommodate is presented in chapter IV. Attention is now directed to the quantitative means by which a State can accomplish such an objective. This chapter focuses on the number of persons who must be accommodated and the facilities needed to serve them. The needs of the economy and of society are considered in chapter VIII.

OVERVIEW

Every State should study continuously the kind, number, and size of public higher education institutions that will be needed to meet the needs of qualified students and at the same time make recommendations as to the general location of such institutions. In conducting the studies involved, three objectives are vital: (1) to provide within the State an enrollment

---

[1] In a democracy, the responsibility for manpower training is met when educational opportunities are readily available, on a free-choice basis, to qualified applicants in all occupations. Severe occupational shortages may justify temporary lowering of admission requirements and increasing financial aid to encourage enrollment in certain fields, but ultimately reliance must be placed on a labor market that adjusts to supply and demand.

capacity for anticipated student attendance in each area of recognized program need, (2) to encourage institutional development and growth consistent with assigned differential functions, and (3) to expand existing facilities and initiate new programs in such a way as to enhance geographical accessibility and effective program clustering. Insuring enough places—when and where needed—for every able and interested person and providing the kind of programs required involve a complex set of projections and analyses. Such complexity requires that the major pertinent studies be delineated first. Once the entire operation and sequence are explained, details can be filled in. The ensuing studies, somewhat simplified, constitute the major elements.[2]

State-level studies:

1. Review national and State trends and goals related to higher education to identify conditions and policies that will likely affect the direction and objectives of program and capacity planning. This review should result in a statement of intent and assumptions upon which projections and recommendations can be based.

2. Establish the general magnitude and progressive structure of State higher education enrollments by projecting statewide enrollments by level of instruction.

3. Study college student migration, the major objective being to predict the amount and direction of interstate college migration in order to ascertain its effect on State enrollments.

4. Convert State totals into enrollment projections by type and control of institution, by level of instruction, and by migration status.

5. Study the distribution of present and future high school graduates and their college attendance rates in the various counties and economic areas of the State. Such an analysis can provide the geographical data required for college expansion and new college location to be undertaken in response to local enrollment potentials and accessibility needs.

Area and institutional studies:

6. Project the enrollments of individual campuses, using differential area attendance rates. (If potential enrollments exceed current institutional capabilities, see the three options for accommodating additional enrollments in studies nos. 7 and 8.)

7. Study the following options for accommodating additional student enrollments: (a) redirecting students and (b) increasing the capability of existing institutions. The

---

[2] The studies and analyses proposed in this chapter have been developed from a review of procedures employed by State planning agencies as well as by individuals. The overall approach, however, is most closely patterned after that used by California in preparing the 1960–75 Master Plan for Higher Education. See *Institutional Capacities and Area Needs of California Public Higher Education, 1960–1975*, prepared for the Liaison Committee of the Regents of the University of California and the State Board of Education and for the Master Plan Survey Team by the Technical Committee on Institutional Capacities and Area Needs (Lloyd N. Morrisett, chairman), University of California, Berkeley, February 1961.

second option can be accomplished by extending instructional time, initiating year-round operation, increasing annual growth rate, or, if necessary, raising enrollment ceilings.

8. Identify the need for additional higher education centers. If existing campuses cannot accommodate enrollees or area educational needs are unmet, new institutions must be planned. Sparsely settled areas may be served by cable TV or radio, by extension classes, or by funding student commutation and board-and-room expenses.

The preceding eight studies are discussed individually in the ensuing sections of this chapter. Together they constitute the total frame-work within which a State can expect to meet the higher education program and capacity needs of its citizens. Perspective and overall direction can be achieved if this outline and sequence are kept in mind. Perspective can also be gained from the graphical summary in figure VII-1. It illustrates some

Figure VII-1. — Illustrative distribution patterns of State level enrollments in higher education

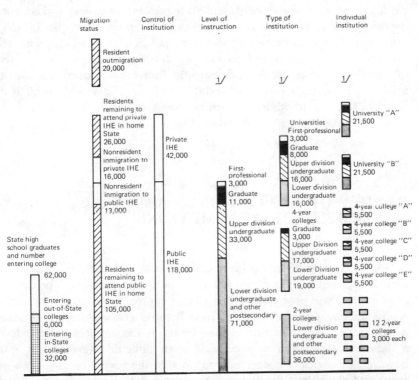

1/ Private sector not subdivided by level, type, or individual institution. IHE = institution of higher education.

of the various types of enrollment distribution patterns measured and projected in studies nos. 2, 3, and 4.

Projection Methodology

The methodology for projecting State enrollment *totals* is presented in appendix A. Special procedures to project enrollments for individual campuses, taking into account variations in area attendance rates, are discussed in a later section of this chapter. Even with the most exacting techniques, however, predicting college enrollments is a hazardous undertaking because of the number, variety, and uncertainty of the variables involved. Since it is impossible to foresee everything that will influence enrollment rates in the years ahead, the usual procedure is simply to make a projection based on a continuance of present trends, presuming that at some later point in the projection period a general leveling off of enrollment rates will occur as the potential maximum is approached. Those assumptions bearing directly on enrollment projection that should be spelled out include the following: expected rates of total State population growth and economic development; high school retention rates and geographic distribution of graduates; future anticipated admission policies, curriculums, and such other factors affecting enrollments as overall college entrance rates, patterns of student residence, attendance rates at individual institutions, and the ability of institutions to accommodate everyone who would enroll if any or all of these assumptions were to become fact.

REVIEW OF STATE GOALS AND STATEMENT OF ASSUMPTIONS

Goal-oriented direction is especially necessary to guide the planning of such fundamentals as institutional capacities and locations. The acid test of planning these program elements is, of course, the degree to which the results achieve the desired objectives. Because goals in higher education generally declare intent rather than establish specific achievement levels, a definitive evaluation of success is often difficult. Nevertheless, goals, however ideologically conceived, do provide the necessary direction, purpose, and sometimes the parameters required for systematic progressive planning.

Some commonly stated higher education goals relevant to education program planning are:[3]

1. To provide, insofar as practicable, equal and open educational opportunity beyond high school through (a) programs fulfilling all (qualified) persons' needs for economic and social self-sufficiency, (b) equalization of cost and geographical accessibility throughout the State, and (c) elimination of financial barriers.

2. To identify and encourage all capable youths to continue their education beyond high school, with opportunities not restricted by race, creed, or national origin.

3. To establish a system of post-high school education through graduate and professional levels that will meet State and national needs for trained manpower and higher educational services.

4. To foster continued growth in extent and quality of research and development by State colleges and universities to meet State and national requirements.

5. To contribute to the well-being of the community.

6. To foster diversity and flexibility among and within institutions, while observing the need for differential functions in order to avoid unnecessary duplication and to conserve resources.

7. To facilitate and encourage private colleges and universities to assume as large a share as feasible in meeting present and future higher educational needs. To foster an integrated system of public and private institutions with concomitant responsibility on the part of both sectors.

8. To maintain sufficient faculty, facilities, and budgetary support to meet the State's total higher education needs, both quantitative and qualitative.

9. To utilize fully and efficiently the available resources at privately and publicly controlled colleges and universities.

10. To give continuing emphasis and encouragement toward improving the quality and academic excellence of all instructional programs. To sustain academic freedom.

These objectives or themes are referred to not only in this chapter, but throughout the book as well. They represent the major principles which guide many States in the expansion and development of higher education. (Criteria and principles to be followed when determining the need for *additional* public institutions are presented in a later section of this chapter.)

Like many other variables affecting estimates of program needs, State educational goals, together with policies for their attainment, are subject to change. Thus assumptions must be made with regard to both anticipated changes and continuance of existing conditions. Unless there is clear evidence of changes in either intended goals or policy, it is generally assumed that declared positions governing State higher education will

---

[3] These statements incorporate in condensed form the higher education goals frequently found in State master plans and supporting documents. See, for example, *Goals for Higher Education in New Jersey*, *The Regents Statewide Plan for the Expansion and Development of Higher Education, 1964* (New York), and *The Role and Scope of Oklahoma Higher Education*.

remain unchanged. It is also generally assumed that the status quo will be maintained for variables whose future influence cannot be anticipated. Areas in which assumptions may be made include the economic conditions of the State and the Nation, the political and military situation of the country, college entrance rates, the role of private institutions, patterns by which individual institutions attract students, statewide capacity, and willingness to meet physical plant needs.

ESTIMATING THE PROGRESSIVE
LEVELS OF STATEWIDE ENROLLMENT

No single characteristic is more common to or more descriptive of educational systems than their progressive structure. As instruction gradually deepens and intensifies at successive academic levels, student attrition occurs; thus, at the doctoral and postdoctoral plateau only a relatively few outstanding scholars remain. In view of this fact, the best way to envision future higher educational program needs is to examine the progressive structure of student enrollments. Three basic questions should be asked: (1) In the foreseeable future, how many persons will there be in the State who can successfully *begin* an education beyond high school? (2) How does this total reservoir of human talent compare in size with the actual number of beginning resident students likely to enroll? and (3) What total enrollments, by level of instruction, can be expected as a result of the anticipated number of beginning students?

To answer these questions, the specific populations to be measured and projected (with emphasis on the public sector) are the following:

a. Resident 17-year-olds (separate counts by sex recommended for this population and for others)
b. State high school graduates
c. First-time enrollment of residents attending all colleges anywhere
d. First-time enrollment of residents who attend public institutions of higher education (IHE) in their home State
e. Total first-time student enrollment (fall) in State public IHE
f. Sophomore class enrollment (spring) in State public IHE
g. Junior class enrollment (fall) in State public IHE
h. Bachelor's degrees granted by State public IHE
i. Graduate enrollment in State public IHE
j. First-professional enrollment in State public IHE (students enrolled in a professional school or program that required at least 2 or more academic years of college work for entrance and a total of at least 6 years for a degree).

Using the aforementioned data, the retention rates shown below may be calculated and utilized in studying the progressive nature of a State's public educational system. Trends in these rates, as well as interstate and national comparisons, can be useful in that they suggest fundamental changes both in the composition of student enrollment and in the State's educational structure. Some data and retention measures of this type on a national level, appear in table VII-1.

High school graduation rate........   High school graduates as a percent of population age 17 (b/a)

Overall college entrance rate......   First-time enrollment of residents attending all colleges anywhere as a percent of high school graduates (c/b)

Retention rate of State public IHE........................   First-time enrollment of residents attending State public IHE as a percent of first-time enrollment of residents attending all colleges anywhere (d/c)

Lower division retention rate of State public IHE.............   Sophomore class enrollment (spring) as a percent of first-time enrollment (fall) (f/e)

Upper division retention rate of State public IHE.............   Bachelor's degrees granted as a percent of junior class enrollment (fall) (h/g)

Graduate enrollment rate of State public IHE....................   Graduate enrollment as a percent of bachelor's degrees (i/h)

First-professional enrollment rate of State public IHE............   First-professional enrollment as a percent of bachelor's degrees (j/h)

The ratios are largely self-explanatory. How their meaning can be interpreted is illustrated by consideration of a single measure—the overall college entrance rate. The precise number of people within a given population who have the ability and desire to benefit from some form of postsecondary education cannot be determined. Views on the subject vary widely, but estimates have been rising. Much of the actual increase in college entrance rates during past years can be attributed to the geographic and economic accessibility of community colleges. Because these colleges provide a bridge between high school and 4-year institutions, they serve as an enticement to youths who might not otherwise pursue postsecondary education. Another factor affecting the increase in college attendance is the broadly accepted proposition that a college degree is necessary to future success and security.

Table VII-1.—Progressive structure of enrollments and trends in retention rates in higher education: 1960–80

Characteristic	Fall 1960	Fall 1970	Percent change, 1960 to 1970	Fall 1980 projected	Percent change, 1970 to 1980
	Thousands			Thousands	
Population age 18 (nearest birthday).....	2,789	3,826	37	4,074	6
High school graduates...	1,971	3,036	54	3,340	10
Percent of 18-year-olds graduating from high school..............	69.6	77.2	—	83.7	—
Percent of high school graduates going on to college..............	51.6	62.3	—	72.3	—
First-time undergraduate degree-credit enrollment...............	923	1,775	92	2,427	37
Undergraduate degree-credit enrollment......	3,227	7,020	118	10,551	50
Non-degree-credit enrollment............	206	661	221	1,227	86
Bachelor's degrees awarded............	370	825	123	1,275	55
Bachelor's degrees as a percent of undergraduate degree-credit enrollment............	11.5	11.8	—	12.1	—
Master's degrees awarded............	81.7	224.0	174	395.9	77
Master's degrees as a percent of bachelor's degrees..............	22.1	27.2	—	31.0	—
Doctor's degrees awarded............	10.6	32.0	202	68.7	115
Doctor's degrees as a percent of master's degrees..............	12.9	14.3	—	17.4	—

Source: Kenneth A. Simon and Martin M. Frankel, *Projections of Educational Statistics to 1980–81*, U.S. Department of Health, Education, and Welfare, Office of Education, U.S. Government Printing Office, Washington, D.C., pp. 9–10.

How can a State interpret the college entrance rate of its own youth? An examination of the statistics in peer States will suggest potential enrollment possibilities. (The procedures to be followed are described in chapter II.) Certain States have been trailblazers as far as full utilization of their human educational potential is concerned. They are the ones that have transformed *mass* higher education into *universal* higher education. Trow has described the trend as follows: ". . . In the upper middle classes, and in states like California, the proportion of youngsters going on to some form of postsecondary education is already over 80 percent. For youngsters in those places and strata, universal higher education is here: nearly everybody they know goes on to college."[4] The high college-entrance rate in such instances is generally the result of (1) a high-quality elementary-secondary school system in which the majority is well prepared for college entrance, and (2) the presence of a network of low-tuition open-door community colleges. Based on statistics from Arizona, California, New York, Washington, and Wyoming, a 70- to 75-percent entrance rate for resident high school graduates attending all colleges anywhere appears to represent the maximum level currently obtainable. Any State, by comparing its own entrance rate with these indicators of college-going potential, can judge its own deficiencies, if any, in providing postsecondary schooling opportunities.

RESIDENCE AND MIGRATION
OF COLLEGE STUDENTS

The general attractiveness and accessibility of a State's colleges and universities are important in the retention of resident students; accessibility also plays a significant role in attracting nonresident students. These phenomena are subjects for study under the general heading, "Residence and Migration Analysis," a topic concerned with the effect of educational, economic, and demographic factors on student movement patterns. In concert, these factors determine the number of resident students in a given State who pursue their higher education in that State and the number who enroll elsewhere.

For too long the value of migration analysis has been clouded by seemingly endless definitions involving every conceivable component of student movement. Now, largely due to penetrating studies by sociologist Calvin Schmid and others, the essential ratios have been extracted and given the prominence they deserve. In this brief introduction, attention is focused on those migration indicators considered most significant in State-level planning.

---

[4] Martin Trow, "Reflections on the Transition from Mass to Universal Higher Education," *Daedalus*, Winter 1970.

Migration Components and Measures

Seven components are present in student migrations. Illustrated in figure VII-2, they are as follows:

    A. The total number of State-resident students who attend all colleges located any where. (A student is considered a resident of the State in which he maintains his permanent home.)
    B. The number of student residents who attend public institutions in their home State
    C. The number of student residents who attend private institutions in their home State
    D. The number of student residents who attend public institutions in other States
    E. The number of student residents who attend private institutions in other States
    F. The number of nonresident students who attend public institutions in the State
    G. The number of nonresident students who attend private institutions in the State.

To discount the effects of absolute size and thereby facilitate comparisons among populations of different sizes, "rates" are used to report the degree to which a given phenomenon occurs within a source population. A description of the more commonly employed rates and ratios[5] follows.

1. *Overall college-entrance rate:* First-time undergraduate residents of a State attending *all* colleges anywhere as a percent of State high school graduates (A/high school graduates). This rate indicates the extent to which high school graduates have been prepared for college and the accessibility and quality of postsecondary educational opportunities within the State, and, to a lesser extent, within the region and Nation.

2. *College-entrance rate within a State:* First-time undergraduate residents of the State attending public (private) institutions of higher education (IHE) in their home State as a percent of high school graduates (B or C/high school graduates). This rate indicates the relative role State institutions play in providing opportunities for residents to begin their postsecondary education within the State.

The following indexes are generally applied separately to categories of students classified according to institutional control (public or private), level of instruction (first-time undergraduates, undergraduates, graduates, and first-professional) and, in some instances, by type of institution (2-year college, 4-year college, and university). In the ensuing descriptions, the public sector will be used for illustrative purposes. All level-of-instruction and type-of-institution categories have been subsumed within the term "student" in order to eliminate needless repetition and allow for economy of presentation.

---

[5] As suggested by Calvin Schmid (see bibliography), the term *rate* will be applied whenever the measure involves the concept of a "source" or "risk" population; that is, when the population in the denominator is the source of the population in the numerator. If a source population is not involved, the term *ratio* will be used.

Figure VII-2. — Migration components and measures

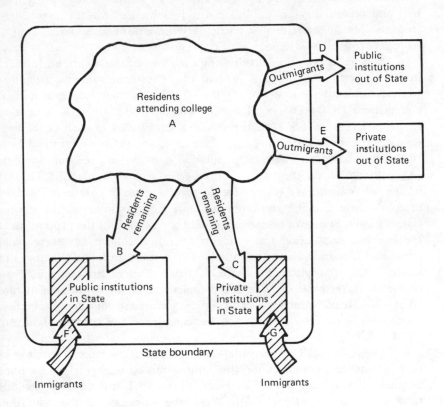

Residents attending college = Residents remaining + outmigrants
$$A = (B + C) + (D + E)$$

Overall college entrance rate   A/high school graduates

For the public sector:
    College entrance rate within State   B/high school graduates
    Retention rate   B/A
    Inmigration ratio   F/(B + F)
    Outmigration rate   D/(B + D)
    Net migration F-D   Gross migration F + D
    Efficiency ratio   (F-D)/(F + D)
    Enrollment resident ratio   (F + B)/(B + D)

3. *Retention rate:* Student residents remaining in their home State to attend (public) institutions as a percent of all resident students attending all colleges anywhere (B/A). This rate suggests the relative role (public) institutions in the State play in providing educational opportunities to State residents.

4. *Inmigration ratio:* Nonresident inmigration of students attending (public) institutions in State as a percent of total student enrollment in State

(public) institutions (F/B+F). This ratio suggests the relative attractiveness and accessibility of (public) institutions in the State to nonresident students. This measurement is particularly important to States seeking to increase or decrease attendence of nonresidents.

5. *Outmigration rate:* Students leaving their home State to attend (public) institutions out of State as a percent of all resident students attending (public) institutions anywhere (D/B+D). The outmigration rate and its complement (B/B+D) reveal less information than does the retention rate (B/A). The *relative* attractiveness and accessibility of each of the four enrollment choices open to residents are most accurately determined by a comparison based on a *common* population source—viz., resident students (A), rather than on the basis of two *different* sector populations, (B+D) for the public sector and (C+E) for the private sector populations. Furthermore, the true drawing and retention powers of public or private institutions within a State can be measured only on the basis of the proportion of the *total* risk population (all residents attending college anywhere) who enroll and remain in these institutions. The best indication of the power of public institutions within the State to attract resident students who have *already chosen the public sector* is the complement of the outmigration rate (B/B+D). (If both the public and private sectors are considered together, the outmigration rate (D+E)/A is the complement of the retention rate (B+C)/A.)

6. *Efficiency ratio:* The percentage of net migration (inmigrants minus outmigrants) to gross migration (inmigrants plus outmigrants)—a measure originally devised and labeled by Henry Shryock.[6] In the public sector this ratio would be (F−D)/(F+D). When the efficiency of the migration between two areas is high, the net migration between the two areas is strongly directional. States with high positive efficiency ratios attract many more students from out of State than they lose to other States. States with high negative efficiency ratios lose a large number of students to other States and attract few inmigrants.

7. *Enrollment-resident ratio*: Total enrollment (both residents and nonresidents) attending (public) institutions in the State as a percent of all resident students attending (public) institutions anywhere (F+B)/(B+D). This ratio indicates the number of students a particular State educates compared to the State's total number of student residents. Ratios larger than 100 indicate that the State is educating not only its own resident college students but also those from other parts of the country. Ratios of less than 100 indicate that the State is educating fewer than its share of the Nation's students in relation to its respective resident student population.

---

[6] Henry S. Shryock, Jr., "The Efficiency of Internal Migration in the United States," *Proceedings, International Union for the Scientific Study of Population*, Vienna, Austria, 1959 pp. 685–94.

Migration Analysis

Although there are many ways to illustrate the important aspects of migration, the following procedures are generally used to study its impact on individual States and on regions:

1. Make a total student head count to establish the absolute magnitude or frequency of any given migration phenomenon. (For the years 1963 and 1968, selected residence and migration data of college students by level of attendance are presented in tables D-1 and D-2 in appendix D.)

2. Use previously described rates and ratios to identify the degree to which given migration phenomena occur among "source" populations. Since such indexes are free from the effects of size, they may be compared with like data from different States or regions to determine relative standings and identify possible standards or benchmarks. The data may be presented in tabular form (see table VII-2) or graphically, either by geographical distribution (see figure VII-3) or as a frequency histogram (see figure VII-4).

3. Study the flow of students from one region to another or from State to State by graphically plotting migration "streams" that identify the direction, volume, and efficiency of student movement. (Five examples of the best graphics of this type, prepared by Calvin Schmid and others,[7] are shown in figures VII-5 to VII-9.)

4. Examine changes in migration patterns that have occurred over time to determine significant trends. This type of analysis is especially meaningful if the situation reveals rapid migration "gains" or "losses."

5. To determine the relative "attractiveness" of States to nonresident students, use a "migration matrix," originally devised by Schmid.[8] It controls, to some degree, distance and population size and summarizes net migration. (For examples, see tables VII-3 and VII-4.) A plus sign (+) indicates that the row State draws more migrants from the column State than it sends to the column State. Thus a plus sign signifies a positive net migration to the row State. The number of plus signs in each row is indicated by the figures on the right, or matrix scores. These numbers serve as relative measures of the attractiveness and accessibility of higher education institutions in each State and indicate, to a lesser extent, the possible absence of mobility among student residents in each State.

6. Use factor analysis to identify the social, economic, and demographic variables which underlie college student migration. The objective is to determine the educational and other characteristics in a State that attract

---

[7] Schmid, Calvin F., and others, *Migration of College and University Students in the United States*, University of Washington Press, Seattle, 1968.

[8] Ibid., p. 109.

college students, as well as the conditions which discourage resident attendance. The best work in this area has been performed by Schmid.[9] Factors he uses to measure the attractiveness of areas include the following: (1) emphasis on public education, de-emphasis on private education, (2) private institutions with limited enrollment, (3) limited public facilities in relation to a large college-age population, (4) high-ranking socioeconomic urban areas, and (5) limited private education in less populous States. Schmid also examines the "intervening" distance to ascertain the degree to which it deters interstate movement of college students. According to his findings, the majority of student migrants move relatively short distances; as the distance from home to college increases, the volume of migration declines, rapidly at first, then more slowly.

Schmid's work shows illustrations of the aforementioned analyses on a national scale. His separate related study conducted in Washington State is also recommended since it can serve as a guide for similar analyses in other States.

---

[9] Ibid., pp. 131–74.

Table VII-2.—Migration measures for resident and nonresident degree-credit students at State public and private institutions of higher education, by level of attendance: Fall 1963, 1968

State	Overall college entrance rate		College entrance rate within State			
	First-time undergraduate residents of State attending college anywhere as a percent of high school graduates col. (4)÷col. (17)		1st-time undergraduate residents remaining in home State to attend public or private IHE as a percent of high school graduates			
			Public inst. col. (1)÷col. (17)		Private inst. col. (18)÷col. (17)	
	1963 (Rank)	1968 (Rank)	1963 (Rank)	1968 (Rank)	1963 (Rank)	1968 (Rank)
	1	2	3	4	5	6
United States[1]	51% (22-25)	58% (23-24)	31% (24-25)	40% (21)	11% (14-20)	9% (12-15)
Alabama	32 (51)	47 (41-42)	19 (37-41)	35 (31-33)	7 (31-36)	6 (32-39)
Alaska	47 (28-33)	50 (35-36)	13 (48-49)	17 (51)	7 (31-36)	6 (32-39)
Arizona	61 (6-8)	88 (1)	52 (2)	79 (1)	0 (50-52)	1 (49-50)
Arkansas	47 (28-33)	54 (28-29)	29 (28)	38 (26-29)	11 (14-20)	8 (16-25)
California	80 (1)	75 (3)	71 (1)	66 (2)	6 (37-39)	5 (40-44)
Colorado	55 (14-15)	61 (19-20)	41 (9-11)	50 (7-8)	3 (46-47)	2 (47-48)
Connecticut	55 (14-15)	67 (8-9)	14 (48-49)	26 (41-42)	17 (5)	13 (4-6)
Delaware	45 (37-40)	48 (39-40)	19 (37-41)	23 (45)	4 (44-45)	8 (16-25)
Dist. of Columbia	61 (6-8)	81 (2)	7 (52)	38 (26-29)	24 (2)	10 (11)
Florida	61 (6-8)	65 (11)	41 (9-11)	49 (9-12)	6 (37-39)	6 (32-39)
Georgia	35 (48-49)	41 (48-49)	19 (37-41)	27 (40)	9 (23-27)	6 (32-39)
Hawaii	48 (27)	64 (12-15)	27 (31-32)	41 (18-20)	5 (40-43)	6 (32-39)
Idaho	62 (5)	62 (16-18)	36 (18)	38 (26-29)	11 (14-20)	12 (7-10)
Illinois	63 (3-4)	68 (7)	34 (20)	43 (15)	15 (6-7)	12 (7-10)
Indiana	44 (41)	46 (43-44)	28 (29-30)	32 (34-35)	9 (23-27)	8 (16-25)

Table VII-2.—Migration measures for resident and nonresident degree-credit students at State public and private institutions of higher education, by level of attendance: Fall 1963, 1968—Continued

State	Overall college entrance rate: First-time undergraduate residents of State attending college anywhere as a percent of high school graduates col. (4) ÷ col. (17)		College entrance rate within State: 1st-time undergraduate residents remaining in home State to attend public or private IHE as a percent of high school graduates			
			Public inst. col. (1) ÷ col. (17)		Private inst. col. (18) ÷ col. (17)	
	1963 (Rank)	1968 (Rank)	1963 (Rank)	1968 (Rank)	1963 (Rank)	1968 (Rank)
	1	2	3	4	5	6
Iowa	47 (28–33)	53 (30)	21 (35–36)	30 (38–39)	15 (6–7)	12 (7–10)
Kansas	54 (16–19)	64 (12–15)	39 (15)	49 (9–12)	7 (31–36)	8 (16–25)
Kentucky	47 (28–33)	49 (37–38)	28 (29–30)	35 (31–33)	12 (12–13)	8 (16–25)
Louisiana	46 (34–36)	49 (37–38)	37 (16–17)	42 (16–17)	5 (40–43)	3 (46)
Maine	31 (52)	34 (51–52)	16 (44–45)	19 (49)	5 (40–43)	5 (40–44)
Maryland	51 (22–25)	52 (31–32)	27 (31–32)	32 (34–35)	10 (21–22)	5 (40–44)
Massachusetts	56 (12–13)	66 (10)	15 (46–47)	24 (44)	27 (1)	28 (1)
Michigan	45 (37–40)	51 (33–34)	33 (21–22)	41 (18–20)	7 (31–36)	6 (32–39)
Minnesota	45 (37–40)	52 (31–32)	30 (26–27)	39 (22–25)	8 (28–30)	7 (26–31)
Mississippi	52 (21)	64 (12–15)	40 (12–14)	52 (5–6)	8 (28–30)	7 (26–31)
Missouri	50 (26)	56 (26)	31 (24–25)	41 (18–20)	9 (23–27)	7 (26–31)
Montana	60 (9)	58 (23–24)	40 (12–14)	44 (14)	7 (31–36)	4 (45)
Nebraska	54 (16–19)	59 (21–22)	37 (16–17)	42 (16–17)	9 (23–27)	7 (26–31)
Nevada	70 (2)	54 (28–29)	49 (3)	39 (22–25)	0 (50–52)	0 (51–52)
New Hampshire	39 (44–45)	45 (45)	17 (42–43)	21 (46–48)	4 (44–45)	8 (16–25)
New Jersey	53 (20)	59 (21–22)	15 (46–47)	21 (46–48)	12 (12–13)	9 (12–15)
New Mexico	47 (28–33)	50 (35–36)	32 (23)	37 (30)	2 (48–49)	2 (47–48)

	(5)			(4)	(3)
New York	47 (28–33)	71 (5)	16 (44–45)	39 (22–25)	18 (4)	17 (3)
North Carolina	36 (47)	41 (48–49)	19 (37–41)	25 (43)	13 (9–11)	12 (7–10)
North Dakota	51 (22–25)	62 (16–18)	40 (12–14)	52 (5–6)	2 (48–49)	1 (49–50)
Ohio	45 (37–40)	51 (33–34)	23 (33–34)	35 (31–33)	13 (9–11)	8 (16–25)
Oklahoma	54 (16–19)	62 (16–18)	41 (9–11)	49 (9–12)	7 (31–36)	8 (16–25)
Oregon	54 (16–19)	64 (12–15)	35 (19)	50 (7–8)	11 (14–20)	6 (32–39)
Pennsylvania	39 (44–45)	43 (46)	10 (51)	21 (46–48)	19 (3)	13 (4–6)
Rhode Island	46 (34–36)	67 (8–9)	17 (42–43)	30 (38–39)	14 (8)	19 (2)
South Carolina	34 (50)	39 (50)	14 (47–49)	18 (50)	13 (9–11)	13 (4–6)
South Dakota	51 (22–25)	55 (27)	33 (21–22)	39 (22–25)	9 (23–27)	8 (16–25)
Tennessee	42 (42)	46 (43–44)	23 (33–34)	31 (36–37)	11 (14–20)	9 (12–15)
Texas	57 (10–11)	61 (19–20)	42 (5–8)	49 (9–12)	11 (14–20)	8 (16–25)
Utah	56 (12–13)	57 (25)	42 (5–8)	45 (13)		9 (12–15)
Vermont	35 (48–49)	34 (51–52)	19 (37–41)	15 (52)	3 (46–47)	7 (26–31)
Virginia	46 (34–36)	47 (41–42)	21 (35–36)	26 (41–42)	10 (21–22)	7 (26–31)
Washington	57 (10–11)	73 (4)	42 (5–8)	62 (3)	8 (28–30)	5 (40–44)
West Virginia	38 (46)	42 (47)	42 (5–8)	31 (36–37)	6 (37–39)	6 (32–39)
Wisconsin	41 (43)	48 (39–40)	30 (26–27)	38 (26–29)	5 (40–43)	5 (40–44)
Wyoming	63 (3–4)	70 (6)	45 (4)	55 (4)	0 (50–52)	0 (51–52)

[1] United States total includes enrollments in armed services schools in the United States and outlying areas (Guam, Puerto Rico, and the Virgin Islands) not listed separately.

NOTE.—Data are from appendix D. Heading descriptions—e.g., col. (1) ÷ col. (4)—refer to columns identified in parenthesis in appendix D, tables D-1 and D-2. Letter descriptions are identified in figure VII-2.

Table VII-2.—Migration measures for resident and nonresident degree-credit students at State public and private institutions of higher education, by level of attendance: Fall 1963, 1968—Continued

State	FIRST-TIME UNDERGRADUATE STUDENTS			
	Retention rate of resident students		Inmigration ratio of nonresidents	
	Residents remaining in home State to attend public IHE as a percent of all residents attending all colleges anywhere B/A or (1)/(4)		Nonresident inmigration as a percent of total State public IHE 1st-time undergraduate enrollment F/(B+F) or (2)/(3)	
	1963 (Rank)	1968 (Rank)	1963 (Rank)	1968 (Rank)
	7	8	9	10
United States	60% (27)	68% (30–32)	10% (34–35)	8% (36–40)
Alabama	56 (30)	75 (16–20)	11 (32–33)	8 (36–40)
Alaska	29 (47–48)	37 (50–51)	18 (11–12)	13 (16–20)
Arizona	86 (2)	90 (1)	23 (7)	16 (10–12)
Arkansas	62 (25–26)	71 (25–26)	10 (34–35)	9 (32–35)
California	88 (1)	88 (2)	4 (48–49)	3 (50)
Colorado	75 (6–8)	82 (6–7)	22 (8)	19 (6)
Connecticut	25 (51)	39 (49)	8 (39–40)	8 (36–40)
Delaware	43 (43)	47 (43–44)	33 (3)	29 (2)
Dist. of Columbia	12 (52)	47 (43–44)	45 (1)	1 (52)
Florida	67 (20–21)	75 (16–20)	6 (44)	8 (36–40)
Georgia	54 (32–34)	68 (30–32)	15 (20)	13 (16–20)
Hawaii	55 (31)	63 (34)	13 (25–27)	9 (32–35)
Idaho	58 (29)	61 (36–37)	12 (28–31)	11 (24–28)
Illinois	53 (35–36)	64 (33)	2 (51)	2 (50–51)
Indiana	62 (25–26)	69 (28–29)	13 (25–27)	11 (24–28)
Iowa	45 (41–42)	56 (38)	14 (21–24)	10 (29–31)
Kansas	72 (13–14)	76 (15)	14 (21–24)	11 (24–28)
Kentucky	59 (28)	70 (27)	21 (9)	13 (16–20)
Louisiana	80 (3)	86 (34)	5 (45–47)	6 (42–45)
Maine	51 (39)	54 (41)	18 (11–12)	17 (8–9)
Maryland	52 (37–38)	62 (35)	9 (36–38)	11 (24–28)
Massachusetts	27 (49)	37 (50–51)	3 (50)	4 (48)
Michigan	74 (9–11)	81 (8)	9 (36–38)	6 (42–45)
Minnesota	67 (20–21)	74 (21–22)	5 (45–47)	5 (46–47)
Mississippi	77 (5)	82 (6–7)	11 (32–33)	8 (36–40)

Table VII-2.—Migration measures for resident and nonresident degree-credit students at State public and private institutions of higher education, by level of attendance: Fall 1963, 1968—Continued

State	FIRST-TIME UNDERGRADUATE STUDENTS			
	Retention rate of resident students		Inmigration ratio of nonresidents	
	Residents remaining in home State to attend public IHE as a percent of all residents attending all colleges anywhere B/A or (1)/(4)		Nonresident inmigration as a percent of total State public IHE 1st-time undergraduate enrollment F/(B+F) or (2)/(3)	
	1963 (Rank)	1968 (Rank)	1963 (Rank)	1968 (Rank)
	7	8	9	10
Missouri	63 (24)	73 (23)	12 (28–31)	12 (21–23)
Montana	68 (19)	75 (16–20)	9 (36–38)	11 (24–28)
Nebraska	69 (16–18)	75 (16–20)	5 (45–47)	10 (29–31)
Nevada	70 (15)	72 (24)	7 (41–43)	16 (10–11)
New Hampshire	45 (41–42)	46 (45–46)	31 (4)	22 (3)
New Jersey	29 (47–48)	34 (52)	4 (48–49)	7 (41)
New Mexico	69 (16–18)	75 (16–20)	25 (6)	16 (10–12)
New York	33 (46)	55 (39–40)	1 (52)	2 (50–51)
North Carolina	53 (35–36)	61 (36–37)	16 (16–19)	14 (14–15)
North Dakota	79 (4)	83 (5)	14 (21–24)	12 (21–23)
Ohio	52 (37–38)	69 (28–29)	12 (28–31)	9 (32–35)
Oklahoma	75 (6–8)	78 (14)	12 (28–31)	10 (29–31)
Oregon	64 (23)	79 (11–13)	13 (25–27)	9 (32–35)
Pennsylvania	26 (50)	48 (42)	7 (41–43)	5 (46–47)
Rhode Island	37 (45)	45 (47)	17 (13–15)	15 (13)
South Carolina	41 (44)	46 (45–46)	26 (5)	21 (4)
South Dakota	65 (22)	71 (25–26)	16 (16–19)	12 (21–23)
Tennessee	54 (32–34)	68 (30–32)	16 (16–19)	14 (14–15)
Texas	74 (9–11)	80 (9–10)	8 (39–40)	6 (42–45)
Utah	75 (6–8)	79 (11–13)	17 (13–15)	13 (16–20)
Vermont	54 (32–34)	43 (48)	40 (2)	40 (1)
Virginia	46 (40)	55 (39–40)	17 (13 15)	18 (7)
Washington	74 (9–11)	86 (3–4)	7 (41–43)	6 (42–45)
West Virginia	69 (16–18)	74 (21–22)	16 (16–19)	17 (8–9)
Wisconsin	73 (12)	80 (9–10)	14 (21–24)	13 (16–20)
Wyoming	72 (13–14)	79 (11–13)	20 (10)	20 (5)

Table VII-2.—Migration measures for resident and nonresident degree-credit students at State public and private institutions of higher education, by level of attendance: Fall 1963, 1968—Continued

State	UNDERGRADUATE STUDENTS			
	Retention rate of resident students		Inmigration ratio of nonresidents	
	Residents remaining in home State to attend public IHE as a percent of all residents attending all colleges anywhere B/A or (5)/(8)		Nonresident inmigration as a percent of total State public IHE undergraduate enrollment F/(B+F) or (6)/(7)	
	1963	1968	1963	1968
	11	12	13	14
United States	58% (30–31)	66% (31–32)	10% (40)	9% (38)
Alabama	60 (25–26)	75 (17–19)	13 (31–33)	10 (35–37)
Alaska	34 (47)	39 (48)	17 (13–16)	21 (5–7)
Arizona	88 (1)	89 (1)	19 (10)	17 (11–12)
Arkansas	62 (22–24)	69 (26–28)	11 (35–39)	11 (30–34)
California	85 (2)	87 (2)	4 (48–50)	4 (48–49)
Colorado	71 (13–14)	81 (4–6)	25 (5–6)	22 (4)
Connecticut	30 (49)	37 (49)	5 (46–47)	8 (39–41)
Delaware	43 (44)	50 (43)	32 (3–4)	29 (2)
Dist. of Columbia	21 (52)	29 (52)	42 (1–2)	2 (51–52)
Florida	62 (22–24)	71 (22–23)	6 (43–45)	7 (42–43)
Georgia	59 (27–29)	70 (24–25)	16 (17–24)	14 (18–21)
Hawaii	59 (27–29)	63 (33–34)	16 (17–24)	18 (8–10)
Idaho	55 (33–34)	62 (35)	15 (25–29)	13 (22–26)
Illinois	46 (39–40)	56 (36–37)	4 (48–50)	3 (50)
Indiana	60 (25–26)	67 (29–30)	15 (25–29)	13 (22–26)
Iowa	44 (42–43)	52 (40–41)	16 (17–24)	12 (27–29)
Kansas	72 (10–12)	77 (14)	14 (30)	13 (22–26)
Kentucky	59 (27–29)	67 (29–30)	20 (9)	18 (8–10)
Louisiana	78 (3)	83 (3)	5 (46–47)	6 (44–45)
Maine	54 (35–36)	55 (38)	16 (17–24)	15 (15–17)
Maryland	46 (39–40)	56 (36–37)	11 (35–39)	11 (30–34)
Massachusetts	23 (51)	34 (50)	3 (51)	4 (48–49)
Michigan	72 (10–12)	80 (7–10)	11 (35–39)	8 (39–41)
Minnesota	67 (18–21)	73 (20–21)	6 (43–45)	7 (42–43)
Mississippi	76 (5–6)	80 (7–10)	13 (31–33)	10 (35–37)

Table VII-2.—Migration measures for resident and nonresident degree-credit students at State public and private institutions of higher education, by level of attendance: Fall 1963, 1968—Continued

State	UNDERGRADUATE STUDENTS			
	Retention rate of resident students		Inmigration ratio of nonresidents	
	Residents remaining in home State to attend public IHE as a percent of all residents attending all colleges anywhere B/A or (5)/(8)		Nonresident inmigration as a percent of total State public IHE undergraduate enrollment F/(B+F) or (6)/(7)	
	1963	1968	1963	1968
	11	12	13	14
Missouri	57 (32)	70 (24–25)	15 (25–29)	13 (22–26)
Montana	69 (16)	75 (17–19)	15 (25–29)	12 (27–29)
Nebraska	67 (18–21)	73 (20–21)	17 (13–16)	11 (30–34)
Nevada	72 (10–12)	71 (22–23)	11 (35–39)	17 (11–12)
New Hampshire	45 (41)	45 (46)	32 (3–4)	25 (3)
New Jersey	32 (48)	32 (51)	4 (48–50)	5 (46–47)
New Mexico	73 (9)	79 (11)	23 (8)	14 (18–21)
New York	37 (46)	52 (40–41)	1 (52)	2 (51–52)
North Carolina	55 (33–34)	63 (33–34)	16 (17–24)	16 (13–14)
North Dakota	77 (4)	81 (4–6)	16 (17–24)	13 (22–26)
Ohio	54 (35–36)	66 (31–32)	11 (35–39)	11 (30–34)
Oklahoma	75 (7–8)	78 (12–13)	12 (3–4)	11 (30–34)
Oregon	67 (18–21)	80 (7–10)	15 (25–29)	10 (35–37)
Pennsylvania	26 (50)	47 (45)	7 (42)	5 (46–47)
Rhode Island	39 (45)	40 (47)	16 (17–24)	15 (15–17)
South Carolina	44 (42–43)	48 (44)	24 (7)	21 (5–7)
South Dakota	62 (22–24)	69 (26–28)	18 (11–12)	14 (18–21)
Tennessee	58 (30–31)	69 (26–28)	17 (13–16)	15 (15–17)
Texas	75 (7–8)	78 (12–13)	6 (43–45)	6 (44–45)
Utah	76 (5–6)	80 (7–10)	17 (13–16)	12 (27–29)
Vermont	49 (37–38)	51 (42)	42 (1–2)	33 (1)
Virginia	49 (37–38)	54 (39)	16 (17–24)	16 (13–14)
Washington	71 (13–14)	81 (4–6)	8 (41)	8 (39–41)
West Virginia	68 (17)	75 (17–19)	18 (11–12)	21 (5–7)
Wisconsin	67 (18–21)	76 (15–16)	13 (31–33)	14 (18–21)
Wyoming	70 (15)	76 (15–16)	25 (5–6)	18 (8–10)

Table VII-2.—Migration measures for resident and nonresident degree-credit students at State public and private institutions of higher education, by level of attendance: Fall 1963, 1968—Continued

State	GRADUATE STUDENTS			
	Retention rate of resident students		Immigration ratio of nonresidents	
	Residents remaining in home State to attend public IHE as a percent of all residents attending all colleges anywhere B/A or (9)/(12)		Nonresident inmigration as a percent of total State public IHE graduate enrollment F/(B+F) or (10)/(11)	
	1963	1968	1963	1968
	15	16	17	18
United States	47% (32)	53% (31)	25% (33)	24% (33–36)
Alabama	57 (20–21)	64 (20–21)	32 (22–23)	22 (38–41)
Alaska	25 (47–50)	16 (51)	31 (24–25)	55 (2)
Arizona	90 (1)	87 (1)	22 (41)	27 (29–30)
Arkansas	57 (20–21)	48 (38)	23 (37–40)	31 (21–24)
California	67 (7)	65 (16–19)	16 (46)	16 (44–46)
Colorado	50 (28–29)	67 (11–12)	46 (3)	39 (10–13)
Connecticut	28 (43–44)	45 (40–41)	12 (47)	14 (48)
Delaware	61 (13–16)	56 (27–28)	43 (7–9)	48 (3–5)
Dist. of Columbia	0 (52)	0 (52)	0 (52)	0 (52)
Florida	34 (39)	52 (32–35)	45 (4)	22 (38–41)
Georgia	43 (34)	57 (26)	35 (17–18)	31 (21–24)
Hawaii	71 (4–5)	83 (2)	43 (7–9)	27 (29–30)
Idaho	33 (40)	34 (47)	29 (27–28)	39 (10–13)
Illinois	44 (33)	44 (42)	27 (31)	28 (25–28)
Indiana	65 (8–9)	65 (16–19)	40 (12–13)	39 (10–13)
Iowa	42 (35)	51 (36)	62 (1)	48 (3–5)
Kansas	69 (6)	66 (13–15)	23 (37–40)	35 (18–19)
Kentucky	59 (18–19)	61 (23–24)	20 (42)	23 (37)
Louisiana	59 (18–19)	68 (7–10)	18 (44–45)	16 (44–46)
Maine	25 (47–50)	54 (30)	26 (32)	15 (47)
Maryland	26 (45–46)	38 (44–45)	42 (10)	31 (21–24)
Massachusetts	25 (47–50)	21 (49–50)	9 (49–50)	22 (38–41)
Michigan	81 (2)	82 (3)	19 (43)	22 (38–41)
Minnesota	63 (12)	63 (22)	44 (5–6)	40 (8–9)
Mississippi	54 (25)	61 (23–24)	24 (34–36)	28 (25–28)

Table VII-2.—Migration measures for resident and nonresident degree-credit students at State public and private institutions of higher education, by level of attendance: Fall 1963, 1968—Continued

State	GRADUATE STUDENTS			
	Retention rate of resident students		Inmigration ratio of nonresidents	
	Residents remaining in home State to attend public IHE as a percent of all residents attending all colleges anywhere B/A or (9)/(12)		Nonresident inmigration as a percent of total State public IHE graduate enrollment F/(B+F) or (10)/(11)	
	1963	1968	1963	1968
	15	16	17	18
Missouri	35 (37–38)	45 (40–41)	33 (20–21)	36 (15–17)
Montana	49 (30)	56 (27–28)	29 (27–28)	35 (18–19)
Nebraska	60 (17)	67 (11–12)	28 (29–30)	25 (31–32)
Nevada	55 (22–24)	70 (6)	31 (24–25)	24 (33–36)
New Hampshire	28 (43–44)	21 (49–50)	36 (16)	48 (3–5)
New Jersey	35 (37–38)	38 (44–45)	9 (49–50)	12 (49)
New Mexico	77 (3)	75 (5)	34 (19)	31 (21–24)
New York	29 (42)	33 (48)	3 (51)	7 (51)
North Carolina	65 (8–9)	68 (7–10)	41 (11)	39 (10–13)
North Dakota	51 (27)	52 (32–35)	37 (14–15)	46 (7)
Ohio	50 (28–29)	58 (25)	24 (34–36)	24 (33–36)
Oklahoma	71 (4–5)	64 (20–21)	28 (29–30)	28 (25–28)
Oregon	61 (13–16)	78 (4)	33 (20–21)	20 (42)
Pennsylvania	14 (51)	49 (37)	18 (44–45)	16 (44–46)
Rhode Island	26 (45–46)	66 (13–15)	24 (34–36)	11 (50)
South Carolina	55 (22–24)	55 (29)	23 (37–40)	33 (20)
South Dakota	38 (36)	52 (32–35)	40 (12–13)	40 (8–9)
Tennessee	61 (13–16)	68 (7–10)	23 (37–40)	24 (33–36)
Texas	64 (10–11)	68 (7–10)	11 (48)	18 (43)
Utah	64 (10–11)	65 (16–19)	30 (26)	28 (25–28)
Vermont	30 (41)	35 (46)	37 (14–15)	37 (14)
Virginia	25 (47–50)	43 (43)	35 (17–18)	25 (31–32)
Washington	52 (26)	52 (32–35)	44 (5–6)	47 (6)
West Virginia	61 (13–16)	65 (16–19)	32 (22–23)	36 (15–17)
Wisconsin	55 (22–24)	66 (13–15)	43 (7–9)	36 (15–17)
Wyoming	48 (31)	46 (39)	53 (2)	57 (1)

Table VII-2.—Migration measures for resident and nonresident degree-credit students at State public and private institutions of higher education, by level of attendance: Fall 1963, 1968—Continued

State	FIRST-PROFESSIONAL STUDENTS			
	Retention rate of resident students		Inmigration ratio of nonresidents	
	Residents remaining in home State to attend public IHE as a percent of all residents attending all colleges anywhere B/A or (13)/(16)		Nonresident inmigration as a percent of total State public IHE 1st-professional enrollment. F/(B+F) or (14)/(15)	
	1963	1968	1963	1968
	19	20	21	22
United States	32% (27–30)	35% (28–31)	17% (22–23)	18% (26)
Alabama	48 (13)	53 (11)	23 (16–17)	24 (16–19)
Alaska	0 (45–52)	0 (45–52)	0 (45–52)	0 (45–52)
Arizona	37 (23)	52 (12–14)	12 (32–33)	14 (32)
Arkansas	62 (2–3)	60 (6)	2 (44)	10 (38–40)
California	34 (26)	38 (22–24)	13 (28–31)	12 (33–34)
Colorado	36 (24–25)	36 (26–27)	40 (3–4)	32 (6–9)
Connecticut	26 (35–36)	22 (40)	13 (28–31)	11 (35–37)
Delaware	0 (45–52)	0 (45–52)	0 (45–52)	0 (45–52)
Dist. of Columbia	0 (45–52)	0 (45–52)	0 (45–52)	0 (45–52)
Florida	22 (37–38)	32 (32–33)	14 (25–27)	6 (41–42)
Georgia	46 (15–17)	35 (28–31)	18 (20–21)	12 (33–34)
Hawaii	5 (44)	0 (45–52)	38 (5)	0 (45–52)
Idaho	71 (1)	18 (42)	18 (20–21)	33 (5)
Illinois	22 (37–38)	26 (37–38)	3 (43)	5 (43–44)
Indiana	62 (2–3)	67 (3)	9 (36–37)	10 (38–40)
Iowa	52 (8–9)	56 (8–9)	24 (15)	24 (16–19)
Kansas	52 (8–9)	48 (15–16)	23 (16–17)	15 (28–31)
Kentucky	55 (6)	68 (2)	25 (11–14)	30 (10–11)
Louisiana	40 (21–22)	38 (22–24)	5 (40–42)	5 (43–44)
Maine	8 (43)	20 (41)	7 (38)	32 (6–9)
Maryland	31 (31)	31 (34)	25 (11–14)	21 (24)
Massachusetts	0 (45–52)	0 (45–52)	0 (45–52)	0 (45–52)
Michigan	53 (7)	62 (4–5)	26 (8–10)	23 (20)
Minnesota	46 (15–17)	47 (17)	17 (22–23)	15 (28–31)
Mississippi	26 (35–36)	48 (15–16)	14 (25–27)	10 (38–40)

Table VII-2.—Migration measures for resident and nonresident degree-credit students at State public and private institutions of higher education, by level of attendance: Fall 1963, 1968—Continued

State	FIRST-PROFESSIONAL STUDENTS							
	Retention rate of resident students				Inmigration ratio of nonresidents			
	Residents remaining in home State to attend public IHE as a percent of all residents attending all colleges anywhere B/A or (13)/(16)				Nonresident inmigration as a percent of total State public IHE 1st-professional enrollment. F/(B+F) or (14)/(15)			
	1963		1968		1963		1968	
	19		20		21		22	
Missouri	47	(14)	40	(21)	28	(7)	30	(10–11)
Montana	20	(40)	25	(39)	11	(34)	26	(13–15)
Nebraska	51	(10–11)	57	(7)	14	(25–27)	15	(28–31)
Nevada	0	(45–52)	0	(45–52)	0	(45–52)	0	(45–52)
New Hampshire	0	(45–52)	0	(45–52)	0	(45–52)	0	(45–52)
New Jersey	36	(24–25)	13	(43)	10	(35)	22	(21–23)
New Mexico	19	(41)	42	(19–20)	13	(28–31)	22	(21–23)
New York	10	(42)	12	(44)	6	(39)	6	(41–42)
North Carolina	32	(27–30)	36	(26–27)	13	(28–31)	20	(25)
North Dakota	41	(19–20)	32	(32–33)	19	(19)	32	(6–9)
Ohio	32	(27–30)	35	(28–31)	9	(36–37)	16	(27)
Oklahoma	41	(19–20)	35	(28–31)	16	(24)	27	(12)
Oregon	57	(5)	44	(18)	25	(11–14)	26	(13–15)
Pennsylvania	0	(45–52)	26	(37–38)	0	(45–52)	22	(21–23)
Rhode Island	0	(45–52)	0	(45–52)	0	(45–52)	0	(45–52)
South Carolina	40	(21–22)	56	(8–9)	5	(40–42)	11	(35–37)
South Dakota	29	(33–34)	29	(35)	36	(6)	36	(3)
Tennessee	60	(4)	52	(12–14)	25	(11–14)	32	(6–9)
Texas	50	(12)	54	(10)	5	(40–42)	11	(35–37)
Utah	46	(15–17)	52	(12–14)	26	(8–10)	24	(16–19)
Vermont	29	(33–34)	28	(36)	69	(1)	74	(1)
Virginia	32	(27–30)	42	(19–20)	52	(2)	40	(2)
Washington	42	(18)	38	(22–24)	26	(8–10)	26	(13–15)
West Virginia	51	(10–11)	62	(4–5)	22	(18)	24	(16–19)
Wisconsin	30	(32)	37	(25)	12	(32–33)	15	(28–31)
Wyoming	21	(39)	71	(1)	40	(3–4)	35	(4)

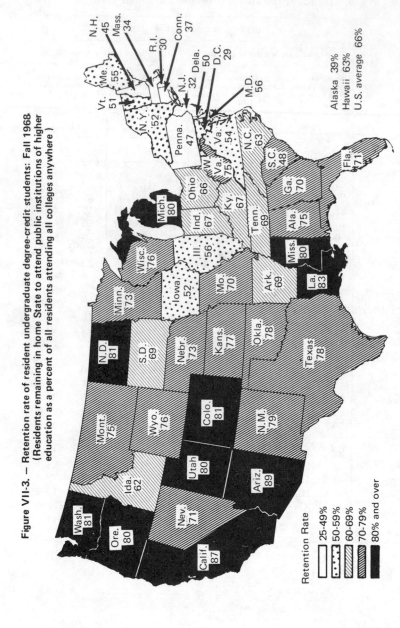

Figure VII-3. — Retention rate of resident undergraduate degree-credit students: Fall 1968
(Residents remaining in home State to attend public institutions of higher
education as a percent of all residents attending all colleges anywhere)

Retention Rate

25-49%
50-59%
60-69%
70-79%
80% and over

Alaska 39%
Hawaii 63%
U.S. average 66%

Source: George H. Wade, Residence and Migration of College Students, Fall 1968, Analytic Report, U.S. Department of Health, Education, and Welfare,
Office of Education, U.S. Government Printing Office, Washington, D.C., 1970.

Figure VII-4. — Distribution of States for selected migration measures: 1968

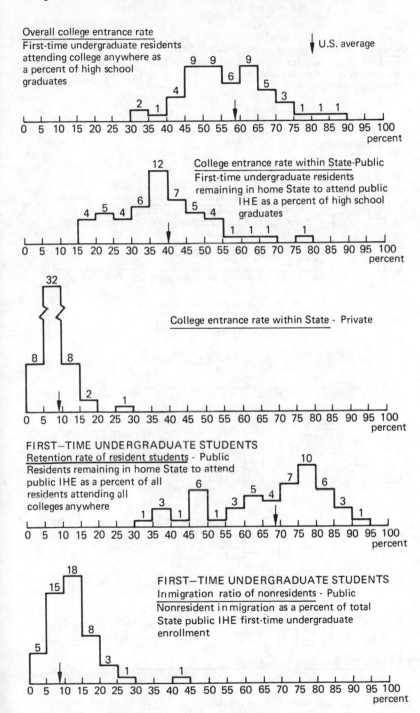

Figure VII-4. — Distribution of States for selected migration measures: 1968 — continued

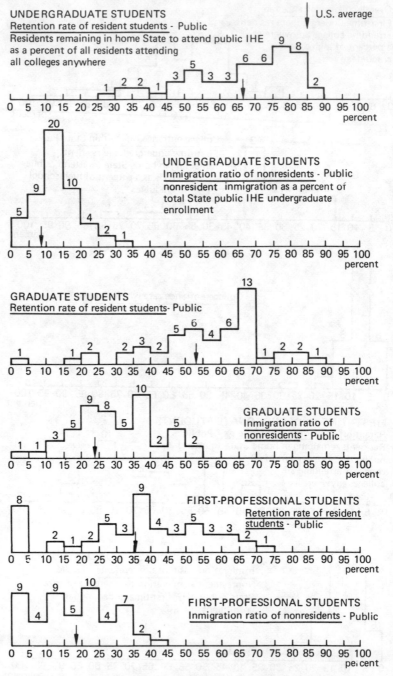

Source: George H. Wade, Residence and Migration of College Students, Fall 1968, Analytic Report, U.S. Department of Health, Education, and Welfare, Office of Education, U.S. Government Printing Office, Washington, D.C., 1970.

Figure VII-5. — Major streams of net migration, undergraduate students, public institutions: 1963

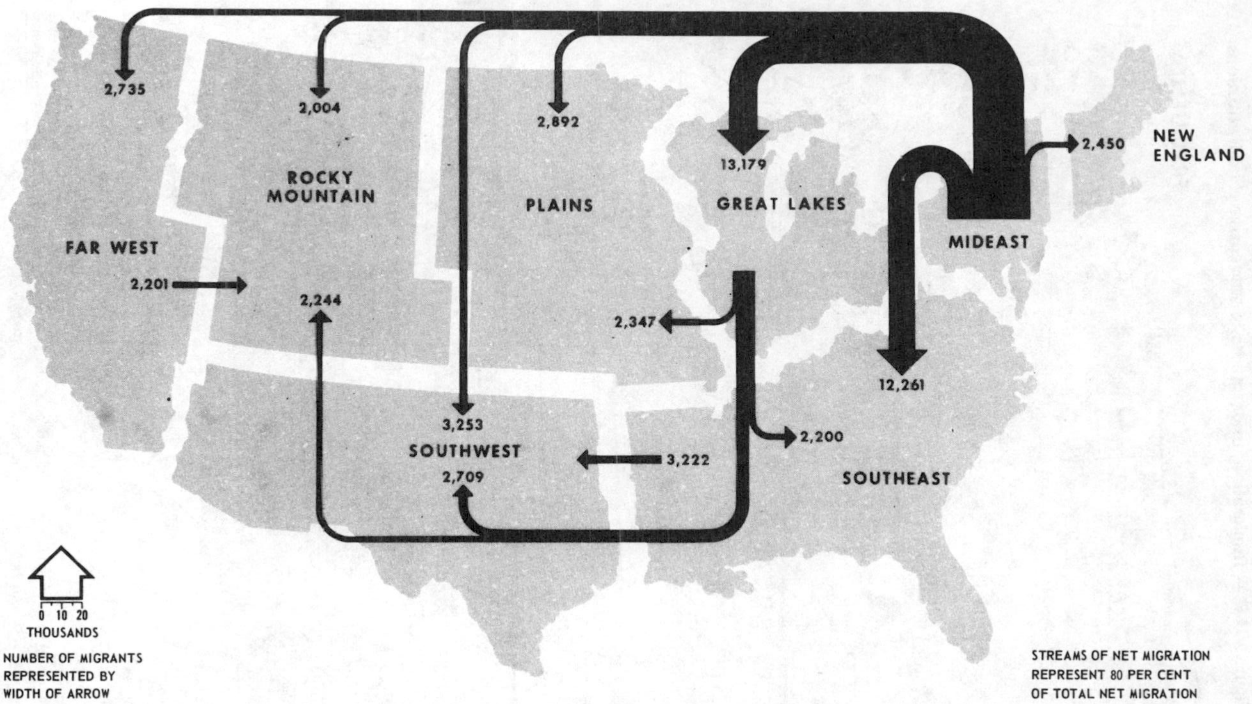

STREAMS OF NET MIGRATION
REPRESENT 80 PER CENT
OF TOTAL NET MIGRATION

NEW ENGLAND

2,450

MIDEAST

12,261

SOUTHEAST

13,179 GREAT LAKES

2,200

2,347

3,222

PLAINS

2,892

SOUTHWEST

3,253

2,709

ROCKY MOUNTAIN

2,004

2,244

FAR WEST

2,201

2,735

THOUSANDS
0 10 20

NUMBER OF MIGRANTS
REPRESENTED BY
WIDTH OF ARROW

Reproduced by permission from Calvin F. Schmid and others, Migration of College and University Students in the United States, University of Washington Press, Seattle, 1968, p. 43.

Figure VII-6. — Inmigration, undergraduate students, public institutions: 1963

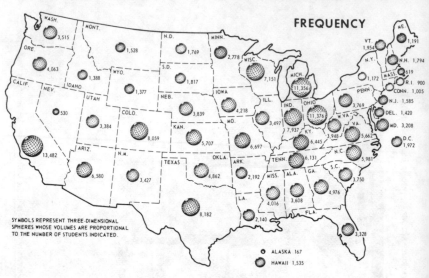

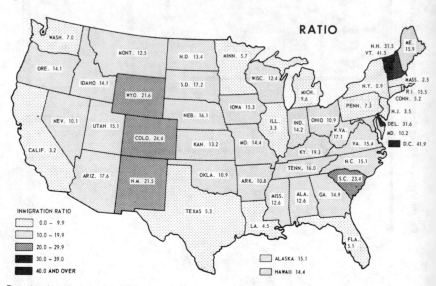

Reproduced by permission from Calvin F. Schmid and others, Migration of College and University Students in the United States, University of Washington Press, Seattle, 1968, p. 34

Figure VII-7. — Outmigration, undergraduate students, public institutions: 1963

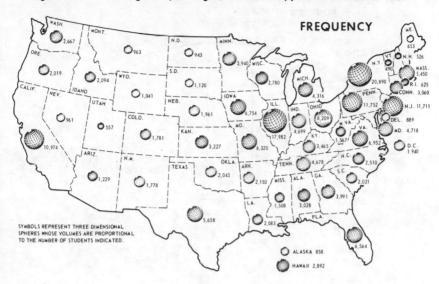

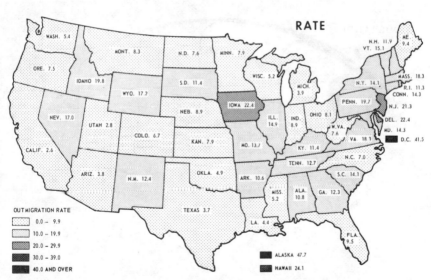

Reproduced by permission from Calvin F. Schmid and others, <u>Migration of College and University Students</u> <u>in the United States</u>, University of Washington Press, Seattle, 1968, p. 32.

Figure VII-8. — Migration streams, undergraduate students, public institutions, Washington: 1963

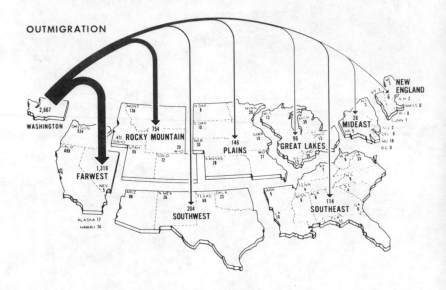

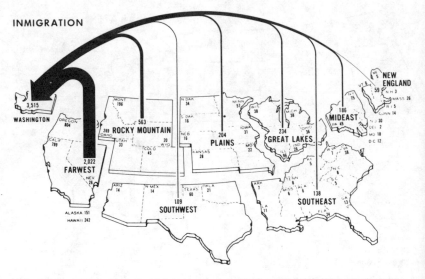

Reproduced by permission from Calvin F. Schmid and others, <u>Migration of College and University Students:</u>
<u>State of Washington,</u> Washington State Census Board, Seattle, 1967, p. 10.

Figure VII-9. — Migration efficiency, undergraduate students, public institutions: 1963

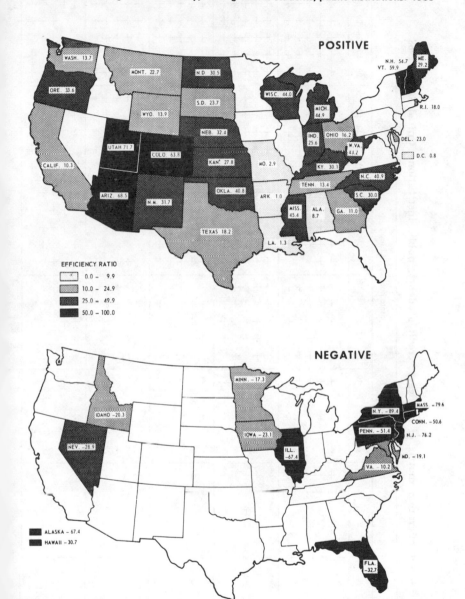

Reproduced by permission from Calvin F. Schmid and others, <u>Migration of College and University Students in the United States</u>, University of Washington Press, Seattle, 1968, p. 37.

Table VII-3.—Net migration matrix of all degree-credit students, public institutions: United States, 1968

State number (column)

No.	Name	1	2	3	4	5	6	7	8	9	10	11	12	13	14	15	16	17	18	19	20	21	22	23	24	25	26	27	28	29	30
1.	Arizona		+	+	+	+	+	+	+	+	+	+	+	+	+	+	+	+	+	+	+	+	+	+	+	+	+	+	+	+	+
2.	Colorado				+	+	+		+	+	+	+	+	+	+	+	+	+	+	+	+	+	+	+	+	+	+	+	+	+	+
3.	Washington				+	+		+		+	+	+	+	+	+	+	+	+	+		+	+	+	+	+	+	+	+	+	+	+
4.	Oklahoma					+	+	+	+	+	+	+			+	+		+	+	+	+	+	+	+		+	+	+	+	+	+
5.	Texas						+			+	+	+	+	+	+	+		+	+	+	+	+	+	+	+	+	+	+	+	+	+
6.	New Mexico		+		+	+			+	+	+	+	+	+	+	+	+	+	+	+	+	+	+	+	+	+	+	+	+	+	+
7.	Utah			+	+	+	+			+	+	+	+	+		+	+	+	+		+		+	+	+		+	+	+	+	+
8.	Indiana							+		+			+		+	+	+	+	+	+	+			+		+	+	+	+	+	+
9.	Kansas					+			+			+	+	+	+	+	+	+	+	+	+	+	+	+		+	+	+	+	+	+
10.	Wyoming									+			+		+		+	+		+	+	+	+	+		+	+	+	+	+	+
11.	Montana				+	+	+		+		+		+	+	+		+	+	+	+	+	+	+	+	+	+	+	+	+	+	+
12.	California				+			+				+			+		+		+	+	+		+	+	+	+	+	+	+	+	+
13.	Michigan						+		+		+					+	+	+	+		+	+			+	+	+	+	+	+	+
14.	Nebraska											+	+	+			+			+	+		+	+		+	+	+	+	+	+
15.	Oregon														+		+	+		+	+		+	+	+	+	+	+	+	+	+
16.	Hawaii					+	+	+					+		+	+		+	+	+	+	+	+		+	+	+	+	+	+	+
17.	Idaho														+		+			+	+			+		+			+	+	+
18.	Missouri						+		+					+		+	+	+								+		+	+	+	+
19.	N. Carolina																					+	+		+	+	+		+	+	+
20.	Iowa																+		+	+						+	+	+		+	+
21.	Kentucky	+							+							+	+			+	+				+			+			+
22.	Tennessee						+		+	+						+		+		+		+			+						+
23.	Wisconsin										+								+			+								+	
24.	Arkansas				+			+										+	+		+			+		+			+	+	
25.	Mississippi																		+		+						+	+	+	+	+

26. Louisiana
27. Georgia
28. Minnesota
29. Alabama
30. N. Dakota

31. S. Dakota
32. Nevada
33. S. Carolina
34. Florida
35. W. Virginia

36. Alaska
37. Ohio
38. Virginia
39. Illinois
40. Maryland

41. N. Hampshire
42. Vermont
43. Delaware
44. Maine
45. Rhode Island

46. Connecticut
47. Pennsylvania
48. Massachusetts
49. New Jersey
50. New York
51. D.C.

+ Indicates that the row State draws more migrants from the column State than it sends to the column State.

* Designates number of States in which immigrants exceed outmigrants.

Source: George H. Wade, *Residence and Migration of College Students, Fall 1968, Analytic Report,* U.S. Department of Health, Education, and Welfare, Office of Education, U.S. Government Printing Office, Washington, D.C., 1970.

Table VII-3.—Net migration matrix of all degree-credit students, public institutions: United States, 1968—Continued

State (row) No.	Name	31	32	33	34	35	36	37	38	39	40	41	42	43	44	45	46	47	48	49	50	51	Matrix scores*	Net migrants
1.	Arizona	+	+	+	+	+	+	+	+	+	+	+	+	+	+	+	+	+	+	+	+	+	50	+10,949
2.	Colorado	+	+	+	+	+	+	+	+	+	+	+	+	+	+	+	+	+	+	+	+	+	47	+14,797
3.	Washington	+	+	+	+	+	+	+	+	+	+	+	+	+	+	+	+	+	+	+	+	+	46	+6,719
4.	Oklahoma	+	+	+	+	+	+	+	+	+	+	+	+	+	+	+	+	+	+	+	+	+	43	+5,648
5.	Texas	+	+	+	+	+	+	+	+	+	+	+	+	+	+	+	+	+	+	+	+	+	43	+8,901
6.	New Mexico	+	+	+	+	+	+	+	+	+	+	+	+	+	+	+	+	+	+	+	+	+	42	+1,798
7.	Utah	+	+	+	+	+	+	+	+	+	+	+	+	+	+	+	+	+	+	+	+	+	42	+4,307
8.	Indiana	+	+	+	+	+	+	+	+	+	+	+	+	+	+	+	+	+	+	+	+	+	40	+12,215
9.	Kansas	+	+	+	+	+	+	+	+	+	+	+	+	+	+	+	+	+	+	+	+	+	40	+5,287
10.	Wyoming	+	+	+	+	+	+	+	+	+	+	+	+	+	+	+	+	+	+	+	+	+	39	+844
11.	Montana	+	+	+	+	+	+	+	+	+	+	+	+		+	+	+	+	+	+	+	+	38	+850
12.	California	+	+	+	+	+	+	+	+	+	+	+	+	+	+	+	+	+	+	+	+	+	37	+12,378
13.	Michigan	+	+	+	+	+	+	+	+	+	+	+	+	+	+	+	+	+	+	+	+	+	37	+17,029
14.	Nebraska	+	+	+	+	+	+	+	+	+	+	+	+	+	+	+	+	+	+	+	+	+	37	+1,732
15.	Oregon	+	+	+	+	+	+	+	+	+	+	+	+	+	+	+	+	+	+	+	+	+	33	+4,723
16.	Hawaii	+	+	+	+	+	+	+	+	+	+	+	+	+	+	+	+	+	+	+	+	+	32	+626
17.	Idaho	+	+	+	+	+	+	+	+	+	+	+	+	+	+	+	+	+	+	+	+	+	32	−365
18.	Missouri	+	+	+	+	+	+	+	+	+	+	+	+	+	+	+	+	+	+	+	+	+	31	+5,851
19.	N. Carolina	+	+	+	+	+	+	+	+	+	+	+	+	+	+	+	+	+	+	+	+	+	31	+9,292
20.	Iowa	+	+	+	+	+	+	+	+	+	+	+	+	+	+	+	+	+	+	+	+	+	30	−3,117
21.	Kentucky	+	+	+	+	+	+	+	+	+	+	+	+	+	+	+	+	+	+	+	+	+	30	+6,290
22.	Tennessee	+	+	+	+	+	+	+	+	+	+	+	+	+	+	+	+	+	+	+	+	+	30	+6,581
23.	Wisconsin	+	+	+	+	+	+	+	+	+	+	+	+	+	+	+	+	+	+	+	+	+	30	+13,880
24.	Arkansas	+	+	+	+	+	+	+	+	+	+	+	+	+	+	+	+	+	+	+	+	+	29	+45
25.	Mississippi	+	+	+	+	+	+	+	+	+	+	+	+	+	+	+	+	+	+	+	+	+	29	+2,692

State number (column)

No. & State	Net	N	I	II	III	IV	V
26. Louisiana	+1,900	27	++++	+++++	+++++	+++++	++++
27. Georgia	+4,189	26	+++++	+++++	+++++	+++++	+++
28. Minnesota	+1,241	26	+++++	+++++	+++++	+++++	+++ +
29. Alabama	+2,811	24	+++++	+++++	+++++	+++++	++
30. N. Dakota	+1,191	23	+++++	+++++	+++++	+++++	
31. S. Dakota	+868	22	+++++	+++++	+++++	++++	+
32. Nevada	−192	20	+++++	+++++	+++++	++	
33. S. Carolina	+1,748	20	+ +++	+++	+++	++ ++	
34. Florida	−3,125	16	+++++	+++++	++	+	
35. W. Virginia	+6,420	16	+++++	+++++	++++		
36. Alaska	−885	15	+++++	+++++	++	+++	
37. Ohio	+8,092	14	+++++	++++	+++ +		
38. Virginia	−1,183	14	+++++	+++ +	++		
39. Illinois	−23,193	12	+++++	+++++	+	+	
40. Maryland	+1,085	11	+ + +	++		+	
41. N. Hampshire	+1,176	11	++++	+++		+	
42. Vermont	+1,595	11	++++	+ +	+ + +		
43. Delaware	+1,346	8	+++++	++	+		
44. Maine	+330	7	+ +++	+			
45. Rhode Island	+209	6	++ ++		+		
46. Connecticut	−2,608	5					
47. Pennsylvania	−17,280	5					
48. Massachusetts	−7,967	3					
49. New Jersey	−27,002	1					
50. New York	−35,286	1					
51. D.C.	−3,838	0					

Table VII-4.—Net migration matrix of all degree-credit students, private institutions: United States, 1968

State (row)		State number (column)																													
No.	Name	1	2	3	4	5	6	7	8	9	10	11	12	13	14	15	16	17	18	19	20	21	22	23	24	25	26	27	28	29	30
1.	D.C.	+	+	+	+	+	+	+	+	+	+	+	+	+	+	+	+	+	+	+	+	+	+	+	+	+	+	+	+	+	+
2.	Utah			+	+	+	+	+	+	+	+	+	+	+	+	+	+	+	+	+		+	+	+	+	+	+	+	+	+	+
3.	Massachusetts			+	+	+	+	+	+	+	+	+			+	+	+		+	+	+	+	+	+	+	+	+	+	+	+	+
4.	Tennessee				+	+	+	+	+	+		+	+	+	+	+	+	+	+	+		+	+	+	+	+	+	+	+	+	+
5.	Missouri							+	+			+		+	+	+	+	+	+	+	+	+	+	+	+	+	+	+	+	+	+
6.	N. Carolina					+	+	+	+	+	+	+	+	+	+	+	+	+		+	+	+	+	+	+	+	+	+	+	+	+
7.	Indiana			+					+	+	+		+	+	+		+	+		+	+		+	+	+	+	+	+	+	+	+
8.	N. Hampshire			+	+	+			+		+	+	+	+	+	+	+			+		+	+	+	+	+	+	+	+	+	+
9.	Nebraska					+			+	+		+	+	+		+		+		+		+	+	+	+	+	+		+	+	+
10.	Louisiana													+	+	+				+			+	+	+	+	+	+	+	+	+
11.	Texas						+	+	+	+	+	+	+	+	+	+	+	+	+	+	+	+	+	+	+	+	+	+	+	+	+
12.	Colorado								+		+		+				+		+	+	+	+	+	+	+	+	+	+	+	+	+
13.	Iowa							+						+	+	+		+		+		+	+	+	+	+	+		+	+	+
14.	Oklahoma																		+			+	+	+	+	+	+	+	+	+	+
15.	Arkansas																						+			+	+	+	+	+	+
16.	Kansas	+	+	+		+		+		+	+	+	+	+	+		+	+	+	+	+	+			+	+	+	+	+	+	+
17.	Vermont												+	+			+				+		+		+	+			+	+	+
18.	Kentucky										+	+	+						+	+		+				+	+	+	+	+	+
19.	California											+		+	+										+	+		+	+		+
20.	Rhode Island																								+		+		+	+	+
21.	Idaho											+	+	+	+		+	+	+	+	+	+		+	+	+		+	+		+
22.	Wisconsin												+						+								+		+	+	
23.	Georgia													+		+					+		+				+		+	+	
24.	Minnesota												+			+			+				+				+		+	+	
25.	Florida															+							+			+	+		+	+	+

	26. Illinois 27. S. Dakota	28. Michigan 29. Ohio 30. Alabama	31. Oregon 32. Virginia 33. Montana 34. Washington 35. S. Carolina	36. New Mexico 37. Mississippi 38. New York 39. Pennsylvania 40. Connecticut	41. W. Virginia 42. Maine 43. Maryland 44. N. Dakota 45. Arizona	46. Hawaii 47. Delaware 48. New Jersey 49. Alaska 50. Nevada 51. Wyoming
			+++		+	
	+++ +	+		+		
	+ +		++	+ +	+	
	+	++ +	++ +	+		
	+	+		+		
		+	+ +	+		
	+			+	+	
	++ +	+	+++			
	++ +		+	+	+	
			+	+	++ +	
		+ +	+	+	+	
		+	+ +	+		
	++			+	+	
				+		
		+				
		+	++	+		
	+					
		+	+			
			+			
	+					

+ Indicates that the row State draws more migrants from the column State than it sends to the column State.

* Designates number of States in which inmigrants exceed outmigrants.

Source: George H. Wade, *Residence and Migration of College Students, Fall 1968, Analytic Report*, U.S. Department of Health, Education, and Welfare, Office of Education, U.S. Government Printing Office, Washington, D.C., 1970.

Table VII-4.—Net migration matrix of all degree-credit students, private institutions: United States, 1968—Continued

No.	Name	State number (column) 31	32	33	34	35	36	37	38	39	40	41	42	43	44	45	46	47	48	49	50	51	Matrix scores*	Net migrants
1.	D.C.	+	+++++	+++++	+++++	+++++	+++++	+++++	+++++	+++++	+++++	+++++	+++++	+++++	+++++	+++++	+++++	+++++	+++++	+++++	+++++	+	50	+41,331
2.	Utah					+++++	+++++	+++++	+++++	+++++	+++++	+++++	+++++	+++++	+++++	+++++	+++++	+++++	+++++	+++++	+++++	+	47	+13,679
3.	Massachusetts	+++++	+++++	+++++	+++++	+++++	+++++	+++++	+++++	+++++	+++++	+++++	+++++	+++++	+++++	+++++	+++++	+++++	+++++	+++++	+++++	+	46	+45,773
4.	Tennessee	++															+++++	+++++	+++++	+++++	+++++	+	45	+13,638
5.	Missouri	++	+++++	+++++	+++++	+++++	+++++	+++++	+++++	+++++	+++++	+++++	+++++	+++++	+++++	+++++	+++++	+++++	+++++	+++++	+++++	+	43	+11,281
6.	N. Carolina	+++++	+++++	+++++	+++++	+++++	++++	+++	+++++	+++++	+++++	+++++	+++++	+++++	+++++	+++++	+++++	+++++	+++++	+++++	+++++	+	43	+14,502
7.	Indiana	+++++	+++++	+++++	+++++	+++++		+									+++++	+++++	+++++	+++++	+++++	+	41	+14,586
8.	N. Hampshire	+++++															+++++	+++++	+++++	+++++	+++++	+	40	+3,574
9.	Nebraska	+++															+++++	+++++	+++++	+++++	+++++	+	39	+5,333
10.	Louisiana																+++++	+++++	+++++	+++++	+++++	+	38	+3,349
11.	Texas	+	+++++	+++++	+++++	+	+++++	+++	+++++	+++++	++	+++++	+++++	+++++	+++++	+++++	+++++	+++++	+++++	+++++	+++++	+	37	+4,759
12.	Colorado	+++	++			+++											+++++	+++++	+++++	+++++	+++++	+	35	+3,099
13.	Iowa	+++															+++++	+++++	+++++	+++++	+++++	+	35	+9,129
14.	Oklahoma	+++	+++++	+++++	+++++	++++	++++	+++	+++++	++	+++++	+	++++	+++++	+	+++++	+++++	+++++	+++++	+++++	++	+	35	+1,008
15.	Arkansas	+	+++++	++++	+++	+++	++++	++++	++++	+	+++++	++	+++	+++++	++	+++++	+++++	+++++	+++++	+++++	+	+	32	-4,674
16.	Kansas	+++	+++++	++	+++	++++	+					+	+++		+		+++++	+++++	++	+++++		++	32	+1,258
17.	Vermont		+++++				+++			++		++			++		+++++	+++++		+++++			32	+4,684
18.	Kentucky	+	+++++	++			+++	+++	+++++	+	+++++	++	+++	+++++	++	+++++	+++++	+++++	++	+++++	+	++	31	+2,754
19.	California		+++++														+++++	+++++	++	+++++	+	++	30	+938
20.	Rhode Island						+										+++++	+++++		+++++			29	+3,346
21.	Idaho	++	+++++		+++++	+++	+	++++	++++	+++++	+++	+++++	+++	+++++	++++	+++++	+++++	+++++	+++++	+++++	+++++	+	27	-1,488
22.	Wisconsin	+	+++++	+	+++++		+++				+		+				+++++	+++++	++	+++++		+	27	+3,065
23.	Georgia																+++++	+++++		+++++			26	+1,738
24.	Minnesota																+++++	+++++		+++++			25	+2,846
25.	Florida										+						+++++	+++++		+++++		+	24	-516

No.	State	Net	Rank	Pattern
26.	Illinos	−8,558	24	++++ ++++ + ++ +++ +
27.	S. Dakota	+874	24	++++ ++++ +++++ + + + +
28.	Michigan	+686	21	+++++ +++++ + +++ +++ +
29.	Ohio	+3,044	21	+++++ ++ + + ++ ++++ +
30.	Alabama	−145	20	+ +++ +++++ +++ + ++ + +
31.	Oregon	+210	18	++++ + +++ ++++ +++ +
32.	Virginia	−12,949	17	+++++ ++ ++ ++++ ++ +
33.	Montana	−2,009	16	++++ + ++ + + + +
34.	Washington	−1,010	16	+ +++ ++ + + ++ + +
35.	S. Carolina	−1,697	15	+++++ + + + + +
36.	New Mexico	−1,327	14	++ ++ ++ ++ + ++
37.	Mississippi	−1,362	13	+++++ ++ + + +
38.	New York	−18,990	13	+++++ + + + + ++ +
39.	Pennsylvania	+7,672	13	++ + +++++ + +++
40.	Connecticut	−18,216	12	+++ + + + +
41.	W. Virginia	+3,457	12	++ ++ + +
42.	Maine	+544	10	+ +++ + + +++ + +
43.	Maryland	−16,069	10	++++ + + + +
44.	N. Dakota	−1,843	10	++++ + ++ + +
45.	Arizona	−3,929	4	+ +++ + +++
46.	Hawaii	−3,138	4	
47.	Delaware	−1,856	3	
48.	New Jersey	−71,027	3	
49.	Alaska	−767	2	
50.	Nevada	−1,454	0	
51.	Wyoming	−1,586	0	

ESTIMATING THE DISTRIBUTION PATTERNS OF STATE ENROLLMENT POTENTIAL

In discussions thus far, no reference has been made concerning the subdivisions within statewide enrollments. Yet, if the public and private sectors are to share the responsibility for higher education and if the programs of the various types of institutions are to be coordinated, a finer resolution of enrollments is necessary. The task is to identify trends in the various distribution patterns of enrollment potential in order (1) to provide a realistic statewide picture of changing enrollment patterns and their implications and (2) to enable colleges to plan their programs and enrollment capacities as realistically as possible.

The commonly used enrollment classification categories are as follows:

1. *geographic coverage*—statewide, economic area, individual institution

2. *student population*—total, male, female, special group

3. *control of institution*—public, private

4. *type of institution*—2-year junior college, 4-year senior college, university

5. *level of instruction*—freshman, sophomore, junior, senior, first-level graduate, second-level graduate, first-professional (groups may be combined if less detail is required)

6. *student migration status*—residents remaining in the State and nonresident inmigration (resident outmigration on a statewide basis may also be considered)

7. *professional discipline*—by profession as required.

Figure VII-10.—Estimated undergraduate degree-credit enrollment in all institutions of higher education, by institutional control and by migration status: 1958-78

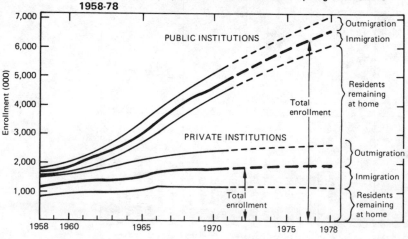

Figure VII-11.— Estimated graduate enrollments in all institutions of higher education, by institutional control and by migration status: 1958-78

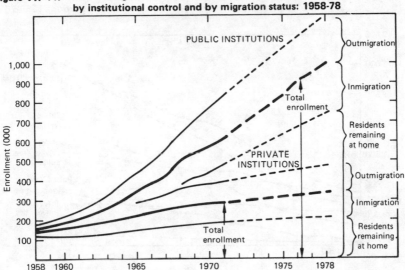

Source: Kenneth A. Simon and Martin M. Frankel, Projections of Educational Statistics to 1980-81 (1971 edition), U.S. Department of Health, Education, and Welfare, Office of Education, U.S. Government Printing Office, Washington, D.C., 1972, and unpublished USOE data.

On a statewide basis, enrollment estimates for individual categories may be made either by totaling the separate projections reported by individual institutions or by extrapolating recent enrollment distribution trends and applying the resultant percentages to a projection of total statewide enrollment. (Projection methodology for State totals, introduced at the beginning of this chapter, is discussed in detail in appendix A. Methodology for projecting enrollments at individual institutions is described later in this chapter.)

To conduct an initial State-level study of enrollments in either the public or private sector, the total State student population must be classified by type of institution, level of instruction, and student migration status:

	Type of institution	*Level of instruction*	*Migration status*
1.	2-year college	undergraduate	resident
2.	"	"	inmigrant
3.	4-year senior college	undergraduate	resident
4.	"	"	inmigrant
5.	"	graduate	resident
6.	"	"	inmigrant
7.	university	undergraduate	resident
8.	"	"	inmigrant
9.	"	graduate	resident
10.	"	"	inmigrant
11.	"	first-professional	resident
12.	"	"	inmigrant

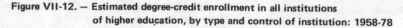

Figure VII-12. — Estimated degree-credit enrollment in all institutions of higher education, by type and control of institution: 1958-78

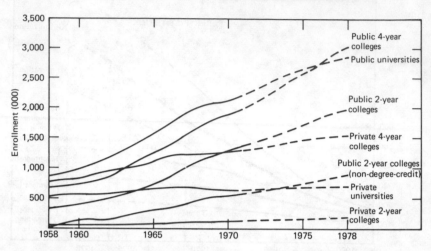

Figure VII-13. — Estimated degree-credit enrollment for public 4-year institutions, by level of instruction and by migration status: 1958-78

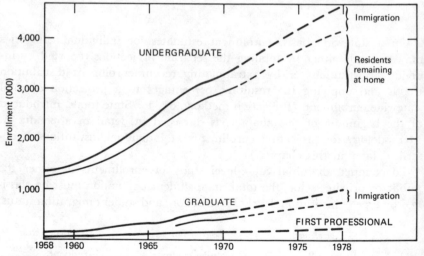

Source: Kenneth A. Simon and Martin M. Frankel, Projections of Educational Statistics to 1980-81 (1971 edition), U.S. Department of Health, Education, and Welfare, Office of Education, U.S. Government Printing Office, Washington, D.C. 1972, and unpublished USOE data.

These enrollments may be studied and compared in a variety of combinations. On a statewide basis, the distribution analyses commonly used are:

1. Institutional control and migration status of enrollments for each level of instruction (see figures VII-10 and VII-11).
2. Institutional type and control of enrollments for each level of instruction (see figure VII-12).

3. Level of instruction and migration status of enrollments for each type of institution (see figure VII-13). This breakdown should also be determined for each institution individually.

It should be emphasized that the three foregoing analyses represent an attempt to estimate, on the basis of past trends and available facilities, the size of potential student enrollments at different levels of instruction and the student distribution pattern among the three types of institutions. The data thus developed provide a general basis not only for coordinating expansion plans among institutions at the State level but also for developing facilities at a pace consonant with expected enrollment changes.

The *geographical* distribution of college enrollment potential, an important factor, is considered in the next section. Among other things, the geographical distribution of college entrance rates serves (1) as a means by which individual institutions can more precisely identify their enrollment potential and expansion requirements and (2) as the basis by which State planning agencies can identify unmet area needs and determine whether or not additional higher education centers will be required.

GEOGRAPHICAL ANALYSIS OF POTENTIAL ENROLLEES

To plan intelligently the expansion of State colleges and universities and to create new educational centers, consideration must be given to the current and projected geographical distribution of a State's high school graduates[10]—the primary source of first-time enrollees. A study of this potential can enable statewide planners to expand colleges in such a way as to provide geographical accessibility to a maximum number of potential enrollees, thereby ensuring that the educational needs of all concerned are judiciously met. It also will enable them to prevent an unwarranted proliferation of institutions.

As a general rule, universities draw their freshmen from a wider geographic area than do 4-year senior colleges, and students at senior colleges, in turn, represent a wider geographic area than do those at 2-year colleges. Naturally, the area served by community colleges is limited, since a major reason for their existence is to serve students who live within commuting

---

[10] Because of available census data, college-age population (18 through 21) is often used as the base measurement of enrollment potential. However, because high school graduates are the *immediate primary* source of first-time college enrollees, their total is the most accurate single indicator of enrollment potential and, whenever possible, should be used in preference to college-age population.

distance. There are other equally compelling reasons, however, why accessibility is critical at the 2-year college level. There is, for example, considerable evidence to the effect that 2-year colleges, more than either 4-year colleges and universities, motivate high school graduates to continue their education (see chapter III). It should also be recognized that the existence of a local State college or university does not always ensure full educational opportunity to the youth of a given community. Four-year colleges and universities do not—and should not—provide the 2-year terminal occupational programs and other unique services offered by community and junior colleges. Moreover, since both 4-year colleges and universities are selective in admissions, neither fulfills the educational needs of those young people capable of pursuing courses beyond high school yet not qualified to enter 4-year institutions.

Owing to the highly localized mission and support bases of community colleges, study of the geographical location of potential enrollees should be made for areas not larger than counties, or in some instances, metropolitan centers.[11] The number of high school graduates in each county can be estimated by projecting the share or proportion of the State's total number of high school graduates for each county and multiplying these shares by the projected State total high school graduate population.[12]

To estimate the future number of high school graduates in each county is difficult because the socioeconomic forces that determine the rates of migration into, out of, and within a State cannot be easily predicted. For example, the relocation or construction of new industry in rural areas may cause a migration to these previously sparsely settled locations. The movement of residents from the cities to suburbs may decline as urban renewal takes place and as travel time reaches unacceptable limits. Since the rate of growth or decline will never be uniform in all counties and communities within a State, accelerated trends, where expected, should be part of any projection analysis.

To obtain a thorough geographical description of potential college enrollments, the following measurements of high school graduates by county should be determined by both historical count and projection: (1) absolute number (and total by sex, if possible) to indicate relative magnitude of first-time college enrollment potential; (2) rates of increase over time to indicate relative growth in potential; (3) number per 100-square-mile

---

[11] If the potential enrollment of a possible *new* college is being estimated, the number of high school graduates surrounding the location of the proposed college must be identified in finer geographic detail than by county area—normally within successive 10-mile commuting zones.

[12] This procedure is carefully described and examples are given in A. J. Jaffee, *Handbook of Statistical Procedures for Long-Range Projections of Public School Enrollment*, U.S. Department of Health, Education, and Welfare, Office of Education, U.S. Government Printing Office, Washington, D.C., 1969, pp. 44–53. (See appendix A for annotation.)

Figure VII-14 — Demographic factors associated with college enrollment potential

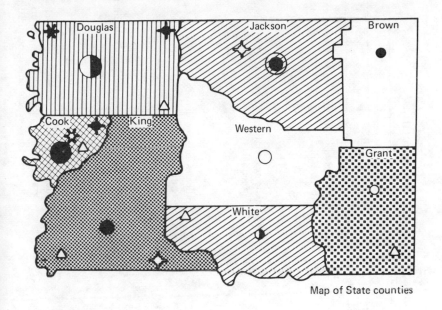

Map of State counties

LEGEND

College entrance rate of high school graduates:

70% and over ▨   50% to 59% ▨   30% to 39% ▨
60% and 69% ▨   40% to 49% ▨   0% to 29% ☐

Location of institutions by type and control:

	Public	Private
University	✾	✸
4-year college	✧	▲
2-year college	△	▲

Number and growth rate of high school graduates:

Number of high school graduates in 1 year	Percentage growth during past 5 years			
	0% to 9%	10% to 19%	20% to 29%	30% and over
Less than 1,000	○[1]	◐	●	◉
1,000 to 2,499	○	◐	●	◉
2,500 to 4,999	○	◑	●	◉
5,000 and over	○	◐	●	◉

[1]Circle areas are proportional to number of high school graduates.

Table VII-5.—Demographic factors associated with college enrollment potential

Measurement and year	State total	Jackson	County or economic area		
			Smith	Brown	Grant
Number of high school graduates			Indicates absolute magnitude of enrollment potential.		
1960	48,000	1,900			
1965	53,000	2,100			
1970	57,000	2,900			
1975	60,000	3,600			
Percentage increase over 1960			Indicates relative growth rate of enrollment potential.		
1960	—	—			
1965	10%	10%			
1970	19	50			
1975	25	90			
Number per 100-square-mile area			Indicates relative density of enrollment potential.		
1960	80	54			
1965	89	60			
1970	95	82			
1975	100	102			
Percentage of state total			Indicates shift in concentration of enrollment potential.		
1960	100%	4%			
1965	100	4			
1970	100	5			
1975	100	6			
College entrance rate			Indicates preparedness of high school graduates and accessibility to appropriate post-secondary educational opportunities.		
1960	48%	38%			
1965	52	45			
1970	56	47			
1975	59	48			

Minority population measurements		Special ethnic considerations.	
Family income		Index of family ability to pay student college expenses.	
1960	$ 6,857	1960	$5,379
1965	7,995	1965	5,975
1970	9,123	1970	6,457
1975	10,467	1975	7,895

area to indicate relative density of potential; (4) percentage distribution among all counties to indicate geographic shifts in college enrollment potential; (5) college entrance rate to indicate preparedness of high school students to enter college and the accessibility of suitable postsecondary educational opportunities; (6) special counts relating to minority populations; and (7) family income or other desired socioeconomic factors. Both graphical and tabular presentations of these data are shown in figure VII-14 and table VII-5.

Any geographic analysis of college enrollment potential and the related factor, adequacy of educational opportunity, usually takes the form of county-by-county comparisons. Such comparisons reveal growth and shifts in the high school graduate population that should be taken into account in estimating future college-capacity requirements. If spatial segregation of minority racial groups exists, it should be studied in order to determine the possible impact of growth and shifts in residential patterns. Even more important than the aforementioned factors, however, are the college entrance rates of high school graduates in the various areas.

There are various reasons why the number of high school graduates who go to college varies from county to county. Whether or not a county is predominantly rural or urban seems to have an effect on college-going rates, as do per capita income, the quality of the elementary-secondary school system, and parental attitudes toward the advantages of a college education. Although a clear-cut attendance pattern seldom emerges, a dominant factor influencing college attendance appears to be student proximity to a college. In view of this fact, comparisons of local college entrance rates may be used to tentatively identify geographical areas where educational opportunities appear to be inadequate. Once an initial identification has been made, a detailed study of the need for possible new community colleges or other centers of higher education should follow. (The procedures involved in such a study are discussed later in this chapter.)

PROJECTING CAMPUS ENROLLMENT POTENTIAL BY AREA ATTENDANCE RATES

The responsibility for determining the total college enrollment potential within a given State rests with the State planning-coordinating agency. In addition to expanding existing facilities or establishing new ones, or both, planning requires that projections be made of enrollment potentials for each individual institution. Such projections, although they may be performed at the State level, are generally an institutional responsibility.

The "cohort-survival" or grade progression technique and the "ratio" method of projecting college enrollments at the State and national level (see appendix A) are generally unsatisfactory for institutional forecasts, the reason being that institutional enrollments, as opposed to State totals, depend on geographic distribution of the population in the vicinity of the campus location. Attendance rates generally decline rapidly as distance and commuting time from the campus increase. This is particularly true at 2-year community colleges, somewhat less so at 4-year senior colleges and universities. For example, it is quite possible for community colleges and senior colleges in large metropolitan areas to draw up to 90 percent of their enrollment from students living within a 30-mile commuting radius. Since neither the cohort-survival or ratio method of projecting enrollments normally refines source population to account for this phenomenon, it is necessary to apply geographically differentiated attendance rates of high school graduates to modified cohort-survival procedures.[13]

In estimating college enrollment potential based on area attendance rates, the enrollment base of State high school graduates is the primary factor. The methodology is suitable only for institutions that primarily serve State resident high school graduates and plan enrollments proportional to this primary population source. High school graduates are considered in both their magnitude and geographic location. Enrollment potential estimates are based on the attendance rates of high school graduates in successive irregular residence zones concentric with the college location. The fact that attendance rates decline in successive residence zones accounts for the strong influence that proximity to an institution exerts on student attendance. The perimeter or boundary lines identifying the successive zones are constructed in each case to represent relatively constant rates of attendance. Expansion factors for continuing and returning students, for freshman transfers, and for nonresident immigrants from outside the State are used to estimate total first-time enrollment. Total first-time enrollment can then be expanded to total undergraduate enrollment at all class levels.

This methodology, illustrated in figure VII-15, involves the following five steps:

1. From institutional enrollment data, determine geographic distribution and numerical trends among first-time resident students according to the location of their residence within the State at the time of high school graduation. Depending on the degree of precision desired, the distribution may be established according to (a) suc-

---

[13] The methodology for estimating potential enrollments on the basis of geographic distribution of high school graduates surrounding college locations is described in *Institutional Capacities and Area Needs of California Higher Education 1960–1975*, op. cit. These concepts, subsequently employed in various forms by other States, serve as the basis for the methodology presented here.

Figure VII-15. — Illustrative analysis of campus enrollment potential, by differential attendance rates

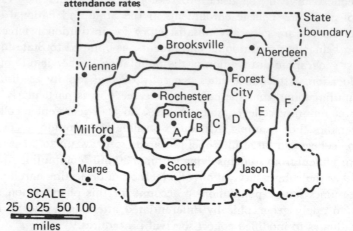

Geographic distribution of enrollment factors, actual count, Pontiac (4-year) College: Year 1 and projected year 6.

Residence zone (based on county boundaries)	High school graduates		Average attendance rate		First-time resident students (2) x (4) (3) x (5)	
	Actual year 1	Projected year 6	Actual year 1	Projected year 6	Actual year 1	Projected year 6
(1)	(2)	(3)	(4)	(5)	(6)	(7)
A	1,826	2,350	29.4%	31.0%	537	728
B	4,871	4,900	9.2%	12.0%	448	588
C	6,345	5,750	5.2%	5.5%	330	316
D	9,110	11,250	3.1%	4.5%	282	506
E	23,471	24,300	2.0%	2.0%	469	486
F	17,489	17,000	1.5%	2.0%	262	340
				Total	2,328	2,964

	Actual year 1	Projected year 6
First-time resident students	2,328	2,964
Ratio of first-time students to first-time resident students	1.057	1.083
First-time students	2,461	3,210
First-time students plus first-time enrollment for 3 previous sucessive years	8,221	11,865
Ratio of total undergraduate enrollment to first-time enrollment over 4 successive years	.968	.971
Total undergraduate enrollment	7,958	11,521

cessive irregular residence or commuting zones concentric with the institution's location or (b) on a county-by-county basis. (Details of zone construction are discussed in the ensuing section.)

2. From the geographical attendance pattern, determine for each zone the relationship between the number of resident first-time students enrolled and the total number of high school graduates, i.e., the average attendance rate. Extrapolate these relationships for the projection period, using any of the methods for this purpose discussed in appendix A.

3. To obtain the projected number of potential first-time resident college students, apply the ratios obtained in step 2 to the estimated number of high school graduates in each zone for the projection period.

4. Using projected migration-resident ratios, convert the annual number of first-time resident students during the projection period to first-time enrollment, including nonresident inmigrants.

5. Compute for each year the ratio of actual total undergraduate enrollment to the first-time enrollment for that year and the 3 successive previous years. Use the projected values from this conversion ratio to calculate the total undergraduate enrollment for each year in the projection period.

If projections of individual institution enrollments are prepared at the State level, the following sixth step is recommended:

6. When the sum of the projected enrollments for individual institutions varies from State totals, modify the parts to conform to totals.

Design of Residence Zone Boundaries

The majority of first-time freshmen at public colleges consists generally of recent graduates of high schools located either near institutions of higher learning or scattered throughout the State. It would be a tedious task for a college to project its enrollment by separately estimating the likely input from each of these many sources. To simplify the process, high schools with similar enrollment potential should be grouped together and the resultant groups treated as single sources. The geographic area in which all high schools within a single group are located is designated a "residence zone."

The geographic pattern and attendance rates at locations from which a college draws its students are influenced by many factors. Among the more important are the following: the educational programs, level of instruction, and entrance requirements of the college; the degree to which enrollment potential is distributed in the immediate and surrounding vicinity; the availability of dormitories; variations in commuting time resulting from the existence or nonexistence of a surrounding road network, public transportation, and terrain barriers; alternative educational opportunities; and various socioeconomic factors that encourage or deter attendance. By grouping high school locations with similar attendance rates, it is possible to establish geographical zones of student residence in which the combined effect of these factors on student academic interest and ability is relatively uniform.

Differential functions established for institutions have resulted in the combination of some of these factors. In the public sector, for example, a single university and a few widely separated 4-year colleges usually are sufficient to serve all students within a single State. Since such institutions accommodate a large number of students from a wide geographical area, the competition between institutions to attract local students is practically nonexistent. The opposite is true at community colleges serving commuter students and at institutions located near one another in large metropolitan areas. Because these institutions generally serve a small, concentrated area, competition for students is likely to be intense. These two situations— a large statewide area versus a small city or community area—require that different residence zone boundaries be created if the geographic pattern of attendance rates is to be accurately determined.

Inasmuch as students attending institutions serving large areas come from widely scattered areas, the distribution of attendance rates need not be analyzed with precision. For projection purposes, it is generally sufficient to identify the location of the high schools from which first-time enrollees have been graduated on a county-by-county basis. The county in which the institution is located is considered the primary zone of potential enrollment. Additional residence zones are established by identifying and grouping counties in which the attendance rates of freshmen are similar. If distance from the campus is the principal determinant, residence zones generally consist of successive rings of contiguous counties, with ring midpoints at progressively greater distances from the campus. Exceptions to this rule occur in locations in which atypical attendance rates are caused by the presence of other educational institutions or by poverty, terrain barriers, etc. (The use of this county-by-county method to define residence zone boundaries is illustrated in figure VII-15.)

The foregoing methodology provides neither details concerning the geographic location of high school graduates nor differences in attendance rates *within* the various counties. Such detail is required, however, to determine the enrollment potential of institutions that serve small areas and draw their students from a relatively concentrated population source. In such instances, a majority of students generally commute from a few surrounding counties; therefore, the area of significant enrollment potential does not extend beyond a reasonable travel distance.

To establish differential attendance rates within small geographical areas, it is necessary to define relatively narrow residence zones based on the locations of *individual* high schools, the graduates of which comprise the majority of first-time students at the college in question. The zone boundaries may be established on a scale road map (illustrated in figure VII-16) by constructing lines which enclose the locations of all high schools with attendance rates between specified limits, e.g., zone "A," containing all high schools from which 60 to 90 percent of the graduates attend the college in question; zone "B," 50–59 percent; zone "C," 40–49 percent; and so on. To determine the institution's first-time student enrollment potential, the average attendance rates from previous years are projected into the future and applied to the projected number of high school graduates for each zone.

Residence zone boundaries established on the basis of commuting distance or time are especially applicable to colleges serving a high concentration of commuter students whose attendance depends primarily on proximity to the college and on commuting time. The enrollment potential of proposed new colleges can be projected by examining the attendance rates at existing colleges. The term "commuting zone" normally identifies the relatively small geographic area immediately surrounding a given college—specifically, the area from which students can commute at the least cost, in terms of room and board and travel time and expense. A majority of sources indicate that the one-way commuting distance for the majority of students should be under 30 miles.[14]

Many factors other than distance, however, affect commuters: the density or sparsity of the population in a given area, road conditions, traffic congestion, availability of rapid-transit facilities, and climate. To account for these factors, commuting distance should be calculated not in terms of specific mileage but in travel time. A total of 40-to-45 minutes in transit each way is generally considered an acceptable maximum. A student traveling 40 miles over an expressway, for example, probably would not spend any more time commuting to college than a student covering 5 miles through congested city streets. Depicting a commuting zone based on travel time will, of course, result in an irregular boundary line (see figure VII-16).

To estimate enrollment potential based on the commuting zone approach, draw a scale map showing successive commuting zone boundaries representing 10, 20, and 40 minutes of travel time to the campus (or other time values suggested by local conditions). The attendance rate for each zone can then be established—i.e., the percentage of high school graduates in the zone who enter the college as first-time students. To obtain the projected number of potential first-time resident students attending the college during the projection period, project these rates, and as previously explained, apply them to the corresponding estimated number of future high school graduates in the zone.

---

[14] A 1967 survey of California State college students revealed the following distribution of average commuting distances: 0–1 mile, 20.1 percent; 1–9 miles, 39.5 percent; 10–19 miles, 24.4 percent; 20–29 miles, 10.1 percent; 30 or more miles, 6.0 percent.

Figure VII-16. — Residence/commuting zones

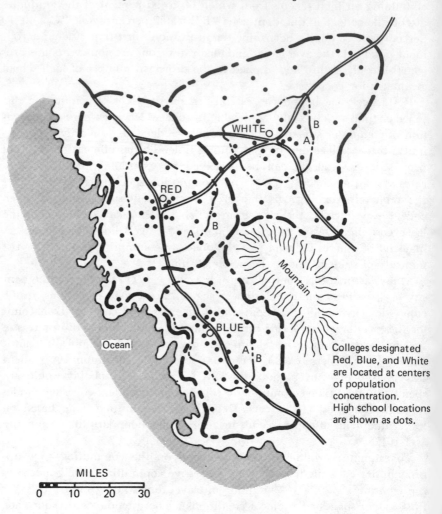

Colleges designated Red, Blue, and White are located at centers of population concentration. High school locations are shown as dots.

Zone boundaries group high school locations with similar attendance rates. If boundaries are based on commuting time, major highways and terrain must be taken into account. Overlapping areas served by two or more institutions are split evenly.

If commuting zones overlap within metropolitan areas, similar institutions located near one another must compete for the same students. In such cases, potential enrollments may be divided equally between two institutions, on the premise that if students are given a choice between equal commuting distances, they will divide evenly in their choice of institution.

PLANNING THE ENROLLMENT
CAPACITY OF EXISTING INSTITUTIONS

In previous sections of this chapter, projection of State and institutional enrollments and an analysis of their growth and distribution have been discussed. By analyzing projected enrollment figures, it is possible to identify geographically the potential program needs in a given State and to ascertain those existing facilities that should be expanded, as well as the locations for additional educational centers. When enrollments exceed institutional capacities, there are three options which individually or in combination can provide the means whereby additional students can be accommodated.

The first option is to direct applicants from colleges at which demand exceeds existing facilities to institutions which can accommodate more students. A second option is to increase the capacity of existing institutions. This may be done in any of the following ways: by extending the hours of instruction or by operating on a year-round basis; by increasing the annual enrollment growth beyond the figure previously established; or by raising the maximum enrollment ceiling set by individual institutions. The third option is to establish new colleges.

Generally it is more feasible to accommodate expanded enrollment by options one and two. Establishing new campuses is usually justified only by a combination of circumstances, of which an increase in enrollment is but one. Other conditions that lend support to establishing a new institution include low overall college entrance rates relative to potential, the distance students must travel to reach existing institutions, unmet program needs, and possible savings in instructional costs. The rather complex analysis required in any comprehensive study of the need for additional educational centers is the subject of the final section of this chapter.

At the State level, the first step in planning the enrollment capacity of existing institutions is to identify anticipated capacity deficiencies. Such deficiencies are measured by comparing projected potential enrollments with student capacities that will exist in State colleges and universities at the time of completion of new construction. These information, together with recommendations for appropriate adjustments, should be made available by each institution. Tabular presentation of these data can then be summarized, as illustrated in table VII-6, and used as a worksheet to determine a program of future action.

Because different amounts of space are required for different levels of instruction, projected enrollments and student capacities submitted by individual institutions must be identified at least by level of instruction. For example, if an institution offers a comprehensive program of graduate

Table VII-6.—Worksheet of projected enrollments, institutional capacities, and recommended action: State colleges and universities

	Total enrollment	Lower division	Upper division	Graduate	First professional
All institutions					
Projected enrollment	118,000	71,000	33,000	11,000	3,000
Capacity	100,800	62,000	28,000	8,700	2,100
Deficiency	17,200	9,000	5,000	2,300	900
Recommended action:					
1. Redirect students[1]	0	0	0	0	0
2. Increase capacity of existing institutions					
a. Extend instructional time	2,820	1,020	1,000	800	—
b. Year-round operation	4,825	2,500	2,325	—	—
c. Increase annual growth[2]	4,225	2,000	1,675	250	300
d. Increase ceilings[2]	1,850	—	—	1,250	600
3. Establish new campuses[2]	3,480	3,480	—	—	—
All 4-year senior colleges					
Projected enrollment	39,000	19,000	17,000	3,000	
Capacity	30,550	15,000	13,550	2,000	
Deficiency	8,450	4,000	3,450	1,000	
Recommended action:					
1. Redirect students	(+)210	(+)870	(−)380	(−)280	
2. Increase capacity of existing institutions					
a. Extend instructional time	1,280	820	270	190	
b. Year-round operation	4,825	2,500	2,325	—	
c. Increase annual growth[2]	2,135	1,550	475	110	
d. Increase ceilings[2]	420	—	—	420	
3. Establish new campuses[2]	—	—	—	—	
Senior college "A"					
Projected enrollment	5,500	2,000	3,000	500	
Capacity	4,800	1,940	2,600	260	
Deficiency	700	60	400	240	
Recommended action:					
1. Redirect students	(−)60	(−)60	—	—	
2. Increase capacity of existing institution					
a. Extend instructional time	150	—	150	—	
b. Year-round operation	—	—	—	—	

Table VII-6.—Worksheet of projected enrollments, institutional capacities, and recommended action: State colleges and universities—Continued

	Total enrollment	Lower division	Upper division	Graduate	First professional
c. Increase annual growth[2]	490		250	240	
d. Increase ceilings[2]	—	—	—	—	
3. Establish new campuses[2]	—	—	—	—	
Senior college "B"					
University "A"					
All 2-year colleges					

[1] Summation of redirected students from (−) institutions to (+) institutions must equal zero.
[2] Requires construction of additional facilities.

studies, its classrooms and laboratories will be used by fewer students than if it concentrates on undergraduate work. Hence, if comparisons are to be meaningful, institutional capacities and potential enrollments must be based on the same level of instruction.

When the number of students desiring to enroll exceeds the capacity of institutions of higher education, continuing students should receive priority over new enrollees. There should, however, be a plan for accommodating the latter. They should be directed first to campuses that are the least crowded or that are planning immediate expansion. Insofar as possible, these students should be able to enroll at institutions near a location of their first choice; they may, however, have to accept their second, or even third choice. Those least inconvenienced by failure to be accepted by their first choice will be freshmen planning to live in a dormitory on a campus at a considerable distance from their home.

The second option—increasing the enrollment capacity of existing institutions—may be accomplished either by constructing additional classrooms and laboratories, together with such associated support facilities as dormitories, offices, parking lots, etc., or by more fully utilizing existing facilities. The usual way to increase the utilization or efficiency of instructional facilities is to extend the hours of instruction to late afternoon, evening, and Saturday morning. Although this action appears relatively simple, it requires a careful analysis of both instructional costs and the overall effect on scheduling effectiveness, as well as considerations involving transportation, safety, and morale. Sometimes a more effective way to obtain greater utilization of facilities is to encourage as many students as possible to attend summer sessions. In the interest of economical operation, attention must be given to maintaining a balanced enrollment between courses offered during summer sessions and those offered during the rest of the year.[15]

Existing institutions that plan to increase their enrollment capacity by constructing additional facilities may have to reassess their desired annual rate of growth or, if already at a planned optimum or maximum size, decide whether to maintain or raise the ceiling. The rate of campus growth should not adversely affect educational programs; i.e., it should not prevent the hiring of qualified faculty or interfere with either the organization and development of courses and curriculum or with necessary supporting services. The fact that some institutions have met almost incredible expansion demands suggests that, with adequate planning, colleges and universities can cope efficiently and effectively with rapid enrollment expansion.

If an increase in the planned optimum enrollment of an institution is being considered, extreme caution must be exercised. Such a decision should be made only after extensive deliberation, for the consequences are far-reaching and irrevocable. While some States have issued recommendations regarding the optimum size for various types of institutions, the danger of applying uniform standards to *all* colleges and universities should be apparent. Factors influencing optimal size can vary significantly from campus to campus. They include institutional objectives, internal organization, breadth and depth of program, student peer group and student-faculty relationships, availability of space at site, possible economies-of-scale, and the availability of monetary resources. (The problem of institutional size and the central issue of coherency are delineated in chapter VI.)

IDENTIFYING THE NEED FOR ADDITIONAL HIGHER EDUCATION CENTERS

Consideration should be given to establishing new higher educational centers when any of the following conditions exist: If program needs are unmet; if a considerable number of students live in areas far removed from a college or university; if enrollment potential exceeds the optimum or maximum capacities of existing institutions; or if per student costs can be substantially reduced. Before new centers are established, attention must also be given to other factors—namely, the geographical areas to be served

---

[15] For a complete discussion of space utilization analysis and scheduling procedure see chapter X. Further discussion of year-round plant operation is presented in chapter XIII.

commuting distances, lead time required to establish a program, and site acquisition.

In any study of this complexity, the principles and assumptions that appear to define and govern recommended action must be determined in advance. In the ensuing section of this chapter, such principles, as well as some of the considerations essential to site selection, are discussed. Finally, the survey requirements and criteria needed to identify the conditions under which public 2-year colleges can be established with a reasonable assurance of success are reviewed.

Principles for Establishing New Centers

The criteria and principles recommended by various California planning groups[16] are notable for their completeness. Slightly modified, they can be summarized as follows:

1. Optimum use should be made of State higher education resources in relation to the greatest relative need, both geographically and functionally.

2. To avoid unnecessary duplication, differentiation of functions of the three segments of public higher education—2-year colleges, 4-year colleges, and university campuses—is imperative.

3. Basic to effective program expansion is the assumption that adequate 2-year college facilities will be provided through local initiative and State assistance prior to the establishment of additional 4-year institutions or universities.

4. The financing of new publicly supported institutions should be so arranged that it in no way interferes with the needs, including necessary improvement, or expansion of existing ones.

5. It is not in the public interest to extend publicly supported institutions to the degree that they jeopardize the continued operation of long-established private ones that are serving the community well.

6. In considering the need for additional public institutions, the particular needs of localities should not be overlooked yet the general interest of the State should be paramount. Therefore, in determining the need for additional 2-year college facilities and the location of new 4-year colleges and university campuses, the following are most important:

   a. The number of high school graduates, the location of existing institutions, and the relation between the student capacity of these institutions and the estimated enrollment in the geographical area served by each

   b. The number of potential students within reasonable commuting distance of each of the proposed sites (to insure that a maximum number of students can attend)

   c. The size of potential enrollments (to insure that per capita costs may be kept at a minimum)

   d. The need to enroll more students than can be accommodated by existing 2-year colleges, 4-year colleges, and universities

---

[16] Coordinating Council for Higher Education, *California's Needs for Additional Centers of Public Higher Education*, Sacramento, 1964, p. 10.

    e. The need to provide additional educational opportunities for students in counties beyond reasonable commuting range of existing colleges who might not be able to obtain a college education

    f. The need to include all high school districts within a 2-year college district (to insure that the largest possible number of young people in the State have an opportunity to pursue a postsecondary education and to equalize the burden for support of lower division education throughout the State).

Selecting Locations for New Colleges

One of the more obvious places to locate a new college is in an area in which a substantial number of students are "isolated" from educational opportunities, i.e., beyond a reasonable commuting distance from an existing college. Student isolation, while most prevalent in rural counties, also exists in large metropolitan areas, especially if public transportation is either inadequate or time-consuming and if potential students cannot afford to live away from home. Since geographic accessibility is a desired objective, colleges established in isolated areas should be located within commuting distance of the maximum number of projected high school graduates. Attendance rates at proposed colleges are generally based on those of similar existing colleges.

If the enrollment potential in an isolated area exceeds the ultimate capacity of nearby institutions, establishing a new campus should be considered—provided the potential enrollment is consonant with the minimum size warranted by unit-cost factors. In addition, the potential enrollment base should be sufficiently large to warrant a new college but should not in any way drastically affect attendance rates at nearby institutions. In some instances the rate of growth of enrollment potential in an area may be an important factor, since considerable time may elapse between authorization, financing, building, and occupancy of new facilities. Another factor to be carefully considered in connection with establishing a new campus is the availability of both financial and community support.

Past experience indicates that if new colleges are located close to centers of potential student population, the number of high school graduates attending college will usually increase substantially. Obviously, even after a new college is established in the immediate vicinity, a certain number of high school graduates will continue to attend other colleges in the general area. In other words, it can be assumed that attendance rates at a given college will not be drastically lowered if a new college is established within a reasonable distance. However, too-close proximity and/or too much similarity in curriculum and tuition can cause keen competition for students on the part of rival institutions. In such instances, while a redistribution or shift in enrollment can be expected, the overall enrollment for the area probably will not increase significantly. The potential enrollment in overlapping commuting zones, representing areas within which the great est competition between several colleges will occur, may be divided equally between the colleges on the basis that approximately 50 percent of the students who live within an area equidistant from two institutions will attend one and 50 percent will enroll at the other.

Estimating the enrollment potential for new colleges is only the first step in determining the most appropriate sites. Many additional factors must be critically examined before there can be reasonable assurance that a new college will be successful. The evaluation guidelines are usually stated as criteria. But there is no *one* set of criteria which can be applied satisfactorily to public or private colleges throughout the United States. It is generally agreed, however, that an examination of locations at which colleges have failed can at least decrease the odds against failure. Data concerning past experiences in this area await intelligent interpretation and application to specific and unique State and county situations.

Survey and Criteria for Establishing Public 2-Year Colleges

Many State studies and a few national ones have developed criteria to assist in identifying the necessary conditions under which a 2-year college can be established with a reasonable assurance of success. The foremost conclusion which may be drawn from a review of these criteria is that, while they are important, their application alone cannot guarantee success. The most important prerequisite for success is a careful and detailed comprehensive survey of the geographic area and constituency to be served by the proposed college, followed by sound and objective planning.[17]

Too frequently, survey procedures to determine whether or not a proposed district meets the standards inherent in the criteria do not provide the detail necessary for effective planning. A notable exception is the survey format proposed by the Missouri Commission on Higher Education.[18] An indication of the scope and content of the more than 60 items surveyed can be ascertained from the 12 subject headings:

1. Socioeconomic and population descriptions of the proposed district
2. Maps showing topography, road systems, population centers and main commuting routes to a proposed campus
3. Followup studies of high school students in previous years
4. Prospective community junior college students

---

[17] The California experience indicates that a lead time of 6 to 8 years from the date of authorization to admission of the first students is desirable in the planning of any public higher education institution. This lead time may be cut from 2 to 4 years if a new community college is established in a district in which one or more community colleges exists.

[18] Missouri Commission on Higher Education, *Final Report: Missouri Public Junior College Study*, Jefferson City, July 1968, pp. 38–41.

5. Programs needed in the community junior college district
6. Post-high school programs now in the area to be served
7. Programs of high school level in the area
8. Facilities and/or sites available which may be used either temporarily or permanently by the college
9. Guidance facilities now available
10. Teaching staff available
11. Community attitudes—evidence of community support, hostility, or indifference
12. Extent of local resources for financing the community junior college.

Among the primary reasons why new 2-year colleges fail are that they open without reasonable assurance of sufficient enrollment, community support, and financing, or that they do not meet educational needs. In addition to these factors, there are other aspects that should be examined: the availability and selection of qualified faculty, the prospect for educational leadership (essential to both community interest and financial support), the planning of the program and facilities, and the availability of facilities and/or sites that may be used either temporarily or permanently by the college.

Minimum and potential enrollments. While authorities do not agree on the minimum starting enrollment (and appear to be raising their estimates), few recommend that a 2-year college open with less than 200 students. Most cite a potential enrollment of 400 full-time students by the end of 5 years as necessary to provide adequate program breadth for a 2-year college. At the upper end of the scale, the decision in some States is that a minimum of 900 to 1,000 students[19] should be the goal if a comprehensive community college and community service program are to succeed. Needless to say, in establishing minimum enrollment guidelines there must be a concomitant attempt to relate recommended enrollments to the breadth and depth of the envisioned *program*. In sparsely populated areas, for example, it may be necessary to accept only a few students and provide a limited program.

Although different methods can be used to estimate potential enrollment, the most reliable estimates are based on high school enrollment or number of high school graduates and persons 18 or 19 years old in the area. Whatever college enrollment potential is planned, the 3-year high school population must be at least twice as large as the expected college enrollment (attendance rates will vary greatly, depending on population density, proximity to other educational institutions, and the overall college attendance rate). In every instance, attendance ratios must be based on the experience of existing 2-year colleges in the State. It is strongly recommended that instead of applying a single ratio to the total popula-

---

[19] California and Michigan, respectively, among others.

tion of the entire district to be served by the proposed college, that different ratios be used for successive commuting zones.

Evidence of local interest. Community support for a proposed college is difficult to ascertain, yet some indicators of community attitude do exist. These include (1) the petition activity and local vote count in States that require enabling legislation for 2-year colleges; (2) community initiative in conducting a local study of need; (3) the plans and/or expectations on the part of high school seniors to attend a community college, if known; (4) amount raised through contributions and pledges; (5) the number of civic, educational, and service groups to adopt motions supporting the idea of a community or junior college; and (6) reports in the news media relative to support for establishing such a college.

Unmet student needs and proximity to other institutions. The educational needs of potential students can be determined by surveying not only local high school students and their parents but also area college students currently attending college elsewhere. Local firms should be surveyed to determine the extent of training needed by employees and the training required for all occupations in the area. It should be obvious that educational programs at one institution should not duplicate those at a nearby institution. Although other types of institutions may be located in the area, the role of the 2-year college is usually complementary. Conceivably, a junior college or a 2-year technical school might justifiably be opened within a block of a liberal arts college, particularly in densely populated areas. Another need met by 2-year colleges is that they offer an opportunity for an advanced education to many students who cannot afford to attend high-tuition institutions, even though such may be located in the area. In States in which differentiated requirements for admission have reduced competition for students among the different types of institutions, proximity may be a relatively less important factor overall.

Extent of local financial resources. It should not be surprising that there is considerable variation of opinion regarding what a minimum support level should be. Some institutions rent facilities or share them—in part or in full—with high schools. Unit costs fluctuate according to the variety of course offerings, the size of the institution, the salaries of staff and administrators, the quality of the guidance program—all are involved in per student costs.

The income and proportional amounts expected from tuition, district, county, and State funds also vary widely. There is a consensus that student tuition and fees should be kept low. In one survey[20] the preponderance

---

[20] D. G. Morrison and S. V. Martorana, *Criteria for the Establishment of 2-Year Colleges*, U.S. Department of Health, Education, and Welfare, Office of Education, U.S. Government Printing Office, Washington, D.C., 1961, p. 41.

of opinion favored one-third of current operational costs as the maximum tuition a public 2-year college should charge students. The wide variance in tax rates and in the proportion that assessed value bears to real value precludes suggesting a specific assessed valuation to be used as a measure of the financial support which a community might provide a proposed public 2-year college.

In summary, each State and even each county must make its own estimates not only of the expenditures necessary to operate a proposed 2-year college but also of the income expected from each source. An illustration of the budget computations used to estimate revenue necessary for operation follows:

1,000 FTE (full-time-equivalent) students × $900 (estimated per
    student expenditure requirements) $900,000

1,000 FTE students × $300 yearly tuition and fees $300,000
    (one-third operational costs)

1,000 FTE students × $360 State aid (40 percent of $360,000
    operational costs)

                                   Subtract $660,000

Amount of money to be raised from local taxes $340,000

    by property tax: $340,000 ÷ $1,000,000 assessed
                valuation = 34 cents per one hundred
                dollars (3.4 mil) assessed valuation

    or by local tax levy: $340 per FTE student

Total plant requirements equal 1,000 FTE students × 100 square
    feet per student × $40 per square foot $4,000,000

BIBLIOGRAPHY

Coordinating Council for Higher Education, *Meeting the Enrollment Demand for Public Higher Education in California Through 1977: The Need for Additional Colleges and University Campuses*, Sacramento, 1969, 216 pp.

This report, the second to be prepared for CCHE, is one of a series of statewide studies dealing with the need for and location of new public higher education facilities. In the first-study, *California's Needs for Additional Centers of Public Higher Education*, 1964, attention was primarily directed to an examination of the following: the principles and criteria to be explored in establishing area needs; State population growth patterns and corresponding higher education enrollment trends; the planning status of new centers by independent colleges and universities; the pattern of junior college distribution in the State; the need for new 4-year college facilities and university campuses.

The second study, which continues and expands these investigations, focuses on measures which alone, or in combination, can enable a State higher education system to accommodate increased enrollments through more efficient use and development of *existing* colleges and campuses.

Among the measures given particular attention are the following: redirecting students to institutions with available physical capacity, accelerating expansion at campuses that have not yet reached their maximum enrollment potential, and increasing the number of students to be accommodated on a given campus.

Morrison, D. G., and S. V. Martorana, *Criteria for the Establishment of 2-Year Colleges*, U.S. Department of Health, Education, and Welfare, Office of Education, U.S. Government Printing Office, Washington, D.C 1961, 101 pp.

Although some of the recommendations in this reference may be out of date, they represent the results of the only comprehensive survey regarding conditions necessary to assure success of new 2-year colleges. Criteria examined include: minimum and potential enrollments, financial support, accessibility of location to students, evidence of local interest, unmet student needs, and proximity to other institutions of higher education. Statutory and regulatory criteria are also reviewed.

Schmid, Calvin F., Charles S. Gossman, Charles E. Nobbe, Theresa J. Patricelli, and Thomas E. Steahr, *Migration of College and University Students in the United States*, University of Washington Press, Seattle, 1968, 180 pp.

This volume is considered the single best available study of college and university student migration. Praise is due the authors for emphasizing the results of their research while at the same time not burdening the reader with minutiae. Tables of absolute numbers are included only in instances in which head counts are meaningful. In all other instances, informative migration rates, ratios, and indexes are tabulated and graphed in such a way as to present clear and coherent summaries of findings.

The report is divided into two major parts. The first is concerned with the identification and analysis of migration patterns. Separately, for both the public and private sector at State and regional levels, the migration patterns of undergraduate students, graduate students, and first-professional students are examined individually. Of exceptional interest and value is the chapter containing an analysis of historical trends in student migration from 1938 to 1963. The second part of the study is devoted to an analysis of the social, economic, demographic, and educational factors related to student migration. One of the major objectives of the analysis is to develop a method for predicting the number and direction of interstate college migrants.

Schmid, Calvin F., Vincent A. Miller, and William S. Packard, *Enrollment Statistics, Colleges and Universities, State of Washington, Fall Term 1966*, Planning and Community Affairs Agency, Olympia, 1967, 56 pp.

Schmid, Calvin, and Wayne W. McVey, Jr., *Growth and Distribution of Minority Races in Seattle, Washington*, Seattle Public Schools, Seattle, 1964, 62 pp.

Schmid, Calvin F., Charles S. Gossman, Charles E. Nobbe, Theresa J. Patricelli, and Thomas E. Steahr, *Migration of College and University Students, State of Washington*, Washington State Census Board, Seattle, 1967, 65 pp.

Among the many excellent studies of basic enrollment data and related demographic statistics conducted by different States, the three prepared by Schmid and others for the State of Washington are outstanding. The volume concerning college and university enrollment statistics is notable for its clarity, brevity, and careful attention to precise data classifications. The migration study parallels at the State level Schmid's national study previously cited. As with the national study, graphical presentations effectively convey important elements of migration processes. The volume also includes information not commonly found in State studies: demographic data dealing with special populations.

The monograph that Schmid and McVey have prepared on the growth and distribution of minority races in Seattle includes demographic technology and interpretation that should be of value to State planners interested in undertaking similar types of investigations.

Technical Committee on Institutional Capacities and Area Needs (Lloyd N. Morrisett, chairman), *Institutional Capacities and Area Needs of California Public Higher Education 1960–1975* (prepared for the Liaison Committee of the Regents of the University of California and the State Board of Education and for the Master Plan Survey Team), University of California, Berkeley, 1961, 137 pp.

This comprehensive study is of exceptional value as a guide for analyzing current college enrollment capacities at the State level and determining the need for additional facilities and faculty to accommodate projected enrollments. Many subsequent California studies in this area have been prepared, but this one remains the single best instructional source on the topic. It includes chapters on institutional capacities, the utilization of physical plants, enrollment projections and needs for new colleges, faculty demand and supply, and possible locations of new colleges and their probable effects on existing institutions.

Wade, George H., *Residence and Migration of College Students, Fall 1968*, vol. 1: *Basic State-to-State Matrix Tables* and vol. 2: *Analytic Report*, U.S. Department of Health, Education, and Welfare, Office of Education, U.S. Government Printing Office, Washington, D.C., 1970, 71 pp. and 87 pp., respectively.

Detailed tabular data on student migration for fall 1968 are supplemented in the *Analytic Report* with computed ratios and graphics.

Chapter VIII

MEASURING PROFESSIONAL MANPOWER SUPPLY AND DEMAND

Attention is directed in this chapter to measuring society's need for the trained manpower output of colleges, particularly the demand and supply in professional occupations.

Although a free society does not countenance programing students into specific occupations, when certain manpower shortages occur, institutions are obligated to review their policies and capacities to determine what action, if any, they can take to encourage students to enter those occupations in which shortages exist. The task of analyzing professional manpower demand and supply rests with State higher education planning agencies. The course of action they follow can have a pronounced effect on the health, employment, and general welfare of the public to which they are responsible.

In what fields are personnel shortages or surpluses of direct concern to colleges and universities? Four criteria may be used: (1) Does entrance into the occupation require specialized college training? (2) Are employee qualifications and training requirements so unique that personnel trained in related fields cannot be transferred to the occupation? (3) Is the occupation sufficiently important to society that even a personnel shortage of minor proportions warrants prompt remedial action? (4) Has there been a history of shortages or surpluses in the occupation?

Clearly the major occupations with which higher education must concern itself are the professions—career fields whose chief, if not exclusive, source of manpower is college graduates. The professional fields that commonly experience shortages and consequently are subject to continual supply and demand study are teaching, the natural sciences, engineering, and health. To these may be added law, psychology, social work, and more recently, computer programing. Still another demand-supply area requiring the attention of higher education is that involving technicians, preparation for which requires 2 or more years of postsecondary study. Shortages in these fields, while usually of less severe consequence to the economy than shortages in the professions, warrant the attention of higher education because, to a high degree, colleges control the supply of technically trained personnel.

Once an existing or expected occupational shortage is identified, there are a number of ways in which colleges and universities can try to increase the personnel supply. More students may be motivated to enter under-staffed fields if the economic and job advantages are well demonstrated and publicized. Guidance and counseling may also encourage individuals with qualifying aptitudes and abilities to select careers in which shortages exist. Some potential applicants do not choose to enter certain professions because of rigid qualifying requirements, excessively long courses of study, or an inflexible curriculum. If entrance and curriculum requirements were eased and preparation time shortened, graduate and professional study could be made considerably more attractive. Experiments with a shortened program (7 years) leading to a medical degree have proven successful, thereby suggesting the feasibility of such an approach. In another direction, the supply of college trained people in specific occupations may be increased, of course, simply by increasing college enrollments overall. If any of the aforementioned methods result in expansion or shifts in enrollments, institutional capacities must be correspondingly adjusted.

METHODS OF ANALYSIS

The apparatus of supply and demand is immensely complicated. The immediate factors affecting the quantity of manpower available and required are commonly known: wages, working conditions, prices, industrial techniques, and the consumer market. Less directly, supply and demand are also influenced by the composition of the labor force, the status of the economy, geography, worker mobility, market regulations, and advertising. These factors dictate that the methods of analysis in any study of supply and demand necessarily involve simplified approaches to the subject. Such approaches differ principally in defining what constitutes a labor shortage.

The circumstances which govern the applicability of a given definition include (1) availability of data, (2) need for a projection versus an estimate of the immediate situation, (3) need for an actual measurement versus an indication of a shortage, and (4) the most appropriate level of application—e.g., national, regional, State, county.

In the ensuing sections, five methods of analyzing the manpower supply and demand in professional occupations are presented, together with illustrative data. The five methods are (1) job vacancy survey, (2) supply lag theory, (3) occupational ratio, (4) expenditure ratio, and (5) social need theory. A final section deals with the special case of estimating faculty supply and demand.

Since the job vacancy survey is the most straightforward and encom-

Table VIII-1.—Characteristics of five methods for analyzing manpower supply and demand

Method	Projection period for which best suited		Market level for which best suited		Nature of measurement			
	Short-range	Long-range	State or local	National or regional	Directly measures shortages reported by employers	Measures shortage relative to standard	Measures demand only; separate supply study required	Shortage indicator only
Job vacancy survey	X		X		X			
Supply lag theory	X			X				X
Occupational ratio		X	1	X			X	
Expenditure ratio		X		X			X	
Social need theory	X		X			X		

[1] If data are available, the occupational ratio method may also be applied to State or local markets.

passes the basic theory used by economists to explain supply and demand in the labor market, it is discussed first. Characteristics of the five methods are shown in table VIII-1.

THE JOB VACANCY SURVEY

The popular conception of a labor shortage is that the number of jobs exceeds the number of workers available *at the prevailing wage*. In a free market, such an imbalance usually does not persist over a long period of time because (1) some employers are able to attract additional employees by raising salary schedules, and (2) firms unable to offer higher wages reorganize their operation in such a manner as to continue with the same number of workers. As a result of higher salaries and reorganization, the supply of workers is increased and the demand reduced. Eventually supply and demand become equal, but more workers are being paid higher salaries.

This brief description of supply and demand can be more easily understood if depicted in graphical terms. Supply and demand schedules (curves) are shown in figure VIII-1. The supply curve represents the number of workers willing to work at given wage levels. The demand curve represents the number of workers that employers are willing to hire at these wage levels. No labor shortage exists as long as the supply of workers (q_1) willing to work at the prevailing wage (w_1) equals the demand for workers at that wage. This balance or equilibrium is represented by the intersection of the supply curve (S) with the demand curve (D) at E_1. What happens when employers demand more workers at the same wage—i.e., when the demand curve shifts to the right from D_1 to D_2? Employers seek to hire—at the prevailing wage—q_3 number of workers instead of q_1. Since workers at this wage are not immediately available—i.e., no immediate shift occurs in the supply curve because of the time required for job training—a *temporary* shortage of workers equal to quantity q_3 minus quantity q_1 exists.

Although the supply-demand situation is out of balance, in the absence of wage and worker restrictions, both employers and workers are able to reestablish an equilibrium. Employers will begin to solve their worker shortage by gradually increasing wages and gradually reducing the number of workers they are willing to hire—illustrated in the figure by the dash-arrow path paralleling the demand curve D_2. As wages rise, more workers will seek jobs and will be hired; i.e., the supply of workers will move along the supply curve, as indicated by the dotted arrow path. Eventually a new equilibrium will be reached (E_2) in which the numbers of workers supplied and demanded, q_2, are equal, but at a new and higher wage, w_2. Thus whenever demand increases, a shortage of workers can be expected to

Figure VIII-1. — Operation of labor supply and demand in a free market

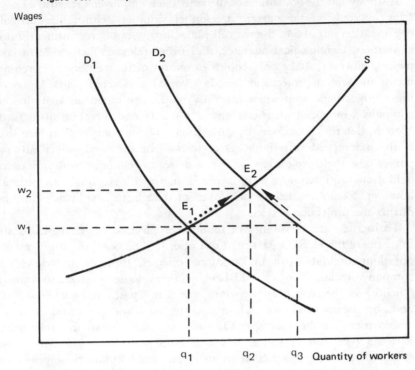

persist until a new equilibrium is reached. Similarly, a temporary shortage of workers can occur as the result of a reduction in supply at every wage level—i.e., a shift in the supply curve to the left. Such a shift, however, is rare.

As previously described, the job vacancy survey is a method of measuring labor shortages when the demand for labor exceeds the supply at the prevailing wage. The survey thus assesses only immediate or temporary shortages based on employer estimates of their immediate and future employee needs in those occupational categories in which they are interested.[1] In most studies of this type, questionnaires are mailed to a cross section of employers. They are asked the number of individuals they employ in specific occupations, current staffing requirements, and the number of employees they expect to employ in the foreseeable future. Sometimes they are also asked to estimate their replacement needs and hiring practices with respect to graduates of various types of training and educational institutions.

---

[1] An approximate measure of current labor shortages can be obtained from Help Wanted ads in newspapers and technical journals. An index of engineers and scientists developed from this source is prepared by Deutsch, Shea & Evans, Inc., a manpower advertising agency in New York City.

A survey has the advantage of utilizing each employer's extensive knowledge not only of the current personnel situation within his particular organization but also of the overall plans for personnel recruitment, future expansion, technological changes, and other relevant factors. Most companies, however, make only rough estimates of future personnel requirements and seldom project their needs beyond a period of 5 years. Moreover, these projections, even when carefully made, are based on an individual company's independent assessment of the rate and direction of its future growth, determined in part by an estimate of the company's future share of the market. More reliable estimates can be obtained only if all companies base their projections on the same set of economic assumptions and definitions and follow a standardized methodology. Such an estimate, however, would not include employment data from new firms established during the projection period.

To increase the credibility of manpower surveys, the Bureau of Labor Statistics of the U. S. Department of Labor has, on occasion, supplemented questionnaire data with information collected through interviews with company officials. The general BLS objective is to demonstrate to company officials, on the basis of survey data, the firm's past employment statistics and, by means of charts and tables, the past and projected growth of employment in the industry. Officials are also shown the relationship between past and projected ratios of employees being studied to total employment in their particular industry and are told how these projections were derived and on what assumptions they are based. With this information as a point of reference, officials are better equiped to estimate their company's present and future employment trends in relation to overall industry trends. Such supporting material, BLS believes, substantially enhances the credibility of any projections furnished by the companies.

THE SUPPLY LAG THEORY

The supply lag theory recognizes that repeated increases in demand followed by minimal increases in supply will result in a continuing series of temporary labor shortages accompanied by rising wages. Blank and Stigler, early proponents of this theory, have stated that a series of temporary shortages will persist "when the number of workers available (the supply) increases less rapidly than the number demanded *at the salaries paid in the recent past.*"[2] If employers seeking to hire more workers raise salaries, these

---

[2] David M. Blank and George J. Stigler, *The Demand and Supply of Scientific Personnel,* National Bureau of Economic Research, Inc., New York, 1957, p. 24.

wage increases, in turn, may be used as a shortage indicator. It should be noted that part of the supply lag in the professions—following an increase in salaries—is due mainly to the extended time (often years) required to train new employees and also to imperfect market information and labor immobility.

The supply lag theory as an indicator of labor shortages is illustrated in figure VIII-2. The demand for a given occupation in any year is represented by D, the supply schedule by S. Subscripts denote the year. It is assumed that the number of workers supplied and the number required depends only, or at least approximately, on the salary level. During any given year D_1 and S_1 will intersect to establish the number of workers employed in the occupation q_1, and wage rate, w_1. Over a period of time a series of intersection points will appear, the trace (T) of which represents the historical trend in wages. If demand increases (shifts to the right) faster than supply, shortages will be indicated by a rise in the trace of intersection points; i.e., in a general rise in wages over time. If the supply increases faster than demand, the trace will fall, indicating decline in wages and a series of temporary surpluses of workers.

If changes in salary are to provide insight into the adequacy of supply in a

Figure VIII-2. — Supply and demand schedules illustrating the supply lag theory

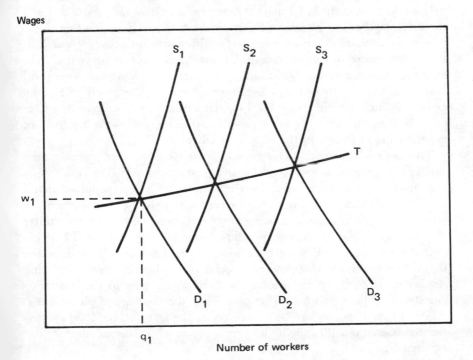

given occupation, they must be considered in relation to salary changes in other professions requiring similar training and, to a lesser extent, to the general trend for all salaries and wages. By such relative comparisons, certain common factors may be canceled out—i.e., price inflation, general competitiveness in the labor market, overall economic growth, and wage trends common to particular occupational groups.

Salary comparisons among different related occupations to determine relative upward or downward trends and, hence, continuing shortages or surpluses can be made in a number of ways. The easiest method is to plot the data for different related occupations in order to compare salary trends visually. Percentage increases in salaries from a base period may be calculated and compared; a comparison can also be made between the ratio of earnings in one occupation with that in another. Annual percentage changes in salaries may be computed and compared. Whatever statistical techniques are used, any significant upward trend in wages in one occupation *relative* to others requiring similar training (the absolute differential between occupational wages must be ignored) indicates that demand is increasing faster than supply. As a result, temporary manpower shortages for that occupation can be expected in the market place. Salary data in table VIII-2 for some professional occupations and a related plot, figure VIII-3, illustrate the supply lag approach to supply-demand analysis.

Imperfections in the labor market may prevent the supply of workers and the price mechanism (wages in this case) from properly responding to increases in demand. One type of market imperfection occurs when constraints are placed on the labor supply. If new employees are prevented from entering an occupation in which more workers are needed, employers will raise wages in an attempt to alleviate the shortage. The result will be an artificially high absolute wage level for one occupation in comparison with other occupations that require equivalent training and skills but are not experiencing restraints in the supply of labor.

The foregoing suggests that *differences in the absolute level* of wages among similar occupations, as well as *relative changes* in wages over time (the supply lag theory), may, under certain circumstances, reflect supply-demand conditions. The validity of this premise rests with soundness of judgment; in other words, the occupations being compared must be sufficiently similar that no significant differences in salary levels among them would be expected if the labor market were without defects. For example, some allege that the high salary level of physicians, relative to other professions requiring similar training, is indicative of a shortage due in part to the restrictive enrollment policies of medical schools. That the shortage of physicians is related to such policies can be supported by the fact that the level of physicians' salaries is artificially high in comparison with those in other similar occupations.

Another form of market imperfection is collusion on the part of employers

Figure VIII-3. — Salaries of selected professions and other occupations: 1948-72

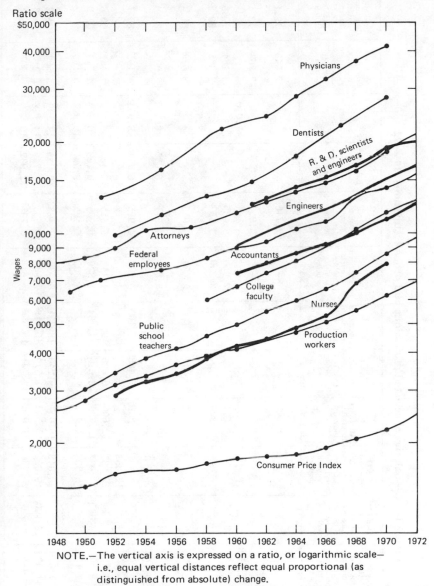

NOTE.—The vertical axis is expressed on a ratio, or logarithmic scale—
i.e., equal vertical distances reflect equal proportional (as
distinguished from absolute) change.

Source: See table VIII-2.

to fix wages at a level below what would exist in a free market. When this
practice occurs, a low salary level does not indicate a surplus of workers. In
fact, when wages are controlled, no assessment of their level or movement
is valid for purposes of interpreting supply and demand. Again using the

Table VIII-2.—Salaries of selected professions and other occupations: 1948-72

Year	Physicians (self-employed) median net income before income tax	Dentists (self-employed) median net income before income tax	R.&D. scientists and engineers (nonsupervisory) with doctoral degree	Attorneys in private industry	Accountants in private industry	Engineers in private industry	Nurses (generalized staff nurse in public health agencies)	Public school classroom teachers	Full-time faculty all ranks IHE, median salary	Federal employees GS-12	Production workers, all private nonagriculture payrolls	Consumer Price Index 1967 equals 100.0
1948				8,003			—	2,710			2,548	72.1
1950	13,150			8,349			—	3,050		6,400	2,763	72.1
1952		9,961		9,021			2,850	3,485		7,040	3,154	79.5
1954	16,017	11,533		10,258			3,250	3,867			3,355	80.5
1956				10,425			3,404	4,055		7,570	3,678	81.4
1958	22,100	13,366		10,792			3,881	4,571	6,015	8,330	3,904	86.6
1960		14,747	12,353	11,596	7,488	9,100	4,202	4,995	6,711	8,955	4,195	88.7
1962	24,300		12,931	12,696	8,028	10,152	4,442	5,515	7,486	9,475	4,467	90.6
1964	28,380	18,020	14,087	13,728	8,616	11,184	4,829	5,995	8,163	10,250	4,749	92.9
1966	32,170	22,850	15,397	14,751	9,202	12,022	5,305	6,485	9,081	10,927	5,139	97.2
1968	37,620		16,848	16,057	10,240	13,381	6,938	7,423	10,235	13,389	5,602	104.2
1970	41,500	28,100	19,020	18,789	11,379	15,116	7,986	8,635	11,745	14,192	6,212	116.3
1972	—	—	20,676	21,076	12,704	16,656	—	9,705	12,932	15,866	6,907	125.3

Sources

Physicians: American Medical Association, *Medical Economics*.

Dentists: American Dental Association, *Survey of Dental Practice*.

R. & D. scientists and engineers: 1961–1968, Los Alamos Scientific Laboratory of the University of California, Wage and Salary Department, *National Survey of Professional Scientific Salaries*.

    1968–   Battelle Memorial Institute, Columbus Laboratories, *National Survey of Compensation Paid Scientists and Engineers Engaged in Research Development*.

Attorneys: 1948–1954, *Survey of Current Business*.

    1957–58, U. S. Treasury Department, Internal Revenue Service, *Statistics of Income*.

Attorneys: 1960–   ⎫

Accountants and auditors: ⎬ U. S. Department of Labor, Bureau of Labor Statistics, *National Survey of Professional, Administrative, Technical, and Clerical Pay*. Weighted averages of mean annual salaries.

Engineers: ⎭

Nurses: American Nurses' Association, *Facts About Nursing, A Statistical Summary*.

Public school instructional staff: National Education Association Research Division, *Economic Status of the Teaching Profession*.

College and university faculty: National Education Association, Research Division, *Economic Status of the Profession*.

Federal employees: U. S. Civil Service Commission.

Production workers: U. S. Department of Labor, Bureau of Labor Statistics, *Employment and Earnings*. Annual earning estimates computed by NEA Research Division from weekly earnings shown in report.

Consumer Price Index: U. S. Department of Labor, Bureau of Labor Statistics.

medical profession as an example, the argument has been made that nurses' salaries have remained relatively low in the past because hospitals have allegedly agreed not to pay wages above a certain level.[3] If the allegation is true, salary data cannot be used to determine the status of supply and demand in the nursing profession. What is important in this context is not the validity of these contentions but the consequence that market imperfections may have on wage levels. It should also be kept in mind that while the supply lag theory employs only relative changes in wage levels over time, the level of wages may (if there are restraints on supply) be used as a labor-shortage indicator.

One advantage of analyzing wages to determine labor shortages is that no manpower census is required, only wage data. However, in order to maintain consistency and comparability between occupations and over the time span of a given study, care must be exercised in defining occupations and salaries. An inherent disadvantage of using a wage analysis is that the shortage is not quantified, i.e., no physical count is made of the number by which demand exceeds supply. The supply lag theory, which only provides an indication of past and current shortages, is most appropriately used for analysis of national supply and demand.

THE OCCUPATIONAL RATIO METHOD

The hypothesis that underlies the occupational ratio method of projecting long-range demand is that statistical relationships between employment in a given occupation and total employment in a given sector can be analyzed and utilized in making projections. The soundness of this hypothesis rests upon the degree to which total employment in any given sector has a causal or logical and reasonably stable relationship to employment in any one of a number of occupational subcomponents. Since each industry has a unique occupational structure, it is reasonable to expect there will be a close relationship between the number of workers in a given occupation

---

[3] One economist has described the nursing labor market as oligopsonistic, i.e., a market dominated by a few major buyers who can, if they agree, control the salaries of nurses. It is contended that hospitals are aware of the differences between the higher wage necessary to attract additional nurses and the marginal factor cost of paying that wage to all nurses employed. Furthermore, hospitals are also conscious of the impact their wage decision will have on the decision of other medical institutions in their area.

See Donald E. Yett, "The Causes and Consequences of Salary Differentials in Nursing," paper presented to the annual meeting of the Western Economic Association, Berkeley, Calif., Aug. 26, 1966.

and total employment in that industry. The success of the method depends on the accuracy with which this relationship can be projected and, even more basically, on the degree to which an accurate independent projection of total employment in the sector is possible.

In deriving projections of overall employment in a given sector, the factors which must be taken into account are growth in population and in the labor force, shifting consumer preferences, and technological developments.[4] These types of employment projections are frequently prepared by the Bureau of Labor Statistics for such sectors as government and colleges and universities and for such industries as mining, construction, manufacturing, transportation, and public utilities.[5] Since the factors affecting employment of scientists and engineers, for example, are far different in educational institutions from what they are in private industry and in government agencies, individual projections must be made for these and other major sectors of the economy.

The procedure to be followed requires that employment data for the occupation under consideration be related (in terms of a ratio) to total employment in the sector over a sufficient period to permit an analysis of trends and extrapolation into the future. By applying the projected occupational employment ratios to projections of total employment within the sector, it is possible to derive an approximation of future employment levels (demand) in any given occupation. (For an illustration employing this approach to estimate the long-range demand for scientists and engineers, see table VIII-3.) Because factors influencing demand for personnel differ

---

[4] For example, underlying Bureau of Labor Statistics projections for the *demand* for college-trained manpower are the following economic, political, and technological assumptions:

The institutional framework of the economy will not change radically during the 1970's. There will be full employment in 1980, with the unemployment rate ranging between 3 and 4 percent. The United States will no longer be fighting a war, but the still-guarded relationship between major powers will permit no major arms reduction. Defense spending, however, will be reduced from the peak levels of the Viet Nam conflict. Economic, social, technical, and scientific trends will continue, including public values placed on work, education, income, and leisure. Fiscal and monetary policies and an active manpower program will result in a satisfactory balance between low unemployment rates and relative price stability without reducing the long-term economic growth rate.

[5] For discussion of the sources and methods used by BLS in deriving projections of total employment by sector, see U. S. Department of Labor, Bureau of Labor Statistics, *Tomorrow's Manpower Needs: National Manpower Projections and a Guide to their Use as a Tool in Developing State and Area Manpower Projections*, Bulletin 1606 (4 vols.), U. S. Government Printing Office, Washington, D. C., 1969.

For projection data; see *The U. S. Economy 1980: A Summary of BLS Projections*, Bulletin 1973, U. S. Department of Labor, Bureau of Labor Statistics, U. S. Government Printing Office, Washington, D. C., 1970.

Table VIII-3.—Illustrative employment data and projected demand for scientists and engineers in selected industries

Industry	Total employment		Scientists and engineers as a percent of total employment					Employment of scientists and engineers	
	yr 4	yr 16 projected	yr 1	yr 2	yr 3	yr 4	yr 16 projected	yr 4	yr 16 projected
Mining	647,600	833,400	2.3	3.5	4.0	4.7	9.5	30,500	79,500
Construction	1,298,500	2,008,600	3.9	5.5	3.1	4.1	5.3	53,700	110,600
Manufacturing	15,830,400	20,643,500	2.7	3.7	3.3	3.5	5.3	568,000	1,140,000
Transportation, communication, and public utilities	3,800,100	4,418,600	1.5	1.9	1.4	1.6	1.9	59,500	84,800
Engineering and architectural services	185,200	238,000	—	—	30.4	30.3	30.3	56,100	72,100
Medical and dental laboratories	12,300	15,600	—	—	7.9	8.0	8.4	1,000	1,300
Miscellaneous business services	296,400	377,800	—	—	1.5	2.3	3.3	7,000	12,300
Nonprofit organizations	26,300	34,300	—	.7	22.9	—	22.9	6,000	7,900
Other manufacturing	6,475,800	8,640,000	.3	.7	.4	.4	.6	26,300	52,700

among occupations and according to the exact type of function performed within each occupation, it is important that the occupation under consideration be finely detailed.

It must be borne in mind that when the foregoing ratios are employed to derive projections, actual employment represents demand. It may be necessary to revise the size of the labor force of an industry and the occupational mix to account for possible changes in the productivity or utilization of personnel. In addition, vacancies created by deaths and retirements must be estimated separately.

A number of techniques can be used to develop State and area occupational employment projections. Local employment in an industry can be compared over time with national employment in the same industry; a trend in the relationship can then be determined by computing for each year the local industry employment as a percentage of the industry's employment nationwide. In geographical areas in which local and national employment trends are not closely related, regression techniques may be used to account for growth factors originating within the area. State and area occupational projections may be developed through the use of national industry-occupational matrices. Details of how national manpower data may be used to develop State and area manpower requirement projections are published by the Bureau of Labor Statistics.[6]

ESTIMATING MANPOWER SUPPLY

The occupational ratio method determines only the *demand* for manpower; to measure shortages, an estimate of *supply* must be ascertained. The expenditure ratio method (discussed in the ensuing section) also requires a separate estimate of supply. Supply projections are usually made to estimate the levels of supply that would result if no corrective steps were taken—through vocational guidance or increased training program enrollments—to adjust supply to prospective demand. Determining projected supply usually involves those persons employed in a given occupation as well as those unemployed *qualified* persons *seeking* employment in the same occupation. Excluded are qualified "potential" workers who choose not to work in the occupation.

---

[6] See U. S. Department of Labor, Bureau of Labor Statistics, *Developing Area Manpower Projections*, vol. 1 of *Tomorrow's Manpower Needs*, op. cit.

The general formula for supply-demand analysis is:

$$\text{Demand} - \text{Supply} = \text{Manpower Requirements}$$

Demand for manpower is created by:
    (1) new jobs due to growth and technology
    (2) deaths and retirements
    (3) transfers and promotions to other occupations

Supply for manpower is created by:
    (1) new entrants from training programs
    (2) unemployed workers seeking work in the occupation
    (3) entrants from other occupations
    (4) immigrants.

The factors that immediately influence the number of new entrants into an occupation are: (1) the ease with which jobs can be obtained, as determined by whether a shortage exists or not, and (2) wage differentials. Over the long run, the availability of educational opportunities, student financial aid, and the length of training required have an important bearing on the supply of new entrants. The social status of the occupation is also a factor. Since most though not all of the increment in the annual supply of professional personnel is derived from college graduates, secondary factors are especially important and their control by colleges and universities has much to do with governing the adequacy of supply in the professions. In developing supply projections, specific assumptions must be made concerning each factor and its effect on supply.

The usual procedure in developing supply projections consists of three basic steps:[7]

First, a current supply estimate is established as the base of the projection. The current supply in a given occupation equals actual current employment and the number actively seeking employment in that occupation. The current supply is different and less than the "potential" supply, which includes all workers who could perform the type of work in question but who decide to work in another occupation or not to work at all.

Second, the annual number of entrants from all sources is ascertained for the period that the projection is to cover. College graduates make up, by far, the largest portion of new entrants into the professions. The estimates of entrants from college are based on three factors: (1) projections of new

---

[7] Adapted and condensed from procedures described in two sources: Neal Rosenthal, "Projections of Manpower Supply on a Specific Occupation," *Technical Note*, reprint no. 2512 from the *Monthly Labor Review*, November 1966, U. S. Department of Labor, Bureau of Labor Statistics; U. S. Department of Labor, *Developing Area Manpower Projections*, op. cit.

college graduates in each field, (2) estimates of the proportion of new college graduates in each degree field who enter the field immediately after receiving their degree, and (3) estimates of the proportion of these graduates not employed in the field at the time they receive their degrees. Projections of graduates, by sex, in individual fields of study are made continuously by the U.S. Office of Education on the basis of past trends within the total school population enrolled or graduated in each course.[8] These projections assume that the inclination of students to enroll in the various courses will follow past trends.

Since not all who complete a specialized training program enter the field for which they have been prepared, estimates must be made of the proportion who actually do. Estimates of such proportions are generally derived from follow-up studies of recent graduates.[9] Such studies can also provide estimates of the number of entrants with degrees in other fields who enter the occupation in question. Finally, an adjustment must be made to reflect the number of graduates, who, while attending school, were employed in the *same* field of work they entered directly following graduation. The latter cannot be considered new entrants.

Although graduates who enter professional occupations immediately after completing college represent a major source of supply, new entrants also include workers from related occupations, persons (other than students) not previously in the labor force, and immigrants. Estimates of new entrants from each of these smaller sources may be made separately and aggregated to develop a total. For most occupations, however, the information necessary to develop such independent estimates is lacking, and an alternative method must be used: a net estimate of all other entrants combined, based on an analysis of past data.

The third and final step in developing projections of total annual supply is to add the base current supply to the yearly estimate of new entrants and deduct annual occupational losses from each group—losses resulting from transfer to other fields of work, from retirement, and from death. Transfers may be measured either by a follow-up study of persons completing training for an occupation or of a large group of individuals currently employed in an occupation.[10] Estimates of occupational losses resulting from death and retirement are developed by applying empirically derived separation rates

[8] See U. S. Department of Health, Education, and Welfare, Office of Education, *Projections of Educational Statistics to 1980–81, 1971 Edition*, U. S. Government Printing Office, Washington, D. C., 1972.

[9] Two major follow-up studies by the National Science Foundation provide data in developing such estimates: *Two Years After the College Degree—Work and Further Study Patterns*, and *Education and Employment Specialization in 1952 of June 1951 College Graduates*.

[10] The first method is illustrated in the National Science Foundation publication, *Two Years After the College Degree—Work and Further Study Patterns;* the second, in the *Postcensal Survey of Professional and Technical Personnel*.

to the age distribution of the occupation. Separation rates resulting from retirements and deaths are available from a series of tables of working life prepared by the U. S. Department of Labor.[11] These tables depict, through successive ages, the experience of an initial cohort of 100,000 births. Among all occupations, retirement and death rates for men range from about 1 percent to more than 3 percent, depending upon the age composition. For women, the rate ranges from 3 to 5 percent.

In estimating demand, allowance should be made for improvements in worker utilization that could result in a lower demand than that indicated in first approximations. The problem of projecting supply is also compounded by the fact that significant numbers of persons without college degrees may enter certain professions, with little information available on the number involved.

THE EXPENDITURE RATIO METHOD

Another factor that bears a causal or logical relationship to employment levels is the amount spent to purchase goods and services in a given sector or industry. There is a direct connection between dollar expenditures and employed manpower. When levels of employment in different occupations are related to total expenditures within the industry, projections of this ratio can be applied to alternative estimates of future dollar expenditures based on expected national and industrial growth. The validity of this type of approach rests fundamentally on the accuracy with which total future expenditures in any given sector can be estimated and on the relevancy and stability of employment levels to these expenditures.

Although expenditures in many areas are probably related to the volume of production and manpower requirements, management decisions to increase production depend on a variety of factors difficult to measure and project. Among them are the amount of return on investment expected, the attractiveness of alternative allocations of resources, and the impact of competition. Assuming that the problems involved in evaluating these factors are surmounted and that projections of expenditures are derived, it is still necessary to know something of how the funds are to be allocated; specifically, the amount to be devoted to facilities, equipment, and personnel. Further, it is necessary to know what changes can be anticipated in worker productivity due to technological advances. These are only a few

---

[11] See U. S. Department of Labor, Manpower Administration, *The Length of Working Life for Males, 1900–1960*, Manpower Report no. 8, 1963.

of the problems involved in developing projections of future employment levels on the basis of total expenditures in a given industry. Nevertheless, this general approach appears to be theoretically defensible and, in some instances, it is the only feasible method.

Predicting future expenditures in any given sector is usually accomplished by determining the relationship between sector expenditures and the gross national product (GNP). Since considerable effort is made by many institutions to project this basic measure of U. S. national productivity, any consistent relationship between expenditures in a given sector and the GNP immediately assumes much of the accuracy (or inaccuracy) inherent in the GNP prediction itself. Alternative estimates of GNP based on different

Table VIII-4.—Illustrative projection of biomedical research expenditures and relation to gross national product and professional manpower

Year	GNP (billions)	Biomedical research		Professional manpower	
		Amount (millions)	Percent of GNP	Total number	Expenditure per worker
1	$257.6	$124	.05		
2	256.5	147	.06		
3	284.8	161	.06		
4	328.4	175	.05		
5	345.5	197	.06		
6	364.6	214	.06		
7	364.8	237	.07		
8	398.0	261	.07	18,600	$14,000
9	419.2	312	.07		
10	441.1	440	.10		
11	447.8	543	.12		
12	483.7	648	.13		
13	503.7	845	.17	39,700	21,000
14	520.1	1,045	.20		
15	560.3	1,290	.23		
16	590.5	1,486	.25		
17	632.4	1,652	.26		
18	683.9	1,841	.27	64,000	30,000
19	743.3	2,050	.28		
20	785.0	2,280	.29		
PROJECTED					
23	886.0	2,900	.33	71,000	41,000
28	1,077.0	5,500	.51	100,000	55,500
33	1,310.0	9,700	.74	130,000	75,000
38	1,594.0	15,700	.98	150,000	104,500

NOTE.—Historical amounts in actual dollars; projected amounts in constant year 20 dollars.

assumptions are available,[12] and the user can select the estimate most consistent with his own set of assumptions.

Use of the expenditure ratio methodology to project professional manpower requirements for biomedical research is illustrated in table VIII-4. The procedure followed consists of: (1) determining the probable rate of growth in biomedical research expenditures by projecting the relationship of this research to the gross national product; (2) determining the probable increase in expenditures per professional worker (in this instance, estimated to be six percent per annum), and (3) calculating future employment requirements by dividing projected expenditures for biomedical research by projected expenditures per professional worker.

THE SOCIAL NEED THEORY

Previously discussed methods of manpower analysis—job vacancy survey, supply lag theory, occupation ratio, and expenditure ratio—rely on a free market to ensure optimal resource allocation and to establish equilibrium between manpower supply and demand. The social need theory differs from these economic-oriented methodologies in that it is based on a moral or value approach. It proposes that a "shortage" exists in any occupation whenever fewer persons than *ought* to be are employed. The theory is based on the premise that certain enterprises in this society (particularly those providing public services) require a certain number of staff members if they are to operate effectively and in the best interests of the public and the economy. Thus a teacher shortage, as defined by this concept, would mean that from a pedagogically desirable viewpoint too few qualified teachers are teaching too many students. In the case of medical doctors, a shortage, according to the social need theory, occurs whenever there is an insufficient number of physicians to provide adequate and proper medical services for the existing population, i.e., when some health needs are not met.

As pointed out by Alice Rivlin and others, the meaning of a labor shortage in the aforementioned sense must be carefully distinguished from the economist's meaning (unfilled positions at current salaries)—if for no other reason than the fact that solutions to the shortage differ. Unfilled positions at current salaries will eventually be filled by a freely operating market mechanism. However, a shortage defined on the basis of social need will not disappear by normal market action because a shortage so identified is based on a value judgment rather than on employer or consumer demand.

---

[12] See U. S. Department of Commerce, Office of Business Economics, *Survey of Current Business*, U. S. Government Printing Office, Washington, D. C.

A shortage based on social need will be alleviated only when public demand is sufficient to bring about an increase in pay and thereby attract an increased supply. A doctor shortage or a teacher shortage, for example, will abate only if society decides to devote more resources to educating and hiring doctors and teachers. Whether or not society will take such action depends on how much value it receives from these services as against the amount received from alternative expenditures.

The staffing requirement of a given occupation, based on social need, is generally expressed in the form of a ratio indicating the number of qualified workers required in that occupation relative to a selected population base serviced by the occupation. Examples of such ratios are 1 elementary school teacher per 25 pupils, 100 physicians per 100,000 population, 2 to 3 supporting technicians per engineer, 25 general duty nurses per 100 hospital patients, etc. In each instance, the designated population base supposedly represents the principal recipients of the services provided by the occupation; therefore, it is, in effect, an indirect measure of worker "productivity." It may also be viewed as a unit "load" measurement.

The most serious limitation of the social need theory lies in the fact that any single group receiving services does not accurately represent all of the multiple populations benefiting from those same services. Probably the most valid use of this theory is when it is applied to the teaching profession. According to recommended class sizes, elementary-secondary school teachers are expected to instruct approximately 25 pupils per class. With 50.4 million pupils in grades K-12 in 1973, approximately 2.0 million teachers would be needed. (The actual number was 2.3 million.) In most other categories, however, determining the relationship between personnel requirements and population served is more difficult. In some instances, special variants must be introduced. For example, the requirements for policemen must be based on variations in local crime rates, as well as the size of the population served. In general, the base population and desired personnel ratio can be determined without too much difficulty in pro fessions such as teaching and health, which independently provide direct services to individuals. Such is not the case, however, for professions that combine with other occupations to produce varied and interrelated services. In such instances—attorneys, for example—identifying an individual load measure may be impossible.

Assuming that the difficulties of devising a population load measurement can be surmounted, there are three types of standards that may be used to determine staffing adequacy. The simplest approach is to assume that the manpower staffing-to-load ratio of a base year is adequate and that present or estimated future ratios below the one established represent shortages. This assumption, usually made in the absence of any better criterion, does not take into account measured increases in the productivity of the occupation or any possible changes in demand. A second standard that may be

Table VIII-5.—Illustrative ratios of physicians to population and effective buying income per capita, by county group

County group within State	Number of physicians (M.D.'s) per 100,000 population					Effective buying income per capita (in dollars)				
	State "A"	State "B"	State "C"	State "D"	U.S.	State "A"	State "B"	State "C"	State "D"	U.S.
Greater metropolitan	NA	NA	NA	145.4	195.4	NA	NA	NA	$2,461	$2,526
Lesser metropolitan	156.4	126.5	179.5	148.0	145.3	$2,134	$2,082	$2,521	2,026	2,070
Adjacent to metropolitan	65.2	40.3	71.7	101.3	85.6	1,381	1,408	1,668	1,784	1,65
Isolated semirural	120.5	98.7	91.4	93.4	94.2	1,693	1,815	1,755	1,733	1,551
Isolated rural	44.7	50.2	60.0	67.8	53.0	1,516	1,268	1,416	1,619	1,207
Total	91.3	82.1	117.9	114.2	142.9	1,513	1,644	1,984	1,918	2,059

NA = not applicable.

used, based on analytical study of worker productivity, defines an optimal staffing-to-load ratio that provides adequate, effective, and efficient service. Except for classroom teachers, however, few if any studies of productivity in the professions have been conducted; therefore, no standards of this type are available. Even if such studies were made, it is unlikely that a consensus could be achieved as to what constitutes adequate and proper staffing. One reason is that manpower-productivity analysis is further complicated by geographical and economic factors affecting staffing requirements. Thus, complexity and insufficient research in the case of the productivity standard and oversimplification in the case of the base year standard prevent either of these measures from adequately serving as a benchmark for the social need theory. The third approach, relative comparison, is a feasible and acceptable alternative.

The relative comparison approach provides a yardstick for occupational shortages by noting relative differences in manpower staffing levels at comparable geographical locations where the governing factors appear similar. The relative comparison approach is based on the assumption that, under a set of similar circumstances, manpower staffing requirements *"ought"* to be the same at different locations; that only achievement will differ. It is also assumed, with some reservation, that the highest staffing level achieved will be adequate and acceptable.

The inherent advantage of this approach is that since the major causal factors remain relatively constant, many circumstances affecting manpower demand are accounted for. Reasonable comparisons provide reasonable measures of shortages that are at once both realistic and meaningful. In table VIII-5, for example, consider the adequacy of physician staffing in State "B" compared with that in three other States whose buying income per capita is similar. Comparison suggests that a standard of 100 physicians per 100,000 population ratio would be reasonable. If this standard is accepted, a shortage of approximately 20 physicians per 100,000 population exists in State "B" (pop. 687,000). To alleviate this shortage, 140 additional physicians properly distributed throughout the State are required. Analysis as detailed or more detailed than this may be conducted for any professional staffing-load ratios, subject only to data limitations.

ESTIMATING FACULTY SUPPLY AND DEMAND—A SPECIAL CASE

The demand for faculty is most frequently estimated on the basis of assumed student-faculty ratios—an approach employing the social need theory. If only an indication of present and impending shortages is desired, a survey may be used. One conducted nationwide to measure the relative scarcity of faculty in 23 disciplines reported seven factors—each either a cause or a result of excess demand.[13] Surveys of local needs, within a State for example, may be less complex, but because the differences in manpower shortages among the various disciplines are substantial, each discipline must be considered separately.

Before discussing the procedure to be followed in estimating faculty needs based on assumed student-faculty ratios, it is important to recognize the assumptions on which such a projection is based. It is equally important to understand the need to establish clear definitions of faculty and students and the need to provide detailed breakdown of data by instructional level and discipline. As with any projection, the accuracy of estimating the number of faculty needed depends on whether or not certain assumptions become actualities. The two most critical assumptions—because they vary and are subject to error—are the expected student-faculty ratio and the trend in total enrollment. Other assumptions are generally less critical since in most instances it is assumed that the existing situation will not change enough to significantly affect the estimates. Assumptions of the latter type are usually made regarding admission and retention policies, distribution of institutional course offerings and levels of instruction, provision for new facilities, proportion of staff involved in research, appointment standards, and annual rate of staff loss.

Because faculty needs may be most readily acted upon when the number involved are identified by discipline and level of instruction, demand estimates should provide separate projections for junior colleges, senior colleges, and universities (lower division, upper division, and graduate levels), as well as for major subject fields (California, for example, uses 2 subject fields). Such detail may appear excessive, but it is necessary because enrollment trends and student-faculty ratios vary greatly in such aspect as instructional level and discipline.

Lastly, the validity and usefulness of faculty-need estimates are seriously jeopardized if terms are not properly defined. Enrollments must be measured according to full-time-equivalents, with careful weighting of degree credit and non-degree-credit status. Since the student-faculty ratio expresse the expected balance between students and faculty in the classroom, th ratio is suitable only for projecting *teaching* faculty who devote most of thei

---

[13] See David G. Brown, *The Mobile Professors*, American Council on Education Washington, D. C., 1967, pp. 10–14. The seven scarcity indicators surveyed wer (1) starting salaries of newly graduated Ph.D.'s, (2) extent of salary increases, (3) salari paid to full professors in 1962–63, (4) academic rank of newly graduated Ph.D.'s, (5) u filled positions as a percentage of all positions, (6) percentage of newly graduate Ph.D.'s entering college teaching, and (7) expansion demand as a percentage of hiring.

time to instruction. Faculty required to conduct research or perform other activities may be determined as a proportion of the projected needs for full-time-equivalent teaching staff.

Although many variations exist, a typical procedure for estimating future teaching faculty needs is as follows:

1. Obtain for at least the past 5-year period the number of student credit hours classified by level of instruction (lower division, upper division, master's, and doctor's), type of institution (junior college, senior college, university), and field of study.

2. Convert the number of student credit hours in each field of study and at each level of instruction to percentages of the total instruction at each type of institution. Thus for 1 year at all senior colleges, 10,000 credit hours of English instruction at the lower division level might equal 5 percent of the total instruction (200,000 credit hours) offered.

3. On the basis of past trends and stated assumptions, project the future share (percentage) of total instruction expected in each field-level combination. For the example in step 2, the past trend in lower division English instruction may warrant a 6- or 7-percent increase in the future.

4. For each type of institution, project *total* enrollment during each year of the projection period. Convert to full-time-equivalent students and, in turn, to total instructional load in student credit hours (one FTE student is usually equal to 12 to 15 credit hours).

5. To determine projected instruction loads, apply the projected share percentages in each field-level combination (as determined in step 3) to projections of total instruction load.

6. For each type of institution, subject field, and level of instruction, determine planned future student-faculty ratios in terms of student credit hours of instruction per FTE teaching faculty member.

7. The number of FTE teaching faculty required in each discipline, by level of instruction and type of institution, can now be determined by applying the student-faculty ratios to the number of student credit hour instructional loads predicted in step 5.

8. New annual staff requirements can be expected to equal new additional staff requirements based on enrollment as calculated in step 7, plus replacement of yearly staff losses through resignation, retirement, or death.

The data basic to estimating the future supply of faculty are less complete than are those for demand. The principal gap is in the lack of data regarding the definite number with graduate degrees in a given field who will teach in colleges and universities. At the State level this data gap is particularly wide due to the difficulty of estimating the number of faculty who enter from out of State. Any State estimating the future potential supply of faculty should first ascertain its major sources of recruits. Such an estimate can most easily be accomplished by surveying faculty members and studying trends. A State may determine, for example, that 60 percent of its faculty are graduates of public and private institutions within the State and that 30 percent are graduates of public institutions in three adjoining States. A potential total supply of faculty members can then be calculated by weighting the projected number of graduates from each source. Comparison of past faculty employed, by type of institution, with potential estimated supply will reveal trends in the ratio of potential supply to actual employment. The resultant ratio can be projected and applied to the expected numbers of graduates from the various sources.

The supply of faculty members determined in this manner is based on three critical assumptions:

1. The proportion of graduate degrees from each source and in each subject field awarded in the past will remain constant.
2. In each subject field the percent of degree holders who enter college teaching will remain the same.
3. The State will continue to recruit from the major sources of supply at approximately the same rate (in proportion to the number of graduates) as it has in the past.

BIBLIOGRAPHY

Altman, Stuart H., *The Structure of Nursing Education and its Impact on Supply* (reprint), The Urban Institute, Washington, D. C., 1970, 22 pp.

Blank, David M., and George J. Stigler, *The Demand and Supply of Scientific Personnel*, National Bureau of Economic Research, Inc., New York, 1957, 200 pp.

Blumberg, Mark S., *Trends and Projections of Physicians in the United States*, Carnegie Commission on Higher Education, Berkeley, Calif., 1971.

Engineering Manpower Commission of Engineers Joint Council, *Demand for Engineers and Technicians—1968*, New York, 1969, 40 pp.

Fein, Rashi, *The Doctor Shortage: An Economic Diagnosis*, The Brookings Institution, Washington, D.C., 1967, 199 pp.

Simon, Kenneth A. and Martin M. Frankel, *Projections of Educational Statistics to 1980–81*, U.S. Department of Health, Education, and Welfare, Office of Education, U.S. Government Printing Office, Washington, D.C., 1972, 176 pp.

U.S. Department of Health, Education, and Welfare, Public Health Service, National Institutes of Health, *Resources for Medical Research: Biomedical Research Manpower for the Eighties*, Report No. 11, U.S. Government Printing Office, Washington, D.C., 1968, 119 pp.

U.S. Department of Health, Education, and Welfare, Public Health Service, National Center for Health Statistics, *Health Resources Statistics, 1970*, U.S. Government Printing Office, Washington, D.C., 1971.

U.S. Department of Labor, Bureau of Labor Statistics, *College Educated Workers 1968–80* (Bulletin 1676), U.S. Government Printing Offiice, Washington, D.C., 1970, 25 pp.
  —*Ph.D. Scientists and Engineers in Private Industry 1968–80* (Bulletin 1648), 1970, 20 pp
  —*Technician Manpower 1966–80* (Bulletin 1639), 1970, 28 pp.
  —*The U.S. Economy in 1980: A Summary of BLS Projections* (Bulletin 1673), 1970, 59 pp
  —*Tomorrow's Manpower Needs: National Manpower Projections and a Guide to their Use as a Tool in Developing State and Area Manpower Projections* (Bulletin 1606), 4 vols. 1969.

Chapter IX

COLLEGE AND UNIVERSITY LIBRARIES

In view of the tremendous increase in published works[1] and the greater demand for library services, without corresponding increases in staff and budget, pressure for changing outmoded operational procedures is mounting. What can be done to update them is discussed in this chapter.

The four library operations chosen for discussion are: (1) selecting the collection, (2) providing access to the collection, (3) sharing of resources through interlibrary cooperation, and (4) evaluating the adequacy of the collection size. (Library financing and formulating library budgetary requirements are discussed in chapters XII and XIV, respectively.)

SELECTION

The most valuable function that librarians perform is that of selecting the collection. This task demands continuity as well as detailed professional screening—responsibilities shared with faculty. To select books intelligently, one must not only be thoroughly familiar with the disciplines involved but must also recognize the reference and research needs of the faculty, the special requirements of graduate students, and the basic needs of undergraduates. Furthermore, knowledge of the holdings of those libraries within the interlibrary loan system should be sufficiently broad to

---

[1] In 1972 alone, 26,868 new titles were published in the United States, 5,000 to 6,000 of which were likely to be sufficiently serious or scholarly to merit consideration as additions to the college undergraduate library. The increased publication rate has resulted in university and research libraries doubling in size every 15 to 12 years. See Fremond Rider, *The Scholar and the Future of the Research Library, Problem and Its Solution*, Hadham Press, New York, 1944. Dunn and others, in analyzing 58 research libraries, confirm this rate of doubling by projecting growth patterns from 1951 to 1980. See Oliver Charles Dunn, W. F. Seibert, and Janice A. Scheuneman, *The Past and Likely Future of 58 Research Libraries, 1951–1980: A Statistical Study of Growth and Change*, University Libraries and Audio Visual Center, Purdue University, Lafayette, Ind., 1966.

avoid duplication. Under these conditions, it is difficult to visualize accomplishing the selection process other than by a personal appraisal of each title by members of the library staff and faculty.

If title-by-title selection is to be preserved in preference to blind "bulk" buying, new selection methods must be introduced. A multiapproach that appears to be workable consists of (1) discriminating use of "core collections" for establishing and reviewing the library base; (2) a greater role in book selection by the librarian and book jobber, with increased reliance on approval orders; and (3) more extensive and organized use of review material, such as proof slips, *Choice*, *Booklist*, catalogs, etc.

Core Collection and Package Buying

The American Library Association has declared that a 2-year institution of up to 1,000 students (full-time equivalent) "cannot discharge its mission without a carefully selected collection of at least 20,000 volumes, exclusive of duplicates and textbooks."[2] In the fall of 1970, 301 junior colleges, 130 4-year institutions, and 40 universities had collections of less than 20,000 volumes (see figure IX-1). Many of these institutions were new colleges that quite literally required "instant" libraries, but any institution experiencing rapid enrollment growth will find it difficult to maintain an adequate collection. Either starting or expanding a college library is a very expensive process. Books in print cost an average of approximately $13 each (1972), and processing can add more than half again as much to this amount. Thus the problem of rapidly acquiring literally thousands of basic titles is compounded by the disparity between high prices and a limited budget. A solution that is gaining acceptance, particularly among new institutions attempting to establish an opening-day collection, is "package" buying of "core collections."

The concept of a core collection, or basic list of references considered essential and commonly required by many college libraries, offers exceptional opportunities for savings. Both a list of books published in past years and a list of new publications constitute finite sets that can be mass-produced at a low unit cost and sold as packages. Such packages, which may feature inexpensive reinforced paperbacks and Perma-Bound editions, generally arrive fully processed and shelf-ready.

---

[2] Association of College Research Libraries (ACRI) Committee on Standards, Felix E. Hirsch (chairman), "Standards for Junior College Libraries," *College and Research Libraries*, vol. 21, May 1960, pp. 200–06.

As a substitute for quantity recommendations—later ALA guidelines advocate a collection showing that materials are "relevant to the various ages, cultural backgrounds, intellectual levels, developmental needs, and vocational goals represented in the student body."

Figure IX -1. — Distribution of colleges and universities by number of volumes held at end of year and by institutional control, type, and size: 1970-71

Key: Universities _1_   4-year colleges (1)   2-year colleges 1

PUBLIC

Number of institutions by volumes held at end of year

Enrollment	Less than 5,000 volumes	5,000 to 9,999	10,000 to 19,999	20,000 to 34,999	35,000 to 59,999	60,000 to 99,999	100,000 to 199,999	200,000 to 499,000	500,000 to 999,999	1,000,000 or more volumes
10,000 or more		1	(1)	2	14	14	2 _5_ (13)	_17_ (32)	27 (3)	_34_
5,000 to 10,000	1		3	15	41	13 (4)	1 2 (53)	_1_ 19 (28)	4 (2)	
2,500 to 5,000		1	16	68 1	36 (2)	2 (23)	1 10 (45)	2 (6)		2
1,000 to 2,500	1 _1_	20 _1_	64 _8_	105 _8_ (2)	20 _7_ (22)	1 _2_ (29)	1 (13)	1 (4)		
500 to 1,000	6	19 3 (1)	63 _10_ (3)	32 6 (4)	2 (7)	3 (6)	1 2 (3)			
Less than 500	3 _1_	23 4 (1)	13 _9_ (4)	4 5 (7)	3 (3)	(2)				

PRIVATE

Number of institutions by volumes held at end of year

Enrollment	Less than 5,000 volumes	5,000 to 9,999	10,000 to 19,999	20,000 to 34,999	35,000 to 59,999	60,000 to 99,999	100,000 to 199,999	200,000 to 499,000	500,000 to 999,999	1,000,000 or more volumes
10,000 or more						1	(2)	_3_	_9_	_11_
5,000 to 10,000	2	(1)		_1_		1	1 (10)	8 (7)	6 (1)	_9_ (1)
2,500 to 5,000				1 (3)	1 (6)	(13)	1 (31)	6 (9)	1 (2)	(1)
1,000 to 2,500	(2)	2 (4)	2 (4)	10 (8)	7 (33)	1 (136)	2 (97)	(27)	(2)	
1,500 to 1,000	4 (3)	4 (5)	11 (9)	16 (31)	6 (123)	(110)	1 (28)	(6)		_1_
Less than 500	7 (16)	9 (21)	1 28 (56)	32 (59)	11 3 (68)	(35)	(16)	(2)		

Source: Stanley V. Smith and Joel Williams, _Library Statistics of Colleges and Universities, Institutional Data, Part A, Fall 1971_, U.S. Department of Health, Education, and Welfare, Office of Education, U.S. Government Printing Office, Washington, D.C., 1972.

Package buying of large standardized sets[3] of books rests entirely on the assumption that every well-endowed college library contains a similar core collection of publications so valuable that if a significant number were missing the educational program would suffer. The listing is generally compiled by distilling shelf lists of recognized superior college library collections and by using bibliographies. Final selection is left to the judgment of panels of experts typically composed of subject specialists, faculty members, and librarians.

Probably the most persuasive argument in favor of the core concept is the fact that substantial "overlap" exists in the collections of similar types of institutions. The extent of the "overlap" or "commonality" in acquisitions has been documented in several studies. In one, conducted at five university libraries in the District of Columbia (American University, Catholic University, George Washington University, Georgetown University, and Howard University), a random sample of 200 currently published books formed the basis of investigation. The percentages of this sample of 200 acquired by each institution were, respectively, 57.5, 47.0, 32.5, 50.0, and 37.0.[4] If libraries at universities with goals more similar than those in the District of Columbia had been selected, the percentage of duplication would possibly be even higher.

The feasibility and the desirability of compiling standard lists have been repeatedly demonstrated.[5] Some of the more popular core collection listings relevant to college libraries are:

Books for College Libraries—A selected list of 53,400 titles of interest to an undergraduate community, based on the initial selection made for the University of California's New Campuses Program by Melvin J. Voigt and Joseph H. Trez, American Library Association, 1967. The list, which encompasses all fields of knowledge, includes essential titles for the general collection as well as some scholarly monographs, important out-of-print titles, and original paperbacks. A second edition of *Books for College Libraries,* citing 40,000 titles, is now being prepared by *Choice* and the Associa-

---

[3] On a more restrictive basis, subject modules can be identified for common curriculum areas and graded lists developed to accommodate budgetary limitations.

[4] *A Feasibility Study for a Joint Computer Center for Five Washington, D.C. University Libraries: Final Report,* Consortium of Universities of Metropolitan Washington, D.C., 1968.

[5] For a compendium that comprehensively reviews the current status and future outlook of bibliography, see Robert B. Downs and Frances B. Jenkins, "Bibliography: Current State and Future Trends, Parts 1 & 2," *Library Trends,* vol. XIV, January and April 1967.

For standard works of reference and for bibliographic tools, see Constance M. Winchell, *Guide to Reference Books* (8th ed.), American Library Association, Chicago, 1967.

tion of College Research Libraries and is scheduled for publication in spring 1974.

Books for Junior College Libraries—A list of approximately 15,000 titles carefully selected for transfer and liberal arts students at junior and community colleges. An initial selection of approximately 40,000 titles was made, based on the shelf lists of three junior colleges (in different geographic areas) with recognized outstanding collections. A corps of more than 300 consultants—subject specialists, faculty members, and librarians—assisted in the final selections under the direction of James W. Pirie of the American Library Association, 1969.

Junior College Library Collection—A core for the junior college library consisting of 17,500 titles. Edited by Frank Bertelan, Bro-Dart Foundation, Newark, N.J., 1968.

Choice "Opening Day" Collection—More than 2,000 essential in-print and out-of-print books for the undergraduate library.

Xerox College Library Enrichment Collection—A list of 9,000 titles to enrich the "Opening Day" Collection, based on *Choice* reviews beginning with vol. 1, 1964. Of the total, 3,000 titles are the cumulation of the 1964–68 annual "Outstanding Academic Books" bibliographies. The balance was selected by University Microfilm staff librarians from *Choice* reviews from January 1964 through December 1969. Twenty-two special subject and survey bibliographies appearing in *Choice* from 1964 through 1969 were also studied prior to selecting and compiling this collection.

Law Books Recommended for Libraries—A list of 40,000 titles representing a "cooperative evaluation of the best in legal literature," by the Association of American Law Schools (1967). Each title is identified with a symbol to indicate the size of the library for which it is recommended, and periodic supplementary lists are planned.

Although the primary purpose of the aforementioned lists is to serve as a guide to core selections, they may also be used for package acquisitions. However, if these lists are used as a basis for mass purchases (by a new library, for instance) the librarian must be familiar not only with his own library needs and aims but also with the relationship between the institution's programs and curriculum and the collection's content. A librarian may find it necessary to conduct a title-by-title review of collection lists to consider the merits of each book against the library's needs (rather than the indiscriminate purchase of an entire collection).

Approval Order Plans

It is too early to make an overall assessment of single-source order approval plans. Certainly the fact that the number of libraries adopting such plans is increasing is evidence that dealers can rapidly supply books, within stipulated categories, on the basis of standing orders. Moreover, by not selecting and ordering books title-by-title, and through single billing and centralized cataloging, dollar savings can usually be effected. Yet standing-order book buying may prove disappointing in certain respects. Unless the dealer scrupulously follows the library's instructions, a sizable number of books may have to be returned. Contrary to the agreement, the dealer may ship older titles, duplicates, serials as opposed to monographs, material from nondesignated categories, textbooks, reprints, etc. It is also possible that the approval plan service may not supply *all* books needed. Unless the dealer provides an advance list of books to be shipped, whether or not a particular title will be included cannot be known for certain prior to receipt of said book. Also, unless books are received with a Library of Congress proof slip, some difficulty in identification may be experienced.[6] Since these drawbacks appear more mechanical than conceptual, the promise of greater efficiency in ordering procedures is obviously present. What is of greater concern and the subject of some debate is the effect of approval buying on the selection process itself.

The traditional book selection policy as practiced by many academic institutions consists of individual title-by-title selection based on review media and/or proof slips. The librarian, who is finally responsible for the book buying program, usually handles a majority of all book selections. In large institutions, the librarian has the assistance of a number of subject specialists on the library staff. The average college, however, does not have such specialized personnel; consequently, initiating book orders is the responsibility of the faculty, members of which are given the specific responsibility of selecting books in their respective fields. Within the funding limits of each department, their recommendations are generally honored.

The intrinsic worth of this individual, personalized method of book selection is that it brings to the process the specialized knowledge of persons who are cognizant of the holdings in the respective library divisions and the contribution each contemplated new addition may be expected to bring to a given subject. Furthermore, faculty and library staff are in a position to be familiar with holdings at nearby libraries that can be obtained through interlibrary loan.

---

[6] These and other problems may not be typical, but they are part of a brief but disappointing experience at the Oklahoma State University Library. See Roscoe Rouse "Automation Stops Here: A Case for Man-Made Book Collections," *College and Research Libraries*, vol. 31, May 1970, pp. 147–54.

To the extent that selection is made by machines or by persons off-campus, the professional responsibilities of librarians and faculty may be eroded. Certainly the danger exists that some very inappropriate and lopsided collections will result.[7] However, approval-order plans should not be thought of as incompatible with traditional methods of selection. Approval plans can contribute to the efficiency of ordering and to some extent can perform the initial selection function. And since review and final selection of books received still must be done by the librarian and faculty, these functions can be performed as well with an approval plan as without one. Most will agree that a better job of selection can be done with the book in hand than from a short annotation, review, or proof slip. Furthermore, for those items which do not appreciably strengthen the collection, the return privilege may always be exercised.

In summation, the potential advantages of approval ordering are clear: (1) significant reduction in search, selection, and ordering costs, (2) rapid, automatic service, (3) guaranteed continuous conformity with the selection profile, and (4) under certain circumstances, reduced bookprocessing costs. If these advantages are to be fully realized, it is essential that libraries exercise great care in identifying and refining their acquisition policy and selection profile. Furthermore, institutions must continuously monitor the service if consistent conformity with selection specifications is expected. While approval-order plans may well provide definite financial advantages and savings in time for already overburdened library staffs, they do not exempt the library staff and faculty from concurrent selection responsibilities.

Review Media

Among a number of guides for current selection, only one, *Choice*,[8] is designed specifically for the college library. Other review media include *Booklist, Current Content, Library Journal, Publishers' Weekly, Wilson Library Bulletin, RQ, Subscription Books Bulletin, New York Review of Books, The New*

---

[7] To determine whether or not reader usage of books varies according to the method by which they are selected, a recent study was conducted at four senior colleges. The findings were that (1) the circulation of titles selected by approval blanket-order plans was lower than that for titles selected by faculty and (2) titles selected by librarians were more in demand than titles selected by faculty. While certainly not conclusive, this study suggests the problem of acquiring books by approval-plan selection procedures. See G. Edward Evans, "Book Selection and Book Collection Usage in Academic Libraries," *The Library Quarterly*, vol. 40, no. 3, July 1970, pp. 297–308.

[8] *Choice*, Richard Gardner, ed., published by the Association of College and Research Libraries, a division of the American Library Association, 50 East Huron St., Chicago, Ill. 60611, monthly (July/August combined issue).

York Times Book Review, and various scholarly journals.[9] All are valuable as guides, but *Choice* is indispensable as the one regular, definitive, and authoritative source of new English-language titles that have been screened as potential undergraduate library additions.[10] *Choice*, with over 6,000 subscribers, was initiated in 1964 to update the selections reflected in *Books for College Libraries*.

In 1972, *Choice* received approximately 1,500 new titles and reprints a month from publishers. After being evaluated by the editor, Richard Gardner, in consultation with five assistant editors, titles are selected for their value to a given subject-matter bibliography and to the intended college audience. All selections are reviewed by a working staff of over 3,000 college and university professors. These reviews, published monthly in *Choice*, numbered 6,561 in 1972. "Review-on-Cards," purchased by 600 subscribers, affords a convenient means for distributing review information to department heads and faculty charged with selection responsibilities.

At 1972 prices, the yearly total of 6,561 titles reviewed by *Choice* would cost about $85,000. Public universities, with few exceptions, spend considerably more than this amount for new acquisitions, as do most public 4-year institutions with graduate programs (see figures XIV-4 and -5, chapter XIV). On the other hand, this level of expenditure is beyond the acquisition budget of most public 4-year institutions without graduate programs and of public junior colleges (see figures XIV-6 and -7). While *Choice* is highly selective, it is by no means a final screening for smaller institutions, many of which operate close to the minimum $42,000 budget for current acquisitions determined by Massman and Patterson.[11]

Choice does publish a more selected list of titles, "Outstanding Academic Books." Only 11 percent of the monographs reviewed in 1972 were included in the "Outstanding" list, yet the editors repeatedly caution that nonselective purchases of the entire collection will result in some superfluous acquisitions.

BIBLIOGRAPHIC ACCESS

Almost as important as selecting the collection is the task of relating library resources to the reader's needs. This process requires that the con-

---

[9] Reprint catalogs, foreign listings, publishers' lists and newsletters, and Library of Congress proof slips provide general information on current titles.

[10] While serving principally as a selection and review medum for college libraries, *Choice* is widely used by public, research, and high school libraries.

[11] See Virgil F. Massman and Kelly Patterson, "A Minimum Budget for Current Acquisitions," *College and Research Libraries*, vol. 31, March 1970, pp. 83–88. The 1972 budget was obtained by multiplying the Massman and Patterson 1967 budget of $26,000 by the ratio of 1972 to 1967 book prices ($12.99/$7.99 = 1.62).

tents of the collection be indexed or cataloged. An index card for each volume contains a capsule description of significant features and of content. Further, each volume is assigned a classification number to provide a subject-grouping order for shelving and filing and to identify location for retrieval. The end product of the cataloging process is a set of indexed catalog cards for each item, arranged by author, title, and subject. When filed alphabetically, the cards comprise a dictionary catalog affording multiple access to any specific item.

Cataloging

Centralized cataloging is a monument to persistence, patience, and an extremely sound concept. The question of cooperative cataloging was first raised by Melvil Dewey at the 1876 convention of librarians in Philadelphia—the convention which led to the founding of the American Library Association. By 1898 only one small-scale cooperative cataloging program was in operation. But the fact that the Library Bureau was providing a few major research libraries with printed cards of a selected list of periodicals was proof that such a scheme was practical. The real breakthrough came in 1901 when Herbert Putnam, Librarian of Congress, announced that the Library was prepared to distribute copies of its cards to libraries desiring them.[12]

Extensive development of the Library of Congress (LC) card service in the years since 1901 has made it the most effective centralized cataloging agency in the world. Yet as late as 1965, the Library was not able to provide cards for almost half the books acquired annually by major research and university libraries. That same year, the problem was forcefully brought to the attention of Congress by the Association of Research Libraries and other organizations. The result was enactment of title II-C of the Higher Education Act of 1965, providing for an effective centralized cataloging program. John W. Cronin, formerly director of the Library of Congress Processing Department, heralded the news in these words: "For the first time in the history of civilization, a program has been evolved which presents the potentials of developing a central source of bibliographic information on all materials of value to scholarship published throughout the world.[13]

With the legislative authority provided by title II-C, the Library of Con-

---

[12] For the history of centralized cataloging, see John M. Dawson, "A History of Centralized Cataloging" and William S. Dix, "Recent Developments in Centralized Cataloging," *Library Resources and Technical Services*, vol. 11, no. 1, Winter 1967, pp. 28–32 and 32–35.

[13] John W. Cronin, "The National Program for Acquisitions and Cataloging," *Library Lectures*, no. 6, Louisiana State University, Baton Rouge, 1968, pp. 10–24.

gress initiated in fiscal year 1966 and implemented in fiscal year 1967 the National Program for Acquisitions and Cataloging (NPAC). With NPAC funds, the Library increased its cataloging and support staff (by 400), arranged to "share" the cataloging data of the national bibliographies of 23 foreign countries, altered its procedures to speed up book selection and ordering, established nine shared cataloging offices abroad, and instituted an extra shift to accelerate the production of printed cards. The multiple benefits of this program to college and university libraries, as well as to all libraries, are well known; however, so rapidly has the program developed that there is not yet a wide awareness of some aspects of the service.

In fiscal year 1972 the Library of Congress cataloged 243,753 titles, a 122-percent increase over the number prepared in 1965, the year preceding initiation of the program. Also in 1972, 122 million catalog cards were distributed to more than 30,000 subscribers. Almost 7,000 subscribers received the Library's book catalogs, the *National Union Catalog*, the *Library of Congress Books: Subjects*, and the *New Serial Titles*. The *National Union Catalog* contains, in addition to cataloging information, a record of holdings at major research libraries in the United States. A total of 14 million proof sheets covering the entire Library of Congress cataloging output was also disseminated in 1972.

This increase in Library of Congress cataloging output has quite literally eliminated the cataloging task as a basic function at a majority of college and university libraries. To be sure, libraries still need to adapt Library of Congress cards to fit variant editions, and there are a wide variety of publication forms (periodicals, serials, documentary, and reports) that the Library of Congress catalogs only partially or not at all. Nevertheless, the coverage is quite comprehensive. Consider these recent reports by large university libraries:

Princeton, with 2.1 million volumes, finds that LC covers 65 percent of all monographs acquired by the university; Indiana University, with 2.46 million volumes, receives 80 percent coverage within 6 months for all current acquisitions; the University of Michigan, with 4 million volumes, reports 73 percent coverage; the University of Iowa, with 1.4 million volumes, 70 percent; and Pennsylvania State University, with 1.3 million volumes, 80 percent.

For college libraries with smaller collections and fewer annual acquisitions, the cataloging coverage by the Library of Congress should be adequate. In addition, the LC copy saves each library a substantial proportion of the processing costs[14] accruing from original cataloging and related

---

[14] The University of California at Berkeley estimates processing costs at $8.44 a title. For nine campuses, the University of Colorado calculates an average cost of $4.50 a

tasks. And because the use of the LC service involves primarily clerical personnel, professional catalogers can concentrate on "original" materials and on reducing backlogs.

Until NPAC is fully funded, the major problem remaining will be to reduce the time lag between the date of publication of a given work and its availability to subscribers of the LC catalog card. Some libraries feel that the waiting period (up to 6 months in some cases) is justified and delay processing of new acquisitions until the LC card arrives. Libraries may, of course, print their own cards from LC proof sheets. The time lag will be shortened when sufficient LC funds permit the recruitment and training of more qualified catalogers and speedier acquisition of published works.

Classification

The printed cards now available from the Library of Congress are so comprehensive, are provided on such liberal terms, and are of such excellent quality that any library would be foolish not to consider them as the basis for its catalog. Yet, because of the usual permanency of the original choice, or, if reclassification is undertaken the arduous, time-consuming, and costly task involved, extreme care must be exercised in choosing a classification system. To provide some clarity and insight regarding choice of a classification system, it is helpful to identify the essential circumstances that in most instances appear to be decisive in choosing one scheme over another. Critical in this regard are recent decisions by the Library of Congress which have tended to diminish in importance certain factors which previously were believed to be of prime if not overriding importance.

There has been a recent tendency for college libraries, both new and established, to adopt the Library of Congress Classification (LCC or LC) in preference to the Dewey Decimal Classification (DDC or DC). The only statistics available to document this trend are for junior colleges. Of the 225 new junior colleges established between 1960 and 1966, 38.2 percent originally started with or later adopted the LC system. In 1961, on the

---

title, the same figure Arthur D. Little, Inc., reported in a feasibility study for a centralized processing center for the State University of New York. See Ferdinand F. Leimkuhler and Michael D. Cooper, *Cost Accounting and Analysis for University Libraries*, Research Program in University Administration, University of California, Berkeley, 1970, p. 22; Lawrence E. Leonard, Joan M. Maier, and Richard M. Dougherty, *Colorado Academic Libraries Book Processing Center Study*, Norlin Library, University of Colorado, Boulder, 1968, p. 76; and Arthur D. Little, Inc., *A Plan for a Library Processing Center for the State University of New York*, Report to the Office of Educational Communications, State University of New York, New York, November 1967, p. 8.

other hand, only 3.5 percent of all junior colleges used the LC system.[15] LC and DC usage among all colleges and universities in the United States, as of 1967, is shown in table IX-1. The dominance of the Dewey system is clearly evident, but because it originated earlier (in 1876 versus 1901 for LC), neither its prevalence nor the recent and enthusiastic swing to LC should lead one to infer the superiority of one system over the other.

Many fine points can be raised in making relative comparisons of the merits of the Dewey versus the Library of Congress classification systems. The librarian confronted with the problem of having to make a choice will need to review critically the literature on this subject.[16] Neither scheme is perfect nor ever will be. Both DC and LC provide relative book-to-book location and are practical as bookshelving devices. In a fundamental sense, the two are more similar than they are dissimilar. If proper perspective is to be maintained in evaluating the truly distinguishing properties of the two systems, their common virtues and faults should be appreciated. Understanding how DC and LC are alike is particularly important at this juncture since certain previous major distinctions have almost disappeared. The minor differences remaining are primarily those concerned with centralized cataloging, automation, and schedule revision.

Before the National Program for Acquisitions and Cataloging was established, a valid and heavily weighted argument in favor of LC was its superior *economy* in classification. Since Library of Congress cards are prepared for the LC catalog, they contain the LC classification notation. Prior to 1965, DC numbers were also used, but on a somewhat erratic basis. From a high of 99-percent coverage in 1934 (42,314 titles), the number decreased to about 26 percent in 1964 (21,977 titles). As a result, colleges and universities using the DC classification system and availing themselves of the Library of Congress cataloging service had to add the DC classification on most cards containing lesser known titles. The cost of this operation was approximately $1.50 per volume. It is likely that this additional classification expense plus the fear that fewer DC numbers

---

[15] Desmond Taylor, "Classification Trends in Junior College Libraries," *College and Research Libraries*, September 1968, pp. 351–56.

[16] For example, see ALA, RTSD, Classification Committee Report, May 15, 1964, "Statement on Types of Classification Available to New Academic Libraries," *Library Resources & Technical Services*, vol. 9, Winter 1965, pp. 104–11.

Howard F. McGaw, "Classification: A Bibliography," *Library Resources & Technical Services*, vol. 9, Fall 1965, pp. 483–88.

Jean M. Perrault, ed., "Reclassification: Rationale and Problems," *Proceedings* Conference on Reclassification, University of Maryland, 1968.

Richard H. Schimmelpfeng and C. Donald Cook, eds., *The Use of the Library of Congress Classification*, American Library Association, Chicago, 1968.

William J. Welsh, "Considerations on the Adoption of the Library of Congress Classification," *Library Resources & Technical Services*, vol. 11, Summer 1967, pp. 345–53.

Table IX-1.—Classification system used by college and university libraries: Fall 1967

		Total		Public		Private	
		Number	Percent	Number	Percent	Number	Percent
All institutions	DC	1,408	68.4	542	67.5	866	68.9
	LC	496	24.1	226	28.1	270	21.5
	Other	157	7.6	36	4.5	121	9.6
Universities	DC	71	48.6	35	46.7	36	50.7
	LC	56	38.3	30	40.0	26	36.6
	Other	19	13.0	10	13.3	9	12.7
4-year institutions with grad. programs	DC	304	60.0	133	68.2	171	55.0
	LC	149	29.4	53	27.2	96	30.8
	Other	53	10.5	9	4.6	44	14.2
4-year institutions without grad. programs	DC	524	71.4	67	67.0	457	72.0
	LC	159	21.6	29	29.0	130	20.5
	Other	51	6.9	4	4.0	47	7.4
2-year institutions	DC	509	75.5	307	70.7	202	83.8
	LC	132	19.6	114	26.2	18	7.5
	Other	34	5.0	13	3.0	21	8.7

NOTE—DC = Dewey Decimal Classification.

LC = Library of Congress Classification.

"Other" includes a substantial number of institutions in the process of converting to the Library of Congress Classification.

Source: Bronson Price, *Library Statistics of Colleges and Universities: Data for Individual Institutions, Fall 1967*, U.S. Department of Health, Education and Welfare, Office of Education U.S. Government Printing Office, Washington, D.C., 1968.

would be placed on LC cards in the future persuaded librarians to adopt LC. It was also feared that DC notations would not be a component part of the Machine-Readable Cataloging Project (MARC), essentially an automated process at the Library of Congress that records and distributes bibliographic data on magnetic tapes. Fortunately, neither fear was realized.

Today DC is being assigned to virtually all current nonfiction titles published in the United States in any language or published anywhere in English. The DC notation now appears on approximately 40 percent of all Library of Congress cards (80,462 titles in 1972), and the Library intends to increase the number gradually to the maximum permitted by funding. Current estimates are that 90 percent or more of LC cards used by 2-year institutions, 60 to 90 percent by 4-year institutions, and 40 to 80 percent by universities carry DC. Thus the greater frequency with which LC numbers appear on Library of Congress catalog cards over DC numbers is gradually diminishing. For small libraries at least, original DC classification requirements are minimal. As far as the MARC project is concerned, the bibliographic data include DC numbers.

After 20 years of rapid updating, the Dewey system has emerged on a par with LC insofar as anticipated revision requirements are concerned. In some areas, such as science and life sciences, Dewey appears more up to date. LC is considered by some librarians to be superior in the social sciences, but the 18th edition of Dewey may change such opinions. Both systems are continually updated quarterly or periodically.

Quite certainly the inherent imperfections of any classification system require that schedules be continually changed to accommodate new material. Maintaining the integrity of a classification number that would perpetuate, in many instances, outmoded concepts defeats the proper function of the catalog—i.e., to reveal through classification a logical and systematic profile of scholarship as currently understood. That continued relocations are necessary to reflect current knowledge and emerging concepts is inevitable. Neither the Dewey nor the Library of Congress classification system eliminates this responsibility.

From the foregoing observations, neither the Dewey nor the Library of Congress classification system appears more advantageous for centralized cataloging and automation, nor is one system less subject to revision than the other. In view of the fact that these factors have influenced many libraries to reclassify, what conditions now recommend one system or the other? At the risk of incurring the indignation of advocates on both sides and also at the risk of oversimplifying, it is suggested that only three institutional circumstances should be recognized as decisive: existing classification, ultimate collection size, and style or manner of reader usage.

Conversion Versus Retention. As explained in the ensuing sections, the relative merits of the DC and LC systems, except for the large research or specialized library, are slight indeed. For the great majority of colleges and universities with well-established general collections, conversion from one to the other should be ruled out on the premise that any possible advantages gained through reclassification are not likely to offset the expense, extended time commitment (often running into years), inconvenience, and arduous labor involved. In most instances the outlay for reclassification is simply not worth the return, particularly when compared with the alternative of collection improvement. For the very large library reclassification is usually a practical impossibility, although some very large libraries (e.g., Cornell, Stanford, and Dartmouth) have converted. For the small college library there is little to justify converting from Dewey to LC unless the card system is worn out and must be replaced. The most likely candidates for conversion to LC are the medium-sized libraries that expect to grow significantly and the specialized libraries that require highly refined classification. Even in these cases, reworking the catalog should be undertaken only when it is an absolute necessity.

Collection Size. Libraries of all sizes use both LC and DC. Some 2-year institutions with fewer that 10,000 volumes find that "LC is not too expensive for a collection of any size." The University of Illinois, with over 4.7 million volumes, uses Dewey with apparent ease. What, then, is the relationship between size of collection and system preference? Obviously no rigid rule applies, but generally the simplicity and ease of interpretation of Dewey is preferred by libraries under 200,000 volumes, and, as the library grows, the elaborate LC system is more satisfactory. It is generally recommended for collections of more than 500,000 volumes.

Small libraries desiring the simplicity of broad classification are well served by Dewey, a system that allows abridgment of numbers to indicate broad subject areas. When a collection needs to be subdivided, the subject matter can be further refined by the simple addition (gradually if desired) of figures to the classification notation already assigned.[17] On the other hand, because the full LC notation must be used at all times, it is not particularly suitable for a library seeking simplicity. To eliminate any LC figures changes the meaning of the classification, whereas abridging a number in the Dewey system merely broadens its significance. Abridging the DC system also permits a library that wishes to disregard certain DC form subdivisions to arrange the works falling within a given form in any manner it wishes—alphabetically by author, for example.

The more elaborate Library of Congress Classification is designed to bring together all books on very detailed subjects. The system's comprehensiveness and flexibility are of recognized value to large research and specialized libraries that require fine (close) classification of many detailed subjects. But since the system does not as a rule follow a logical pattern, it

---

[17] Since a library is almost certain to grow, it is better to subdivide, when in doubt, in order to provide for future divisions that will likely be required.

cannot be easily expanded, certainly not without rearranging books already classified. Dewey, on the other hand, can be expanded only through further breakdown of existing classes, by subclassification, or by renaming and reassigning classes. Dewey has, of course, been expanded to include as much detail as LC; more in such areas as the life sciences, fewer in literature. The LC scheme often appears to be much more detailed than DC because it enumerates every subdivision as many times as may be necessary; Dewey, with its facility for building numbers, does not. Perhaps the real advantage LC offers the large library is its individualized treatment of specialized topics. Because the subdivisions have been varied to fit a particular subject, it has met with substantial favor among scholars and researchers.

Style of Reader Usage. When open shelves and self-service are important, the easily mastered enumerative and positional decimal classification of Dewey facilitates the search for material. The highly elaborate and more synthetic notations of LC, on the other hand, are not necessarily related to preceding or following classes; they follow many variant systems. Such a pattern often makes browsing a difficult and frustrating experience. The consolidated DC index and its "Users' Manual", neither of which is currently available for LC, make it still easier for the reader to search out material on his own. In all fairness it should be pointed out that the mnemonic features of the Dewey system are of less consequence in the large research library where shelf browsing is not of primary importance. Furthermore, the LC notation tends to become more or less mnemonic as the user becomes familiar with it. Regardless of which classification system is used, only through a well-designed catalog, with its analytics and multiple-subject entries, can the total resources of a library be made accessible.

From this brief discussion one might become skeptical about claims made for either classification system. Skepticism is proper, for whether or not the values gained from revising the catalog justify the work involved remains an issue difficult to resolve. Neither classification is completely satisfactory.[18] Fortunately, most colleges and universities find themselves at ease with whatever system they employ.

---

[18] All books are not confined solely to one subject; some cover several subjects or are concerned with relationships between subjects. An attempt to shelve books according to subject can, therefore, never be more than partially successful. An early study by Grace Kelley (*The Classification of Books*, H. W. Wilson, New York, 1937) examined the extent to which material concerning definite subjects was grouped together on the library shelves. The investigation dealt with both Dewey and Library of Congress systems. Approximately one-third of the material found to be grouped together was classified by a specific subject; one-third was classified by broader but related categories and located nearby; and one-third, for various reasons, was classified in other ways and physically separated from the specific subject location.

INTERLIBRARY RESOURCE SHARING

While the scope of interlibrary cooperation is broad, the sharing of resources is undoubtedly the most important single element.[19] Those libraries that share the extensive collections of general and specialized libraries provide their patrons with access to resources far beyond what would otherwise be immediately available. In practice interlibrary cooperation generally includes: (1) distribution to participating libraries of some form of union catalogs or lists; (2) accelerated receipt, processing, and delivery of requested material; and (3) coordinated efforts to establish fields of special responsibility and to provide for preacquisition agreements and assignments. Of these three aspects, the second—accelerated receipt and delivery arrangements—has recently been developed and tested in projects worth the attention of every librarian. For State higher education planners especially, the University of Minnesota's (U. of M.) MINITEX program[20] is worth noting. While unique, the arrangements being tested at Minnesota can probably be adapted by any State system.

The 4-year MINITEX (Minnesota Interlibrary Teletype Exchange) project, initiated in December 1968, was designed to obtain information on expediting interlibrary requests through teletype communication, custom handling, and rapid delivery arrangements. Information was also sought regarding the kinds of local library needs that could be met effectively through loans from the U. of M.'s extensive collection. Yearly progress reports provide realistic evidence that the project has been successful.

The 66 institutions participating in the MINITEX experiment represent those desiring access to U. of M. resources: private colleges, State colleges, junior colleges, university branches, and public libraries. The communication network consists of a teletype installation in each participating library by which requests for books or periodicals can be instantaneously transmitted to the Minnesota library. As soon as such requests are received, project personnel locate the desired publications and mail them to the library submitting the request. Books are sent on loan, while journal or serial articles are furnished in photocopy (the original journals remain on campus for use of U. of M. library patrons).

---

[19] A second important area of interlibrary cooperation is central processing. When a high proportion of overlap in book requirements exists among participating institutions, use of such a system can effect savings in unit costs of approximately 30 percent. See Lawrence E. Leonard, Joan M. Maier, and Richard M. Dougherty, *Colorado Academic Libraries Book Processing*, Center Study, Norlin Library, University of Colorado, Boulder, 1968.

[20] See Edward B. Stanford, "University Library Undertakes MINITEX Interlibrary Service Project," *Minnesota Libraries*, vol. 22, no. 8, Winter 1968, and *MINITEX: Progress Report, 1971–72*, University of Minnesota, Minneapolis, October 1972.

During 1972 a total of over 70,000 requests were received from the participating libraries. The highest number of requests received from a single library was 5,300. More than 75 percent of the requests were processed (i.e., either an asked-for item or a report was transmitted) within 24 hours, and requesting libraries received the material within 2 days. Delivery was made by United Parcel, 1st-class mail, and private courier. The total cost of the service, including central staff salaries, teletype expense, photocopy, and delivery charges, is estimated to average $2.00 per item. This represents the lowest cost and shortest turnaround time yet reported by any comparable interlibrary service.

Approximately 80 percent of the requests were filled by photocopies; the remaining 20 percent by original copies (books, documents, etc.). Faculty members, the major users of the service, accounted for 51 percent of the requests during the 1st year, followed by undergraduate users (28 percent) and graduate users (15 percent). As might be expected, the service was utilized primarily by those involved in research and teaching (49 percent and 17 percent of all requests, respectively). Requests for the purpose of college course study accounted for 15 percent of the total; for graduate study, 9 percent. Approximately 15 percent of the items requested could not be supplied immediately or within a few days. In the majority of cases, the item was not owned by the U. of M. library or a participating library; the other reasons were: "volume in use or missing," "material designated as noncirculating," "volume at bindery," or "citation incomplete or incorrect."

The eminently successful Minnesota project clearly demonstrates both the value and technical feasibility of library-sharing at the State level. Other projects of this type are even more ambitious. The New York State Interlibrary Loan network (NYSILL) includes approximately 700 participants from the 22 public library systems.[21] Establishing so large a chain of library resources is complicated, yet a study of this and other pioneering systems can provide valuable background data for States planning to initiate a library-sharing network.

COLLECTION SIZE

The *number* of books in an academic collection measures in part the library's ability to support and stimulate the educational program. In

---

[21] See S. Gilbert Prentiss, "The Evolution of the Library System (New York)" in *Library Networks—Promise and Performance*, Leon Carnovsky, ed., The Thirty-third Conference of the Graduate Library School, July 29–31, 1968, The University of Chicago Press, pp. 78–79.

judging the adequacy of a collection, primary emphasis should properly be placed on the *quality* of the holdings and their *propriety* to the users' needs. The aphorisms that books need to be "carefully chosen" and that the collection must be judged "in terms of the college program" express the basic philosophy that guides most evaluation efforts. Yet beyond these considerations, an adequate collection should be one in which the actual number of books is appropriate for intended educational purposes.

A relatively recent formula that has been developed for this purpose estimates the size for minimal adequacy in a far more convincing fashion than do subjective criteria. Although the formula needs to be improved, it can in its present form be a useful device for persuasively demonstrating to planning, budgeting, and appropriating bodies the necessity for a specific number of volumes.

The formula, originated by Verner W. Clapp, when he was president of the Council on Library Resources, Inc., and Robert T. Jordan, staff associate, appears in its entirety in the September 1965 issue of *College and Research Libraries*, no. 26 (corrigenda at Id 27:72, January 1966). For its quality element, the formula presumes that the subject matter covered has been carefully chosen; in other words, that the selection has been made from book-selection lists and specialized subject bibliographies customarily used for this purpose. All values are considered averages, and no factor represented in the formula is operative in isolation; i.e., the various component requirements are meaningful not as independent entities, but only in concert with the entire collection. Except for seldom-used research and graduate material, it is presumed that most of the holdings will be full-size, i.e., not reduced. Fully cataloged material on microfilm is measured in volumes, as though it were in printed form. The title-volume ratio for books is 1:1.2; for periodicals, 1:15.

The formula for estimating the size of the liminal adequacy of the collections at senior college and university libraries[22] involves the following factors and supporting rationale:

1. *Basic collection for an undergraduate library:* 50,750 volumes. This number is based on the collections of the Universities of Michigan[23] (56,550 volumes) and California[24] (55,000 volumes). A basic list, it contains 35,000 book titles (42,000 volumes), 250 periodicals (3,750 volumes), and 5,000 documents. The Michigan list includes 245 periodicals and the California list 900, of which the 300 most used cover a period of 20 or more years. The recommended figure of 250 periodicals represents 50 percent of the titles listed in the *Readers' Guide to Periodical Literature*, the *International Index*, and the *Applied Science and Technology Index*. The 5,000 documents include the most

---

[22] A special formula is provided for junior and community college libraries.

[23] University of Michigan Undergraduate Library *Shelf List* (revised edition), University Microfilms, Inc., Ann Arbor, Mich., 1964.

[24] University of California at San Diego Library. Lists of books selected for the libraries of three new University of California campuses.

important publications of the U.S. Congress, the Bureau of the Census and other Federal agencies, the United Nations and its specialized agencies, the 50 States, etc.

2. *Supplement for faculty needs:* 100 volumes per FTE faculty member. An enrichment amounting to 50 titles (e.g., 3 per year for 16 years), one periodical subscription, and 25 documents per faculty member would seem to be minimum.

3. *Supplement for student enrollment:* 12 volumes per FTE student. To meet the additional demand of a larger student body, 12 volumes per student is suggested.

4. *Supplement for undergraduate honors or independent study program:* 12 volumes per enrolled student. This figure is considered a minimal enrichment to support the resource needs of these programs.

5. *Supplement for fields of undergraduate concentration:* 335 volumes per "major" subject field. "Basic lists" for "major" fields typically include at least 2,000 or more titles. A modest 17 percent of this number should supplement the basic collection, which rarely totals more than several hundred titles in any one field.

6. *Supplement for fields of graduate concentration—master's work or its equivalent:* 3,050 volumes per subject field. For the "basic lists" requirements in the various academic fields, this number is deemed average.

7. *Supplement for fields of graduate concentration—doctoral work or its equivalent:* 24,500 volumes per subject field. Because these volumes represent but a fraction of the literature on any but the most recently developed subject, they will cover only the most recent aspects of a subject.

When applied to selected senior colleges, the requirements of the Clapp-Jordan formula are more demanding for institutions offering many graduate programs and less demanding for those offering only a few than are the Standards for College Libraries of the Association of College Research Libraries (ACRL); namely, increments of 10,000 volumes, in addition to the basic collection of 50,000, for each 200 students beyond an initial 600. In another area, selected State universities, some collections recommended by Clapp and Jordan will not suffice for the number of doctoral fields offered.

In conclusion, it appears that the Clapp-Jordan formula systematically accounts for the measurable factors upon which minimum collection size should depend. Other variables, which may be controlling but cannot be measured (methods of instruction, availability of suitable places for study on the campus, intellectual climate, and proximity to other libraries), obviously cannot be incorporated in the formula. In view of these shortcomings, it has been suggested that considerable additional research be undertaken to determine precisely which factors, and the respective weight of each, affect book needs in particular academic situations.[25]

[25] For later developments, see H. William Axford, "An Approach to Performance Budgeting at the Florida Atlantic University Library," *College and Research Libraries,* vol. 32, no. 2, March 1971, pp. 87–104; and R. Marvin McInnis, "The Formula Approach to Library Size: An Empirical Study of Its Efficacy in Evaluating Research Libraries," *College and Research Libraries,* vol. 33, no. 3, May 1972, pp. 190–98.

BIBLIOGRAPHY

Axford, H. William, "An Approach to Performance Budgeting at the Florida Atlantic University Library," *College and Research Libraries*, March 1971, pp. 87–104.

This article summarizes the 1969 reorganization of the FAU library following an indepth examination of operational problems. A detailed cost study is analyzed, and both the Clapp-Jordan and University of Washington formulas for budgeting, together with a modified formula, are described. A program performance budgeting system is now employed by the Florida State university system.

Braden, Irene A., *The Undergraduate Library*, American Library Association, Chicago, 1970, 158 pp.

Based primarily on personal interviews and a study of office files, this book describes six separately housed undergraduate libraries at Harvard and Cornell and the Universities of Michigan, South Carolina, Indiana, and Texas. Each library is described in terms of background history, development, financing, the book collection, and staff. In each case, the operation of the library and how and to what extent it is used are delineated. Six objectives of the undergraduate library are presented and an attempt is made to describe how closely each library adheres to them. The six are: (1) open access to the collection, (2) centralized and simplified services to undergraduate students, (3) selection of the collection for undergraduate use, (4) design of the library as an instructional tool, (5) special services to undergraduates, and (6) design of the library building, with the express needs and habits of undergraduates in mind. The final chapter compares the major differences and similarities among the six libraries.

Branscomb, Harvie, *Teaching With Books: A Study of College Libraries*, Shoe String Press, Inc., Hamden, Conn., 1964, 239 pp.

The fact that this book is a reprint of the 1940 original attests to the durability of Dr. Branscomb's advice. His theme is the educational effectiveness of the college library—from the point of view (and the problems) of college presidents and faculty. The author brings to a host of library topics insight and a depth of understanding rarely matched in library literature. Beginning with a delineation of undergraduate use of the library, he discusses the significance of reading and study in the education process, contending that "The library will be used heavily only when books become the major instruments by which the educational program is carried on." The remainder of the volume is concerned with important issues that libraries must face if they are to attract readers. Topics include: some responsibilities of the college president, making books accessible, books in residence halls, what books the library should buy, and the costs of library service.

Dunn, Oliver Charles, W. F. Seibert, and Janice A. Scheuneman, *The Past and Likely Future of 58 Research Libraries, 1951–1980: A Statistical Study of Growth and Change* (4th issue), University Libraries and Audio Visual Center, Purdue University, Lafayette, Ind., 1968, 70 pp.

In this statistical study of 58 member libraries of the Association of Research Libraries (ARL), the authors emphasize identifying trends in predicting future characteristics and growth. The analyses and predictions are based on data collected over a 14-year period (1950–51 through 1963–64) and over a 3-year follow-up period (beginning in 1964–65) during which subsequent information was compared with predictions. The major analyses developed from these data include (1) determination of the average annual levels of the descriptive statistics (e.g., collection size, acquisitions, total expenditures) and projection of these to predict their future levels; (2) determination of the annual rank or standing of each library with respect to each descriptive statistic; and (3) a calculation of the annual correlation between each pair of statistics. The past and future levels of the several descriptive statistics have been analyzed not only for the total or undifferentiated group of ARL libraries but also for several subgroups.

Lyle, Guy R., *The Administration of the College Library*, The H. W. Wilson Company, New York, 1961, 419 pp.

All aspects of college library administration are treated in this volume: organization, personnel, selection, acquisition, cataloging and classification, circulation and reference, financial administration, building and equipment, public relations, and evaluation.

Marshall, John David, ed., *The Library in the University*, The University of Tennessee Library Lectures 1949–1966, The Shoe String Press, Inc., Hamden, Conn., 1967, 304 pp.

Each of the 18 essays in this volume was first presented as a University of Tennessee Library Lecture. All solid contributions, they deal with specific problem areas: book classification, research collections, divisional organization in the university library, sources of support for college libraries, and the public relations role of a university librarian. The durability of the series is due in a large measure to the care with which the subjects have been chosen and to the expertise of the authors.

Moore, Everett LeRoy, *Junior College Libraries: Development, Needs, and Perspective*, ACRL Monograph no. 30, American Library Association, Chicago, 1969, 104 pp.

Nineteen papers submitted by program participants at the 1967 Conference on Junior College Libraries, jointly sponsored by the American Library Association and the American Association of Junior Colleges, are included. The major topic areas are: library needs in the development of the new campus, library support of instruction, the library and research, library education and personnel, the library and information retrieval, and library facilities and equipment.

Palmer, David C. ed., *Planning for a Nationwide System of Library Statistics*, U.S. Department of Health, Education, and Welfare, Office of Education, U.S. Government Printing Office, Washington, D.C., 1970, 117 pp.

This report by the Library Administration Division of the American Library Association contains the opinions and recommendations of a group of experts on the needs for and uses of library statistics and also the methods for establishing an efficient nationwide data-collection system. General position papers deal with library statistics from the perspective of the professional librarian and the Federal and State governments. Other papers delineate specific statistical concerns of public libraries, school libraries, college and university libraries, State libraries, special libraries, and Federal libraries.

Sheehan, Sister Helen, *The Small College Library* (revised ed.), Corpus Books, Washington, D.C., 1969, 232 pp.

A handbook of administration and methods applicable to a small collection and a small staff, this volume offers straightforward practical advice in all areas of librarianship. According to the Introduction, "Emphasis throughout is on the best use of available resources, efficiency, and simplification of methods in all library operations, and economy and imagination in expenditure of income." A listing of the contents indicates the scope of coverage: staff, finances, book selection and ordering, periodicals, audiovisual materials, technical processes, readers' services, public relations, evaluation, and accrediting. The first and last chapters deal with the library's place in the college and with planning a new library. Appendixes include a librarian's book shelf, sample budgets and forms, addresses, standards, and a library evaluation questionnaire. Most reviewers agree that in one way or another this book is of value to *every* librarian.

Turner, Edward F., Jr., *A Study of the Implications of Modern Technology for Small College Libraries*, Office of Education Project No. 7–0910, U.S. Department of Health, Education, and Welfare, Office of Education, Bureau of Research, Washington, D.C., 1969, 131 pp.

This study was undertaken to ascertain the extent to which the tools of modern technology can be applied to help solve the problems of small college libraries. The author and his collaborators (Stanley McElderry and William Kurth) provide a clear perspective of the requirements of the college library and alternative solutions for meeting these requirements. Two chapters deal with the uses of technology in identifying and acquiring new information most relevant to the library's purpose. The authors also devote two chapters to the special problems of providing bibliographic and physical access to a collection. The report concludes with a summary that identifies areas requiring further investigation, and a series of recommendations.

U.S. Department of Health, Education, and Welfare, Office of Education, *Library Statistics of Colleges and Universities—Institutional Data;* and *Library Statistics of Colleges and Universities—Analytic Report*, U.S. Government Printing Office, Washington, D.C.

These reports, usually issued annually, present individual institutional data and summary or aggregate statistics for nearly all U.S. college and university libraries. Statistics reported include those relevant to the library collection, library staffing, regular staff salaries, hours of assistance and wages of hourly staff, and operating expenditures by function.

Wilson, Louis R. and Maurice F. Tauber, *The University Library: The Organization, Administration, and Functions of Academic Libraries* (2d ed.), Columbia University Press, New York, 1956, 641 pp.

This volume treats all aspects of university library administration: organization, personnel, selection, acquisition, cataloging and classification, circulation and reference, financial administration, building and equipment, public relations, and evaluation.

Chapter X

SPACE MANAGEMENT
AND PROJECTION

Amid the flux of continuous enrollment expansion and relentless demands for more meaningful education, one fact is clear: Higher education faces the challenge of solving many and varied problems, not the least of which is systematic planning of new facilities and controlled utilization of existing space.

Planning, as well as designing, constructing, and financing physical facilities—particularly large-scale building programs within the framework of a State system of higher education—is a responsibility often assumed by State boards and coordinating councils. When these tasks are undertaken by the institutions themselves, however, the State's role may be substantially lessened, generally limited to plant inventory and utilization studies. But whatever the division of responsibility, the key to effective mobilization of resources and employment of professional talent to accomplish the identified tasks is a well-defined understanding of the principles, procedures, and tools that guide and serve day-to-day operations. Toward this end, a condensed yet reasonably comprehensive review of facility-planning procedures and methods is presented in this chapter and in chapter XI, "Campus and Building Planning."

The content of this review has been selected to meet orientation requirements of general planners at the State level. Persons seeking more indepth treatment of the subject should consult the suggested technical references listed in the bibliography. Regardless of the kind of information needed, all planners should recognize that the devices and procedures outlined here do not represent final solutions to the overall problem of meeting facility needs. The fact is that there can be no final solutions.

Providing adequate physical plant facilities is one of the greatest problems of higher education today—a problem that can never be definitely and finally solved because education is not a static process. The student population grows, its makeup alters, and its demands on the educational plant change. Equally important, teaching methods alter and improve and subject matter fields expand, requiring new kinds and amounts of space and equipment. Techniques of research—the increasingly vital product of our colleges and universities—are in a constant state of change, and new public services are created, demanding new solutions to space problems.[1]

---

[1] William T. Middlebrook, *How To Estimate the Building Needs of a College or University*, University of Minnesota Press, Minneapolis, 1958, p. 3.

OVERVIEW

The basic foundation on which operating principles are established and analytical tools identified is a clear delineation of objectives. In the process of planning for the construction and use of facilities there are four principal objectives:

Space management and projection of needs—

(1) To provide adequate and appropriate facilities to meet present and future educational program needs and enrollment

(2) To secure overall efficiency in construction, utilization, and operating costs

Space design and campus planning—

(3) To provide the kind of physical atmosphere most conducive to the teaching-learning process

(4) To provide effective campus design and development and, at the same time, achieve architectural harmony.

In practice, equal weight cannot always be given to each of these four objectives. It is axiomatic that such qualifying factors as time, quality, and budget may require that priorities be established to ensure that funds are expended in such a manner that overall returns to higher education will be maximized.

The science of managing and projecting space is essentially one of determining how well existing facilities are being used and should be used and estimating present and future facility requirements.[2] The procedures, definitions, and forms used in conducting the many studies involved have been developed over a number of years by many individuals and institutions. The first major efforts were the 1954–55 "California and Western Conference Cost and Statistical Study" (chapters V and VI) and the 1957 *Manual for Studies of Space Utilization in Colleges and Universities* by John Dale Russell and James I. Doi, published by the American Association of Collegiate Registrars and Admissions Officers. These landmark pioneer surveys were followed by numerous others, some of which are cited in the bibliography. The most recent contributions are manuals on facility planning and management prepared by the Western Interstate Commission for Higher Education (WICHE) and a facility inventory and classification manual issued by the U.S. Office of Education.

In the past, the most critical and detailed analysis of space dealt mainly with scheduled utilization of classrooms and class laboratories. The primary

---

[2] Not included in this review are routine studies of the condition of existing facilities and special problems of financing planned construction. Both studies, however, are often incorporated in discussions of space management and projection.

reason for this focus was the ease and attractiveness of statistically analyzing scheduled space. But there was also another contributing element: the mistaken idea that college and university campuses consist mostly of classrooms and laboratories. Actually, any justification for this focus lies in the fact that colleges and universities consider their key function one of instruction, and, in fulfilling this obligation, efficient design and scheduling of classrooms and laboratories is usually more important than the planning and use of other types of plant facilities. This assumption is particularly true during times of burgeoning enrollment. However, on most campuses the fact remains that many segments of the physical plant (on the average, about two-thirds) serve purposes other than those directly related to the instructional process; specifically, research, office, general, auxiliary, and residential purposes (see room-type distribution of space, figure X-1). Recognition by educators of the fact that so much noninstructional space exists has led to increased interest in its proper design and utilization. As a result, space is now classified for utilization study into two major categories: instructional facilities with scheduled use (classrooms and class laboratories, for example) and support facilities not normally scheduled for instructional occupancy (offices, libraries, residential housing, etc.).

Current analysis of space and its projection consists of four principal operations:

(1) *Classification and inventory* of existing facilities to determine what is presently available and what condition it is in

(2) Establishing *space standards* to serve as design and scheduling benchmarks for utilization evaluation

(3) *Utilization study* to measure and evaluate current use-efficiency in order to recommend improvements

(4) *Projection* of immediate and future facility needs.

The facilities inventory is a continuing data-gathering process to identify, on a building-by-building, room-by-room basis, the amount, type, use, and condition of existing building space. Such information is required to assess present and future space needs accurately. To simplify comparisons and analyses, facilities should be classified and inventoried according to a uniform system compatible with that devised by the National Center for Higher Education Management Systems at WICHE.[3]

Space standards provide design information and define optimum levels of utilization, both of which are prerequisites not only for appraising the

---

[3] Leonard C. Romney, *Higher Education Facilities Inventory and Classification Manual* (prepublication draft), Higher Education Facilities Services, Inc., Raleigh, N.C., February 1973, 156 pp.

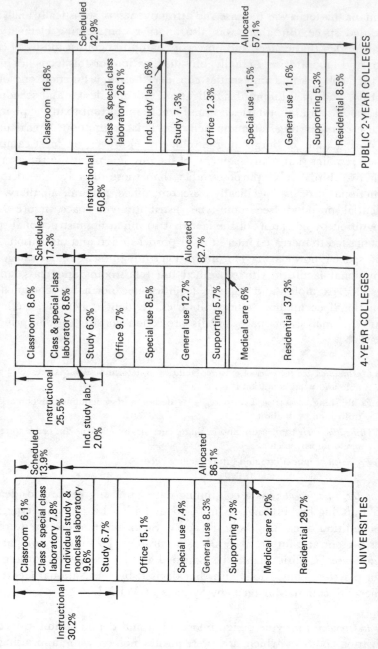

Figure X-1. — Percentage distribution of assignable areas in buildings of institutions of higher education, by type of facility: September 1970

PUBLIC 2-YEAR COLLEGES

Scheduled 42.9%
Allocated 57.1%
Instructional 50.8%

Classroom 16.8%
Class & special class laboratory 26.1%
Ind. study lab. .6%
Study 7.3%
Office 12.3%
Special use 11.5%
General use 11.6%
Supporting 5.3%
Residential 8.5%

4-YEAR COLLEGES

Scheduled 17.3%
Allocated 82.7%
Instructional 25.5%

Classroom 8.6%
Class & special class laboratory 8.6%
Ind. study lab. 2.0%
Study 6.3%
Office 9.7%
Special use 8.5%
General use 12.7%
Supporting 5.7%
Medical care .6%
Residential 37.3%

UNIVERSITIES

Scheduled 13.9%
Allocated 86.1%
Instructional 30.2%

Classroom 6.1%
Class & special class laboratory 7.8%
Individual study & nonclass laboratory 9.6%
Study 6.7%
Office 15.1%
Special use 7.4%
General use 8.3%
Supporting 7.3%
Medical care 2.0%
Residential 29.7%

Source: Higher Education Facilities Services, Inventory of Physical Facilities in Institutions of Higher Education, Fall 1970 and Fall 1971 (preliminary data), Raleigh, N.C., 1972.

adequacy and utilization of existing facilities but also for estimating additional space needs. The most frequently employed standards are those that prescribe optimum values to determine how often rooms should be used, what the occupancy should be when in use, and how much floor area is required—e.g., the number of square feet per classroom chair. Standards should not be based on average or existing practice; rather, they should represent recommended conditions determined by careful mechanical design and utilization study.

A *space utilization study* evaluates how efficiently existing facilities are being used by comparing measured current-usage rates with prescribed standards. These comparisons show whether students, faculty, and staff can be accommodated in existing facilities through improved scheduling of classes and room use or whether additional facilities are required. The major means for improving utilization is to *schedule* existing classrooms and class laboratories so as to minimize *total* operating costs (capital and instructional), while, at the same time, maintaining course selectivity[4] and observing institutional class-size policies. In some instances, when room use is extended by scheduling late afternoon, evening, and Saturday classes, the result will be smaller classes and increased unit costs for teaching. In other instances, however, room use can be substantially increased without any significant reduction in class size. Whatever the circumstances, a comprehensive approach to scheduling of classes is recommended—an approach in which the least-cost objective and academic requirements are appropriately balanced according to institutional priorities.

Projection of facility needs is based on current capacity, anticipated utilization levels, estimated enrollment, expected expenditures and income, and building and campus design.

DATA REQUIREMENTS

Although there are varying reasons for blueprinting and measuring physical facilities, the four principal ones are to provide:

(1) The required data and base information for determining current and projected space requirements,

(2) The data base necessary to conduct facility utilization studies,

---

[4] Course selectivity refers to the scheduling of classes in such a way that all students can pursue their academic work with as few delays, conflicts, and nonpreferred time choices as possible.

(3) Normative data to assist in setting standards for improving the functionality and design of facilities, and

(4) A record of existing space for use in scheduling classrooms and class laboratories and assigning allocated space.

Some of the required data concern *buildings* as entities and are collected and classified accordingly. A majority of the data, however, will pertain to individual *room* details. The information and measurements appropriate to buildings and rooms include the following:

Building Data—

Identification: *building number, name, date of initial occupancy,* location, number of floors, type of construction

Financial: *actual capital investment, estimated replacement value, source of funds,* construction costs, furnishing costs, other costs

Space measurement*: *gross area (square feet),* assignable area, custodial area, circulation area, mechanical area, construction area

Condition: *detail as desired*

Room Data—

Identification: *room number and building number* or name, *institutional organizational-unit, type-of-room use,* program**

Space measurement*: *assignable area, number of stations,†* teaching facilities, room dimensions, equipment arrangement, and other design considerations.

NOTE.—Data considered essential are in italics; other items listed are deemed optional.

* Recommended by the WICHE classification system.

† Stations are usually located only in classrooms, class laboratories, study and seminar rooms, study areas, open-stack study rooms, offices, conference rooms, and assembly areas.

Numerous forms and procedures have been suggested for the efficient collection, filing, and updating of required data.[5] The mechanics of conducting the space inventory consist solely of measuring and recording data in accordance with a given space-classification system. In addition

---

[5] See, for example, John Dale Russell and James I. Doi, *Manual for Studies of Space Utilization in Colleges and Universities,* American Association of Collegiate Registrars and Admissions Officers, Athens, Ohio, 1957.

John V. Yurkovich, *A Methodology for Determining Future Physical Facilities Requirements for Institutions of Higher Education* (U.S. Office of Education Contract No. OE-5 10-291), University of Wisconsin, Madison, 1966.

Planning and Management Systems Division, Western Interstate Commission for Higher Education, *Higher Education Facilities Planning and Management Manuals* (7 vols.), Boulder, Colo., 1971.

to reporting accuracy, the most critical element in establishing usable inventory data is the space-classification system itself. Such a system must be applicable to both a small institution and a complex university, uniform for comparisons among institutions and for compiling State totals, and comprehensive. The WICHE classification system meets these requirements.

SPACE CLASSIFICATION

The diversity and complexity of modern college and university campuses obviously require a systematic approach to facility planning and management. The key to such a system is an orderly classification of facility information—one which ensures the identification, collection, and organization of data for a variety of uses. Requirements inherent in comparative study and aggregate analysis further suggest the need to adhere to common standards and definitions when classifying and reporting facilities information.

Because of the need for standardization, use of the WICHE classification system is recommended. It provides for detailed space definitions and for groupings into more general categories; it is generally compatible with most existing institutional systems; and it arranges classifications in such a way as to facilitate space projection. A general description of the WICHE system follows.

The objective of classifying facility information is to establish distinguishable and useful categories of data that can be independently analyzed and for which reasonable and justifiable standards can be determined. To achieve this objective, classifying facility information primarily by use of the space involved has proven the most advantageous. In adopting this approach, the WICHE system employs three principal dimensions for identifying and classifying space. (See figure X-2.)

Space is first classified on a building basis by *building area type* (see figure X-3). The entire gross area of the building (all areas on all floors within the *outside* faces of exterior walls) is identified according to one of five basic purposes served: (1) *assignable* area functionally usable for principal activities; (2) *circulation* area used for physical access to rooms; (3) *mechanical* area designed to house mechanical equipment, utility services, and public toilet facilities; (4) *custodial* area used for building protection, care, maintenance, and operation; and (5) *construction* area—e.g., exterior walls not usable because of certain structural features of the building. The latter four are identified collectively as the *nonassignable* area. Since in most instances only the assignable area is subject to further classification and detailed analysis, accurate measurement of this particular area is critical. Generally the ratio of assignable area to gross area ranges from .45 to .95, depending on the type of facility. Overall, an institution is likely to have an assignable-to-gross ratio of 50 to 65 percent.

The additional ways of classifying space apply only to assignable areas and are used solely to describe *rooms* and to distinguish one from another. Classification of assignable areas according to room characteristics is usually adequate to answer the basic inventory question, "How much of each kind of space exists?" Rooms are first identified by the *organizational unit* or basic component of the college or university to which it is assigned. Such identification (by the institution) is usually on a departmental basis for academic units (English Department, Physics Department, etc.) and generally parallels typical budget categories for administrative units (Office

Figure X-2. — Schematic outline of WICHE space classification system

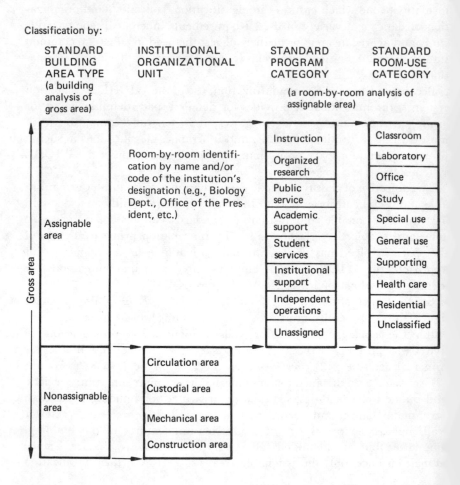

Figure X-3. — Illustration of building area types

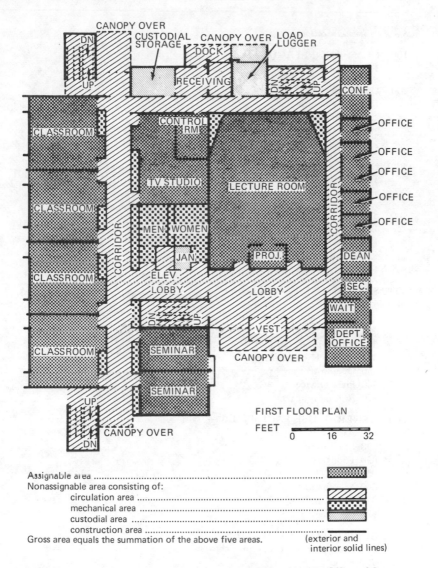

FIRST FLOOR PLAN

Assignable area ....
Nonassignable area consisting of:
     circulation area ....
     mechanical area ....
     custodial area ....
     construction area ....
Gross area equals the summation of the above five areas.   (exterior and interior solid lines)

Source: This illustration is adapted from a series developed by the Office of Space Utilization, Michigan State University, Lansing.

Table X-1.—Abbreviated outline of WICHE standard room-use categories and program classification

---

Standard room-use categories

100 CLASSROOM FACILITIES
       110 Classroom[1]

200 LABORATORY FACILITIES
       210 Class laboratory[1]
       220 Special class laboratory[1]
       230 Individual study laboratory[1]
       250 Nonclass laboratory[1]

300 OFFICE FACILITIES
       310 Office[1]
       350 Conference room[1] (Office related)

400 STUDY FACILITIES
       410 Reading/study room
       420 Stack
       430 Open-stack reading room
       440 Study service

500 SPECIAL USE FACILITIES
       510 Armory[1]
       520 Athletic/physical education[1]
       523 Athletic facilities spectator seating
       530 Audiovisual, radio, TV[1]
       540 Clinic[1] (Nonmedical)
       550 Demonstration[1]
       560 Field service
       570 Animal quarters[1]

600 GENERAL USE FACILITIES
       610 Assembly[1]
       620 Exhibition[1]
       630 Food[1]
       650 Lounge[1]
       660 Merchandising[1]
       670 Recreation[1]
       680 Meeting room[1]

700 SUPPORTING FACILITIES
       710 Data processing/computer[1]
       720 Shop[1]
       730 Storage[1]
       740 Vehicle storage[1]
       750 Central food stores
       760 Central laundry

800 HEALTH CARE FACILITIES
       810 Patient bedroom
       820 Patient bath

See footnote at end of table.

Table X-1.—Abbreviated outline of WICHE standard room-use categories and program classification—Continued

---

    830 Nurse station
    840 Surgery
    850 Treatment
    860 Service laboratory
    870 Supplies
    880 Public waiting
    890 Service

900 RESIDENTIAL FACILITIES
    910 Individual sleep/study
        911 Sleep/study without toilet/bath
        912 Toilet/bath
        913 Sleep/study with toilet/bath
        914 Sleep/study service

    920 Housekeeping
        921 House
        922 House service
        923 Apartment
        924 Apartment service

000 UNCLASSIFIED FACILITIES
    050 Inactive area
    060 Alteration or conversion area
    070 Unfinished area

Standard program classification

1.0 Instruction
    1.1 General academic instruction
        1.1.0100 Agriculture & natural resources
        1.1.0200 Architecture and environmental design
        1.1.0300 Area studies
        1.1.0400 Biological sciences
        (continued detailed listing through 1.1.5500)
    1.2 Occupational and technical instruction
        (1.2.0100 through 1.2.5500 as in 1.1 above)
    1.3 Special session instruction
        (1.3.0100 through 1.3.5500 as in 1.1 above)
    1.4 Extension instruction
        (1.4.0100 through 1.4.5500 as in 1.1 above)

2.0 Organized research
    2.1 Institutes and research centers
        (2.1.0100 through 2.1.5500 as in 1.1 above)
    2.2 Individual and project research
        (2.2.0100 through 2.2.5500 as in 1.1 above)

See footnote at end of table.

Table X-1.—Abbreviated outline of WICHE standard room-use categories and program classification—Continued

---

3.0 Public service
    3.1 Continuing education
        (3.1.0100 through 3.1.5500 as in 1.1 above)
    3.2 Community service
        (3.2.0100 through 3.2.5500 as in 1.1 above)
    3.3 Cooperative extension
        (3.3.0100 through 3.3.5500 as in 1.1 above)

4.0 Academic support
    4.1 Libraries
    4.2 Museums and galleries
    4.3 Audiovisual services
    4.4 Computing support
    4.5 Ancillary support
    4.6 Academic administration & personnel development
    4.7 Course and curriculum development

5.0 Student Service
    5.1 Social and cultural development
        5.1.72 Intercollegiate athletics
    5.2 Supplementary educational service
    5.3 Counseling and career guidance
    5.4 Financial aid
    5.5 Student Support
        5.5.730 Supporting services (Student housing is 5.5.7330.)

6.0 Institutional support
    6.1 Executive management
    6.2 Fiscal operations
    6.3 General administrative services
    6.4 Logistical services
    6.5 Physical plant operations
    6.6 Faculty and staff services
        6.6.7300 supporting services (Faculty and staff housing is 6.6.7330.)
    6.7 Community relations

7.0 Independent operations
    7.1 Institutional operations
    7.2 Outside agencies

0.0 Unassigned
    0.1 Capable of use
    0.2 Incapable of use

---

[1] Indicates that there is an additional service category, e.g., "115 classroom *service*," associated with the basic room-use category.

Source: Leonard C. Romney, *Higher Education Facilities Inventory and Classification Manual* (prepublication draft), Higher Education Facilities Services Incorporated, Raleigh, N.C., February 1973.

of the President, Registrar, Physical Plant, etc.). Classification by organizational unit is designed to provide for the allocation of rooms according to the institutional units being served. However, if a room is a multiple-use facility, it may be difficult to classify it by organizational unit. Rooms which serve a variety of organizational units should be *collectively* allocated according to hours of use, budgetary support, or other appropriate pro rata considerations.

The second and third ways of classifying rooms—by room use and by program—should follow the *standard* categories developed by the WICHE system and outlined in table X-1. The *use* of a room, its most distinguishing characteristic, simply identifies the room according to its designed purpose or how it is actually used. For classification purposes, the term "program" refers to "those identifiable sets of related activities that can be grouped together because of common, broadly defined goals and objectives." The program classification provides a framework by which to organize and analyze room data to determine how facilities are distributed among different kinds of activities or functions.

SPACE MEASUREMENTS
AND STANDARDS

Because space standards are model values for measurements relating to station design, room scheduling, and occupancy rates, they are used as *guides* by planners and architects to estimate total space needs and to appraise use efficiency in existing facilities. Although standards may be based on current or past use of space, it is preferable that they reflect optimum conditions that have been determined scientifically. For purposes of comparison, textbook or theoretical values are sometimes useful as guides or benchmarks; however, from a practical standpoint, *each institution should establish its own workable values*, based on derived rates of utilization and on existing and planned room design. But even tailored standards should not rule out creative and functional design considerations.

Space standards recommend values for three independent *average measurements*:[6]

(1) *Station area* in square feet [A_s]
(2) *Room use in hours* scheduled per week [H_r]
(3) *Station-occupancy percentage* for rooms used [P_s].

---

[6] The symbols used, developed in consultation with James F. Blakesley, are similar to those presented in *Composite and Elemental Space Measures*, Purdue University, Lafayette, Ind., 1965.

Station area measurements may be developed for most room types, whereas room use and station-occupancy measurements can be applied only to rooms *scheduled for use*. When calculating averages for rooms scheduled for use, station area and room use averages should be based on rooms actually used rather than on all inventoried rooms; otherwise, averages will not be consistent with related station-occupancy measurements. In determining averages for all three measurements involving rooms with scheduled occupancy, rooms in reserve, rooms being remodeled, and rooms used exclusively for special short-term purposes should be *excluded*. The overall assessment of utilization, however, should take into account all available facilities, including the amount of space not in use.

Because each *station area* [A_s] is a *design* factor, it is important that standards be based on detailed studies conducted by qualified environmental engineers. What the station area measures—for various room types—is the average amount of immediate floor space (and average associated service area) per station. Station area standards may be developed for rooms with scheduled occupancy (classrooms, laboratories, etc.), and also for rooms without scheduled occupancy (allocated space): offices, library stack areas, dormitory rooms, and the like.

The type of station involved depends on the function of the room. A *student* station in a classroom, for example, is a chair, a seat, or a laboratory desk. The student station area is the floor area required to accommodate one student during an instructional period, plus a proportion of the related instruction area, closets, or other ancillary service areas. An *office* station generally consists of a desk, a chair, and other essential office equipment. The office station area is the immediate floor area needed to accommodate one faculty or staff member, plus required space in any associated service areas, e.g., file rooms, closets, supply cabinets, etc. Station areas are always expressed in assignable square feet (ASF). A 600-square-foot classroom with 40 student chairs and an associated service and instruction area of 100 square feet would contain 700 ASF and a 17.5 ASF per student station. Standards for station areas should be based, if possible, on detailed design studies conducted by persons knowledgeable in human environment engineering.

Room use [H_r] measures the number of hours (periods) per week that a room (or the average for a group of rooms) is scheduled to be occupied by a class.[7] A room is considered to be in use whenever an organized class, regardless of its size, is scheduled to meet. Room use standards have gen

---

[7] This measurement is independent of any institutional variation in the length of an academic week. What is considered a "normal" week varies among institutions; therefore, if sound comparisons are to be made, room use expressed as a percentage of "normal" week of fixed time should be avoided.

erally been developed only for rooms serving functions that require scheduled occupancy—classrooms and class laboratories, for example. In many institutions such rooms represent less than one-fourth of the total building space. Standards for room use are expressed in class hours or periods per week. To ensure scheduling efficiency, thereby minimizing capital and instructional costs yet maintaining course selectivity and departmental class-size policies, room use standards must be determined carefully and scientifically.

Station-occupancy percentage $[P_s]$ measures the average percentage of stations occupied in rooms with scheduled usage. The percentage occupancy indicates the relationship between average class size (number of students) and average room size (number of stations).[8] As with room use measurements, occupancy levels reflect scheduling practice; therefore, they apply only to rooms with scheduled occupancy.

---

[8] The station-occupancy percentage reports average class size (divided by average room size) based on *total* student-contact hours. It therefore provides at best only a rough indication of the "fit" between class size and room size. An accurate and preferred measure of "fit" is a weighted average of the percent station use of each room during each hour of room use. This distinctive measurement, it should be pointed out, *cannot* serve as a mathematical calculation in the utilization index.

To illustrate how the two measurements differ, what follows is a sample calculation for 10 classrooms used a total of 200 hours a week:

Room number	Student stations	Student-contact hours
#1	100 seats × 1 room = 100	80 students × 25 hrs. = 2,000
#2–#6	60 seats × 5 rooms = 300	40 students × 100 hrs. = 4,000
#7–#10	30 seats × 4 rooms = 120	10 students × 75 hrs. = 750
	Total 520	Total 6,750

Average room size = 520/10
= 52 seats

Average class size = 6,750/200
= 33.75 students

Percent station occupancy = ave. class size/ave. room size = 33.75/52 = 65%

Room number	Percent of stations occupied	Weight according to hours of room use relative to total classroom hours
#1	80 students/100 seats = 80.0%	× 25/200 = 10.0%
#2–#6	40 students/60 seats = 66.6%	× 100/200 = 33.3%
#7–#10	10 students/30 seats = 33.3%	× 75/200 = 12.5%
		55.8%

Weighted average of the percent station use of each room for each hour of room use (a measurement of "fit" between class size and room size).

In addition to the three independent space measurements (station area, room use, and station-occupancy percentage), a derived measurement commonly employed is *station use* $[H_s]$, measured in hours scheduled per week. Station use is the average number of hours per week (usually referred to as weekly student hours, WSH) that room stations are scheduled to be used by students. Station use equals the product of room use $[H_r]$ and station-occupancy percentage $[P_s]$. For example, if a single room with 40 student stations is scheduled for 30 class hours a week ($H_r = 30$) and the *average* scheduled number of students (class size) in the room during the week is 20, the station-occupancy percentage $[P_s]$ will equal the average scheduled class size divided by the number of student stations ($20/40 = 50\%$). Station use $[H_s]$, equal to the product of $[H_r]$ and $[P_s]$, would be $30 \times .50 = 15$ hours per week, or 15 weekly student hours (WSH).

In evaluating efficient use of rooms *scheduled* for occupancy and projecting future needs, the three independent measurements are combined in a formula to equal a composite space factor or *utilization index* (UI). The UI is expressed in assignable square feet (ASF) per weekly student hour (WSH).

$$UI = \frac{A_s}{H_r \times P_s} \quad \text{also} \quad UI = \frac{A_s}{H_s}$$

A classroom with a student station area of 15 ASF that is scheduled for 30 class hours per week and has a station occupancy of 50 percent will have a utilization index of 1.0 ASF per WSH.

$$UI = \frac{15}{30 \times .50} = 1.0$$

With regard to teaching laboratories, the utilization index or space factor will be substantially larger in value because a greater area per student station is required. For example: $A_s = 48$ ASF, $H_r = 20$ hours per week, and $P_s = 60\%$.

$$UI = \frac{48}{20 \times .60} = 4.0 \text{ ASF per WSH}$$

The *allocation ratio* $[AR]$ of average net-assignable square feet of space (including service area) per user unit (the person or object employing or occupying the space in question) is a measurement recommended for evaluating the efficient use of rooms *without* scheduled occupancy and also for projecting the need for such space. Some examples of allocation ratios commonly employed are the following: ASF of office space per FTE staff member, ASF of study space per FTE enrollment, and ASF of library stack area per volume.

For a summary of space-measurement definitions and formulas and for a graphical illustration of their mathematical relationship, see figure X-4.

Figure X-4 — Graphic illustration of the mathematical relationship between space measurements for scheduled classrooms and class laboratories

Summary of Space Measurements and Formulas

A_s = Station area in assignable square feet (ASF)

H_r = Room use in hours scheduled per week

P_s = Station occupancy percentage for rooms used

H_s = Station use in hours scheduled per week or weekly student hours (WSH)

$\quad\quad H_s = H_r \times P_s$

UI = Utilization index in assignable square feet per weekly student

$\quad$ hour (WSH) $\quad UI = \dfrac{A_s}{H_r \ \times \ P_s}$ or $UI = \dfrac{A_s}{H_s}$

AR = Allocation ratio in assignable square feet per using unit

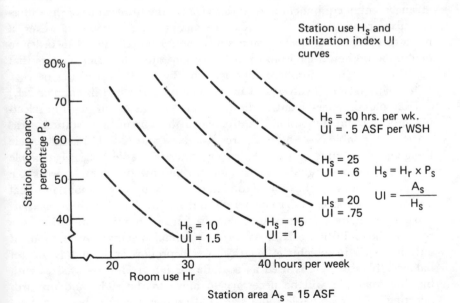

Station use H_s and utilization index UI curves

H_s = 30 hrs. per wk.
UI = .5 ASF per WSH

H_s = 25
UI = .6 $\quad H_s = H_r \times P_s$

H_s = 20 $\quad UI = \dfrac{A_s}{H_s}$
UI = .75

H_s = 10
UI = 1.5

H_s = 15
UI = 1

Station occupancy percentage P_s

Room use Hr

Station area A_s = 15 ASF

NOTE.—The foregoing six space measurements (A_s, H_r, P_s, H_s, UI, and AR) constitute the basic input for utilization studies and projection of facility needs. If data cannot be collected in detail, certain general indexes may be used to provide limited information pertaining to facility utilization. One general measurement is the total ASF for a given type of facility—classrooms per FTE student, for example. A second general measurement is the mix-ratio of various categories of space, such as the ratio of classroom area to total area. Since program emphasis varies greatly among institutions, mean values for these general measurements can seldom be realistically compared. Moreover, short cuts such as these merely provide evidence of over- or under-utilization; they do not reveal space-design or scheduling factors indicated by the six principal recommended measurements.

Establishing Station-Area Standards

The principal design element of the utilization index (UI) and the allocation ratio (AR) is station area [A_s], or average immediate area and service area per occupant or using unit. Station area standards for various room types should be based on optimum design rather than on past or present use patterns. For existing rooms, optimum design can be achieved through space-layout on module studies that determine the most effective arrangement of equipment and stations within the limitations of the different space configurations and areas. In planning new rooms, however, a more comprehensive space-design study should be conducted in order to determine optimum environmental conditions and all design factors that contribute to an atmosphere conducive to the teaching-learning process. (The many factors involved in space design are discussed in chapter XI.)

Examples of space-layout studies that can serve as useful *guides* in selecting proper room dimensions, equipment arrangement, and station areas are shown in table X-2 and in figures X-5, X-6, and X-7. Using as a guide the given chair dimensions and spacing pattern in table X-2, it is possible to select the most suitable classroom dimensions, based on a workable compromise between the desired total number of stations per room, minimal average station size, and room width and length. The curve of *minimum* assignable square feet per station for the various number of stations per room is shown in figure X-5. As a rule, minimal spacing can be obtained only in rooms in which the length-to-width proportion is unduly out of balance. If table X-2 is used as a guide for integrating room sizes with building plans, it will be necessary to move to the right and upward, selecting a few reasonable room sizes and proportions at only a slight increase in average station size. As figure X-5 indicates, the smaller the room, the larger the area required per station. It follows, then, that smaller institutions, which tend to have fewer pupils per class and, consequently,

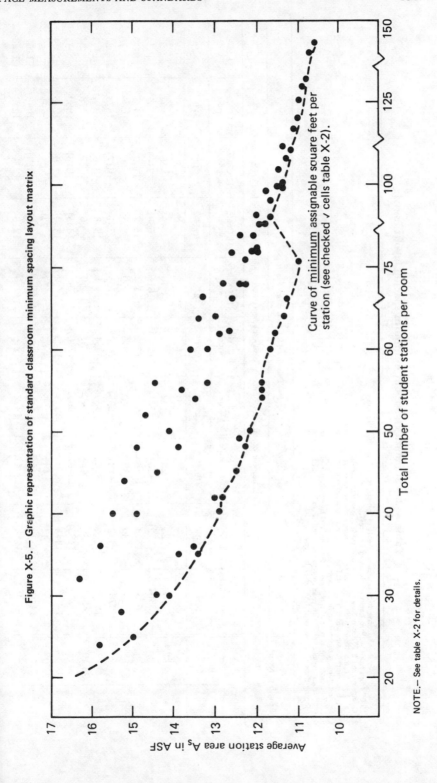

Figure X-5. — Graphic representation of standard classroom minimum spacing layout matrix

Average station area A_s in ASF

Total number of student stations per room

Curve of minimum assignable square feet per station (see checked ✓ cells table X-2).

NOTE.— See table X-2 for details.

Table X-2.—Standard classroom minimum spacing layout matrix

Conventional arrangements of tablet-arm chairs¹ in solid rows

1. 10'0" from front wall to backs of chairs in first row.
2. Chairs spaced 3'2" from back to back, and on 2'2" centers laterally.
3. (a) Less than 8 chairs wide: 6'0" total aisle, measured from center of chair.
   (b) 8 or more chairs wide: 8'0" total aisle, measured from center of chair.
4. Second door, if more than 50 stations.
5. 3'0" lateral aisle at rear of flat floor, if 2 doors and more than 7 chairs wide.
6. 0'6" from backs of chairs in rear row to rear wall if no lateral aisle at rear.
7. Sloping floor (i.e., stepped) behind eighth row.

Tabulated for each room width

Total number of stations (Number of assignable square feet) Assignable square feet per station

Length of room		5 Chairs wide 14'8"	6 Chairs wide 16'10"	7 Chairs wide 19'0"	8 Chairs wide 23'2"	9 Chairs wide 25'4"	10 Chairs wide 27'6"	11 Chairs wide 29'8"	12 Chairs wide 31'10"	13 Chairs wide 34'0"	14 Chairs wide 36'2"
No. of rows	Feet inches										
4	22'6"²	20³ (330) 16.5	24 (379) 15.8	28 (428) 15.3	32 (521) 16.3	36 (570) 15.8	40 (619) 15.5	44 (668) 15.2	48 (716) 14.9	52 (765) 14.7	56 (814) 14.5
5	25'8"²	25³ (376) 15.0	30 (432) 14.4	35 (488) 13.9	40 (595) 14.9	45 (650) 14.4	50 (706) 14.1	55 (761) 13.8	60 (817) 13.6	65 (873) 13.4	70 (928) 13.3
6	28'10"²	30³ (423) 14.1	36 (485) 13.5	42 (548) 13.0	48 (668) 13.9	54 (730) 13.5	60 (793) 13.2	66 (855) 13.0	72 (918) 12.8	78 (980) 12.6	84 (1043) 12.4
7	32'0"²	35³ (469) 13.4	42³ (539) 12.8	49 (608) 12.4	56 (741) 13.2	63 (811) 12.9	70 (880) 12.6	77 (949) 12.3	84 (1019) 12.1	91 (1088) 12.0	98 (1157) 11.8

		40[3]	48[3]	56[3]	64	72	80	88	96	104	112
8	35'2"	40[3] (516) 12.9	48[3] (592) 12.3	56[3] (668) 11.9	64 (815) 12.7	72 (891) 12.4	80 (967) 12.1	88 (1043) 11.9	96 (1119) 11.7	104 (1196) 11.5	112 (1272) 11.4
9	38'4"	45[3] (562) 12.5	54[3] (645) 11.9	63[3] (728) 11.6	72 (888) 12.3	81 (971) 12.0	90[3] (1054) 11.7	99 (1137) 11.5	108 (1220) 11.3	117 (1303) 11.1	126 (1386) 11.0
10	41'6"	50[3] (609) 12.2	60[3] (699) 11.7	70[3] (789) 11.3	80 (961) 12.0	90[3] (1051) 11.7	100[3] (1141) 11.4	110[3] (1231) 11.2	120[3] (1321) 11.0	130 (1411) 10.9	140[3] (1501) 10.7
11	44'8"	55[3] (655) 11.9	66[3] (752) 11.4	77[3] (849) 11.0	88 (1035) 11.8	99[3] (1132) 11.4	110[3] (1228) 11.2	121[3] (1325) 11.0	132[3] (1422) 10.8	143[3] (1519) 10.6	154[3] (1615) 10.5

[1] This matrix is designed for tablet-arm chairs with a sideways center-to-center spacing of 26", and an overall front-to-back chair dimension (from the back of the chair to the edge of the tablet arm) of about 28". By spacing these chairs 3'2" from back to back, the recommended minimum back-to-arm spacing of 10" is provided.

[2] Deduct 2'6" (and correspondingly from square footage) if no lateral aisle.

[3] Curve of minimum assignable square feet per station (see plot, figure X-5).

Source: Originally devised in 1948 by Donovan Smith for the University of California; further developed by Edward Rodgers.

Figure X-6. — Layout study showing the potentialities of a 140-square-foot faculty office

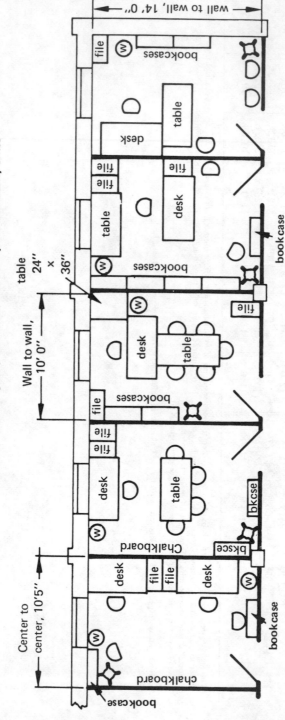

NOTE. — Furniture-arrangement flexibility is built in two ways: by providing wall space on the window side of the room and by placing electrical outlets on both sides on each window and on the opposite wall.

Source: Robert V. Walen, Memorandum to Chief Campus Offices, University of California, Office of Architects and Engineers, October 20, 1959.

For another faculty office study, see C. R. Carpenter and others, A Faculty Office Study: Design and Evaluation, Division of Academic Research and Services and Department of Physical Plant Planning and Construction, Pennsylvania State University, University Park, December 1961.

Figure X-7. — Layout study for seminar and conference rooms showing minimal
areas and dimensions for various arrangements of standard 2½ -foot
by 5-foot tables

(Each occupant is provided not less than 4 square feet of table area; student stations
equal number of chairs, less one for instructor.)

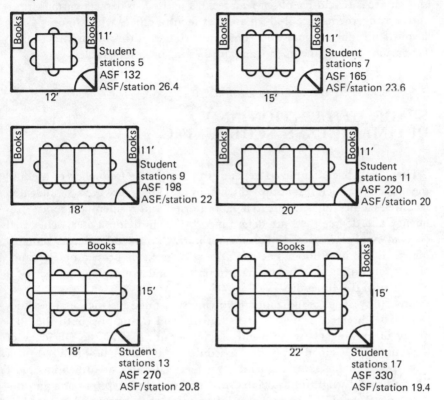

NOTE. — In planning seminar and conference room layouts, adequate consideration
should be given to door and window requirements; also to placement of
blackboards. Except in square rooms (where location of windows and
doors is optional), a preferred practice is to place windows (high or low)
along the entire length of one of the major-dimension walls, and doors
(or door) on the opposite wall. With regard to blackboards, the best
arrangement is to place one across from the minor-demension wall and/
or behind the instructor's chair. In the case of mathematics and science
seminar rooms, however, the second blackboard is usually attached to the
major-dimension wall adjacent to the door or between doors.

The square footages indicated provide ample room, in most instances, for
the addition of 15" deep bookcases along one wall. If bookcases are to be
installed (particularly along major-dimension walls), it is recommended
that the "push-out" clearance between the chairs and bookcases be examined and, if necessary, that 12" to 15" be added to the room dimensions.

Source: Adapted, with modification, from Robert F. Walen, "Seminar and Conference Room Facilities",
a paper prepared for the Planning Analysts' Conference, University of California at San Diego,
Dec. 8-9, 1966.

a need for relatively smaller room sizes, will have a greater area per station than will larger schools.[9]

The space-layout studies in figures X-6 and X-7 are designed to assist in the selection of room sizes and dimensions, together with corresponding station areas (exclusive of service areas). Figure X-6 depicts various furniture arrangements in a 140-square-foot faculty office, while figure X-7, a layout study for seminar and conference rooms, illustrates minimal areas for various arrangements of standard $2\frac{1}{2}$ foot by 5 foot tables.

SPACE UTILIZATION AND OPTIMAL CLASS SCHEDULING

How well space is utilized depends in part on the frequency of use and the degree to which it is occupied when in use. For many types of allocated facilities—faculty offices, research laboratories, and residential rooms—frequency and degree rates are determined by the individual user. Scheduled occupancy of classrooms and class laboratories, on the other hand, is determined by the institution. The potential savings from proper performance of this scheduling justify an institution's giving continuous and critical attention to this function.

Any study of space utilization involving scheduled instructional facilities should be directed primarily at measuring and evaluating both the adequacy of existing classrooms and class laboratories and the efficiency of their use. To begin this process, scheduling data must be analyzed on a room-by-room basis; subsequently, the derived rates of utilization must be evaluated in light of associated instructional and capital costs and desired operating effectiveness. From information obtained, it will be possible to determine whether the expected number of students can be accommodated in existing facilities or whether changes in scheduling or additional facilities will be required.

More specifically, the immediate and primary purpose of the utilization-scheduling function as it applies to instructional facilities is to *schedule* the use of existing instructional space in such a manner as to minimize *total operating costs* (capital and instructional) and meet the *academic requirements*

---

[9] The following comparison of classroom area per FTE student by campus size is reported for Indiana colleges and universities: Campus enrollment 500 or less, 26.9 square feet per FTE student; enrollment 501–750, 21.2 sq. ft.; enrollment 751–1,500, 18.9 sq. ft.; enrollment 1,501–5,000, 17.3 sq. ft.; enrollment over 5,000, 10.3 sq. ft. See James F. Blakesley, Paul C. Bayless, W. Charles Sherwood, and Frederick H. Wolf, *Indiana Facilities Utilization Survey for Colleges and Universities, Fall 1967*, Indiana Advisory Commission on Academic Facilities, Bloomington, 1968, p. 57.

of course selectivity and class-size policies. Schedules so developed provide data for three additional aspects of physical plant design and expansion: (1) correcting imbalances in the number and size of rooms in relation to class-size distribution; (2) pinpointing specific building- and room-type needs in conjunction with developing a comprehensive program of plant expansion, and (3) justifying capital-outlay appropriation requests and any priorities that may have been established for new buildings.

NOTE.—While basic to the accomplishment of these purposes, the mechanics of measuring existing levels of space utilization are not reviewed in this publication. For detailed procedures on this facet of utilization study, see Planning and Management Systems Division, WICHE, *Higher Education Facilities Planning and Management Manuals,* op. cit.

In this presentation, the discussion is limited to the two competing objectives involved: (1) the scheduling of instructional space so as to maintain course selectivity and adhere to class-size policies, and (2) the scheduling of instructional space in such a way as to minimize total operating costs.

The second objective—scheduling instructional space to minimize total operating costs—is a complex task that includes a number of controversial priority considerations. Both capital and instructional costs are involved; however, the space measurements that directly influence capital requirements provide the best springboard for discussion. From the formula for the composite utilization index $UI = A_s/(H_r \times P_s)$, it can be seen that lower UI values, and, hence, increased utilization or reduced capital costs, can be obtained in three ways:

(1) The size of the student station $[A_s]$ may be reduced;
(2) The number of hours rooms are scheduled per week $[H_r]$ may be increased (also year-round operation may be introduced); or
(3) The station-occupancy percentage $[P_s]$ may be increased by a schedule that better matches average class sizes and average room-seating capacities.

Class Scheduling To Meet Academic Requirements

In planning master class schedules, course selectivity should be a prime consideration. Another factor to be considered is that classes should conform as nearly as possible to the size patterns and policies recommended by each department for various subject offerings.

Class size is a policy matter to be decided by each institution and individual department on the basis of educational philosophy and program requirements and on the basis of available staff and space resources. Course selectivity, on the other hand, may be approached on a more mechanical basis by observance of certain scheduling rules. The following scheduling practices are designed to provide course selectivity yet minimize conflicts:

1. Broad distribution of courses over the hours of the day and days of the week reduces the number of courses taught at the same time and thereby increases the number of courses from which a student may choose. Conversely, concentrating courses during a few hours in the academic week reduces course selectivity.

2. To the extent that the academic program permits, conflicts may be limited by reducing the total number of courses offered during a semester, an action whereby the number of courses taught concurrently is also reduced.

3. The more courses individual students request, the more likely that conflicts will occur. Curriculums designed to reduce the average number of courses students are required to take will reduce scheduling conflicts.

4. To reduce the many conflicts that large classes create, such classes should be scheduled at a time when few other courses are offered (normally during nonpremium hours).

5. When all students in a certain group—freshmen or selected majors, for example—are enrolled in the same or nearly the same curriculum, block-scheduling by groups can reduce conflicts. If a block of students is following a similar course pattern, scheduling becomes less of a problem.

6. Student scheduling (involuntary assignment of students to various sections of multisectioned courses) can be an effective method to balance class sizes, regardless of the hours at which the classes are offered. If student scheduling is adopted, legitimate special requests—those arising from participation in athletics or other extracurricular activities, job requirements, or commuting problems—should be honored. Furthermore, even if no special request is involved, students registered for multisection courses should be given an equal chance of being assigned to any section.

7. A program of early registration gives students an opportunity to become aware of existing course conflicts and make necessary adjustments.

Utilization Efficiency and Station Design

Very little saving in capital cost[10] can be obtained by improving classroom utilization through a reduction in student station area [A_s], nor is such a reduction generally recommended. Space economies should be made strictly in accordance with specifications set forth by optimal model design. For example, only so many chairs can be crowded into a room without reducing the amount of space essential for aisles and a comfortable seating arrangement. However, better seating efficiency can result from the construction of larger rooms. Lecture halls with auditorium-type seating may require only 9 feet per station, in contrast to the 20-to-25 square feet per station necessary in small seminar rooms.

A value of 15 square feet per station, including service area, is often used—although seldom justified—as a standard for projecting classroom space. Each institution, however, should determine and justify its own value, based on detailed station-design studies.

---

[10] Instructional costs are not a factor in station area design.

Scheduling Room Use To Minimize Total Costs

Any study of increasing utilization through expanded room use should involve not only an effort to minimize capital outlay but also a series of judgments and priorities related to associated instructional costs and scheduling effectiveness. Under certain circumstances, scheduling of classes during the late afternoons, evenings, and Saturdays may result in reduction in class sizes at those times, and also in higher teaching costs which may more than offset any reduction in capital costs. In other circumstances, however, an institution may expand its class schedule without reducing class size and thus effect a saving in both instructional and capital costs. In this section, the scheduling of room use to minimize total costs, under both sets of circumstances, will be reviewed. Whatever the scheduling situation, it is important that, over and above the cost factor, academic considerations should be foremost. It is essential that course conflicts be minimized and class-size policy be observed.

Different campus situations obviously present substantially different opportunities for expanding room use. Some of the factors involved are relatively fixed, the result of program emphasis and the relationship between the institution and the community. Others, particularly those pertaining to institutional priorities, may be changed as circumstances require. These two contrasting situations may be summarized under the headings *structured* and *flexible*.

	Situation description	
Factors	Structured	Flexible
1. Ability of students to attend classes on an expanded schedule. Attitude of institution toward honoring student preferences.	Mainly resident and part-time *students who can easily accommodate an expanded schedule*. Institution and staff predisposed to expand schedule.	Mainly commuter students or students who, because of a substantial extracurricular program, *prefer or require classes during premium hours*. Institution and staff predisposed toward "free" afternoons.
2. Standardization of curriculum.	Relatively *fixed*, with many required courses and few electives. Block-scheduling possible	*Tailored* to meet individual needs, with many options and electives. Block scheduling seldom possible.
3. Course distribution requirement (selectivity).	Structured curriculum, with limited substitutions. Courses not easy to cancel, postpone, or take out of sequence. *Courses are broadly distributed throughout day; selectivity high.*	Flexible curriculum, with many opportunities for course substitutions. Courses easily canceled without serious consequences. *Course distribution concentrated in morning and afternoon; relatively low selectivity tolerated.*

| | Situation description | |
Factors	Structured	Flexible
4. Number of different courses offered each semester, relative to student load.	*Relatively low.*	*Relatively high.*
5. Class-size variance.	*Relatively low.*	*Relatively high.*
6. Class-size policy.	*Strict adherence*, limited in part by fixed laboratory space.	*Flexible*, depending on student demand. Many opportunities for very large classes.
7. Student registration for multisection courses.	*Students assigned* involuntarily to sections. Many multisection courses offered with large enrollments involved.	*Student choice*. Few multi-section courses offered.

The structured situation provides optimal conditions for minimizing classroom and class laboratory space needs by means of expanded room use without concurrent reduction in class size or an increase in teaching costs. When students and faculty are willing and able to attend classes throughout the day and when the curriculum includes many required courses that must be broadly scheduled in order to avoid conflicts, the scheduling of classes during late afternoons, evenings, and Saturdays is feasible; in fact, if instructional facilities are limited, such scheduling may be necessary.[11] Little, if any, reduction in class size should be expected at these odd hours if students have limited opportunity to substitute morning classes and are discouraged from delaying or taking courses out of sequence. Those institutions deciding to extend the class day should be prepared to solve such concomitant problems as staffing, use of auxiliary facilities, library hours, safety, and parking.

An outstanding example of maximum utilization of instruction facilities is the one followed by Purdue University. This institution operates on a 55-hour week, beginning at 7:30 a.m. and ending at 5:20 p.m., with 5 hours of classes offered on Saturday mornings. Since residence dining halls serve from 10:30 a.m. to 12:45 p.m., scheduling of classes even during the lunch hour is possible. Students are involuntarily assigned to

---

[11] On a broader time span, room use may be increased by lengthening and balancing the school year: adopting a three-term (trimester) or four-quarter system, for example. Year-round operation of facilities not only extends room utilization for 3-plus months but also makes possible more equitable distribution of students each term or quarter. If year-round operation is to be worthwhile, however, a substantial number of students must be encouraged to attend summer sessions. For further discussion of this topic, see chapter XIII.

multisection courses, with allowance made for student preference of instructor and involvement in extracurricular activities. Examinations, tutoring sessions, and some regular classes are scheduled in the evenings.[12]

Purdue's pattern of instructional facility use is impressive. During the 1971–72 academic year, classroom utilization averaged 36 hours per week; station occupancy for rooms in use, 66 percent. Based on a station area of 15 ASF, this represents a utilization index (UI) value of .63 ASF per WSH. Since class size (an average of 28 students) did not decline during nonpremium time periods, instructional costs per weekly student hour remained relatively fixed.

Few institutions will ever need to maximize the use of their facilities to the extent that Purdue has. Nevertheless, the Purdue system demonstrates that space requirements and capital costs can be drastically reduced without lowering academic standards. The broad time span over which courses at Purdue are distributed provides maximum course selectivity. Furthermore, instructional costs are held to a minimum without increasing recommended class size or reducing the total number of courses offered.

Institutions operating with the type of *structured* situation described earlier should explore the possibility of adopting some of the scheduling methods employed by Purdue to minimize total operating costs.

If an institution is disposed towards holding most of its classes during morning and early afternoon hours and if its situation approximates that described as *flexible*, instruction costs may be high and can be expected to figure prominently in any consideration of optimum room use.[13]

For a variety of reasons, extending room use by scheduling courses during nonpremium time periods may result in smaller classes and increased teaching costs. Within the framework of a flexible curriculum, many students who prefer morning classes will try to avoid taking electives during nonpremium times by registering for only those courses (probably second-choice electives) offered in the morning or early afternoon. Other

---

[12] For a detailed explanation of the Purdue University student-scheduling system, see Victor A. Abell and G. E. Morgan, *Purdue Academic Student Scheduling (PASS)*, Purdue University Press, Lafayette, Ind., 1965; Victor A. Abell, J. F. Blakesley, G. E. Morgan, and W. C. Sherwood, *A Comprehensive University Scheduling System (CUSS)*, Purdue University Press, 1965; and James R. Marshall and G. E. Morgan, *Examination Scheduling Procedure (ESP)*, Purdue University Press, 1969.

[13] Argument for conducting the kind of utilization study that reveals the relationship between room use and instruction costs has long been advanced by Donovan Smith. See "Space Standards and Concepts of Efficiency in the Planning and Operation of Capital Plant for Higher Education," an unpublished staff paper, University of California; also, "Optimal Class Scheduling," paper presented at the 55th annual meeting of the American Association of Collegiate Registrars and Admissions Officers, Dallas, Tex., Apr. 21–25, 1969.

students will defer taking required courses scheduled in the late afternoon or on Saturday in the hope that at a future date they will be able to take such courses at a more convenient hour. Still others—students involved in extracurricular activities, those who hold part-time jobs, and those who must commute long distances—will be able to attend only those classes held during morning and early afternoon hours.[14] Finally, some students (particularly women), because of concern for personal safety, will refuse to attend evening classes.

Thus it can be seen that when room use is extended by scheduling classes during nonpremium hours, the average class size may be so significantly reduced and unit teaching costs so significantly increased that any resultant capital-cost saving is nullified.

In view of the foregoing, figure X-8 and table X-3 have been prepared to illustrate and clarify a method of determining optimum room use that minimizes total operating costs.[15] In the upper graph of figure X-8, curve B shows that by extending the number of weekly class hours for which instructional facilities are used [H_r], the total number of required classrooms is reduced; hence, a capital-cost saving. Curve A reflects what often happens when attempts are made to extend room use by scheduling classes during nonpremium hours; namely, a significant decline in mean class size and a corresponding increase in average teaching costs. Optimum class scheduling occurs when the total capital- and teaching-unit costs (curve A plus B) are minimized; in this example, it occurs at $H_r = 26$ hours per week (see vertical arrow).[16]

In the lower graph of figure X-8, the decline in station-occupancy percentage (P_s) as room use (H_r) is increased is indicated by the solid-line curve. Dash-line curves represent constant values for station use (H_s) and the utilization index (UI), for various values of room use and station-occupancy percentages. In this example, total average costs are minimized at a room use (H_r) level of 26 hours per week and a corresponding station-occupancy percentage of 54.4 percent. Operating at this point results in station use (H_s) equal to 14.1 hours per week and a utilization index (UI) value of 1.06 assignable square feet per weekly student hour (ASF per WSH).

As shown in table X-3, in order to increase class size and reduce room use, the number of classes per week must also be reduced. Unless many

---

[14] These conditions apply particularly to full-time students; many part-time students actually prefer evening and Saturday classes.

[15] The example data should not be interpreted as normative.

[16]In a strict sense, this is a cost-effectiveness analysis rather than a cost-benefit analysis. Since returns are not measured, no attempt can be made—as is done in a cost-benefit analysis—to maximize benefits by operating at the point at which *marginal costs equal marginal returns*. In the absence of economically measurable returns, the optimum operating point occurs when *average costs* are minimized.

Figure X-8. — Example illustration of cost effectiveness analysis to determine optimal room use under conditions identified as flexible

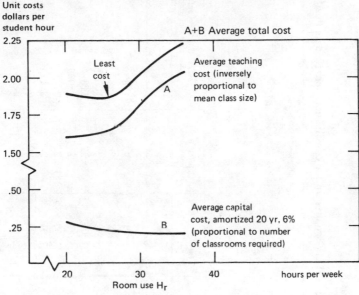

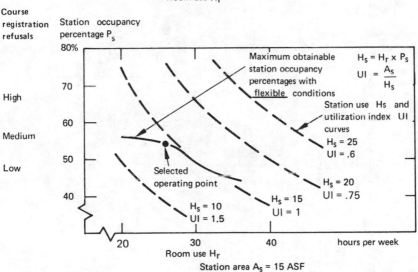

NOTE. — See table X-3 for data and computational details.
See text for conditions identified as flexible.

Table X-3.—Example of utilization rates and unit costs for general classrooms under conditions identified as flexible

Enrollment: 6,667 full-time students
Average weekly student load: 15 WSH
Total campus weekly student hour load: 100,000 WSH
Room use (col. 1) × mean class size (col. 2) × number of classrooms required (col. 3) = 100,000 WSH
Mean room capacity: 50 student stations
Station occupancy percentage P_s = mean class size divided by mean room capacity.

WSH = weekly student hours
ASF = assignable sq. ft.

Room use $[H_r]$ hrs. per week	Mean class size and station occupancy percentage P_s in ( )	Number of classrooms required	Number of classes held per week col. 1×col. 3	Average unit costs		
				Teaching[1] $ per student hour	Capital[2] $ per student hour	Teaching and capital $ per student hour
(1)	(2)	(3)	(4)	(5)	(6)	(7)
20	28.0 (56.0%)	178	3,560	1.61	.28	1.89
22	27.8 (55.6%)	164	3,608	1.62	.26	1.88
24	27.6 (55.2%)	151	3,624	1.63	.24	1.87 } least cost range
26	27.2 (54.4%)	141	3,666	1.65	.22	1.87
28	26.1 (52.2%)	137	3,836	1.72	.215	1.935
30	24.7 (49.4%)	135	4,050	1.82	.21	2.03
32	23.5 (47.0%)	133	4,256	1.91	.205	2.115
34	22.7 (45.4%)	130	4,420	1.98	.205	2.185
36	22.0 (44.0%)	126	4,536	2.04	.20	2.24

Parameters:

General:
Conditions approaching those identified as *flexible.*

Average teaching costs:

Faculty salary[3] for 30-week academic year: $12,000.

Teaching load: 11 class hours per week.

Teaching cost per class hour: $36.40 + 25% for administration, supplies, etc. = $45.

Classroom data and average capital costs:

Mean room capacity: 50 student stations.

Average area per station: 15 ASF.

Capital outlay per ASF: $55.

Capital outlay per room: $41,200.

Amortized 20-year period at 6% .... $3,600 per year

Maintenance & operation per classroom per year: $1.50 per ASF×750 ASF $1,100

Total yearly cost per room $4,700

Weekly cost per room (30 weeks)[1] .... $ 157

NOTE.—See figure X-8 for graphic presentation. See text table for conditions identified as *flexible*.

[1] Teaching cost per student hour = $\dfrac{\$45 \text{ per class hour}}{\text{mean class size}}$.

[2] Capital cost per student hour = $\dfrac{\$157 \text{ per room per week} \times \text{number of rooms}}{100{,}000 \text{ WSH}}$.

[3] Faculty salary should reflect reimbursement for all professional and administrative tasks related to teaching and student-centered activities.

multisection courses are offered,[17] the result will be a reduction in the number of courses offered. It follows then that institutions operating on a morning and early-afternoon class schedule basis can offer fewer courses during each semester than institutions (with the same number of students) scheduling classes over a broader time span. In considering both academic standards and total costs, institutions may choose to meet curriculum course-offering requirements and, at the same time, operate at room use levels higher (to provide more courses) than those indicated solely by cost considerations.

Increasing Station Occupancy To Minimize Capital Costs

Space requirements are reduced when station occupancy [P_s] is improved by more closely matching class size with room capacity.[18] There is a limit, however, to a feasible level of occupancy. At some point the cost of the complex task of closely matching class sizes and room capacities may become prohibitive.

More important, the higher the occupancy level, the less flexibility there is to cope with unexpected overenrollment or other emergency situations. In the event more students register for courses than the scheduled rooms can accommodate, some institutions (particularly those with rapidly increasing enrollments) find that it is less expensive in the long run to operate at lower station-occupancy rates and permit the overflow to be accommodated in existing classes rather than to schedule additional class sections.

In addition to cost and flexibility considerations, two other factors limit the amount by which station-occupancy rates can be increased. The first is the relatively fixed size of classrooms resulting from the delay between the planning of new construction and actual completion. This condition means that an institution must face the fact that a time lag will constantly interfere with the goal of providing classrooms of the size needed to meet changing enrollment and curriculum requirements.

The second factor limiting the degree to which station occupancy can be increased is that of class-size variance. When class sizes vary greatly from expectations—as in the case of the *flexible* situation—high average station occupancy can be obtained only by refusing to permit substantial numbers of students to register for courses when actual class size exceeds

---

[17] Multisection courses usually account for no more than one-fourth of the total number of course offerings.

[18] See footnote 8 for limitation of station occupancy as a measure of "fit" between class size and room capacity.

scheduled room capacity, or, alternatively, to offer smaller sections at less desirable times, with resultant low station-occupancy rates and increased costs.

When class-size variance is high, station-occupancy percentages of 45 to 55 percent are generally considered maximum. On the other hand,

Figure X-9. — Distribution of number of class-period meetings per week, by size of class in relationship to capacity of room in which classes are held

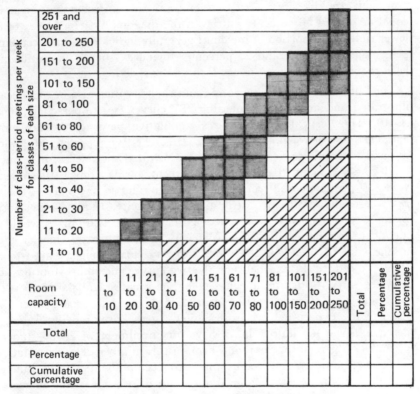

Station percentage occupancy P_s

P_s generally 50% or greater

P_s generally 25% to 50%

P_s generally 25% or less

Source: Adapted from John Dale Russell and James I. Doi, Manual for Studies of Space Utilization in Colleges and Universities, American Association of Collegiate Registrars and Admissions Officers, Ohio University, Athens, Ohio, 1957, p. 74.

if class sizes can be controlled through student scheduling, or accurately predicted (in the case of a rigid curriculum and stable enrollment), the matching of class sizes with room capacities is easier; therefore, station-occupancy rates as high as 60 to 65 percent are possible.

To visualize the existing "fit" between class sizes and room capacities, institutions can plot a chart similar to the graph in figure X-9. On completion, such a chart will give an approximate visual indication of the variation in occupancy rates by room capacities and class sizes.

Entries indicate the distribution of the number of class-period meetings per week by size of class in relation to room capacity in which the classes are held. In the gray area, station-occupancy percentages generally equal or exceed 50 percent. Entries in the diagonally striped area of the lower right-hand portion of the chart generally indicate station-occupancy percentages not exceeding 25 percent. Obviously, such a low utilization level requires review if space use is to be upgraded.

The "fit" between class size and room capacity may also be graphically illustrated and analyzed by plotting "S" curves (see upper chart, figure X-10). The vertical axis measures cumulative percent; the horizontal axis, class size or room capacity. The *class-size* curve represents the teaching and scheduling program. The case illustrated shows that, in terms of total classes scheduled per week, 8 percent enroll from 1–10 students, while 30 percent enroll from 1–20 students. The second curve, *room capacity*, presents classroom distribution by capacity. If all stations in all rooms were occupied during scheduled classes, the two curves would be identical; but the fact that room capacity must be greater than or equal to class size accounts for the room capacity curve being placed to the right. To reduce the gap between the two curves and improve utilization, it is necessary to identify at what point the greatest imbalances between class size and room capacity occur. Graphically, it occurs where the *slopes* of the two curves are least similar. In the situation illustrated, 35 percent of the scheduled classes have an enrollment of 20–30 students, yet only 7.5 percent of the rooms contain this number of student stations. There are also too few rooms that can accommodate 30–40 students, and there is an excess of large rooms. Fifteen percent of the rooms seat from 50–60 students, while only 3 percent of the classes include this many students. Such a comparison permits the pinpointing of specific imbalances, which, in turn, can be rectified by improved scheduling, subdividing large rooms, and constructing more appropriately sized rooms.

The lower chart in figure X-10 depicts the degree of classroom utilization by size. The utilization index [UI] is plotted for various categories of classroom sizes. High values denote poor overall room use in the size category indicated.

Figure X-10. — Graphic representation of classroom use

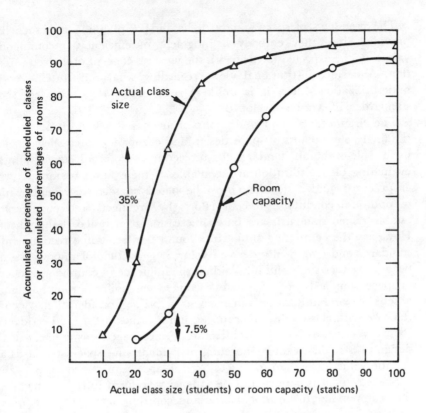

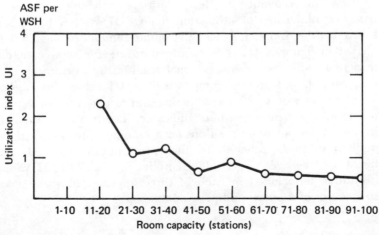

Source: Adapted from State of Illinois Board of Higher Education. State-Wide Space Survey,
August 1968, p. 42, fig. 7.

SPACE STANDARDS DATA

The usefulness of space standards lies in the planning guidance they provide. Since they embody a judgment of efficiency, recommended values can be expected to vary with the viewer's concept of desired utilization. And since institutional views regarding what constitutes over- or underutilization differ, it is unlikely that universally accepted space standards will ever be developed.

The circumstances and philosophy of an individual institution remain the final determinants of space design and occupancy rates. Nevertheless, useful rule-of-thumb standards for projecting space requirements and for evaluating plant utilization are available. If these standards are to serve as practical guideposts, they must be based on scientific identification of optimum conditions. Recent efforts by architects and engineers to establish such standards are based increasingly on tested design theory. However, the continuing similarities found between some recommended standards and empirically derived values suggest that planners have not been altogether successful in avoiding the influence of common practice.

Space standards are of greatest value when uniform room design is acceptable and utilization efficiency is a prime consideration. Such is the case with classrooms, laboratories, library stack areas, and residential rooms. When creativity in architecture is encouraged—as is likely in the design of a student center, museum, or gymnasium—space standards are of little value other than to suggest overall area requirements.

Space standards data should be sufficiently refined to reflect the effects that campus size, institutional type and control, and program emphasis will have on recommended design and class scheduling. On a statewide basis, measurements of utilization index (UI) values have been published by the Indiana Advisory Commission on Academic Facilities.[19] Shown in figure X-11, they clearly illustrate the significant differences in actual utilization of instructional facilities by institutions of different size, control, and program emphasis. The UI values for classrooms and class laboratories at 47 participating institutions are arranged in rank order, with percentile positions indicated. The two outside columns contain the aggregate score positions for a number of institutional groupings public institutions, private institutions, institutions over 5,000 enrollment liberal arts colleges under 2,000 enrollment, etc. The UI value of each institution is included in each of three appropriate groupings: campus size, source of support, and program emphasis.

---

[19] Blakesley and others, *Indiana Facilities Utilization Survey for Colleges and Universities Fall 1967*, op. cit. pp. 101, 121.

Figure X-11. — **Percentile ranking of utilization index UI values for classrooms and class laboratories on all campuses, Indiana colleges and universities: October 1967**

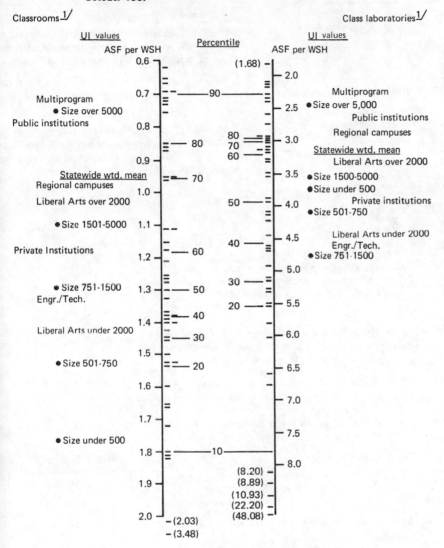

[1]UI values in assignable square feet per weekly student hour are based on all daytime and evening instruction in classrooms or class laboratories actually being used. Area does not include service areas or unused rooms.

Source: Adapted from James F. Blakesley, Paul C. Bayless, W. Charles Sherwood, and Frederick H. Wolf, Indiana Facilities Utilization Survey for Colleges and Universities, Fall 1967, Indiana Advisory Commission on Academic Facilities, Bloomington, 1968, pp. 101, 121. Similar values for 1970-71 are unpublished.

Table X-4.—General range of design and utilization space standards for classrooms and class laboratories

Classrooms

Room use [H_r]   = 30 hrs. per week for 7 a.m. to 5 p.m. daytime use; 30–36 hrs. per week, with night classes. (Larger schools tend to make greater use of rooms.)

Station-occupancy percentage [P_s] = 50%–66% (varies only slightly among campus-size groups).

Station area [A_s]   = 12–18 ASF per station (generally inversely proportional to average room capacity). (Smaller schools generally have smaller classrooms with a higher average area per station.)

Class laboratories

Room use [H_r]   = 15–25 hrs per week[1]
Station-occupancy percentage [P_s] = 60%–80%[1]
Station area [A_s]

Individual station laboratory   30–32 ASF per station

provides a single desk, table, bench, listening station, etc., per student (commerce and business, speech, military science, drafting, sociology, etc.).

Small instruments laboratory   48–50 ASF per station

provides experimental work area and storage for a minimal amount of small equipment (anthropology, botany, journalism, zoology, music, etc.).

Standard laboratory   65–70 ASF per station

provides experimental work area and substantial storage space for tabletop equipment and material (horticulture, physics, urban planning, geography, chemistry, architecture, etc.).

Floor equipment laboratory   100–112 ASF per station

provides extra work area and space for such items as metalworking machines, kilns, stoves, etc. (ceramic engineering, dramatics, home economics, etc.).

Heavy equipment laboratory   160 ASF per station

provides a large amount of experimental (or storage) space for such large items as turbines, animals, material-testing machines (veterinary medicine, mechanical engineering, civil engineering, mechanics, etc.).

NOTE.—Standards represent recommended *institutional average* values for all inventoried classrooms, class laboratories, and service areas, including unused rooms.

[1] Institutions having a large proportion of lower division and less specialized laboratories with high student demand usually maintain higher utilization rates.

ASF = Assignable square feet.

Source: Based on a review of State and institutional facility planning and survey documents.

Table X-5.—Example of space standards for faculty and administrative offices

Standards by office type[1]

	Square feet
President	300
Deans	200
Associate deans and division chairmen	180
Department heads, librarians, and coordinators	150
Standard office	110
2-occupant	160
3-occupant	250
Group offices (per occupant)	80
Secretary-receptionist	160
2-occupant	160
3-occupant	230
4-occupant	300
Student assistants (each)	60

Fileroom (with workspace): $\frac{2}{3}\times$linear feet of files$\times 10 =$ area, or 10 square-feet per file
Fileroom (without workspace): $\frac{2}{3}\times$linear feet of files$\times 6 =$ area, or 6 square-feet per file

Standards by amount of furniture[1]

Private offices: If the furniture covers less than 25 square feet, the office size should be from 80 to 100 ASF; if it covers from 25 to 35 square feet, the office size should be from 100 to 120 ASF; if more than 35 square feet, the office size should be from 120 to 140 ASF. For department heads with a four-to-eight-station work-conference table, the office size should be from 160 to 180 ASF.

A guide for floor space covered by office furniture is as follows: a $30'' \times 60''$ desk or table should be allotted $12\frac{1}{2}$ square feet; file cabinet, desk chair or bookcase, 3 square feet each; side chair, 2 square feet; wardrobe or storage cabinet, $4\frac{1}{2}$ square feet.

Collegewide basis[2]

As a planning factor, 135 ASF per FTE staff or faculty member requiring office space provides private faculty offices of about 120 square feet; larger areas for offices occupied by department heads and for conference rooms, reception, file, and storage areas. Note that 140 ASF per FTE staff is also frequently used as a planning factor.

---

[1] Standards for California State Colleges set by Coordinating Council for Higher Education, *Space and Utilization Standards*, California Public Higher Education, Sacramento, September 1966, pp. 69–70.
[2] State of Illinois Board of Higher Education, *Statewide Space Survey*, Springfield, Fall 1967, p. 83.

On a national basis, information is not available for this type of space-data cross classification; therefore, only a simple range of values can be presented in this handbook. Furthermore, many so-called standards are based on normative practice; consequently, it is difficult to distinguish empirically derived values from standards based on analytical design and scheduling research. For all of these reasons, standards in tables X-4, X-5, and X-6 are presented as tentative guides; in no instance should

Table X-6.—Example of space standards for libraries

Book storage

    0.10 assignable square feet per bound volume for stack and openstack areas, including card catalog area

    .025 ASF for unbound volumes

Reading stations

    25 to 30 assignable square feet per reading station (includes immediate station area and direct access area only)

Number of reading stations as a percentage of 8 a.m.-to-5 p.m. FTE enrollment

    20–30 percent, depending on number of commuter students

Library service area

    Basic complement of 400 ASF plus 100 to 150 ASF per FTE staff member, or 10 to 15 percent of total library ASF

NOTE.—Space measurements for library facilities are remarkably lacking in uniformity. Among peer institutions, maximum reported values for stack areas per volume exceed four times the minimum requirements. Much of this variation is due to differences in "lead" time (excess capacity built into an individual facility to accommodate future capacity requirements) resulting from the practical exigencies inherent in campus planning and development. Since libraries exhibit less uniformity than classroom buildings and residence halls, they are generally unique to each campus, designed not according to a standard pattern but evolved from subjective efforts to fulfill the special needs of a given institution.

Source: Based on a review of State and institutional facility-planning and survey documents.

For formulas and tables on structural column spacing, ceiling heights, floor areas, reader accommodations, book storage, and card catalogs, see Keyes D. Metcalf, *Planning Academic and Research Library Buildings*, McGraw-Hill Book Co., New York, 1965, appendix B.

they be adopted by an institution or a State without careful study and justification.

PROJECTING INSTITUTIONAL SPACE REQUIREMENTS

The method of projecting institutional space requirements is simply a process of applying selected space standards to projected user-loads. To determine new construction, existing space is subtracted from the overall requirements. The validity of the final dollar estimate depends on the appropriateness of selected space standards, the accuracy of projecting user-loads, and the accuracy of estimated architect and construction costs.

The general procedure by which institutions can project scheduled and allocated space requirements is outlined in this section. The column numbers, which refer to those in table X-7, should be consulted in order to clarify the step-by-step procedure.

1. List in the table stub (unnumbered first column) all room use—including institutional level, organizational unit, and subject field—that require separate projections based on distinctive space standards and input data.

SPACE STANDARDS:

2. For *scheduled space*, enter institutional values for standards of room use (H_r), station-occupancy percentage (P_s), and station area, including service area (A_s), in columns 1, 2, and 4, respectively. Calculate the value for station use (H_s), then enter in column 3.

3. For *scheduled space*, calculate the value for the utilization index (UI) and enter in column 5.

For *allocated space*, enter institutional values for the allocation ratio (AR) in column 5.

SPACE REQUIREMENTS:

4. Enter the expected user-load in column 6.

For *scheduled space*, user-load is measured in weekly student hours (WSH). This entry is based on current and past records of WSH, by room type and organizational unit, and, when necessary (as in the case of class laboratories), by subject field. Projected FTE enrollment should first be converted to WSH, then, on the basis of present patterns and expected trends and changes in curriculum emphasis, the total WSH should be apportioned among classrooms and various types of class laboratories. (For methods of projecting college and university enrollments, see appendix A).

For *allocated space*, the expected user-load to be entered in column 6 is measured in the same units as reported in the allocation ratio, i.e., FTE faculty, library volumes, etc.

5. Calculate and enter in column 7 space requirements equal to user-load (column 6) multiplied by the appropriate utilization index or allocation ratio (column 5).

6. In column 8 enter existing space plus that already scheduled for construction. Outmoded and structurally unsafe facilities should be excluded.

7. Calculate and enter in column 9 new construction requirements equal to total space requirements (column 7), less existing and previously planned space (column 8).

BUILDING REQUIREMENTS:

8. Group and proportion those selected room-type space requirements that constitute likely building totals and enter in column 10. Since most unit-cost factors are based on the gross square feet (GSF) of buildings,

Table X-7.—Worksheet to illustrate a method for projecting scheduled and allocated space requirements

Institution type and control: 4-year public college
Student level: undergraduate
Projected enrollment: year 2—2,500 FTE students
year 7—5,350 FTE students

Room use (Listing should include organizational unit, student level, and subject field, when required.)	Space standards				
	For scheduled class space only				Utilization index $UI = \dfrac{A_s}{H_s}$ or Allocation Ratio AR
	Room use [H_r]	Station-occupancy percentage [P_s]	Station use [H_s] $H_s = H_r \times P_s$	Station area [A_s] (including service areas)	
	(1)	(2)	(3)	(4)	(5)
Classrooms	30 hours per week	60%	18 hours per week	15 ASF	.83 ASF per WSH →
[Separate listing of classroom requirements by department should be entered here]					
Class laboratories					
Psychology					
Lower Division	26	80%	20.8	40	1.92 ↑
Upper Division					
Business					
Lower Division					
Upper Division					
[Additional entries for all types of class laboratories by subject field must be added to equal total requirements]					
Offices					
Faculty (one occupant)					140 ASF per FTE faculty member ↑
(Additional office entries as required)					
Study Facilities					
Closed stack					.08 ASF per volume →
(Additional study facilities entries as required)					
Special-use					
General-use [Allocated space entries as required]					
Medical care					
Residential					

Table X-7.—Worksheet to illustrate a method for projecting scheduled and allocated space requirements—Continued

Space requirements

Expected (year 7) user load	Space requirements (year 7) UI×WSH or AR×user-load	Existing space and space scheduled for construction (year 2)	Required new construction (year 2 to year 7) (7)–(8)
(6)	(7)	(8)	(9)
→56,000 WSH (70%)[1]	46,500 ASF	25,500 ASF	21,000 ASF
→3,200 (4%)	6,150	4,100	2,050
Total class laboratories	75,000	35,000	40,000
→300 FTE faculty	42,000	20,000	12,000
→180,000 volumes	14,400	5,600	8,800

Building requirements

Grouping of room type space requirements to equal building requirements		Building efficiency and unit project costs	Total project costs
(10)		(11)	(12)
Building #1		Building efficiency	Building #1
Classrooms 32%	13,500		
Class labs. 32%	13,500	$\dfrac{ASF}{GSF}=60\%$	$3,900,000
Research labs. 10%	4,500		
Faculty offices 12%	5,000	Unit project costs	
Study facilities 7%	3,000	= $55 per GSF	
Other 7%	3,000		
Total 100%	42,500 ASF		
Building #2			
Classrooms 14%	7,500		
Class labs. 50%	26,500		
Research labs. 9%	5,000		
Faculty offices 13%	7,000		
Supporting facilities 8%	4,000		
Other 6%	3,000		
Total 100%	53,000 ASF		

NOTE.—Space standards are dependent on a number of variables, including the type, control, and size of an institution, the student level, and the subject fields offered. Since example data are to illustrate and clarify the nature of entries and computations, they *should not* be considered normative or standard.

WSH = weekly student hour.   GSF = gross square feet.
ASF = assignable square feet.   FTE = full time equivalent.

[1] Total WSH (80,000) equals expected (year 7) FTE undergraduate enrollment (5,350) multiplied by the average WSH per FTE student (15). User-load for general classrooms is expected to be 70 percent of total WSH, or 56,000 WSH.

to arrive at new construction costs it is necessary to convert room-type space requirements in ASF to building requirements in GSF. This complex operation consists of first arranging room-type space needs into suitable departmental and subject-field composites and second, combining these groupings into building totals reflecting the necessary complexity and mix to achieve intended building and program purposes. These ASF building-space requirements can then be easily converted to GSF and the appropriate unit cost applied.

9. For the types of buildings planned, in column 11 enter factors to convert ASF building requirements to GSF; also enter GSF unit-construction costs. These values should be based on both recent construction experience and expected trends.

The relationship of assignable area, nonassignable area, and gross area can be expressed either as an *add factor* or as *building efficiency*. The add factor is the ratio of nonassignable area—circulation, construction, mechanical, and custodial—to assignable area expressed as a percentage.[20]

Building efficiency is the ratio of assignable area to gross area, expressed as a percentage. Using guideline values developed from initial studies by Bareither and Schillinger,[21] the relationships for nonresidential buildings can be illustrated as follows:

Assignable square feet			100,000
Add factor:	Custodial	0.4%	
	Mechanical	8.2 (3–14% range)	
	Restrooms	1.4	
	Circulation	16.0	
	Construction	14.0	
		40%	
Nonassignable square feet			40,000
Gross square feet			140,000
Nonresidential building efficiency			$\dfrac{100,000}{140,000} = 71.4\%$

10. To calculate total project costs, divide the ASF building requirements in column 10 by the expected building efficiency and multiply by the unit cost in column 11.

---

[20] For building-area definitions, see section "Space Classification."

[21] Harlan D. Bareither and Jerry L. Schillinger, *University Space Planning*, University Press, Urbana, Ill., 1968, p. 95.

BIBLIOGRAPHY

Bareither, Harlan D., and Jerry L. Schillinger, *University Space Planning*, University Press, Urbana, Ill., 1968, 153 pp.

The authors have written a basic reference covering methodology, unit areas, and utilization rates. Included is an analytical method to define, analyze, and project space requirements systematically. Explicitly identified are the underlying factors and recommended values that can be altered by the user within the framework of a proposed "numeric method". Numerous charts, tables, and architectural drawings supplement the text. Also included is an extensive appendix illustrating the complete planning process for an academic building. This book will be particularly useful to institutions that have not established a basis for projecting space requirements objectively.

Blakesley, James F., Paul C. Bayless, W. Charles Sherwood, and Frederick H. Wolf, *Indiana Facilities Utilization Survey for Colleges and Universities*, Fall 1967, The Indiana Advisory Commission on Academic Facilities, Bloomington, 1968, 272 pp.

A superior utilization study of the physical facilities of Indiana colleges and universities, this volume contains space-inventory summaries for both residential and nonresidential areas, with emphasis on the nonresidential. Comparisons are made on a group basis by campus size, program emphasis, or source of support. Where appropriate, comparisons are made with facility studies from other States. The depth of analysis and the clarity of presentation make this State utilization study a model in its field.

California Coordinating Council for Higher Education, *A Comparison of the Trimester and Four Quarter Calendars for Year-Round Operation of Public Higher Education in California*, Sacramento, 1964, 43 pp.

This work is directed specifically to the question: "What type of calendar is preferable for year-round operation of higher education facilities?" The text suggests that the trimester arrangement is more advantageous with respect to providing for faculty sabbatical, accelerating graduation, and minimizing recordkeeping. The four-quarter calendar is seen to be more advantageous with respect to effecting flexibility in faculty and/or student options, achieving a consistently balanced enrollment, and sustaining articulation with secondary schools and among other institutions of higher education. Any differences in operational costs—excluding capital outlay—between the four-quarter system and the trimester were judged not of sufficient magnitude to warrant rejection of the former.

California Coordinating Council for Higher Education, *Inventory and Utilization Study for Public Higher Education, Fall 1969*, Sacramento, January 1971.

Illustrative of the many outstanding State facility surveys, the California study is directed to the following purposes: (1) determining current availability of higher education facilities, (2) determining current efficiency of use of these facilities, (3) evaluating existing and proposed utilization standards, (4) relating utilization rates to operation costs and capital outlay, and (5) refining capital outlay decisions through model simulation.

Among many other State studies providing useful guidance, two of the more analytical investigations include Paul C. Bayless, James F. Blakesley, W. Charles Sherwood, and Frederick H. Wolf, *Future Space Requirements for Indiana's Institutions of Higher Education,* The Indiana Advisory Commission on Academic Facilities, Bloomington, 1970, 94 pp., and W. Charles Sherwood, *Indiana's Four State-Supported Universities*, 1967–69 Biennial Capital Appropriations Study, Purdue University, Lafayette, April 1966, 85 pp.

California Coordinating Council for Higher Education, *Space and Utilization Standards, California Public Higher Education*, Sacramento, 1966, 78 pp.

A manual of classroom, laboratory, library, and office space standards, this work contains material obtained, in part, from an extensive 1963 analysis of the three segments of the California public higher education system: public junior colleges, State colleges, and the University of California. Class laboratory standards are divided by subject fields into lower division and upper division. This work also includes a summary of existing utilization rates for classrooms and laboratories in the three public segments.

Colorado Commission on Higher Education, *Planning Guidelines for Construction of Facilities at the State-Supported Colleges and Universities in Colorado*, Denver, 1968, 49 pp.

This pamphlet contains a tabular presentation of 17 building standards and utilization factors useful as guidelines in planning higher education facilities; specifically, utilization standards, unit space allocation factors, various planning ratios, optimum scheduling guides, and special planning criteria for classrooms, class laboratories, research laboratories, offices, libraries, and other specific room types.

Doi, James I., and Keith Scott, *Normative Data on the Utilization of Instructional Space in Colleges and Universities*, American Association of Collegiate Registrars and Admissions Officers, Athens, Ohio, 1960, 24 pp.

Intended as a supplement to the Russell-Doi *Manual*, this pamphlet presents normative data collected from 217 colleges and universities surveyed in the fall of 1959. Four measures of utilization for both general classrooms and class laboratories are illustrated, with the data arranged by percentile rank and by institutional type, size, and control categories. Selected space-allocation factors, such as square-feet-per-student-station, are presented in similarly organized tables.

Higher Education Facilities Services, Inc., *Inventory of Physical Facilities in Institutions of Higher Education, Fall 1970*, and *Fall 1971* (preliminary data), Raleigh, N.C., 1972, 225 pp.

This national census of college and university facilities contains an exceptional amount of detailed data. Assignable area is presented by State, type and control of institution, enrollment size of institution, organizational unit, type of room or facility, and median and selected percentiles per full-time-equivalent student. Other tables show number of beds in dormitories and residence halls; number of family dwellings, by design capacity and fall occupancy; number of dining seats in residence halls; and average assignable area per bed, dwelling, or seat.

For a 1958–60 national survey of historical interest, see E. Eugene Higgins and Mary Fuller, *College and University Facilities, Survey, Part 3: Inventory of College and University Physical Facilities*, U.S. Department of Health, Education, and Welfare, Office of Education, U.S. Government Printing Office, Washington, D.C., 1965, 575 pp.

Jamrich, John X., *To Build or Not To Build—A Report on the Utilization and Planning of Instructional Facilities in Small Colleges*, Educational Facilities Laboratories, New York, 1962, 38 pp.

Except for the fact that this report presents information solely pertaining to smaller colleges, it is similar (the author claims it is a direct descendant) to the classic Russel-Doi *Manual*. In addition to an entire range of facts about the use and extent of instructional space, the work also includes normative material on enrollment trends, curriculums, faculty, salaries, teacher-student ratios, class size, and financing. A "do-it-yourself" space-utilization workbook, which may be detached from the main body of the report, contains normative figures on individual forms, thus facilitating the making of comparisons with institutional data.

Pinnell, Charles, and Michael Wacholder, *Guidelines for Planning in Colleges and Universities* (5 vols.), The Coordinating Board, Texas College and University System, Austin, 1968.

The authors discuss procedures and recommendations intended to serve as guidelines for institutional planning. The method they describe focuses on the creation of a system that integrates management and program planning, physical plant planning, and financial planning into a single overall process. The system permits institutions to identify what is innovative and unique about their educational program and objectives and to plan in depth within the context of their objectives. Specific details about the techniques of management and financial planning and various aspects of physical plant planning appear in volumes 2 and 3. Volume 4, "Facilities Studies," presents techniques for estimating institutional facility requirements. Numerous formulas and specific numerical values provide the key to workable and meaningful procedures.

Planning and Management Systems Division, Western Interstate Commission for Higher Education, *Higher Education Facilities Planning and Management Manuals* (7 vols.), Boulder, Colo., 1971.

These seven manuals in a looseleaf binder are intended to be used as handbooks from which institutional planners may select those facilities planning methodologies appropriate to particular needs. Manual One, which contains an overview of the complete set, includes an introductory discussion of the facilities planning cycle and an essay on the possible effects that changing instructional techniques may have on the facilities planning process. Manuals Two through Five describe the procedures for evaluating and projecting the requirements for various types of space: classroom and class laboratory facilities, office and research facilities, academic support facilities (library, audiovisual, exhibition), and general support facilities (athletic, recreational, residential). Manual Six contains a description of those detailed program planning and analysis procedures that yield the input for the facilities planning process. This manual also includes a proposal for systemwide facilities planning criteria appropriate to statewide or system-level evaluation of the output of institutional facilities planning systems. Manual Seven contains pertinent general reference material: a glossary, bibliography, index, and table of contents.

Romney, Leonard C., *Higher Education Facilities Inventory and Classification Manual* (prepublication draft), Higher Education Facilities Services Inc., Raleigh, N.C., February 1973, 156 pp.

Designed primarily to assist colleges and universities in the classification of building-inventory data, this manual delineates a classification system that identifies building-area categories and classifies assignable space by room use and program. Detailed appendixes include building-data collection forms, room-inventory forms, and space-category codes and definitions. The manual serves not only as the basis for uniform reporting of facilities inventory data to State and Federal agencies but also as a guide for establishing a data collection system within institutions.

Russell, John Dale, and James I. Doi, *Manual for Studies of Space Utilization in Colleges and Universities*, American Association of Collegiate Registrars and Admissions Officers, Athens, Ohio, 1957, 130 pp. (Out of print)

Considered a pioneer in its field, this book features detailed instructions and procedures to guide college and university administrators in making space-utilization studies. Included are directions and forms for the collection, analysis, and interpretation of data. Units and measures involved in space-utilization studies and space-classification categories are defined. The Doi-Scott supplement to this manual updates the normative data.

Yurkovich, John V., *A Methodology for Determining Future Physical Facilities Requirements for Institutions of Higher Education* (Project No. 2920, Contract No. OE-5-10-291), University of Wisconsin, Madison, 1966, 174 pp. (Order by number ED-10850 from ERIC Document Service, Bell and Howell Company, 1700 Shaw Avenue, Cleveland, Ohio 44112.)

The body of the report is devoted to the many considerations inherent in the development of a space-management and planning program. It not only presents an overview of the total methodology but also describes each specific system involved. The appendixes contain detailed guides for conducting a physical facilities inventory and/or a room-utilization study, also instructions for projecting enrollment and structuring the required computer systems.

Chapter XI

CAMPUS AND BUILDING PLANNING

There is little of what is happening on the campuses of U.S. colleges and universities that cannot be described as near radical change. The immense task of accommodating 9.5 million students by 1974 is, of course, the immediate cause of much that is visibly new on campuses. Less tangible are changes in the students themselves, particularly their critical, questioning concern about the quality and relevancy of higher education. As a result of both the increase in enrollment and the newly expressed demand for excellence, curriculum and teaching methods are undergoing a mild revolution: More tuned-in courses are replacing traditional ones and sophisticated electronic and automated machines are introducing greater efficiency and effectiveness.

Amid the growth and ferment, one might expect that at least the physical structure of campuses—the buildings and the land—would remain fixed in form and function. But changes are occurring here, too. Buildings are being erected in new places and in new arrangements and for different and variable functions. Examples are the communications-lecture-hall-center and the modular library. What is newer than the flight-deck principle of laboratory research space? How old is the cluster concept of grouping colleges? It is probably not too great a generalization to say that much of the growth and change and innovation taking place in higher education today is being accurately embodied and permanently recorded in the new kinds of buildings and campuses that are being created.

The importance of excellence in campus buildings and campus design is obvious, regardless of functional effectiveness, return on investment, or esthetics. A badly designed building or an improperly planned campus is a serious handicap to both students and faculty; good buildings, effectively related, can contribute to the intellectual health of the entire institution. Buildings of any type—good or bad—are not only expensive but long-lasting. The deficiencies of a poorly designed building, if forced on each new generation of faculty and students, compound the consequences of initial mistakes. It is evident, then, that planning is of critical importance. Both the design and arrangement of new buildings require greater

467

consideration of future needs than any other aspect of planning for higher education, because decisions, once made, are more permanent than those pertaining to nonphysical components.

Despite the critical nature of campus and building planning, most new college facilities can only be described as merely adequate; they project little of the excellence which current architectural knowledge allows. One reason is that planners rarely are afforded opportunities to work closely with architects.[1] Also, on most campuses there is not enough new construction to provide planners much practice in campus design and building planning. As a partial substitute for personal experience, this chapter summarizes some of the best practices in campus and building planning. Attention is focused on fundamentals. Information concerning the many technical details involved may be obtained by consulting works listed in the bibliography.

PLANNING FOR GROWTH—THE OVERALL PROCESS

Creating new campuses and expanding present physical facilities are a weekly if not an everyday occurrence. From 1965 to 1970, an average of 76 new institutions (mostly community colleges) were established each year, a rate of three every 2 weeks. Capital outlay expenditures during the 5 years 1968–72 averaged $3.8 billion per year. At $50 per square foot, 70 percent of this expenditure for new construction would mean 53 million square feet of new space each year, an area equivalent to 23 football fields per week.

Quite naturally, physical plant construction means a preoccupation with building materials. But an institution planning for growth must also be concerned with educational ideas and values as well as financial considerations. The overall process in planning for growth then involves three elements: (1) program or academic planning to guide and direct the undertaking, (2) the physical plant itself, and (3) budget requirements. Each element will, of course, be materially affected by a time factor. Thus phasing or scheduling is an essential aspect of each element.

Program or Academic Planning

It should be obvious that the intentions of an institution should serve as a basis for physical development. As with any organization charting

---

[1] Notable exceptions are the massive multibillion-dollar construction programs which require continuous and extensive interaction between campus planners and architects.

its course, the first steps a college or university must undertake in planning its expansion are to carefully review its past history and realistically appraise its present status and goals. With this background and some foresight an attempt can be made to project a desired future role.[2]

Broadly interpreted, determining both institutional objectives and procedures for attaining them is synonymous with program planning. A final conclusion cannot be made regarding what constitutes desirable and realistic objectives until past and present operations have been rigorously appraised and carefully formulated conclusions drawn about future intentions. These tasks are difficult and can best be accomplished by a planning team. Central members on any team assembled to coordinate the effort are the college president, the chief campus planner, selected administrative officers, department and faculty representatives, student representatives, and ad hoc specialists as required.

To be complete, the program plan should cover all facets of institutional endeavors. It should include commentary on such major components as the instructional programs to be pursued; emphasis to be given each student level; admission policy; desired flexibility; projected enrollments and requirements for faculty and staff; institutional organizations; research, public service programs, and community relations; library operations; student services and housing; and faculty recruitment and housing. Emphasis throughout should be given to specifying end objectives clearly, recognizing restraints and opportunities, and considering likely policy and strategy. As these concerns are examined and goals and standards established, the planning team will be able to undertake with confidence the more pragmatic task of translating broad guidelines into specific campus and building requirements, budget considerations, and time schedules.

Physical Plant

Most planning efforts focus on physical facilities, as well they might, for the latter represents the translating of objectives and projections, blueprints, and statistics into tangible forms. For purposes of organizing

---

[2] How to determine what a college should be and do is well illustrated in the plans for beginning Hampshire College as expressed by Pres. Franklin Patterson. The working papers ". . . examine the present context of circumstances in which a new college will be built, projects Hampshire's role as an agent of change, defines an organized vision of liberal education for a new era, establishes the groundwork of the College's academic program, outlines in provisional but illustrative detail the nature of the Hampshire curriculum, . . . describes the community of Hampshire College, and forecasts the financial requirements and operations of the new institution." Franklin Patterson and Charles R. Longsworth, *The Making of a College*, Massachusetts Institute of Technology Press, Cambridge, 1966, p. xi.

plant planning procedures, it is desirable to proceed on two levels: *campus planning*, in which overall physical development—the perfection of campus function, physical environment, and community relationships—is structured according to college goals, and *building planning*, in which the educator-planner defines in detail the function and physical needs of buildings and works with the architect to translate these ideas and concepts into a graphic, coordinated design.

Financial Aspects

Planning for the financing of new construction should achieve a balance between what is to be done and how much money is available to do it. This process involves forecasting plant needs, based on program goals and projected enrollments, and translating these needs into a schedule of dollar outlay. The means of payment must then be ascertained; if it appears that there will be an imbalance between expected cost and income, either the objectives must be altered or additional funding must be obtained.

The entire process of financial planning and decisionmaking is discussed in detail in a number of recent publications.[3] A system for projecting space needs is presented in chapter X; chapter XII deals with financing. One special point, however, is worthy of mention at this point. A great deal of misunderstanding and wasted time can be avoided if, at the outset, the architect is given a clear and firm idea of exactly how much the institution intends to spend. In the view of one contemporary authority, Donald Canby, "More than one client has shortchanged himself by cannily setting aside a secret contingency fund and thus imposing a needless limitation on both the architect and the building. Others have wasted their own time and the architect's by talking big at the outset, then spending small when the chips are down."[4] Canby goes on to say that most design decisions require that a three-way balance be struck among initial cost, eventual cost, and the cost of money (interest).[5] The architect can help strike a balance, but only if he knows the client's complete financial picture.

Only when the overall planning process is understood can the concentrated attention essential to physical plant planning be realistically dis-

---

[3] See, for example, Charles Pinnell and Michael Wacholder, *Guidelines for Planning in Colleges and Universities*, vol. 2, "Management and Financial Planning," Coordinating Board, Texas College and University System, Austin, 1968.

[4] Donald Canby, *Your Building and Your Architect*, American Institute of Architects, New York, n.d., p. 8.

[5] If physical facilities are to house new or enlarged programs, provisions for financing increased faculty and staff salaries and operating costs must be arranged concurrently with those for capital investment.

cussed. In this chapter three aspects are considered. First, an introduction to campus planning, wherein it is suggested that, in creating total environment as an instrument of institutional policy, the importance of the campus is much greater than the sum of its parts. This macro-approach directs attention to the spatial and functional relationships among buildings and their exteriors rather than to their internal design. In the second section, planning the design of individual buildings is examined, with special attention given to establishing the proper client-architect relationship and to preparing educational specifications—those specifications that convey to the architect the educator's concept and understanding of the kind of building required, the people and functions to be served, and any aspects of the institutional program or philosophy which may influence design. The third section includes general reminders of the ways in which the architectural character of space—shape, lighting, color, climate, and acoustics—can provide an atmosphere conducive to the teaching-learning process. These environmental-design details are intended primarily for reference purposes.

CAMPUS PLANNING

Campus planning, essentially an orderly process of designing physical facilities based on the college or university educational program objectives and policies, must take into account all factors which may affect the final result. While the goal of campus planning is perfection of the total physical environment, attention should be focused principally on outside space rather than on building interiors.

Recognizing the many and varied problems inherent in campus planning, one authority describes the scope and character of physical plans in these terms:

> . . . physical plans must be both general and specific; they must be concerned with immediate requirements as well as long-range considerations; they must cover the campus and environs as well as specific building sites, and they must implement today's educational goals while at the same time encourage if they can, but not hinder, new objectives. Plans—as an instrument by which the campus administration can make good decisions—should reflect the institution's point of view on land-use development, incorporate the widest range of opinions as to how the institution should grow, but restrict such opinions to reasonable alternatives. Plans should aid the architect in successfully completing his commission, give design form to the entire campus, serve as symbol for friends and alumni to support emotionally and financially. Plans must be practical and plans must be imaginative.[6]

---

[6] Richard P. Dober, *Campus Planning*, Reinhold Publishing Co., New York, 1963, p. 45.

This chapter will not cover in detail the many analytical studies which collectively constitute comprehensive campus planning. Rather, it is the intention, in a limited discussion, to outline the procedure and convey an appreciation of the nature of the activities involved, as well as the approaches currently advocated and practiced.

Procedure

The very visible and exciting graphic and physical products of campus planning tend to draw attention away from the concepts involved. Therefore, before describing the problem-solving procedures of campus planning, a few ground rules are in order.

At the outset, it must be understood that the role of the educator in campus planning is to envision the perceptual quality of the campus and its elements and not to interfere with the architect's task of creating the physical design. It is the nature of the physical elements that form the campus—their interrelationships, spatial organization, character, and growth pattern—to which the educator must direct his attention. The resulting philosophy, concepts, and schemes—the *design vocabulary* as labeled by the State University Construction Fund of New York—establish the environmental objectives that form the basis for the architect's design. Without such a reference point, the architect's efforts will be all but rudderless.

As long as an institution survives, campus planning is a perpetual activity. It should be viewed as a continual round of creating, revising, modifying, and updating. An occasional flurry of interest, producing a single concept, for example, of how the campus will look in the year 1985, usually lacks realistic direction and the sustained support required for complete implementation. On the other hand, a more leisurely yet continuous and concerted planning approach, with realistically phased implementation, is much more likely to result in steady, progressive perfection of the campus environment.

The importance of the latter approach cannot be overemphasized. What phased planning accomplishes is decisionmaking in logical sequence, thereby permitting review, agreement, and commitment before proceeding. If campus planning is unstructured, there is a tendency for those involved to wander haphazardly, skip elements, argue needlessly, and retrace steps. For an activity as complex and often controversial as campus planning, systematic phasing is an absolute necessity.

Finally, if campus plans are to be carried out effectively, they must be enforced on a day-to-day basis. Such enforcement ranges from thoroughly familiarizing the architect with the plans and securing his understanding and endorsement, to processing requests for space-allocation changes. If plans are to be authentically and rigorously implemented, authority must be vested in one or more persons whose decisions are final.

With regard to the procedural aspects of campus planning, the State University Construction Fund of New York suggests that the following guidelines can provide an effective interchange of findings and recommendations between the architect and the educational planner:[7]

—Clarify and interpret education, site, and building program objectives,
—Evaluate the significance of research conclusions on alternative plan proposals, and
—Arrive at planning conclusions and recommendations.

To achieve these objectives, a number of interrelated and interdependent planning activities and a sequence of decisions are mandatory. They may logically be divided into three major phases:

Phase I, *Preparatory Survey and Recommendations*, consists of an initial reconnaissance of program, site, and economic feasibility problems, also recommended solutions. Activities are devoted principally to the tasks of identifying, analyzing, and evaluating basic complex campus requirements. The survey phase involves collecting a considerable amount of material on all aspects of campus development, then analyzing this data as comprehensively as possible to permit, in phase II, the discussion, development, and approval of a systematic working concept of the campus environment.

Phase II, the *Conceptual Plan Development* stage, involves indepth consideration of all aspects of campus requirements considered in the survey phase for the purpose of evolving a proposed campus environment. The conceptual plan should combine the institution's educational philosophy and curriculum, topography, climate, spatial sequences, adjacent land development, program for expansion, and vehicular and pedestrian circulation, into a unified visual concept. The plan should also outline the relationships of campus functional areas to one another and to the community. A preliminary schematic working plan serves primarily as a guide for locating specific buildings.

Phase III consists of refining the implementation plan, or *Final Design Drawings*, in such a way that more detailed technical development will not require any radical revision of functional concepts.

---

[7] As a result of extensive experience in planning more than two dozen campuses for the State University of New York, the Fund has been able to define and refine the process of campus planning into a compact yet complete and orderly procedure. For details, see State University Construction Fund, *A Guide for Campus Planning*, Albany, N.Y., 1967.

Phase I—Preparatory Survey and Recommendations

Phase I, an initial reconnaissance and data-gathering effort, includes the making of initial recommendations to produce the necessary basic information required to develop a physical plant plan. This phase encourages the architect and planner to review all assumptions and input factors before developing proposals. Investigation and recommendations should pertain to three areas: educational program, site analysis, and economic considerations.

The purpose of the *educational program* analysis is to set forth those aspects of an institution's role and scope that may influence the concept and development of the physical plant. The main focus of the presentation should be to list, for a variety of topic areas, associated program policies and objectives, current operating principles, assumptions, possible existing problems, and preliminary recommendations relevant to campus planning. Topics to be considered should include the philosophy and purpose of the campus, the educational programs to be offered and degrees awarded, the anticipated enrollment and student-faculty ratio, and the relationship of the institution to the community. A list of buildings scheduled for construction and their respective target dates should also be prepared, together with the institution's viewpoint toward housing, traffic flow and parking, communications, and any other aspect of the campus plan about which the institution feels its commentary would be helpful in guiding the architect.

A summary of conclusions resulting from the educational program analysis can be communicated by words, descriptions, timetables, and/or graphic devices (see figure XI-1). Drawings, which should depict the required relationships between various facilities and activity areas in a manner unrelated to existing features of the site, should also set forth schematically the major functional and circulation elements, major access points, and the significant relationships of each to adjacent areas.

Site analysis, the second component of phase I, establishes the influence of regional, community, and campus environments vis-a-vis campus development; also, the effect of the proposed campus on the community and region. The conclusions reached may be effectively communicated in a graphic summary (see figure XI-2).

The regional study should identify present and future forms of transportation, public facilities, institutions of learning (as feeders, competitors, and/or supporting resources), and all major development plans within the region that could affect the physical environment of the planned institution or its student population. Regional research obviously should always precede selection of the site for a new campus.

Community analysis, which follows the regional study, should include

Figure XI-1. – Ideal functional diagram

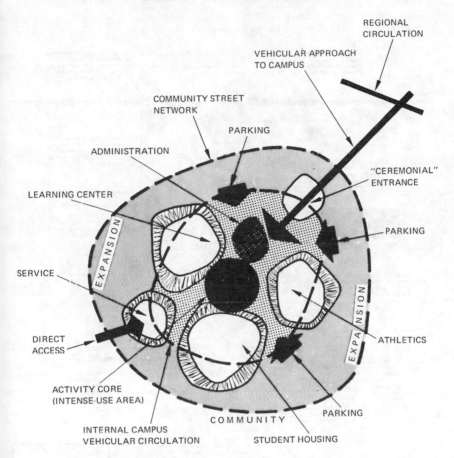

Source: State University Construction Fund, A Guide for Campus Planning, Albany,
N.Y., 1967, p. 3.

a discussion and evaluation of the effects on campus plans of urban circulation, adjacent land use, major utility facilities, location of cultural and recreational facilities, interaction of institution with community, existing zoning, future community land use, etc. Noteworthy observations and recommended action or conclusions should be summarized.

On a larger scale, the campus and environs portion of site analysis should list all natural and man-made features and their possible effect on building location, traffic circulation, parking, campus expansion, and placement of utilities. Adverse noise levels or air pollution should be carefully noted. Such geographical features as vistas or historical sites are highly relevant; early awareness of their existence makes it possible

Figure XI-2. — Summary of site conclusions

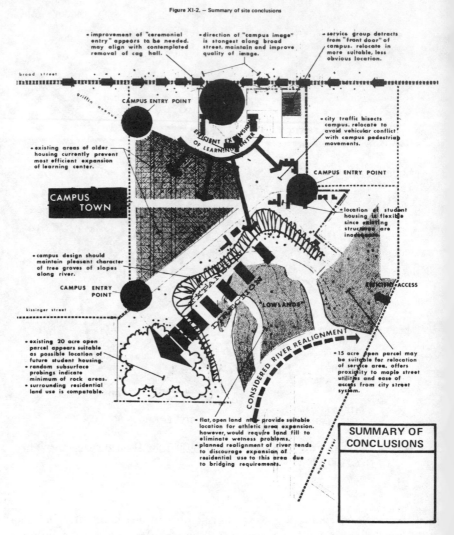

Figure XI-2. — Summary of site conclusions

• improvement of "ceremonial entry" appears to be needed. may align with contemplated removal of cag hall.

• direction of "campus image" is stongest along broad street. maintain and improve quality of image.

• service group detracts from "front door" of campus. relocate in more suitable, less obvious location.

broad street

CAMPUS ENTRY POINT

griffin avenue

• city traffic bisects campus. relocate to avoid vehicular conflict with campus pedestrian movements.

EFFICIENT EXPANSION OF LEARNING CENTER

• existing areas of older housing currently prevent most efficient expansion of learning center.

CAMPUS ENTRY POINT

CAMPUS TOWN

• location of student housing is flexible since existing structures are inactive.

• campus design should maintain pleasant character of tree groves of slopes along river.

CAMPUS ENTRY POINT

RESTRICTED ACCESS

kissinger street

EXPANSION RESTRICTION

LOWLANDS

• existing 20 acre open parcel appears suitable as possible location of future student housing.
• random subsurface probings indicate minimum of rock areas.
• surrounding residential land use is compatable.

CONSIDERED RIVER REALIGNMENT

• 15 acre open parcel may be suitable for relocation of service area. offers proximity to maple street utilities and ease of access from city street system.

• flat, open land may provide suitable location for athletic area expansion. however, would require land fill to eliminate wetness problems.
• planned realignment of river tends to discourage expansion of residential use to this area due to bridging requirements.

maple street

SUMMARY OF CONCLUSIONS

Source: State University Construction Fund, A Guide for Campus Planning, Albany, N.Y., 1967, p. 9.

to use them to enhance the esthetic and environmental quality of the campus.

The general scope of the preliminary *economic analysis*, the third component of phase I, is to estimate a meaningful budget for the visualized campus plan. Initial "ball-park" cost estimates should be made for acquisition of land, construction, and landscaping. Alternative forms of construction and their economic advantages should also be noted. The overall process will probably require surveys of regional construction costs. The objective of the estimate is to roughly determine the financial feasibility of the plan relative to expected budgetary limitations.

Phase II—Conceptual Plan Development

The purpose of the second phase is to examine, for the purpose of arriving at a consensus, the basic environment of the campus proposed by the architect, together with his rationale for the design. The kind of environment proposed, described in terms of its educational, social, recreational, and perceptual ingredients, should be based on the conclusions developed during the analysis of the educational program, site, adjacent land use, expansion program, circulation patterns, etc. Sketches, perspectives, photographs, and working models should be used to support and illustrate the concepts developed. (For a sample sketch, see figure XI-3.)

Major components of the conceptual plan are:

1. A study of *density, land coverage, and scale* in order to establish the best possible combination of these factors to produce the desired environment.

2. A *perspective plan*, aerial photo, or model to show the concept of the plan and its major identifiable elements, including the campus core; the various subareas defined by building groups and open space; linkages between core and subareas, between subareas, and the total open space as a system, both developed and natural, in relation to all buildings.

3. A *schematic working plan* to serve primarily as a guide for locating specific campus buildings. It should show the location of specific structures within functional areas; the relative size, shape, and location of athletic and parking areas; various circulation patterns, including major and minor roads and walks; and the most significant landscape elements: water sites, space-defining plants, shrubbery, trees, etc., treatment of major grade changes and large paved areas. Individual construction projects, along with proposed land acquisition, should be identified in order of development.

4. *Functional relationships* between campus activities: How the campus functions should be organized by its form, as defined by buildings and open space, and its relationship to the surrounding community and region.

5. The *mode of expansion* that will best achieve program plans yet permit orderly campus growth without sacrificing either functional or esthetic quality of the environment. To minimize disruption of campus activities, construction should be scheduled by zones.

6. *The campus circulation system:* The major flow of pedestrian, bicycle, and vehicular traffic should be delineated. Included should be identification of streets, roads, service and parking areas, intersections, etc., plus systems for visitor orientation and direction and traffic control, together with signs and signals to be used and how they will achieve desired goals. (Eye-level sketches of typical locations can be used to indicate the relationship between signs and signals and surrounding site objects.)

Figure XI-3. — Conceptual plan

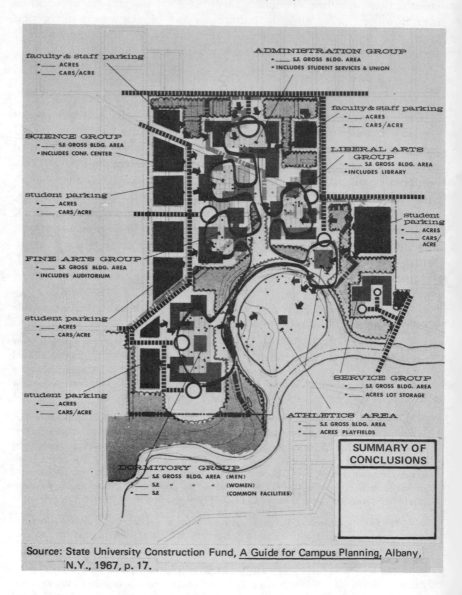

Source: State University Construction Fund, <u>A Guide for Campus Planning</u>, Albany,
N.Y., 1967, p. 17.

7. *Spatial quality* (degree of openness or enclosure): the general size, shape, and
location of outdoor areas as defined by the ratio of ground area to building area and
of building height to distance between buildings; by percentage of space devoted to
roads and parking, planting and grading; by the structures themselves; and by light,
shadow detail, etc. All campus open spaces should be defined and arranged not only
according to purpose and overall design, but also to functional sequence and appearance.

8. *Outdoor design features:* Specific description and drawings of any outdoor features considered pertinent to the campus design; relationship of campus to topography and other natural features; building appearance and massing; outdoor night lighting; surface materials and patterns, colors; the nature and character of such additions as pools and fountains, sculpture, flags, banners, etc.; and plants and plant massing to be used in landscaping.

Phase III—Final Design Drawings

This phase consists of preparing and presenting the final design drawings and implementation data for the campus plan. The drawings, substantially the plan itself, should be of such refinement that more detailed technical development (e.g., engineering drawings) will not require any radical revision of functional concepts. Although the drawings represent modification, refinement, and elaboration of the conceptual development plan, they should be consonant with phase II decisions regarding program objectives, planning principles and assumptions, the total land acquisition program, etc. They should be accompanied by a brief statement of the concept, development objectives, and planning principles that form the basis of the design.

The plans, sketches, models, or other means employed to illustrate the design should be presented in such a way that each major element—(1) spatial form, (2) architectural form, (3) traffic and parking, (4) utilities, (5) grading, (6) landscaping—and the relationships between each over the time of the planning period are clearly shown. The analysis upon which the plan for each element is based should be apparent. Whenever possible, each of the series of design drawings should be prepared as an overlay that can be placed on a basic map showing such existing details as topography and natural features; structures with finished floor elevations; roads, walks, terraces, and existing paving; service areas; tree massing; grid coordinates; and property lines.

The master drawing, actually a refined design of the campus as it will look at the end of the proposed development period, should include such details as space arrangement, building location, traffic and parking, land contour, landscaping, and new or remodeled structures. The master drawing should be supplemented by perspective and sectional sketches and models. In addition, six supplementary drawings should indicate the steps by which various elements of the basic plan are to be realized. Each of these should contain a delineation of existing conditions, planned development, and phasing.

1. The *spatial form* should show existing and proposed organization of outdoor space, the size of each space and the linkages between, and the character of the elements defining open spaces.

2. The *architectural form* should analyze existing and proposed buildings

in terms of location, floor elevations, general condition, architectural quality, functional use, materials, height, and location of entrances and service areas.

3. The *traffic and parking* drawings should identify (concurrently existing and proposed) community, campus, and pedestrian circulation patterns and the relative-use intensity of various routes and parking areas. Critical grade hazards and inefficient methods currently being used to control traffic should be noted.

4. The *utilities* drawing should portray (existing and proposed) conditions and locations of utility systems, including storm and sanitary sewers, natural gas conduit, power and electric lines, heating, communications, clock, temperature control, fire alarm, etc. The source and distribution of these utilities, whether it is on or off the campus, should be indicated.

5. The *grading* plan should indicate subsurface conditions and proposed new contours; also, spot elevations for parking areas, buildings, retaining walls, roads, walks, and steps.

6. The *landscaping* study should evaluate existing plants, shrubbery, and trees in terms of quality and conservation. The plan for the future should indicate location, type, and relative size of materials; also, the functional use of each, whether for windbreak, environmental enhancement, shading effect, etc. A statement of the overall effect to be achieved should be included.

Design Guidance

If the complex activities of campus planning are to proceed in an orderly and progressive manner, some form of systematic structuring is required. Since any arrangement and ordering of tasks serves only to guide human thought and energy, by itself, systematic structuring is an empty framework. The vital commodities missing are the talents and skills of architect and educator. No procedure or process, however grandly designed, can be a substitute for the intelligence and creativeness required of those who participate in campus planning.

Much of the skill needed in campus planning is supplied by the architect and others expert in allied fields of specialization. But the educator makes a serious mistake if he relies exclusively on the professional skills of these individuals, for it is the interactions between client and architect and between client and consultant that determine whether or not the final design is educationally functional as well as technically sound. The educator, of course, must be well versed in the art of campus planning and must have a basic concept of what the campus environment should be.

Experience is by far the best teacher, but few educators have an opportunity to plan more than one campus. Consequently, about the only advice that can be offered them is to (1) read all that is available on the subject of campus planning, (2) seek and listen to advice from all qualified sources, and (3) visit as many campuses as possible to learn what has been done and what mistakes should be avoided.

An outstanding example of how much know-how can be acquired if the right source is tapped are the findings of William W. Caudill, former chairman of the Department of Architecture at Rice University (Houston, Tex.), principal member of Caudill, Rowlett and Scott, and a speaker at the 1964 WICHE Sixth Annual Institute on College Self-Study. Caudill's theorems and design premises, while not beyond challenge, are worthy of the attention of planners and architects pursuing excellence and utility in building and campus design. Substantially abbreviated, they are as follows:[8]

Theorem 1: In the planning of a new campus or the development of an old one, whether or not the right kind of physical environment is created will depend on the subdivision and organization of space.

The key problem of campus planning is how most effectively to subdivide outside space (the space that flows around and over buildings), using buildings as space dividers.

Good buildings with effectively designed *interiors* should be so arranged as to give *exterior* space a degree of spatial order.

Theorem 2: Buildings are important, but not as important as the students, their professors, and the educational program.

The most important thing about higher education—or secondary or elementary, for that matter—is the *student*.

If the students, teachers, and program (in that order) are basically good, good citizens can be turned out—even if the facilities are only adequate. On the other hand, how nice to have excellence in all four areas, which includes inspirational space and up-to-date teaching equipment.

Theorem 3: Only through a simultaneous consideration of function, form, and cost can a really effective campus plan, college building, or item of educational equipment be realized.

If thinking is limited to function and form, a thoroughly programed project and a beautifully conceived design can result, but if the cost is

---

[8] William W. Caudill, "Housing the Educational Program: The Physical Plant as Educational Environment," in *Long-Range Planning in Higher Education*, Owen A. Knorr, ed., Western Interstate Commission for Higher Education (WICHE), Boulder, Colo., 1965, pp. 53–63.

exorbitant, time and effort are wasted. The same is true when function and cost turn out big "uglies." There are too many academic junkyards now. And finally, if only form and cost are considered, we could produce something that in some eyes might be very beautiful and very cheap, but if it does not perform with educational efficiency, then neither the campus, the building, nor the equipment will be praiseworthy. Function, form, and cost are inseparable; they must be considered simultaneously.

Premise 1: The campus and each of its buildings should be planned more for flexibility than for exactitude.

A successful educational plant must grow and change. Accordingly, the physical plant must possess the quality of expansibility, convertibility, and versatility. Since it is inevitable that educational functions will change, buildings must be able to conform effectively and economically to these changes.

Premise 2: A university or college is more than the sum of its parts. Since the various departments, schools, and institutions that form a university must do a better job collectively than separately, the architecture must aid, not hinder, the task.

A university should possess what its name implies—wholeness, educationally and architecturally. Each department or school must operate on the assumption that collectively it can do a better job than separately, and the design of its buildings must be based on the same premise. Buildings should dwell together in unity with their neighbors. Campus buildings should speak to each other with understanding and sympathy.

Premise 3: A university plant should reflect the excitement of learning that can only be found in a pure form of democracy.

The one place in the world for free thinking and democratic action should be on the university campus. Should such freedom not be reflected in the buildings and the grounds? College buildings should portray the most advanced thinking. They should have a certain degree of independence yet be cognizant of the others. The greatest buildings on earth should be on the campus. Unfortunately, they are not.

Premise 4: There should be no crystallized form for university architecture.

Nothing is wrong if it is done right. Every campus has different problems. The organizations differ; the architectural forms differ. The only possible thing that can be constant is the approach to planning university buildings and grounds. Styles and fads decay with time. But the approach—and particularly the trilateral approach (a balance between function, form, and cost)—flourishes with time.

Premise 5: The architectural structure must respond to the educational structure.

A university plant is the largest and most expensive teaching machine on earth. It has a job to do—primarily to help the professor teach—and it should do it well. But the job will change from year to year. In fact, it should change from place to place; standardization of education can smother progress. It makes no sense for States to require every one of their institutions to conform to a common pattern.

Premise 6: The campus should have a unifying element.

On a unified campus with 30 or 40 buildings, there are many different building types and many kinds of architecture, yet the campus has unity. Why? What overrides the buildings? Is the landscape strong enough to do it? Sometimes, yes. In most cases, however, what overrides the buildings is organized outside space—the outside rooms, the vistas, and the surprises around the corner. The most important element at Harvard is the Harvard Yard, not the buildings that form it. At Cornell, the hills and the trees are the overriding elements. At Oklahoma State, the heights of the buildings, the common materials, and the distances between the buildings seem to be the overriding and unifying element. Sometimes age is the great unifier. Time blends stone and brick; old trees and vines do also.

In building a new campus or a new portion of an old one, unity can be achieved with materials, building heights, architectural forms, especially roof forms, and a constant scale.

Scale concerns not only the details of buildings but their placement. Professional planners talk in terms of "pedestrian scale," which helps unify a campus, and "automobile scale." When buildings are more than one-half mile apart, a campus ceases to have a pedestrian scale.

Premise 7: Every campus needs a symbol.

Northwestern has Lake Michigan; Cornell has rolling hills overlooking Lake Cayuga. Wisconsin University, too, has a lake. M.I.T. has the Charles River. Colorado University has magnificent mountains as a backdrop. A college in western Colorado has its own natural pedestal: a dramatic mesa. These God-given symbols do a better job than any man-made symbols can ever do. But man-made symbols are also necessary. Texas University has a library tower, Washington University in St. Louis has a sallyport, and Duke has a magnificent chapel.

But these are more than symbols. They serve as unifying elements and give a certain visual order to the hodgepodge of buildings. Lakes, rivers, and mountains give personality to campuses. Unquestionably, the campus planner should capitalize on the uniqueness of the natural environment.

Premise 8: Zoning should not be a sacred cow.

There is nothing wrong with zoned colleges. But zoning is not the only way to arrange buildings. A college can be completely devoid of zones in the classical sense. For lack of a better phrase, the design can be called "scrambled zoning."

This technique consists primarily of a main academic street, patterned after one in an old German town, where people work, live, and eat in buildings lining the street. The residential halls—like city apartments—are dispersed along this street. So are the dining halls, the classrooms, and sections of the library. The academic street can be a most exciting place during both day and night. It is a pedestrian street; therefore there are rentable spaces for commercial shops. This is urban planning in the truest sense.[9]

Premise 9: Reserve some campus space on which cars are not allowed.

Many campuses are so large that students must drive cars to get from class to class. Although cars should not be banned from use on such campuses, there should be a no-car land, a place where cars cannot even be seen. If the campus is so large students cannot walk to and from campuses, there should be a campus within a campus, designed for people—not automobiles. Such an arrangement would not only eliminate the confusion of traffic, but also the noise of motors and the smell of exhaust fumes. The following are a few ways in which a pedestrian campus can be achieved:

—Create a perimeter road around the campus to permit city traffic to flow around rather than through the campus.

—Bar all automobiles, except service or emergency vehicles, from certain campus areas.

—If city traffic must cross the campus, submerge busy streets to unify space and to help eliminate any conflict between pedestrian and vehicular flow.

—Use parking as a transition from vehicular to pedestrian flow.

The concept of the pedestrian campus is sound. Before the renowned architect Eero Saarinen died in 1961, he challenged his colleagues to build university campuses comparable to the monasteries of the Middle Ages: the only beautiful, respectable pedestrian places left.

Premise 10: Every campus building should be generic.

Not only should each building be flexible but each should have a certain generic quality. An engineering building should "look, act, and feel" like an engineering building—not like an embassy in India or a State capitol in North Carolina. A veterinary medicine building for small animals should be what it is, not a twin of a building for humanities. A library is a library, but since there are different kinds of libraries, all libraries should not look or function alike. They should, however, look like libraries.

Premise 11: The process of learning must encompass many activities,

---

[9] It should be noted that a three-dimensional zoning concept, as opposed to the more traditional two-dimensional one, facilitates the "scrambling" of activities by structuring housing vertically.

which, if effective, should relate not only to the intelligence, the motivation, and the state of development of the learner but also to the physical
environment of the learning task.

The design of the physical environment of the learning task is often
neglected yet science has established a close correlation between the amount
of work people do and where they do it. It stands to reason that a student
sitting in an unbearably hot, stuffy room listening to a lecture on cryogenics
would not learn as much as he would in a cool, comfortable space. Unfortunately, most college buildings have been planned to impress people
from the outside, not necessarily to provide comfort for the users.

Creative Planning Ideas

Some of the excitement of creative campus planning can be gathered
from the imaginative ideas being expressed publicly. The following design ideas were discussed at a conference on campus planning sponsored
by the School Planning Laboratory, School of Education, Stanford University.[10]

—By lifting large buildings off the ground on stilts and by landscaping the rooftops
of low structures located within heavily trafficked areas, it is possible to increase
campus open space while increasing density.

—In developing a high-density campus, a key notion involves the distinct separation
of those functions with much personnel movement from those with little traffic.
The most frequented spaces (classrooms, lecture halls, and coffee shops) should be
at ground level or below in a sprawling layer of space continuously linked together,
but perforated with courtyards. Functions that require a large volume of building
space but attract relatively little traffic (library stacks, dormitories, and laboratories)
should be located above ground level. Activities requiring little intercommunication
or traffic can be assigned to towers. Ground level or subterranean space can be
used to house activities that must be linked together.

—If several buildings are separated by city streets (at urban colleges, for example),
they can be linked by over-the-street bridges at second- and third-floor levels.

—If student lounges, game rooms, and activity centers are not compressed into a
single area but are scattered about the campus, they will not only be more convenient to individual students but serve as a social adhesive as well.

Because of the constantly changing nature of university society, any
artificial constriction of movement, either academic or physical, will prove
all too soon to be out of date and possibly impede future development
plans. What can be done instead is to institute a continuous teaching environment with a physical form that permits accretion and internal change
while encouraging maximum communication among all constitutent parts.

---

[10] John Beynon, *Campus Planning: Review and Preview*, Educational Facilities Laboratories, Inc., New York, July 1963, pp. 4–8.

Representatives of Casson and Conder, a British architectural firm, when presenting this idea at Birmingham, England, in 1958, identified some of the principles that suggest how it can work in an existing institution:

—Do not spread unnecessarily; a university should express itself as an entity by means of a compact and coherent layout.

—Keep open the possibility of access to long-term sites.

—Use the principle of the "joker"; allow undifferentiated space within areas set aside for specialized activities, this for sudden and previously unknown expansion.

—Use the principle of courtyard planning; completion of space by space; contrasting space to space.

—Discourage architecture that imposes obligations. Except where there is obvious justification and certainty of the completion of an effect, design without dependence on symmetry and center-lines.

—Use the natural given personality of the site; demand that each building contribute to the special quality of the whole and not be something apart.[11]

To further their idea, Casson and Conder propose the street-deck principle of expansion. They exploit the natural fall of the land by providing two buildings, one above the other, separated by an open pedestrian street deck.

BUILDING PLANNING

Planning the construction of a new building is a vast, complicated, and tremendously important task involving many persons. What prevents the task from overwhelming the planners is the critical influence that the relatively simple client-architect relationship exerts on the final outcome. Significantly enough, the combination of the right architect and a knowledgeable client, effectively interacting and following a master plan for campus development, is a reasonable guarantee that the job will be accomplished to everyone's satisfaction. Toward this end, three elements are required. First, the architect must be suitable—in the sense that he believes in the client's overall plan, is trusted by the client, and possesses the talent and technical capability essential to the assignment. In addition, the architect and the client must be able to cooperate in a forthright and direct manner to produce that special amalgam of understanding, enthusiasm, and talent required for joint participation in creative effort. Second, the client should be an expert in his profession and should actively

[11] Quoted in Richard P. Dober, *The New Campus in Britain: Ideas of Consequence for the United States*, Educational Facilities Laboratories, Inc., New York, 1965, p. 35.

express himself and participate with the architect in identifying needs and translating them into physical facilities. Third, these two most important people must be able to sit down and mutually accomplish what can best be described as a melding of visions.

How can these three requirements of the desired client-architect relationship be achieved? While there is no easy way to select an architect, some of the general rules which should be followed and pitfalls which may be avoided are summarized in the section entitled "Planning Pointers." Another section, "New Ideas for Campus Buildings," includes examples of the type of information with which the educator-planner must be familiar if he is to be a knowledgeable client. Choosing the right architect and being knowledgeable, actually secondary activities of the client, help pave the way and support his most important function: effectively communicating with the architect. From the client's point of view, this process of communication is generally referred to as "building programing."

Programing

Building programing is a process of continuing deliberation between the client and the architect. In the course of this process the client conveys his needs, preferences, and concepts of an intended building program; he also ensures that the dialogue is correctly interpreted in the working documents. The written portion of this communication process, commonly called the "educational specifications" or more accurately the "building design program," consists of descriptions, instructions, and suggestions relative to the proposed construction prepared by the client in advance of the architectural planning process.

In serving his client, the architect seeks to achieve a desirable balance among four principal elements: *function* (what the building should do); *technology* (how the building should be built and how its interior environment should be controlled); *economics* (opportunities and restraints imposed by the budget), and *esthetics* (what the building should look like). How this balance is accomplished in the final design plans is largely a matter of how well the client expresses his preferences and how effectively the architect carries out these preferences and employs the vision essential to creating true design quality.

All things being equal, the client gets as good a building as he can communicate to the architect. No two architect-client relationships are the same, but if something worthwhile is to emerge both parties must jointly participate in the creative effort. The client, who in the college context can be many different people—president, administrator, planner, faculty member, etc.—brings to the table a unique operational approach. He knows better than anyone else the life of the college, the kind of routine that is desired, and the type of facilities best suited to this pattern. Clients can and should express themselves in all areas where their needs, individual tastes, and reactions can affect the final design.

The architect will want the client to express thoroughly and completely his needs and wants. Only when the architect has a clear and firm idea of exactly what is needed can he use his talent to create the desired physical environments. Needless to say, any architect worth his salt is not going to let his talent be hamstrung by a domineering client. Yet on occasion an architect, in an attempt to please, will suppress his own views, thereby becoming merely a draftsman. With the right architect, a client need seldom fear that he may exert too much control in presenting his views. Rather, he must avoid too timid an approach.

Much of the communication between architect and client is through conferences and informal discussions. The architect and planning team members should become first-name friends. Only by so doing can the exchange and interaction required for effective negotiation be accomplished.

Prior to the talking stage, however, the client must prepare, with deliberate thought, a written document known as "educational specifications" or a "building design program."

Educational Specifications

The term "educational specifications," while overly precise, is so commonly employed by educators and architects that it, rather than the less-popular but more accurate description, "building design program," is used in this work. Both terms refer to the inexact process of translating educational function into criteria for physical form. Through words and diagrams the specifications attempt to identify (1) those institutional goals and philosophy that may influence facility design, (2) the people and functions to be accommodated, and (3) the kind of environment the educator-planner feels is required. The tone of the specifications should suggest what the facilities should *do* rather than what they should *be*. Emphasizing intended *performance* clearly places the specifications within the purview of the educator and leaves the specifics of the physical solution primarily to the architect.

The scope of the specifications statement may range from strictly technical instructions to a general background statement of the academic requirements that must be considered in the design of the environment. The topics are generally those which, by virtue of the institution's interest, knowledge, or special needs, warrant clarification and discussion with the architect. Although translation details are usually left to the expertise of the architect, the institution should feel free to comment on any and all aspects of building design since the educational specifications, to a large degree, constitute the ". . . basis for providing a building that works in every sense."[12]

---

[12] Peter D. Paul, "Expressing Educational Requirements," *AID Journal*, July 1967.

Figure XI-4. — Illustrative matrix of educational specifications

Specification topic	Level or focus of commentary							
	Campus or institution	Total building	Organizational division within building	Space or room-type areas within building				
				Classrooms	Teaching laboratories	Faculty offices	Administrative offices	Other room types
	(1)	(2)	(3)	(4)	(5)	(6)	(7)	(8)
1. Identification								
2. Role, justifica- tion, & priorities								
3. General a. Philosophy b. History c. Policy d. Practice								
4. Architectural excellence								
5. Ecological considerations (site planning)								
6. Functional requirements a. Activities b. Relationships c. People (1) Students (2) Staff (3) Others d. Flexibility								
7. Space requirements a. area b. Spatial relationships								
8. Environment a. Quality b. Layout c. Material d. Lighting & color e. Acoustics f. Thermal								
9. Technical a. Equipment and furnishings b. Electrical c. Mechanical and plumbing								
10. Miscellaneous								

Good educational specifications are said to be characterized by[13]:

—A statement of program needs (details of design methods remain the prerogative of the architect)
—Clarity and conciseness
—A position which encourages creative thinking and cooperation
—Complete coverage of the scope of immediate and future educational needs (to insure the planning of adaptable and functional facilities)
—Content based on a fully defined curriculum
—Inclusion of the views of the education profession, particularly the faculty
—Avoidance of rigid prescription
—A constant outlook for creating flexibility and adaptability.

---

[13] Adapted from Dwayne E. Gardner, "Do's and Don'ts of Educational Specifications," *American School Board Journal*, vol. 148, June 1964, pp. 17–19.

Over the years, colleges and universities have prepared a vast number of educational specifications with varying degrees of success. Useful as models are those workable procedures that have been slowly developed through multiple application and continual review and upgrading. The architectural design programing procedures at the University of Utah, for example, demonstrate how a carefully prepared format may be used to present "all available information concerning the needs which must be fulfilled and the functions which are essential to the proposed building."[14]

In preparing the following composite outline, a number of formalized and tested procedures for building programing have been reviewed. The list is not necessarily complete for every building program nor is it suitable for every type of facility, yet it does suggest the nature and scope of topics most frequently cited in the better written educational specifications. Four levels of commentary are required: (1) campus or institutional, (2) total building, (3) organizational divisions which can be logically grouped together because of their functional and operational similarities, and (4) room-type areas. The resulting matrix of information is illustrated in figure XI-4.

1. Identification

Each level of commentary—campus, building, the organizational division, and space within the building—should be carefully established by name and such other identifying factors as location, organizational status, definition, components, jurisdiction, etc.

2. Role, justification, and priorities

The role of the project in the overall campus design should be briefly explained and justified. Justification may be made on the basis of necessary organizational structure or in terms of expected contribution or functional requirements.

In the likelihood that available funds prove inadequate to complete the facilities as originally envisioned, a statement of priorities and modifications to be followed as monetary constraints are encountered is valuable in giving structure to what otherwise might become a chaotic and undisciplined situation.

3. General

In this area, attention should be given to enumerating those elements of institutional philosophy, history, policy, and practice likely to give general direction and guidance to planning and design efforts. Some of the elements, best expressed in terms of the campus as a whole or the total building program, need not be detailed

---

[14] Bruce H. Jensen, *Architectural Design Programming Guide*, Campus Planning Department, University of Utah, Salt Lake City, n.d., p. 2.

for individual room types. Examples of topics which may be discussed include:

—Educational objectives and academic philosophy
—Recent discernible trends in curriculum offerings, course content, enrollments, etc.
—General learning climate desired
—Relationship between student and teacher in the classroom
—Emphasis to be placed on computer-assisted instruction and audiovisual aids
—Faculty-staff relationships
—Relationship of departments to building, departments to institution, building to institution, etc.
—Student-faculty relationship outside the classroom
—Length of instructional day
—Overall flexibility of curriculum
—Academic and administrative organization concepts
—Receptivity of institution to innovation and change
—Student life on campus (degree of privacy afforded, freedom allowed, resident versus commuter, institutional student services provided, etc.)
—Position toward principle of clustering versus integrating different institutional functions
—Scale of institutional operations (expected total enrollment, student-faculty ratio, growth rate, proportion budgeted for organized research, etc.)
—Community service function of institution.

4. Architectural excellence

The construction boom on college campuses has created an exceptional opportunity for good architecture. Whereas a typical campus plan formerly was implemented over a period of many years on a piecemeal building-by-building basis, entire new campuses are now being erected all at once. Now, too, large additions are being made to rapidly expanding existing plants. Such larger scale construction has caused college administrators to take a more careful look at the need and desirability of extending quality to include beauty and excellence. Increasingly it is being recognized that architectural form can express a great deal about the beliefs and central values of an institution. Educators realize that distinguished-looking buildings reflect their own as well as the architect's ideals. Institutions that strive for high standards in education can hardly settle for less than superior campus architecture.

The contributions of design excellence are implicit in the remarks by Harold B. Gores, president of the Educational Facilities Laboratories, at a recent design awards ceremony.

—A good college building first of all contributes effectively to the learning process. In addition, it performs the tasks assigned to it and can meet, with equal facility, future needs.
—A graceful and sensitive educational building can endow its neighborhood with a measure of dignity and delight.
—Buildings of dignity provide the community with pleasure and pride in achievement.
—Superior campus design helps establish an overall climate of excellence which shapes and supports the expectations and efforts of students and faculty.

—The lasting physical nature of U.S. colleges serves as an enduring symbol of national culture. Also, and more importantly, college buildings transmit the values of this culture to succeeding generations.[15]

There is, of course, no set pattern of excellence in the arts; excellence in architecture has great diversity. Other than whatever is designed be functionally useful, there are no restrictions, no limits. No hard-and-fast rules govern those who strive for design excellence. Instead, they are guided by an appreciation of excellence and the ability to recognize superior design quality.

Educators and planners who aspire to the highest standards of architecture can begin by studying and visiting those campuses on which superior designs have been created. Educational facilities deemed outstanding are often cited for awards.[16] Architectural excellence on campuses is also frequently reviewed, although too often in terms of purely physical criteria, in such journals as *Architectural Record* and *Architectural Forum*.

In any study of superior architecture, attention must be given to more than external form. Since beauty of form and design is most easily recognized, there is a tendency to express appreciation of architecture in terms of the visible physical features. Yet excellent architecture has other qualities. Among these are functional efficiency and the degree to which the design suits its environment. The components of a building and its surroundings should of course be fully integrated to produce a comfortable and harmonious whole. Flexibility and low cost, as well as completion of the job on time, are also elements of architectural excellence. Possibly even lack of distinction may be important. Consider an unobtrusive boiler house: An architecturally excellent one would not be noticed.

5. Ecological considerations (site planning)

Each building must of course be designed in harmony with the overall campus master plan.[17] Consequently, the master plan and its relationship to individual buildings under consideration should be discussed first, followed by a detailed review of the environmental factors that may influence the design. Topics likely to be important are traffic circulation and parking, main traffic arteries, topography, drainage, major utility lines, adjacent buildings (proximity, height, exterior architecture, etc.), tree groupings, and potential expansion areas. Where applicable, the effect of construction on existing buildings and their functions and on campus traffic should be discussed.

---

[15] U.S. Department of Health, Education, and Welfare, Office of Education, *Excellence in Design—A New Potential on the American Campus*, U.S. Government Printing office, Washington, D. C., 1967, pp. 9–11.

[16] For example, 29 award-winning projects (out of 258 entries) are described in the U.S. Office of Education publication, *1966 Design Award Program*. (See bibliography for details.)

[17] Conditions of contiguous surroundings affecting building design are usually described in the overall campus plan. Because of the importance of conveying, from the outset, a complete and accurate picture of the *total* scene, one campus architect feels that during the early stages all drawings should include adjoining buildings and other existing structures.

6. Functional requirements

a. Activities: The function the building will serve is probably more important to design than all other factors combined. The best possible design will be forthcoming only if the architect has a sensitive understanding of the activities which are to take place in each space of a given facility. Both the overall education program scheduled for the building as a whole and the activities to take place in each major division and area should be explained in detail. The educator has no greater responsibility than the careful preparation of these specifications.

b. Relationships: A description of the functional, administrative, and spatial interrelationships within not only levels but also superior and subordinate elements that may have a bearing on the organization of space, communications, and traffic patterns. Diagrams may be useful to supplement the description.

c. People: A description and count of the faculty, administrative staff, and students who will occupy the space under consideration, together with peak load data and any other relevant information that will assist the architect to completely understand the nature of the occupants and their use of the building.

d. Flexibility: Some indication of anticipated variations in teaching materials and techniques and in class size that may require multi-use or convertible space. Attitudes toward open space, utility chases and cores, and the use of movable partitions; consideration to be given to acoustics and visual division of space; and future developments that may require changes or render existing designs obsolete.

7. Space requirements

a. Area: A list of the number of required rooms by type and size (assignable area). Desired ratio of building area types; for example, assignable square feet to gross square feet (one ratio for the entire building is usually adequate).

b. Spatial relationships: Both verbal and diagrammatic descriptions of the functional and physical relationships between spaces within an entire building, within each department, and between rooms of various types; and circulation pattern requirements.

8. Environment

For each room type, a general description is needed of the atmosphere or character of the space in terms of its shape, materials, lighting, color, acoustics, and thermal requirements (see last part of this chapter for a detailed discussion of these factors). Items which should be described include:

a. Quality: Any special quality, feeling, or character that the space should convey to the occupant.

b. Layout: Recommendations and restrictions regarding room dimension or shape, number of student stations and station locations; special requirements for window and door locations; and preference for flat, stepped, or sloped floors. Unless special requirements or restrictions are involved, details should be omitted. An exception: the results of detailed layout studies that take into account the activity, occupants, equipment, and need for functional flexibility (see chapter X).

c. Material: A delineation of special requirements for finishes and surface treatment of walls, floors, ceilings, and working surfaces. Do they need to be resistant to chemicals? Scratch resistant? Nonreflecting?

d. Lighting and color: Specifications for natural and artificial light, type (fluorescent or incandescent), direct or indirect, location, lumination level, desired contrast; identification of visual work surfaces to be most brightly illuminated; areas where glare and shadows must be eliminated; special locations for switches, and what colors if any are to be used in designated locations.

e. Acoustics: Specifications for distribution of reflective and absorptive materials, sound isolation between spaces, sound systems, and other special needs.

f. Thermal: Requirements for temperature, humidity, air circulation, and odor control.

9. Technical

An itemized list of technical requirements for individual areas. The following should be included where applicable:

a. Equipment and furnishings: Equipment is generally viewed as all fixed items (e.g., cabinets and sinks) and items with major utility connections (e.g., shop machines and scientific apparatus), while furnishings consist mainly of furniture and such appointments as draperies, carpeting, wastebaskets, etc. Overall considerations may include commentary on quality and cost, durability, ease of cleaning, standardization, portability, adaptability, and adjustability. Special attention should be given to descriptions of educational display systems, both nonprojected (chalkboards, tackboards, models, modular demonstration carts) and projected (motion pictures and television).

b. Electrical: Number, location, height above floor, and voltage for electrical outlets. Location and source for sound, television, telephone, and intercommunication system outlets.

c. Mechanical and plumbing: Air-conditioning and ventilation requirements; plumbing outlets, drains, etc.; special requirements for radiation shielding, electronic influence control, and infectious disease isolation.

10. Miscellaneous

Specifications for any number of additional design features, including provisions for the handicapped, fire-prevention apparatus, storage areas, building security alarm systems, safety devices, emergency lighting, vibration control, etc. A check of local building codes will often reveal other special requirements. If consideration is to be given to modular design (orderly organization of components by means of a common dimensional unit wherever practical), recommendations should be included in this section.

Planning Pointers

There is no single correct way to plan a building—some general rules perhaps a few warnings, but no magic formula guaranteeing success. No even all questions can be anticipated. But answers to some of the most frequently asked are worthy of attention. In selecting the following tips or guides from a number of sources, only those ideas and recommendations that appear to be particularly sound have been included. The list is not meant to be all-inclusive.

Choosing an architect. In regard to the crucial choice of an architect, formal architectural competition, while not overly popular, is the one cut-and-dried method which may be worth the trouble. Using the American Institute of Architects' (AIA) code for competitions, the client hires a professional advisor, appoints a jury, and invites architects to submit designs based on preannounced specifications. In his booklet, *Your Building and Your Architect*, Donald Canby states, ". . . the formal competition is the nearest thing to a surefire system for attaining superior architecture—a system that lets the client see a facsimile of the product before a designer is selected and provides a panel of experts to guide the choice. It is especially well-suited to public projects; it is, after all, a particularly democratic way to pick architects, and it also takes some of the political pressure off the public client. Most important, it often leads to a freshness and excitement not often found in public buildings."[18] One drawback: The expensive and time-consuming task of submitting an entry sometimes tends to eliminate the busier, better known firms that simply do not have time to speculate. Probably the most obvious reason to consider architectural competition is that it provides an opportunity to search for interesting and unconventional approaches to relatively simple projects.

Visiting other campuses in search of ideas. Just about everyone agrees that austerity in planning can be costly in the long run. Visits to other campuses are frequently bypassed because of their cost. Such an attitude is false economy. The planner who firmly intends to have a good building erected and is willing unabashedly to pick the brains of accessible experts, visit new campus buildings, and systematically record his observations will reap ideas that far outweigh travel expenses. On any tour, functionalism should be probed: How and why is the building performing better or worse than expected? What innovative ideas are working well, which ones are not? Information on costs of construction, furnishings, and equipment can be most useful. Arrangements should be made to interview the campus planning officer, the architect, the contractor, faculty members, students, and sometimes maintenance staff members to ascertain viewpoints on what went right and what went wrong. Such a procedure may seem tedious, but the more knowledge a planner obtains the less likely he will be to make mistakes in his own planning process.

---

[18] Canby, *Your Building and Your Architect*, op. cit., p. 2.

Appraising existing buildings. "As part of the site analysis on your own campus, any existing buildings on the site should be appraised and their potential utility for the college carefully estimated. In considering such facilities there is a strong temptation to equate 'existing' with 'permanent.' Such a temptation should be carefully avoided. Many years of 'making do' with a white elephant may use up more in maintenance funds and psychic energy than would a completely new structure."[19]

Controlling costs. The importance of cost control cannot be overemphasized. Estimated project costs must be not only completely and accurately defined but also include escalation factors in accord with the construction schedule and expected completion date. The job of the architect, as expressed by one observer, is to "place things in proper perspective, to scale the project to the allocated budget and to explain that the client cannot expect the Taj Mahal for $3 a square foot." Frequently this process may require that the client adjust his thinking in terms of size of the building or in terms of materials or building methods to be used. It is essential that both the architect and client talk about the same building and not try to fool one another as to their true intentions. The client and architect should carefully review the project budget, for once a contract is signed the architect should be expected to accept budget restraints as a design objective. The architect, preferably with the help of a qualified cost consultant, should develop a cost breakdown at the end of each major design stage, then, in consultation with the client, determine whatever revision or updating may be necessary. Throughout the design stage, the agreed-upon budget can be maintained by constantly reviewing changes and additions. Frank Grad & Sons of Newark, N.J., call this "the 'creep' stage, for all those little things creeping in can be the greatest factor affecting costs."

Conducting reviews. Constant review through all stages should be the operational slogan. Each stage—programing, schematic, design development, contract documents, final cost estimate, and construction—demands the careful attention of planner, architect, and administrator if appropriate adjustments are to be made and actions kept in line with agreements. At the completion of each stage, it is probably desirable that a cost estimate be made, together with evaluation and approval of any consequential program changes. Approval signatures are useful to verify agreements. Part of this review is simply explaining and clarifying what is going on, particularly as it relates to final construction. From experience, planners

---

[19] Community College Planning Center on Community College Facilities, *Planners and Planning*, School of Education, Stanford University, Stanford, Calif., 1966, p. 40.

have found that the more inexact the review process, the more misunderstanding and misinformation develop, and consequently, the more dissatisfaction among those involved. Double-checking can help prevent numerous small mistakes that could be made if a review of all of the thousands of details is left to the architect. Keeping everyone informed and checking regularly are the best ways to insure a building consistent with everyone's understanding of its function, design, and cost.

Saving time. With escalating land prices and construction costs, saving time means saving money. One California district is reported to have saved the equivalent of the cost of an entire building by carefully selecting and purchasing a campus site ahead of time. At an annual escalation of 5 percent, a 1-year delay in a $4 million facility project would mean the loss of $200,000. This amount, converted to building area, represents the loss of approximately one faculty office each week or enough money to furnish one faculty office generously for each day of delay. In view of the importance of streamlining planning and saving time, Bruce H. Jensen of the University of Utah makes the following suggestions:

—Keep the decisionmakers and planners in close touch. A good organizational arrangement is to have the administrator and planner only one step away from the university president or chancellor.

—Anticipate the prerequisites. Use the fiscal plan to anticipate when to start preparing a building design program or educational specifications. As soon as approval to proceed with the project is given, the completed design program should be ready for immediate use by the architect. If possible, involve the architect in the programing stage.

—Anticipate special needs and approvals such as city zoning, preferred access routes, State, county, and city roads and freeways and their capacities, sewer and storm drainage connections and capacities, electrical substation capacities, etc. Lead time is important. At the present time, delivery on some electrical materials, for example, can be as much as a year or more.

—Don't let what can be labeled the slow "*institutional tempo*" cause the program to suffer. There can be a tendency in large institutions to feel no urgency for prompt decisions. The attitude of "what you can't do today can wait until tomorrow" will cost the expansion program money.[20]

Engineering design. The importance of good engineering design in modern educational buildings is not always recognized. In a science building, for example, the heating, ventilating, and air-conditioning can quite easily amount to 25 percent or more of the building dollar. Similarly, the plumb-

---

[20] Bruce H. Jensen, "Administrative Responsibilities During Plant Expansion," in *Challenging a New Future*, paper presented at the 1969 College and University Conference and Exposition sponsored by *American School and University*, Buttenheim Publishing Company, New York, 1969, pp. 33–38.

ing can account for another 15 percent, the electrical portion for 12 percent, and the structural portion for another 15 to 20 percent. Since these percentages will total considerably more than half of the total expenditure, engineering design is of vital importance. Consequently, the planner should know the capabilities of the engineering organization to be associated with the project as well as he knows the abilities of the architect.

Preparing contract documents. It is generally agreed that the greatest weapon in administering the construction phases of a project is a good set of contract documents. In developing the drawings and specifications the architect and his consultants should try to anticipate problems and develop criteria, stipulations, and systems to protect the client in the event of difficulties and misunderstandings. After the contract is signed, the contractor—because he is in the driver's seat—is in a position to call for cost hikes. To maintain original budget figures, therefore, it is helpful in most instances to specify unit prices in the contract. All-round, sound advice regarding construction cost-control, particularly useful during the preparation of drawings and specifications, should be obtained directly from the contractors.

Concerning the format of specifications, George S. Campbell & Associates of Chattanooga, Tenn.,[21] recommends the "or approved equal" type in which all substitutions are submitted and acted upon before the bid date. This procedure not only provides the client with the maximum advantages competitive bidding offers, but also eliminates conflicts over approval of substitutions that can arise between construction and design teams after the contract price has been fixed.

A specification cannot be written which is long enough, detailed enough, or accurate enough to make a crook honest; on the other hand, an honest contractor does not need five volumes of specifications to force him to perform honestly. Consequently, specifications should be kept as succinct as possible. They should include drawing schedules as well as catalog names, numbers, and performance data. In other words, only those items of workmanship technique and methods should be included that experience has indicated need to be spelled out in order to get the desired job done.

Selecting a contractor. The ins and outs of single and multiple bidding and contracting are exceptionally complicated and fraught with pitfalls, unresolved issues, and legal nuances. One of the few documents which attempts to evaluate objectively alternative procedures and make recom-

---

[21] George S. Campbell, "Specializing for Workable Mechanical Specs," *American School and University*, vol. 41, no. 3, November 1968, pp. 31, 56, 58.

mendations has at this time a restricted distribution. This study provides a compelling line of reasoning for a single responsible director as provided by a single contract system. Especially when projects are large and complicated, the need of a single administrative authority to oversee proper, efficient, and timely completion of work appears evident.

With regard to selecting a contractor through open competitive bidding, the following advice is available:

> The system of open competitive bidding is a traditional part of the romance of construction. It is free enterprise at its freest and most frantic form. It virtually assures the client of getting the lowest available price tag on his building. It also has a great deal to do with the fact that Dun & Bradstreet reports a ratio of net profit (on sales) of only 1.18 percent among building contractors.
>
> If wide-open bidding is a perilous gamble for many contractors, it also has its risk aspects for client and architect. The lowest bid is seldom the most realistic one, and a builder in danger of losing his shirt can find room for costly extras in even the most tightly drawn contract documents. More important, it makes price the prime basis of selection, eliminating the opportunity to weigh the contending contractor's comparative abilities to turn out quality work.[22]

The author goes on to suggest that by limiting the number of contenders to a select list, the benefits of competition can be retained and the contractors can be screened in advance. This may mean ". . . looking into the success of the contractor's past projects, the size and length of service of his work force, his reputation as an administrator of construction and even the kind of equipment in his corporation yard." The client may also protect himself by requiring each contending contractor to submit a deposit with his bid. If the low bidder for some reason decides to withdraw, the client is entitled to retain the deposit. The successful bidder normally is required to post a performance bond to ensure that the work will be finished even if he goes out of business, and often a labor and material bond guaranteeing payment for supplies and subcontractors is also mandatory. Standard bonding forms have been drawn up by the AIA

New Ideas for Campus Buildings

"Innovative" is a term very often used to describe education practices. However exaggerated its use, nowhere is it more applicable than in describing the ideas and changes taking place in campus building design. The most creative work on a campus today may well be the most recently constructed building—replete with modern technology and architectural surprises, which, if not responding to changes in the academic process, are literally reshaping it.

---

[22] Canby, *Your Building and Your Architect*, op. cit., pp. 12–13.

Educational Facilities Laboratories, Inc. (EFL), a nonprofit corporation helping American schools and colleges with building and equipment problems, has, since its founding in 1958, been a leader in disseminating information about all that is new and creative in facilities design. EFL publications constitute virtually a library of aids for solving space-design problems. While no review can do justice to the many new ideas in building design, a selection of some recent developments should suffice to stimulate further investigation. The following sampling of design ideas has been drawn mainly from EFL publications, particularly from *Bricks and Mortarboards* (1966), a catalog of exciting new practices in campus building.

—The problem of inadequate sound isolation has been solved by new operable walls which reduce noise transmission between class areas to the point that activities in one area rarely distract classes on the other side of the partition. Operable walls may cost much more than permanent walls, but their installation, by permitting an increase in the utilization rate or providing additional classrooms, can make them an unqualified bargain.

—The School of Business at the University of Indiana plans what it calls the "10 by 10 classroom" in which students will be almost completely surrounded by learning stimuli. Swivel seats, arranged in 10 rows of 10 chairs each, will permit students to rotate 360 degrees to view the chalkboards, tackboards, and projection screens arrayed along three walls, as well as follow the instructor and his assistant as they move around a three-sided platform.

—In the new physical sciences lecture hall at the University of California at Berkeley, physics and chemistry demonstrations may be set up backstage ahead of classtime, then mechanically propelled on a revolving stage to the front of the lecture room. Such an innovation prevents large lecture halls from remaining empty while apparatus from previous classes is removed and a new demonstration prepared.

—With the growing emphasis on individualism, carrels and other individual study units are being provided for library users. Since it has been determined that students prefer not to sit at flat tables in the middle of a large reading room, library study space should be scaled down to accommodate individuals or small groups.

—The modular library has directly challenged the notion that human beings are uncomfortable in rooms with low ceilings. According to Keyes D. Metcalf, librarian emeritus of Harvard and dean of library construction consultants, the death knell of the high ceiling came when Princeton conducted an unusual experiment. In preparing to erect a modular library, he says, "Princeton built a two-bay mock-up with a fake ceiling and cranked it up and down. Librarians, students, architects, college presidents, faculty members, and others were asked to holler when they felt uncomfortable. It was found that users were comfortable when the ceiling was lowered to 8'4" in a room as large as 25 by 36 feet." Today most modular libraries limit the height in reading areas to 8'6".

—More attractive and comfortable libraries are being created by the use of high-quality furniture purchased from fine furniture houses rather than traditional standard pieces featured by library suppliers. Fabric or leather-covered armchairs, coffee tables, couches, and table lamps can be seen with increasing frequency in alcoves, lounges, or lobbies of newer libraries. The concern for comfort is also evident in the increasing use of rugs. Not only is carpeting much more comfortable to walk on but it can provide color and acoustical control. The initial cost of carpeting is still higher than that of other kinds of floor covering, but maintenance costs are significantly lower. A cost analysis prepared for the John Crerar Library at the Illinois Institute of Technology showed that the most expensive grade of carpeting would be cheaper to buy and maintain—over a period of less than 8 years—than all other types of floor covering. The carpeting had a life expectancy of 15 years.

—Architect H. H. Peter Klein of Bedford, Massachusetts, a World War II pilot, views the needs of a science building as analogous to those of an aircraft carrier. "The flight deck of an aircraft carrier," says Klein, "must be completely open and empty." These are precisely the requirements of lab space in a science building. If space is to be fully available for any kind of use, it must be open and uninterrupted. Partitions that may be removed and used elsewhere can serve as dividers.

ENVIRONMENTAL DESIGN

To a greater extent than perhaps any other type of institution, colleges and universities need to create environments suitable to living and work. The largely indoor pursuit of teaching and learning requires that the character of instructional space—its shape, climate, lighting, color, acoustics, and seating—be conducive to the highest levels of communication and mental productivity. In addition to a healthy atmosphere, interior spaces should also provide both flexibility and versatility.

Lighting and Color

The goal of room lighting is simply to allow occupants to see effectively without undue distraction. The level of illumination must be adequate to permit all concerned to perform efficiently essential visual tasks. The overall quality of lighting should help create a comfortable and pleasing environment.

For the planning generalist interested in good lighting who wishes to avoid the specialized theories of lighting and psychophysics, the following principles convey in layman's terms the basic thesis upon which good lighting is based:

—We see better the more light we have, up to a point, but this light must be free from glare.

—We see better if the main visual task is distinguished from its surroundings by being brighter, or more contrasting, or more colorful, or all three. It is therefore important to identify the main focal points and build up the lighting from their requirements.

—We see better if the things we have to look at are seen in an unobtrusive and unconfusing setting, neither so bright nor so colorful that it attracts the attention away, nor so dark that work appears excessively bright with the result that the eyes are riveted on the visual task. Good lighting therefore provides a moderate and comfortable level of general lighting, with preferential lighting on the work. This can be called *focal lighting*.

—The surroundings should be moderately bright, and this should be achieved by combination of lighting and decoration.

—No source of light should be a source of glare discomfort. Excessively bright areas should never be visible. Windows should be provided with curtains, blinds or louvres to be brought into use when the sky is very bright.

—Plenty of light should reach the ceiling, in order to dispel any feeling of gloom, and to reduce glare.

—Sources of light should be chosen to ensure that the color rendering which they give is satisfactory for the situation in which they will be found.

—Care should be taken to eliminate any discomfort from flickering light sources.

—A dull uniformity should at all costs be avoided. Small brilliant points of light can give sparkle to a scene without causing glare.

—The lighting of a building should be considered always in relation to its design and in particular to the scheme of decoration to be installed. On no account should lighting be considered to be merely a matter of windows or fittings. The whole environment enters into a good lighting installation.[23]

While there must be adequate interior light for clear vision, color and brightness of the surroundings are largely responsible for beauty of appearance and a feeling of comfort. Color is not simply a matter of personal preference but relates to function. If color distracts rather than aids vision, if it causes undue eye strain, impairs human performance, or otherwise impedes the efficient conduct of work, it should not be used.

The proper scientific control of color, while not governed by academic rules, is subject to the following principles:[24]

—Excessive contrast in the field of view is inimical to good, comfortable vision and should be avoided.

—Where the field of view is varied in color and brightness, within moderate limits, vision is at its best.

—Brightness and warmth of color (red), which has a centrifugal effect, tends to draw attention to the environment and to stimulate muscular reaction. Since all sensations are enjoyed best in moderation, color should seldom be brilliant or severe. Where it is, the environment becomes too dominating.

—Softness and coolness of color (green, blue) has a centripetal effect, removes outside distraction, and is conducive to mental concentration.

—When a task requires chief attention to the environment, high levels of illumination and brightness in the surrounding area will condition the human organism accordingly. The attention and interest of the room occupant will be *outward*.

—When a task requires concentrated visual and mental attention at fixed points, more subdued brightness in the surrounding area may accomplish the best results. If critical seeing tasks are performed, supplementary localized illumination may be

---

[23] R. G. Hopkinson, *Architectural Physics: Lighting*, Her Majesty's Stationery Office, London, England, 1963, p. 125.

[24] Assembled from Faber Birren, *Color for Interiors: Historical and Modern*, Whitney Library of Design, New York, n.d.

added. In such a setting, attention and interest will be away from the environment and to the job at hand, and man's body and eyes will be psychologically and optically well adjusted.

—Brightness and color are closely related. Writing surfaces should not be glossy white (producing glare) or too dark (contrasting with writing paper). Light matte surfaces with reflection in the 50–60 percent range are best.

—Light and color are interrelated. The color tint of a light source must shift from warm to cool with increased intensity if a pleasant or natural appearance for surface color in the field of view is to be assured. The colors of an environment will appear normal (1) when the tint of the light source is warm at low levels, (2) yellowish at slightly higher levels, and (3) white or bluish at high levels.

—In very dim light the true values of dark colors will be lost more or less completely. If the environment is designed for soft light there is little sense in using dark colors. Dark colors, in fact, may "fall apart" and grow muddy. It is wholly incongruous to pick colors in bright light and expect them to appear the same under dim light. The color white is an exception. As long as the eye is able to see, a white surface will always appear white—from a fraction of a footcandle to high into the hundreds of footcandles.

—In purely casual or recreational areas, almost anything in the way of color in the surrounding area may be tried.

Interior Climate

It is generally recognized that high temperatures and humidity produce physiological and psychological stress that accelerates fatigue, causes people to work more slowly, exert greater effort, and make more mistakes. The classroom climate in particular should be carefully controlled not only to provide physical comfort but also to serve as a positive factor in the learning process by engendering alertness and attention. To maintain such a climate, the air must be treated to simultaneously controlled temperature, humidity, cleanliness, and circulation.

A person is thermally comfortable when there is no strain on the body to reduce or increase heat loss. Since the level of physical activity determines the rate of heat generation within the body, it is a major factor in determining comfort levels. The body attempts to maintain a constant temperature; in so doing it must dispose of heat primarily through convection losses to the surrounding air, through heat and water vapor added to air involved in respiration, and through evaporation of perspiration from the skin. Three factors influence body heat loss: air temperature, relative humidity, and air motion. Under conditions of high temperature, high humidity, and low air flow, the body becomes overheated, and in its attempt to induce evaporation by pouring out perspiration, discomfort ensues. Body adjustments leading to thermal discomfort are unnecessary when the air temperature is lower than that of either the skin or clothing-surface temperature, and the moisture content and circulation of air permit evaporative and convective heat losses.

A varied range of air temperature, relative humidity, and air motion can produce comfort conditions. Experiments with a large number of people have demonstrated that within a relative humidity range of 30 to 70 percent and an air movement of 15 to 25 feet per minute, the winter comfort zone temperature range is from 63 to 71 degrees, with 97 percent of those participating feeling comfortable at 66 degrees. The summer comfort zone ranges from 66 to 75 degrees, with 98 percent feeling comfortable at 71 degrees. To insure the maintenance of these comfort conditions in large, fully occupied, well-lighted classrooms, the air must be sufficiently cooled and dehumidified to offset the high latent heat produced by both the people and the lights.

Whenever large numbers of people are assembled in an enclosed space for appreciable periods of time, sufficient fresh air and its proper distribution are a primary problem. The chief purpose of ventilation is to disperse body odors by replacing stale air with fresh, either by bringing it in from the outside or by recirculating it. Seating area ventilation requirements are usually set by codes that call for 10 to 15 cubic feet of fresh air per minute per person as a minimum in a large space. Sufficient movement of fresh air is essential to assist in the evaporation of skin moisture. To circulate air without producing drafts, it is advisable to introduce cool fresh air at or near the ceiling and exhaust it at lower levels.

Acoustics[25]

Good acoustics are critical to all teaching-learning situations that by nature produce noise and by necessity require quiet. Even more than lighting, good acoustics result from basic design decisions made very early in the planning process; "tacking up" acoustical materials after the fact is rarely if ever satisfactory.

Architectural acoustics are basically concerned with two objectives: (1) providing good hearing conditions within a given space by controlling the direction, impact, and duration of sound waves, and (2) providing a satisfactory acoustical environment by creating barriers against unwanted sounds originating outside the space. Any noise which does intrude should be of a general character, unintelligible, and without easily identifiable components.

The first objective is chiefly concerned with *absorption and reflection* of sound waves within the space itself; the second, with *isolation* of sound by preventing its transmission through materials or open spaces. Accomplish-

---

[25] The major content of this section has been condensed and adapted from Center for Architectural Research, School of Architecture, Rensselaer Polytechnic Institute, *New Spaces for Learning: Designing College Facilities To Utilize Instructional Aids and Media* (revised), Troy, N.Y., 1966, pp. 61–64.

ing these objectives depends not only on room shape but also on the choice and judicious use of acoustical materials. Both are important in the design of learning spaces.

Sound absorption and reflection. The quality of hearing as applied to sounds originating within the room itself is governed by the size and shape of the room, the location and volume of the sound, and the reflection characteristics of materials in the room. Reflection, in turn, depends on the ability of materials to absorb sound energy. Hard, dense materials absorb very little sound; rather, they reflect nearly all the sound waves that strike them. Soft, porous materials, on the other hand, absorb a high proportion and reflect little.

In designing rooms for good hearing, the objective is to so disperse the reflective and absorptive materials within the room that all occupants will receive as nearly as possible an agreeable volume of sound. The most important single factor is the control of reverberation (sound persistence after cessation of the original source). In "live" classrooms, where sounds reverberate, speech is often difficult to understand because listeners experience difficulty in separating syllables. Further, if room noise is high, more effort is necessary to project speech. Reverberation within a room can be controlled by the amount and placement of absorptive material within it. To effect proper sound absorption and reflection, the following design principles should be observed:

—To amplify and disperse the original sound, surfaces relatively close to the sound source should be reflective.

—To minimize the rebound of sound energy that causes delayed repetition, surfaces behind the audience and facing the sound source should be absorptive.

— In order to increase the amount of beneficially reflected sound, ceiling surfaces should be flat and of hard reflective materials. Since a reflective ceiling facilitates the flow of sound from a speaker located anywhere on the floor to all persons within the room, its use is recommended for discussion areas. Curved ceiling surfaces should be avoided because they focus rather than disperse sound.

—Nonparallel walls, converging in the direction of the sound source, are preferable to parallel walls. They improve sound dispersion and tend to reduce the length of the reverberation period.

—Reflecting surfaces, whether on walls or ceilings, should be large, not small flat planes. The minimum width recommended is from 3 to 4 feet, with 10 feet or more preferred. Because small surfaces absorb only sound waves of high frequency (and short wave length), they cause sound distortion; conversely, large surfaces absorb sounds of all common frequencies and wave lengths.

—An acoustically absorptive floor covering reduces within-room noise, thereby contributing added sound absorption.

Sound isolation. Although isolation problems stem mainly from construction of walls, floors, and ceilings *between* spaces, they may also result from the equipment in a room. It is in partitions in particular that the lack of adequate isolation is generally most evident, and current interest in light-weight, flexible partitions has highlighted this fact.

Any openings in an intended sound barrier constitute *leaks*—leaks that have the same significance as those which occur in waterproofing. An effective barrier to sound transmission must be airtight. All sound energy that strikes a void, however small, penetrates that void. A 1-inch-square hole will leak as much sound as a 100 square foot wall with a 40 decibel transmission-loss rating.

In unoccupied classrooms the acceptable noise level is about 40 decibels for ordinary lecture rooms and as low as 35 decibels for language, music, and other rooms in which a quiet environment is especially desirable. The noise-insulation factor needed to insure these degrees of quietness will depend on the location of each room within the building and on the magnitude and nature of the noise in the immediate vicinity, both within and outside the building. An important consideration in acoustical isolation is the level of background noise within learning spaces. A high level of continuous background noise, such as may be present in city offices, serves to mask many of the minor acoustical intrusions which, in quieter surroundings, might be intolerable. Since the normal level of background noise in learning spaces is generally low, it may be advisable to introduce background noise through a mechanical system.

The basic rules of sound isolation are simple:[26]

—Separate noise sources from areas requiring quiet by the greatest practical distance.

—Plan buildings or rooms not particularly susceptible to noise to serve as screens or baffles for noise sources.

—Locate rooms from which noise may originate on any part of the site where there is likely to be noise from other (exterior) sources; conversely, locate rooms which must be quiet in a quiet part of the building.

—If possible, locate machinery and any other noise sources that radiate sound within a building in the basement. Since structural materials are likely to be heavier and therefore more sound-insulating at this level, vibrations will be absorbed by the earth on which the building stands.

—Remember that an open window or a flimsy door in a heavy and otherwise highly sound-insulating wall will reduce the overall insulation.

Seating

A student in the classroom is properly seated if he has a clear view of the instructor, is provided with a suitable writing surface and a place for book storage, is reasonably comfortable, and is so situated that persons going to

[26] P. H. Parkins and H. R. Humphreys, *Acoustics Noise and Buildings*, Praeger Publishers Inc., New York, 1958, pp. 190–91.

and from adjacent seats will not disturb him. A number of other criteria are involved, including esthetic and economic considerations, but these functional aspects are the most important.

Guided by functional criteria and also by such aspects as mechanical simplicity, ease of cleaning, and economy of space, the architectural research staff of the School of Architecture, Rensselaer Polytechnic Institute, has devised a method for rating generic seating types.[27] The highest score is accorded a combination consisting of a continuous writing counter and movable chairs. Next in value and closely rated are the two-man counter unit with adjustable pivotal seats, the continuous counter with fixed pivotal seats, and the fixed seat with movable tablet area. At the time of the study (1964), available designs for the fixed seat with movable tablet arm failed to meet Rensselaer's standard for adequate writing space (approximately 12 inches deep by 24 inches wide). In the interim several new, improved designs have been placed in production, all of which have been approved. A chart showing different types of fixed seating, together with writing surface areas and required floor space, is shown in figure XI-5.

In designing seating arrangements and corresponding room layouts, particularly in areas involving audiovisual equipment, good vision and hearing are primary objectives. The four major viewing factors to be taken into account are as follows:[28]

1. If distortion is to be avoided, the viewing angle of the image surface should not be greater than 50 degrees from perpendicular (for particular combinations of screens, projectors, and lenses, it may be necessary to reduce the angle). This maximum viewing angle determines the effective left-right width of seating. By tilting the center of viewing surface slightly away from the audience (see figure XI-6), the front-row seating width may be substantially increased.

2. The minimum viewing distance depends on image size. Instructors using a blackboard generally prefer to be separated from the class by at least 8 feet. Films, slides, and TV projected on a screen should not be viewed from a distance closer than twice the width of the screen. TV receivers should not be viewed closer than four times the screen width.

3. The distance at which an image can be clearly seen determines maximum viewing distance. At 8 feet, the minimum symbol height normally readable is $\frac{1}{4}$ inch; at 16 feet, $\frac{1}{2}$ inch; at 32 feet, 1 inch; the larger the symbol height, the greater the distance can be. The maximum viewing distance for films, slides, and projected TV is 6 to 10 times the image width; for TV receivers, 12 times image width; and for overhead projectors, 3 to 6 times image width.

4. The vertical viewing angle (the horizontal angle at the viewer's eye level to the top of the image surface) should not exceed 30 degrees.

A fan-shaped classroom provides optimum viewing conditions. A care-

---

[27] Architectural Research Staff of the School of Architecture, Rensselaer Polytechnic Institute, *Design Criteria For Learning Spaces*, Troy, N.Y., n.d., pp. 18–23.

[28] Center for Architectural Research, op. cit., pp. 41–42.

Figure XI-5. — Seating types

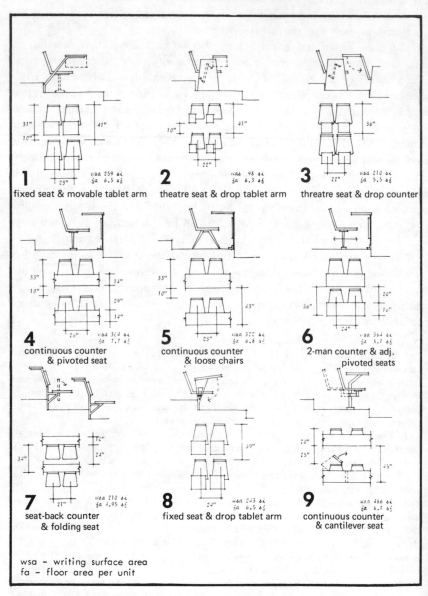

1   fixed seat & movable tablet arm

2   theatre seat & drop tablet arm

3   threatre seat & drop counter

4   continuous counter
    & pivoted seat

5   continuous counter
    & loose chairs

6   2-man counter & adj.
    pivoted seats

7   seat-back counter
    & folding seat

8   fixed seat & drop tablet arm

9   continuous counter
    & cantilever seat

wsa - writing surface area
fa - floor area per unit

Source: Center for Architectural Research, School of Architecture,
          Rensselaer Polytechnic Institute, New Spaces for Learning:
          Designing College Facilities to Utilize Instructional Aids and
          Media (revised), Troy, N.Y., 1966, p. 73.

Figure XI-6. — The fan-shaped classroom

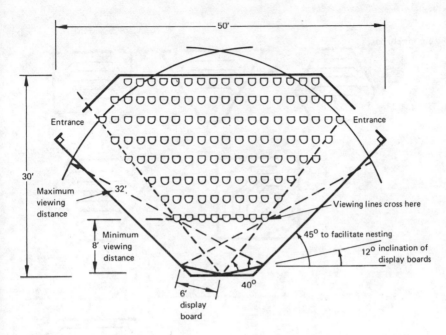

Seating capacity: 120*.
Room area: 1,000 sq. ft.
Net assignable sq. ft. per station: 8.3
*Local building codes stipulate the
number of seats permitted per row
between aisles.

Based on design studies by the Center for Architectural Research, School of Architecture,
Rensselaer Polytechnic Institute, Troy, N.Y.

fully designed hexagon or fan-shaped room, as shown in figure XI-6, offers
the following advantages:

—It virtually eliminates angular distortion and provides both minimum and
maximum viewing distances. To improve viewing further, particularly in very
large rooms, it is feasible to introduce seating at different levels and offset seating.

—The shape tends to focus student attention on the front where instruction and
visual presentations take place.

—Nonparallel walls improve the acoustics.

—Access is provided at the rear; circulation paths are minimal but adequate.

—Station area is adequate; wasted space minimal.

—The 45-degree walls facilitate clustering or nesting.

The foregoing precepts become more critical as room capacity increases.

In addition to the advantages already mentioned, fan-shaped rooms

Figure XI-7 — Room shapes and arrangements

Room Shapes:

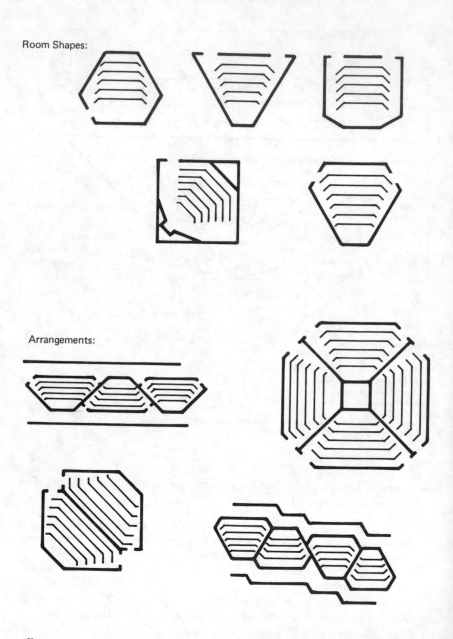

Arrangements:

offer many opportunities for creative internal configurations and may suggest some interesting overall building layouts. The odd-shaped left-over spaces can prove useful for storage, display preparation, etc. Some of the possible room shapes and arrangements are schematically illustrated in figure XI-7.

Figure XI-7. — Room shapes and arrangements — **continued**

Arrangements:

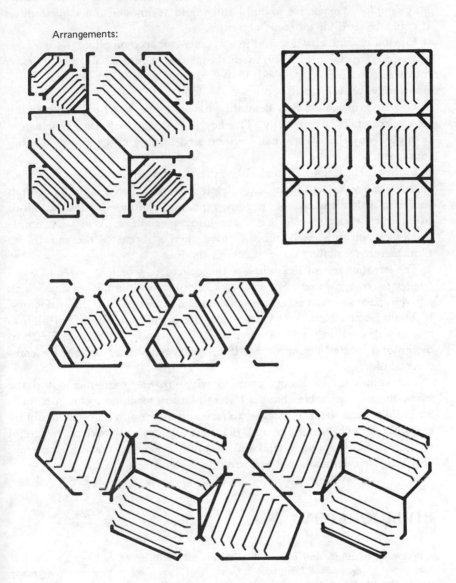

Flexibility

The dictionary defines flexibility as "capable of conforming to changing or new situations." As applied to the design of educational facilities, however, the meaning is broader in scope. Flexibility can, in fact, mean a wide variety of things.

Obviously it denotes *variable functionalism*. A laboratory equally suitable to chemistry, biology, or physics is flexible. Flexibility is particularly desirable when the space involved—a laboratory, auditorium, or fieldhouse, for example—is expensive to build and would at times be unoccupied unless it could be used for different activities.

Flexibility can also mean the capacity to accommodate *variations in class size*. To divide and subdivide large rooms into small ones quickly, movable curtains may be used; if speedy conversion is not essential, partitions may be relocated.

For the growing college, flexibility means *expansibility*: enlarging buildings horizontally or vertically. The key is to design the original structure in such a way that its size can be increased in a natural manner at minimum cost.

Many teachers think of flexibility in terms of possible *variations in teaching materials and techniques*. Such flexibility is exemplified in a communications center in which it is possible to film, tape, and computerize instruction or to conduct a variety of other programing specialities. At a very simple level, flexibility means being able to darken a room for the showing of films merely by pulling down blackout shades.

The greatest test of flexibility is the degree to which it *provides for unforeseen future developments*. For example, should the situation arise in which a given space as designed or constructed is not needed or is unsatisfactory, it should be possible to convert or renovate it, easily and economically, to suit any desired use. And in an urban setting it should be possible to so design and locate buildings that, if necessary, they may be sold for commercial use.

The knowledge explosion, coupled with growing enrollments and the sweeping, unpredictable changes taking place in teaching techniques, calls for buildings that lend themselves to new and different uses. Such flexibility can only be achieved by sound planning—planning based on a careful study of the past, present, and future—and by designs that will meet not only expected demands but also unforeseen needs.

BIBLIOGRAPHY

Berlowitz, Manfred, and Eugene E. Drucker and William H. Scarbrough, *Thermal Environment of Educational Facilities: A Guide for Planners and Administrators*, Syracuse University Research Institute, School of Architecture, Syracuse, N.Y., 1969, 110 pp.

The authors present, in a concise, condensed form, information concerning the need for and techniques of good thermal environmental design. Chapter I on fundamentals defines and describes the thermal environment, its elements, and the factors that influence it. A review of some research studies appears in chapter II, also some conclusions based on the effects of thermal environment on comfort, human performance, and academic achievement. Chapter III provides realistic, up-to-date school design criteria for temperature, humidity, etc. The inherent characteristics of each of the school "plan types" is generally related to the thermal systems in chapter IV. Chapters V and VI provide the basis for understanding and evaluating various thermal systems and fuels; brief mention is made of several relatively new and important concepts. An index and bibliography are included.

Birren, Faber, *Color for Interiors—Historical and Modern*, Whitney Library of Design, New York, n.d., 210 pp.
Of greatest interest to facility planners is the author's explanation of functional uses of color in modern interiors and the reasons certain colors should or should not be used for certain specific purposes. Many subtle taboos normally not recognized, as well as positive facts about the relation of color to the human body and to the psyche, are presented. Color charts classified by historical periods contain 238 paint samples.

Canby, Donald, *Your Building and Your Architect*, The American Institute of Architects, New York, n.d., 16 pp.
This brief work delineates an informed architectural critic's candid view of how the interests of both the prospective building owner and the professional architect can best be served. A wealth of experience is summarized in Canby's answers to such questions as how to pick an architect, what architects do and the fees they charge, how to turn a problem into a set of plans, how to proceed from concept to construction, and how to transform a set of drawings into a building.

Center for Architectural Research, School of Architecture, Rensselaer Polytechnic Institute, *Educational Facilities with New Media*, National Education Association, Washington, D.C. 1966, 230 pp.
Three reports directed toward one objective: "optimizing the conditions for learning by providing the environments most conducive to learning when learning media are employed in the educational process." Report A, "A Guide for Policy Makers," discusses the role of learning media, its status and trends, its implications for planning, and the programing process which translates educational needs into a definition of a building. Report B, "A Guide for the Design Professions," written especially for architects, planners, and design specialists, as well as planning committees, presents design criteria for various types of learning spaces. Report C, "A Technical Guide," concerned with details of design relating to acoustics, climate, furniture, projection equipment, controls, etc., is intended for architects, engineers, equipment and furniture suppliers, and instructional media specialists.

Center for Architectural Research, School of Architecture, Rensselaer Polytechnic Institute, *Modular Coordination and School Design*, Troy, N.Y., 1967, 102 pp.
This report investigates the potential importance of modular planning and coordination in school design. Modular design is defined as "orderly planning, so arranged as to make logical and extensive use of a repetitive module or dimension of at least a foot or more." The study objectives are to determine the current status of modular coordination as an influence in building design; to investigate current attitudes on the part of the building fraternity with respect to the modular concept; to evaluate, in general terms, its significance and merits; and to assess its implications particularly in reference to the design of school buildings. For the nonarchitect, this study explains clearly the merits, problems, and status of modular coordination and summarizes effectively the current "state of the art."

Center for Architectural Research, School of Architecture, Rensselaer Polytechnic Institute, *New Spaces for Learning: Designing College Facilities to Utilize Instructional Aids and Media* (revised), Troy, N.Y., 1971, 137 pp.

The purpose of this report is to "assist in developing optimum environments by defining the design criteria which will provide an atmosphere most conducive to learning." Attention is focused principally on new concepts of space types and their design for the efficient and effective use of new instructional aids and learning media appropriate to large group instruction. Programing and flexibility in planning are discussed along with design factors for lighting, display systems, acoustics, climate, and seating. In addition to informative design technology, the volume presents 12 design studies, a case study, and a useful discussion of a new building type—the communications center. The excellence and importance of this report, first published in 1961, is suggested by the fact it has been revised (1966) and is now in its third printing.

Clearinghouse on Educational Facilities, Educational Resources Information Center (ERIC), the University of Wisconsin, Madison.

"A clearinghouse of information about sites, buildings, and equipment used for educational purposes; included are the efficiency and effectiveness of relative activities such as the planning, financing, constructing, renovating, maintaining, operating, insuring, utilizing and evaluating of educational facilities." Abstracts of subject-area information are published monthly in *Research in Education* (RIE). Publications are mainly bibliographies, annotated reference lists, and state-of-the-art papers. The ERIC Document Reproduction Service (EDRS) sells reports cited in RIE in either microfiche or facsimile form. The current EDRS contractor is the National Cash Register Co., 4936 Fairmont Ave., Bethesda, Md. 20014.

Community College Planning Center on Community College Facilities, *Planners and Planning*, Stanford, Calif., 1966, 64 pp.

This booklet offers community college planners practical and procedural suggestions and guidelines for designing and constructing a physical plant that meets the complex functional demands required of a community junior college. A desirable approach to planning, including the role of various participants, is suggested; also, recommendations on how to prepare the master plan and related documents. Chapter III includes a wealth of ideas and guides to help solve specific problems that have been faced by others.

Dober, Richard P., *Campus Planning*, Reinhold Publishing Corp., New York, 1963 314 pp.

The author states that the objective of this book is "to suggest ways and means by which the development of campuses can be controlled so that functional goals can be aesthetically expressed with the least compromise to the past, the present and the future." The material is organized into three sections. The first defines and fully describes campus planning and the evolution of the campus as a design form. Section two describes each of the constituent physical parts of the campus in functional and esthetic terms. Section three, which presents the steps and procedures necessary for preparing campus plans, contains extensive illustrations of how old campuses can be expanded and new ones developed. The photographs of good architecture, the historical prospectus, and the full spectrum of case examples help make this volume of unusual interest and value.

Dober, Richard P., *The New Campus in Britain: Ideas of Consequence for the United States*, Educational Facilities Laboratories, Inc., New York, 1965, 71 pp.

The author, well known for his book, *Campus Planning*, examines current physical developments in Great Britain to discover ideas and approaches pertinent to the American scene. The report begins with a discussion of four different housing patterns.

Examples of how Britain has intelligently exploited the urban environment point the way to design which might well be considered in similar circumstances in the United States. The author believes that Britain's major contribution to university development is the continuous teaching environment which is ". . . a physical form that preserves communication and contact between all parts of the institution while allowing external accretion and internal change." Other topics discussed include the use of a flexible prefabricated system of college construction; the preservation of amenity in recent designs through ". . . a genuine regard for scale, materials, and site planning," and the "omniflexibility myth." Illustrated case studies on eight campuses comprise the final section.

Educational Facilities Laboratories, Inc., *Bricks and Mortarboards—A Report on College Planning and Building*, New York, 1966, 168 pp.

In this volume is a collection of five articles by professional writers who bring together the best available information on what is happening in the four major types of campus buildings—the classroom, the laboratory, the library, and the dormitory—and in campus design itself. The writers toured the United States to talk with educators, planners, architects, and other professionals. Their findings offer rare insight into the ways in which college buildings are being designed to accommodate the new procedures and technology reshaping the academic process.

Educational Facilities Laboratories, Inc., Duke University, and Caudill Rowlett Scott, *Information Needs: For Planning Physical Facilities in Colleges and Universities* (4 vols.), New York, 1969.

The broad purpose of this series of four volumes is to describe techniques that will assist institutions of higher education in dealing with the problems of physical facilities planning. The first volume, devoted to an overview of information needs, suggests an approach to the collection of appropriate activity and facility information. The second volume provides guidance for establishing a room-inventory system for use in reporting to outside agencies and internal management. The third volume discusses the structure of a computer-based mathematical model that could be used to simulate an institution's use of physical facilities. The fourth volume contains a description of a measurement system that can gauge the level of space-demanding activities and a list of guidelines that can be employed to ascertain the requisite detailed information for assessing activity levels.

Fitzroy, Dariel, and John Lyon Reid, *Acoustical Environment of School Buildings*, Educational Facilities Laboratories, Inc., New York, 1963, 128 pp.

The trend toward more open interior spaces in recently constructed school buildings has suggested the need to determine the minimum acoustical separation necessary to allow a group or an individual to work effectively. While that determination served as the starting point for this investigation, field measurement and study have been directed toward identifying *all* criteria for the design of the acoustical environment in the classroom. The "Analysis and Conclusions" section, a complete and informative discussion of classroom acoustics, presents both basic theory and experimental data that enable educators, architects, and planners to become more conversant with the acoustical problems of the learning environment.

Haviland, David S., and William F. Winslow, *Designing for Educational Technology—A Guide to the Available Resources*, Center for Architectural Research, School of Architecture, Rensselaer Polytechnic Institute, Troy, N.Y., 1971, 14 pp.

This reprint from the *AIA Journal* is a resource document designed to guide the architect through available reference material on planning and designing for educational technology. The planning, programing, schematics, and design development of instructional media are discussed for various types of space—large, small, and medium-group, independent study, special-purpose, flexible and open-plan, and resource. A 79-entry bibliography includes a directory of sources.

Hopkinson, R. G., *Architectural Physics: Lighting*, Her Majesty's Stationery Office, London, 1963, 360 pp.

In this source book on lighting the author discusses those principles pertinent to the needs of the human being in his environment. The first part of the book gives a general account of the technical basis for lighting design. Chapters deal with psychophysics, vision and buildings, calculations of daylight and artificial lighting quantity, glare and visual discomfort, supplementary lighting, and reflectance and color. The second part of the book—the collected papers—describes the contribution of the Building Research Station "school" to the development of a scientific basis for essentially subjective aspects of lighting technology in buildings.

McCormick, E. J., *Human Factors Engineering*, McGraw-Hill Book Co., New York, 1964, 653 pp.

A survey book, this volume deals with the task of "designing things so people can use them effectively and creating environments that are suitable for human living and work." Part IV, entitled "Space and Arrangement," guides the educational facility planner seeking information on work space and seating design, also on the proper arrangement of displays, controls, and other elements within work-space layouts.

McGuffey, Carroll W., *Selected References for Planning Higher Education Facilities*, Council of Educational Facility Planners, Columbus, Ohio, 1968, 95 pp.

Careful annotation of nearly 200 selected references makes this bibliography particularly valuable. Entries are organized into five major categories and subdivisions: I. Orientation to Educational Facility Planning. II. Developing a Master Plan for Plant Expansion—long-range planning for facilities development, population projections, utilization of existing facilities, estimating space needs, selecting and planning educational facility sites. III. Planning the Individual School—educational specifications, the planning of individual buildings. IV. Planning the Technical Aspects. V. Administering the Plant Expansion Program—planning, financing, cost and economics. While not intended as a complete survey of current literature, this compilation is probably as extensive as any presently available.

Metcalf, Keys D., *Planning Academic and Research Library Buildings*, McGraw-Hill Book Co., New York, 1965, 431 pp.

Considered the major reference work in library planning, this comprehensive manual deals with problems directly or indirectly connected with the planning and construction of academic and research libraries. The detailed treatment given to library planning is indicated by the following partial chapter listing: library objectives and their relation to aesthetic problems, quality of construction, function, and cost; financial matters; the modular system; problems relating to height; traffic problems; accommodations for readers and staff; housing the collections; lighting and ventilation; planning preliminaries, first steps, and the final plan; the program for assignable space requirements. Appendixes are devoted to formulas and tables, a selective annotated bibliography, and a glossary.

Parkins, P. H., and H. R. Humphreys, *Acoustics, Noise and Buildings*, Frederick A. Praeger, New York, 1958, 331 pp.

A complete and comprehensive guidebook to the technical problems of acoustics, this work includes material on the nature of sound, the behavior of sound in rooms, the design of rooms for speech, general principles of sound insulation and noise control, and much more. Over 100 diagrams, charts, and illustrations supplement the text. The two authors, one a scientist and the other an architect, have combined scientific theory and practical design in a thoroughly practical reference.

Pinnell, Charles, and Michael Wacholder, *Guidelines for Planning in College and Universities* (6 vols.), Coordinating Board, Texas College and University System, Austin, 1968.

The authors employ the latest techniques of scientific management to develop a total system concept of institutional planning as well as logical systematic procedures for a continuing planning process. The planning effort is divided into three major phases: management and program planning, physical plant planning, and financial planning. The first volume is entitled "The Planning System"; additional volumes, "Planning Techniques." The latter deal with management and financial planning and three areas of physical plant planning—land use and traffic, facilities studies, and utility studies. A sixth volume, developed by the architectural firm of Caudill, Rowlett and Scott in Houston, provides guidelines for the implementation of building programs.

Rice University Department of Architecture, *10 Designs: Community Colleges*, Houston, Tex., 1962, 100 pp.

This unusual and stimulating book delineates the remarkable accomplishment of creating exciting and worthwhile community college designs in a 10-day Design Fete at Rice University. Ten talented architects and teams of five students each were assigned the task of finding architectural solutions for 10 hypothetical, but typical, community college locations. Their proposals are presented in drawings, plans, sketches, and models, augmented by calculations and graphs showing projected growth. The solutions and new concepts should generate real excitement and enthusiasm among architects and educators who are seeking inspiration and encouragement in planning future community colleges.

Riker, Harold C., with Frank G. Lopez, *College Students Live Here: A Study of College Housing*, Educational Facilities Laboratories, Inc., New York, 1961, 152 pp.

Topics covered in this comprehensive study of college housing include the kinds of people to be housed and their needs, different kinds of housing and their characteristics, specific spaces and equipment that enable housing units to function effectively, how housing should be planned and by whom, and the financing of a housing program. Extensive use is made of designs and pictures to illustrate points developed in the text. A final section includes a portfolio of recent college housing projects that have been reasonably successful in overcoming specific problems.

Rork, John, and Leslie Robbins, compilers, *Casebook on Campus Planning and Institutional Development*. U.S. Department of Health, Education, and Welfare, Office of Education, U.S. Government Printing Office, Washington, D.C., 1962, 162 pp.

A comprehensive and factual account of the steps taken and the obstacles faced by 10 institutions planning for campus growth. Specific cases deal with founding an institution at a new location in completely new buildings, relocating an existing institution, and planning institutional expansion on a permanent campus site. The personal backgrounds of the authors account for the different points of view expressed.

Society for College and University Planning and Educational Facilities Laboratories, *Planning for Higher Education* (newsletter), New York.

This newsletter, currently published six times a year, includes two to five articles per issue on a variety of information concerning all aspects of higher education planning. Some recent topics dealing with campus and building planning are entitled "Campus Form and Community Tension." "The 'Temporary' Facilities Syndrome," "Stockton: Campus Planning by Increments," "Professional Self-Concept and Campus Planning," and "Educational Innovation and Space Management."

State University Construction Fund, *A Guide for Campus Planning*, Albany, N.Y., 1967, 40 pp.

Based on experience gained in planning 21 campuses for the State University of New York, this guide presents an orderly procedure for the development of comprehensive long-range physical campus plans. The procedure is outlined in detail and each component is illustrated by some type of graphic presentation as well as by examples of the type of information to be included. It is the opinion of this reviewer that *A Guide for Campus Planning* contains the most complete and carefully structured procedure currently published.

U.S. Department of Health, Education, and Welfare, Office of Education, *1966, Design Award Program*, U.S. Government Printing Office Washington, D.C., 1966, 79 pp.

This publication discusses distinguished college facilities that ". . . reflect careful analysis of the needs of a modern educational program, the changing nature of those needs, and designs that both meet today's requirements and are adaptable to unknown future requirements." Included are 29 award winners (out of 258 entries) in five categories: general classroom buildings; science and laboratory buildings; libraries; graduate schools, including schools of architecture, law, fine arts, etc.; and long-range campus development plans. Each award entry, illustrated by photographs, plans, or models, is described by the architect. Comments by the head of the award-winning institution and the jury are also included. This reference work is one of the few available for planners seeking examples of acknowledged excellence in college facilities design.

University Facilities Research Center, *Monograph Series:* "Plumbing Fixture Requirements in University Instructional and Research Buildings," "Horizontal and Vertical Circulation in University Instructional and Research Buildings," "Parking Programs for Universities," "Space for Audio-Visual Large Group Instruction," "University Research Buildings for Short-Term Grant Programs," "High-Rise or Low-Rise? A Study of Decision Factors for Residence Hall Planning," and "Central Food Stores Facilities," Madison, Wisconsin, 1960–61.

The seven pamphlets are concerned with basic design questions. Findings are organized to aid in the planning and designing of future college and university facilities. Among the objectives of the Research Center is "the isolation of planning and design criteria problems, followed by the finding or developing of measures for design—all to the end of permitting the best possible use of the university and college construction dollar." This series of reports is of particular value because of the attention focused on individual aspects of design and on execution of new facilities. The result is that solutions rather than generalized approaches are offered.

Chapter XII

FINANCING HIGHER EDUCATION—
STATUS AND ISSUES

The considerable attention currently being paid to the financial plight of colleges and universities suggests the urgency of the present situation. While various aspects of the financial crisis affect the public and private sector and different types of institutions in different ways, the number of similarities is sufficient to warrant a general discussion of the most important aspects of higher education *financing*. The intent is to provide a fairly comprehensive *abstract* of those statistical facts and issues that are relevant to the financing of undergraduate education. (Not examined are the special problems of graduate education, research, and plant investment or such distinctive economic aspects of higher education as the rate of return on education, the redistribution of income, the distribution of educational capital, and details of specific solution proposals.)

Although it is not readily apparent, available literature suggests that there is a great deal of continuity to much of the analysis of higher education financing. To identify and establish this continuity, an effort has been made to establish a sound and consistent framework that includes the major findings and observations of many noted economists and financial experts.[1] This eclectic approach is intended to provide a reasonable comprehensive and balanced survey.

In this handbook the subject of financing higher education appears in two chapters. This one contains an overview of the current financial status of America's colleges and universities and the nature and causes of the financial difficulties, together with some possible remedies. Trends and projections for financing higher education at the national level are reviewed, and the distinctive income and expenditure patterns of universities, 4-year colleges, and 2-year colleges within the public and private sectors are examined. From this background, attention is shifted to the national objectives of higher education and the central issue of who should pay the costs. Chapter XIII provides a closer look at the response by and

---

[1] Among the experts whose works the author has found especially helpful are Roger E. Bolton, Howard R. Bowen, William G. Bowen, Roger A. Freeman, W. Lee Hansen, Seymour E. Harris, Selma J. Mushkin, Alice M. Rivlin, and Theodore W. Schultz.

capacity of government and institutions to alleviate the present financial stress.

INTRODUCTION

Four times as many dollars were spent for current operations in higher education in 1972–73 ($30.2 billion) as were spent a decade ago ($7.7 billion in 1962–63). This increase represents a growth rate of 14 percent a year or nearly double the 7 percent growth rate of the Nation's gross national product (GNP) during the same time period. Yet, despite this exceptional growth and the tremendous amount of money being expended, there is great concern for the financial well-being of colleges and universities.

Current Financial Difficulties

The Nation's commitment to universal higher education is proving to be an exceedingly expensive venture. Because of the changing age composition of the population and the expectation that more youths will attend college, higher education enrollments are growing faster than the economy in general. Thus for over a decade there has been a decline in the ratio of gross national product to total college enrollment. To maintain quality and program level in the face of this declining support capacity, it has been necessary and natural to allocate an increasing proportion of the Nation's wealth to higher education. Few will question the capacity of the economy to support higher education, but as a greater share of the wealth is required, the claim on resources is increasingly difficult to justify.

Although society is willing and able to devote a greater share of national resources to higher education, the commitment is proving to be a challenge because per student costs are rising. This increase in unit costs is basically the result of the fact that educational productivity has not kept pace with national economic growth. As the economy grows, teacher salaries must be raised, and, in the absence of improved efficiency in providing instruction, the inevitable result is a rise in the cost of education per student. Inflation, or the cost of money, has further increased costs. The combined result has been an estimated $5\frac{1}{2}$ percent yearly decrease in the true purchasing power of each dollar invested in higher education.[2] College and university budgets would have to be increased annually by this amount simply to offset rising prices.

---

[2] For an explanation of the annual $5\frac{1}{2}$ percent deflation factor, see appendix B Higher Education Price Indexes.

At the core, then, of the financial crisis facing higher education are (1) an enrollment growth that exceeds growth in national wealth, (2) rising unit costs that make education an ever more expensive operation, and (3) increasing competition for funds as higher education seeks a greater share.

How well has higher education fared financially in recent times? During the decade of the 1960's, there was a gigantic increase in absolute quantity while quality remained unchanged. Enrollment doubled and the capacity-burden ratio (i.e., the financial resources available relative to student enrollment load) declined from $164,608 of gross national product per full-time-equivalent student in 1960 to $143,789 in 1970. In addition, unit costs for instruction and related supporting activities increased 60 percent—twice the increase in the cost of living over the same time period as measured by the Consumer Price Index. Within this same 10-year period, the allocation of national wealth for student-related expenditures was doubled—from .695 percent of the GNP in 1960 to 1.425 percent in 1970. As a result, real unit investment in higher education grew modestly— from $1,465 per student in 1960 to $1,606 per student in 1970, or less than 1 percent yearly over the decade.[3]

During the late 1960's, as budgets continued to expand, college and university revenue sources simply could not provide the funds required. The three main reasons were that Federal and State Governments altered their priorities; stock market uncertainties discouraged individual dona-tions; and foundations transferred their attention from higher education to the problems of the cities and the environment. Institutions felt that if tuition were raised, educational aristocracies might result—student bodies comprised of the rich and/or those poor enough to merit grants.

There now exists in higher education what is popularly called a financial "depression." A growing number of institutions are reporting a financial situation that ranges from "stand-still" budgets to "hovering on the brink of financial disaster." For many, deficit spending has become the rule rather than the exception. A survey conducted during the summer of 1970 by William W. Jellema for the Association of American Colleges reveals that many institutions—both private and public—are in financial trouble. Extrapolating data from the 507 colleges surveyed, Jellema estimates that 365 of the 762 private 4-year accredited colleges have exhausted their liquid assets; moreover, if they continue current deficit operations, they will be forced to declare bankruptcy within 10 years. According to Jellema,

---

[3] In a study prepared for the Carnegie Commission on Higher Education, June O'Neill found that the investment in higher education per student credit hour in constant dollars did not change from the mid-1950's to the late 1960's. See June O'Neill, *Resource Use in Higher Education: Trends in Output and Inputs, 1930 to 1967*, Carnegie Commission on Higher Education, Berkeley, Calif., 1971.

"Behind these mounds of grotesque deficits lie the broken remains of curtailed operations, of abbreviated departments, of decimated academic programs, of faltering plans and languishing aspirations, of innovation untried and of creativity curbed."[4]

Nearly two-thirds of the public institutions responding to a survey by the National Association of State Universities and Land-Grant Colleges[5] reported "stand-still" budgets, or less, for 1971–72. Twenty-eight of the 55 respondents reported that State appropriations had been increased by less than 10 percent over the previous year, and nine institutions said their appropriations had actually declined since 1970–71. Because higher education costs are rising at an estimated 5 percent annually, unless State support matches this rate the financial position of public colleges and universities can only worsen.

Despite this real evidence of financial trouble in many colleges and universities, Alice Rivlin and others are of the opinion that no *general* crisis exists.[6] Rivlin does, however, point out that *some* institutions are suffering from cutbacks in Federal research programs or federally funded graduate programs. She also notes that some State-supported institutions are victims of smaller-than-usual increases in State appropriations, and that others, especially private colleges and universities, are overextended. Even more institutions are suffering from the combined effect of recession and inflation. Still, not all institutions are in financial difficulty; many are soundly financed and optimistic about the future. Furthermore, national higher education statistics reveal a pattern of financial stability with the possibility of slight gains in the future. Thus it appears that the financial problems facing higher education, while widespread, are particular rather than universal, prevalent in a majority of institutions, less prevalent in others, and nonexistent in a comparatively few.

According to Earl F. Cheit, an institution is judged *in financial difficulty* ". . . if its current financial condition results in a loss of services that are regarded as a part of its program *or* a loss of quality."[7] He found that the resources of almost three-fourths of the 41 schools he studied were inadequate or would soon be inadequate to support their defined mission at the stated academic quality level. It is certainly not difficult for an institution to find itself in this position. At many older institutions the increase in rank

---

[4] *The Chronicle of Higher Education*, vol. VI, no. 1, Sept. 27, 1971, p. 4.

[5] Office of Research, National Association of State Universities and Land-Grant Colleges, "For Your Information," Circular No. 169, Oct. 28, 1971.

[6] Testimony by Alice Rivlin of the Brookings Institution before the Special Education Subcommittee, Education and Labor Committee, U.S. House of Representatives, April 1971.

[7] Earl F. Cheit, *The New Depression in Higher Education*, Carnegie Commission on Higher Education, McGraw-Hill Book Co., New York, 1971, p. 36.

of faculty has resulted in higher salaries without any real change in program or outside salary competition.[8] Other institutions face rising costs for fixed commitments and unforeseen costs occasioned by earlier growth and expansion. Still others are under the financial stress imposed by expanded programs or by a commitment to programs they cannot cut back or terminate. Finally, many institutions cannot balance their budget because income sources have not been sufficiently responsive in supporting needed programs.[9]

In summary, the current situation in higher education financing is one of multiplicity and variance—in cause, consequence, and remedy. Institutions are being affected differently and are reacting differently. Governments, foundations, and corporate and private donors view their roles with little uniformity. Furthermore, the situation is continually changing. As with all phenomena, however, certain predominant threads are discernible. The problems, if not equally shared, are clearly definable. Their causes are evident, and there are multiple approaches to a solution.

Student Education Expenditures

Current operating expenses constitute the most serious worry for college administrators. Nonrecurring capital outlay for new building construction, while requiring some kind of extraordinary financing, does not, as a rule, pressure for balance between income and expenditure. Each year, however, colleges and universities must have enough current fund income to meet commitments for programs and services. Faculty and staff salaries and operating expenses related to instruction continue to be the largest items in college budgets, costing more than $14 billion a year. Not only is it difficult to raise funds for these expenditures, but Federal support is practically nonexistent.

The financial squeeze in higher education is a consequence of the continuing imbalance between *unrestricted* current income (generally unspecified as to use) that is available for educational purposes and outlays for instruction and related supporting activities. These outlays, or "student education expenditures," consist of the following current fund educational and general expenditure accounts: (1) instruction and departmental research, (2) extension and public service, (3) libraries, (4) physical plant operation and maintenance, and (5) administration and student services.

Most colleges and universities can clearly distinguish between student

---

[8] It should be noted that the opposite may be true at rapidly expanding institutions if the addition of mostly young faculty tends to lower the overall salary level.

[9] See Frederick E. Balderston, "Varieties of Financial Crisis" in *Universal Higher Education: Costs and Benefits*, American Council on Education, Washington, D.C., 1971, pp. 67–70.

education and supporting activities funded by unrestricted revenue and those service and commercial components of current operations purchased by individuals or for which payments are made by organizations through grants, contracts, or other means. To focus attention on basic higher education financial problems and to avoid distortion by including nonrelevant factors, the financing of all self-supporting services and commercial activities of colleges and universities, as well as student aid, have been *excluded* from this analysis.[10] Not included are sponsored research, separately budgeted programs such as workshops and college work-study programs, major public service programs such as federally funded R. & D. centers, hospitals, auxiliary enterprises, and sales and services of educational departments. The component of administration and physical plant operation related to the research function should technically also be excluded from the analysis. The reasons it is not are (1) the difficulty of estimating research "overhead" and (2) the relatively small amount involved (except for universities).

This approach to analyzing higher education financing results in the pairing of revenue and expenditures as follows:

Unrestricted* income from:	*Student education expenditures for:*
Student tuition and fees	Instruction and departmental research
Federal Government appropriations	Extension and public service
State & local govt. appropriations	Libraries
Endowment income	Physical plant operation and maintenance
Private gifts and grants	Administration and student services

* Includes some restricted income for student education expenditures—e.g., endowment income and gifts designated for particular professorships or academic departments.

Financial Problems, Causes, and Remedies—an Overview

Before proceeding with a detailed analysis of higher education financing, some key elements can be summarized: specifically, the problems, causes, and remedies.

---

[10] It should be pointed out that the so-called "self-supporting" services and commercial activities of colleges and universities are also in financial difficulty. When a service no longer pays for itself, the institution may elect to make up the deficit or cut back operations and relocate personnel. Either practice adds to overhead costs. If it is decided that a service should be phased out, the start up costs, which may have been high, are sacrificed. At large universities with many diversified operations the lack of outside funding to support research and other special services has led to many difficult decisions regarding program continuation and has contributed greatly to the overall financial difficulties being experienced.

Problems. The financial difficulties of higher education may be described as follows:

1. Beginning in the late 1960's, many colleges and universities began to experience *increasing difficulty in balancing income with expenditures.* For a variety of causes, this cost-income squeeze now threatens the solvency or growth of many institutions. Among those most severely affected are the large research universities and the small liberal arts colleges. The big universities have suffered from a reduction in Federal research money and at the same time have faced rising costs in educational technology, e.g., expensive laboratory equipment, audiovisual aids, and books and periodicals. Some small colleges simply lack the personnel necessary to marshal resources required for sound financing. A special problem of Catholic colleges has been the decline in membership of Catholic teaching orders. The limited offerings at other small colleges no longer attracts students who seek a more comprehensive curriculum. Among institutions experiencing financial difficulty the problem ranges from a small deficit to a virtual fight for survival. Dozens of colleges have closed and many others have merged with neighboring institutions. If present trends continue, the situation promises to deteriorate even further. Thus the new "depression," red-ink operations, and deficit financing are omens of a continuing financial problem in higher education.

2. Unique to private colleges, but of serious consequence to the entire education community, is *the disadvantage that independent institutions face in competing for students as a result of the tuition gap between the public and private sector.* Tuition at independent colleges and universities, which in 1962–63 averaged 4.2 times that at public institutions, has been inching upward. In 1972–73 it was 4.9 times as high. While private colleges have much to offer a student in terms of ideology, religion, student body, or special atmosphere, the price tag is too high for many students and their families.[11] As a result of high tuition, there has been a decline in the *proportion* of students attending private institutions of higher education (*total* enrollment in the private sector is increasing only about $1\frac{1}{2}$ percent yearly). In the early 1950's, public and private institution enrollments were about evenly divided; in 1972, the public sector enrolled nearly 75 percent of all students. Faced with vacant spaces, many private colleges have had to lower their admission standards and freeze faculty salaries. Such actions are bound to be reflected, sooner or later, in the one quality of which private colleges have long been proud, namely, the high caliber of both faculty and students.

---

[11] The remarkable fact is that so many small private colleges flourish despite high tuition. Their most precious asset is a uniqueness that enables them to attract students despite overwhelming competition from the public sector.

3. Although the situation is improving, *opportunities for a college education are still greater for the rich than for the poor.* While factors other than family finances may be important determinants of who goes to college—such factors as ability, the family's willingness to spend money for a higher education, commitment on the part of the student to attend, etc., are often of overriding importance—a student from an upper income family has a greater chance of matriculating than does a student from a low-income family, even if they have substantially equal ability.[12] This inequality in educational opportunity is due in large measure to insufficient public support.

4. Nearly all observers recognize the fact that *the quality of higher education could be substantially improved.* While there is some hope for the future, there has been little improvement in the constant dollar investment in education per student during the past 15 years. With the number and complexity of collegiate functions steadily increasing, with graduate work assuming increased importance, and with little evidence of accompanying increases in productivity or efficiency, it is apparent that real unit expenditures must increase if academic quality is to improve. That such has not been the case suggests the possibility of adverse effects on the quality of education, especially undergraduate education.

The following collateral issues associated with these four basic problems have further complicated the financial scene.

5. Many educational administrators express *dissatisfaction with current methods of financing colleges and universities.* The case has been summarized by John Millett:

It is a wearing business constantly to cultivate all available sources of philanthropic

---

[12] Many empirical studies have explored the ability to pay as a contributing factor to college attendance. Perhaps the most important evidence has been obtained from Project Talent, sponsored by the U.S. Office of Education. This survey clearly showed that college attendance by high school graduates within given ability-achievement groups is positively related to socioeconomic status and that college dropout rates are higher among those with lower income. Based on this evidence, total years of college attendance are more skewed to upper income groups than data on entering students would indicate.

A more recent Census Bureau report sheds light on another important dimension: the influence of family income on the *quality* of college education a student is likely to receive. (See U.S. Bureau of the Census, *Current Population Reports*, Series P-20, No. 183, "Characteristics of Students and Their Colleges," October 1966, U.S. Government Printing Office, Washington, D.C., May 22, 1969.) The data show that youths from the poorest families are underrepresented in college while youths from the richest are overrepresented; also, that students from high-income families attend colleges reporting higher freshman aptitude scores than do students from low-income families. It should be pointed out that these higher "quality" institutions are not necessarily the most expensive ones.

support: annual alumni giving, corporation contributions, gifts and bequests of friends, church support, foundation assistance. The college and university president must be a perpetual beggar if he is to find the current operating income and the capital funds needed to ensure institutional well-being. Some surcease from this continual solicitation would be welcome indeed to most educational administrators.[13]

6. Continuously debated in the world of higher education is *the question of the desirable level of student charges*. The answer to how much of the cost of higher education should be borne by students and how much by society depends on one's judgment as to the relative benefits derived by each and whether one views education primarily as a public service or a personal desire. Proponents on both sides have legitimate arguments, and, as expected, the range of tuition charges varies widely. Any precipitate change in this area is unlikely, but as the issue is further debated, modest and gradual shifts in the proportion of costs borne by the student versus those borne by society may occur. Over the past 5 years, however, no discernible trend toward such a shift in either the public or private sector has been noted.

7. Concomitant with the need for additional government support of higher education is *the problem of how public funds may be most effectively distributed*. At issue is whether aid should go to institutions or to students. Persons in favor of institutional aid argue that the subsidy should be in the hands of educators because they are in a position to enhance the quality of education. Those in favor of grants to students argue that student aid would maximize the scope of choice open to enrollees and would subject institutions to healthy competition. Giving aid to students also bypasses the troublesome issues of public policy and constitutional doctrine raised when a government subsidy is given directly to church-related institutions.

Causes. The financial crisis in higher education and its correlated problems stem from the difficulty that colleges and universities are experiencing in securing the necessary funds to provide not only academic quality but equal educational opportunity. This imbalance, basically due to a disproportionate growth in the factors affecting financial strength, is widening the gap between annual income and expenditures. The essential elements that have caused institutional funding needs to rise are growing student enrollment, expanding institutional functions, and rising instructional costs. On the other side of the equation, a fourth factor, the financial capacity of funding sources, has not kept pace with needs.

1. *Growth in enrollments.* In the decade of the 1960's, full-time-equivalent enrollment in higher education more than doubled. Such unprecedented

---

[13] John D. Millett, "The Role of Student Charges" in *Financing Higher Education: 1960–70*, Dexter M. Keezer, ed., McGraw-Hill Book Co., New York, 1959, p. 164.

growth was the result of an increase in the college-age population (18 through 21-year-olds) from 9.5 to 14.5 million and the continual rise in the percentage of Americans entering college. The fact that a larger percentage of young people than ever before are attending college is, of course, a consequence of efforts to achieve greater equality of access to higher education. However, when enrollment is viewed as a measure of financial burden, rapid growth becomes more a challenge than an achievement. The challenge can be observed in the fact that enrollment growth in higher education exceeds that of one of the common measures of ability to pay—the Nation's gross national product. Now that enrollments are rising more slowly, by 1976 the capacity-burden ratio should improve.

2. *Growth in functions.* In addition to increased enrollment, colleges and universities have had to cope with the knowledge explosion. Both the range and the specialization of instruction have had to be expanded, with greater attention being given to graduate and professional programs, and new research being directed toward civic and social problems. This steady growth in the number and complexity of functions has had the effect of continually redefining the role of higher education in society. Thus higher education today is a *new* product, inherently more expensive than it was in the past.[14]

3. *Rising Costs.* The factor having perhaps the most devastating effect on the financing of higher education is the continual rise in the cost of education—a rise resulting primarily from increases in faculty and research staff salaries.[15] Concurrent with a continual growth in the U.S. economy has been a continual increase in the quantity of goods produced per unit of labor. These increases in productivity determine proportional increases in real wages and salaries paid, not only in sectors where productivity has increased but also in sectors where productivity fails to increase. Despite the fact that higher education is a sector in which production techniques have changed very little, if salaries of faculty members do not keep pace with those in other occupations, teachers will be tempted to leave the educational labor force to earn higher salaries in some other field.[16] Since a salary increase for teachers is not offset by an increase in

---

[14] With real unit investment in higher education remaining relatively constant, an increase in the cost of certain functions, such as graduate education, means that other functions, such as undergraduate education, must be performed at a lower cost.

[15] See Fritz Machlup, *Education and Economic Growth*, University of Nebraska Press, Lincoln, 1970, pp. 92–98.

[16] Teachers' salaries have at times risen even faster than other salaries. During the 1960's, for example, rapid expansion in student enrollment caused the demand for faculty to exceed the supply.

productivity per worker, the cost of educational services per student increases year after year.

In a growing economy, the necessity of raising the *real earnings* of faculty, despite the absence of technological improvement in education, is not a consequence of inflation. The fact that government fiscal and monetary policies are conducive to continual inflation of incomes and prices chiefly affects the *money cost* of education. The rate of monetary inflation must be added to the rate of increase in real earnings of faculty to equal the total rise in the costs of providing education.

The Price Index for Higher Education (see appendix B) indicates that a $5\frac{1}{2}$-percent yearly increase has occured during the past 6 years. Four percent represents an increase in the physical productivity of the economy passed on to higher education in the form of higher salaries; $1\frac{1}{2}$ percent is due to monetary inflation.

4. *Capacity and effort of primary funding sources.* The chief financial burden for public higher education has been borne by State and local governments. Appropriations to public universities and 4-year colleges from these two sources have accounted for about 71 percent of total unrestricted revenues during the past 6 years; for public 2-year colleges, the percentage has been 80 percent. Many States would find it difficult to provide higher levels of support, both because of tax base limits and because public funds are needed for other essential services. Further expansion of the State support role might also result in an excessive dependency by institutions on this single revenue source. For these reasons, much attention has been directed toward tuition charges (they now provide about 20 percent of the unrestricted revenue in the public sector). Many believe that public responsibility for equal educational opportunity would not be diminished if tuition charges were keyed to family income. For those who feel that well-to-do families should assume a larger share of the cost, higher tuition is the most realistic approach to improving the financing of public institutions.

The private sector has for some time been overly dependent on a single revenue source—tuition. Tuition and fee payments amount to 66 percent, 74 percent, and 76 percent of total unrestricted educational and general revenues for private universities, 4-year colleges, and 2-year colleges, respectively. These percentages, which have been relatively stable over the past 6 years, probably will not rise appreciably in the foreseeable future. The question is: To what degree can private institutions increase tuition charges and still remain competitive with their public counterparts? Currently, tuition at private institutions averages 4.9 times that charged by public institutions. Because of this price differential, the private sector can attract the best students and faculty only by offering a high quality education. Any substantial reduction in this quality may cause private institutions to price themselves out of the market.

Remedies. As with any acute financial crisis, alleviating those fiscal problems threatening the solvency or growth of colleges and universities will require major readjustments. Naturally those adjustments that cause the least inconvenience and interference with personnel and programs are tried first. When more stringent efforts are indicated, goals and plans may have to be seriously curtailed. New ways to increase revenue must be explored, together with the means to allocate resources better within the system. But if present cost and income problems continue, even these methods will not suffice. The severity and consistency of the problem may be such that a long-range solution will require that society spend a substantially greater proportion of its earnings on education—perhaps through Federal assistance. It may further require a breakthrough in educational technology to improve productivity. These two solutions, in combination, will mean investing proportionally more physical capital (machinery, books, equipment) in higher education and less human labor so as to increase both educational capacity and efficiency.

There are five major means by which the higher education community and the Nation can ease financial difficulties and create stronger financial support.

1. *Introduce economies* (improving instructional productivity is considered separately). Colleges can effect savings and improve efficiency in a variety of ways (see chapter XIII). The rationale for economizing should be to secure greater returns in essential program areas, with less investment, while maintaining planned quality.

2. *Tap existing revenue sources more fully and develop new sources.* No one seems to doubt seriously the intent of citizens to continue to devote a growing share of national income to higher education. Relative to GNP, the amount required from the public is small. With student enrollment growth tapering off, the capacity-burden ratio should improve. Based on past trends, the major sources of support—State appropriations in the public sector and tuition charges in the private sector—will likely grow at the same rate as higher education costs. Consequently, their percentage share of total unrestricted revenue should remain fairly stable. To improve resources per student, the potential sources not yet fully tapped (tuition in the public sector and State subsidies in the private sector, for example) will need to be exploited. It will also be necessary to obtain income from such "new" financing sources as charging the consumer the full cost for public services provided.

3. *Improve the effectiveness of resource allocation and introduce more budget flexibility.* Better methods are required for determining financial needs and allocating resources. Administrators at many institutions are searching not

only for more rigorous means to review priorities and measure quality, performance, and output, but also for better procedures by which to allocate funds internally. (See chapter XIV.) Shifting fiscal responsibility to lower local levels (together with increased accountability) and avoiding excessive budgetary controls, red tape, and inflexibility are necessary if administrators are to have the freedom they need to make resources available for immediate priorities.

4. *Increase and broaden Federal funding.* In view of the resources available from the graduated income tax, the Federal Government is one, and perhaps the only, source capable of supporting higher education at a growth rate *exceeding* cost increases. Currently, the Federal proportionate share of student education expenditures is exceedingly small, the reason being that most Federal funding is categorically restricted to research, student aid, and facility construction. If Federal funding is to be broadened, it must do more than supplement existing revenues. Toward this end, the Carnegie Commission's recommendations[17] include, among others, the following, sometimes conflicting, objectives for Federal Government aid: it should draw forth rather than merely replace State and private support; it should improve equality of educational opportunity; it should rely on open competition in student choice of field and institution; it should encourage diversity; and it should maintain among distinguished institutions a margin for excellence. Widely discussed and highly controversial approaches to Federal funding include a massive program of grants and loans to individual students to enable them to pay higher tuition, across-the-board grants to institutions, and tax credits to parents of children in college.

5. *Improve teaching productivity.* Although more difficult than the other approaches, improvement in instructional productivity offers a major opportunity for basic restructuring of educational costs. One method being used to lower classroom costs is to increase the student-faculty ratio—by increasing class size, requiring more independent work by students, increasing the faculty teaching load, etc.[18] On a larger scale, greater efficiency can be expected from such major reforms as the establishment of regional examining universities and regional television colleges.[19] While both of these innovations have possibilities, implementation is likely to be slow

---

[17] Carnegie Commission on Higher Education, *Quality and Equality: New Levels of Federal Responsibility for Higher Education*, McGraw-Hill Book Co., New York, 1968, p. 15.

[18] See chapter XIII for a discussion of ways to raise the student-faculty ratio.

[19] For a delineation of new teaching techniques and new types of institutions, see U.S. Department of Health, Education, and Welfare, Office of Education, *Report on Higher Education*, Frank Newman, chairman, U.S. Government Printing Office, Washington, D.C., 1971, pp. 61–86.

and may prove disappointing. One reason—and the most important—is the difficulty of applying technological advances to the personal process of teaching and learning. Education by television may provide the great breakthrough. But in the foreseeable future, the great bulk of students will continue to acquire a higher education through instruction by individual teachers and oncampus experiences.

TRENDS AND PROJECTIONS AT THE NATIONAL LEVEL

A brief statistical account of the financing of student education expenditures in U. S. higher education during the past decade, together with a future projection, will help establish the important dimensions of financial need and accomplishment. Discussion will be limited to the five factors governing the aggregate financing of higher education: gross national product, college-age population, college attendance ratio, higher education price index, and percent allocation to higher education.

The equation for the financing of student education expenditures in higher education at the national level is:

CAPACITY-BURDEN RATIO $\times$ ALLOCATION $\times$ PURCHASING POWER

$$= \text{ACHIEVEMENT (in constant dollars)}$$

$$\frac{\text{Gross national product}}{\begin{array}{c}\text{College-age} \quad \text{College} \\ \text{group} \quad \times \text{attendance} \\ \text{ratio}\end{array}} \times \text{Percent allocated to higher education} \times \frac{100}{\begin{array}{c}\text{Higher} \\ \text{education} \\ \text{price index}\end{array}}$$

$$= \text{Student education expenditures per FTE student (in constant dollars)}$$

An indicator of the capacity of the country to pay for higher education is the *gross national product*, a comprehensive measure in dollars of the Nation's total annual production of commodities and services.

The *college attendance ratio* measures college enrollment relative to a source group and reflects the rate at which youths enter college. When multiplied by the principal source population,[20] the *college-age group* of 18- through 21-year-olds, the product equals full-time-equivalent (FTE) college enrollment.

---

[20] According to October 1970 census data, students 18 through 21 years of age comprise 60 percent of the total college enrollment.

The ratio of GNP to FTE college enrollment is the CAPACITY-BURDEN RATIO.

The reciprocal of the *higher education price index* (HEPI) (see appendix B) is a PURCHASING POWER or deflation factor that eliminates the influence of changes in the prices of current operating inputs of colleges and universities. The HEPI is used to convert actual dollar amounts in any given year to their equivalent in 1967 dollars, i.e., dollars of constant purchasing power.

The *percent allocated to higher education* is that proportion of the GNP allocated to institutions of higher education for student education expenditures. The ALLOCATION ratio can be considered as a measure of the priority that the economy attaches to financing student instruction and related higher education supporting activities.

Student education expenditures are those current-fund educational and general expenditures by colleges and universities for instruction and related supporting activities—expenditures for instruction and departmental research, extension and public service, libraries, physical plant maintenance and operation, and general administration and student services. Student education expenditures in constant dollars per FTE student, a measure of relative fiscal ACHIEVEMENT, indicates the *commitment* of funds to support higher education at desired quantity and quality levels.

Statistical Data

Statistical data for the finance equation are presented in table XII-1 and graphically illustrated in figure XII-1. According to the formula, calculation of student education expenditures for the years 1964, 1971, and 1976 (Beta projection) are as follows:

1964:
$$\frac{\$631.7 \text{ billion}}{11,319,000 \times .375} \times \frac{100}{90.8} \times .918\% = \$1,503 \text{ student education}$$
expenditures per FTE student

1971:
$$\frac{\$1,050.4 \text{ billion}}{14,864,000 \times .477} \times \frac{100}{132.3} \times 1.449\% = \$1,621$$

1976: (Projection Beta)
$$\frac{\$1,474 \text{ billion}}{16,602,000 \times .542} \times \frac{100}{165.0} \times 1.700\% = \$1,687$$

The annual growth rates for the five variables and for student education expenditures from 1964–71, together with example projections for 1971–76, are as follows:

Factors in equation for finance	Annual growth rates in factors			
		Example projections 1971–1976		
	1964–1971	Alpha	Beta	Delta
GNP	7½%	6%	7%	8%
Percent allocated	6¾%	2%	3¼%	4½%
College-age group	4%	2¼%	2¼%	2¼%
College attendance ratio	3½%	2½%	2½%	2½%
HEPI	5½%	4½%	4½%	4½%
Student education expenditures in constant dollars per FTE student	1%	−1½%	¾%	3%

TECHNICAL NOTE.—Equations with variables at different interest rates require *separate* interest calculations for each variable involved. In this case, however, there is a rapid method of calculating the *approximate* interest rate of an equation result: The approximate annual rate of growth of student education expenditures per FTE student is equal to the *sum* of the annual growth rates for the factors in the *numerator* of the equation (GNP and percent allocated) *minus* the annual growth rate for the factors in the denominator of the equation (college-age group, college attendance ratio, and HEPI). Thus, for the period 1964–71 this calculation would be $7½\% + 6¾\% - 4\% - 3½\% - 5½\% = 1¼\%$; and for the period 1971–76 (Beta projection) $7\% + 3¼\% - 2¼\% - 2½\% - 4½\% = 1\%$. By means of this method, the annual rate of increase for student education expenditures in constant dollars per FTE student can be easily approximated for any assumed values of the five variables in the equation.

The mathematical justification for the aforementioned approximation method is as follows: For compound interest rate i, the equation for the sum S, or amount to which the principal P will accumulate in n equal conversion period or time units, is $S = P(1+i)^n$. If a and b represent the annual interest rate or rates of growth of the two principal factors, A and B, and n is equal to the number of years involved, the equation will be

$$S = A(1+a)^n \times B(1+b)^n$$

for $n=1$, $S = AB(1+a+b+ab)$

$$S \approx AB(1+a+b)$$

where a and b are small (less than 10 percent) $a \times b$ is close to zero in value.

To approximate the growth rate of the ratio, $S = A/B$, the equation will be:

$$\frac{S = A(1+a)^n}{B(1+b)^n}$$

for $n=1$, $S = \dfrac{A}{B}\left(1 + \dfrac{a-b}{1+b}\right)$

$$S \approx \frac{A}{B}(1+a-b)$$

where a and b are small (less than 10 percent) $1+b$ is close to unity.

Figure XII-1. — Selected statistics on the financing of higher education: 1958-76

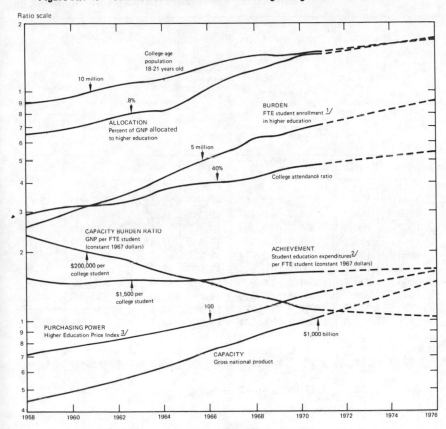

[1] Full-time-equivalent (FTE) student enrollment equals full-time enrollment plus one-third part-time and extension enrollment.

[2] Student education expenditures are those current-fund educational and general expenditures for instruction and departmental research, extension and public service, libraries, physical plant maintenance and operation, and general administration and student services.

[3] See appendix B.

NOTE.— The vertical axis is expressed on a ratio, or logarithmic scale- i.e., equal vertical distances reflect equal proportional (as distinguished from absolute) changes.

Analysis of Trends

The trend for financing higher education during the 1964–71 period can be briefly summarized as follows:

During the 8 years in question the capacity-burden ratio in constant dollars of GNP per FTE student fell from $163,695 to $111,880. The decline occurred because the combined growth in the college-age group

Table XII-1.—Selected statistics on the financing of

Year (also academic year beginning)	Total population incl. Armed Forces abroad (millions) July 1	CAPACITY Gross national product		Enrollment potential— college-age population (18–21 years) July 1	College attendance ratio (6)÷(4)	BURDEN FTE student fall enrollment[1] in higher education	
		Amount (billions)	Per capita (2)÷(1)			Number	Per 1,000 capita (6)÷(1)
	(1)	(1)	(3)	(4)	(5)	(6)	(7)
1958	174.9	$447.3	$2,557	8,909	29.4%	2,620,000	15.0
1960	180.7	503.7	2,787	9,549	32.0	3,060,000	16.9
1962	186.5	560.3	3,004	10,761	32.3	3,480,000	·18.7
1964	191.9	631.7	3,292	11,319	37.5	4,250,000	22.1
1966	196.6	749.9	3,814	12,887	39.8	5,126,005	26.1
1967	198.7	793.9	3,995	13,633	40.6	5,539,222	27.9
1968	200.7	864.2	4,306	14,342	42.0	6,024,199	30.0
1969	202.7	930.3	4,590	14,199	45.0	6,382,618	31.5
1970	204.9	976.4	4,765	14,540	46.7	6,790,509	33.1
1971	207.0	1,050.4	5,074	14,864	47.7	7,096,444	34.3
Projected							
Alpha							
1976	214.5	1,405	6,550	16,602	54.2	9,000,000	42.0
Beta							
1976	214.5	1,474	6,872	16,602	54.2	9,000,000	42.0
Delta							
1976	214.5	1,543	7,193	16,602	54.2	9,000,000	42.0

[1] Full-time-equivalent (FTE) enrollment equals full-time enrollment plus one-third part-time and extension enrollment.

[2] Current fund educational and general expenditures for instruction and departmental research, extension and public service, libraries, physical plant maintenance and operation, and general administration and student services.

[3] For description of the Higher Education Price Index see appendix B.

(4 percent annually), the college attendance ratio ($3\frac{1}{2}$ percent annually), and inflation ($5\frac{1}{2}$ percent annually) exceeded growth in the GNP ($7\frac{1}{2}$ percent annually). Stated differently, the financial capacity to support higher education (GNP), in terms of the true purchasing power of colleges and universities, did not increase as fast as enrollment. Owing to the increased percentage of GNP allocated to higher education during this period (from .918 percent in 1964 to 1.449 percent in 1971, education expenditures in constant dollars per FTE student rose slightly from $1,503 in 1964 to $1,621 in 1971. Faced with a rapidly declining capacity-burden ratio, the Nation has been forced to allocate larger amounts to higher

higher education in the United States: 1958–76

Year (also academic year beginning)	CAPACITY-BURDEN RATIO GNP per FTE student		ALLOCA-TION to higher education—student education expenditures as a percent of GNP (11)÷(2)	ACHIEVEMENT Student education expenditures[2] academic year			Higher Education Price Index[3] 1966–67 =100 academic year
	Actual dollars (2)÷(6) $(8) \times \frac{100}{(14)}$	Constant dollars (1967 prices)		Amount (thousands)	Per FTE student		
					Actual dollars (11)÷(6)	Constant dollars (1967 prices) $(12) \times \frac{100}{(14)}$	
	(8)	(9)	(10)	(11)	(12)	(13)	(14)
1958	$170,725	$237,778	.648%	2,900,000	$1,107	$1,542	71.8
1960	164,608	210,766	.695	3,500,000	1,144	1,465	78.1
1962	161,006	191,219	.785	4,400,000	1,264	1,501	84.2
1964	148,635	163,695	.918	5,800,000	1,365	1,503	90.8
1966	146,293	146,293	1.029	7,717,317	1,506	1,506	100.0
1967	143,323	135,980	1.152	9,146,492	1,651	1,566	105.4
1968	143,455	128,199	1.233	10,658,032	1,769	1,581	111.9
1969	145,755	122,175	1.323	12,309,209	1,929	1,617	119.3
1970	143,789	112,687	1.425	13,910,893	2,049	1,606	127.6
1971	148,017	111,880	1.449	15,224,000	2,145	1,621	132.3
Projected Alpha 1976	163,372	99,013	1.600	22,480,000	2,498	1,514	165.0
Beta 1976	171,395	103,876	1.700	25,058,000	2,784	1,687	165.0
Delta 1976	179,419	108,739	1.800	27,774,000	3,086	1,870	165.0

education not only to provide essential services but also to maintain quality.

For the 6-year period 1971–76, three example projections are offered—Alpha or "pessimistic," Beta or "middle course," and Delta or "optimistic." Of the five determinant factors in the equation, the two most difficult to project with accuracy are the gross national product and the percent allocated to higher education. The three projections are based on different estimates of the annual growth rates for these two factors only. Within each projection, the *same* estimated values are employed for the annual growth rates of the other three factors—college-age group ($2\frac{1}{4}$ percent), college attendance ratio ($2\frac{1}{2}$ percent), and the higher education price index ($4\frac{1}{2}$ percent).

The college-age group for the immediate future can be projected with precision since students in this category have been born and accurate mortality rates are available. Of striking significance is the fact that the yearly growth rate of this principal source of college enrollments will *decline* from the 4 percent recorded during the 1964–71 period to $2\frac{1}{4}$ percent during 1971–76. Thus *potential* college enrollments, while continuing to grow, will increase at only about half the previous rate.

A long-range prediction of college attendance rates is more difficult to make, but a key guideline is available. As an ever-greater percentage of youths enter college, it is expected that the yearly growth will begin to decline as the level of maximum development of human resources is approached. In other words, it is expected that the time series of entrance rate values will eventually become asymptotic to an entrance rate level representing the greatest possible percentage of youths beginning post-secondary education that can reasonably be expected, given the normal distribution of ability.[21] The rapid expansion of educational opportunities in the past decade suggests that there will be significantly lower gains in the college-going rate of high school graduates in the 1970's. For the aforementioned reasons, the college attendance ratio is projected to show an increase of $2\frac{1}{2}$ percent yearly for the period 1971–76, as opposed to $3\frac{1}{2}$ percent for 1964–71.

As a result of a decline in the growth rates among both the college-age population and the number attending college, the increase in total FTE enrollment (the higher education burden) is expected to be $4\frac{3}{4}$ percent yearly, a substantial decline from the $7\frac{1}{2}$ percent annual rate during the 1964–71 period. Another factor likely to brighten future financial prospects, although of substantially less importance, is the possibility of a slight decline in the rise in prices. During the 1964–71 period, the higher education price index rose $5\frac{1}{2}$ percent yearly (compared to the nearly 4 percent annual increase in the consumer price index during the same time period). A $4\frac{1}{2}$ percent yearly increase is projected for 1971–76. The reduction is predicated on the basis of the following four factors: (1) a shift from a sellers' to a buyers' market in academic personnel, with a concomitant effect on faculty salary increases; (2) pressure on educational institutions to reduce instructional budgets and to forego or greatly limit salary increases; (3) renewed efforts on the part of administrators to heighten productivity by increasing class sizes and reducing student-faculty ratios; and (4) continued efforts by the Federal Government to control prices and reduce inflation.

As previously explained, the three projections differ only in the estimated values of the gross national product and the percent allocated to higher education. For projection Beta, if the gross national product continues to grow at an annual rate of 7 percent, as it has in the recent past,

---

[21] In some States, the college entrance rate among high school graduates may well reach the 80-percent level.

and reaches $1,474 billion by 1976, an allocation of 1.7 percent to higher education will raise student education expenditures in constant 1967 dollars to $1,687 per FTE student. This amount, which is slightly higher than the $1,606 per student in 1970, can be achieved—provided all other factors are correctly projected—by increasing the share of GNP allocated to higher education by 3¼ percent yearly. The annual rate of increase of this share during the 1964–71 period was 6¾ percent.

INSTITUTIONAL STATUS AND TRENDS

At the national level, adequately detailed data concerning institutional financial practices have not been available until recently. The fact that data now exist makes possible more rigorous and accurate analysis of those income sources that pay for various institutional expenditures. Since many college and university expenditures are allocated to functions only indirectly related to each other, it is critical that the various incomes and expenditures be accurately *sorted and matched*. Only by so doing will it be possible to determine exactly who is paying for what.

Since 1965–66, the U. S. Office of Education has used the Higher Education General Information Survey (HEGIS) to collect on a yearly basis financing data from colleges and universities. The finance components of this survey are significantly more comprehensive than those gathered in the past, particularly in that they provide a detailed separation of institutional revenues by *intended use*. An analysis of these data for 6 academic years, 1965–66 through 1970–71, is presented in this section.

Financial Health

The financial health of any institution is usually difficult to determine with precision. The easily calculated price-earnings ratio for the common stock of corporations—measuring owner confidence in potential earning power—is not available from colleges or universities. As nonprofit organizations, institutions of higher education typically set the level of their operations and expenditures to coincide with the amount of income received; consequently, their budgets are generally "balanced." In straitened circumstances an institution may respond by cutting back its programs, but such action will not be readily apparent in a financial statement. Institutional officials recognize of course that abandoning or reducing educational programs, lowering standards of excellence, limiting research and public service activities, and adopting other restrictive measures are sirens of financial distress. But despite the din, the balance sheet is likely to remain "balanced." Because expenditures are ordinarily cut to match available funding, a cost-income squeeze will not often be recognized by "red ink" operations. A more subtle indicator must be used.

A valuable measure of institutional financial strength is the *trend of unit expenditures for student education in constant dollars*, together with a related income analysis. Expenditures for student education measure the financial resources available to an institution for its primary function of instruction and for such directly related supporting activities as extension and public service, administration, library operations, and plant operation and maintenance. On a unit basis, and reported in dollars of constant purchasing power, analysis of student education expenditures over time reveals the financial ability of an institution *to maintain the quality level of a basic educational program*. A decline in quality so measured or improvement at a rate substantially lower than that of peer institutions is a sign of possible financial deterioration. Since unit expenditures may also decline as a result of improved efficiency in operations, such improvement should be kept in mind when dealing with individual institutions.

Because an institution's funding level does not permit it to *raise* the quality of its instructional program or *expand* its offerings does not mean that the college or university is in financial difficulty. Neither should the *temporary* sacrifice of *marginal* programs or "belt-tightening" be considered evidence of financial trouble. Only when an institution is forced to lower the quality of its basic educational program can it be said that a fundamental and critical financial crisis exists.

The revenue side of the ledger can also reveal why a financial problem exists. Only those unrestricted revenues, generally unspecified as to use, with which an institution finances student education expenditures should be considered. Trends in the mix of incomes and in per student amounts in constant dollars indicate the stability, growth, or decline of a given source. Evaluation can also be made by comparing per student amounts with those at other peer institutions.

Although the aforementioned approach to financial analysis is relatively straightforward, income and expenditure data can be easily misinterpreted unless certain guidelines are observed. Briefly summarized, they are as follows:

> 1. Expenditures should be classified and grouped according to the functions they serve. The five major budgetary functional classifications in higher education that require *separate* financial analysis are (a) student education (consisting of instruction and departmental research, extension and public service, libraries, physical plant operation and maintenance, and general administration and student services); (b) organized research; (c) auxiliary enterprises; (d) student aid; and (e) plant additions.

2. Comparisons of income with expenditures should involve *related* revenue sources and expenditure categories; i.e., only incomes designated or used for a given function should be compared with expenditures for that function.[22]

3. Terms used in the collection and analysis of financial statistics should be *explicit* and *consistent* over time.

4. The distinctive financial patterns of the public and private sectors, as well as those of universities, 4-year colleges, and 2-year colleges, require that higher education financing be analyzed by *type and control* of institution. Whenever possible, the financing of undergraduate and graduate education should also be analyzed separately. In individual institutional analysis, peer group comparisons are important.

5. Meaningful comparisons can be made only on the basis of *relative* measurements — e.g., input-output ratios, amounts per student, unit costs.

6. To indicate the amount of real resources involved, not inflationary factors, relevant *price indexes* should be used whenever possible.

In the following analysis of the status and trends of institutional financing, the aforementioned guidelines have been applied to data at the national level. Although it is intended that the conclusions reached accurately reflect the composite financial situation of all institutions, it is a fact that conditions at individual colleges are not necessarily represented by the group average. For this reason, no inference regarding an individual institution should be drawn from the national data.

Income and Expenditure Patterns

The finances reviewed in this chapter deal only with student education expenditures and related unrestricted revenues. Summary data for 1970–71 are shown in table XII-2. An outline of recognized trends is presented in table XII-3. Detailed data for 1965–66 through 1971–72, by type and and control of institution, are presented in appendix C.

Examination of education revenue reveals few surprises. Immediately notable is the traditional sharp difference in reliance by public and private institutions on State and local government appropriations (over 70 percent versus 4 percent or less, respectively) as opposed to tuition and fees (approximately 20 percent versus 65–75 percent or more, respectively). At private institutions endowment income and private gifts and grants account for 20 to 26 percent of the revenue available for general use; at public institutions the same sources account for less than 2 percent of the revenue received. The Federal Government's role in both sectors is small,

---

[22] This procedure is difficult to follow if the funding of one function also supports another. For example, sponsored research partially supports graduate education, most notably by defraying salaries of faculty who both teach and do research and by covering the cost of equipment used in both teaching and research.

consisting primarily of various types of funding programs for land-grant institutions.

As can be seen in table XII-2, the unrestricted revenue available for general use in each instance nearly matches student education expenditures. In the private sector, the significant role of tuition and fees as the principal source of revenue for student educational expenditures should be noted. Tuition and fees pay for 76.2 percent of student education expenditures at private 2-year colleges; for 74.2 percent at private 4-year colleges; and for 66.0 percent at private universities. That tuition and fees account for nearly *three-fourths* of the income for instruction and related supporting activities at private institutions is not generally known or appreciated.

With regard to student education expenditures, only a few facts are relevant to any discussion of finance. One is that private institutions spend more than do their public counterparts. They provide considerably more student services and maintain a larger administrative overhead than do their public counterparts. Three factors contribute to larger administrative expenditures by private colleges and universities: (1) need for more staff members to raise funds; (2) generally higher salaries paid administrative officers; and (3) diseconomies of scale because of smaller enrollments.[23] The fact that private institutions spend more for supporting activities than do their public counterparts does not mean that they spend less for instruction. Larger overall budgets permit private universities to spend substantially more for instruction: $1,892 compared to $1,370 at public universities. Although private 4-year colleges spend a smaller proportion of their budget on instruction than do public 4-year colleges (49 percent compared to 60 percent), both spend the same amount per student, $1,054. Private 2-year colleges spend 42.8 percent of their budget, or $641 per student, on instruction, while public 2-year colleges spend 61.8 percent, or $800 per student.

A final but important difference in the expenditure patterns of private and public institutions is that the former spend about 2.7 times more on student aid grants than do the latter. The difference in the amount of student aid is, however, far smaller than the differential in tuition between the public and private sectors. At all types of institutions, expenditures for student aid grants exceed revenues designated for this purpose. One reason is that institutions frequently do not report tuition and fee remissions as student aid income, or report the use of surplus auxiliary enterprise income to aid students. Another reason is that government appropriations not designated for student aid but used for this purpose are frequently reported only as educational and general revenue.

---

[23] The estimated *median* enrollments in private and public institutions, fall 1971, were: universities, 8,600 and 21,000, respectively; 4-year colleges, 800 versus 4,700; and 2-year colleges, 350 versus 2,000. (See chapter VI for a discussion of economies of scale.)

Table XII-2.—Unrestricted educational and general revenues, student education expenditures, and student aid grants revenues and expenditures, by control and type of institution, amount per FTE student and percent of total: 1970–71

| | Universities | | | | 4-year colleges | | | | 2-year colleges | | | |
| | Public | | Private | | Public | | Private | | Public | | Private | |
	Amount per FTE student	Percent	Amount per FTE student	Percent	Amount per FTE student	Percent	Amount per FTE student	Percent	Amount per FTE student	Percent	Amount per FTE student	Percent
Unrestricted educational and general revenues	$2,468	100.0	$2,926	100.0	$1,819	100.0	$2,139	100.0	$1,398	100.0	$1,447	100.0
Student tuition and fees	583	23.6	1,931	66.0	375	20.6	1,587	74.2	208	15.0	1,103	76.2
Federal Govt. appropriations	96	3.8	102	3.5	124	6.8	35	1.6	54	3.9	37	2.6
State & local govt. approp.	1,736	70.3	120	4.1	1,311	72.1	25	1.2	1,130	80.8	21	1.4
Endowment income	26	1.1	415	14.2	2	.1	155	7.2	1	.1	33	2.3
Private gifts	28	1.1	359	12.3	7	.4	338	15.8	4	.3	254	17.5
Student education expenditures	$2,457	100.0	$3,252	100.0	$1,759	100.0	$2,151	100.0	$1,294	100.0	$1,499	100.0
Instruction & dept. research	1,370	55.8	1,892	58.2	1,054	60.0	1,054	49.0	800	61.8	641	42.8
Extension and public service	240	9.8	43	1.3	27	1.6	18	.8	26	2.0	10	.7
Libraries	121	4.9	204	6.3	96	5.5	116	5.4	53	4.1	65	4.3
Physical plant operation & maint.	292	11.9	420	12.9	232	13.2	293	13.6	140	10.8	243	16.2
Gen. admin. & student services	433	17.6	693	21.3	350	19.9	671	31.2	275	21.2	540	36.0
Student aid grants revenues	$ 120	100.0	267	100.0	71	100.0	143	100.0	35	100.0	69	100.0
Federal Government	71	59.2	116	43.4	42	59.2	58	40.6	23	65.7	38	55.1
State & local government	17	14.2	14	5.2	20	28.2	18	12.6	7	20.0	10	14.5
Private gifts and grants	24	20.0	57	21.3	7	9.9	34	23.8	3	8.6	14	20.3
Endowment income	6	5.0	54	20.2	—	—	25	17.5	—	—	3	4.3
Other student aid grants	2	1.6	26	9.7	2	2.8	9	6.3	1	2.9	4	5.8
Student aid grants expenditures	175	—	481	—	89	—	257	—	36	—	94	—

Source: Data from appendix C.

Table XII-3.—Trends in unrestricted educational and general revenues and in student education expenditures, by control and type of institution: 1965-66 through 1970-71[1]

	Public			Private		
	Universities	4-year colleges	2-year colleges	Universities	4-year colleges	2-year colleges
Unrestricted educational and general revenues						
Major sources of income (average values)	State & local govt. 70% Tuition 22%	State & local govt. 72% Tuition 20% Federal (−)	State & local govt. 80% Tuition 15%	Tuition 65% Gifts and endowment 27%	Tuition 73% Gifts and endowment 25%	Tuition 77% Gifts and endowment 19%
Changes in relative importance of income sources	Tuition (+) Federal (−)		Stable	Stable	Stable	Stable
Student education expenditures						
Changes in relative importance of expenditure categories	Admin. (+) Extension and public service (−)	Stable	Admin. (+) Extension and public service (−)	Stable	Admin. (+)	Admin. (+) Instruction (−)
Change in real purchasing value of expenditures per student	+1%/year	+4%/year	+5½%/year	+2%/year	+2½%/year	+3½%/year

[1] Analysis of data in Appendix C.

Income and Expenditure Trends

Institutional finances for the 6 academic years 1965–66 through 1970–71 can be generally described as stable. In the private sector and at public universities, revenue in constant dollars per student increased between 1 and 3 percent annually. At public 4-year colleges the annual increase was 4 percent and at public 2-year colleges it was $5\frac{1}{2}$ percent. The relative contribution of each income source remained remarkably stable over the 6-year period, except that the Federal share of revenue declined slightly at public universities and 4-year colleges.

In both sectors expenditures for student education in constant dollars increased at approximately the same or at a slightly greater rate than did revenues. The most significant improvement in real value of expenditures per student was obtained by public 2-year colleges ($5\frac{1}{2}$-percent annual growth), public 4-year colleges (4-percent annual growth), and private 2-year colleges ($3\frac{1}{2}$-percent annual growth). A noticeable trend in expenditure composition during the 6 years was the modest increase in the amount spent for general administration and student services[24] by public universities and 2-year colleges and by private 4-year and 2-year colleges. In some instances, this increase was paralleled by a proportional decline in the relative amounts allocated to instruction or to extension and public service.

Details regarding patterns and trends of college and university expenditures, as well as a projection of traditional sources of income, are available in several studies.[25] Some of these direct attention to *total* current fund incomes from all sources and to *total* educational and general expenditures, including organized research, auxiliary enterprises, student aid, etc. The analysis of the more restricted incomes and expenditures in this chapter provide conclusions with regard to the relative roles of various income sources and various expenditure patterns that differ from those resulting from studies of the *total* finances of colleges and universities.

---

[24] Student services include those provided by the registrar, admissions office, deans of students and of men and women, guidance and testing programs, health service, financial aid, and by institutional subsidies to student activities.

[25] For an extended analysis of institutional finances during the period 1959–60 to 1966–67, see Ernst Becker, "The Financing of Higher Education: A Review of Historical Trends and Projections for 1975–76" in *Trends in Postsecondary Education*, U.S. Department of Health, Education, and Welfare, Office of Education, U.S. Government Printing Office, Washington, D.C., 1970, pp. 97–180.

See also numerous papers on institutional finance by the Joint Economic Committee, Congress of the United States, *The Economics and Financing of Higher Education in the United States*, U.S. Government Printing Office, Washington, D.C., 1969.

Future Prospects

What are the possibilities for an increase in constant dollars per student? An assessment by sources follows.

Student fees. In the private sector, tuition revenue pays nearly three-fourths of the costs of educating students. Tuition at private institutions is four to five times that charged by public institutions, and were it to be increased, private colleges and universities could price themselves out of existence. In the public sector, on the other hand, if tuition were doubled (and enrollments remained unchanged), the total revenue available for instruction and related supporting activities would be increased by about 12 percent. If aid to needy students were substantially expanded or charges were based on parental income or to the postcollege income of students, the tuition increase per se would be more acceptable to the general public. (For additional information on this topic, see the ensuing section on the role of tuition in financing higher education.)

Philanthropic gifts and endowment. Private funding through philanthropic gifts and the earnings from such gifts (endowment) is a significant revenue source only in the private sector.[26] It is generally agreed that the potential for private funding is practically unlimited. The task involved in securing such gifts is, however, difficult and time-consuming. During the above-mentioned 6-year period income from gifts and endowment in the private sector kept pace or exceeded only slightly enrollment growth and cost increases. Any optimism regarding the continued support of private higher education through philanthropic gifts must be based on an expansion of fund-raising efforts, together with a change in the attitude on the part of corporations, alumni, church groups, and foundations. The picture would also be brighter if fewer gifts were designated for peripheral endeavors and more for the support of education in general.

As for endowment income, future prospects are somewhat bleak. In view of the irregular fluctuations of the stock market, the fact that revenue from endowments has kept pace with the increasing costs of higher education is in itself remarkable.[27]

State and local governments. The bulk of funds to support publicly controlled institutions comes from State governments; for public 2-year colleges, the

---

[26] An exception: those public universities aggressively seeking private donations.

[27] See Charles D. Ellis, "Let's Solve the Endowment Crisis," *Harvard Business Review*, March–April 1970, pp. 92–102; and William L. Cary and Crag B. Bright, *The Law and the Lore of Endowment Funds*, The Ford Foundation, New York, 1969.

primary source is municipal government. Increased support from tax sources will depend mainly on the fiscal capacity and taxing effort of the various States. Although additional taxation is not feasible in certain States, others are in a position to secure much additional revenue by exploiting tax sources not now fully utilized. (For details, see the section entitled "State Fiscal Measures and Support of Higher Education," Chapter XIII.)

Federal Government. For many years the Federal Government has supported colleges and universities by allocating funds to research, facility construction, and student aid. Many argue that support of selected activities compounds rather than eases the financial difficulties of colleges and universities. With the exception of student fellowship grants that provide additional program funds, many Federal grants actually increase administrative overhead costs. What colleges and universities appear to need is broad, unrestricted support—money to be used for basic educational and general purposes. Were sufficient funds to be so allocated, colleges and universities could be free of the burden of soliciting funds. If the Education Amendments of 1972 are funded, the Federal Government will for the first time on a large scale begin to provide cost-of-education payments. (For a discussion of the 1972 Amendments, see chapter XIII.)

Although the Federal Government can bear the burden of increased support for higher education more easily than can either State or local governments, direct support of institutions poses some difficult questions. How can funds from the Federal Government be used to support privately controlled—in many cases church-related—colleges and universities and how can funds be equitably distributed among institutions? One feasible means would be through a massive Federal student aid program. Opinions are sharply divided on the relative desirability of expanding Federal support in this direction as opposed to across-the-board grants to institutions. Such other considerations as educational opportunity, preserving competition among institutions, survival of the private sector, and effectiveness of resource allocation add to the complexity of the question of Federal involvement. (These issues are examined in chapter XIII.)

Alternative income sources. Relief from financial stress may be secured by developing alternative sources of income. While there are few truly "new" sources for financing higher education, there are many means from which additional institutional income can be derived. A 1968 study in California[28] identified a number of seldom-used income sources, most of which

---

[28] California Coordinating Council for Higher Education, *Study of Income for Public Higher Education*, Sacramento, Calif., 1968, pp. 15–35.

are in the form of charges to recover the costs of services provided to both the public and to students. A partial list of these income-producing sources follows:

1. Patent royalties
2. Copyright income
3. Agricultural extension charges
4. Charges for general extension and adult education
5. Charges for public use of library facilities
6. Charges for use of institutional facilities and/or services to the general public.
7. Charges for agricultural research
8. Land development
9. Increased gift and grant solicitation from nongovernmental sources
10. Revised fee charges for noninstructional services to students
11. Routine laboratory charges
12. Earmarking of special governmental revenues for higher education
13. A higher education lottery
14. Student fees for academic facilities
15. Charges for faculty time devoted to individual research projects
16. Charges to industry for general research
17. Hiring fees
18. Fees for licensing practitioneers in professional occupations
19. Loans for current operations.

PUBLIC INVESTMENT AND NATIONAL OBJECTIVES

Public investment in higher education should be recognized as one of a number of alternatives to be considered on the basis of comparative rates of return. Although there is no satisfactory way to measure either the nonmonetary return to students or the social benefits to society from higher education, it is relatively easy to make a strong case for additional funding based on expressed public interest for more and better colleges and universities. However imprecise the response, educators must continually ask and be prepared to answer the question: Is the additional expenditure for higher education worth the additional return compared to that which might be received from an equal expenditure on some other public enterprise?

It is not necessary at this point to assess the cost of or return from alterna-

---

[29] See for example, Mary Jean Bowman, "Economics of Education"; Christopher Jencks, "Social Stratification and Higher Education"; and Theodore W. Shultz, "Resources for Higher Education: An Economist's View" in M. D. Orwig, ed., *Financing Higher Education: Alternatives for the Federal Government*, American College Testing Program, Iowa City, 1971.

tive public activities. Such information is in the domain of economists and political scientists.[29] However, the issue cannot be totally ignored. A premise regarding society's commitment to higher education must be assumed as the framework for developing national education objectives. The prevailing attitude among most Americans appears to be that stated by Rivlin and Weiss: "The nation can afford, in addition to meeting other social goals, to improve its higher education system, and that improvement implies more students (especially more low-income students), gradually increasing resources per student, and a consequent increase in the proportion of our national resources flowing into higher education."[30] On the basis of this assessment, it would follow that the search for solutions to financing higher education will receive the political and cultural support of society.

Conclusions about finance should flow logically from the aims of higher education. Much of the controversy over funding is due to a lack of agreement on basic objectives or to differences in value or weight which society attaches to each. The relative emphasis to be given each objective is a matter of compromise among competing and often conflicting goals. Nevertheless, there does appear to be some general agreement among most Americans regarding the objectives toward which the national effort in higher education should be directed. These objectives have been most clearly stated by Howard R. Bowen. A condensed version of his "aims of higher education" and some of their financial implications follow.[31]

1. *Equality of opportunity.* Young people, regardless of circumstances, should have access to as much higher education as they are capable of assimilating. Equality of opportunity is based on the idea that it will not only benefit individuals but, by increasing both the number of educated persons and the number of professional and skilled workers, will also enrich the culture and foster economic growth. Since the innate ability to do intellectual work at the college level is widely distributed among the population and the higher education system is an efficient device for discovering talent and sorting people according to their interests and abilities, it would appear that colleges and universities, if they are to help young people prepare for careers in which they can be productive and happy, will need to open their doors to larger numbers of students. If equality of opportunity is to become a reality, the traditional emphasis on low tuition and student financial aid must, of necessity, continue.

---

[30] Alice M. Rivlin and Jeffrey H. Weiss, "Social Goals and Federal Support of Higher Education—the Implications of Various Strategies" in *The Economics and Financing of Higher Education in the United States,* op. cit., p. 549.

[31] Howard R. Bowen, "Finance and the Aims of American Higher Education" in *Financing Higher Education: Alternatives for the Federal Government,* op. cit., pp. 157–63.

2. *Varied programs and diversity.* Institutions and instructional programs should be able to accommodate persons of different abilities and interests. In other words, the system as a whole should be fitted to the students rather than the students to the system.

3. *Student freedom.* Students should be free to choose institutions which best suit their abilities and tastes. Financial aid to students, therefore, should be provided, at least in part, by sources other than the institutions themselves. Furthermore, such financial aid should be of the kind that permits freedom of choice.

4. *Academic freedom.* Colleges and universities should enjoy not only freedom of thought and expression but also substantial freedom to choose the subjects to be taught, the research and scholarship programs to be undertaken, and the public services to be offered. Academic freedom also presupposes a substantial amount of unrestricted funds, diversity in sources of support, and a varied pattern of support and control among institutions.

5. *Efficiency.* Because of the social benefits accruing from higher education, it is undoubtedly in the interests of society for colleges and universities to provide more instruction, research, and public services than individuals or agencies would demand if they were required to pay the full cost. Since it would not further the interests of efficiency to permit the public to determine either the curriculum or the tuition, the task must be left to scholars, students, and public officials. And if they are to make the proper decisions, they must be given the financial freedom to make independent choices. If members of the higher education community are to be responsible to the deep and long-range interests of society, they must of course realize the enormous responsibility that is theirs.

6. *Equity.* A goal of increasing public concern is fairness in assessing the costs of higher education, particularly between taxpayers and donors, who represent "society," and students and their families, who are the principal individual beneficiaries. That students and their parents are conscious of the benefits they receive from higher education is evident in the fact that most of those able to pay for higher education are willing to do so. Society, in turn, recognizes and expects to pay for those aspects of higher education that benefit everybody. While it is extraordinarily difficult to calculate the returns to each beneficiary, the goal should be to proportion the burden of financing fairly—according to relative benefit and responsibility.

7. *Advancement of civilization.* Because institutions of higher education are centers of *learning*, they exert considerable influence on the cultural,

political, and economic aspects of society. As the foundation of civilization, colleges and universities serve as repositories and guardians of accumulated knowledge and wisdom; they advance fresh ideas and provide new interpretations of old values; they are the main source of knowledge concerning science and technology; they offer meaningful esthetic, moral, and social criticism; they are patrons of the arts and literature; they promote national health and safety; and they provide an invaluable nucleus of talent for the study and resolution of a multitude of social problems. As educational institutions, colleges and universities benefit society in a number of ways: educated men and women improve the quality of life by providing enlightened and humane social, political, civic, and intellectual leadership; the home, church, government, and the community are all enhanced by the influence that colleges and universities exert; and educated and professionally trained men and women not only increase the productivity of labor and capital but favorably affect national economic growth and further national goals by contributing new ideas, new technology, and new ways of doing things.[32]

WHO SHOULD PAY? THE ROLE OF TUITION AND RELATED ISSUES

At the heart of the wide-ranging debate over student charges, which in large part determines who pays for higher education, is the question of whether opportunity for educational development is primarily a social necessity or whether it is the fulfillment of an individual desire. If viewed as a social necessity, higher education deserves the maximum public expenditure necessary to support it. If, on the other hand, higher education is considered primarily an opportunity that benefits an individual, then it can be considered a service to be paid for by consumers.

In the United States, higher education has traditionally been regarded as a social responsibility. Both public and private institutions exist in order that all youths of ability can be accommodated. The public concern for higher education is acknowledged by the financial support given colleges and universities, not only by government but by the private sector. The fact that higher education is considered a social necessity has not meant, however, that colleges and universities could not charge tuition to cover part of their operational costs.

---

[32] For a study of the benefits of higher education, see Stephen B. Witney and others, *A Degree and What Else: A Review of the Correlates and Consequences of a College Education*, McGraw-Hill Book Co., New York, 1971.

Close examination of the problem of financing higher education generally leads to the conclusion that there is no one best source of income. Higher education requires support from various income sources: from students, government, corporations, alumni, foundations, churches, etc. The area of disagreement arises over the amount to be supplied by each source. In particular, the controversy centers on what proportion of educational costs should be borne by students and their families and what proportion by society.

There are a number of incontrovertible observations regarding the role of tuition in higher education that must be recognized:

1. Tuition charges are an important source of financing, particularly for private institutions. But, since student charges have increased substantially in the past 20 years, what must be resolved is how much increase, if any, there should be in the future.

2. The present funding of higher education, generally speaking, is inadequate to maintain quality and to provide for expansion; consequently, educational administrators must continually solicit additional funds. Moreover, they must search for new sources of revenue.

3. Changes in higher education financing are likely to be evolutionary rather than revolutionary. The dual-pricing system—low tuition in the public sector and high tuition in the private sector—can be expected to continue in the foreseeable future.

4. Higher education benefits cannot be measured exactly nor can their relative proportion be determined. Therefore, any attempt to proportion costs equitably in terms of benefits received must be based on estimates.

5. Any system to finance higher education, however conceived, must contend with those inequities that stem from the differing abilities of families and students to pay. For affluent families that seek an expensive college education for their children, the ratio of educational costs to benefits is likely to be higher than average. If equal educational opportunity is to be provided for students from low-income families, generous subsidies are required, in the form of either repayable loans or monetary grants. For students with a limited ability to pay, the ratio of educational costs to benefits will, therefore, likely be lower than average.

6. When higher education resources are limited, a conflict can be expected regarding the goals relating to equality of educational opportunity; equity in allocating costs; diversity of programs and institutions; and quality, efficiency, and balanced budgets. In particular, if equality of educational opportunity is to be achieved, equitable payment cannot be expected from poor students. Any effort to achieve efficiency in higher education would doubtlessly eliminate many small institutions, which, because of the variety of choice they provide the student, should be preserved. Increasing the number of students from low-income groups may make it more difficult to increase the average quality of education for *all* students. These kinds of conflicts suggest that the real difficulty in establishing an overall strategy for financing higher education lies in determining and securing agreement over the *relative* emphasis to be given each goal.

7. Concerning the higher education finance role of the student and his family,

there appears to be wide agreement on several propositions.[33] First, there seems to be no debate on the presumption that the student himself should bear the full cost of any unrecovered loss of earnings due to his devoting time to higher education.[34] Second, the student should contribute as much as possible through part-time work, though such work should not unduly interfere with either his studies or his participation in meaningful extracurricular activities. Third, the family, according to its ability, should contribute toward an undergraduate's living costs and incidental expenses. Fourth, some form of student aid should be available—either grants or long-term loans—to cover living expenses and other college costs for which a family cannot afford to pay. Finally, instructional costs should be distinguished from expenses for research and public service not closely related to instruction, and the latter should not be financed through tuition but through taxes and private gifts.

On the basis of these general observations, most of the arguments concerning the financing of higher education can be said to focus on the answers to four questions:

1. What fraction of total educational costs should be borne by the student and his family and what proportion by society?

2. Should the public subsidy to higher education go primarily to institutions or to students?

3. Should subsidies to students be primarily in the form of loans or grants?

4. How can private colleges and universities be preserved?

A review of the alternative responses to these questions and the supporting rationale is presented in later sections. As a preparatory step, however, it is necessary to identify higher education costs and the actual proportion currently being provided by the various income sources.

The Costs of Higher Education and Who Now Pays

On a unit basis, the costs of higher education in any given year can be defined as the value of all resources devoted in that year to the education of a full-time student enrolled in a college or university.[35] These costs may be divided into three components: (a) the value of the time the student spends in acquiring an education—i.e., the earnings he foregoes while

---

[33] See Howard R. Bowen, "Who Pays the Higher Education Bill?" in *Financing Higher Education: Alternatives for the Federal Government*, op. cit., p. 288.

[34] Poor youths who are needed at home, either to work to support the family, or to care for younger children, elderly parents, etc., should be entitled to receive a subsidy to compensate them for earnings foregone while attending college.

[35] Not included are such indirect costs as the loss of return on alternative investments of capital used in higher education and the loss by local governments of property taxes on school land.

attending college; (b) incidental expenses for books, supplies, transportation, etc.; and (c) expenditures by the institution for instruction and related supporting activities. The two last-named components constitute the direct costs of higher education.[36]

Although a college degree significantly increases a student's *lifetime* earnings, while he attends college he foregoes whatever income he could have earned through full-time employment. For the average college student, this loss of income is estimated to be approximately $4,680 per year.[37]

The second major cost element, incidental expenses related to college attendance, includes books, supplies, equipment, transportation, and (perhaps most important) living expenses. (The normal costs of living that a student would have incurred had he not attended college are *not* included.) Incidental expenses vary greatly among students and institutions, but at 4-year public institutions they are estimated to be $263 yearly; at private colleges and universities, $491.

The third cost element includes expenditures by the institution for instruction and related supporting activities. Previously discussed, they consist of expenditures for instruction and departmental research, extension and public service, libraries, physical plant operation and maintenance, and general administration and student services. They are estimated to be $2,153 yearly at public 4-year institutions and $2,539 at private 4-year institutions.

Costs on a per student basis and estimates of payment by source for the public and private sector are presented in tables XII-4 and XII-5, and in figure XII-2. While based on the best available data, the statistics are, nevertheless, estimates that suggest only the general magnitude and proportions involved. The fact they are not precise does not, however, preclude some general conclusions:

    1. By recognizing as an *indirect cost* the value of a student's time, the principal costs of higher education are those associated with the student, not the institution. As the following summary indicates, when costs are broadly defined in terms of all resources employed and foregone, students and their families are responsible for at least three-fourths of the costs of higher education.

---

[36] See Bowen, "Who Pays the Higher Education Bill?" op. cit., pp. 282–85.

[37] Over a 4-year period as a Federal employee, a youth capable of a higher education could earn an average annual salary of $6,000 to $7,000. The Federal salary schedule is reasonably competitive with that of private enterprise. Of course some youths not attending college, especially women, might not be employed. Assuming 15 percent unemployment, a reasonably conservative estimate of the earnings the average college student foregoes would be $5,250 to $5,850. Students who work part time or during the summer earn from $585 to $1,175; their net unrecovered loss is, therefore estimated to be approximately $4,680.

Higher Education Costs

Student's payment for:	Public	Private
Incidental expenses	$ 263	$ 491
Tuition not covered by grants	287	1,328
Unrecovered loss of foregone income	4,680	4,680
	$5,230 or 74%	$6,499 or 84%

Society's payment* for:		
Institutional student education expenditures not covered by tuition	$1,866 or 26%	$1,211 or 16%
Total	$7,096 student	$7,710 student

* In the public sector, primarily through taxes; in the private sector, primarily from philanthropic gifts.

2. When only the *direct costs* of higher education are considered—i.e., resources actually utilized—the situation changes substantially. A student and his family pay 60 percent of direct costs in the private sector but only 23 percent in the public sector (see figure XII-2).

3. *Society's support* to private institutions through direct aid and student grants covers only 48 percent of *student education expenditures* ($1,211/$2,539). Private institutions must rely on *tuition* payments (less grants) to finance 52 percent of their direct costs ($1,328/$2,539), while tuition at public institutions pays for only 13 percent of these costs ($287/$2,153). The extent to which private colleges and universities rely on tuition is, in large part, the basic cause of their financial plight.

4. *Direct support to institutions* (not in the form of tuition payments financed by student aid grants), which the private sector receives mainly from gifts and endowment income, amounts to $743 per student; in contrast, State government support of public institutions is double this amount, or $1,550 per student.

5. *Student aid grants* to finance the direct costs of higher education in the private sector are double what they are in the public sector.

Financial Support Received by Students[38]

Students attending private institutions spend about 70 percent more for their education and living expenses than do students attending public

---

[38] For details on the impact of financial barriers, enrollment patterns and family income, the financial costs of college, how people pay for college, and financial aid resources and their distribution, see W. Lee Hansen, "An Examination of Barriers to College Attendance" in *Trends in Postsecondary Education*, op. cit., pp. 31–55.

For a recent survey of the educational interests, aspirations, and finances of college sophomores, see Elizabeth W. Haven and Dwight H. Horch, *How College Students Finance Their Education*, College Scholarship Service of the College Entrance Examination Board, Princeton, N.J., 1972.

Table XII-4.—Illustrative costs of higher education and related sources of payment at public-4-year institutions; dollar amounts per student and percent distribution: 1970–71

Total Cost of education and living expenses	$8,617 (100%)			
A. *Cost of higher education*		7,096 (82%)		
1. Direct cost:			2,146 (28%)	
(a) Incidental student expenses[1]				263 (3%)
(b) Institutional student education expenditures[2]				2,153 (25%)
2. Indirect cost: unrecovered loss of foregone income[3]		1,521 (18%)		
B. *Normal living expenses*[4]			4,680 (54%)	
Payment for out-of-pocket costs (direct cost plus normal living exp.)	$3,937 (100%)			
A. *Sources of student support*		2,235 (57%)		
1. Family			895 (23%)	
2. Student			1,176 (30%)	
(a) Self-employment				649 (16%)
(b) Spouse's employment				64 (2%)
(c) Savings				293 (77%)
(d) Repayable loan				170 (4%)
3. Society (grant)			164 (4%)	
B. *Sources of support to institution from society*[5]		1,702 (43%)		
1. Federal Government appropriations			117 (3%)	
2. State and local government appropriations			1,550 (39%)	
3. Endowment income			17	
4. Private gifts			18	
Payment for direct cost of higher education	$2,416 (100%)			
A. *By student and family, less normal living expenses*		550 (23%)		
1. Tuition (less grant received, $450–$164)			287 (12%)	
2. Incidental expenses			263 (11%)	

E. *By society*

1. Government	1,866 (77%)	1,667 (69%)
2. Endowment income		17 (1%)
3. Private gifts		18 (1%)
4. Grant to student		164 (7%)

[1] Expenses for books, supplies, transportation, dormitory, etc., beyond normal living expenses.

[2] Student education expenditures for instruction and departmental research, extension and public service, libraries, plant maintenance and operation, and general administration and student services.

[3] Full-time employment income foregone by student due to college attendance, less student's part-time earnings.

[4] Living expenses that the student would have incurred even if he had not attended college.

[5] Excluding tuition and fees paid by student sources of support.

Table XII-5.—Illustrative costs of higher education and related sources of payment for private 4-year institutions; dollar amounts per student and percent distribution: 1970–71

Total cost of education and living expenses	$9,231 (100%)			
A. *Cost of higher education*				
1. Direct cost:		7,710 (84%)		
(a) Incidental student expenses[1]			491 (5%)	
(b) Institutional student education expenditures[2]			3,030 (33%)	2,539 (28%)
2. Indirect cost: unrecovered loss of foregone income[3]			4,680 (51%)	
B. *Normal living expenses*[4]		1,521 (16%)		
Payment for out-of-pocket costs (direct cost plus normal living exp.)	$4,551 (100%)			
A. *Sources of support to student*		3,808 (84%)		
1. Family			1,673 (37%)	
2. Student			1,667 (37%)	
(a) Self-employment				795 (17%)
(b) Spouse's employment				88 (2%)
(c) Savings				386 (8%)
(d) Repayable loan				398 (9%)
3. By society (grant)			468 (10%)	
B. *Sources of support to institution from society*[5]		743 (16%)		
1. Federal Government appropriations			53 (1%)	
2. State and local Government appropriations			47 (1%)	
3. Endowment income			263 (6%)	
4. Private gifts			380 (8%)	
Payment for direct cost of higher education	$3,030 (100%)			
A. *By student and family, less normal living expenses*				
1. Tuition (less grant received, $1,796–$468)		1,819 (60%)	1,328 (44%)	
2. Incidental expenses			491 (16%)	

B. *By society*	1,211 (40%)	
1. Government		100 (3%)
2. Endowment income		263 (9%)
3. Private gifts		380 (13%)
4. Grant to student		468 (15%)

[1] Expenses for books, supplies, transportation, dormitory, etc., beyond normal living expenses.
[2] Student education expenditures for instruction and departmental research, extension and public service, libraries, plant maintenance and operation, and general administration and student services.
[3] Full-time employment income foregone by student due to college attendance, less student's part-time earnings.
[4] Living expenses that the student would have incurred even if he had not attended college.
[5] Excluding tuition and fees paid by student sources of support.

Figure XII-2. — Estimated payments by source of direct costs of higher education per student for public and private 4-year institutions: 1970-71

Private 4-year institutions

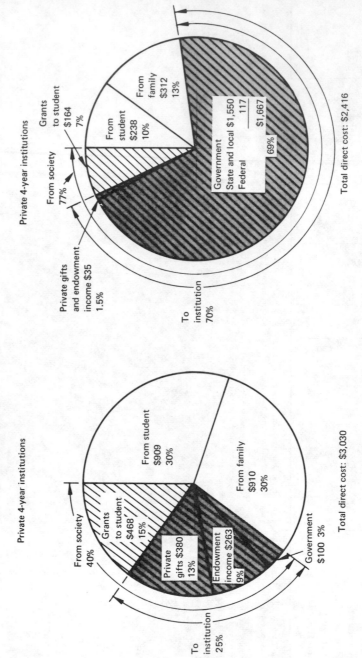

Private 4-year institutions

Grants to student $164 7%

From family $312 13%

From student $238 10%

From society 77%

Government
State and local $1,550 117
Federal $1,667
69%

Private gifts and endowment income $35 1.5%

To institution 70%

Total direct cost: $2,416

From student $909 30%

From family $910 30%

From society 40%

Grants to student $468 15%

Private gifts $380 13%

Endowment income $263 9%

Government $100 3%

To institution 25%

Total direct cost: $3,030

Note. — Direct costs of higher education include student incidental expenses related to college attendance and institutional student education expenditure; unrecovered loss of foregone income and normal living expenses are not included.

institutions. The higher out-of-pocket costs in the private sector are due primarily to the higher tuition charged. The breakdown of estimated student expenses at 4-year institutions, 1970–71, is as follows:[39]

Student out-of-pocket expenditures for	*Public*	*Private*
Incidental expenses	$ 263	$ 491
Tuition	450	1,796
Normal living expenses	1,521	1,521
	$2,234	$3,808

To pay these expenses, students rely on three principal sources: (1) their family; (2) part- or full-time employment, savings, and/or loans; and (3) grants or scholarships. Data recently available from the American Council on Education make it possible to estimate the relative amount received by freshmen from each of these sources *by parental income level.* (See table XII-6 and figure XII-3.) These figures represent estimates from questionnaire data and are not intended to reflect precise amounts.[40] The dollar amounts are for 4-year institutions only.

Despite shortcomings in the estimating procedure and in the ACE data themselves, it can be assumed that the general pattern of support which emerges is reasonably accurate. Additional ACE data suggest that, with some exceptions, the pattern for freshmen is also fairly typical for upper-

---

[39] For illustrative purposes estimates are based on unpublished Office of Education data. They compare favorably with those published in an Educational Testing Service report prepared for the College Scholarship Service of the College Entrance Examination Board. Based on information gathered from 3,000 full- and part-time students who were sophomores in the 1969–70 academic year, the average cost of 1 year at a public college was $1,869; at a private college, $3,329.

[40] The ACE questionnaire asked students to indicate one of four possible responses for each source of financial support: (1) not a source, (2) minor source, 1–25 percent, (3) minor source, 26–50 percent, and (4) major source, over 50 percent. For purposes of deriving the single values presented here, the four responses were assumed to represent the following *average* relative contributions: (1) 0 percent, (2) 5 percent, (3) 30 percent, and (4) 60 percent. For the various parental income levels, the total percentage distribution from all sources should equal 100 percent. Using this weighting, the totals ranged from a low of 78.4 percent to a high of 117.2 percent. Each distribution was corrected to total 100 percent, as shown in table XII-6.

It should be pointed out that in the ACE survey many students, either through inability or unwillingness, failed to identify accurately the interval representing their family income. Agnes Martinko, educational research associate with the Department of Public Instruction, Harrisburg, Pa., found that only 51 percent of the students responded accurately to this question. The degree of accuracy, according to her study, diminished considerably at income intervals above $15,000.

Table XII-6.—Estimated percentage distribution by source of financial support used by freshman students to pay for college and living expenses during academic year 1969, classified by level of parental income

Public institutions

Income source	All incomes	Parental income								
		Less than $4,000	$4,000–$5,999	$6,000–$7,999	$8,000–$9,999	$10,000–$14,999	$15,000–$19,999	$20,000–$24,999	$25,000–$29,999	$30,000[1] or more
Family	37.0	20.8	22.5	24.1	29.3	36.4	44.1	38.1	60.8	48.0
Summer employment	18.1	17.7	19.6	22.0	20.8	19.7	16.2	19.3	12.3	10.0
College employment	9.0	12.4	12.3	9.2	10.7	9.4	7.3	9.0	3.8	4.6
Spouse employment	2.5	3.3	2.8	3.0	2.0	2.2	2.7	4.8	1.3	2.6
Savings, investments	12.3	12.8	14.2	16.0	14.3	13.1	11.6	10.4	8.1	5.0
Repayable loan	6.9	10.6	7.8	8.2	7.8	7.0	5.5	3.8	3.1	12.0
Grant	10.0	18.5	14.9	12.0	10.1	8.4	8.6	11.4	3.9	14.5
Other	4.2	3.9	5.9	5.5	5.0	3.8	4.2	3.2	6.7	3.3
Total	100.0	100.0	100.0	100.0	100.0	100.0	100.0	100.0	100.0	100.0

Private institutions

Income source	All incomes	Less than $4,000	$4,000–$5,999	$6,000–$7,999	$8,000–$9,999	$10,000–$14,999	$15,000–$19,999	$20,000–$24,999	$25,000–$29,999	$30,000 or more
						Parental income				
Family	39.7	14.7	21.9	22.8	28.4	38.4	50.3	61.7	63.8	70.7
Summer employment	13.2	13.6	15.0	15.2	15.1	14.1	12.5	10.2	9.2	7.7
College employment	5.4	10.1	7.2	7.0	5.7	5.3	5.1	3.5	3.0	3.1
Spouse employment	1.9	3.3	1.6	1.8	1.9	1.9	1.9	1.4	3.0	2.2
Savings, investments	9.0	6.5	9.1	10.7	10.2	9.9	8.3	6.6	7.0	7.1
Repayable loan	9.3	14.8	13.2	13.2	12.4	9.5	6.1	3.7	4.8	2.3
Grant	17.3	31.6	27.0	22.8	22.2	16.8	11.8	9.8	6.1	3.8
Other	4.2	5.4	5.0	6.5	4.1	4.1	4.0	3.1	3.1	3.1
Total	100.0	100.0	100.0	100.0	100.0	100.0	100.0	100.0	100.0	100.0

[1] No satisfactory explanation was given for the inconsistency in data reported by freshmen from families with incomes of $30,000 or more.

Source: Estimates interpreted from data provided by the American Council on Education.

classmen.[41] As is well known, the family is most frequently relied upon to support a student attending college. At all parental income levels, the family contributes nearly 40 percent of the total support received by a student in both the public and private sectors. As would be expected, however, the family contribution is highly dependent on parental income level—more so in the private than in the public sector. Based on a smoothly drawn curve (rather than on the actual irregular plot), the family contribution in the public sector increases from approximately 21 percent of the total (a contribution of $400) if parental incomes are less than $6,000 yearly to nearly 55 percent ($1,050) when incomes are $30,000 or more. In the private sector the range is from approximately 15 percent ($488) to a remarkable 70 percent ($2,280).

While family ability to pay probably increases geometrically, or at a *faster* rate relative to increases in parental income,[42] the actual curve of family contributions increases at a *declining* rate relative to parental income. Thus, it would probably be more equitable if the curves showing family contribution in figure XII-3 were concave upward rather than convex upward. The situation as it now exists supports the contention that under present arrangements, middle-income families, compared to high-income families, are forced to pay an inequitably large share for student education and living costs. This inequity could be corrected by establishing a sliding scale of tuition charges based on student and family ability to pay. To achieve a concave upward curve, it would be necessary to raise substantially the tuition charged students from high-income families. Since the demand for higher education is generally believed to be somewhat more inelastic among high-income families than among medium- and low-income families (i.e., relatively more insensitive to price), higher tuition would pose no serious threat to attendance by high-income students. If the demand for higher education is more elastic (i.e., more sensitive to price differentials) among low-income families, it would be necessary to establish modestly progressive tuition charges at lower family income levels so as not to discourage attendance by low-income students.[43] What would likely occur would be that no tuition would be charged at the lowest family income levels.

---

[41] In comparison with seniors, freshmen in both the public and private sectors relied somewhat *more* on family income (particularly if parental income was at a lower level) and on grants, and substantially *less* (about half) on employment earnings. In the private sector, freshmen relied *less* on summer employment earnings than did seniors. No other significant differences were discernible, and those noted did not appear of a sufficient magnitude to preclude utilizing the freshmen pattern for *all* students.

[42] See model of the expected contribution from parents, chapter IV.

[43] For studies on the elasticity of demand in higher education, see John Bishop, *The Private Demand for Places in Higher Education*, Panel for Student Financial Need Analysis, College Scholarship Service, Princeton, N.J., 1973.

Figure XII-3. — Estimated percentage distribution and amount per student, by source of financial support used by freshmen students to pay for college and living expenses during academic year 1969, classified by level of parental income

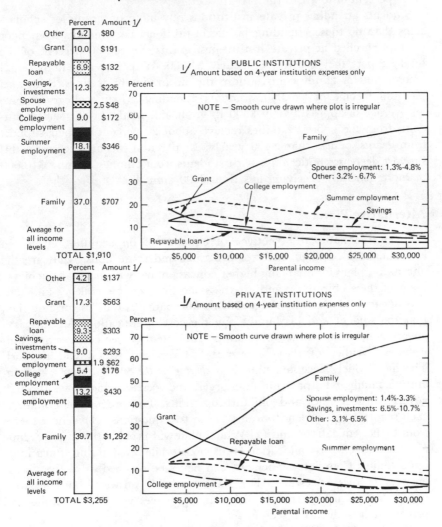

	Percent	Amount 1/
Other	4.2	$80
Grant	10.0	$191
Repayable loan	6.9	$132
Savings, investments	12.3	$235
Spouse employment	2.5	$48
College employment	9.0	$172
Summer employment	18.1	$346
Family	37.0	$707
Aveage for all income levels		
TOTAL	$1,910	

PUBLIC INSTITUTIONS
1/ Amount based on 4-year institution expenses only

NOTE — Smooth curve drawn where plot is irregular

Family

Spouse employment: 1.3%-4.8%
Other: 3.2% - 6.7%

Grant

College employment

Summer employment

Savings

Repayable loan

$5,000 $10,000 $15,000 $20,000 $25,000 $30,000
Parental income

	Percent	Amount 1/
Other	4.2	$137
Grant	17.3	$563
Repayable loan	9.3	$303
Savings, investments	9.0	$293
Spouse employment	1.9	$62
College employment	5.4	$176
Summer employment	13.2	$430
Family	39.7	$1,292
Average for all income levels		
TOTAL	$3,255	

PRIVATE INSTITUTIONS
1/ Amount based on 4-year institution expenses only

NOTE — Smooth curve drawn where plot is irregular

Family

Spouse employment: 1.4%-3.3%
Savings, investments: 6.5%-10.7%
Other: 3.1%-6.5%

Grant

Repayable loan

Summer employment

College employment

$5,000 $10,000 $15,000 $20,000 $25,000 $30,000
Parental income

Source: Estimates interpreted from data provided by the American Council on Education.

Funds earned, saved, or borrowed by a student to finance his education and living expenses are sizable—amounting on the average to approximately 48.8 percent of the total support of students at public institutions, and 38.8 percent of those at private colleges and universities. At all parental income levels the student contribution amounts to $932 in the public sector and $1,264 in the private sector. The student contribution, which is highest at low parental-income levels, declines gradually as parental income and the family's contribution increases. The combined student and family contribution is $1,639 (86 percent of total) in the public sector and $2,556 (78.5 percent of total) in the private sector.

Students attending private institutions rely more on grants or scholarships than do those attending public institutions. For students from poor families enrolled at private institutions, grants average 30 percent of the total support they receive, or nearly $1,000. With increases in parental income and/or family contribution, the aid gradually declines. Still, at a parental income of $20,000, students attending private colleges receive an average of approximately $300 in grant aid. In the public sector, students from the poorest families receive about 20 percent of their support from grants, or less than $400 yearly. As parental income increases, this support decreases noticeably, with students from families earning $10,000 or more generally receiving less than $200 annually.

Alternative Plans

Given the national objectives of equality of opportunity, equity in allocating costs, and diversity of programs and institutions, what are the alternative plans for financing higher education that will ensure the achievement of these objectives, and, at the same time, enable colleges and universities to balance their budgets? One alternative is full-cost pricing, i.e., that the student and his family pay the cost of education. Another is a government subsidy that would support a system of free colleges and universities. Neither of these extremes has received widespread support. The most widely accepted plan is a *sharing of the cost* between a student and his family, who pay tuition charges, and society, which pays through government subsidies and philanthropic gifts. The proportional share of each segment will depend on answers to two questions: (1) Who benefits from higher education? and (2) Which plan will provide the most revenue and the most effective allocation of resources while maintaining educational opportunity? Complete agreement can never be reached as to the "best" answers to these questions. For some workable answers, however, one need only examine current policies and practices within the public and private higher education sectors.

The low tuition and high government subsidy prevalent at public institutions are based on the premise that the external or social benefits produced by higher education warrant substantial government investment. Low tuition provides equality of opportunity yet ensures some degree of equity of payment through the progressive income tax system.[44] Financ-

---

[44] See footnote 51 for limitations on the ability of the progressive income tax system to provide equity of payment for education.

ing of private institutions is based on the premise that the student directly and personally derives the greatest benefit from a higher education; therefore, the individual enrollee should assume most of the costs. As in the public sector, equity of payment for social benefits is obtained through the progressive tax system. Society also contributes through philanthropy, with alumni in effect "repaying" their alma mater for individual benefits accrued as a result of their education. Scholarships and loans are provided students who cannot afford the high tuition.

Any plan of financing higher education must be such that it encourages *growth* to the point at which the marginal social and individual benefits combined are equal to the marginal benefits derived from investment in other public and private goods and services. No one expects that this goal can be achieved if the public approach succeeds at the expense of the private approach or vice versa. Both must be so structured that together they provide a diversity of educational programs and the fair competition essential to a healthy growing enterprise. But what the future course of each should be is uncertain—a decision made especially critical by current financial problems. And what is appropriate Federal financial strategy? In succeeding sections, these topics and the issues involved will be discussed. The order of presentation will be as follows: (1) the case for high tuition, (2) grants versus loans, (3) the case for low tuition, and (4) subsidies to institutions or aid to students. A summary of some of the main features of alternative financial approaches to tuition is presented in table XII-7.

The Case for High Tuition

The case for high tuition rests on the logic, and during financial difficulty on the apparent necessity, of tapping fully every source benefiting from higher education. The position taken by proponents is that the price of higher education should be commensurate with the benefits derived and the ability to pay. It is argued that the benefits from higher education accrue primarily to students and their parents; therefore, instructional costs should be paid primarily through tuition. Equal opportunity is provided, in part, by offering grants or loans to students with low incomes. If a limited amount of tax revenue is available, those favoring high tuition contend that it is better to subsidize low-income students, many of whom could otherwise not afford to go to college, than to subsidize through low tuition above-average-income students who can afford to go to college and would do so even without the subsidy. In effect, then, the higher tuition is charged only to those who can afford it and are willing to pay.

The private sector of higher education operates primarily on this basis, with students and their parents paying on the average $1,819, or approximately 60 percent of the direct costs of education—i.e., institutional

Table XII-7.—Descriptive summary of two basic plans for financing higher education

	Low tuition plan	High tuition plan
Description	Institutions receive large government subsidies approximating full cost of education. Major payment by society through progressive tax system.	Institutions charge tuition approximating full cost of education. Generous aid provided needy students by government and philanthropic sources. Major payment by students and their families with middle and high incomes. Society pays through progressive tax system.
Equity: Benefactor believed to receive greatest returns from education and therefore is most responsible for its cost.	*Society at large* Payment made through progressive tax system according to earning level. College graduate and nongraduate taxed alike; graduates average larger payments due to greater lifetime earnings.	*Students* Middle- and upper income students and their families pay more through tuition and taxes. Students from low-income families pay substantially less.
Equality: Equal educational opportunity among all income levels	Low-cost education provided indiscriminately for all. Aid often not sufficient to cover *total* expenses required by needy students.	Needy students must receive generous aid. Insufficient aid severely limits opportunity for qualified low-income students. Opportunity for middle- and high-income students limited only by willingness to pay (according to financial ability) and/or to borrow.
Market action: Student choice of college is less dependent on ability to pay. Stimulates fair competition among institutions.	Low-tuition public institutions compete fairly within State for resident students. Low-tuition institutions have competitive advantage in a dual-pricing system. Con-	High-tuition private institutions compete fairly among themselves to the extent equal student aid is provided. If tuition were raised in the public sector, the negative effects of dual

Table XII-7.—Descriptive summary of two basic plans for financing higher education—Continued

	Low tuition plan	High tuition plan
	tinuation of dual system hastens growth of public sector and forces some private institutions to close	pricing would be reduced. Substantial student aid improves competition among sectors.
Resource allocation	Allocation of resources based on judgment of institutional administrators, faculty, and government officials attempting to maximize returns to society and to the individual student. Inefficient from standpoint of providing equal subsidy to all students regardless of need.	Allocation based on student preference to maximize direct benefits to himself. May result in institutions catering to student buyer. Efficient from standpoint of providing greatest amount of aid to students most in need.
Redistribution of income effects	Mainly redistributes income *within* family income classes in favor of students attending low-tuition colleges.	Redistributes income from families and students with high incomes to families and students with low incomes.
Total public support level required	Relatively high, since government subsidy provides nearly free education to all, including those who could afford to pay.	Relatively low, since tuition payments by students serve as a primary source of income.
Government control	Restrictive controls can be attached to government subsidies to institutions. Certain institutions can be favored by nature of support formula.	Less control by government; however, institutions may be pressured to respond to student preferences.
Administrative costs	Lower administrative costs due to relatively small number of total U. S. colleges and universities receiving institutional subsidies.	Higher costs as a result of directly aiding many thousands of students.

student education expenditures and incidental student expenses. Those who advocate raising tuition in the public sector propose no decrease in existing levels of government subsidy and philanthropic support but suggest that substantial increases in total funding will come from additional income contributed by students who can afford to pay. The direct costs of higher education in the public sector are approximately $2,416 per student, of which approximately $550 or 23 percent is paid by the student and/or his family for tuition and incidental expenses. If student and family payments were doubled, revenues for direct costs in the public sector would be increased by 23 percent (from $2,416 to $2,966). Of the additional tuition revenue collected, a proportion would be used for scholarships to help capable students who lack the money to attend college. If this added revenue were not used to ensure entry to those who deserve it, the case for higher tuition would be seriously weakened.

What is the rationale for the argument that because students and their families are able to pay for higher education they should do so? First, it should be recognized that despite recent progress in this country to extend educational opportunities, vastly unequal participation in higher education continues. In 1972 only 19 percent of persons between 25 and 29 years of age had completed 4 or more years of college. Furthermore, benefits from higher education are more personal—dependent as they are on individual ability and initiative—than are benefits from such tax-supported public services as elementary and secondary education, fire and police protection, and sewage and highway service. Thus, while everyone gains to some degree by the presence in society of college-educated men and women, the value accrues primarily to the individual participant, and these participants are a minority of the population. Therefore, so the argument goes, since higher education benefits only a few, it should be paid for primarily by the individual participant, according to his ability to pay, rather than by the general public. The fact that the increase in per capita income has far exceeded most increases in tuition, the argument continues, makes it possible for many more people to afford to go to college.

Advocates of high tuition as well as those who favor low tuition agree that it would be desirable for the beneficiaries of higher education to pay the costs according to the value received. But there is disagreement on the degree to which benefits are shared by a student, his parents, and society. Because no precise answer concerning equity is possible, the debate will continue. College-educated students obviously derive material gains through larger lifetime earnings as well as through intellectual and cultural satisfactions. College attendance as a transient experience is enjoyed by most students and is, therefore, worth something in itself to participants. Society also gains from the presence of college-educated persons. Some of these benefits are tangible and can be documented: the lower crime rate and fewer auto accidents among college-educated persons, the enhancement of most professions resulting from formal training, etc. But, as with the nonpecuniary benefits to the student, most benefits to society are illusive and almost always related to education through correlation rather than through a causal basis. Despite vaunted claims concerning the enormous value of a college education, it is extremely difficult to demonstrate precisely those values that are exclusively the result of the college experience and those that might have been acquired without it.[45] And, of course, no price tag can be attached to the cultural and citizenship attitudes attributed to college attendance. Such intangibles make it impossible to draw any realistic comparison between the relative gains to society and to the individual. As an example, consider that the degree earned by a medical doctor is worth to society every cent of the educational cost, while, at the same time, the $1.5 million lifetime income of a physician is worth to him personally all tuition costs. The benefits of education to society and to the individual far exceed its cost, not only in medicine but in many other professions, and either beneficiary would, or at least should, be willing to pay the entire bill. How then can payment for higher education be divided equitably?

On the problem of equity, proponents of higher tuition suggest that since the student most directly and fully benefits from an education, determination of his fair share of the cost can best be resolved by letting market action in the sale of education set prices on a competitive basis. Students, they contend, would be willing to pay for their education (as they pay for any other service) in some proportion to the benefits they expect to receive. Society, as a secondary beneficiary, would be willing to support higher education, they argue, to the extent of the unpaid balance. Furthermore,

---

[45] Keniston and Gerzon cite four major conflicts with the assumption that observed differences between graduates and nongraduates can be causally attributed to higher education. First, college graduates as a group share a number of characteristics, apart from attendance at college, that may have important and truly causal relationships to factors that empirically differentiate them from non-college-educated individuals. Second, those who enter college are demonstrably different from those who do not. In view of the fact that college attenders, when compared to nonattenders of equal ability and background, possess a distinctive set of psychological characteristics and motivations, the problem of attributing differences between graduates and nongraduates to the effects of college becomes even more complicated. A third difficulty lies in the vagueness of the so-called "college experience" concept. Because different kinds of colleges may have different effects on students, studies that merely contrast graduates with nongraduates inevitably obscure these effects and therefore may be misleading. Fourth, the most intractable methodological problem springs from the *interaction* between freshman characteristics and college characteristics. Since students apply selectively to colleges, the correlation between freshman characteristics and college characteristics creates great difficulty in identifying those differences in the graduates of each college that are clearly attributable to the special characteristics of that college. See Kenneth Keniston and Mark Gerzon, "Human and Social Benefits" in *Universal Higher Education: Costs and Benefits*, op. cit., pp. 44–47.

they say, if students and their parents were confronted with prices that more fully reflect the true cost of education, high school graduates would find it easier to make decisions about the type and location of a college they plan to attend. If such were the case, more efficient resource allocation could result.

In the public sector, higher tuition would reduce some of the unfair aspects resulting from the existing dual-price system. Even though students from low- and middle-income families might derive more benefit from an education acquired at a private—as opposed to a public —college or university, the majority cannot afford to pay the high tuition at private institutions. Consequently, they are forced, solely because of their economic status, to matriculate at those public colleges or universities which charge low-to-moderate tuition. If tuition at both private and public institutions of higher learning were approximately the same, a student's choice could be based on factors far more meaningful than cost.

In summary, the basis for arguments favoring high tuition include the following: (1) Since the student is the one who derives the greatest benefit from a college education, he should pay as much for such an education as he is able to. (2) Government and philanthropic support of higher education, together with high tuition, would maximize the total revenue available to operate colleges and universities. (3) Funds derived from high tuition could increase the number of grants and loans available to needy students and thereby enhance the ideal of equal educational opportunity for all. (4) High tuition would provide greater market action and stimulate healthy institutional competition. (5) Because high tuition more closely approximates the cost of providing a higher education, it could effect a more efficient use of resources. (6) High tuition, together with generous aid to needy students, would tend to redistribute income from the wealthy to the poor.

Grants Versus Loans

Currently, needy students receive slightly more financial support from grants and scholarships than they do from loans.[46] Because of student preference for an outright grant of money, as opposed to a long-term loan, grants can be expected to continue as the more widely preferred form of student aid. Yet, increasing scarcity of resources may dictate that student

---

[46] Among sophomores attending college in 1969–70, the percentage of income received from grants and loans at all colleges was 10 percent and 9 percent, respectively. At public 4-year institutions, the percentages were 9 percent and 10 percent; at private 4-year institutions, 15 percent and 11 percent, and at public 2-year institutions, 6 percent and 8 percent. See Haven and Horch, *How College Students Finance Their Education*, op. cit., p. 10.

preference can no longer be the dominant factor governing aid policy. In the past 10 years student borrowing has increased rapidly, mainly because of federally supported programs. If the financial situation of colleges and universities grows worse and if tuition rates rise still further, the need for student aid will increase substantially. The preferable form of this expanded aid has been the subject of considerable study and not a little controversy.[47] Much of the argument centers on how the benefits of higher education are viewed, particularly on whether the public or private sector is favored.

Those who view higher education as primarily benefiting the individual expect the student to pay a substantial part of the cost—by borrowing if necessary. While some individuals may be reluctant to assume a debt for this purpose, careful consideration of the returns from higher education can justify borrowing.[48] On the other hand, those who view the benefits of higher education as primarily societal in nature are apt to feel that the public should bear the major cost of higher education, either by providing free or low-cost public higher education to all or by providing students with grants that enable them to attend more expensive private institutions. There are those who believe that ". . . no student who is willing to work a reasonable amount and to live modestly should have to go deeply into debt to secure an education."[49]

Generally speaking, private institutions, in order to compete for able students, must provide more grants, loans, and work opportunities than their public counterparts. Since grants reduce immediate out-of-pocket costs, they are the most effective means of attracting students. Loans, while less attractive, also help private institutions compete; moreover, they are less costly. As long as the dual-pricing system exists, there can be little doubt that the private sector, to preserve its competitive position, cannot cut back its program of student grants.

It is probably recognized by most educators that heavy institutional reliance on loans is a serious obstacle to low-income students capable of and desiring to attend college. "No matter how readily available the loans

---

[47] For three different approaches in one book, see W. Lee Hansen and Burton A. Weisbroad, "A New Approach to Higher Education"; Robert W. Hartman, "Student Loans for Higher Education"; and Howard R. Bowen, "Who Pays the Higher Education Bill?" in *Financing Higher Education: Alternatives for the Federal Government*, op. cit., pp. 117–42, 177–99, and 281–98, respectively.

[48] Borrowing is made more attractive by the Government's making available subsidized loans at lower rates of interest than would be charged in the free capital market, with longer repayment periods or with the start of repayment delayed. For some technical features of various forms of "favorable" loans, see Roger E. Bolton, "The Economics and Public Financing of Higher Education: An Overview" in *The Economics and Financing of Higher Education in the United States*, op. cit., pp. 80–92.

[49] Bowen, "Finance and the Aims of American Higher Education," op. cit., p. 158.

or how generous the terms, to ask young persons from low-income and/or minority backgrounds to assume indebtedness of $5,000, $10,000, or $20,000, to acquire a formal higher education presents a formidable barrier. The plan might not frighten away middle-income people, but it would surely deter low-income students."[50] Repayment of loans is also a factor. A student from a high-income family as a rule can end his college career with little or no debt, whereas a student from a low-income family must repay the money he has borrowed following graduation—when he is least able to do so.

Whatever one's philosophical view concerning who should assume the costs of a college education, consideration of the relative advantages and disadvantages of loans versus grants tends to support certain conclusions. Grants, not loans, best offset hindrances to equal educational opportunity among low-income and disadvantaged students. Supplemented by whatever a student and his family can reasonably pay, a grant should permit him to attend any public institution or any of the more moderately priced private institutions. As long as the dual-pricing system exists, the number and amount of grants should be such that private institutions can remain competitive. To the degree that resources are scarce and funding is not adequate to provide complete educational opportunity through grants, greater reliance must be placed on loans. In some instances it may be necessary to encourage certain students to borrow so that the college or university can extend its limited grant funding to as many needy students as possible. To promote flexibility in choice of college, ease budgets, and cover any unusual expenses, loans should always be readily available to every student. Undoubtedly some kind of promotional campaign will be required to convince students and their parents of the worthwhileness of postfinancing a higher education.

ADVANTAGES	DISADVANTAGES
Loans	
1. Borrowing is consistent with the view that higher education is primarily a private good that should be paid for by a student user.	1. Students may be reluctant to assume a long-term debt in order to finance their education.
2. Loans help the public sector, since students reluctant to borrow are inclined to attend low-cost public institutions rather than borrow to attend high-cost private institutions.	2. Loans do not provide equal opportunity: low-income students tend to be reluctant to assume debts and find it difficult to repay borrowed money.

---

[50] Bowen, "Who Pays the Higher Education Bill?", op. cit., p. 292.

ADVANTAGES	DISADVANTAGES
3. For the same annual expenditure, loans obtain more capital to aid more students than do grants.	3. If financed by government borrowing, loans increase inflationary pressures.

Grants

1. This form of aid is consistent with the view that higher education is primarily a social service that should be paid for by the public.	1. Grants require the expenditure of more current income to support a given number of students than do loans.
2. Grants enable private institutions to be more competitive by counteracting the price differential between the public and private sectors.	2. If not carefully monitored, grants may support other-than-needy students.
3. Grants are more effective in attracting to college students from poor families.	
4. If employed as a scholarship, grants can be used to encourage academic achievement.	

The Case for Low Tuition

Traditionally, public higher education has been financed through low tuition and substantial government support. At public 4-year institutions, students and their parents pay only about 23 percent of the direct costs of education and State governments pay a major portion of the remaining costs. Defenders of low tuition or no tuition emphasize the large social benefits accruing from higher education and minimize the substantial gains to the individual. They also contend that whatever benefits the individual receives from higher education are paid for dearly by the earnings that the student forfeits while attending college.

Low tuition is advocated as the best means of facilitating college attendance by qualified young people from low-income families. High tuition, it is argued, is inimical to the basic concept of equal opportunity. Unless more grants are made available in the future, tuition will continue to be a significant barrier to college attendance by young people from low-income families.

Low or zero tuition for everyone implies a substantial level of government support. Following graduation, the student, together with other members of society, pays a share of this support through the progressive income tax. This delayed payment is judged preferable to charging high tuition at a time when a student is least able to afford to pay for it. Furthermore, the college graduate reimburses society to some extent for a higher education by the fact that out of his larger lifetime earnings he pays higher State and Federal taxes than does the lower salaried nongraduate.[51] If society at large is the greatest beneficiary of higher education and if ability to pay should govern the burden placed on each member of society, then it logically follows that low tuition and the graduated income tax constitute the most equitable financing system.

In summary, the low-tuition argument is based on the following rationale: (1) Since society benefits greatly from higher education through broad economic, social, and cultural advancement, society should bear a significant portion of the cost of such education. (2) Based on ability to pay, higher educational costs are most equitably shared by society through the progressive tax system. (3) Since high tuition is seldom sufficiently offset by student aid grants, low tuition provides more equal educational opportunity.

Subsidies to Institutions or to Students

Direct aid to students and the subsidizing of institutions, both traditional in American higher education, have basic merits. Public institutions have traditionally been in a position to charge very low tuition because they have been directly subsidized by society—predominately by State governments. Private colleges have done all that they possibly can through grants and loans to make it possible for students to afford the higher fees they charge. The continuing vitality of this kind of pluralism attests to the real value of both approaches. Controversy arises not over any attempt to restructure higher education drastically but over whether the major thrust of *additional* support, particularly at the Federal level, should be in the form of aid to institutions or to students. It is the need for further support that gives impetus and special importance to a study of the rationale supporting the two alternatives.

The position one takes with respect to aid to institutions versus aid to students must generally parallel the stand taken on high versus low tuition and on the concept of who benefits from higher education. Aid to institutions provides quality education at bargain prices to all comers, regardless of their financial status (unless the aid is predicated on an institution enrolling low-income students). Institutional aid is supported by those

---

[51] It should be pointed out that only to the degree that education, income, and tax burden are correlated does the progressive income tax system provide for equity of payment for education received. It is the State governments that primarily support public higher education and their tax plans are generally not progressive or are imperfectly so. Also, a person's income level is attributable only in part to the amount or the cost of education received. Finally, the income tax cannot be considered an equitable "user tax" since the person who does not receive a higher education pays the same as the person who does.

who believe that society at large is the greatest beneficiary of higher education and should therefore assume most of the cost involved. The essential features of the institutional aid plan are: (1) direct support of institutions by Federal, State, and local governments in an amount approximating total operational costs; (2) low tuition to provide equal educational opportunity for all students; and (3) payment for higher education primarily by society as a whole through a progressive tax system based on income. In the United States, the financing of public higher education is accomplished essentially in the foregoing manner.

The public system of financing is open to criticism by anyone who feels that the student benefits most from his education and should therefore pay nearly all of the actual costs, and that whatever public aid is given should be directed primarily to low-income and disadvantaged groups. Especially critical are those who believe that public institutions do not enroll a proportionate share of either black or extremely disadvantaged students. Because public institutions have low student-aid budgets, they cannot cover the living and incidental expenses of students from the very poorest families.[52] Those placing emphasis on individual benefits from higher education believe in the soundness of a financing plan that is characteristic of private higher education: (1) high tuition approximating the full cost of instruction; (2) equitable payment by the student (and his family) according to ability; and (3) generous aid to needy students in order to provide equal educational opportunity.

Aside from the aforementioned irreconcilable differences arising out of philosophical beliefs regarding the benefits of education and equitable payment, there are other considerations in assessing the relative merits of student aid versus institutional subsidies. A major issue centers on which practice results in the most efficient allocation of resources. Supporters of student aid contend that higher education resources are most effectively allocated through a market in which institutions fairly compete for the student consumer.[53] Student aid enhances the role of the market, propon-

---

[52] The argument is made by some observers that private institutions *better* serve minority groups than do public institutions. Consider the following statement: "The willingness of many 'private' institutions, at considerable sacrifice, to base undergraduate financial assistance on total need and to create in effect a sliding-scale tuition system supplemented by subsistence grants accounts for the anomaly that these institutions have student bodies more representative of the income structure of society than do most of their 'public' counterparts whose low-tuition policies are defended as more 'democratic.'" See David Truman, "Autonomy with Accountability," a contribution to a symposium on "Financing Higher Education" in *The Public Interest*, Spring 1968, p. 106.

[53] For a strong and persuasive argument that student aid and market action are means of placing American higher education on a sound financial basis, see Michael Clurman, "Does Higher Education Need More Money?" in *The Economics and Financing of Higher Education in the United States*, op. cit., pp. 632–51.

ents say, because it enables students to choose the most satisfactory educational package and price-benefit ratio and does not force any student to make a selection based on individual financial resources. When tuition fees more nearly approximate actual educational costs, students are further encouraged to seek a more expensive higher education only if they expect more valuable additional benefits. Selective buying in a competitive market, enhanced by student aid and coupled with prices more nearly covering costs, provides conditions in which students are most able and most likely to try to maximize the immediate direct benefits accruing from their educational expenditures. A competitive market would also serve as a powerful incentive to college administrators to provide the type of education sought by the consumer or face the loss of the institution's most important source of income. Thus higher education resources would be allocated by institutions responding to student preferences and by students seeking to maximize their direct educational benefits. Proponents of the market system believe it would eventually result in optimal allocations.

In rebuttal to the market argument, persons who favor institutional subsidies believe that the allocation of public funds is best left to institutional trustees and faculty—not to students. In other words, the institution should decide the kind of clientele it wishes to serve, the nature and quality of the program it offers, and the tuition it charges. Since not every institution will follow the same pattern, a wide variety of choices will be available to the student, thereby enabling him to exercise his right of selection.[54]

The social responsibilities of education, it is argued, are undoubtedly better served by more instruction, research, and public service, in varying proportions, than would be demanded by either individuals or agencies if they were required to pay the full cost. Under a system in which students

---

[54] Roger E. Bolton argues that there may be little difference in the effect on higher education *quality* whether aid is given to institutions or to students. Each institution receiving aid can use the funds either to raise the quality of its educational package or to maintain quality at a given level and lower tuition charges, or choose to employ a combination of the two. Since not every institution will follow the same course, students will be provided with many options. If students receive aid directly, they have a choice between using it to reduce out-of-pocket expenditures or to purchase a higher quality, more expensive education. Some will prefer to follow one course, some the other; many will use the money to acquire both. Again, a wide variety of quality-price combinations will result. "We would expect the same diversity of results to occur as under institutional aid, therefore, a family desiring a higher quality will likely find it under either kind of aid, and so will a family desiring a lower price."

"This leads to the conclusion that if most institutions would choose to upgrade quality, as proponents of institutional aid assume they would, it would be because *most families are happy with the outcome and would choose higher quality if aid were given directly to them*. In a system where there is competition for students, this is the only explanation why most institutions would feel they can get away with raising quality." See Bolton, "The Economic and Public Financing of Higher Education: An Overview," op. cit., p. 70.

would pay tuition nearly equal to the cost of instruction and government agencies and business would pay contractually for research and other services, colleges and universities would be obliged to offer services only on the basis of what the consumer deems they are worth. But student consumers and research buyers are not necessarily the individuals most capable of making sound decisions as to what should be taught and what should be studied and researched. Therefore, there is an inherent danger in permitting student preferences to influence unduly institutional programs and policies.

Few would argue that it is not in the best national interest to make available certain unrestricted funds to college and university administrators to be allocated *within* their institutions as they see fit.[55] There is considerably less agreement that the Government is as capable of making an equitable and efficient division of educational resources *among* institutions. It would be exceptionally difficult to design an aid formula combining the necessary criteria and weighting of factors so as simply to raise the overall level of higher education funding without significantly altering the present competitive structure. Furthermore, institutional aid is not necessarily intended to preserve the existing hierachy of academic wealth and quality. But in what manner and to what extent can the quality of higher education and its structure best be altered? If the competitive advantage of low-cost public institutions is to be improved, a formula for aid based on enrollment and growth will serve this purpose. A formula for aid predicated largely on institutional quality, such as the number of advanced degrees or research contracts, would channel disproportionate amounts of money into the best and most expensive universities and particularly into the ranking private universities. It is unlikely that an aid formula would seriously be considered if it favored any single group of institutions at the expense of others. To win general acceptance among competing recipients, a formula would have to contain several different criteria and be of such complexity as to prevent favoritism. That such a formula could be devised by govern-

---

[55] The position of certain national educational associations on this issue is clear. In a joint statement, the American Association of State Colleges and Universities and the National Association of State Universities and Land-Grant Colleges stated that "the greatest unmet need in the federal support of higher education in the country today is an institutional support program such as that outlined through which *flexible, predictable* funds can be made available to the colleges and universities on a *continuing* basis." American Association of State Colleges and Universities and National Association of State Universities and Land-Grant Colleges, *Recommendations for National Action Affecting Higher Education*, Washington, D.C., 1968, p. 7.

In a similar vein, the American Council on Education has declared: "We believe that beyond adequate funding for existing programs, the principal unfinished business of the Federal government in the field of higher education is the necessity to provide support for general institutional purposes." American Council on Education, *Federal Programs for Higher Education: Needed Next Steps*, Washington, D.C., 1969, p. 17.

mental bureaucracy is unquestioned; that the resulting "equitable" sharing of aid would constitute the most effective allocation of resources, however, is highly doubtful.

As many economists have noted, no one, especially formula writers, can be sure which trade-offs between alternative educational investments will result in the most effective allocation of resources. Is it preferable to have small colleges or large universities? Should more money be spent on faculty salaries or teaching machines? Should classes be larger or smaller? Should available funds be spent to aid disadvantaged students or to purchase computers? Opponents of institutional aid believe that centralized allocation of educational resources

> . . . generally turns out to be a clumsy and ineffective device lacking most of the subtlety and respect for small distinctions which makes a market such a sensitive mechanism for satisfying individual preferences.
>
> A closely related drawback of aid by formula is that in an area in which our goals are as subtle and complex as they are in higher education it will be difficult to design a formula which rewards and encourages educational excellence without simultaneously encouraging an educational system which strives to excel partly in sterile formula beating.[56]

Summary. A number of observers have stated that the heart of the controversy surrounding the future role of the Federal Government in financing higher education is the priority to be given to direct, noncategorical aid to institutions as opposed to that given to students. In the following summary of the contended advantages of each approach, it is apparent that desired goals can be achieved in both instances and that decisionmakers would find it difficult to make a full commitment to either plan. As with so many issues in higher education, a compromise solution or dual approach will prove most satisfactory—one that secures in part the particular benefits attributed to each plan and ideally maximizes total returns or at least encourages continued competition until such time as the superiority of one plan or the other is clearly demonstrated.

To sum up, the most frequently cited advantages of aiding students are the following: Such aid (1) encourages efficient allocation of resources according to the student preference to maximize his desired benefits; (2) promotes freedom of choice and educational opportunity by reducing restraints imposed by financial need, particularly for disadvantaged students; (3) enhances market action that promotes healthy competition, educational diversity, and also lessens the effects of the differential subsidies presently enjoyed by public institutions; (4) is consistent with the belief that students benefit most from higher education and therefore should pay, in accordance with their ability, most of the costs; and (5) requires a

---

[56] Clurman, "Does Higher Education Need More Money?", op. cit., pp. 642–43.

formula less difficult to devise than one which would subsidize institutions in such a manner as to best meet society's higher education goals.

The advantages cited for directly subsidizing institutions are that such financing (1) encourages efficient allocation of resources according to the judgment of government officials and college administrators as to how society and students are best served; (2) provides educational opportunity for *all* students by making possible low tuition charges; (3) allows colleges and universities to achieve a certain amount of flexibility and freedom from market pressures; (4) is consistent with the belief that society benefits most from education and therefore should pay most of the costs through a progressive tax system; and (5) involves lower administrative costs because institutions, not students, are the recipients.

BIBLIOGRAPHY

American Council on Education, *Universal Higher Education: Costs and Benefits*, Washington, D.C., 1971, 186 pp.

This book contains high-quality papers by 12 authors well known for their professional approach to higher education. The contents and authors are as follows: "Pressures, Benefits, and Options," Louis Hausman; "Economic Benefits of Universal Higher Education," W. Lee Hansen and David R. Witmer; "Human and Social Benefits," Kenneth Keniston and Mark Gerzon; "Varieties of Financial Crisis," Frederick E. Balderson; "Public Financing of Higher Education," Selma J. Mushkin; "Student Financial Aid," Allan M. Cartter; "More for Less: Higher Education's New Priority," Virginia B. Smith; "Two Models of Open Enrollment," A. J. Jaffee and Walter Adams; and "Another Approach to Higher Education," Alexander M. Mood.

Bowen, Howard R., *The Finance of Higher Education*, Carnegie Commission on Higher Education, Berkeley, Calif., 1968, 36 pp.

In this short essay the author argues strongly for a plan that ". . . would allow the institutions to progress, that would open up opportunity for all, that would afford reasonable equity in finance, and that would safeguard the legitimate interests of both private and public institutions." He calls for grants to all bona fide students that would be based on the difference between minimal college costs and the amount that parents and students could assume (to be determined by a means test). In addition, students would have access to loans, without a means test, to take care of "extras"—costs over and above those provided by grants or supplied by parents. Institutions would receive unrestricted grants by which the Federal Government would share in future increases in total costs and per student costs. In discussing the future, the author concludes that ". . . tuitions in public colleges and universities should be low or, better, non-existent; and that tuitions in private institutions must and can be higher than in public institutions, but also should be held to moderate levels."

Chambers, M. M., *Higher Education: Who Pays? Who Gains?*, The Interstate Printers & Publishers, Inc., Danville, Ill., 1968, 302 pp.

This stimulating volume, described by the author as "a subjective essay dealing with comprehensive concepts," leaves little doubt about M. M. Chambers' stand on many issues. Without apology, he speaks of his need to inject his opinions on issues when complete "objectivity" is impossible. He conceives his function "as interpretative and tendentious in an area involving great issues not susceptible of resolution by other means." There are not too many topics in higher education financing that Chambers does not probe. Beginning with an argument for a pluralistic system of higher education, he brings his seasoned judgment to bear on such subjects as the meaning of "efficiency," financing academic facilities, endowment, the amount students should pay, tax credits for tuition payments, differential tuition fees, philanthropy, State tax support, statewide "coordination" in public higher education, Federal involvement, and higher education and economic growth. For those interested in the financing of higher education, this volume of personal "observations, careful thought, and best judgment" offers a refreshingly individualistic approach.

Cheit, Earl F., *The New Depression in Higher Education*, Carnegie Commission on Higher Education, McGraw-Hill Book Co., New York, 1971, 169 pp.

The growing financial problems in higher education and the desire of college presidents and other administrators to learn more about how individual institutions are coping with them motivated the Carnegie Commission to sponsor this study. The investigation involved 41 case studies based on "on site" interview reports and appropriate financial records. The sample selected for the study represents several types of institutions: public and private, universities, liberal arts colleges, comprehensive colleges, and 2-year institutions. It was found that 29 of the institutions (71 percent) either were headed for financial trouble or were already in financial difficulty. An institution was considered to be headed for financial trouble if, at the time of the study, it had been able to meet current responsibilities but could neither ensure that it could much longer sustain current program and quality standards nor plan to support evolving program growth. Colleges and universities forced to reduce services or eliminate important educational programs were considered in financial difficulty.

On a nationally weighted basis, the institutions discovered to be heading for financial trouble represented 42 percent of U.S. institutions (1,000) accounting for 54 percent of the students. Again on a weighted basis, slightly less than one-fifth, or 19 percent of the institutions, accounting for 24 percent of the students, were in financial difficulty.

In addition to revealing the magnitude of the current depression in higher education, Professor Cheit calls attention to the nature and impact of the financial problems as they affect institutions of various types, and to the response being made by these institutions. The author's case-study examination of expenditure patterns, income factors, and administrative practices enables the reader to obtain a down-to-earth perspective of a variety of financial problems and how they may be most effectively solved. The study also presents views of school administrators concerning public policy toward financing higher education.

College Entrance Examination Board, *The Economics of Higher Education*, New York, 1967, 89 pp.

This collection of papers was originally presented at the College Scholarship Services' third colloquy on the topic, "The Economics of Higher Education." Although a mere listing of the papers and their authors does not do justice to the volume, it does provide an insight into the scope of this work. They are as follows: "The Economics of Higher Education," Seymour E. Harris; "Pricing Problems for Higher Education," Allan M. Cartter; "Student Diversity and National Goals in Higher Education," Fred L. Glimp; "Investment in Higher Education and Its Returns," Peter P. Muirhead; "Higher

Education: State and Local Governments," Selma J. Mushkin; "Aiding Higher Education Through Income Tax Credits," Roger A. Freeman; "An Argument Against Tax Credits in Higher Education," H. Edwin Young; "Long-Term Credit: Implications for Colleges and Universities," Jack B. Critchfield; "Monetary Policy and the Financing of Higher Education," Eliot J. Swan; and "Student Aid: Will Uncle Sam Make All the Ends Meet?" Robert N. Kreidler.

Council for Financial Aid to Education, Inc., *Handbook of Aid to Higher Education by Corporations, Major Foundations, and the Federal Government*, New York, 1973.
A comprehensive guide to the types and sources of aid to higher education, this volume is divided into five parts. Part I outlines tested areas of corporate grants and pinpoints some of the more creative corporation grants. Part II sets forth information on the higher education grant programs of 23 major foundations. Part III outlines, agency by agency, the grant programs of the Federal Government and the amounts obligated. Part IV lists each State's tax-fund appropriation for higher education operating expenses and includes information on State aid to private institutions, student aid, and the State coordinating or governing agency. Part V contains information on 36 national educational associations, their membership and purpose, and other relevant details. Supplements at 6-month intervals provide new information.

Danière, André, *Higher Education in the American Economy*, Random House, New York 1964, 206 pp.
A substantial study of the economics of education, this text covers a wide range of topics in a detailed and penetrating manner. Separate chapters are devoted to pricing at cost, educational productivity, market imperfections, decreasing costs and joint production, research, planning, free education, competition, and efficiency. The author's approach is to clarify the issues, identify the crucial problems involved, and, by application of economic analysis, formulate some conclusions and reforms. Danière's unique contribution in this book is his crisp and rigorous approach, liberally supported by near-incontestable economic logic.

Freeman, Roger A., *Crisis in College Finance? Time for New Solutions*, Institute for Social Science Research, Washington, D.C., 1965, 243 pp.
Although the author has lately written on another related topic—Federal assistance to higher education through income-tax credits—his 1965 arguments for Federal support tax relief and higher tuitions and his conservative position on who should go to college, on faculty productivity, and on space utilization remain valid.

Fromkin, Joseph, *Aspirations, Enrollments, and Resources*, U.S. Department of Health, Education, and Welfare, Office of Education, U.S. Government Printing Office, Washington, D.C., 1970, 151 pp.
This study attempts to estimate the Federal resources required to fulfill American aspirations for postsecondary education. The vigorous analysis, documentation, and statistical treatment go far beyond typical efforts by the Federal Government in this area. Part I of the study discusses the possible benefits of postsecondary education and examines the revolution in demand for higher education, particularly the increase in number of poor youngsters eager to attend college. On the assumption that these aspirations of the poor will be met, the demand for postsecondary education is projected to 1976. Part II summarizes such aspects of postsecondary institutions as course offerings, cost of instruction, educational costs, etc. An analysis of institutional characteristics in relation to admission policies and student subsidies is also presented. Part III deals with two issues that cut across the financial and attendance patterns previously de-

scribed: graduate education and the pros and cons of general aid to institutions. Part IV is devoted to the financial needs of students and institutions and the various alternative levels of Federal aid to higher education. The eight appendixes provide technical support for the text.

Hansen, W. Lee, and Burton A. Weisbroad, *Benefits, Costs, and Finance of Public Higher Education*, Markham Publishing Co., Chicago, 1969, 114 pp.

The authors begin by presenting a conceptual framework for making choices: the issues involved, related questions regarding the benefits and costs of higher education, and an explanation of some major conceptual distinctions, e.g., efficiency effects versus equity effects, private effects versus social effects, etc. The second chapter focuses primarily on estimates, in monetary terms, of some of the important benefits of higher education as they apply to the State of California. Empirical estimates are made of the apparent increase in labor productivity resulting from higher education, as indicated by the significant differential in earnings of college graduates as compared with high school graduates of the same age, sex, and color. An adjustment is made to account for differences in ability. In chapter III, a study of the forms and magnitudes of the private and social costs of higher education in California, the proportion of costs borne by students, parents, and taxpayers is examined, together with what the effects, if any, would be of alternative means of sharing costs. Chapter IV discusses the way in which benefits and costs of public higher education in California are distributed. The conclusion is that the distribution of subsidies provided through public higher education is exceedingly unequal. The agenda for research in Chapter V emphasizes the kinds of information that would be most useful for further quantifying the benefits and costs of public higher education in a particular State.

Harris, Seymour E., *Higher Education: Resources and Finance*, McGraw-Hill Book Co., New York, 1962, 713 pp.

Clearly, Professor Harris has made a major contribution by writing a book which, it is reasonable to say, has no peer in terms of coverage, depth, detail, and practical worth. The writings of Seymour Harris on the economic issues of higher education have long been noted, and it is fortunate that an opportunity was extended him by the Ford Foundation to conduct such a full and comprehensive study. The length of the book may overwhelm some readers, but each of the 53 chapters is relatively short and sufficiently self-contained to permit independent consideration. To accommodate the casual reader, a 170-item summary of conclusions and points of emphasis is included.

Part 1 consists of three introductory chapters. The first delineates some historical trends; the second projects the higher education budget to 1970; and the third discusses trends in enrollment, income, endowment, scholarships, and faculty structure for a selected group of 100 institutions. Parts 2 to 4 treat cost factors, including scholarships and loans. Part 5 examines State aid to higher education through measurements of burden, capacity, effort, and achievement. In part 6, Harris stresses the declining significance of endowment-fund income in the face of rising enrollments, the increasing importance of other sources of income, and spiraling cost and income levels. He also examines management mistakes and proposes accounting methods that could bring larger returns from endowment. Also included are the results of a questionnaire addressed to the 50 most heavily endowed higher education institutions. The subjects dealt with in part 7 are costs and economies. The final part of the book is devoted to faculty economic status. Harris bases his treatment of many topics on questionnaire responses and on visits to over 100 colleges and universities.

Hudgins, Garven, and Ione Phillips, *People's Colleges in Trouble. . . A Financial Profile of the Nation's State Universities and Land-Grant Colleges*, Office of Research and Information,

National Association of State Universities and Land-Grant Colleges, Washington, D.C., 1971, 26 pp.

As recently as 1967 not a single public university in the country was operating with a deficit; between 1969 and 1970, however, 12 public universities ended the year with insufficient funds to meet expenses. This alarming finding and others, based on a survey of the financial status of 78 multicampus State universities, are discussed by the authors. Sixty-nine of the 78 universities that reported having taken one or more economy measures to help stem the tide of rising costs, saved money by deferring maintenance, eliminating new programs, and instituting faculty/staff freezes and cutbacks. Forty-four adopted standstill budgets (an average annual increase of less than 10 percent for operations). According to the authors, these economy measures represented a step backward. The report also includes a discussion of State appropriations, student fees, the student share of instructional costs, low tuition, private gifts, and Federal support.

Jellema, William W., *Redder and Much Redder: A Follow-Up Study to "The Red and The Black,"* Association of American Colleges, Washington, D.C., 1971, 17 pp.

A supplementary report, this study covers the financial status of private colleges and universities for fiscal 1970, projections for fiscal 1971, and financial prospects through 1973. An earlier report, *The Red and The Black,* by the same author, presented financial data for 1968 and 1969 and projections for 1970 and 1971. The two reports paint not only a bleak picture of recent deficit operations (the actual average deficit for 507 institutions in 1970 was $131,000) but also a depressing prospect for the immediate future. Whereas the earlier report found that many institutions were looking forward to an improved financial position, most now predict that they will suffer deeper deficits. "Behind these mounds of deficits" the author writes, "lie the broken remains of curtailed operations, of abbreviated departments, of decimated academic programs, of faltering plans and languishing aspirations, of innovation untried and of creativity curbed." A significant feature of the book is an especially informative discussion of why the very small private colleges are experiencing financial difficulty. He cites many reasons, including the fact that smallness is no longer prized by a majority of Americans. Consequently, while the small college is praised and its virtues extolled, it is the large and complex institution that is favored, partly because of the variety and anonymity it offers. Jellema also points out that "Since it is also a characteristic of very small colleges that they tend to have small endowments, a drop in enrollment means that the cost per remaining student rises more precipitously than in larger institutions and must either be reflected in increased tuition or in institutional deficits." The report includes institutional forecasts for 1972–74 and a lengthy discussion regarding what may happen to higher education if the deficit level of 1968–69 or 1970–71 continues.

Jenny, Hans H., and G. Richard Wynn, *The Golden Years: A Study of Income and Expenditure Growth and Distribution of 48 Private Four-Year Liberal Arts Colleges, 1960–1968,* The College of Wooster, Wooster, Ohio, 1970, 217 pp.

This study describes and evaluates in considerable detail the growth and structure of income and expenditures of a sample of 48 small, private 4-year liberal arts colleges. Because the study centers on the period from 1959–60 through the end of fiscal year 1967–68, a time of remarkable growth, the impending financial crisis is only foreshadowed. The highly informative conclusions may well be fairly representative of what has happened to all private undergraduate 4-year colleges. The authors warn, however, that the indicators are not intended as *normative* guides to *future* resource allocation. As might be expected, the sample produced very pronounced quantitative differences, yet on a college-by-college basis, trends led to the authors' conclusion that ". . . the basic principles which guide the allocation of resources do not seem to have undergone any significant changes during the period studied." Growth in total student expenditure of 5.7 percent was found to be larger than the real cost growth of 1.8 to 2.6 percent. "The student or his family may have been paying 7.6 percent more tuition each year, but he was buying only from 1.8 to 2.6 percent more education," according to the authors. Other areas explored in the study include the solvency of the institutions surveyed, the aggregate growth of income and expenditures, the effects of inflation, the distribution patterns of income and expenditures, enrollment size and growth of income and expenditures, and the gap between income specifically designated for student aid and actual expenditures for student aid. Tables containing key annual data for each college in the sample are included.

(The College of Wooster has announced an updated edition of *The Golden Years* by Jenny and Wynn entitled *The Turning Point—A Study of Income and Expenditure Growth and Distribution of 48 Private Four-Year Liberal Arts Colleges, 1960–1970.*)

Joint Economic Committee, Congress of the United States, *The Economics and Financing of Higher Education in the United States*, U.S. Government Printing Office, Washington, D.C., 1969, 683 pp.

This book approximates an encyclopedia on the economics and financing of higher education, and the introductory overview paper alone (by Roger E. Bolton) is one of the more comprehensive studies available in this field. The papers in part II examine two of the issues most basic to formulating economic policy in higher education: the efficiency of expenditures and the distribution or equity impact of costs and benefits. Part III, which focuses on economic efficiency considerations, examines the factors that determine the quality of education offered by colleges and universities and discusses the several factors that influence short-run and long-run variations in institutional costs. The role of enrollment growth and class size are considered as are the centralization of university functions and the year-round use of university facilities. A rather long-run perspective is examined in the part IV appraisal of the future structure of higher education. The social and political forces that influence this structure are assessed in the context of campus unrest. A series of projections into the latter part of the 1970's is presented for such pertinent higher education variables as enrollment, staff, expenditures, and degrees granted. Because of the significant portion of total higher education income expended on faculty salaries, one of the papers in this section is devoted to the academic labor market. The two topics in part V deal with the implications of increasing demands, higher costs, and pressures for change being felt by private colleges and universities. The first topic, based on a sampling of private universities, examines the trends in expenditures and income over the past decade. The second topic includes estimates of future expenditures reported by 30 private colleges. The final section of the book, part VI, which deals with the financing of higher education in the decade of the 1970's, includes presentations that explore the prospects for financing higher education from sources other than the Federal Government and examine the major issues and various questions that arise in connection with Federal aid to higher education. The subject matter covered includes the basic decisions that must be made in determining the optimum form of Federal aid; the benefits and costs of a number of forms of student aid; the major findings of the Carnegie Commission on Higher Education; and strategies for securing Federal aid.

Authors include Roger Bolton, Howard Bowen, William Bowen, Allen Cartter, André Danière, Paul Feldman, Roger Freeman, Lee Hansen, Seymour Harris, Hans Jenny, Clark Kerr, Selma Mushkin, Alice Rivlin, and many other nationally known experts in the economics field.

Keezer, Dexter M., ed., *Financing Higher Education 1960–70*, McGraw-Hill Book Co., New York, 1959, 304 pp.

Owing to the high caliber of the contributors and to the fact that they focus on broad financial issues rather than on current statistics, most of the papers in this 14-year-old volume are still timely. They deal with such continuing problem areas as long-range planning, student costs, the role of research, opportunities for better institutional management, and conflict and cooperation in higher education.

Machlup, Fritz, *Education and Economic Growth*, University of Nebraska Press, Lincoln, 1970, 106 pp.
This is a book, written with clarity and depth, to be treasured. One need not be an economist to understand Fritz Machlup's presentation. In 106 pages he provides the reader with an appreciation and knowledge of how educational efforts promote economic growth and provide social and private benefits. Part II of the book is devoted to the demand for education and part III to the cost of education. Machlup explains that the continuing increase in the per student cost of education is not so much a consequence of inflation, which it is often presumed to be, as the inevitable result of economic growth and an absence of technological improvement in higher education. A clear understanding of these circumstances will bring about fuller realization of the critical need to increase educational productivity as the only possible escape from ever-increasing costs.

Mertins, Paul and Norman Brandt, *Financial Statistics of Institutions of Higher Education: Current Funds, Revenues, and Expenditures 1969–1970*, U.S. Department of Health, Education, and Welfare, Office of Education, U.S. Government Printing Office, Washington, D.C., 1972.
The financial statistics of institutions of higher education—current fund revenues and expenditures, physical plant assets, endowment, and student charges—are published annually and biannually by the U.S. Office of Education. The series itself provides an invaluable source of financial data to facilitate analysis by type and control of institution and by interstate comparisons. Beginning with fiscal year 1965–66, the Office of Education used a new questionnaire—part of the Higher Education General Information Survey (HEGIS)—to collect financial statistics. Since that time it has been possible to classify income sources according to intended use of revenues and function of expenditures. This refinement contributes materially to identifying which sources are paying for what. The 1969–70 publication contains the following summary tables: current fund revenues and expenditures by control, region, and State; current fund revenues by source, control, and level of institution; and current fund expenditures by function, control, and level of institution. For each State and region, current fund revenues by source and expenditures by function are presented by level of institution and by control.

O'Neill, June, *Resource Use in Higher Education*, Carnegie Commission on Higher Education, Berkeley, Calif., 1971, 106 pp.
This technical report is concerned with trends in effort and productivity on the part of U.S. higher education between 1930 and 1967. An exceptionally valuable contribution is the central finding that there was virtually no change in costs per student credit hour in *constant* dollars between the mid-1950's and the late 1960's. In other words, during this period the amount of *real* resources used to produce a credit hour remained fairly constant. Although this fact might have been conjectured from knowledge that the technology of producing education does not lend itself to cost-saving innovations, the phenomenon must be documented if educators are to fully appreciate and respond to the consequences of higher education being a constant-cost industry.

Orwig, M.D., ed., *Financing Higher Education: Alternatives for the Federal Government*, The American College Testing Program, Iowa City, Iowa, 1971, 390 pp.

This well-organized volume is described in the introduction as presenting various viewpoints on aspects of three broad questions: (1) What are the issues that should be considered in outlining a strategy for the financing of higher education? (2) What are the alternative strategies that can be employed and what does each have to recommend itself? and (3) What is the role of the Federal Government in financing higher education? Each of the 13 papers summarizes or includes most of the major ideas associated with a particular point of view; represents a landmark study on an important problem; or presents a fresh, innovative, and relatively uncirculated proposal for the financing of higher education. Part One includes papers that discuss the economic and social background within which a financial strategy can eventually evolve. Part Two examines three general strategies for financing higher education, and Part Three discusses the five programs most frequently proposed as ones which the Federal Government should support more generously. Part Four provides a current perspective on the present and future prospects for the financing of higher education. The final chapter, written by the editor, is an effective summary and appraisal of the issues raised in previous sections of the book.

U.S. Department of Health, Education, and Welfare, Office of Education, *Trends in Postsecondary Education*, U.S. Government Printing Office, Washington, D.C., 1970, 261 pp.

Two papers in this collection deal with the financing of higher education. In examining the financial barriers to college attendance, W. Lee Hansen reviews the impact of these barriers and ways to offset them. He also discusses enrollment patterns and family income, the financial costs of college, how people pay for college, and financial aid resources and their distribution. In order to highlight the interrelationships among financial need, college costs, and financial aid, based upon 1966–67 data, he divides institutions into several broad classes. The paper by Ernst Becker concentrates primarily on an analysis and review of financial trends in higher education from 1959–60 to 1966–67 and develops projections of expenditures for 1975–76. The carefully prepared tabular data represent one of the better summaries of institutional income and expenditure data based on U.S. Office of Education statistics.

Chapter XIII

GOVERNMENT SUPPORT
AND INSTITUTIONAL ECONOMIES

Almost all colleges and universities recognize the need to secure more effective government financing—at the Federal, State, and local level—and to use existing financial resources more efficiently. Although the Federal Government currently finances many facets of higher education, increased funding and new forms of aid will be needed if the dual objectives of maintaining academic quality and expanding educational opportunity are to be met. There is little doubt that a national commitment to greater and more equal educational opportunities will bring about more Federal support of higher education. But if Federal participation is to add to the vitality and effectiveness of colleges and universities, it must be restructured. Some of the methods by which the Federal Government currently supports higher education and may modify and expand that support are discussed in the second part of this chapter.

The major financial contribution of State and local governments to higher education is not fully appreciated. Seven out of 10 students currently attend public institutions that receive three-fourths of their unrestricted revenue for instruction and related supporting activities[1] from State and local governments. Even when the private sector is included, State and local government funding accounts for 50 percent of the amount used for student education expenditures. Comparative measures of State and local fiscal capacity and effort, discussed in the third part of this chapter, are designed to inform educators of the capacity of their governments to obtain resources for public purposes, as well as to indicate how much of this capacity such governments are actually using. (Chapter II should be consulted for a discussion of how fiscal measures can be used to analyze State financing of public higher education involving such other factors as student *burden*, *allocation* to higher education, and financial support *achievement*.)

---

[1] Such revenue finances expenditures for instruction and departmental research, extension and public service, libraries, physical plant operation and maintenance, and general administration and student services. See chapter XII.

The financial gap between the actual cost of operating a college and the revenue received may be closed by lowering costs as well as by raising revenues. Colleges and universities that are either in financial trouble or heading toward it must be concerned with employing all available resources in the most effective, least wasteful manner possible. Less costly techniques must be sought that will enable a given institution to achieve its goals and at the same time preserve quality. The last section of this chapter stresses the importance of effective management and planning and describes some of the economies college administrators are introducing to stretch limited budgets.

FEDERAL SUPPORT OF HIGHER EDUCATION

Persistent financial problems in higher education have brought nearly general agreement that the Federal Government, in one way or another, must become more involved if lasting solutions are to be found. The Federal Government is, of course, already deeply involved. The issue is really how Federal funding can be more effectively structured and expanded to meet the continuing needs of colleges and universities and their students.

Level and Nature of Federal Support

To date most Federal aid has been channeled into three areas: students (grants, fellowships, and loans); research; and facility construction. Concentration in these areas, it is argued, has been necessary to meet special needs. If this trend continues, however, it may aggravate rather than relieve the financial difficulties plaguing higher education. Furthermore, Federal support has tended to be concentrated in the major universities. Under existing restrictions, institutions most in need are often ineligible for Federal support. Moreover, categorical restrictions usually prohibit those institutions receiving funds from using them for the most urgent needs. For these and other reasons, there is growing support in the educational community for across-the-board grants to be used as an institution chooses.

Federal financial involvement in higher education is extensive and varied. Table XIII-1 presents a summary of Federal revenues received by colleges and universities for fiscal year 1971. The vast bulk of this money (approximately 70 percent) was allocated to colleges and universities with the stipulation that they perform specific services or provide special training in accordance with contractual agreements. The other 30 percent was

Table XIII-1.—Federal revenues received by institutions of higher education: Fiscal year 1971

	Amount (millions)	Percentage
Educational and general		
Appropriations to land-grant institutions and for other educational and general purposes	$567.4	11.5
Sponsored research (includes $306.7 million recovery of indirect costs)	1,783.2	36.2
Sponsored programs: training programs, workshops, work-study programs, etc. (includes $77.9 million recovery of indirect costs)	878.8	17.8
Student aid	375.8	7.6
Major services		
Hospitals	36.9	.7
Research & development centers	739.7	15.0
Facilities and equipment (includes $197.9 million for research facilities)	548.2 (est.)	11.1
	$4,930.0	100.0

Source: Paul F. Mertins and Norman J. Brandt, *Financial Statistics of Institutions of Higher Education: Current Funds Revenue and Expenditures, 1970–71*, U.S. Department of Health, Education, and Welfare, Office of Education, U.S. Government Printing Office, Washington, D.C., 1973.

divided between aid to students (7.6 percent); construction of facilities (11.1 percent); and medical and graduate education, land-grant programs, ROTC activities, and other specific purposes (11.5 percent). Only a small fraction was available for general institutional operations and undergraduate education. Thus, while educational and general expenditures for instruction and related supporting activities total nearly $14 billion a year (1971) and despite the fact that money to support these basic functions is the most difficult to raise, the Federal Government provides virtually no support for them.

There are three major reasons why general Federal support of higher education is not forthcoming: a belief that the States and the private sector, not the Federal Government, should assume the primary responsibility for higher education; congressional reluctance to make money available without specifying in considerable detail how it should be spent; and the controversy over the interpretation of the First Amendment clause prohibiting government support of religious institutions. To include private church-related institutions in a general Federal aid program would violate a tenet, held by a large segment of the American people, concerning the separation of church and state. Yet, to ". . . deny those institutions Federal benefits would [confront] most of them with the alternative of either severing their religious ties and turning secular or withering until they are forced to close their doors."[2]

(In the next section some of the issues concerning public aid to private colleges are discussed, together with existing State programs supporting private higher education. Such a discussion is necessary because any evaluation of alternative methods of Federal funding of higher education must include the private sector.)

Public Support for Private Institutions[3]

Student aid for the purpose of providing equal educational opportunity and expanding accessibility to and choice of an institution of higher learning is a widely accepted and prevalent form of public support—one that benefits all colleges and universities. Such aid is not intended to enhance private institutions directly, but to the extent that it enables students to matriculate at a college of their choice, its impact neutralizes the tuition differential between the public and private educational sectors and thereby strengthens the competitive position of private institutions. Tax credits for parents of college students also serve to stimulate enrollment at private institutions. For that matter, any nonrestrictive student support program can exert a positive influence on enrollment in the private sector; consequently, it is widely accepted as an instrument for social improvement.

Much more controversial are public programs of *direct* support to private institutions. State and Federal grants and loans for capital construction and operating budgets, project and service contracts, and tax exemptions come under this category. Such programs are frequently criticized as devices for transforming private institutions into public ones without literally doing so. In addition, such direct support is highly susceptible to constitutional challenge and may introduce elements of government initiative and control. Most controversial of all direct support programs are the so-called bloc grants that involve per student allocations for institutional operating budgets. Since there are no contracted direct benefits from this type of general support, it is most difficult to justify in terms of serving State residents.

---

[2] Roger A. Freeman, "Federal Assistance to Higher Education Through Income Tax Credits," in *The Economics and Financing of Higher Education in the United States*, a compendium of papers submitted to the Joint Economic Committee, Congress of the United States, U.S. Government Printing Office, Washington, D.C., 1969, p. 668.

[3] The primary source for this material is William H. McFarlane, *State Support for Private Higher Education*, Southern Regional Education Board, Atlanta, Ga., 1969.

A pivotal issue in the legal problems surrounding direct public aid to private institutions is the church-state controversy. The Federal approach has proved to be much more flexible than that used by most States. The Supreme Court, while upholding the general intent of the First Amendment in maintaining separation between church and state, has, in specific cases, moved in the direction of finding exceptions to the "establishment" clause. One Supreme Court test for "exceptive instances" is the rule of "secular legislative purpose." If the primary purpose and effect of a law is to benefit the public welfare in a way that is not possible through other means, the law will be regarded as constitutional even though it confers some additional but incidental benefits on persons or institutions of a particular religious persuasion. Opponents of public support programs attack "secular legislative purpose" and related theories on the ground that such reasoning could justify the expenditure of public funds for any and all educational purposes. In July 1971, by a 5–4 margin, the U.S. Supreme Court upheld the constitutionality of Federal construction grants to church-related colleges, provided the buildings financed with government funds be used for secular purposes. "The crucial question," said Chief Justice Warren E. Burger in delivering the Court's majority opinion, "is not whether some benefit accrues to a religious institution as a consequence of the legislative program, but whether its principal or primary effect advances religion."

Whatever the outcome of the legal and other issues, administration of Federal and State support programs poses problems. The use of public funds in the public interest requires fiscal accountability to the government source, a fact that often generates sensitive concern about the delicate balance between institutional autonomy and government responsibility. At the State level, the greater support of private institutions has raised questions regarding the willingness of these institutions to accept whatever associated coordinating and accountability procedures are deemed necessary.[4] Furthermore, the degree to which private institutions are likely to become interdependent with public institutions in return for financial support from State governments is not at all clear. To what extent can private institutions participate in developing a public-private system of higher education and subject themselves to coordination and control, yet

---

[4] An example of the type of "control" that might be imposed on private institutions in return for State aid are those adopted by the American Association of State Colleges and Universities: "That any State providing funds to private colleges should require 'fiscal accountability to the State'; that funds be allocated among public and private institutions 'on the basis of an agreed-upon standard for space utilization and faculty-student ratio'; and that to qualify for State funds, all institutions in a State be 'subject to common standards' except for distinctions based on academic ability and other 'student factors.'"

remain private? The expected difficulties in this area are perhaps even more problematical than the questions raised by political and legal issues.

To note the progress being made and the likely direction of future efforts, it is worth examining some of the existing State support arrangements with private institutions. These include grants and loans to students; appropriations for distinguished professorships, capital improvements, and interinstitutional cooperative associations; contractual agreements for special services; and tax exemptions. Few involve unrestricted operating grants, but as financial difficulties in both the public and private sector worsen, it is expected that requests for such grants will be honored, especially at influential private institutions performing valuable services to the State.

Despite constitutional State prohibitions against direct appropriations of tax funds to private or sectarian institutions, at least 34 States support private higher education.[5] All 34 of these States provide some form of financial aid to students attending private colleges and universities and 20 also provide institutional support. State programs supporting private institutions include aid for construction through tax-exempt bond issues or matching grants (12 States); contractual arrangements for educational services and student enrollment (5 States); and direct grants, with or without restrictions (17 States).

Direct aid by States to private institutions is provided in a number of different ways. Unrestricted grants to *specific* private institutions are given in four States (Alabama, Ohio, Pennsylvania, and Wisconsin). Illinois, Maryland, and Washington very recently adopted programs of direct grants of $100 for each freshman and sophomore holding a State scholarship, and Illinois allocates grants of $200 for each junior and senior who is an Illinois resident. Since July 1, 1971, Maryland has provided direct grants to accredited institutions on the following basis: $200 for each associate of arts degree awarded and $500 for each bachelor's degree, exclusive of those awarded in theology. The new program in Washington State provides up to $100 to private colleges for every full-time undergraduate State resident enrolled.

Five States—Florida, New Jersey, New York, North Carolina, and Michigan—provide subsidies for special programs (e.g. medical and/or nursing; disadvantaged students) offered by private institutions.

In 1972 Minnesota and Oregon joined the list of States that "contract" with private colleges for the education of State residents. Five other States—Alabama, Alaska, Connecticut, New York, and South Carolina—also contract with private colleges for educational services to State residents.

---

[5] From a 1971 survey (updated to 1972) conducted by the Academy for Educational Development, Inc.

MAJOR ALTERNATIVE METHODS
OF FEDERAL FUNDING

The material in this section is largely an adaptation and summary of portions of Wolk's study.[6] Other commentaries on current proposals are readily available.[7] What is included here is a concise description of the various types of government aid to higher education—categorical aid, aid to students, grants to institutions, tax relief, and revenue sharing—plus special attention to some of the relative advantages and disadvantages of each.

Categorical Aid

Until very recently Federal support for higher education has been almost solely in the form of categorical aid, i.e., the allocation of funds earmarked for a specific project. The two areas that have received the bulk of categorical aid are research and building construction. To the extent that research grants represent payment for services rendered, they are not *aid*. In many instances, however, grants do not cover the full cost of the research, and institutions make up the difference.

With regard to Federal contracting of research, the central concern is the concentration of funds at a few hundred major universities (see chapter VI); the imbalance of funding in favor of the sciences; and the neglect of the humanities. Even more important may be the overall impact that Federal research money has had on some institutions of higher learning—encouraging them to become huge conglomerates operating laboratories and administering other projects only tangentially related to teaching. The long-term consequences of Federal involvement are not yet clear, but undoubtedly the role the Government has played has had a profound effect on the structure, function, and governance of American higher education.

It is also significant that the massive amounts spent on research by the Federal Government have distorted and conveyed a false impression of the Federal role in support of higher education. The failure of the Government

---

[6] Ronald A. Wolk, *Alternative Methods of Federal Funding for Higher Education*, Carnegie Commission on Higher Education, Berkeley, Calif., 1968.

[7] See, for example, John P. Mallan, "Current Proposals for Federal Aid to Higher Education: Some Political Implications," in M. D. Orwig, ed., *Financing Higher Education: Alternatives for the Federal Government*, American College Testing Program, Iowa City, 1971, pp. 303–30; also Roger E. Bolton, "The Economics and Public Financing of Higher Education: An Overview," in *The Economics and Financing of Higher Education in the United States*, op. cit., pp. 76–104.

to inform the public that the nearly $2 billion paid colleges and universities must be used for research and research facilities creates an impression that Federal money is paying much more of the operating costs of higher education than is actually the case.

The tremendous jump in student enrollment during the fifties and sixties resulted in a critical shortage of academic facilities. This shortage obviously called for a substantial commitment of government funds to construction. By 1971, Federal support for construction through the Higher Education Facilities Act of 1963 and earlier legislation totaled nearly $2.5 billion in grants and another $1.5 billion in loans. The target year for completing construction of all funded facilities is 1977.

Allocation in the best "public interest" is not always as easy to determine as it was in the case of new facilities. Consequently, proposals for broad Federal aid to institutions—free from so-called restrictions—will likely set the pattern for future Federal support. In this regard it will be necessary for institutions to identify more clearly their mission and the program alternatives and budgeting options to be employed in accomplishing it.

Aid to Students

College students receive financial aid in a variety of forms. Scholarship *grants* provide a student a sum of money, usually with the stipulation that he attend an approved college or university. A grant program can be easily tailored to meet various requirements. If it is a general policy to give more aid to poor students, grants can be awarded accordingly. If the emphasis is on quality education for gifted students, the criteria can be so adapted.

Loans, at low interest rates, are less costly than grants. If students are willing to borrow to finance their education, loans also permit more students to be aided in the long run than do grants.[8] Like grants, loans may be repaid according to family income, ability, or any other criterion. Contingent repayment plans usually stipulate that a student liquidate his loan by paying a certain percentage of his future income (usually in the form of an additional income tax), rather than by repaying the amount of the loan at some fixed rate of interest. If his income is low, the amount repaid will be less than he borrowed. Another variation requires a student, regardless of how much he borrowed, to pay an annual surcharge of 2

---

[8] To determine the total budget level and corresponding mix of student aid programs that provide marginal benefits equal to the marginal value of the "general" Federal budget dollar, see André Danière, "The Benefits and Costs of Alternative Federal Programs of Financial Aid to College Students," in *The Economics and Financing of Higher Education in the United States*, op. cit., pp. 556–98.

percent of his annual income for as long as he earns an income. (For a more complete discussion of loans versus grants and the advantages and disadvantages of each, see chapter XII.)

The *college work-study program*, another form of student assistance, permits students to pay for their education with earnings from part-time employment. The Federal contribution, which amounts to 80 percent of wages paid to students by the institutions, is in effect a Federal subsidy.

Certain provisions of the Education Amendments of 1972 will determine the course of Federal aid to students in the foreseeable future.[9] The legislation provides for a program of basic education opportunity grants, State scholarship incentives, and an expanded insured loan program. The basic educational opportunity grants entitle every undergraduate student in eligible institutions to a Federal grant equal to $1,400 minus the expected family contribution for that student, or one-half of the actual cost of attendance, whichever is less. No grant is given to a student entitled to less than $200. The $200 minimum grant has been criticized as unfair since receipt of even this small amount is deserved by those who qualify and may be material in lessening financial hardship in some cases.

It is estimated that the basic educational opportunity grants will provide between $1.5 and $2.5 billion in new Federal subsidies for higher education. This new Federal program offers aid not only to *all* low-income students but also to many middle-income students as well.

A second major provision of the 1972 Education Amendments—grants to States for State scholarship incentives—specifies that the Federal Government will pay 50 percent of any increase in State scholarship grants during a base year. Such a provision cannot help but make student aid a much more attractive form of State subsidy to higher education. For various reasons, the outlook for the private sector will also undoubtedly improve.[10]

(1) Even if public and private colleges freeze tuition at current levels, a State scholarship program that permits grants to be used at private institutions may induce many more students to attend such institutions;

(2) Private institutions will be able to divert some of their own student aid funds to other purposes;

(3) Some private institutions will be able to raise tuition without experiencing a loss in enrollment because the increased State grants can be used by some students to offset the increase; and

---

[9] For a comprehensive analysis of the Education Amendments of 1972, see Robert W. Hartman, "Higher Education Subsidies: An Analysis of Selected Programs in Current Legislation," in Joint Economic Committee, Congress of the United States, *Higher Education and Manpower Subsidies*, Part IV of *The Economics of Federal Subsidies Programs*, 92d Congress, 2d session, U.S. Government Printing Office, Washington, D.C., 1972, pp. 465–96.

[10] Ibid., p. 481.

(4) As State legislatures shift resources to State scholarship programs and as tuition increases at public institutions, the competitive position of the private sector will be enhanced.

The 1972 Amendments also make it possible for a student to borrow a larger sum, up to $2,500. The Federal Government will pay a student's interest liability provided that the institution in which he is enrolled certifies that he needs the loan. The consequences of this and other provisions will be to encourage an increase in the annual loan volume and to permit many more students who wish to borrow (including those from middle-income families) to do so.

Grants to Institutions

The term "institutional grant," according to current usage, normally means comprehensive, unrestricted support to colleges and universities. The demand for such across-the-board institutional support from the Federal Government has grown as the financial problems of colleges and universities have worsened. Through 1972 the only allocations generally free of Federal restrictive conditions were those made available to either land-grant colleges or "developing institutions" under title III of the Higher Education Act of 1965. The amount was small, in fiscal year 1971 totaling less than $50 million. In accordance with the Education Amendments of 1972, the Federal Government has agreed to provide each institution of higher education with a cost-of-education payment to be used to defray instructional expenses. The amount, determined by formula, ranges from $500 per student recipient of a basic educational opportunity grant to $100 per student recipient, depending on the institution's total undergraduate enrollment. General assistance grants are also being provided graduate schools, and payments to graduate schools will be made to cover the cost of instruction for veterans.

Higher education authorities have long advocated general institutional support by the Federal Government. The most persuasive argument has been that the institutions themselves can best determine exactly how any funds should be spent. Another argument is that the Federal Government is in a position to provide such support:

Federal taxes are more efficient and equitable than are the taxes of the States, and the collection costs are lower, both to the administrative agency and to the taxpayer. Federal taxes conform more nearly than do State taxes to the realities of our national economy and to national markets. It is important, too, that Federal taxes are far fairer in their burden on income than are State taxes, and have fewer adverse economic incentives (on business location, land use, and property investment) built into their structure.

. . .

In a Federal system of government, moreover, it is not efficient to rely exclusively on the States to finance subsidies, for frequently the public benefits are external to the States' boundaries. Federal funding makes for a more equitable allocation of resources.

. . .

States do need help in financing higher education. Their fiscal capacity will not stretch to finance the many requirements for public services and new deficits for student higher education. Even if all of the State allotment funds proposed by the administration in its revenue-sharing proposal were pledged to the student higher education deficit, the amount would still fall short.[11]

If arguments for more Federal institutional support are well understood, the role of Federal aid vis-a-vis State subsidies is not. As a general principle, that portion of the total costs of higher education paid for by each segment of society should be proportional to the share of benefits received. The student's payment should depend on the personal satisfactions and financial rewards he receives. State government subsidies should be proportional to the benefits that accrue to the State (largely external to the individual) as a result of its having more well-educated residents. The Federal Government's share should be proportional to the broad socioeconomic benefits (largely external to the States) attributable to an educated national population. Theoretically, the foregoing division of financing is sound; practically, it is impossible to achieve. Benefits cannot be measured with any precision; moreover, there is a great deal of overlap in benefits derived by individuals and by each level of government. Furthermore, State investment is diminished to the extent that college graduates leave to work or live elsewhere.[12]

As to the manner in which Federal aid might be distributed, many criteria or "load" factors to which the amount could be pegged have been suggested. The principal criteria and their primary consequences have been summarized by Mushkin as follows:[13]

---

[11] Selma J. Mushkin, "Public Financing of Higher Education," in *Universal Higher Education: Costs and Benefits*, American Council on Education, Washington, D.C., 1971, pp. 93–94.

[12] A State that educates a student who subsequently leaves that State loses not only the social and economic benefits that could accrue from his education but also the fiscal benefit from those tax payments that exceed the cost of public services. For a general discussion of the benefits of higher education and a specific case study of the effects of migration (in California), see W. Lee Hansen and Burton A. Weisbrod, *Benefits, Costs, and Finance of Public Higher Education*, Markham Publishing Co., Chicago, 1969.

[13] Mushkin, "Public Financing of Higher Education," op. cit., p. 99.

Criteria or Measure of Fund Allocations	Consequences
All enrollments	Benefits would be greater to public institutions, less favorable to small, high-tuition colleges.
Enrollment of holders of economic opportunity grants and doctoral fellowships	Favors institutions enrolling large numbers of poor students and high school graduates of outstanding ability.
Scholarship supplementation and fellowships	Favors institutions with large student assistance resources and those with strong graduate programs.
Institutional expenditures	Ignores economies of scale; provides a relatively larger part of the funds to relatively rich institutions; may reward inefficiency.
Level and rate of growth of expenditures	Favors relatively rich institutions, those that increase their outlay, and institutions that have received a large amount of research support.
Degrees awarded	Relatively favorable to degree-granting institutions; may be unfavorable to 2-year colleges that do not award degrees.

According to the Education Amendments of 1972, the basic determinant of an institution's share of Federal subsidies is the number of students receiving educational opportunity grants. On this basis, a larger proportion of funds goes to those institutions serving a relatively large number of low- and middle-income students.[14] In examining alternative formulas for general Federal support to institutions, Farrell and Andersen found considerable variation in cost and in administrative complexity but only a slight difference in relative amounts received by institutions classified by type and control.[15] Their conclusion, like that of some others, is that regardless of the formula used, certain institutions will benefit more than others. Inequities cannot be completely eliminated. The "best" formula is one that satisfies most equitably the generally recognized needs of a particular institution.

The most frequently heard argument against more Federal general support of higher education is essentially that inequities result from any

---

[14] For further evaluation of the new institutional assistance provisions, see Hartman, "Higher Education Subsidies: An Analysis of Selected Programs in Current Legislation," op. cit., pp. 488–90.

[15] For a description of five formulas of general Federal support to institutions, see Robert L. Farrell and Charles J. Andersen, "General Federal Support for Higher Education: An Analysis of Five Formulas," in *Financing Higher Education: Alternatives for the Federal Government*, op. cit., pp. 219–268.

broad funding of public institutions by State and local governments. Despite the fact that low-tuition public institutions are an accepted part of American life, their indiscriminate offering of higher education at bargain prices is bound to result in certain inequities.

Public institutions are open to criticism by anyone who feels public aid should discriminate in favor of lower income groups, since almost all generally charge all resident students the same tuition and since they spend very little on student aid, very few public colleges and universities discriminate in that way. They are thus very attractive to middle and higher income families; since many of them are of high quality, and some of the very highest, they are all the more attractive to people who would be willing, if forced to, to pay more for the quality they get. The public institutions have also been criticized for not enrolling their share of black students and of extremely disadvantaged students in general. Their low student aid budgets do not permit them to do that, of course, since even at a low-tuition institution the real costs of attendance are burdensome enough for the very poorest families to require heavy student aid.[16]

Public support of higher education naturally favors those students who attend the most heavily subsidized institutions and who stay in school the longest. If these same students also represent families with high incomes, then public support of higher education, particularly in States with non-progressive tax systems, taxes the poor to help the rich. Of course the net redistribution effect of *all* State taxes paid, compared with all benefits received (not just those from higher education), may in many States be quite favorable to the poor.[17]

In addition to these negative redistribution effects, other reservations concerning substantial extension of Federal general support have been expressed. The Carnegie Commission, for example, suggests that greater Federal support may prompt States to "hold off" final appropriations until they know the amount of operating costs the Federal Government will pay. Lump-sum, across-the-broad grants, the Commission claims, may diminish the basic support of and responsibility for higher education remaining with the States and the private sector. The Commission also

---

[16] Roger E. Bolton, "The Economics and Public Financing of Higher Education: An Overview," op. cit., p. 102.

[17] For studies on the income distribution effects of higher education, see Arthur J. Corazzini, Dennis J. Dugan, Henry G. Grabowski, "Determinants and Distributional Aspects of Enrollment in U.S. Higher Education," *The Journal of Human Resources*, vol. VII, no. 1, Winter 1972, pp. 39–59; W. Lee Hansen, "Income Distribution Effects of Higher Education," *The American Economic Review*, vol. LX, no. 2, May 1970, pp. 335–40; and Hansen and Weisbrod, *Benefits, Costs, and Finance of Public Higher Education*, op. cit. Critical commentary is provided by Joseph A. Pechman in "The Distributional Effects of Public Higher Education in California," *Journal of Human Resources*, vol. V, no. 3, Summer 1970, pp. 361–70.

fears that across-the-board support could interfere with positive change and, as a consequence, adversely affect diversity in higher education. Moreover, such support, in the Commission's view, would quite likely be accomplished at the expense of present Federal aid programs. While the Carnegie Commission believes that the Federal Government should provide substantially more financial aid to higher education, including funds for general support of institutions, its view is that the first priority should be to effect equality of educational opportunity. To this end, the Commission recommends that the Federal Government establish a ". . . program of cost-of-education supplements to colleges and universities based on the numbers of students enrolled in these institutions who hold grants awarded on the basis of financial need."

By way of summary: Certain circumstances and rationale argue strongly in favor of institutional grants as the preferred form of Federal aid. Even though conditions and justifications may not appear equally realistic or sound to all observers, this form of aid, now part of the Federal program of support to higher education, should be understood by educators if it is to be accurately evaluated. As an *added* component to existing Federal aid programs, grants to institutions will provide operating funds that State and local governments and the private sector seem unable to raise. And since certain aspects of higher education are a matter of national concern, they should be a Federal responsibility. In such areas as the cultivation and preservation of diversity, the growth and development of small private colleges and predominantly black student colleges, and the extension of equal educational opportunity, the Federal interest can best be served by strengthening the corporate whole of selective institutions rather than by offering fragmented categorical support of specialized programs. To some degree it is possible to adjust the components of any institutional grant formula to favor those institutions making the social contributions recognized as national in scope. The task, therefore, is (1) to identify those national responsibilities that can best be served through general funds to be used by institutions at their own discretion, and (2) to determine a formula by which the degree to which each institution serves the national welfare can be ascertained. An institution providing multiple services would require a "package" of support, with the amount of each component being determined according to selectivity factors and formula. Whether or not a plan for distributing institutional funds appropriated by Congress will in fact carry out national purposes remains to be seen. Hartman believes that "In the aggregate, it is likely that institutional aid would: (a) lower nominal tuition increases; (b) raise enrollments; and (c) enhance the dollar resources expended per student compared to the state of the world before institutional aid. But the mix of these elements at particular institutions or the overall share of each component in the national total demands a more complete knowledge of how institutions of higher education behave than is presently available."[18]

Tax Relief

The major existing tax relief accruing to universities and colleges is that which exempts them, as nonprofit organizations, from property, income, and capital gains taxes. Indirectly these institutions also benefit from the fact that individuals and corporations can make deductible gifts of up to 50 percent of their adjusted gross income and up to 5 percent of their net income, respectively.

For parents and students, who carry a substantial part of the burden of educational expenses, there is currently little tax relief. A student may claim an exemption on his tax return, and parents who provide half of his support may claim a student as an exemption on their return. In addition, full-time degree candidates are not required to pay taxes on fellowships received.

A tax relief proposal that has engendered considerable excitement is one that would grant students and parents either a tax deduction for educational expenses or a tax credit. If a deduction was permitted, persons with high incomes would derive the greatest benefit. A tax credit would be fairer in that it would permit educational expenses up to a designated maximum to be deducted from the actual tax owed rather than from the tax base. Moreover, a sliding scale would permit greater tax relief credit for initial educational expenditures and less for succeeding amounts. In the case of those low-income individuals who pay no Federal income taxes, a negative income tax credit (in effect, a grant) would be provided.

Opponents of the tax credit proposal argue that institutions would benefit more than would students and parents. Institutions, they point out, by raising fees, could secure all or much of the savings to parents and students. Proponents claim, on the other hand, that since tuition and fees are destined to rise, tax credits will at least offset the increase. They also insist that the tax credit would provide some assistance to institutions in need of financial help. Another major argument by the opposition is that tax credit programs will help the rich more than the poor. In response, proponents declare that tax credits primarily aid the middle-income group; that there are other special programs to help low-income students. Other points being debated are whether tax relief would favor private institutions over public institutions and whether it would transfer control of public

---

[18] Hartman, "Higher Education Subsidies: An Analysis of Selected Programs in Current Legislation," op. cit., p. 4881.

funds to private individuals. Even if a tax relief measure is passed, certain issues would continue to be debated.[19]

Revenue Sharing

By definition, revenue sharing is the return to the States of certain tax monies collected by the Federal Government. In general, revenue sharing calls for a designated percentage of the Federal tax revenue to be distributed to the States by formula. If the formula is based on the amount collected from each State, high-income States with large Federal tax payments would receive the largest shares. If it is based on a per capita distribution in an amount equal to a small percentage of the Federal income tax base, States with the largest population would receive the largest shares. As a general rule, the Federal money returned to the States can be spent at the State's discretion; however, some proposals allow the Federal Government to determine which activities are to be funded.

The logic of revenue sharing is that the greatest financial problems exist at the State level. By returning tax revenue to the States, the Federal Government is providing them with the financial support and control necessary to deal effectively with local problems. Opponents of revenue sharing argue that the States would have enough money to finance their programs adequately if they would overhaul their respective tax systems. Six States do not levy a personal income tax, and the tax rate in many other States is too low to be effective. One question frequently raised concerns the propriety of allocating Federal funds to States without attaching strings or establishing any standards. Former Secretary of Health, Education, and Welfare Wilbur J. Cohen suggests that

> . . . any Federal revenue sharing proposal should include requirements for merit selection of personnel, and ways to effectively trace the Federal funds, and performance or budgeting requirements. The requirements in most pending proposals is that the Federal money be spent or given away in almost any manner whatsoever. Is this a responsible way of developing federalism in terms of effective Federal-State local partnership? Of course not. It would probably result in graft, collusion, misunderstanding, and undermining faith in Federal as well as State and local government.[20]

Federal-State revenue sharing became a reality in 1972 with passage by the 92d Congress of Public Law 92-512. According to the formula adopted, the total revenue sharing funds are initially distributed among States (including their local governments) on the basis of population, weighted by relative income levels (so that the lower the income the greater

---

[19] For additional comment on this topic, see Roger A. Freeman, "Federal Assistance to Higher Education Through Income Tax Credits," op. cit., pp. 665–83.

[20] Letter to *The Washington Post*.

the amount of the aid) and by tax effort. Inherent in the formula is the assumption that Federal aid should increase with the size of a State's population and the degree of poverty of its residents; further, that more Federal aid should be given to those States and local governments that make a relatively greater effort to finance their own needs. Public Law 92-512 stipulates that revenue sharing funds may be used only for specific priority expenditures: public safety, environmental protection, public transportation, health recreation, libraries, social services for the poor or aged, and financial administration. Education, it should be noted, is *excluded* as a priority need.

STATE FISCAL MEASURES AND SUPPORT OF HIGHER EDUCATION

State governments, more than any other single element in American society, have assumed the responsibility of financing higher education. In fact, States, together with local governments, provide as much funding for the educational aspects of the country's colleges and universities as do all other revenue sources combined.[21] (The statistics, which are impressive, are summarized in table XIII-2). In the fall of 1970, 6.79 million full-time-equivalent students were pursuing a higher education in the United States. The number attending public institutions was 4.99 million, or 73.5 percent of the total. The education of these students— nearly three out of four—was financed primarily by State governments, which contributed 64.5 percent of the total unrestricted revenue used for instruction and supporting activities.

Inasmuch as State governments are the primary source of revenue for institutions enrolling seven out of 10 students, it is surprising that greater attention has not been given to the considerable differences in fiscal capacity, effort, and achievement among the States in support of higher education. As an illustration of the existing range of estimated State tax *capacity* in 1966–67, Mississippi had a capacity equal to only 67 percent of the national average while Nevada had a capacity of 187 percent. In terms of *effort* to achieve tax revenue in relation to capacity, Hawaii has been the most successful, with a rate equal to 208 percent of the national average in 1966–67, and New Hampshire the least successful, with a rate equal to only 61 percent. One measure of State *achievement* in financing public

---

[21] Total unrestricted revenue in the public and private sectors in 1970–71 amounted to $13,973,036,000. State and local government funding totaled $7,209,280,000, or 51.6 percent.

Table XIII-2.—Summary of State and local government unrestricted revenues for public higher education: 1970–71

	All public institutions		Public universities		Public 4-year colleges		Public 2-year colleges	
	Amount (000,000)	Percent	Amount (000,000)	Percent	Amount (000,000)	Percent	Amount (000,000)	Percent
Total unrestricted revenues[1]	$9,741	100.0	$4,798	100.0	$2,967	100.0	$1,976	100.0
State government	6,280	64.5	3,363	70.1	2,017	68.0	900	45.5
Local government	830	8.5	11	.2	122	4.1	697	35.3
All other sources	2,631	27.0	1,423	29.7	829	27.9	380	19.2
Number of FTE students fall 1970	4,988,573		1,943,735		1,631,097		1,413,741	

[1] Unrestricted educational and general revenues from student tuition and fees, Federal Government appropriations, State and local government appropriations, endowment income, private gifts.

Source: Paul F. Mertins and Norman J. Brandt, *Financial Statistics of Institutions of Higher Education: Current Funds Revenue and Expenditures, 1970–71,* U.S. Department of Health, Education, and Welfare, Office of Education, U.S. Government Printing Office, Washington, D.C., 1973.

higher education is the amount of State tax funds allocated to higher education operating expenses per resident high school graduate. In 1970, Washington led with $3,587 of State tax funds allocated to public higher education per State high school graduate, while New Hampshire was last, with $961 per graduate.

It is extremely important to the future financing of higher education that differences in fiscal capacity, effort, and support achievement among States be known and appreciated. Such information should encourage those States with untapped fiscal potential and/or below-average effort and achievement to improve their standing. If, for example, the 27 States below the national average in State appropriations for public higher education per high school graduate were to increase their appropriations in 1970 to the national average rate, the total State support of higher education of $6,139 million would be increased by $656 million.

Analysis of State Support

Although there are marked variations in the ways in which States share responsibility with local governments in providing and financing many public services, such is not the case in the financing (through unrestricted revenue) of public higher education. In nearly every instance, the financing of public 4-year institutions is the exclusive responsibility of State governments. The financing of public 2-year institutions, on the other hand, is generally a shared responsibility between State and local governments, with the relative proportional support varying from State to State (the average division, based on national data, is about 55–45). However, the total amount of unrestricted revenue provided by local governments equals only 13 percent of that provided by State governments. Because the role of local governments is so limited, the following analysis of governmental support of public higher education is concerned only with that provided by the State. In those few States in which a substantial share of total public funding of higher education is provided by local governments, composite State-local fiscal measures will give a more accurate picture. (See table XIII-3).

A relatively simple yet useful analysis of State financing of public higher education can be made by studying five factors: student *burden*, fiscal *capacity*, fiscal *effort*, *allocation* to higher education, and financial support *achievement*. The relationship of these factors is shown in the following equation:

$$\frac{\text{Capacity}}{\text{Burden}} \times \text{Effort} \times \text{Allocation} = \text{Achievement}$$

A State's higher education *burden* can be expressed either as a potential or as an actual student load. Since the annual number of students graduat-

Table XIII-3.—Measures of State-local tax capacity and tax effort for States: 1966-67[1]

State	Per capita amounts			Index measures (per capita amounts as percent of U.S. averages)				
	Tax capacity	Tax revenue	Personal income (1966)	Tax capacity	Tax revenue	Personal income (1966)	Relative tax effort[2]	Percent departure of income index from tax capacity index
	(1)	(2)	(3)	(4)	(5)	(6)	(7)	(8)
United States	313	313	2,980	100	100	100	100	XXX
Alabama	219	194	2,055	70	62	69	89	−1
Alaska	311	324	3,473	99	104	117	104	+18
Arizona	298	325	2,561	95	104	86	109	−9
Arkansas	241	200	2,037	77	64	68	83	−9
California	387	417	3,490	124	133	117	108	−7
Colorado	326	345	2,901	104	110	97	106	−7
Connecticut	366	340	3,710	117	109	125	93	+8
Delaware	384	345	3,451	123	110	116	90	−7
Dist. of Columbia	378	341	3,856	121	109	129	90	+8
Florida	325	274	2,654	104	88	89	84	−15
Georgia	249	230	2,371	80	73	80	92	—
Hawaii	310	417	3,090	99	133	104	135	+5
Idaho	286	299	2,408	91	96	81	105	−10
Illinois	357	301	3,555	114	96	119	84	+5
Indiana	311	296	3,056	99	95	103	95	+4
Iowa	325	337	3,013	104	108	101	104	−3
Kansas	328	315	2,895	105	101	97	96	−8
Kentucky	249	212	2,256	80	68	76	85	−4
Louisiana	295	265	2,273	94	85	76	90	−18
Maine	254	267	2,482	81	85	83	105	+2
Maryland	317	326	3,235	101	104	109	103	+8
Massachusetts	305	371	3,291	98	119	110	121	+12
Michigan	326	325	3,258	104	104	109	100	+5

Minnesota	297	354	2,898	95	113	97	119	+2
Mississippi	201	197	1,765	64	63	59	98	−5
Missouri	304	263	2,816	97	84	95	86	−2
Montana	330	308	2,668	105	98	90	93	−15
Nebraska	344	270	2,943	110	86	99	78	−11
Nevada	536	382	3,478	171	122	117	71	−54
New Hampshire	343	278	2,834	110	89	95	81	−15
New Jersey	335	324	3,460	107	104	116	97	+9
New Mexico	293	269	2,360	94	86	79	92	−15
New York	339	469	3,558	108	150	119	138	+11
North Carolina	245	230	2,284	78	74	77	94	−1
North Dakota	287	278	2,441	92	89	82	97	−10
Ohio	314	257	3,089	100	82	104	82	+4
Oklahoma	319	254	2,480	102	81	83	80	−19
Oregon	331	334	2,947	106	107	99	101	−7
Pennsylvania	285	282	2,983	91	90	100	99	+9
Rhode Island	284	297	3,062	91	95	103	105	+12
South Carolina	202	196	2,046	64	63	69	97	+5
South Dakota	284	303	2,471	91	97	83	107	−8
Tennessee	243	212	2,235	78	68	75	87	−3
Texas	307	231	2,577	98	74	87	75	−11
Utah	271	302	2,490	87	97	84	111	−3
Vermont	275	328	2,664	88	105	89	119	+1
Virginia	270	243	2,608	86	78	88	90	+2
Washington	351	370	3,227	112	118	108	106	−4
West Virginia	234	226	2,176	75	72	73	96	−2
Wisconsin	294	363	2,976	94	116	100	124	+6
Wyoming	441	347	2,781	141	111	93	79	−48

[1] For related 1968–69 data, see table XIII-6.

[2] Tax revenue as a percent of tax capacity.

Source: Advisory Commission on Intergovernmental Relations, *Measuring the Fiscal Capacity and Effort of State and Local Areas*, U.S. Government Printing Office, Washington, D.C., 1971, table G-1, p. 120, and table G-4, p. 126.

Table XIII-4.—Measures of State tax capacity and tax effort for States:
1966–67

State	Per capita amounts		Index measures (per capita amounts as percent of U.S. averages)		
	Tax capacity	Tax revenue	Tax capacity	Tax revenue	Relative tax effort[1]
United States........	165	165	100	100	100
Alabama............	120	138	73	84	115
Alaska..............	166	220	101	133	132
Arizona............	157	186	95	113	118
Arkansas...........	129	145	78	88	112
California..........	195	187	118	113	96
Colorado...........	174	171	105	104	98
Connecticut........	193	162	117	98	84
Delaware...........	201	273	122	165	136
Dist. of Columbia....	223	226	135	137	101[2]
Florida............	168	148	102	90	88
Georgia............	140	150	85	91	107
Hawaii.............	147	306	89	185	208
Idaho..............	155	190	94	115	123
Illinois.............	185	134	112	81	73
Indiana............	168	155	102	94	92
Iowa...............	162	168	98	102	104
Kansas.............	165	156	100	95	94
Kentucky...........	134	146	81	88	110
Louisiana..........	171	191	104	116	111
Maine..............	143	144	87	87	101
Maryland..........	169	178	102	108	105
Massachusetts.......	166	177	101	107	106
Michigan...........	174	185	105	112	107
Minnesota..........	163	184	99	112	113
Mississippi.........	110	131	67	79	120
Missouri............	163	135	99	82	82
Montana...........	169	137	102	83	81
Nebraska...........	170	95	103	58	56
Nevada.............	308	201	187	122	65
New Hampshire.....	186	114	113	69	61
New Jersey.........	177	121	107	73	68
New Mexico........	168	204	102	124	122
New York..........	170	226	103	137	133
North Carolina......	133	169	81	102	127
North Dakota.......	150	135	91	82	90
Ohio...............	165	117	100	71	71
Oklahoma..........	168	162	102	98	96
Oregon.............	174	177	105	107	102
Pennsylvania........	153	156	93	95	102
Rhode Island........	158	160	96	97	101
South Carolina......	122	152	74	92	124
South Dakota.......	142	123	86	75	87
Tennessee...........	133	133	81	81	99

Table XIII-4.—Measures of State tax capacity and tax effort for States: 1966–67—Continued

State	Per capita amounts		Index measures (per capita amounts as percent of U.S. averages)		
	Tax capacity	Tax revenue	Tax capacity	Tax revenue	Relative tax effort[1]
Texas............	175	125	106	76	71
Utah............	142	179	86	108	127
Vermont..........	161	193	98	117	120
Virginia..........	142	145	86	88	103
Washington........	175	262	106	159	150
West Virginia.......	127	161	77	98	127
Wisconsin..........	155	220	94	133	142
Wyoming..........	243	175	147	106	72

[1] Tax revenue as a percent of tax capacity.
[2] Treating all nonproperty taxes as "State" and all property taxes as "local."

Source: Unpublished data from the Advisory Commission on Intergovernmental Relations.

ing from high school within the State, per citizen population, is an approximate relative measure of a State's college enrollment potential, it also represents a State's responsibility to resident youth. Actual student load is equal to the full-time-equivalent enrollment in a State's public colleges and universities. A State's fiscal *capacity*, measured in dollars per capita, is the ability of the State to obtain resources for public purposes through taxes. (A complex concept, it is discussed in more detail in the ensuing section.) Fiscal *effort* is a percentage measurement of the amount of a State's capacity the State government is actually using. (Data for the latter two measurements appear in table XIII-4.) The *allocation* factor is the degree or proportion of collected State tax funds allocated to finance the operating expenses of institutions of higher education within the State.[22] The *achievement* index, a product of the capacity-burden ratio multiplied by the effort and allocation factors, reports the dollar amount of State support for institutions of higher education per student (based on either actual or potential enrollment). If measured in terms of actual student enrollment, the achievement index reflects the *commitment* of State tax funds to support public higher education at desired quantity and quality levels. (Quality is reflected only insofar as it is related to dollar input; no adjustment is made for differences among States in efficiency of operation

---

[22] Since the concern is for general State support of public and private *institutions* ($6,377 million in unrestricted revenues for operations in 1970–71), State grants-in-aid to *students* ($99 million in 1970–71) are excluded.

or for variances in salary levels.) If measured in terms of potential enrollment (high school graduates), the achievement index suggests the degree
to which taxes used for higher education reflect the State's potential
responsibility to provide an opportunity for public postsecondary training
for resident youth. (A more thorough explanation of the foregoing factors,
together with procedures for making interstate comparisons of State financial support of public higher education, is presented in chapter II and in
statistical table II-1, columns 11-17.)

The material that follows examines in detail two factors of the equation
for State financing of public higher education: viz., fiscal capacity and
fiscal effort.

Accurately measuring a State's tax capacity is exceptionally difficult,
yet if there is to be any meaningful analysis of a State's ability to support
higher education (and its success), its tax capacity must be calculated.
Most welcome, then, is the 1971 study by the Advisory Commission on
Intergovernmental Relations, *Measuring the Fiscal Capacity and Effort of
State and Local Areas*. The principal source of the sections which follow,
this volume contains the most valid fiscal measures currently available.

State and Local Tax Capacity and Effort

An accurate measurement of the fiscal capability and effort of State
and local governments can be extremely useful to those policymakers
responsible for budgets, taxing, and borrowing. Information concerning
the ability of governments to obtain resources for public purposes and the
extent to which they actually use this ability enables officials to examine
more intelligently the relationship between desired economic development
and existing fiscal practices. State comparisons of fiscal capacity in the
various fields of taxation provide a means whereby legislators can determine whether or not they are making good use of tax sources. Detailed
examination of local capacity measures within a State is essential in any
reevaluation of the State-local tax and allocation system and, for that
matter, in any reassessment of local taxing powers. A State that finds it is
disproportionately strong in State government revenue sources—as compared with local government sources—may consider shifting a larger-
than-average share of financial responsibility to the State government
level.

If State fiscal measures could be compared on a nationwide basis, the
Federal Government would be in a position to select the most deserving
recipients of educational grants. And if grants were adjusted for variations
in fiscal *capacity*, it would be possible to bring into balance the basis by
which State or local areas provide public services. Adjustment of grants
on the basis of tax *effort*, on the other hand, would have as its objective

rewarding and stimulating public spending. For either objective, accurate measures of local capacity and effort are required.[23]

Three Approaches to Measuring Fiscal Capacity

The principal resources available for support of State and local government are the personal income of residents, the natural resources of the State, business activity within the State,[24] and wealth within the State (*stock* of assets—buildings, equipment, inventory, land—and individual and corporate savings). One approach to measuring fiscal capacity directs attention to personal income and the productive achievements of business as the flow of resources most immediately available for taxation. Efforts to measure a "gross State product" of goods and services produced by a State economy are currently in progress.[25] A State's total market activity can be viewed as an aggregate measure of its capacity to pay for public activities from *current productive output*. The principal problem encountered in developing a gross State product is the difficulty of meaningfully allocating to the individual States corporate profits, capital consumption allowances, and indirect business taxes.

A second method of measuring fiscal capacity is to seek acceptable measures of the relative financing capacity of State and local *governments*. In the "representative tax system" approach, as it has been termed, the revenue capacity of a particular area is defined as the total revenue that would result by applying, within the area, the national average rate of each of the numerous kinds of State-local revenue sources. When the tax potential of a given area is based on average nationwide tax rates applied to the existing tax bases within that area, the real world of State-local financing is reflected and the problem of weighting each of several potentially relevant indicators according to their actual relative contributions is solved. The representative system of fiscal capacity analysis is most useful in analyzing how States can increase the funding of public services through

---

[23] The important use of fiscal capacity and effort to adjust grant size suggests the value of recent efforts to define and quantify these measures more accurately. Considerable credit should be given to those who first developed the measures currently employed: L. Laszio Ecker-Racz, Allen D. Manvel, James W. Martin, Charles E. McClure, Selma J. Mushkin, Kenneth E. Quindry, and Alice M. Rivlin, among others.

[24] It should be noted that business activity *within* a State may be used to shift payment of taxes to nonresidents *outside* the State. For example, taxes may be shifted to nonresident consumers through levying sales taxes and severance taxes or to out-of-State suppliers by levying taxes on "imported" products. Such shifting makes resources outside the State available for taxing.

[25] See Harold K. Charlesworth and William G. Herzel, *Kentucky Gross State Product, 1969*, Office of Business Development and Government Services, College of Business and Economics, University of Kentucky, Lexington, 1973.

taxation. For this reason it is explained in some detail in the following section together with presentation of key State fiscal capacity and effort measurements.

The third and simplest approach to fiscal capacity measurement focuses on the ability of the *people* of a State, rather than the government, to support public services. Personal income, within certain limitations, provides an approximate measure of the capacity of State residents to pay taxes. Although taxes are mainly derived from income, individual income earnings are by no means the only (or even the principal) source of State and local taxes. Under existing State and local tax laws, business transactions, certain raw and manufactured products, and corporate income also provide major tax bases. However, if it is intended to determine the ability of *residents* of a State to pay *State* taxes from their *immediate earnings*, then per capita income provides an approximate measurement of this capacity.[26] (Note the limitation to taxes of *resident* citizens as opposed to those of corporations, nonresident tourists, and mineral resources.) Only *State* taxes, which closely relate revenue-raising capability to personal income, should be considered. Because the main impact of the property tax is local, it is not included. Finally, only immediate *earnings*, as opposed to savings and real estate holdings, are interpreted as being readily available for tax payment.

Tax *effort* based on a per capita income measurement of capacity is considered a realistic assessment or index of the immediate contribution residents make in paying certain State taxes directly from earned income, not from savings or invested wealth. An important use for such an index might be the proportioning of Federal aid to States if such aid is to be allocated according to the immediate personal burden which citizens of a State themselves sustain in supporting public services.

The "Representative Tax System"

The Advisory Commission on Intergovernmental Relations first published a report dealing with ways to quantify the relative financing capability and effort of States and their local governments in 1962. An abstract of some portions of the Commission's 1971 report *Measuring the Fiscal Capacity and Effort of State and Local Areas*[27] is presented here.

---

[26] A more valid measure of the ability of residents to pay State taxes would be *net* personal income per capita equal to total personal income, less a minimum expenditure for basic consumption or cost of living.

[27] Advisory Commission on Intergovernmental Relations, *Measuring the Fiscal Capacity and Effort of State and Local Areas*, U.S. Government Printing Office, Washington, D.C., 1971.

The two fiscal measurements employed are defined as follows: *Fiscal capacity* is a measurement of the *ability* of governments to obtain resources for public purposes; *fiscal effort* is a measurement of *achievement* of how much of this capacity governments actually use. It is important to note that fiscal capacity involves the financing capability of *governments* of which the economic well-being of local residents is only a contributing factor. Thus, while there is general similarity in the tax capacity of various States, whether gauged by resident personal income or by the yield of a "representative tax system," some substantial differences occur in individual States. With regard to fiscal effort, what is sought is a measurement of *government use* of its potential financing capacity, rather than a comparison of the burden assumed by the *people*. As in the case of capacity, the two are likely to be related; there are, however, exceptions. Some taxes can be shifted from residents who normally pay them to someone else. For example, an area with a large volume of tourist trade may, through sales taxes, force nonresident visitors to assume a considerable fraction of the financing of public services. In such an area there might be a comparatively high measure of relative revenue effort by the local government, even though—because of the sales tax paid by tourists—the tax burden of local residents is average or even low.

Because of the marked variations in the ways that States share responsibility with their local governments for providing and financing public services, the capacity and effort measures most frequently employed are those reflecting a composite of both levels of government. In public support of higher education, however, the dominant role of State governments requires *separate* State and local government fiscal measures. (Such separate measurements are presented in tables XIII-4 and XIII-5.)

The Advisory Commission's 1971 report is concerned with State and local governments' "general revenue from own sources." In addition to tax revenue, the following are included: fees collected for such governmental services as college tuition and public hospital charges; interest earned on government financial assets; and other miscellaneous nontax revenues. Collectively, these categories supplied nearly one-quarter of the revenue raised by State and local governments from their own sources in 1966–67. However, for the purpose of reviewing the fiscal capacity of State governments to support higher education, it is appropriate to consider only *tax* capacity and effort.

Measuring Tax Capacity and Tax Effort

The "representative tax system" methodology involves the following: (1) determining for each of the various kinds of State and local taxes a national average rate, which, if applied throughout the Nation, would

Table XIII-5.—Measures of local tax capacity and tax effort for States: 1966–67

State	Per capita amounts		Index measures (per capita amounts as percent of U.S. averages)		
	Tax capacity	Tax revenue	Tax capacity	Tax revenue	Relative tax effort[1]
United States........	148	148	100	100	100
Alabama............	98	55	66	37	56
Alaska.............	145	104	98	70	72
Arizona............	141	140	95	95	100
Arkansas...........	112	55	76	37	49
California..........	191	230	129	155	120
Colorado...........	152	174	103	118	115
Connecticut........	173	178	117	120	103
Delaware...........	183	73	124	49	40
Dist. of Columbia....	155	115	105	78	74[2]
Florida.............	157	126	106	85	81
Georgia............	109	80	74	54	73
Hawaii.............	163	112	110	76	68
Idaho..............	131	109	89	74	84
Illinois.............	172	167	116	113	97
Indiana............	143	141	97	95	99
Iowa..............	163	169	110	114	103
Kansas.............	163	159	110	107	98
Kentucky...........	116	66	78	45	57
Louisiana...........	124	74	84	50	60
Maine..............	111	122	75	82	110
Maryland...........	148	148	100	100	100
Massachusetts.......	140	194	95	131	139
Michigan...........	152	139	103	94	92
Minnesota..........	134	170	91	115	127
Mississippi..........	92	66	62	45	71
Missouri............	140	128	95	86	91
Montana...........	160	171	108	116	106
Nebraska...........	175	176	118	119	101
Nevada............	228	182	154	123	80
New Hampshire.....	157	164	106	111	104
New Jersey.........	158	203	107	137	129
New Mexico........	125	65	84	44	52
New York..........	170	243	115	164	143
North Carolina......	112	62	76	42	55
North Dakota.......	137	143	93	97	104
Ohio..............	149	140	101	95	94
Oklahoma..........	151	92	102	62	61
Oregon............	158	157	107	106	100
Pennsylvania........	132	126	89	85	96
Rhode Island........	125	138	84	93	110
South Carolina......	80	44	54	30	55
South Dakota.......	143	180	97	122	126
Tennessee..........	110	79	74	53	72

Table XIII-5.—Measures of local tax capacity and tax effort for States: 1966–67—Continued

| State | Per capita amounts | | Index measures (per capita amounts as percent of U.S. averages) | | |
	Tax capacity	Tax revenue	Tax capacity	Tax revenue	Relative tax effort[1]
Texas..............	132	106	89	72	80
Utah...............	129	123	87	83	95
Vermont...........	114	135	77	91	118
Virginia...........	128	97	86	66	76
Washington........	176	108	119	73	62
West Virginia.......	107	65	72	44	61
Wisconsin..........	139	143	94	97	103
Wyoming..........	198	172	134	116	87

[1] Tax revenue as a percent of tax capacity.

[2] Treating all nonproperty taxes as "State" and all property taxes as "local."

Source: Unpublished data from the Advisory Commission on Intergovernmental Relations.

have produced the same total amount of revenue that State and local governments actually obtained from a particular type of tax in 1966–67 or in any given year; (2) estimating by State the potential yield of each type of tax, if imposed at the aforementioned uniform nationwide rate; and (3) aggregating the potential yield amounts for each State in order to estimate the total tax capacity of a given State. In effect this procedure weights each tax source according to its relative nationwide importance. For example, if an area is "average," in the sense that its economy is a microcosm of that of the entire Nation, 14.6 percent of its estimated tax capacity would be attributable to State general sales taxes, 39.8 to local property taxes, 8.1 percent to State individual income taxes, 5.6 percent to State corporation taxes, etc. The foregoing are the proportions of all State and local government taxes that actually came from these sources in 1966–67.

In estimating the relative tax capacity of particular areas, a nationwide average "rate" for each tax is applied to local tax *base* data. The tax *base* represents the extent of activity in the area subject to the tax. For example, the tax base for the general sales tax is the dollar value of retail sales in the area; for motor fuel tax, the volume of highway fuel consumption; for utility taxes, receipts from electric, gas, and telephone utilities; for individual income, the amount of taxable income in various income classes; for local property tax on farm property, the value of farm realty and selected classes of farm personal property, etc. The most difficult part of measuring tax capacity is determining the appropriate tax base, one reason being that for some tax components no information is available that will serve to determine tax base amounts. In such instances, a stand-in or proxy measure must be used to determine the potential base for a particular tax. The choice of proxy measures has generally been based on the collective judgment of the Advisory Commission's staff, backed by available data and limited testing.

"Tax effort" is an expression of the percentage relation between actual amounts of tax revenue obtained by governments (in 1966–67) and their tax capacity. Actual tax revenue collected *equals* total tax capacity nationwide. Since the nationwide effort measure is 100 percent, the effort measures for various States actually indicate how they compare in tax revenue performance with the national average.

State Comparisons

As depicted in table XIII-3, State *and* local government tax capacity (column 1) in 1966–67[28] ranged from $536 per person in Nevada to $201 per person in Mississippi, a span of 2.7-to-1. Regional influences are apparent: Four of the five States with the greatest taxing capability are in the West (Delaware is the exception), and the five States at the low end of the range are in the South. The data indicate greater variation in tax capacity than in per capita personal income (column 3), which showed a 2.1-to-1 range in 1966—from 25 percent above the national average in Connecticut to 41 percent below the national average in Mississippi (percent values from column 6). As expected, most high-income States are above average in per capita tax capacity, while most low-income States are below average. Such, however, is not always the case, nor are the two relative measures always closely matched; in 24 States the variance is at least 10 percent.

A host of factors contribute to the divergence between relative tax capacity based on the "representative tax system" as opposed to being based on personal income. If mining and tourism are important elements in the economy, a State is likely to exhibit relatively much more tax-raising capability than resident income data would suggest. In such States, the revenue potential of severance taxes (taxes on minerals extracted) and of certain kinds of sales taxes will be greater than the national average. For example, the potential yield of amusement taxes is a very small part

---

[28] Related 1968–69 data are presented in table XIII-6. Although the Advisory Commission on Intergovernmental Relations study presents summary measures for 1968–69, it deals mainly and in detail with data for 1966–67. For current and prospective policymaking purposes, it obviously would be desirable to have up-to-date measures of this kind available on a regular basis.

of the revenue capacity of most States. Nevada, however, is an exception—and for an obvious reason. Although Nevada residents earn only one-quarter of 1 percent of all personal income in the Nation, 5 percent of the entire country's amusement enterprise receipts (as reported by the Census of Business) is earned in this State. Similarly, Texas' share of national severance taxation is seven times that of its residents' proportion of all personal income in the Nation; in Louisiana, the ratio is about 17-to-1; in Wyoming, nearly 20-to-1.

Areas in which agriculture is an important economic element are likely to be relatively better off from the standpoint of the prevailing State-local tax system than resident personal income would indicate. The reasons are (1) the important role of the property tax, which in 1966-67 supplied nearly 40 percent of all tax-source revenue of State and local governments and accounted for a corresponding weight in financing capability; and (2) the fact that modern agriculture is capital-intensive—that is, it involves more property investment per dollar of income than do most other economic activities.

"Relative effort," also shown in table XIII-3, column 7, is used to express, on a percentage basis, the relation between the potential yield of various tax sources at national average rates and tax amounts actually received by State and local governments from corresponding sources in 1966-67.[29] There is a range of 1.9-to-1 in relative tax effort (138/71), from 38 percent above the national average in New York to 39 percent below in Nevada. Regional patterns are far less evident for tax effort than they are for capacity. The States near the top and the bottom of the tax-effort spectrum are widely scattered geographically.

Relative effort varies among States to a far greater extent for particular types or groupings of taxes than for the composite of all taxes. Such a variance is to be expected, of course, since particular taxes represent alternatives of one kind or another; heavy reliance on certain taxes will permit, and is usually associated with, little or no reliance on others. The widely differing reliance on property taxation on the revenue structure of particular States is a case in point. While the extreme interstate range in relative total tax effort is 1.9-to-1, the relative-effort range for property taxes is far broader: 4.2-to-1 or from 55 percent above the national average in Minnesota to slightly more than one-third of the national average in Alabama. Of the 16 States in the South, all except one (Maryland) make below-average use of their property tax capacity, and 12 of the 16 show a lower effort index for property taxes than any other State save New Mexico. Needless to say, "underusage" of the property tax in the South tends to be offset by above-average use of various other revenue sources.

---

[29] Related 1968-69 data appear in table XIII-6.

Table XIII-6.—Measures of State-local tax capacity and tax effort for States: 1968-69

State	Per capita amounts			Index measures (per capita amounts as percent of U.S. averages)				Percent change 1966-67 to 1968-69[1]			
	Tax capacity	Tax revenue	Personal income (1968)	Tax capacity	Tax revenue	Personal income (1968)	Relative tax effort[2]	Per capita tax capacity	Per capita tax revenue	Per capita personal income	Relative tax effort
United States	386	386	3,421	100	100	100	100	23.3	23.3	14.8	—
Alabama	270	227	2,337	70	59	68	84	23.3	17.0	13.7	-5.1
Alaska	403	399	4,146	104	103	121	99	29.6	23.1	19.4	-5.0
Arizona	381	393	3,027	99	102	88	103	27.9	20.9	18.2	-5.8
Arkansas	299	222	2,322	77	58	68	74	24.1	11.0	14.0	-10.5
California	472	547	3,968	122	142	116	116	22.0	31.2	13.7	7.5
Colorado	398	392	3,340	103	102	98	98	22.1	13.6	15.1	-6.8
Connecticut	451	397	4,256	117	103	124	88	23.2	16.8	14.7	-5.4
Delaware	465	377	3,795	120	98	111	81	21.1	9.3	10.0	-10.0
Dist. of Columbia	465	426	4,464	120	110	130	92	23.0	24.9	15.8	1.4
Florida	419	338	3,191	109	88	93	81	28.9	23.4	20.2	-4.7
Georgia	314	273	2,781	81	71	81	87	26.1	18.7	17.3	-5.7
Hawaii	381	492	3,513	99	127	103	129	22.9	18.0	13.7	-4.1
Idaho	338	340	2,668	88	88	78	100	18.2	13.7	10.8	-4.1
Illinois	431	376	3,981	112	97	116	87	20.7	24.9	12.0	3.4
Indiana	375	338	3,412	97	88	100	90	20.6	14.2	11.6	-5.5
Iowa	385	395	3,265	100	102	95	103	18.5	17.2	8.4	-.9
Kansas	405	351	3,303	105	91	97	87	23.5	11.4	14.1	-9.7
Kentucky	312	278	2,645	81	72	77	89	25.3	31.1	17.2	5.1
Louisiana	364	301	2,634	94	78	77	83	23.4	13.6	15.9	-8.0
Maine	316	321	2,824	82	83	83	102	24.4	20.2	13.8	-3.2
Maryland	398	416	3,742	103	108	109	105	25.6	27.6	15.7	1.9
Massachusetts	382	455	3,835	99	118	112	119	25.2	22.6	16.5	-2.0
Michigan	404	439	3,675	105	114	107	109	23.9	35.1	12.8	9.0
Minnesota	367	413	3,341	95	107	98	112	23.6	16.7	15.3	-5.6

Mississippi	252	245	2,081	65	63	61	98	25.4	24.4	17.9	—
Missouri	373	304	3,257	97	79	95	81	22.7	15.6	15.7	−5.8
Montana	391	356	2,942	101	92	86	91	18.5	15.6	10.3	−2.6
Nebraska	416	361	3,239	108	94	95	87	20.9	33.7	10.1	10.7
Nevada	669	475	3,957	173	123	115	71	24.8	24.3	13.8	−.6
New Hampshire	422	325	3,259	109	84	95	77	23.0	16.9	15.0	−4.8
New Jersey	410	411	3,954	106	106	116	100	22.4	26.9	14.3	3.5
New Mexico	355	324	2,651	92	84	77	91	21.2	20.4	12.3	−.9
New York	418	580	4,151	108	150	121	139	23.3	23.7	16.7	.4
North Carolina	308	267	2,664	80	69	78	87	25.7	16.1	16.6	−7.9
North Dakota	352	333	2,730	91	86	80	95	22.6	19.8	11.8	−2.4
Ohio	387	318	3,509	100	82	103	82	23.2	23.7	13.6	.6
Oklahoma	392	290	2,880	102	75	84	74	22.9	14.2	16.1	−7.2
Oregon	401	406	3,317	104	105	97	101	21.1	21.6	12.6	.4
Pennsylvania	350	346	3,419	91	90	100	99	22.8	22.7	14.6	−.4
Rhode Island	355	380	3,549	92	98	104	107	25.0	27.9	15.9	2.1
South Carolina	254	227	2,380	66	59	70	89	25.7	15.8	16.3	−8.0
South Dakota	349	353	2,876	90	91	84	101	22.9	16.5	16.4	−5.2
Tennessee	302	254	2,579	78	66	75	84	24.3	19.8	15.4	−3.2
Texas	388	280	3,029	101	73	89	72	26.4	21.2	17.5	−4.0
Utah	326	337	2,790	84	87	82	104	20.3	11.6	12.0	−7.1
Vermont	339	394	3,072	88	102	90	116	23.3	20.1	15.3	−2.6
Virginia	337	323	3,068	87	84	90	96	24.8	32.9	17.6	6.7
Washington	424	434	3,688	110	112	108	102	20.8	17.3	14.3	−2.9
West Virginia	284	269	2,470	74	70	72	95	21.4	19.0	13.5	−1.7
Wisconsin	358	441	3,363	93	114	98	123	21.8	21.5	13.0	−.2
Wyoming	530	413	3,190	137	107	93	78	20.2	19.0	14.7	−.8

[1] For related 1966–67 data, see table XIII-3.

[2] Tax revenue as a percent of tax capacity.

Source: Advisory Commission on Intergovernmental Relations, *Measuring the Fiscal Capacity and Effort of State and Local Areas*, U.S. Government Printing Office, Washington, D.C., 1971, table G-14, p. 209.

Search for New State Tax Revenue

For a decisionmaker to know that in a general way his State is "poor" in tax capacity is not particularly helpful. On the other hand, it should be helpful if he understands that the relative capacity of his State is much stronger in one type of taxation than in another. The Advisory Commission's report includes fiscal measures that can be useful not only in ascertaining the degree to which the various types of tax capacities are being utilized but also in providing a framework for comparisons with neighboring States. Table XIII-7, prepared by the Advisory Commission, is particularly useful to anyone desiring to estimate which tax sources would bring in the greatest amount of revenue if existing State tax rates were raised to the national average level.

For each State, table XIII-7 shows the following:

(1) Percentage increase in total tax revenue that would have resulted if all "underutilized" tax sources had been raised to the national average level (without reducing rates for other taxes at or above the national average rate);

(2) Number of separate "underutilized" sources;

(3) Major tax classes that appear as part of the "underutilized" group; and

(4) Two types of taxes that would yield the most additional revenue if national average rates were used.

"Unused tax capacity" means the net amount of additional revenue that a State could raise if it utilized *all* of its potential tax resources at the national average rate. There is no such netting of pluses and minuses in table XIII-7; rather, a summation of the minuses, an examination of only those sources in which the effort ratio is below 100. Tax sources representative of effort ratios above the national average are disregarded.

For the same reason, the information provided in table XIII-7 neither indicates which State is "trying harder" (overall tax effort measurements provide this information) nor suggests that every State should use each tax base at the national average tax rate level. It is an illustration of how detailed comparative data may be used by decisionmakers in their search for revenue.

For all States, actual tax revenue in 1966–67 would have been 21 percent higher if each State had used 100-percent effort in those particular sources in which effort was below the national average. Of that potential 21 percent increase in tax revenue, about two-thirds would have come from more intensive use of existing taxes and one-third from an initiation of new taxes. Predictably, general sales taxes and income taxes would have provided most of the additional tax revenue.

In general, States that could add the largest relative amount of funds by further exploitation of certain tax sources are also the States with the lowest overall tax effort ratios. Thus, of the 10 States with the highest revenue-potential percentage in table XIII-7, seven are in the lowest fifth of all States in terms of relative total tax effort. The picture at the other end of the spectrum is similar: Of the 10 States that have relatively the least to gain from more use of "underutilized" tax sources, eight are among the top 10 total-effort States. This general pattern, however, is not always the case. Delaware, for example, has the largest potential revenue percentage, yet has an overall tax effort that is higher than that of 14 other States.

In four States, only one of the eight major tax sources is utilized at a subnormal level. In two of these States the picture is especially dismal, inasmuch as the total tax-effort ratios are already far above average: 121 percent in Massachusetts and 138 percent in New York. The prospects are much brighter elsewhere.

There are three States (New Mexico, Nevada, and Oklahoma) in which seven of the eight major sources are open to further utilization. In Texas all eight major classes are available. In three of these four States, the range of choices is made more attractive by the fact that their overall tax effort index is well below the national average.

Interstate differences in the number of tax classes available for further use are significant. Two States have 16 to 20 options; at the other extreme, one State has only seven. Even though the relative amounts available from these sources vary, a wider range of choices is more welcome than a narrow range.

"Business Taxes" and "Personal Taxes"

In table XIII-8, prepared by the Advisory Commission, certain taxes are grouped under two headings: "business taxes" and "personal taxes." Although three-quarters of all business taxes are collected by local governments in the form of property taxes, any significant policy decisions about these groupings are likely to be made at the State level.

One reason for grouping taxes under these headings is related to industrial development. State and local governments use tax incentives to attract new industry. Another reason for the division is "tax burden." Taxes on business—a corporate income tax or a local property tax on a factory for example—are more likely to be shifted beyond State or local borders than are personal taxes. Economists estimate that part of a business tax may be paid by shareholders (lower profits), part by employees (lower wages and fewer jobs), and part by consumers (higher prices). Thus, Chevrolet purchasers in Des Moines may be contributing to the cost of a school in St. Louis (where a Chevrolet assembly plant is located and where it pays property taxes).

Table XIII-7.—Revenue potential from "underutilized" tax classes, for States: 1966-67

State	Percent addition to actual revenue	Number of tax classes involved[1]	Major tax classes involved							
			Nonfarm residential property	Business property	Farm property	General sales	Individual income & earnings	Motor vehicles	Motor fuel	Corporate income
Alabama	38	10	xx	xx	x			x		
Alaska	32	10	x	xx	x					
Arizona	11	13		xx	xx	xx	xx			x
Arkansas	33	10	xx	xx	x					
California	10	11					xx			
Colorado	10	15			x	x				x
Connecticut	22	10	x	xx		xx	xx	xx	x	
Delaware	51	13	xx	xx	x	xx	xx		x	
District of Columbia	26	8	xx	x		x				
Florida	28	11	xx	x		x	xx		x	x
Georgia	23	11	xx	xx	x			x		
Hawaii	21	13	xx	xx	x			x		
Idaho	17	12	xx		x	x		xx	x	
Illinois	30	10		xx			xx		x	xx
Indiana	18	11							x	xx
Iowa	13	9	xx			xx			x	xx
Kansas	19	13	xx							x
Kentucky	36	10	xx	xx	x		x	x		
Louisiana	32	10	xx	xx	x		xx	x		
Maine	17	8					x	x		
Maryland	10	10			x	xx	xx	x		xx
Massachusetts	14	8				xx		x		xx
Michigan	21	11	x				xx	x		
Minnesota	20	8				xx	xx	xx	x	xx
Mississippi	25	11	xx		xx		x	x	x	

State											
Missouri	24	16	x	xx	x		x		x	x	xx
Montana	31	9	x	xx	xx	xx		x	xx		
Nebraska	49	13	x	x	x	xx	x	x	x		x
Nevada	50	16	xx	x	x	x	x	x	x		x
New Hampshire	47	11				xx	xxx	x	x		x
New Jersey	28	13	x	x	x	xx	xx	x	x	x	x
New Mexico	31	12	xx	xx	x	xx	x	x	x	x	x
New York	6	8						x		x	
North Carolina	29	12	xx	xx	x	x		x	xx	x	x
North Dakota	14	11			x	xx	xx	xx	xx		x
Ohio	32	13	x	x		x	x	x	x		x
Oklahoma	33	14	xx	xx	x		x	x	x	x	x
Oregon	25	11	x			xx		x	x	x	
Pennsylvania	27	10		xx	xx	xx	xx	x			
Rhode Island	17	9					xx	xx			
South Carolina	24	12	xx	xx	x	x	x	xx	x	x	xx
South Dakota	14	11				x	xx	xx	x		
Tennessee	26	13	x	xx	x	xx	xx	xx	x	x	x
Texas	40	16	x	x	x	x	xx	xx	x	x	x
Utah	12	11	xx	xx	xx			x	x		
Vermont	21	7	x	xx	x	xx	x		x	x	
Virginia	32	11	xx	xx	xx		x	x		x	x
Washington	33	11	x	x	x	x	xx		x		x
West Virginia	32	12	xx	xx	x		x	x	x	x	x
Wisconsin	13	10				xx	xx	x	x		
Wyoming	49	14	x				xx	x	x	x	x

NOTE.—The symbol "xx" indicates sources from which the most additional funds could be collected.

[1] Of 20 type-of-tax classes.

Source: Advisory Commission on Intergovernmental Relations, Measuring the Fiscal Capacity and Effort of State and Local Areas, U.S. Government Printing Office, Washington, D.C., 1971, table 25. p. 79.

Table XIII-8.—Capacity and effort measures for "business taxes" and "personal taxes," by States: 1966–67

| States | Percent of estimated total revenue capacity | | | | | Measures of relative effort (percent relation of actual revenue to estimated revenue capacity) | | | | |
| | "Business taxes" | | "Personal taxes" | | | "Business taxes" | | "Personal taxes" | | |
	Including local taxes on farm property[1]	Excluding local taxes on farm property[1]	Total	Local non-farm residential property taxes	Other "personal taxes"[2]	Including local taxes on farm property	Excluding local taxes on farm property[1]	Total	Local non-farm residential property taxes	Other "personal taxes"[2]
United States	20.6	18.0	50.9	15.3	35.6	100	100	100	100	100
Alabama	18.3	15.9	49.4	14.0	35.4	53	57	101	28	131
Alaska	18.2	17.3	36.0	8.8	27.3	79	82	115	93	122
Arizona	19.1	15.2	47.0	13.4	33.6	92	106	108	107	112
Arkansas	21.4	14.7	50.1	13.6	36.5	72	79	87	39	105
California	18.3	16.1	52.4	18.4	34.0	140	141	98	106	94
Colorado	20.5	16.2	48.1	13.4	34.7	115	120	110	126	104
Connecticut	18.8	18.5	58.5	19.8	38.7	108	107	89	119	73
Delaware	20.7	19.6	53.2	16.1	37.1	91	93	92	62	105
Dist. of Columbia	17.5	17.5	60.9	17.9	43.0	88	88	89	72	96
Florida	16.1	14.0	55.2	18.7	36.6	87	86	80	60	85
Georgia	19.0	16.7	50.9	13.2	37.7	85	89	96	60	108
Hawaii	16.9	14.9	49.9	18.0	31.9	70	71	168	62	228
Idaho	25.0	14.6	44.2	8.5	35.7	124	149	100	44	114
Illinois	22.8	19.8	53.3	15.9	37.5	71	62	86	101	80
Indiana	23.2	19.4	49.1	12.2	36.9	91	85	98	104	96
Iowa	25.4	13.4	46.1	12.0	34.1	111	98	100	105	98
Kansas	24.6	16.2	45.1	13.8	31.2	106	104	90	77	96
Kentucky	20.6	16.8	51.7	15.2	36.5	59	61	97	51	116
Louisiana	28.7	26.5	38.6	9.8	28.8	102	109	83	17	105
Maine	17.5	16.3	55.5	15.8	39.7	115	108	102	112	99
Maryland	17.4	16.3	57.4	18.7	38.7	93	94	106	101	108
Massachusetts	18.0	17.9	54.5	16.5	38.1	130	129	115	166	93
Michigan	19.6	18.5	51.9	15.7	36.1	96	94	95	97	94

Minnesota	21.8	16.9	45.6	10.3	35.3	139	139	111	169	95
Mississippi	20.2	14.4	47.4	13.1	34.3	95	119	98	27	126
Missouri	22.3	18.2	52.7	14.1	38.6	72	69	89	85	90
Montana	28.3	15.5	41.8	8.9	32.9	114	143	75	87	72
Nebraska	22.9	11.7	43.5	12.3	31.3	90	68	54	94	38
Nevada	17.7	15.3	55.9	14.2	41.7	78	80	60	60	59
New Hampshire	15.0	14.4	59.8	18.5	41.3	97	94	79	139	52
New Jersey	19.6	19.3	54.9	17.4	37.6	86	85	102	176	68
New Mexico	23.4	18.5	38.6	9.1	29.6	72	85	98	35	118
New York	18.9	18.6	51.4	17.6	33.8	136	135	145	127	155
North Carolina	20.1	17.1	52.4	14.7	37.6	90	95	99	52	117
North Dakota	23.0	9.8	32.8	5.6	27.1	114	120	89	132	80
Ohio	21.4	19.8	52.9	16.1	36.9	90	88	77	85	73
Oklahoma	25.4	19.8	44.5	13.0	31.5	81	87	79	52	91
Oregon	18.9	15.6	49.0	15.0	34.0	126	119	94	99	92
Pennsylvania	22.4	21.6	53.2	14.9	38.3	80	78	107	121	101
Rhode Island	17.5	17.4	54.8	15.7	39.1	112	111	101	130	89
South Carolina	19.4	16.9	49.4	9.0	40.3	97	104	103	30	119
South Dakota	26.3	9.6	40.4	8.3	32.1	114	119	107	181	88
Tennessee	18.9	16.2	49.1	13.4	35.7	81	86	92	75	99
Texas	27.2	22.7	45.1	9.7	35.9	84	90	67	89	61
Utah	21.4	18.2	47.0	14.1	32.8	106	112	113	75	129
Vermont	19.4	16.4	54.2	12.2	41.9	126	117	113	142	105
Virginia	22.0	19.7	68.8	18.7	46.4	72	72	90	57	105
Washington	17.6	15.2	46.9	16.2	30.7	61	55	121	52	157
West Virginia	24.1	23.1	49.7	13.2	36.5	46	45	116	53	139
Wisconsin	19.7	16.8	50.1	14.9	35.2	128	120	123	121	124
Wyoming	31.4	23.6	36.6	9.2	27.3	71	77	64	42	71

1 Comprising corporation taxes, severance taxes, and local property taxes on business property.

2 Comprising general and selective sales taxes, individual income and earnings taxes, and death and gift taxes.

Source: Advisory Commission on Intergovernmental Relations, *Measuring the Fiscal Capacity and Effort of State and Local Areas*, U.S. Government Printing Office, Washington, D.C., 1971, table G-6, p. 130.

Low business taxes attract industry; high business taxes, on the other hand, shift the final payment of taxes to other parts of the country. Depending on which outcome is more desired, a State may decide to increase or decrease business taxes.

SAVINGS THROUGH IMPROVED MANAGEMENT AND ECONOMIES

Financial problems can be eased by seeking additional revenue or making do with existing funds. During the prosperous sixties, public and private monetary support provided the amount required by colleges and universities. Such has not been the case in the 1970's. One reason is the strong feeling among corporate donors, legislators, alumni, and the public that institutions of higher education are not using their resources as effectively as they could. Furthermore, the belief is growing that less costly techniques can accomplish desired educational goals. Thus higher education is faced with obtaining "more for less" through better management of resources and greater economy of operation.

In the broadest sense, sound management to improve efficiency includes designing an educational program that the institution is qualified to offer, establishing better internal organization, recruiting quality staff, planning to achieve objectives, and budgeting to match available income. Institutional management, while certainly important, is beyond the limits of this volume. What will be discussed are those aspects of management specifically intended to eliminate waste and achieve greater productivity.

Resources are most efficiently used when equal returns are obtained from every marginal increment of resources spent, thereby maximizing total returns less total costs. For different institutions, the search for efficiency will mean the use of different tactics.[30] In some instances, more money rather than less will need to be spent to make operations efficient. For the most affluent colleges, economy measures may simply mean "tightening the belt" and/or eliminating "extras." For others, greater efficiency will require fundamental changes in operation. Yet, regardless of financial strength, the intent of management will remain the same: to avoid waste, to increase productivity, and to maintain quality.

Obviously waste can never be sanctioned. Even the most prestigious institutions should recognize that extravagance (a "lush curriculum"

---

[30] For a discussion of efficiency and how it can be improved, see Howard R. Bowen, "Can Higher Education Become More Efficient?" *Educational Record*, Summer 1972, pp. 191–200.

for example) as inimical to long-run interests. Experimentation, innovation, and reform must be continually fostered, not only to increase productivity but also to serve as a tonic for institutional growth and development. Finally, no matter how substantial the "savings," cost reduction at the expense of desired quality and morale are counterproductive. Drastically shortening library hours to cut expenses, for example, is hardly conducive to quality education.

Institutional efforts to cut costs and avoid waste generally meet with little serious opposition as long as they are confined to support functions— e.g., to general administration, student services, and auxiliary enterprises. A review of cost-cutting possibilities, however, suggests that changes in the educational process itself offer the greatest potential for savings. Such changes—experimentation and innovation in academic programs, in instructional techniques, and in the relationship of the student to the institution—involve basic educational philosophy and practice; moreover, they alter personal habits and performance and the way people in an organization relate to one another. Consequently, they are subject to all of the forces that make change difficult. And, according to many researchers, the university, of all organizations, is the most resistant to change. Colleges and universities usually attach far less importance to sound management than do profit-making business enterprises. Thus the traditional reaction by many college administrators to deficit operations has been to turn to new sources of income rather than to improve operational efficiency. For the college president, furthering the educational objectives of the institution (while assuming that revenues will increase) is primary; as a result, little thought is given to increasing institutional efficiency.

Other handicaps experienced by colleges and universities desiring to effect institutional economy have been reported by Virginia Smith.

1. The generally held notion is that institutions which have the highest resource input per student are the highest quality institutions. In higher education we suffer from an inability to find suitable yardsticks for determining quality. Goals have not yet been clearly defined; therefore, measures for ascertaining the extent to which goals have or have not been reached are lacking. In the absence of well-defined goals and measures, the tendency is to assume that high-input institutions must be better and that any reduction in per student cost may actually bring a reduction in quality.

2. Perhaps an even greater deterrent to the introduction of more efficient educational processes is the feeling that attention to costs is somehow not respectable. Only rarely have institutional task forces charged with the task of institutional self-study included any focus on the costs of the proposed reforms. Commonly it is felt that proposals for reforms should not stem from reasons of economy; educational policy should be the sole motivating force.

3. Most tenured and senior faculty in universities are committed to the university setting because of their interests in research. The training received by prospective university faculty does little to stimulate their interest in the educational process as such. Without either a primary commitment to teaching or a background of expertise

or interest in the process, many members of the university faculty, although certainly not all members, have understandably engaged in little activity to improve the educational process.

4. Even if faculty members were to become interested in the relative costs of various educational processes, certain further impediments are inherent in administration in a university or college and in the budgeting process. Program development is often sharply separated from administrative responsibility for securing revenues for the final budget developed. As a result, at the primary unit level, budget construction rarely involves any total analysis of the costs of the program; rather, the budget is simply a statement of justification for additional requirements.[31]

Despite the resistance to change, it is an inescapable fact, whether palatable or not, that colleges and universities, if they are ultimately to solve their financial problems, must direct greater attention to more efficient operating procedures. The purpose of this section is to summarize some of the specific ways in which the principles of sound management may be used by higher education to save money and increase productivity. What follows is a discussion of the immediate response by colleges to financial difficulties, the more comprehensive and permanent reactions, and, finally, adjustments in the educational process itself. The topics are as follows: immediate alternatives, modification of supporting activities, institutional size and plant use, guidelines for management and planning, and improvement of educational productivity. The sources for the recommendations are authors[32] whose publications contain a comprehensive treatment of the subject.

Immediate Alternatives

Faced with financial adversity, the immediate response by many college administrators is to tolerate deficit spending in the hope that the difficulty is only temporary. If the problem persists, the initial adjustments they make are usually those that cause the least interference with institutional programs and activities. By refusing to accept new obligations and by canceling or scaling down future plans, administrators believe that existing patterns will not be radically affected.

---

[31] Virginia B. Smith, "More for Less: A New Priority," in *Universal Higher Education: Costs and Benefits*, op. cit., Washington, D. C., 1971, pp. 137–39.

[32] Most notable, in this instance: Seymour E. Harris, "Financing Higher Education: An Overview," in *The Economics and Financing of Higher Education in the United States*, op. cit., pp. 485–505; Seymour E. Harris, *Higher Education: Resources and Finance*, McGraw-Hill Book Co., New York, 1962, pp. 501–633; and H. J. Heneman, "Opportunities for Improved Management in Higher Education," in *Financing Higher Education 1960–70*, ed. by Dexter Keezer, McGraw-Hill Book Co., New York, 1959, pp. 118–37.

Neither deficit spending nor cutting back on development plans, however, will be sufficient to ward off for any length of time financial losses caused by a fundamental imbalance between basic income and expenditures. Temporary measures offer only a brief respite; more durable remedies are, as a rule, required.

Modification of Supporting Activities

To combat continuing financial pressure, colleges turn first to those adjustments that are the least disruptive and that do not directly concern the instructional program. Reductions and modifications in services not central to the academic program can generally be accomplished without sacrificing either academic quality or institutional morale. And pruning nonessential activities to conserve scarce resources for more important uses provides a basis for an extended list of savings. The Academy for Educational Development has recently published a list of ways in which colleges and universities are saving money. It includes nearly 150 changes in practice in such nonacademic areas as personnel management, administration, maintenance and security, office expenses, purchasing, equipment rental and leasing, travel and meeting expenses, food services, and library administration.[33] Examples include the following: eliminating the use of temporary personnel, reducing the number of secretaries and clerks, reducing the number of athletic scholarships, automating certain routine tasks, controlling the individual portions of food served, eliminating all overtime, discontinuing maid service in dormitories, deferring a tree-care program, postponing publication of a new catalog, and renting or buying less expensive copying equipment. The entire list cannot be duplicated here, but the basis for the economy measures is obvious: Can money be saved on a given activity, service, or item without negative consequences?

The types of changes that institutions are attempting to implement are indicated by the type of actions being taken; namely, actions to eliminate, reduce, defer, replace, simplify, modify, combine or consolidate, stretch, automate, computerize, etc. It is possible, of course, that these and other kinds of dollar savings can convey a sense of automatic benefit which may be misleading; they can even produce undesirable consequences. Efficiency measures adopted too quickly may lead to wasteful use of human resources, to increased future expenditures, and to negative social consequences. To be valid, an efficiency measure must result in less costly operations without producing serious negative effects.

---

[33] "148 Ways Colleges and Universities Are Meeting the Financial Pinch," Management Division, Academy for Educational Development, New York, n.d.

Institutional Size and Plant Use

The high cost of modern construction demands that full utilization be made of existing facilities and that planning new facilities be highly scientific. Although academic requirements must enter into any discussion of plant use, such physical aspects as economies of scale, year-round operation, and excess capacity are of critical importance. An additional consideration, while not as vital, is the obvious saving that can accrue by not constructing buildings for which there is little or no need or facilities for which there is not a great demand.

Economies of scale.—Over 600 institutions of higher education in the United States enroll fewer than 500 students, and 255 enroll less than 200 (fall 1971). While many small institutions, because of their limited curriculum, minimal student services, and restrictive budgets, can function on a relatively low income, they do not necessarily operate efficiently. Provided program scope and quality remain reasonably constant, there is little doubt that some economies of scale do exist as institutions increase their enrollments.[34] In a study limited to public 4-year colleges with similar objectives and operating policies, in one State system there is evidence that institutions with larger enrollments operate at a lower cost.[35] (Further discussion of economies of scale, together with the larger issue of coherence as it is affected by size, is presented in chapter VI.)

Despite the fact that most small institutions could probably operate more efficiently with larger enrollments, the possible erosion of institutional style and educational philosophy deters most of these colleges from actively seeking more students. Many small colleges are technical or special-purpose institutions; therefore, they simply cannot substantially increase enrollment without expanding the curriculum and thereby altering their mission. And even those institutions willing to increase enrollment may not be able to compete successfully for more students because their tuition is high and their curriculum limited.

About the only valid conclusion regarding economies of scale is that per student investment depends principally on educational program and quality, *not* on institutional size. An institution may, however, by deliberate intent, encourage limited enrollment growth so as to benefit from some

---

[34] Economies of scale are usually obscured by variations in expenditures due to differences among institutions in program scope and quality and to changes in these factors as enrollment grows. These inconsistencies make comparisons of unit costs vis-a-vis enrollment among institutions with different or changing academic programs meaningless.

[35] *Meeting the Enrollment Demand for Public Higher Education in California Through 1977: The Need for Additional Colleges and Campuses*, Coordinating Council for Higher Education, Sacramento, 1969, appendix D.

economies of scale without seriously altering its basic mission and operating style.

In concluding this brief discussion on economies of scale, mention should be made of the related question of *pricing*. Economists are frequently tempted to design a model educational enterprise that can be used to identify the price (tuition and fees) of services and the level of enrollment at which marginal costs and marginal revenues are equal, thus maximizing net revenue ("profit"). The greatest difficulty is that of determining the demand that may confront a given college at a given time—i.e., the relationship between student enrollment level and tuition charged. Institutional size and tuition are, of course, established primarily on the basis of educational and social factors, not on the basis of economics. Even though the noneconomic factors cannot be quantified and must therefore be largely ignored, estimates of demand and profit maximizing models are useful in that they suggest the economic implications of decisions regarding tuition and size. Such implications must of course be seriously considered by colleges in financial difficulty. For those wishing to pursue this topic further, recent studies are available.[36]

Excess capacity.—Many contend that classrooms are underutilized, and they are probably right. Yet equating efficient plant use exclusively with classroom occupancy rates is unsound; it fails to take into consideration the fact that more than 80 percent of the space at universities and 4-year colleges is not designed for scheduled occupancy. Included in the nonscheduled occupancy category are libraries, study areas, research laboratories, the book store and student union, residential halls, offices, etc. More efficient use of such space cannot be achieved by revising the curriculum or extending the instructional day, but only by eliminating or modifying costly equipment and furnishings and by designing and locating new facilities in such a way that they can serve multipurpose uses.

Although scheduled instructional facilities represent less than 20 percent of the space on 4-year college campuses (and only about 40 percent at 2-year colleges), the pressure to save money and the apparent ease of increasing scheduled usage have centered attention on the classroom and the teaching laboratory. Certainly sizable economies can be effected by increasing the number of classes scheduled and by a better matching of

---

[36] See Stephen A. Hoenack, "Private Demand for Higher Education in California," in *The Economics and Financing of Higher Education*, op. cit., pp. 375–95; also a related publication by Hoenack and Paul Feldman, "Private Demand for Higher Education in the United States," (Research Paper P-649), Institute for Defense Analysis, Program Analysis Division, Arlington, Va., 1969; and Hans H. Jenny, "Pricing and Optimum Size in a Non-Profit Institution: The University," paper presented at the Annual Convention, American Economics Association, Washington, D.C., Dec. 27–30, 1967.

class sizes with room seating capacities. Yet *ideal* classroom utilization poses many problems. If classes are scheduled throughout the day and week, attendance may decrease during the afternoon hours and on Saturdays because students prefer not only morning classes but also a Monday-through-Friday schedule. Broad scheduling of classes throughout the day will, however, reduce the number of courses taught at a given time, thereby permitting students greater selectivity in choosing courses.

The best way to improve classroom utilization is to match class sizes better with room seating capacities. What this will mean in most instances is larger classes (unless existing classrooms can be subdivided and teaching loads increased) with an attendant potential for a larger student-faculty ratio. The potential financial gain to be derived from such an economy must be considered in light of the effect on both the quality of teaching and the knowledge acquired by students. (These considerations are discussed later in the chapter under the topic "Improvement of Educational Productivity." A thorough analysis of methods for improving space utilization through optimum class scheduling and better "fit" between class sizes and room capacities is presented in chapter X.)

Year-round operation.—One popular recommendation for achieving better utilization of physical facilities is the adoption by colleges and universities of some form of year-round operation. However, many institutions that have adopted year-round calendars report that other adjustments are required which often cannot be effectively made without undermining the whole effort. In essence, neither faculty nor students welcome full-time summer academic work, and, without the wholehearted enthusiasm of participants, it is not possible to conduct a successful summer term. For better or for worse, the lifestyles of faculty and students are geared to a 9-month academic year, with the summer reserved for jobs, vacations, sabbaticals, etc. Faculty view fourth-quarter summer work as "extra" employment, and not all choose to undertake it. Given a choice, students prefer *not* to attend summer sessions. Thus summer enrollment is usually low, and, if a full range of courses is offered, high unit costs are the result. If the number of course offerings is reduced, summer attendance is even less appealing to students.

Year-round operation may take the form of the semester-summer session plan, the quarter plan, or the trimester. Approximately 1,780 institutions operate on the semester system, offering two 17-week semesters and a summer session of from 8-to-12 weeks. Faculties stress that the main advantage of 17 weeks of continuous study is that it permits students to probe deeper into a given subject and allows them more independent study, reading, writing, etc. The principal disadvantages, it is claimed, are the disruption of continuity caused by the Christmas holidays and the fact that because the college year cannot be divided into equal parts, summer terms must of necessity be brief. The quarter plan, in effect at nearly 300 institutions, consists of three 11-week terms plus a summer quarter which may be divided into two 5½-week sessions or scheduled as an 11-week unit. The quarter system provides more flexibility than does the semester plan. Students who wish to experiment with course selection can do so, with the knowledge that if they make a "bad choice," they have not "wasted" half a year. Since the fall quarter ends just before Christmas, they can enjoy the holidays. The main disadvantage of the quarter system is that 10 weeks is often considered too short a period for mastery of subject matter. The trimester plan of three 15-week semesters has been adopted by only about 55 institutions. Its major failing is that it prevents articulation with both of the other educational systems. Also, many students are unwilling to commit their entire summer to study.

The University of California decided in 1966 to begin a year-round operation based on the quarter system. With 40 percent as many students enrolled in the summer quarter as were enrolled during the regular year, it was able to add about 13 percent to its year-round capacity. By 1976, a total increase of $103 million in operating expenses and a total decrease in capital outlays of $208 million are anticipated—a net saving to the California taxpayers of $105 million. A report of the background and record of the implementation of the year-round operation at Berkeley provides a valuable guide to what must be a radical and risky change for any institution.[37]

Guidelines for Management and Planning

The complexity of today's colleges and universities requires sound and effective management. But given the objectives of an institution of higher education, academic matters take precedence over administrative management. Consequently, the chief executive officers of many colleges and universities traditionally have come from the ranks of scholars. Since they have not been chosen for their managerial skill, it has been extremely difficult for them to cope with the multiple responsibilities of the business of operating a college. To obtain the benefits and cost savings of effective management requires, first, that presidents and governing boards recognize that businesslike methods are essential in directing the affairs of institutions of higher education, and, second, that a development and planning staff is needed to provide the skill necessary to conduct internal operations in an efficient and effective manner.

---

[37] Sidney Suslow and Michael J. Riley, *Year-Round Operation at Berkeley, Background and Implementation*, Office of Institutional Research, University of California, Berkeley, October 1968.

Day-to-day management and planning work hand-in-hand. Not all aspects of college operations can be spelled out in detail. In the absence of plans, management must continually review and appraise activities in order to remedy any current deficiencies and to assess consequential trends. Planning, in turn, supports management by providing, when possible, information concerning the implications and consequences of alternative decisions, and, when a course of action is established, a blueprint for implementation. No single activity of college management is more important than planning. Analyzing future goals and programs, projecting requirements for resources, and devising improved operating policies and practices are difficult tasks which require a great deal of thought and effort. But the results are rewarding in that they provide efficient administration and instruction.

There are few affairs of a college or a university not subject to improvement through better management and planning.[38] Some areas in which management policy and planning are recognized as critical and which are of special concern because of their importance to operational efficiency and long-run financial stability are the following:

Defining institutional objectives and responsibilities and clarifying organization to include an honest and complete appraisal of all institutional resources in order to determine their compatibility with the programs offered

Projecting enrollments

Establishing sound budgeting procedures based on a projection of revenues, and determining requirements based on analysis of functions, workloads, and methods

Controlling such activities as sponsored research and auxiliary enterprises to ensure that revenues cover overhead as well as other costs

Checking the propriety of program expansion based on receipt of a "seed money" grant

Monitoring tenure policies and faculty appointments to prevent abuses

Establishing sound wage policies for faculty and other professional staff, with a clear delineation of the principal governing factor (salaries paid by competitors, cost-of-living, average family income, incomes of similar professions, etc.), relation of salaries to years of service, ratio of retirement salary to basic salary, role of tenure in determining salary level, fringe benefits, etc.

Conducting a cost-effectiveness analysis, particularly *within* departments, to determine the relative "expense" of alternative instructional techniques and curriculum design

Exploring *all* avenues for cooperating with other institutions in the following areas: common purchasing and storage, centralized computer and/or business machine center, joint use of library collections, faculty sharing, common use of closed-circuit television, and development of special programs or shared use of equipment and/or personnel.

---

[38] For a more complete discussion of the management aspect, see H. J. Heneman "Opportunities for Improved Management in Higher Education," op. cit., pp. 134–35.

Improvement of Educational Productivity

Changing the educational program and instructional process is one of the most sensitive and difficult ways to attempt to achieve economy. Yet a financial crisis will force an institution not only to examine its central tasks of selecting and instructing students but also to apply modern technology to teaching. If colleges are to cope with further escalation of costs per student, they must increase institutional productivity.

As previously noted, an expanding economy compels colleges to pay higher prices for everything purchased. Yet higher prices are not always offset by corresponding gains in productivity. The principal means of increasing educational productivity and reducing costs is to increase the student-faculty ratio. One of the many obstacles to effecting such an increase is that teaching is a personal matter and therefore difficult to mass produce. There are also limitations on the degree to which the student-faculty ratio can be raised without changing instructional techniques and possibly altering the quality of student education. As Harris[39] has pointed out, raising the student-faculty ratio is also limited by the fact that part of faculty time is allocated to research. The necessity of offering a curriculum covering all or almost all fields is another drawback to increasing the ratio. And even when the ratio is raised, the savings are not directly proportional to the increase since faculty salaries are only part of the total cost of instruction. Another reason why the amount of savings may be less than expected is that the young and lower salaried faculty are the ones most likely to be discharged. Despite the fact that raising the student-faculty ratio is difficult and may bring about only limited savings, if financial pressures continue, this means appears to be the only durable remedy to increase educational productivity. It must, therefore, be seriously considered.

What is involved in raising the student-faculty ratio? Six approaches, with certain reservations, are feasible.[40]

(1) Without appreciably altering teaching methods and loads or the number of courses offered, increase the size of *selected* classes by reducing the number of sections in which the same course is taught. A similar result may be obtained by increasing total college enrollment without increasing the number of classes.

(2) Increase average class size by reducing the number of courses or by *not* offering a full spectrum of studies.

---

[39] Seymour E. Harris, "Financing Higher Education: An Overview," op. cit., p. 490.

[40] Some of these approaches to improving the student-faculty ratio are in six instructional plans recently evaluated by Bowen and Douglass. Their study is of special value in that it provides a comprehensive critical analysis of the different modes of instruction that could be used at a hypothetical small liberal arts college. See Howard R. Bowen and Gordon K. Douglass, *Efficiency in Liberal Education*, Carnegie Commission on Higher Education, McGraw-Hill Book Co., New York, 1971.

(3) Increase faculty teaching load and make judicious use of teaching assistants.

(4) Require students to do more independent work outside the classroom.

(5) Employ one or more new technological devices designed to teach large groups of students.

(6) Institute admission policies that will ensure a high student retention rate.

Larger classes.—It is a rarely contested fact that increasing the size of *selective* classes can result in substantial savings in instructional costs *without* loss in either the quality of teaching or the education received by the student. The key word is "selective." What is advocated and what appears to meet the functional aims of most departments is a combination or mix of class sizes which takes advantage of the best features of each size. Three sizes are involved: the small seminar group of 10 to 15 students, the intermediate class of 30 to 50, and the large lecture class, the size of which is limited only by room-seating capacity.

There should be no intent to eliminate small classes if course content and instructional methods require close communication between students and teacher and among students. In such instances, small student groups are necessary to promote discourse and individual participation. Certain other classes must also be limited in size, i.e., those concerned with particular kinds of laboratory work, with training in skills, with creative study, etc.

Intermediate size classes of 30 to 50 students are not particularly economical, but they are difficult to eliminate, particularly if the institution is small and offers a full curriculum. Classes of this size are necessary if only from 30 to 50 students enroll in a course or if available rooms accommodating this number govern sectioning practices. The number of intermediate-size classes may be decreased by reducing the number of sections offered and by encouraging institutional enrollment growth without corresponding enlargement of the curriculum.

Available evidence suggests that class size, measured in terms of student achievement, is a relatively minor factor in educational efficiency. Both efficient and economical instruction can be provided for classes of 200 or more students when the principal objective is to transmit information rapidly by means of lectures. Large lecture classes by distinguished professors, followed by small seminars, may at times be the best combination.[41]

Proliferation of Courses.—One of the most persistent "diseases" within higher education is proliferation of the curriculum. As subject matter is organized into more fragmented and peripheral divisions, it should be obvious that such specialization will be of critical value or academic

---

[41] For additional discussion of class size, see chapter XIV.

necessity to fewer and fewer students. The higher cost of teaching narrowly limited subjects to a handful of students can hardly be considered as anything other than a waste, particularly at a time when higher education is facing a financial crisis.

The Commission on Financing Higher Education has this to say:

> The greatest extravagance in almost every type of institution from the smallest to the largest lies in the curriculum. This situation usually arises from the absence of even a broad general conception of purpose by which course offerings can be assessed. Partly to meet overrefined needs, partly to attract students, partly to meet competition, real or imagined, institutions have permitted their course offerings to grow more and more numerous, to proliferate far beyond real needs. Too many of our institutions have been victimized by the cult of coverage. . . . many courses, once started, continue a life of their own until they become gnarled branches of the past, left unpruned while new branches of learning grow all around them.[42]

As college administrators know only too well, it is virtually impossible to eliminate a course once it has become entrenched in the curriculum. Offering some courses only in alternate years and consolidating others with offerings at consortium institutions are often acceptable alternatives. The departure of certain faculty members may also provide an opportunity to "weed out" the curriculum. Since most disciplines demand a certain number of required courses, there can be no wholesale slashing of a department's curriculum as long as a given major is offered. Ultimately, it is the faculty who should determine in what manner and to what degree the curriculum can be attenuated.

Faculty load and teaching assistants.—Proposals to reduce instructional costs by revising the faculty work load are not predicated on *increasing* the load, but rather on allocating more faculty time to classroom teaching. Many studies have shown that the average work week of a faculty member is 50 to 60 hours—by any standard, an overlong period. As any academician knows, however, the teaching load of a faculty member represents only a portion of this total. About half of a typical faculty member's work week is spent in scheduled instruction and related duties; the remainder in administrative tasks, research, professional improvement, public service, outside consulting, and numerous other activies connected with his or her position. A recurring question at institutions in financial difficulty is whether the time devoted to these supporting tasks can be justified when more hours spent in the classroom would achieve essential economies.

---

[42] Commission on Financing Higher Education, *Nature and Needs of Higher Education*, Columbia University Press, New York, 1952, pp. 106–07.

Faculty members tend to resist an increase in their teaching load because they visualize themselves not only as teachers but also as scholars. Moreover, scholarship is an indispensable element in the instructional process. The question is: How much research and scholarly study is essential to professional stature and teaching excellence? But who is to answer? More pertinent is the need for an attitudinal change by those colleges and universities that give lip service to the importance of teaching yet continue to reward intellectual or scholarly distinction by reducing the teaching load. It is these institutions that cause many professors to regard a full teaching load as ignominious and, therefore, to employ every kind of stratagem to teach as few hours as possible. Robert Nisbet, in an article entitled "The Future of the University" in *Commentary*, suggests that Harvard, Columbia, Berkeley, and Stanford set a nationwide example by demanding that every faculty member teach a full load—famous scientists and scholars as well as assistant professors. If the central concern of institutions of higher education is teaching, and research is to be related to it, then this proposal must receive serious consideration, whether or not economy is a supporting argument.

The willingness and/or ability of faculty to handle large teaching loads depends, in part, on the availability of assistants. It is much more economical for an assistant than for a faculty member to prepare examinations, grade papers, supervise laboratory work, take attendance, advise students, and perform other routine chores. Effective use of assistants in these areas enables faculty to concentrate on teaching.

The use of graduate assistants as instructors can also save money. There are many situations in the classroom, in the laboratory, and with discussion groups when qualified teaching assistants may be substituted for experienced faculty at less cost and with no loss in quality. In certain instances a graduate student instructor can complement a faculty member. Still, the practice of employing graduate assistants can be fraught with dangers and shortcomings. Too often in the past the teaching assistant has been exploited as a source of cheap labor. Complaints from teaching assistants are numerous: low status treatment, little help or supervision from the senior faculty, unreasonable teaching load that interferes with ontime completion of doctorate, lower pay than that of research assistants, and so on. Complaints also come from students who are dissatisfied because they are denied contact with experienced professors, and also because graduate assistants are chosen with little or no regard for their experience and/or teaching ability.

There is, of course, a legitimate role for teaching assistants—one that is not detrimental either to the quality of teaching or the professional development of the assistants themselves. As a rule, appropriate direction and supervision by the faculty is all that is required. And if assistants are to complete their doctorate in a reasonable length of time, the number of classes they teach and the number of hours they work should be limited. Other specific recommendations to reform and strengthen the teaching assistant system can be found in current literature.[43]

Less Time in the Classroom.—Practices that enable students to pursue their academic studies at a faster-than-normal pace and to earn degrees by spending a minimum amount of time in the classroom certainly save money. Not only are institutional costs reduced, but, more importantly, student expenses are decreased. Traditionally, classroom time has been reduced by permitting students to engage in independent work under faculty supervision. A new idea now gaining momentum is to grant academic credit, on the basis of an examination, for knowledge acquired away from the campus. Credit-by-examination programs are variously known as open universities, external degree programs, and colleges without walls. Heavy reliance is placed on home study (course materials are sent by mail) and on the use of standardized tests. Counseling and tutorial services are generally desired components. Depending on the amount of instruction provided and the total enrollment, such programs can reduce the cost of educating each student by as much as 50 percent. The major reservation of most faculties toward credit-by-exam is the belief that a student who does not attend classes cannot fully comprehend a subject. They caution that the system places too much reliance on the examination; that a test simply cannot adequately measure a student's educational development.

A less controversial idea for reducing classroom time is to substitute more independent work. However, even this plan has its critics. Consider the following summary by Seymour Harris:

> From numerous experiments it is concluded that independent work will prove a failure unless preparation is made for it, that it tends to be more productive if started in the freshman year and continued throughout. On the whole, putting a student on his own for a whole semester without any preparation or guidance is likely to be disastrous. Reducing classes from three to two per week or putting aside a few weeks each semester (the Harvard reading period) for independent work seems to bring better results than a long spell of independent work. Yet the largest economies are to be had by sending the student away for one quarter, thus through a four-quarter system doubling the capacity of the plant (the Oberlin plan). Careful preparation and guidance (e.g., study abroad) may yield a successful quarter-away plan.[44]

---

[43] See, for example, John L. Chase, *Graduate Teaching Assistants in American Universities: A Review of Recent Trends and Recommendations*, U.S. Department of Health, Education, and Welfare, Office of Education, U.S. Government Printing Office, Washington, D.C., 1970.

[44] Harris, *Higher Education: Resources and Finance*, op. cit., pp. 544–45.

A third method of reducing classroom time is to lower the credit-hour requirement, thereby shortening the length of time a student must spend in pursuit of his degree. Some institutions offer a B.A. at the end of 3 years. Thirty-five medical schools now require less than 4 years of study for the M.D. degree. Although this approach will not be successful unless considerable attention is devoted to curriculum design and unless additional resources are provided for adequate planning and development, if such a change is implemented, the savings are substantial, not only to the institution but to the student.

Teaching by television —The potential of television to provide effective instruction at low cost is enormous. The ultimate solution to greater educational productivity may well depend on higher education's seizing the opportunities that this powerful means of communication can provide. What are the characteristics of television that make it so potent a source of instruction? First, the teacher's presence before every class is not required. Second, TV has practically an unlimited capacity to transmit information, both visual and aural. Third, it is possible, by means of film and tape, to store and reuse program lessons. These characteristics make possible two significant economies: (1) an increase in the student-teacher ratio and (2) more far-reaching transmittal of high-quality instruction. There are more advantages and there are also some problems.

1. The transmittal or distribution capabilities of television permit instruction to be delivered to a large and widely scattered audience. A televised program can be heard and seen in physically separated rooms of varied sizes.

2. Film and tape permit repeated showings of the same programs.

3. Television makes it possible for more people to obtain a better view of, say a laboratory demonstration. By means of closed-circuit television, it is possible for 50 to 75 students to view a surgical operation that otherwise could be witnessed by only two or three.

4. Televised instruction is generally of better quality than that presented in the average classroom. Instructors who teach on television usually prepare their lessons with greater care than do others.

5. Television provides many programing possibilities—movies, special laboratory experiments, use of special effects, etc.—that might otherwise be prohibitively expensive.

6. As a mass-teaching device, television provides faculty more time for research and other professional pursuits.

7. Video cassettes permit students to learn at individual speeds, thereby freeing fast learners to pursue other activities.[45]

---

[45] For a discussion of a "video university," one at which video cassettes are used for the bulk of instruction, see Alexander M. Mood, "Another Approach to Higher Education," in *Universal Higher Education: Costs and Benefits*, op. cit., pp. 169–86.

The problems of TV instruction and the reservations regarding its effectiveness include the following:

1. Television requires a substantial investment in hardware and continuing high expenditures for software, i.e., for programs and tapes. Economical use of television requires that the per student cost be less than or equivalent to that of conventional classes. The break-even point for television, or the course enrollment level below which savings are unlikely, may be so large (200 or more students) as to be impractical in many subject areas. Moreover, when facilities are available, large classes in lecture rooms seating, say 600, may be just as effectively and economically taught by the conventional lecture method as by TV.

2. When emphasis is placed on imparting information to students TV has proved as effective as other types of instruction. There is, however, a lack of feedback in televised courses. Thus, if the objective is to teach various types of skills, both manual and mental, or to convey attitudinal development, television may not be the best teaching device. Although students prefer small groups and intimate contact with the faculty, if given a choice, they prefer a master television teacher to a mediocre one in the classroom.

3. Among faculty members, reservations about TV instruction range from distress over the lack of contact with students to fear of a reduction in the number of teachers employed. Since such negative feelings do not encourage faculty participation in television programing, lower morale could result if a majority does not favor TV instruction.

The contribution of television varies greatly with both institutions and subject matter. If its use is to be successful, it should be intergrated with institutional objectives and supplemented by opportunities for faculty-student exchanges. In view of continuous enrollment growth and rising costs, many institutions of higher education should be able to realize large savings by introducing and extending the use of televised instruction. It is indeed fortunate that the usefulness of TV teaching is coinciding with the continuous increase in student enrollment and the increase in faculty salaries, two of the factors that have necessitated the search for greater educational productivity

Deficiencies in admission policies.—Largely because of greater use of seminar-type instruction at upper division and graduate levels and because of normal student attrition, class sizes at upper academic levels are generally smaller and the student-faculty ratio lower. In 1970 the class size enrollment ratios for the 1st, 2d, 3d, and 4th years of college for all institutions of higher education were 2.0; 1.5; 1.1; and 1.0, respectively. To determine if admission criteria are consistent with institutional objectives, colleges and universities should compare their enrollment statistics with these ratios and also with those of peer institutions.

By improving admission policies, institutions can cut costs. The matriculation of a student, which involves testing, record processing, counseling, placement, etc., is expensive. It should be obvious, then, that student dropouts, especially those who leave during their 1st year, are costly. The ratio of "overhead" expense to tuition payment is higher for a dropout than for a full-time student. Careful preliminary screening of prospective students, together with rigid entrance requirements, can materially reduce attrition. (Admission policies are discussed in detail in chapter V.) Among the factors that cause students to leave college include limited finances, change in vocational goals, poor housing, lack of counseling, etc. Correlation studies based on interviews with dropouts can serve as a guide to determine not only the relative importance of these factors but the appropriate corrective action to be taken.

BIBLIOGRAPHY

Advisory Commission on Intergovernmental Relations, *Measuring the Fiscal Capacity and Effort of State and Local Areas*, U.S. Government Printing Office, Washington, D.C., 1971, 209 pp.

Definitive, this study examines ways to quantify (a) the relative financing capability of State and local governments and (b) the extent to which these governments actually utilize this capability. Fiscal *capacity* is identified as the ability of governments to obtain resources for public purposes—their potential to fill the moneybasket. Fiscal *effort* gauges how much of this potential governments are actually using. The study makes use of the "representative tax system" approach by which "the revenue capacity of any particular area is defined as the total amount of revenue that would result by applying, within the area, the national average rate of each of the numerous kinds of State-local revenue sources." State and local financial data are presented for fiscal 1966–67; some updated figures covering fiscal 1968–69 are also included. The information needs that can be served by the data are illustrated by a limited and selective comparative analysis.

Bowen, Howard R., and Gordon K. Douglass, *Efficiency in Liberal Education*, Carnegie Commission on Higher Education, McGraw-Hill Book Co., New York, 1971, 151 pp.

The authors study the possibility of improving educational quality while reducing its cost by examining the educational effectiveness and cost of six different modes of instruction: (1) conventional, with instructors giving lectures and leading discussions, usually before a small group of students; (2) the Beardsley Ruml plan, which includes several very large lecture courses, as well as traditional lecture-discussion and seminar offerings; (3) a carefully devised program of independent study; (4) the David Bakah plan, which offers a highly compressed and relatively unstructured curriculum accompanied by extensive use of tutorials; (5) the Jarold Kieffer plan, calling for individual instruction and extensive use of modern teaching-learning equipment; and (6) an eclectic plan that incorporates certain features of the other five. These plans are examined in the context of a small liberal arts college in terms of their effect on the cost of changes in faculty teaching load, classroom utilization, proliferation of curriculums, distribution of faculty by academic rank, distribution of courses by subject taught, and total college enrollment. Considerable attention is devoted to accounting techniques that provide *comparable* unit costs for each of the six modes of instruction. The authors warn that caution should be used in making comparisons because of the many intangible quality factors involved. Obviously no one method of instruction is best for all subjects, all students, and all professors. While recommending a pattern that combines elements of all plans, the authors suggest that each institution adapt a plan to fit its own needs. Part of the value of this book is that it permits an educator to calculate the costs of the plan he has implemented or plans to implement. Some very interesting theoretical combinations are possible, all based on various assumptions about class size, curriculum proliferation, etc.

Carnegie Commission on Higher Education, *The Capitol and the Campus: State Responsibility for Postsecondary Education*, McGraw-Hill Book Co., New York, 1971, 154 pp.

As with so many Carnegie Commission reports, this one on State responsibilities for planning and providing higher education is packed with information. The chapters are short and tightly written; summary listings are incorporated as a substitute for narrative text. The chapters deal with the following: major themes; the goal and the issues; nature of State responsibility; the governor, the legislature, and higher education; coordination and planning; comparison of State effort; the State and the nonresident student; the State and private institutions; public and private tuition levels; public funds for private higher education; public accountability and institutional independence; and conclusions. Student resident and migration data and State financing statistics appear in the appendixes. This is an exceptionally valuable book which should be on the reading list of members of State boards and commissions charged with responsibility for postsecondary education.

Carnegie Commission on Higher Education, *Institutional Aid: Federal Support to Colleges and Universities*, McGraw-Hill Book Co., New York, 1972, 290 pp.

This report is concerned with institutional support within the totality of Federal aid to higher education. The Carnegie Commission believes that the Federal Government should provide substantially more funds for higher education, including allocations to individual institutions for general support of educational programs. The report sets the principles that should underlie Federal aid to institutions and provides new analytical data about the impact of different formulas on different types of institutions. According to this data, seemingly small changes in a formula make major differences in results, e.g., when allocations are made on the basis of enrollments calculated on a full-time-equivalent basis as opposed to a head-count basis. The components of various institutional grant formulas are described, as well as the amount of total funds distributed to various categories of institutions under six types of formulas. A State or an institutional share of funding is determined not only by the major components included in the formula but also by the definition of the selected components. Since the significant consequences of changes in definition are not usually recognized, the Commission's attention to this detail is well justified.

Formulas that give special preference to small colleges are singled out and examined. The text also covers Federal and State responsibility for higher education, diversity in academic programs, responsiveness to the financial crisis, the resource and tuition gap, Federal support for Federal priorities, cost-of-education supplements and student aid, and administrative and constitutional feasibility. In reporting on the crucial issue of what constitutes a *fair* distribution of Federal funds, the Commission recognizes many facets of the problem and raises a number of questions.

Two-thirds of the book contains appendixes devoted to selected institutional grant proposals and formulas, statements from higher education associations and commissions concerning Federal institutional aid, tables showing allocations of funds according to selected formulas, excerpts from studies revealing the financial conditions of universities and colleges, and other related subjects.

Carnegie Commission on Higher Education, *Less Time, More Options*, McGraw-Hill Book Co., New York, 1971, 45 pp.

This Carnegie Commission report makes recommendations concerning the general flow of students into and through institutions of higher learning and the key role of degrees in this flow. Special attention is given to efficiency, with emphasis on recommendations concerning the number of students in college at any one time, the length of time they spend pursuing undergraduate and graduate education, the options available to students to drop out of college temporarily, and new degree programs. "If the recommendations in this report were widely adopted, the time required to earn degrees in college would be shortened; operating costs could be reduced by 10 to 15 percent a year below levels that would otherwise prevail by 1980 and construction costs of higher education could be reduced by as much as $5 billion during the 1970's; more rewarding alternatives to college attendance would be available during youth; educational opportunities would be more appropriate to lifetime interests and more available to more people; and there would be more opportunities for people to assess their progress, change direction in life, or start a new career—if they wanted to."

Carnegie Commission on Higher Education, *The More Effective Use of Resources: An Imperative for Higher Education*, McGraw-Hill Book Co., N.Y., 1972, 201 pp.

By "more effective use of resources within higher education" the Carnegie Commission means that institutions should (1) carefully analyze the relations between the use of resources and the accomplishment of goals, (2) seek maximum economies with minimal sacrifices in quality, and (3) encourage rapid and flexible adaptation to changes in needs for educational, research, and public service programs. The Commission states that total institutional expenditures should be reduced approximately 20 percent by 1980 (as compared with the costs which would be incurred if the trends of the 1960's were to be continued) if a resource gap and general deterioration in the quality of higher education is to be avoided. The greatest possibilities for savings are (1) reducing the number of students by accelerating programs and by reducing the number of reluctant attenders, and (2) making more effective use of resources. The Commission also notes certain "windfall" changes that will reduce costs, such as the decline in faculty salary increases and the shift of enrollments in the direction of 2-year colleges with some cost savings.

Some key chapters on how costs can be reduced deal with the acceleration and integration of programs, retention rates and the "captive audience," utilization of faculty time, achieving budgetary flexibility, the planning and control of Capital costs, and the management of income and endowment.

Carnegie Commission on Higher Education, *Quality and Equality: Revised Recommendations, New Levels of Federal Responsibility for Higher Education*, McGraw-Hill Book Co., New York, 1970, 37 pp.

This and the earlier (1968) report incorporate the Carnegie Commission's recommendations for the kind and level of Federal support necessary to meet specific higher education priorities during the 1970's. The Commission suggests that the first of these priorities—the removal of financial barriers to college attendance—can be accomplished by a detailed set of proposals centering on three interacting elements: financial aid to students, cost-of-education supplements to institutions, and creation of new places to accommodate all qualified students. The second priority is the reduction or elimination of shortages in the number of professional personnel trained to provide health services. The third priority is the improvement of educational programs, processes, and techniques. Not all will agree with this ordering of priorities, but the carefully developed

Federal funding program by which these objectives can be achieved is an excellent model that can serve as a guide for continued efforts to bring about more effective Federal involvement in higher education.

Chambers, M. M., *Appropriations of State Tax Funds for Operating Expenses of Higher Education, 1971–72*, Office of Institutional Research, National Association of State Universities and Land-Grant Colleges, Washington, D.C., 1971, 28 pp.

This series of reports focuses on *State tax* funds appropriated for *operating* higher education institutions. The appropriations, listed by State and by institution, include those not only for instructional programs but also for research (including agricultural and engineering experiment stations) and for such public services as general extension, adult education, and health care.

Cox, Lanier, and Lester E. Harrell, *The Impact of Federal Programs on State Planning and Coordination of Higher Education*, Southern Regional Education Board, Atlanta, Ga., 1969, 238 pp.

This study is concerned with the new responsibility State governments must assume in coordinating Federal programs and with the impact of these programs on State planning and coordination of higher education. As a basis for the study, information and opinions from officials most directly affected by Federal programs in higher education—governors, statewide governing and coordinating agencies, special State agencies or general academic institutions administering Federal programs, and presidents of senior institutions of higher education—were analyzed.

Some of the questions the study attempts to answer include the following: What has been the effect of Federal programs implemented directly by institutions and of State-coordinated Federal programs on the State planning and coordinating function in higher education? Has the number of direct, categorical-type programs made substantially more difficult the State's efforts to provide reasonably for the educational needs of the State? What should the future direction of Federal programs be in relation to the State? What effect do the State-coordinated Federal programs have on private institutions and what would be the effect on these institutions if State coordination were extended to other Federal programs?

In the current period of reexamination and reappraisal of Federal higher education programs, the opinions of State officials and college and university presidents can be of value to those charged with establishing an appropriate Federal-State relationship.

McFarlane, William H., *State Support for Private Higher Education*, Southern Regional Education Board, Atlanta, Ga., 1969, 28 pp.

This monograph is devoted to a careful and concise study of the restructuring of State systems of higher education to include not only greater overall involvement by the private sector but also public aid for private colleges. The issues are viewed from several perspectives: the need for restructuring State systems in order to effect a better relationship between State systems and private institutions; the need for a more balanced development of educational services among public and private institutions; the problem of removing the major legal and political barriers to public aid for private institutions; and the importance of understanding the variety of approaches open to State support programs. It is hoped that the Southern Regional Educational Board will consider updating this work annually.

Mood, Alexander M., and Colin Bell, Lawrence Bogard, Helen Brownlee, and Joseph McCloskey, *Papers on Efficiency in the Management of Higher Education*, Carnegie Commission on Higher Education, McGraw-Hill Book Co., New York.

This publication integrates four reports emanating from an extensive study of the efficiency of higher education directed by Alexander Mood, director of the Public Policy Research Organization, University of California, Irvine. The four monographs—"Management in Institutions of Higher Education," by Lawrence Bogard; "Can Mathematical Models Contribute to Efficiency in Higher Education?" by Colin Bell; "Allocation of a University's Resources to Instruction," by Colin Bell, Helen Brownlee and Alexander Mood; and "Innovation in Private Colleges and Universities in California," by Joseph McCloskey—will be of most benefit to college presidents, government and foundation officials, and others interested in institutional efficiency.

U.S. Department of Health, Education, and Welfare, Office of the Assistant Secretary for Planning and Evaluation, *Toward a Long-Range Plan for Federal Financial Support for Higher Education*, U.S. Government Printing Office, Washington, D.C., 1969, 73 pp.

This HEW report, prepared in response to a request by President Lyndon B. Johnson, reviews the objectives of financial support to higher education, examines the financial barriers to meeting these objectives, and recommends a program of Federal action. The conclusion is that future Federal aid to higher education should emphasize two major national commitments: promoting equality of opportunity and strengthening graduate education and research. Subjects covered by the chapters include the following: higher educational opportunity, institutional financial strength, the special problems of graduate education, student aid versus institutional aid, and various institutional aid formulas. Recommendations are made concerning ways to improve not only equality of opportunity but also the quality of higher education, graduate education, and research. The report also stresses wise use of institutional resources.

Wolk, Ronald A., *Alternative Methods of Federal Funding for Higher Education*, Carnegie Commission on Higher Education, Berkeley, Calif., 1968, 261 pp.

This book describes the five major alternative methods of Federal funding—categorical aid, aid to students, grants to institutions, tax relief, and revenue sharing—and discusses the advantages and disadvantages of each. The history of Federal support to higher education is also reviewed. The appendixes include texts of important legislative proposals (as of 1968) and related pronouncements by various educational associations.

Chapter XIV

STATE BUDGETING FOR HIGHER EDUCATION

The financial dilemma resulting from a decade of expanding enroll-ments, not always with proportional increases in resources, has forced higher education to adopt new planning and budgeting systems to serve more students at the least possible cost. Broadly stated, colleges and universities, while searching for new, better, and less expensive ways to operate, have had to enhance their judgment and improve decisionmaking by utilizing the most sophisticated budgetary procedures available. From a planning standpoint, this has meant that all possible means of effectively and economically reaching established goals have had to be explored; from a budgeting standpoint, that new allocation procedures have had to be used to channel available funds into alternative and often competing utilization areas.

This chapter is concerned with the rationing of scarce resources among chosen alternatives. Resource allocation is first considered briefly in strictly economic terms of cost-benefit analysis—a rather theoretical approach. The remainder of the chapter deals with practical methods of justifying funding requests and apportioning funds by unit-cost formulas. The methods described seek to allocate limited resources fairly to competing institutions by identifying actual work loads and real deficiencies.

PROGRAM BUDGETING AND REVIEW

In view of the pressure being exerted on higher education to maintain and improve quality in the face of mounting enrollments and increasing costs, the need for economy is manifestly evident. Not only must the efficient and economical use of public funds be demonstrated, but more importantly, such valuable resources as teachers, scholars, and students must be responsibly managed. Citizens and State and local governments have rightly come to expect that public higher education systems be prepared periodically to explain and demonstrate the efficient and eco-nomical use of both public funds and human resources.

The traditional means by which colleges and universities satisfy public curiosity concerning their financial operations is through the budget process. The scope and importance of this activity has grown to such an extent that instead of being a peripheral assignment, it is now the epicenter of management responsibility. Its depth and critical nature are apparent in the following delineation by Melvin Anshen:

> It is the essence of decision making, therefore, to choose among alternative ends and to ration scarce means to their accomplishment. At this level of description, no significant distinction exists between profit and nonprofit organizations, or between private and public organizations. All require the ordering of goals, the analysis of their relative contributions to the great aims of the total undertaking, the development of plans, the measurement of alternative resource inputs and their relation to progress toward objectives, rational choice of feasible ends, allocation of means, monitoring of progress and appraisal of results. The budget process is the activity through which this work is done. The budget is the instrument through which the process is made operational.[1]

To achieve efficiency in implementing the budgetary process, colleges and universities and State higher education systems are adopting a new method called *program budgeting* and establishing comprehensive performance standards or budget formulas and an information system of performance reporting. In so doing, higher education has deliberately shifted its attention from budgetary minutiae to those aspects of the budget that are vital to achieving program goals.

The general idea of program budgeting is that activities can be meaningfully classified according to end objectives and alternative courses of action, then analytically examined in terms of utility and costs. Considerable attention is first given to the formulation of goals, objectives, desired end-products, and programs. What is variously called cost-effectiveness or cost-utility analysis is then employed to estimate the total cost of accomplishing these aims and to select the most efficient approach. Basically, the process consists of ordering and comparing various input-output combinations. The outputs must be so structured that they best reflect major objectives and the inputs—manpower, material, real estate—so ordered that comparisons among a wide range of alternative input-output relationships are feasible and meaningful.

Ideally, program budgeting should encompass all resources involved in attaining future objectives. Similarly, in assessing the degree to which

---

[1] Melvin Anshen, *The Budget as an Instrument for Analysis, Planning, and Management,* RAND Corporation, Santa Monica, Calif., April 1965, p. 1.

these objectives are achieved, all returns must be considered. Highest priority must be given to clear identification of objectives and a singular effort made to quantify them in terms of outputs or number of end-products of specified qualities. In the overall process, the emphasis is not on the traditional *object* classification budgetary approach but on *performance* classification—one that defines various program objectives in budgetary terms to provide a basis for accountability and demonstrated achievement. The most important consequence of adopting such an approach is that it increases the responsibility and accountability of management by establishing an awareness of the contribution and cost of each program under consideration. In other words, it strengthens the organization's capability of directing and changing its own programs and of analyzing expenditure proposals.

In practice, the formulation of budget requests in terms of the foregoing concepts involves the identification and description of proposed inputs and outputs, in budgetary terms, for each major academic and service program and activity. Line-item object classifications are usually not included because their detail distracts from the program's emphasis and tends to forclose the necessary option of studying and using more efficient alternative systems and resource-mixes. Any proposed new programs or improvements in service of monetary significance not only must be presented separately but also justified. If increases in the workload require additional financing to maintain the same level of service, justification is required by formula, ratio, or unit-cost analysis. Whenever significant departures from the previously approved appropriation pattern are made in actual expenditures, reasons for such departures must be explained. In every instance, projected performance must be compared with past performance. Finally, budget requests must always be submitted to reviewing authorities in time for careful study and possible changes *before* final approval action is required.

Under a program budgeting system, anticipated costs by individual campuses are summarized according to program and submitted as budget requests. As a rule, the initial review of such requests is detailed and comprehensive, with each program reviewed in relation to specified goals and expected accomplishments. Because unit costs and measures of productivity are an integral part of this review, they must be presented in the budget request in clear and well-organized language, not as a maze of unrelated figures. Secondary reviews, at higher organizational levels, while of necessity less detailed, can be of value to the review process if they bring the results of special studies to bear upon program requests and effectively comment on inter- and intra-institutional priority needs.

The new approaches being taken with regard to the budget *review* process at the secondary level are exemplified by the role once assumed (now discontinued[2]) by the California Coordinating Council for Higher Education. The Council's budget review, slightly modified for purposes of general applicability, consists of the following elements:[3]

1. *Fulfill the function of commenting on the "general level of support sought"* by presenting the following overall comparisons: interstate comparisons of the general tax burden and ability to pay; interstate and intrastate comparisons of the share of tax resources devoted to public higher education; where feasible, a comparison of functional expenditures at State institutions with those at comparable institutions in other States; and special studies, conducted periodically, of various sources of institutional income.

2. *Perform special studies to evaluate the quality of program and performance budgeting and reporting* through an examination of the budgetary formulas and guidelines used to determine the financial support necessary to maintain continuing programs; place primary emphasis upon the educational validity of the standards in a context outside the annual budget cycle; define the nature of the data to be reported that will most effectively chart actual program performance; and, where applicable, relate results of the studies to program budget proposals.

Continue to consider the philosophy, structure, and procedures of budget development and execution in order to improve relationships between public higher education and State government.

When an area or program in need of reevaluation by the segments (universities, 4-year colleges, 2-year colleges) or individual campuses—rather than by the Council—can be identified, suggest program areas for study.

3. *Comment on or recommend priority groupings among and within the total budget requests* of the segments (or individual campuses); rely and comment on justification information available to these institutions from comparable institutions of higher education nationally.

The nature of the Council's budget review in this regard can be summarized as follows:

(a) *New programs, improved programs and program development.* Relying upon information provided by the segment (or individual campus), the Council will comment on or recommend inter- and intrasegmental (or individual campus) priority groupings. Program development requests will first be examined to ascertain the degree to which each program request conforms to the plan of development accepted by the Council at the time its initiation was authorized in a legislative appropriation. If such requests remain consistent with the accepted plan, they normally will be accorded high priority. As in the past, new and improved program requests will be considered in terms of (1) differentiation of function, (2) the evidence of need for such programs, (3) the probable impact of such programs on existing

---

[2] This budget review role is now largely discontinued for reasons cited in *The Budget Review Role of the Coordinating Council for Higher Education*, CCHE, Sacramento, May 23, 1967. Its discontinuance does not, however, affect the value of the procedure per se. And since a number of the reasons for its discontinuation are not generally applicable in other States (the presence of strong budget review staffs in either or both the executive and legislative branches and a coordinating board dominated by institutional representation), the procedures could conceivably be useful elsewhere.

[3] Coordinating Council for Higher Education (California), *Budget Review in Public Higher Education*, Sacramento, 1965, pp. 21, 22, 28, 29.

institutions, both public and private, and (4) the possible effects of these programs upon subsequent requests for State support.

(b) *Maintenance of continuing programs.* Council comment will be made in this area only when special studies have been completed which are found to affect program proposals of the segments. As noted in item 2, special studies are to be initiated to evaluate the extent and quality of program and performance budgeting and reporting. These studies will examine budgetary standards and guidelines used in determining the financial support necessary to maintain continuing programs. The educational test to be applied is the degree to which the standard meets the programs' budgetary needs. Tests of technical quality will also be applied. The nature of data to be reported to chart the actual program performance will also be defined. All special studies will be performed in a context outside the annual budget cycle.

(c) *Discontinuance and reduction of programs.* Requests of this kind, of course, will be rare and are not likely to be spotlighted in a budget request. Council action in this category will consist of suggesting areas for study by the segments (or individual campuses) themselves, with reports to be submitted to the Council the following year. An area or program appearing in need of reevaluation will be identified and the nature of the reevaluation will be described in terms of background information and pertinent questions.

4. *Changes in funding.* Staff review of proposals for changes in funding will be evaluated on the basis of special studies in such areas as State appropriations, Federal funding, local tax sources, gifts and grants, contract research, tuition, nonresident tuition, charges for auxiliary services, student fees, and so on.

By way of summary, perspective can be given to program budgeting review at the State level if the realities of higher education as an object of systematic analysis are recognized and the particular responsibilities expected of the review understood. The environment of higher education as it affects program budgeting is characterized, as are most social systems, by uncertainty, complexity, and elements that defy measurement. Uncertainty—the inability to fully understand all outcomes arises because all objectives relevant to educational programs can never be accounted for nor can changes in policy or advances in technology be accurately predicted. The budget review officer, who must learn to live with uncertainty, needs to base his decisions on projected estimates of the future without full knowledge of the consequences of his actions.

The complexity of higher education is not difficult to appreciate. A vast number of considerations are involved, including economic, social, and political value choices. There are numerous alternative methods to accomplish presumably similar purposes. Many diverse types of benefits accrue to many different beneficiaries. Relevant factors cannot be squeezed into a single formula; only a few variables can be considered simultaneously. Usually a piecemeal approach is necessary: studying parts of a problem and reporting partial answers.

Many factors and outputs of higher education cannot be measured or cannot be measured on a common scale. Even when given a marketplace value, the price tag cannot always be accepted as a measure of true economic worth. When important variables cannot be quantified, informed and rational judgment must be used in choosing priorities. Even the machinery for making decisions must sometimes be altered.

Given this environment, applying program budgeting to higher education in an orderly and systematic way is formidable indeed. To be realistic, many smaller problems and parts of larger ones must, temporarily at least, be put aside. Possible decisions about some matters will have to be ignored and specific decisions about others taken for granted.

The ordering of future patterns must be given precedence over solving immediate problems or rectifying past mistakes. Since the objectives in higher education are not always known, are often in conflict with one another, and sometimes cannot be agreed upon, the State-level review must be concerned with what ought to be done as much as with how to do it. The overriding concerns of the review should be (1) the marshaling of experience, (2) the sharpening of intuition, (3) the identification of crucial relationships, and (4) the increase of explicitness.

EFFECTIVE RESOURCE ALLOCATION

Without access to unlimited resources, colleges and universities, like all organizations, must choose from a variety of programs and services those which best accomplish their social and cultural purposes. The difficulty of the task lies in selecting criteria or standards by which the "best" or "preferred" or "most rational" use of resources may be measured.

Quite obviously choices may be made either objectively or subjectively, or, more likely, by a combination of both. In reality, most major long-range budgeting decisions must ultimately be resolved primarily on the basis of intuition and judgment—even, in some instances, on the basis of political expediency. There are too many intangibles to allow anything other than experience and intellect to prevail. What, then, is the role of quantitative analysis in budgetary decisionmaking? In sum, the analytical process enables the decisionmaker to sharpen his intuition and judgment by providing cost and utility information for some of the alternatives under consideration.

Three approaches to efficiency analysis may be followed: cost-benefit analysis, systems analysis, and program budgeting. *Cost-benefit analysis*, or, in the higher education context, cost-effectiveness analysis,[4] compares

---

[4] The more common expression is cost-benefit analysis; however, in the field of education, where it is not possible to measure the value of benefits in the marketplace in the same way as costs are measured, the more frequently used term is cost-effectiveness or cost-utility analysis.

quantifiable economic costs with related benefits of alternative investments to determine an expenditure pattern that maximizes the overall output/ input ratio. Economic theory is used to allocate resources to competing programs in such a manner that the ratios of marginal returns to marginal costs for each program are equal, thereby maximizing total returns less total costs. In other words, cost-effectiveness analysis attempts to maximize the current value of all benefits less that of all costs by funding each program to the level at which any additional money added to any program will result in an equal return. The fact that all relevant factors cannot be incorporated in such an analysis is a serious drawback; nevertheless, it is possible to make certain situations subject to analysis that heretofore were commonly subject only to implicit judgments.

Systems analysis is a broad approach toward achieving efficiency in an uncertain environment in which objectives may either not be known or may be subject to change and in which judgment and intuition, as well as quantitative methods, must be relied upon. Representative statistical models are used to study the most crucial relationships, with secondary considerations ignored if their variation has little affect on the outcome. The analysis is a piecemeal approach (involving a few variables at a time) to determine the consequences of alternative courses of action. Working out successive model studies theoretically on paper can be a substitute for experience and may produce reasonable or even good solutions to various problems. The application of systems analysis to the problems of higher education, however, has to date resulted in few significant or practical decisionmaking devices.

Program budgeting, a form of systems analysis, focuses on such outputs as goals, objectives, and program end-products, and employs cost-effectiveness analysis as a means of achieving them. Because significant interdependencies exist between different programs and objectives, it is difficult if not impossible to establish a valid basis for apportioning costs and returns for each individual program. Consequently, program budgeting cannot serve as a workable substitute for judgment in determining program priorities. (The theoretical nature of systems analysis and of program budgeting precludes further discussion within the context of this chapter. Published material on both systems is, however, cited in the bibliography. The papers by Aaron Wildavsky are particularly recommended for initial reading.)

In its purest form, cost-effectiveness analysis, like systems analysis, has had limited practical value when applied to higher education. Yet cost-effectiveness theory is applied repeatedly in the widespread use of formulas to apportion funds according to objective estimates of relative need. The use of *formula budgeting* to estimate budgetary requirements incorporates standard costs and workload factors. Each competing claim, according to its demonstrated need, receives a "fair share" of the budget. Levels of support are based on what is judged to be adequate, or in the case of salaries, acceptably competitive. While no systematic effort is made to obtain optimal allocation by equating marginal returns, formula budgeting does employ this principle of cost-effectiveness analysis by assuming that the workloads of all competing claims are legitimate and, when funded according to actual need, equally productive.

Before beginning the discussion of formula budgeting, the principal topic of this chapter, further orientation concerning cost-effectiveness analysis is in order.

Cost-Effectiveness Analysis

The basic purpose of cost-effectiveness analysis is to obtain objective data that will enable financial planners to choose among alternative ends and to ration scarce resources effectively. The process requires repeated efforts to equalize the value of the last increment of support expended for any program—in other words, to reach the point at which the direction that additional support increases are made makes no difference since all additions will bring equal returns (i.e., the ratio of marginal returns to marginal costs will be the same for each program). Benefits over costs are thus maximized. Within the context of higher education, cost-effectiveness analysis can be applied in a majority of instances only by substituting a model for the real situation. Seldom can cost-effectiveness analysis be expected to provide firm conclusions, yet its role is significant. The great value of cost-effectiveness analysis to higher education is that it promotes *thinking* in terms of goals, alternatives, increments, and comparative payoffs. It encourages a comparison of the payoff (or products) from increments, of resources spent (input) on one program with the payoff realized through applying the same resources to all other programs.

Unfortunately the unassailable logic of equating marginal returns so as to maximize total returns (less costs) has tended to obscure the difficulties of applying theory to reality. The plain fact is that almost all productive effort results in *human* returns that are often decisive but may be neither anticipated nor measured. Such intangibles inevitably defy analytical study, and no matter how significant to the final decision, they cannot be included in the finite calculations of cost-effectiveness studies. Herein lies a great danger (common to all procedures that rely on quantification):

that the limitations[5] of cost-effectiveness, particularly the fact it cannot be used to express properly the importance of all the variables involved, will not be sufficiently recognized. In solving problems, the decisionmaker, particularly anyone in the higher education community, can expect a relatively incomplete set of quantitative calculations on cost and utility. Even a small amount of cost-effectiveness data, however, may provide a sizable payoff by clarifying alternative courses of action.

The following brief outline of procedural steps illustrates how cost-effectiveness theory can be applied to an examination of the relative value of alternative uses of funds in higher education. Additional information can be obtained from references cited in the bibliography.

STEP 1: *Identify a group of programs that share common objectives.* Common objectives provide a frame of reference by which the relative contribution of each program increment can be evaluated in terms of achievement.

STEP 2: *Clarify and define the common objectives operationally in terms by which progress toward their achievement is to be measured.* The basic goals of education—to educate students, to promote research, and to provide public services—are common to many college and university programs. But how is meaningful progress toward achieving these goals to be measured? The tasks of nurturing the human mind and cultivating human talents and skills and the means available to institutions to accomplish these ends are simply too complex and noncorporeal to be measurable (in their entirety) in objective terms by any known instrument of quantification. Also, the ultimate consequences of research usually can be only partially recognized, and only after an extended period of time. Thus it has become necessary to substitute indirect yet clearly distinguishable measures of performance or output. For example, "teaching productivity" in terms of credit-hours taught or number of degrees awarded is frequently (although recognized as inadequate) substituted for measuring the effects that educational programs have on students. Similarly, hours of research performed are commonly substituted for the more realistic, yet impossible to quantify, economic and social returns from research. The crudity of

---

[5] Among the conditions that limit the usefulness of cost-effectiveness analysis are the dependence on a perfect market of competitive conditions and full employment to reflect value through prices. Any imperfection in the market adversely affects the validity of the analysis because it creates an artificial price for goods and services that may vary significantly from their worth to society as valued by consumers in a freely competitive market. Another factor is the question of whose welfare is to be maximized. Among different people there is simply no scientific way to compare losses and gains. Therefore, whenever the end-products concern human benefits, the problem of determining whose welfare is to receive precedence must be resolved by judgment.

such output measures is immediately apparent, and until a better means of measuring *direct* progress toward declared goals is identified, the usefulness of cost-effectiveness analysis to education is limited.

STEP 3: *Define measurable input (cost) factors that may be associated with the aforementioned outputs.* In sharp contrast to the difficulty of quantifying progress toward educational goals or program outputs is the ease by which goods-and-services inputs may be measured on the basis of dollar cost.[6] Yet the problems associated with costing inputs, while not insurmountable, have proven to be a handicap in cost-effectiveness analysis. The problems arise because of inconsistency in definitions, the difficulty in meaningfully organizing or distributing costs, and the technical aspects of collecting and incorporating the data in a useful form.

The accounting system of a typical college or university will generate a large amount of cost data that may be used as a guide in estimating probable future costs. However, few institutions attempt to distribute these costs logically among programs and levels of instruction in a meaningful way. One of the problems is determining the degree to which joint costs should be prorated and charged to each program. Some supporting and administrative activities in themselves constitute distinctive program elements worthy of separate analysis. In other instances, secondary activities common to a number of programs should be prorated and a portion charged to the cost of each program. The conceptual and technical problems inherent in such cost distributions are formidable.[7]

STEP 4: *Compare the ratio of marginal returns to marginal costs in all programs and reallocate or add new funds (within total budget restraints) to high ratio programs until the return/cost ratio for all programs is equal.* This is essentially a process of transferring funds out of low return/cost programs into high return/cost

---

[6] Implicit in using dollar cost to measure inputs is the assumption that prices will be established in a free and open market and thus will reflect true worth or value as appraised by the consumer.

[7] Such problems are being studied by the Western Interstate Commission for Higher Education (WICHE), currently engaged in the design, development, and implementation of management systems generally acceptable to all higher education. One important contribution of WICHE has been a "standard taxonomy or uniform classification system that identifies and categorizes the activities and programs of higher education institutions." (See Warren W. Gulko, *Program Classification Structure*, Technical Report No. 27, National Center for Higher Education Management Systems (NCHEMS) at Western Interstate Commission for Higher Education, Boulder, Colo., 1972.) The use of several of the NCHEMS tools as they relate to a specific institution are presented in *Implementation of NCHEMS Planning and Management Tools at California State University, Fullerton*, NCHEMS at WICHE, Boulder, Colo., 1972.

programs until such shifting is no longer advantageous. Within higher education, maximizing total benefits less total costs by equating marginal returns/costs is a concept likely to provide guidance that is more theoretical than practical. To understand why this is so, one must remember that the results of marginal analysis can enable management to *make* a decision only if *all* outputs (not just a measurable few) are considered. In practically no case in education is a complete measurement of all outputs possible; therefore, marginal analysis can only *assist* the decisionmaker, not make the decision for him. An example will illustrate the inherent dangers. Suppose a cost-effectiveness analysis revealed that the physics department is less productive than other science departments in terms of student-credit-hours per dollar input. On this basis alone, it would be utter nonsense to decide to reduce the budget of the physics department, lower teaching salaries, and increase class sizes in an effort to make the department more competitively productive.[8]

Recognizing the inherent dangers and the limited value and difficulty of performing marginal analysis in the traditional sense, educators have sought a more realistic and practical procedure. Three modifications have been suggested. First, the term "marginal" need not be restricted to a rigorous economic interpretation, i.e., to the *last incremental* units of output and related input. Rather, "marginal" can be viewed as the *difference* in input or output between past and present time periods. These differences result from introducing new programs or making major modifications in existing ones.

Second, new programs or major changes may be evaluated in their entirety as "packages," thereby eliminating the need for a detailed cost breakdown. By combining both the first and second modification, only the *total* costs and returns of *new* or *modified* programs are considered marginal. The quantity and quality level of continuing programs is assumed desirable, and, therefore, to be maintained.

Since only the output/input ratios of new or changed programs are measured and equated, the scope of marginal analysis is reduced and there is no need for comparing marginal returns with those existing programs whose full funding is assumed justified. And since the increment costs and returns being considered are the *whole* inputs and outputs of

---

[8] Too often the "productivity" measures of cost-effectiveness are misinterpreted. They report the cost rate of performing a certain function but do not directly measure efficiency (the degree to which resources are being wasted) or effectiveness (the degree to which a program is accomplishing its goals). The fact that many educational programs requiring expensive equipment, small class sizes, and highly paid faculty have legitimately low production rates (high unit costs) in no way implies that they are either inefficient or ineffective.

new or modified programs, marginal values are represented by the more simply calculated average costs and average returns. Thus the focus is placed on obtaining optimum allocation only among competing new or modified programs on the basis of equating their average output/input ratios.

A third modification that has been suggested is measuring marginal returns in such a way as to determine the *relative emphasis* to be accorded programs or functional aims.[9] Thus, if functional aims can be quantified, they may then be funded in such a manner as to achieve a desired balance. When this balance is obtained, the marginal effectiveness of each program is considered to be equal since the resulting mix of programs is supposedly the best structure to achieve the overall objectives of the institution.

All of the many differing programs of a college or university are to a degree complementary in that all contribute to the quality of performance of each program and to the whole. Consequently, if too great or too little emphasis is given a particular program, not only will the program in question be adversely affected but so also will the performance of the whole institution. Some areas of particular concern are the balance of emphasis between research and graduate instruction, between research and undergraduate instruction, and between undergraduate and graduate instruction; also, the relative emphasis to be given to public service.[10]

As a result of the three aforementioned modifications, marginal analysis becomes a task of examining new programs or proposals in their entirety to ensure that their contributions result in an overall program mix consistent with previously determined relative emphasis. At what exact point an increase in emphasis (funding) of one function ceases to be complementary to another function must be left largely to professional judgment.

STEP 5: *Modify initially specified objectives and criteria if such action is suggested.* The analysis, if thoroughly and imaginatively done, should at times result in improved program objectives or in the criteria (outputs) by which progress toward these objectives is measured.

---

[9] The suggestion that relative emphasis be substituted for program performance (as an intermediate step toward solving the problem of quantification) is proposed by Thierry Koening, Charles McIntyre, and J. C. Scheuerman. See Coordinating Council for Higher Education (California), *November Report on the Level of Support for Public Higher Education 1968–69*, Sacramento, 1967, p. 11.

[10] Ibid., pp. 12–16. The authors present a brief discussion of various balances in program emphasis to support the assertion that interfunctional relationships do exist and that these relationships and long-range aims should not only be defined but also, if possible, quantified.

FORMULAS IN COLLEGE AND UNIVERSITY BUDGETING

Each year colleges and universities must determine their financial needs and present a budget that they can justify. At the State level, governing and coordinating agencies must defend not only the amounts requested but also the equity with which funds are distributed among institutions. While all sources of support—student, alumni, government, public, and corporate—are legitimately concerned with budgetary request, the greatest scrutiny is probably exercised by State legislative appropriations committees. In view of the insistence by State officials and legislators for detailed justification of budget items and the increasing magnitude and complexity of college operations, insofar as possible budgetary "judgments" and "recommendations" must be supported by objective data. One effective means by which objectivity has been introduced to budgeting is through the use of *formulas* that express and interrelate relevant cost and load measurements. Miller defines a "formula" abstractly as:

> an objective procedure for estimating the future budgetary requirements of a college or university through the manipulation of objective (quantitative) data about future programs and the relationships between programs and costs, in such a way as to derive an estimate of future costs.[11]

Budget formulas and cost analysis go hand in hand. Cost analysis measures the current cost of various units of existing programs; formulas extrapolate these cost relationships (with necessary quality and price adjustments) so that, given the expected levels of operation, the costs of future programs can be estimated.

The idea that lengthy and complex financial data can be reduced to a short and relatively simple form by using a formula has considerable appeal. The basic structure of budgeting formulas is in fact simple: standard unit costs are multiplied by projected loads to equal estimated total fiscal support requirements. Such simplicity, however, is deceptive. Among competing institutions with complex and varying educational programs it is difficult to determine what constitutes a true and comparable measure of load. And even though formulas can provide an equitable accounting for certain variances found, introducing flexibility into formula mechanics, especially if some standardization and simplicity are to be retained, is a complicated process. Developing appropriate

---

[11] James L. Miller, Jr., *State Budgeting for Higher Education—The Use of Formulas and Cost Analysis*, Institute of Public Administration, University of Michigan, Ann Arbor, 1964, p. 6.

adaptability in load measurement, and identifying and projecting "fair" or "competitive" costs, are two design features central to formula validity and to the case for or against adopting the formula approach.

Advantages and Uses of Formulas

Budget formulas that provide a systematic means for calculating the resources required by a given program may be used (1) to *project* budgetary needs, (2) to *justify* budgetary requests, (3) to *clarify* the presentation of budgetary information, (4) to *allocate* resources, and (5) to *standardize* budgetary data for comparative analysis.

The advantages of formulas and cost analysis procedures over more conventional subjective approaches to budgeting are:[12]

1. Mathematical precision, logical rationale, objectivity, and adaptability of formulas result in *validity* or soundness of funding proportional to need that is generally superior to educated guesses based on experience and opinion. The use of formulas does not, however, preclude employing value judgments to augment or modify the results of computations.

2. Since formulas are expressed in unit measurements, the projection of financial requirements and allocation of resources is proportional to relative institutional loads rather than based on political or interinstitutional competition. In other words, if budgeting is based on formulas, all institutions are treated in a comparable (*equitable*) manner insofar as the activities or programs are similar and loads and priorities are accurately gauged.

3. Since all requests are structured in a nearly identical manner, formulas facilitate institutional *comparisons*. As long as classifications and definitions remain constant, formulas also facilitate comparisons between one year and the next. When conducting comparison studies, great care must be exercised to insure that only those institutions that closely resemble each other are grouped for like appraisal.

> Through these procedures a large amount of apparently noncomparable information about a number of institutions can be organized in a meaningful way and presented in terms of uniform units of measurement which make comparison possible. Such comparisons are useful for many purposes related both to statewide budgeting and the internal management of individual institutions. Comparisons provide a norm against which the practice of individual institutions can be measured.[13]

4. The use of formulas and the justification of unit cost values based on normative data help ensure adoption of the budget by proper authorities. According to some institution and State officials, more *adequate* support has been secured when requests have been presented in the simple, systematic, and apparently irrefutable way that formula procedures provide.

5. Because cost analysis and formula procedures require systematic presentation of an unusual amount of detailed data and inclusion of criteria for measuring the

---

[12] Based in part on Miller, ibid., pp. 152–57.
[13] Ibid., p. 152.

economy and efficiency of the institution's operation, *evaluation* of institutional performance is encouraged.

6. Since formulas and cost analysis techniques clearly highlight critical components and reduce budget preparation, they provide a relatively uncomplicated and straightforward format for budgetary *presentations*.

7. Cost analysis and formulas have achieved *acceptability* among users who appreciate equitable treatment based on sound rationale.

Criteria for Formula Design

If formulas are to serve as useful procedures for estimating future budgetary requirements, they must be constructed to meet a number of interrelated criteria, the most critical being the following (listed in order of importance):[14]

1. *Validity.* Any formula that does not measure what it purports to measure will be of little value in estimating budgetary needs, and may, if sufficiently inaccurate, perpetuate gross deficiencies, surpluses, and inequities. Formula estimates should be continually compared with actual budgetary patterns and adjusted as required. Only through a rigorous demonstration of validity can institutional officials expect that budget requests will be honored fairly and adequately.

2. *Quantitative definability.* Insofar as practical, formulas and cost analysis procedures should be expressed in measurable terms (subject to physical count) to avoid the bias, errors of judgment, and differences of opinion normally encountered in subjectively derived values. Where judgments are required—as for example in subjectively weighting certain formula factors—every effort should be made to authenticate decisions through empirical evidence. A corollary criterion is that formula units be defined so as to take advantage of readily available data.

3. *Sensitivity to change.* Formulas should be so constructed that, by automatically adjusting resource allocation to account for changes in service demands and growth rates, they are responsive to workload changes. Furthermore, formulas should indicate the effects of changes in such program components as altered emphasis or quality revisions. It should be recognized that in order to be sensitive to change, formulas must be rather complex, a characteristic in direct conflict with the sixth formula design criterion of simplicity.

4. *Adaptability.* Either the mechanics of the formula or its administration should be sufficiently flexible to permit the inclusion of important differences in existing programs, as well as differences among institutions in educational philosophy and operational style. While certain circumstances may require the tailoring of formulas to correspond accurately to an individual institution's needs, care must be exercised to avoid the kind of modification that tends to obscure the common basis of allocation on which equitable treatment is based.

---

[14] These criteria, with a few exceptions, parallel those developed by Miller, ibid., pp. 163–65, and those summarized by the California Coordinating Council for Higher Education, *Instructional Practices and Related Faculty Staffing in California Public Higher Education*, Sacramento, 1967, p. 73.

5. *Comparability.* Formula definitions should be standardized and formula units designed in such a manner as to facilitate comparisons among institutions and programs within the State and with data available from other States. Since comparisons serve as a major indicator of support adequacy, it is imperative that all formula budgetary procedures, terms, definitions, and published data be standardized (preferably on a nationwide basis).

6. *Understandability.* Formula procedures should be sufficiently simple and straightforward that they can be readily understood by users. Simplicity is feasible because the broad estimation purpose of formula budgeting precludes detailed compartmentalization of expenditures. However, if formulas are to be sensitive to load change and adaptable to institutional conditions, complications will necessarily arise. Any oversimplication that destroys formula validity must be avoided. If formulas are to fulfill intended objectives a certain degree of sophistication is required. For example, consideration must be given to important differences between graduate level and undergraduate level, between departments and colleges, and between programs.

Precautions in the Use of Formulas and Cost Analysis

Although there is a tendency on the part of those examining formulas or other kinds of quantification procedures to assume they are valid simply because the precise science of mathematics is involved, it should be understood that common sense and judgment also play an essential role. The reason is obvious: An uncertain and variable relationship exists between precise measurements and the principal objective, namely, the funding of colleges and universities in such a way that collectively they may effectively contribute to the optimum development of society.

While formulas can neither determine policy nor be substituted for judgment, they do have legitimate roles in the decisionmaking process. To provide economic perspective, they should be introduced *prior* to program policy decisions. To the degree that they assist in translating policy into specific program-dollar requirements (if the formula provides such detail), they may serve as an implementing agent *following* the decision. The decisionmaking itself must always be based on multiple considerations, including value judgments and factual data.

There are still other precautions to be taken in making appropriate use of formulas and cost analysis:[15]

1. Formulas are basically a means of *projecting* present ratios and unit costs to estimate *future* budgetary requirements. As with any projection, error occurs when the relationships on which a projection is based change or one or more factors fail to materialize. Accordingly, whenever a formula is used it is important that adjustments be made in the resulting program of funding to account for unanticipated realities. For example, substantially larger enrollments than expected obviously call for appropriately larger instructional budgets than originally estimated. If economies in operating procedures can be anticipated, they should be reflected by budget reductions.

---

[15] Based in part on Miller, op. cit., pp. 155–59.

2. By definition, formula budgeting provides a generalized expression of financial needs, not a detailed breakdown of expenditures. While the formula should closely follow actual patterns of expenditures established by an institution, it is not essential that individual colleges adhere strictly to the specifics of formula allotment when they prepare and execute their actual operating budget. The relative simplicity of formula-type presentations precludes an accounting of every exception or every difference among institutions. Individual colleges and universities are expected to design operating budgets that generally conform to broad expenditure categories, but are under no obligation to conform to a detailed formula breakdown if appropriate institutional action dictates otherwise. When actual expenditure patterns at several institutions deviate widely from those in a formula, the formula norm must be corrected to reflect such patterns realistically.

3. The adoption of a formula or cost analysis procedure requires that participating institutions and State officials relinquish some freedom of action in budgetary matters and give at least tacit approval to formula concepts as the "rules of the game." Such agreement may not be easily secured from college officials who have in the past enjoyed a privileged position with regard to preparing the budget. Nevertheless, if formula budgeting is to be effective, *all* participants must be willing to cooperate by expressing their endorsement of and confidence in the adopted procedures.

To administer formula budgeting, some type of organizational structure is required. Usually it is the State higher education coordinating agency, if such an agency exists, or it may be an organization designated by the State budget office or by an ad hoc committee of representatives from the various institutions involved. Provision should be made for a technically competent staff to conduct necessary studies, devise the formulas and cost analysis procedures, and prepare the budget proposals.

4. Officials should be alert to the influence that formula or cost analysis procedures may have on the organizational structure of a State system of higher education. The continuing need for a budget administrative staff may lead a State to strengthen its coordinating agency. Also, formula or costs analysis reports may, in some instances, indicate needed revision in program assignments at certain institutions.

5. Periodic review of formula cost figures and ratios should be encouraged in order to maintain current input data that invite comparative analyses and to draw attention to variables influenced by time. Because annual or biennial reviews tend to reopen policy questions that otherwise might be looked upon as "settled," they are considered essential by those who challenge existing practices, and desire to reexamine key issues.

6. New programs, often inefficient and unproductive at the outset, have little chance of competing for funds against established programs if money is allotted by a formula based on load or performance. Consequently, funding beyond that provided by the formula must be available to support new programs until they "get on their feet." Such additional funding is especially critical to institutions that have stabilized enrollments and therefore are not entitled to receive increased financial support from formulas that proportion funding to enrollment. It should also be remembered that formula procedures must not overlook the continuing need for support of creative and innovative programs at all institutions.

Types of Formulas and Their Appropriate Use

That formula budgeting is categorical in nature must be recognized. Except in the rare instance when total institutional funding is based on a simple cost-per-student allocation, formula budgeting in higher education provides for *separate* funding computations for *each* of the major functional activities generally agreed upon as requiring individual budget identification. Within the current funds "educational and general" category, the functional accounts that may be funded by formula are general administration, instruction and departmental research, extension and public service, libraries, and plant maintenance and operation.[16] These functional accounts or a modification of them (involving appropriate combinations) are utilized in some manner by almost all types of cost analyses and formula procedures. Functional accounts seldom funded by formula include such largely self-supporting activities as auxiliary enterprises, sales and services of educational departments, sponsored research, and student aid. (The special procedures for determining capital construction needs are discussed in chapter X.)

All formulas for higher education budgeting are based on the simple concept of estimating future requirements by multiplying projected loads by projected unit costs. Variations of this concept result in three "types" of formulas: workload, base, and staffing pattern.

The *workload* or functional formula estimates future expenditures for each activity by projecting a carefully determined load measurement that is relevant to the activity itself and is priced at expected unit costs. For example, library book acquisition expenditures might be represented by the number of volumes to be purchased (the planned total load) multiplied by a representative price (unit cost). Because functional formulas employ the workload factor that most specifically affects the activity involved, they guarantee accuracy. Thus whenever workloads can be measured, this approach is preferred. Obviously, both costs and workload factors must be measured and analyzed in great detail. The fact that preparation time may be lengthened is offset by the fact that accuracy is heightened.

In a *base* formula, expenditures for a particular activity are estimated as a percentage of a given "base," usually the expenditures required for instruction. This approach assumes that the relative expenditures for various budget components bear fairly constant and predictable relationships to one another. For example, *total* library expenditures may be estimated as 7 percent of instructional costs if this percentage existed in the past and is expected to continue in the future.

The most commonly recognized advantage of base formulas—simplicity—is misleading. Mechanically, the formula is simple: Only the instructional expenditure base need be derived in detail by a functional analysis of workload and unit cost factors. Gross amounts for most other

---

[16] For a description of these functional accounts, see George E. Van Dyke, ed., *College and University Business Administration* (rev. ed.), American Council on Education, Washington, D.C., 1968, pp. 232–54.

activities can then be computed simply as percentages of this base. This simplicity, however, is deceptive. If the base formula is to be of value to management as an instrument to focus attention on setting policy rather than as a device to perpetuate existing practice, then the task of determining the relative emphasis to be accorded among programs and functional aims as defined by budgetary proportionment becomes a very difficult task indeed. When allocating funds by a base formula, the relative emphasis to be given to the activity involved in comparison to the base activity must be defined. In other words, it should be possible to defend library funding at 7 percent of instructional expenditures on the ground that such a financial support ratio results in an economically and educationally sound and complementary balance between the library and the instructional programs.

The relative importance that should be given to different programs and functional aims is, of course, a matter of judgment. In applying the base formula approach, however, judgment does not always include careful attention to establishing desired optimum relationships among programs and activities. In addition, percentages derived by computing last year's average are frequently accepted at face value when, in fact, the ratio of funding that will provide the intended emphasis should be explored. If the base formula approach to program budgeting is to be a useful decisionmaking device, the tail must not wag the dog; management must determine the intended emphasis to be accorded various programs instead of permitting programs to be determined solely on the basis of past performance. Whenever allocation involves related programs that can reasonably vie with each other for funding, the base formula approach may be appropriate if care is exercised in determining the relative balance desired among such programs.

The *staffing pattern* formula estimates future salary expenditures by determining the type and number of administrative and functional positions required for the activity being considered and multiplying this number by a corresponding salary schedule. The number of positions may be determined according to 1) the desired ratio of positions to the number of students enrolled or to another workload measure or 2) by developing an appropriate organizational structure and manning table. If the staffing pattern formula is used, the number of staff positions represents the load measurement and the salary schedule provides the unit costs.

If the current workload or the productive effort of human labor cannot be measured, a carefully prepared staffing schedule or manning table is the preferred means by which to estimate salary requirements. The design of the staffing schedule focuses attention on the development and continual appraisal of the organizational structure as well as on a clear delineation of line and staff responsibilities. It is expected that more widespread use of this method of formula budgeting will be made as pressure is exerted on higher education to devise more rigorous means of identifying funding requirements.

FORMULATING INSTRUCTIONAL BUDGETARY REQUIREMENTS

Instruction, the principal function of colleges and universities, is by far the largest and most important budget component. Because it is central to the institution's purpose and also represents the major workload, the instructional function is the raison d'être of college budgeting. Consequently, in the base formula approach to budgeting, instructional costs are the basis on which all other functional allocations are computed. For this reason and because the methods of computing instruction funding are both complex and varied, a clear understanding of the fundamentals involved is essential.

Basic Formulas

For purposes of formula budgeting, instructional expenditures are usually divided into two categories: faculty salaries and departmental operating expenses

(1) Total instructional expenditures = Faculty salary expenditures

+Departmental operating expenses

The faculty consists of all academic ranks (instructor through professor) and may include teaching assistants. Since the workload of faculty consists of research and services to the public, to students, and to the institution, as well as classroom teaching and preparation, faculty salaries represent the amount spent on the total *faculty function*. Teaching salary costs, on the other hand, relate only to instruction.[17]

Departmental operating expenses include expenditures for supplies and travel, the wages and salaries of administrative and technical personnel, and in some cases, expenditures for furniture and equipment installed in classrooms and administrative offices. Since these expenditure items are dissimilar, there is no common workload factor that *directly* affects them all.

---

[17] Teaching salary costs represent a distillation of faculty salary costs following removal of all nonteaching load responsibilities and associated salary reimbursement. Such a refinement is not normally required in State formula budgeting.

In the absence of a dominant single base for measuring workload, several methods can be used to calculate these miscellaneous instructional costs, including previous expenditures, percentage of faculty salaries,[18] and cost per student-credit hour. All are reasonably acceptable, with the percentage of faculty salaries probably preferred. Different percentages should be allowed different types of institutions; at the same time, comparability among like institutions should be maintained.

Essentially all formulas for estimating total yearly faculty salary expenditures attempt to derive a *unit* cost of instruction which, in turn, is multiplied by the projected student enrollment load to equal total funding requirements.

(2) Faculty salary expenditures = Unit cost of instruction

$$\times \text{Projected student enrollment load}$$

The unit cost of instruction equals the mean faculty salary or compensation for the academic year divided by the student-faculty ratio or some variation thereof.[19] Two alternative units of measurement are available: the full-time equivalent[20] (FTE) number of personnel and student-credit hours[21] (SCH). All measurements represent mean values for a *single* term (semester or quarter). The unit cost formula using the FTE measurement is:

(3) $$\frac{\text{Mean salary per FTE faculty per term}}{\text{FTE student-FTE faculty ratio}} = \text{Mean salary per FTE student per term}$$

$$\frac{\$6{,}000/\text{FTE faculty/semester}}{20 \text{ FTE students/FTE faculty}} = \$300/\text{FTE student/semester}$$

Dividing by the credit-hour load per FTE student results in unit costs on a

---

[18] Faculty and staff group insurance and other fringe benefits should be calculated as a percentage of the *total* payroll for all employees eligible to receive these benefits.

[19] It should be noted that the *total* faculty size can always be easily determined by dividing the projected student enrollment by the student-faculty ratio. Formula budgeting places emphasis on determining unit *costs* as opposed to estimating faculty size per se. Final decisions with regard to faculty size are strictly the prerogative of the institution. However, in making this determination, formulas may be used as a guide.

[20] A full-time-equivalent student (or faculty member) is a uniform unit of measurement that represents the normal academic load (work schedule) carried by one full-time student (or faculty member) during a normal academic year.

[21] A student-credit hour (SCH) represents one student receiving instruction for a period of time for which one hour of credit is granted. The total student-credit hours for a course is determined by multiplying the credit-hour value of the course by the number of students registered in that course. The SCH is generally considered the best measure of *instructional* volume or productivity.

SCH basis:

(4) $\dfrac{\text{Mean salary per FTE faculty per term}}{\underset{\text{FTE faculty ratio}}{\text{FTE student-}} \times \underset{\text{per FTE student per term}}{\text{Credit-hour load}}} = \text{Mean salary per SCH}$

$$\dfrac{\$6{,}000/\text{FTE faculty/semester}}{20 \text{ FTE students/FTE faculty} \times 15 \text{ SCH/FTE student/semester}} = \$20/\text{SCH}$$

The student-faculty ratio may be defined in terms of class size, faculty teaching load in credit hours (CH)[22], and student credit-hour (SCH) load as follows:

(5) FTE student-FTE faculty ratio = mean class size $\times \dfrac{\begin{array}{c}\text{Credit-hour teaching load}\\ \text{per FTE faculty per term}\end{array}}{\begin{array}{c}\text{Credit-hour load per FTE}\\ \text{student per term}\end{array}}$

$$20 \text{ FTE students/FTE faculty} = 30 \text{ students} \times \dfrac{10 \text{ CH/FTE faculty/semester}}{15 \text{ SCH/FTE student/semester}}$$

Substituting the definition for the student-faculty ratio in formula (4) results in a variation in the method of computing unit salary costs on a SCH basis:

(6) $\dfrac{\text{Mean salary per FTE faculty per term}}{\text{Mean class size} \times \text{Credit-hour load per FTE faculty per term}} = \text{Mean salary per SCH}$

$$\dfrac{\$6{,}000/\text{FTE faculty/semester}}{30 \text{ students} \times 10 \text{ CH/FTE faculty/semester}} = \$20/\text{SCH}$$

Since the product of mean class size and faculty credit-hour load equals the average number of student-credit hours produced per FTE faculty, it may be considered as a unit teaching *productivity* measure.

Unit instructional costs are governed by both mean faculty salary and student-faculty ratio. The student-faculty ratio, in turn, is dependent upon

---

[22] For formula budgeting purposes, the number of credit hours (CH) of instruction per term is generally recognized as a suitable measure of *teaching* load. It should be remembered that actual classroom teaching encompasses only a part of a faculty member's responsibilities. A more accurate measurement of *teaching* workload takes into consideration the differences in preparation time required for various types of instruction but does not include as an element of faculty workload the credit value given the *student*. For State budgeting purposes, however, these refinements are deemed unnecessary for gross funding allocation purposes and, because they add to processing costs and are likely to restrict institutional control over instructional practices, they may even prove to be undesirable.

class size, faculty teaching load, and student-credit-hour load. The student credit-hour load is an exogenous factor primarily related to academic level: A normal undergraduate load is generally considered to be 15 SCH, master's level 12 SCH, and doctoral level 8 SCH. Thus there are only three variables that an institution can control to influence instructional costs: *mean faculty salary*, *class size*, and *faculty teaching load*. (These three components are discussed separately in succeeding sections.)

As previously stated, *total* salary requirements for the academic year are obtained by multiplying the unit costs of instruction by the projected student enrollment load, either in terms of FTE students or SCH (see formula 2). (See appendix A for enrollment projection methods.) The concept of the FTE student is used because it is widely accepted and can be easily visualized. FTE students may be converted to SCH simply by multiplying the number of FTE students by the mean SCH load per FTE student for 1 academic year—usually 30 semester credit hours or 45 quarter credit hours. Estimating future enrollment levels is highly susceptible to error; therefore, it should be made with great care.

Recommended Student-Faculty Ratio Formula

Within a State system of higher education the formula approach to estimating faculty funding requirements usually determines only the *total* sum of money required to finance faculty salaries for each member institution. The formula is not intended to determine either the manner in which each institution will expend the appropriated funds or establish a faculty staffing pattern. Flexibility and innovation in faculty staffing and program operation must be preserved and encouraged by permitting each institution to exert full discretionary power to modify salaries, load factors, and academic emphasis according to its particular vested interests. Formulas which, because of their complexity and specificity, tend to inhibit institutional flexibility in instructional practices should be avoided. In their place simplified less restrictive formulas should be substituted—even at the risk of a loss in sensitivity and accuracy.

In view of the primary objective of determining adequate funding levels and achieving equitable distribution of funds among institutions, it is recommended that the detail employed in formula budgeting be limited to identifying unit costs simply as the ratio of average faculty salaries to the student-faculty ratio on a full-time-equivalent count basis (see formulas 3 and 4). Since there are legitimate variations in the instructional practices that determine faculty load and, more specifically, teaching load, no single, concise definition or measurement of load is feasible for formula budgeting purposes. On the other hand, for State budgeting purposes the FTE faculty concept is feasible because it does not require a *standardized* expectation regarding the *composition* of faculty workload, only the equating of *total* workloads on a full-time faculty basis without specifically stipulating either average class sizes or faculty workload mix.

What can be determined with reasonable accuracy are inputs of time and cost due primarily (if not exclusively) to either teaching or research. For purposes of unit costs and faculty workload study *within* the institution, this determination is not only desirable but, if teaching loads and opportunities for research are to be correctly balanced, it may be necessary. As a general rule, however, statewide formula budgeting does not require separate allocations for the variety of functions performed by the faculty. Furthermore, detailed specification of teaching loads should be avoided in formula budgeting because it tends to have an inhibiting influence on those member institutions that are inclined to feel compelled to "follow the formula" rather than to tailor their academic program according to their own needs. For example, an institution may decide that it does not have the discretionary power to reduce the formula teaching workload factors and compensate for the difference by increasing class size or reducing faculty salaries.

If an accurate distinction is to be made between the instructional funding requirements among institutions, student-faculty ratios and faculty salaries must be determined *separately* for *each* academic department or college as well as for each instructional level. Composite funding requirements for the institution as a whole can then be determined by totaling departmental needs.

It has been established that average class size and faculty salary, and, to a lesser extent, average faculty teaching load vary significantly by academic program (see table XIV-1) and by level of instruction.[23] To the extent that this variance is caused by legitimate differences in functional aims and instructional requirements, it must be accounted for by distinctive student-faculty ratios. At the very minimum, separate student-faculty ratios (and also faculty salaries) should be established for the five levels of instruction—undergraduate lower division, undergraduate upper division, master's level, doctoral level, and professional level—and for those academic programs in which the instructional methods, research activities, and salary

---

[23] The effect of level of instruction on unit instructional costs is illustrated by a cost study at the University of Michigan. For all schools and colleges, instructional salary costs per student-credit hour by level of students taught were: freshman and sophomore, $12.29; junior and senior, $17.59; graduate M.A. level, $29.00; graduate Ph.D. level, $45.11; and graduate professional level, $25.22. (A student-credit hour represents one student taking a 1 credit course for one term.) Only those salary costs paid for actual time spent in teaching were included. The increased unit costs at higher levels of instruction are due to smaller class sizes and the use of more senior staff members (who earn higher salaries) as teachers. See Paul F. Mertins and Lowell D. Thomas, *Student Credit Hours and Direct Costs in the Schools and Colleges, Fall Term 1966–67*, Office of Institutional Research, University of Michigan, Ann Arbor, March 1967, appendix, p. 2.

Table XIV-1.—University and 4-year-college teaching loads, class sizes, faculty productivity, faculty salaries, and unit costs by principal teaching area

Principal teaching area	Teaching load	Mean class size	Faculty productivity	Teaching faculty salary	Unit cost
	Mean credit hours per faculty primarily teaching		Student credit hours per teaching faculty col. (1)×col. (2)	Academic year mean contract salary	Instructional salary cost per semester credit hr. col. (4) / col. (3)×2
	(1)	(2)	(3)	(4)	(5)
Agriculture and related fields	8	25.9	207	$ 8,475	$20.5
Biological sciences	9	48.7	438	8,685	9.9
Business & commerce	11	28.1	309	8,574	13.9
Education & related fields	11	26.2	288	8,301	14.4
Engineering	8	25.5	204	9,207	22.6
English & journalism	11	27.0	297	7,619	12.8
Fine arts	13	20.5	267	7,549	14.1
Foreign languages & literature	12	19.0	228	7,995	17.5
Health fields	7	45.4	318	7,789	12.2
Home economics	11	22.6	249	7,162	14.4
Law	7	51.4	360	12,914	17.9
Mathematics	11	22.1	243	8,378	17.2
Philosophy	11	31.9	351	8,738	12.4
Physical & health education	11	43.1	474	7,227	7.6
Physical sciences	9	38.3	345	9,213	13.4
Psychology	9	37.0	333	8,994	13.5
Religion & theology	11	35.7	393	7,905	10.1
Social sciences	11	32.5	357	8,546	12.0
All other fields	10	40.8	408	8,704	10.7

Source: Ralph E. Dunham, Patricia S. Wright, and Marjorie O. Chandler, *Teaching Faculty in Universities and Four-Year Colleges, Spring 1963,* U.S. Department of Health, Education, and Welfare, Office of Education, U.S. Government Printing Office, Washington, D.C., 1966.

schedules are sufficiently distinctive to warrant independent treatment. When a public educational system includes a large number of State universities and 4-year colleges that are diverse in function and program, a detailed breakdown by program is usually necessary. The degree of detail generally required is illustrated by the formula devised for the Texas College and University system (see table XIV-2).

In the field of student-faculty ratios, it may never be possible to establish objective "engineered" standards. Yet for budgeting purposes reasonable

Table XIV-2.—Texas recommended formula values for student-faculty ratios, faculty salaries, and unit salary cost rates, by program and level, for universities and 4-year colleges: Fiscal year 1971–72

Program	Undergraduate level			Master's level			Doctoral level		
	Ratio	Salary	Rate	Ratio	Salary	Rate	Ratio	Salary	Rate
Liberal arts	24:1	$12,200	$16.94	13:1	$14,200	$45.51	6:1	$18,000	$166.67
Science	23:1	12,500	18.12	8:1	15,400	80.21	5:1	21,600	240.00
Fine arts	12:1	11,800	32.78	8:1	14,000	72.92	4:1	17,400	241.67
Teacher education	24:1	11,400	15.83	15:1	13,600	37.78	7:1	18,000	142.86
Teacher education and practice teaching	11:1	11,600	35.15						
Agriculture	17:1	12,000	23.53	9:1	14,200	65.74	5:1	19,000	211.11
Engineering	15:1	13,400	29.78	8:1	15,800	82.29	5:1	21,600	240.00
Home economics	17:1	11,400	22.35	11:1	13,800	52.27	6:1	17,000	157.41
Law							30:1[1]	21,000[1]	29.17[1]
Social service	17:1	12,800	25.10	8:1	14,400	75.00			
Library science	21:1	11,200	17.78	11:1	14,000	53.03			
Veterinary medicine									290.32 / 74.73[1]
Vocational training	20:1	10,000	16.67						
Physical training	22:1	10,600	16.06						
Nursing	8:1	11,000	45.83	7:1	12,200	72.62			

	Student-faculty ratio	Average faculty salary	Unit salary cost rates	Student-faculty ratio	Average faculty salary	Unit salary cost rates	Student-faculty ratio	Average faculty salary	Unit salary cost rates
Pharmacy..............	14:1	12,200	29.05	8:1	14,200	73.96	4:1	17,400	241.67
Business administration..	24:1	13,000	18.06	13:1	15,600	50.00	5:1	20,600	228.89
Optometry.............									40.53[1]
Technology............	15:1	11,100	24.67						
Architecture..........	11:1	12,400	37.58	7:1	15,200	90.48			

Note.—Unit salary cost rates = $\dfrac{\text{Student-faculty ratio} \times \text{FTE student credit-hr. load for 9 months}}{\text{(per semester credit hr.)}}$ Faculty includes all academic ranks (instructor through professor) and teaching assistants. Total semester credit hours for the calendar year *times* the above rates equals dollar-funding requirements for departmental faculty salaries.

[1] Special professional level.

A full-time-equivalent (FTE) student credit-hr. load for a 9-month session is defined as (1) 30 semester credit hrs. at the undergraduate level; (2) 24 semester credit hrs. at the master's level; (3) 18 semester credit hrs. at the doctoral level; and (4) 24 semester credit hrs. for law.

Source: Texas Faculty Salaries Formula Study Committee, "Proposed Faculty Salaries Formula for Fiscal 1971–72 and Fiscal 1972–73" (memorandum), Coordinating Board, Texas College and University System, Austin, Nov. 21, 1969, annex A.

standards may be developed through joint study by similar academic departments. Atypical situations must be excluded, and a conscientious effort made to discover values that reflect those *common* instructional practices which best support the basic functional aims of the discipline involved. Recommended values for the student-faculty ratio must be defensible not only in terms of the efficiency and effectiveness of resulting class sizes but also faculty teaching loads. (State and institutional policies and practices pertaining to class sizes and expected faculty workloads are discussed in the ensuing two sections.)

In concluding this discussion of the student-faculty ratio formula for budgeting faculty salaries, the following advantages may be cited as recommendations for its use:[24]

1. The formula is adequate to determine accurately the total sum of money required to finance faculty salaries, yet sufficiently simple to be adapted to the more flexible requirements of instructional practices.

2. By appropriate use of different student-faculty ratios (operationally defined) to account for legitimate differences in functional aims and instructional practices, the formula becomes sensitive to shifts in enrollment among the various academic disciplines. (It must be noted that projecting student enrollment by departments remains a critical problem).

3. Being simple, the formula is easily understood, which promotes its acceptance and provides for relatively easy and inexpensive administration.

4. Use of a simplified formula precludes combining the resource allocation function with program accountability—two distinctly different functions that should be kept separate. Although program cost and performance information which reflects current functional aims and instructional practices is necessary and vital to the continued modification of formula values, the formula allocation process itself should be directed only toward identifying immediate *future* financial needs. The objective of program accountability is to justify *past* expenditures and hopefully provide cost-benefit information for sophisticated future management decisions.

5. Indirectly, the student-faculty ratio prevents an undue proliferation of courses. If courses are added in disproportion to total enrollment growth, the overall student-faculty ratio can be maintained only if the faculty accept either heavier teaching loads or larger than average class sizes.

Class Size

While the student-faculty ratio is proportional to the product of class size and faculty load, class size is by far the more manageable and variable factor in controlling instructional costs. Variations in student-faculty ratios

---

[24] J. C. Scheuerman (see bibliography) has prepared a precise study of instructional practices and related faculty staffing within the California public higher education system. Included are conclusions regarding the relative merits of faculty staffing formulas at the University of California and at the State Colleges. Much of the content of this section is based on Scheuerman's findings and on discussions with Lanier Cox, chairman of the Texas Faculty Salaries Formula Study Committee.

among departments and institutions are most often due to differences in class sizes, not to differences in faculty teaching loads. The latter tend to follow recognized norms that are fairly consistent within a given instructional level. Increasing class size and decreasing unit salary costs proportionately provide an effective yet relatively painless means of controlling per-pupil expenditures. In addition to lowering unit costs, institutions have been encouraged to increase class sizes because of expanding enrollments and greater faculty involvement in activities other than classroom teaching. Thus, mean class size in colleges and universities has tended to gradually increase, especially at those institutions with burgeoning student bodies.

Three factors influence class size: campus size, number of courses offered, and class sectioning practices. The small campus, with its small enrollment and few really large classrooms, finds it difficult to maintain a high average class size and at the same time provide the necessary breadth of course offerings expected. The combination of low enrollment and standard curriculum requirements means that course offerings per student are high and class size correspondingly low. In contrast to some large institutions, small colleges and universities frequently encourage small-group discussion-oriented instructional practices. Because of this difference in educational philosophy, the legitimacy of lower student-faculty ratio recommendations advanced by the departments of small campuses should be recognized. In preparing final values for budgeting purposes, however, the complexity of cross-classifying student-faculty ratios by institutional size should be avoided if possible.

The larger the number of courses an institution offers, the smaller its class sizes will be. The course spread at upper division levels and its attendant influence on class size is usually greater than at lower division levels. In selecting appropriate student-faculty ratios for formula budgeting, departmental recommendations should be supported with evidence that undue course proliferation has been avoided. As previously stated, a fairly stable student-faculty ratio prevents the addition of courses disproportionate to total enrollment growth by forcing the faculty to accept either heavier teaching loads or higher mean class sizes in order to maintain the existing ratio.

Class sectioning, the most important factor in determining mean class sizes, is governed both by academic and cost considerations and by classroom size limitations. In general, courses must be sectioned in such a manner as 1) to allow students course selectivity (thereby enabling them to avoid conflicts and "second" choices) and 2) to conform to prescribed departmental class size and teaching effectiveness policies. In addition to these academic requirements, the size of classes is a factor to be considered if total operating costs, both capital and instructional, are to be minimized. (Class-scheduling procedures designed to meet these multiple objectives, particularly the one to minimize costs, are discussed in chapter X.)

The student-faculty ratio formula (see formula 3 or 4) has been recommended for statewide budgeting of faculty salaries because it is accurate enough for general allocation purposes yet sufficiently nonspecific with regard to teaching load and class size that it does not restrict institutional flexibility in these areas. Thus class size is *not* a direct part of the recommended formula. Yet both class size and teaching load can be examined if formula 5 is used to calculate various possible student-faculty ratios for use in formula 3 or 4. Class-sectioning practices should first be studied in order to determine the optimum *mix* of class sizes that best serves both the instructional objectives of the department concerned and the teaching efficiency of the faculty. The resulting *mean* class size, along with average teaching load, may then become a factor in calculating a tentative student-faculty ratio. However, it is important to keep in mind that no undue pedagogical significance should be attached to mean class size. Determining mean class size is strictly for purposes of initially estimating trial student-faculty ratios; therefore, it may have little in common with either the finally selected ratio or, in the case of a skewed distribution of class sizes, the actual size of most classes.

In general, most departments will find that their functional aims, particularly at the undergraduate level, are best served by a combination of large lecture classes and small discussion sections.[25] Intermediate size classes, often required because of classroom size limitations or minimal course enrollments, are suspect since they discourage discussion and do not maximize the cost advantages of large lecture classes. In a recent review of studies concerning the effect of class size on teaching and learning effectiveness, Wilbert J. McKeachie reached the following conclusions:

> It is commonplace to suggest that the effect of class size depends upon the method used, and it is probably true that the size of the group is less critical for [the] success of [a] lecture, for example, than for that of discussion. Moreover, class size interacts with student characteristics; i.e., small classes are educationally more important for some students than for others. But most important, our analysis of research suggests that the importance of size depends upon educational goals. In general, large classes are simply not as effective as small classes for retention of knowledge, critical thinking, and attitude change.[26]

Support for large classes is based primarily on their economy and on evidence that they maximize a good lecturer's effectiveness in transmitting knowledge, enthusiasm, and an appreciation of the subject matter to students. Empirical research suggests that class size is a minor factor if

---

[25] A class of 10 students is probably sufficiently small to satisfy advocates of close teacher-student relationships. Groups smaller than this should be considered uneconomical.

[26] Wilbert J. McKeachie, "New Developments in Teaching," unpublished paper.

Table XIV-3.—Formula calculations to determine the number of sections in a multisection course

Number of student (S) registrations	Section size policy (P)	Result of calculations (N unmodified)	Number of sections (N)	Average section size High	Average section size Low	Cost per student[1]
10	20	0.95	1		10	$300
15	20	1.20	1		15	200
25	20	1.70	1		25	120
30	20	1.95	1	30.0		100
31	20	2.00	2		15.5	194
50	20	2.95	2	25.0		120
51	20	3.00	3		17.0	176
70	20	3.95	3	23.3		129
71	20	4.00	4		17.8	169
90	20	4.95	4	22.5		133
91	20	5.00	5		18.2	165
110	20	5.95	5	22.0		136
111	20	6.00	6		18.5	162
130	20	6.95	6	21.7		138
131	20	7.00	7		18.7	160
150	20	7.95	7	21.4		140
151	20	8.00	8		18.9	159
170	20	8.95	8	21.3		141
171	20	9.00	9		19.0	158
190	20	9.95	9	21.1		142
191	20	10.00	10		19.1	157
210	20	10.95	10	21.0		143

Formula:

$$\frac{S - 1 + P/2}{P} = N \text{ (whole number only, but not less than 1)}$$

When P (section size policy) $= 20$

[1] It is assumed that the original section of the course costs $3,000 and all subsequent sections cost a like amount.

Source: John E. Swanson, Wesley Arden, and Homer E. Still, Jr., *Financial Analysis of Current Operations of Colleges and Universities*, Institute of Public Administration, University of Michigan, Ann Arbor, 1966, p. 83.

teaching-learning effectiveness is measured in terms of student examination scores (immediate recall) and retention of knowledge for 1 to 2 years.[27] Thus large classes, as a rule, are useful when high rates of information transmission are desired, when small classes are not essential to further educational goals, and when economy is a decisive factor.

The sectioning of courses according to a given class size policy can be accomplished most precisely by the following formula—one that maximizes

[27] W. J. McKeachie, "Research in Teaching: The Gap Between Theory and Practice," in *Improving College Teaching: Aid and Impediments*, background papers for participants in the 1966 Annual Meeting, American Council on Education, Washington, D.C., 1966, pp. 30–32.

the degree to which the average actual section size approaches the recommended section size with any given total number of student registrations.[28]

S = Number of *S*tudent registrations
P = Section size *Policy*
N = Number of sections (using the resultant *whole* number only)

$$\frac{S - 1 + \dfrac{P}{2}}{P} = N$$

Application of this formula to an ascending number of student registrations at an institution with a section size policy of 20 students is shown in table XIV-3. Note that the greater the number of sections, the more likely that the average section size will approximate 20. It is also important to recognize the tremendous reduction in unit cost that occurs when the first section is filled.

Useful class size recommendations are provided in the California State College Faculty Staffing Formula. A "limit" that class size should not exceed is given for each method of instruction; also, a "breaking point" at which, if exceeded by course registrations, a second section will need to be formed. Some suggested sizes are:[29]

	Limit	Breaking point
Classes meeting 1 hour for 1 unit of credit		
Large lecture (for all subjects)	unlimited	
Lecture-discussion (all subjects)	40	50
Lecture (composition and counseling classes, law case study)	30	35
General instruction	25	30
Undergraduate seminars, graduate discussion	20	25
Graduate seminars and honors	15	20
Classes meeting 2 hours for 1 unit of credit		
Art, anthropology, or science activities	24	
Education workshops, science demonstrations	30	35
Physical education or recreation activity	30	40
Speech, drama, and journalism activities	20	25
Remedial instruction	15	20
Laboratories in art, foreign languages, home economics, industrial arts, etc.	physical facilities	
Laboratories in science, psychology, engineering, etc	physical facilities	

---

[28] John E. Swanson, Wesley Arden, and Homer E. Still, Jr., *Financial Analysis of Current Operations of Colleges and Universities*, Institute of Public Administration, University of Michigan, Ann Arbor, 1966, p. 82.

[29] California Coordinating Council for Higher Education, *Instructional Practices and Related Faculty Staffing in California Higher Education*, op. cit., pp. E1-E14.

Classes meeting 3 hours for 1 unit of credit

Coaching intercollegiate sports	20	20
Production courses or workshops in art, drama, journalism, music, debate.	20	20
Major performance group in music	40	50

Faculty Workload

The two fundamental components of unit instructional costs are mean faculty salary and the student-faculty ratio (see formula 3). Inherent in both is the expected faculty workload. If the formula is to be not only sensitive to institutional differences in program emphasis and academic administration but also sufficiently simple to avoid limiting flexibility and innovation, it requires careful definition. The dilemma of achieving budgeting accuracy while permitting flexibility in instructional practices and in faculty activity has been resolved by defining faculty workload in the broad term of full-time-equivalent (FTE) *faculty* as opposed to the more specific measure of expected *teaching* workload.

The total workload of the faculty consists of teaching, preparation for teaching, professional development, research, and service to students, the institution, and the public. A 1963 national study[30] has shown that the "average" faculty member at a university and/or 4-year college spends about half of his 52-hour work week in scheduled instruction and related duties. A breakdown of his time is as follows: an average of 11 hours in the classroom; 6 hours in individual student conferences and administrative tasks; approximately 12 hours in research; about 7 hours in professional activities not related to his faculty position; and the balance in various other activities connected with his position. The university faculty member, because of his greater involvement in research, usually devotes a smaller proportion of time to classroom teaching and related preparation duties than does a 4-year or 2-year college faculty member. It has also been observed that there is a tendency to reduce load requirements for higher ranking faculty and that the larger the institution, the more likely that the classroom teaching load will be smaller.

While there may be more or less generally recognized norms with regard to expected faculty workload, department by department within a given institution, there is no simple description or formula that can make allowances for the many variables involved. Within most colleges, computation

---

[30] Ralph E. Dunham, Patricia S. Wright, and Marjorie O. Chandler, *Teaching Faculty in Universities and Four-Year Colleges, Spring 1963*, U.S. Department of Health, Education, and Welfare, Office of Education, U.S. Government Printing Office, Washington, D.C. 1966, p. 36.

of any of the various quantitative measures of workload will reveal that striking differences exist as to the amount of work among members of the faculty and among departments. In effect, each department, school, or college has its own educational approach designed to achieve its particular instructional objectives. How the faculty is deployed to achieve these objectives must necessarily vary with objectives and curriculum.

Since faculty salary formulas are normally used to estimate *total* salary funding requirements and to distribute monetary amounts equitably among institutions, detail other than that necessary to perform this basic allocation function is unwarranted, particularly if it tends to restrict flexibility in instructional practices. The probability that optimum faculty workload varies with the individual instructor, the department, and the institution makes the fixing of absolute standards impractical and unrealistic.[31] For these reasons, it is neither feasible nor desirable to define faculty workload rigorously for purposes of State formula budgeting.

It seems probable that the best concept of faculty workload for formula budgeting purposes is the full-time-equivalent faculty concept, inherent in the student-faculty ratio, that defines the workload in terms of any combination of activities that adds up to the total work output normally expected of a faculty member employed full time at his job.

In most colleges faculty members are customarily employed with the understanding that service to the institution demands their full time. When the condition of full-time service is met by faculty members, when teaching and other tasks are equitably assigned, and when the overall deployment of faculty achieves desired educational objectives, the number of full-time-equivalent faculty members represents an accurate and useful measure of faculty input for formula budgeting purposes. It follows that the computation of the student-faculty ratio for any given department is simply a process of enumerating full-time equivalents. As previously stated, different teaching approaches as well as mix of students and courses will necessarily result in a legitimate variation in student-faculty ratios by department and level of instruction. It remains for institutions and faculties to develop their own realistic defensible ratios.

The student-faculty ratio formula (see formula 3 or 4) has been chosen for budgeting purposes because it *does not* specify either class size or faculty *teaching* load; nevertheless, in deriving *tentative* ratios, both factors should be examined (using formula 5). Any attempt to define a standard teaching load must take into account differences in the amount of preparation time required not only for various instructional methods but also for subject

---

[31] This view is confirmed by a survey of faculty workload policies and practices across the country. See California Coordinating Council for Higher Education, *Annual Report on Faculty Salaries and Benefits at the California State Colleges and the University*, Sacramento, Dec. 2–3, 1968, pp. 36–37 and appendix D.

matter, as well as differences between the credit-hours assigned to a course and the clock-hours of teaching time involved. If teaching assignments are to be equitable in terms of actual "time on the job," an adjustment must be made for inconsistencies in these factors on a course-by-course basis. The California State Colleges Faculty Staffing Formula includes such a procedure—one which weights course credits to establish equivalency in terms of clock-hours for both preparation and teaching time.[32]

The CCHE formula is based on a 40–45-hour week converted to the equivalent of a 15-unit assignment as follows: 3 unit equivalents (4 to 9 hours a week) for nonteaching assignments normally expected of instructors (college service, student program advising, committee work, administrative duties, extracurricular responsibilities, etc.) and 12 unit equivalents (36 hours a week) of teaching.

Using a "K-Factor" (constant multiplier), the 36 hours a week represented in a 12-unit teaching load are computed for the various types of instruction as follows:

(a) For lecture or discussion-type instruction that requires 1 hour of class time a week for 1 unit of credit: 12 hours a week in the classroom and 24 hours for class preparation, conferences with students, reading student papers, preparing and grading examinations, etc. This allocation is based on the fact that a college teacher normally spends at least 2 hours in supportive work for every hour in class. The 12-credit unit multiplied by the K-Factor of 1 is the equivalent of 12 teaching units.

(b) For activity-type instruction that requires 2 hours of class time a week for 1 unit of student credit: 18 hours in class for every 9 units of student credit and 18 hours out of class checking equipment, instruments, costumes, etc.; guiding and evaluating projects; arranging performances; and conferring with students. The 9-credit unit multiplied by the K-Factor of 1.3 is the equivalent of 12 teaching units.

(c) For science laboratory instruction that requires 3 hours of class time a week for 1 unit of credit: 18 hours in the laboratory for every 6 units of credit and 18 hours for preparation, assembling specimens, setting up and dismantling apparatus, organizing field trips, checking and grading experiments or reports, and conferring with students. The 6-credit unit multiplied by the K-Factor of 2 is the equivalent of 12 teaching units.

(d) For other specialized laboratory instruction (home economics, industrial arts, etc.) that requires 3 hours of class time a week for 1 unit of credit: 24 hours in the laboratory for every 8 units of student credit and 12 hours for outside preparation, student conferences, etc. The 8-credit unit multiplied by the K-Factor of 1.5 is the equivalent of 12 teaching units.

(e) For major sports the amount of coaching time is high when compared to actual units of student credit allowed for the activity. Since State colleges deem coaching of major team-sports and student participation in them essential to the training of physical education teachers, the athletic program is considered a legitimate instructional task. The coach of a major team-sport will spend at least 24 hours a week on

---

[32] California Coordinating Council for Higher Education, *Instructional Practices and Related Faculty Staffing in California Higher Education*, op. cit., pp. E1–E14.

the field or in the gymnasium directing activity for each 2 units of credit and a minimum of 12 hours a week, averaged for the year, in preparation, student contacts, public appearances, and supportive activities. The 2-credit unit multiplied by the K-Factor of 6 is the equivalent of 12 teaching units.

(f) For coaching minor sports and group-performance activities, the coach or instructor will spend at least 24 hours a week directing the sport or activity for each 4 credit units of student credit and at least 12 hours a week in preparation and supportive activities. The 4-credit unit multiplied by the K-Factor of 3 is the equivalent of 12 teaching units.

Instructional Costs and Related Normative Data

The three components of the recommended student-faculty ratio formula—the student-faculty ratio, average faculty salary (compensation), and the combination of these two to equal a unit cost (faculty salary per student)—are the measurements most commonly used by institutions to compare instructional cost factors. While a great many limitations and precautions[33] are involved in the use of these measurements, acceptable comparability of data is usually obtained if comparisons are limited to a peer group of institutions with similar academic programs, objectives, and enrollments.

Actually, instructional costs can be strictly compared only on a *departmental* basis at the same instructional level at institutions of the same type, control, and size. However, differences in institutional *average* instructional costs can be significant, and when they are, may require some explanation or justification—provided the institutions being compared are sufficiently similar. Any study of apparent differences in the relative costs of providing similar programs and services is usually of some value, even if only to support the continuation of existing policy. Such study can also suggest possible goals and benchmarks for measuring progress and indicate recent trends, all of which provide perspective for the reappraisal of policy.

The American Association of University Professors is an excellent source to consult on the matter of instructional costs and related normative data. AAUP findings on the student-faculty ratio, average compensation for full-time faculty, and full-time faculty compensation per student-equivalent for public institutions classified as universities, 4-year colleges, and 2-year colleges, for 1967–68, are presented in figures XIV-1, XIV-2, and XIV-3.

---

[33] One of the most serious limitations is the inaccuracy of basic data—the result of a lack of uniformity in definitions and procedures and in the care exercised in data collection and computation.

Figure XIV-1. — Student-faculty ratio, average compensation full-time faculty, and full-time faculty compensation per student equivalent, public universities: 1967-68

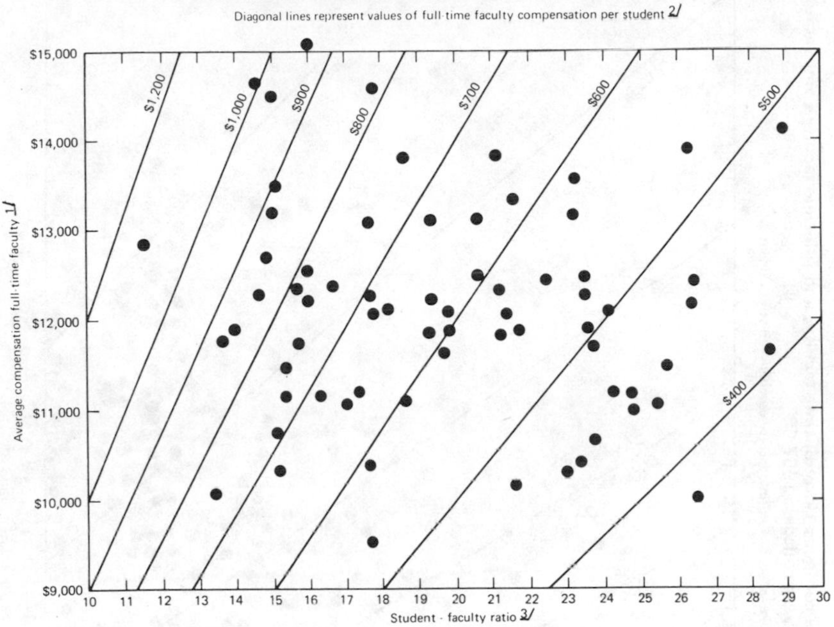

Diagonal lines represent values of full-time faculty compensation per student 2/

Source: William J. Baumol and Peggy Heim, On the Financial Prospects for Higher Education: Annual Report of Committee Z, 1967-68, appendix I and II, American Association of University Professors, Washington, D.C., 1968.

1/For all academic ranks (instructor through professor), average compensation for full-time faculty includes both salaries (adjusted to 9-month basis, when necessary) and countable fringe benifits for 1967-68. Fringe benefits, in general, include only those for which the institution makes a payment of a specified amount on behalf of and for the benefit of the individual faculty member.

2/Full-time faculty compensation per student equivalent was determined by dividing the total outlay for full-time faculty compensation by the number of full-time student equivalents. AAUP warns: "Because of the diversity of situations no attempt has been made to standardize the concept of 'full-time student equivalent'; each institution has applied its own definition. In view of the diversity of standards for full-time student equivalents and the great variety in the types and functions of the institutions included in the tabulations, extreme caution should be used in making comparisons."

3/The student-faculty ratio, not reported in the AAUP report, was derived by dividing the average compensation full-time faculty by the full-time faculty compensation per student.

Figure XIV-2. — Student-faculty ratio, average compensation full-time faculty, and full-time faculty compensation per student equivalent, public 4-year colleges: 1967-68

Diagonal lines represent values of full-time faculty compensation per student 2/

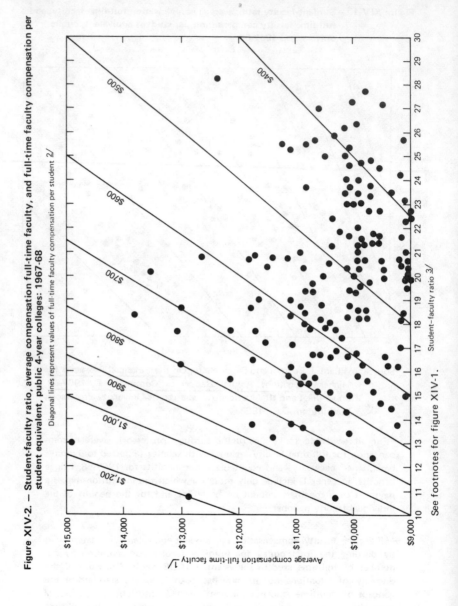

See footnotes for figure XIV-1.

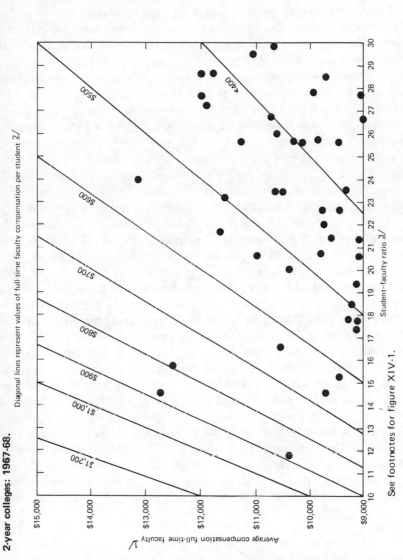

Figure XIV-3. — Student-faculty ratio, average compensation full-time faculty, and full-time faculty compensation per student equivalent, public 2-year colleges: 1967-68.

FORMULATING ADMINISTRATIVE BUDGETARY REQUIREMENTS

The vast range of funding levels for administrative operations gives little evidence that objective procedures are being used to budget this major function. The common methods of comparing administrative and general expense funding levels are on a per student basis, as a percentage of total educational and general expenditures, or as a percentage of instructional costs. Because of the spurious relationships involved (as will be explained), none of these three methods provides a valid basis for establishing a relative measure for comparison purposes. If this shortcoming is recognized, the methods in question, still widely used, can provide at least some indication of the variability present in funding.[34] For example, the per student and percentage-of-instructional-costs ratios (see tables XIV-4 and XIV-5) show that remarkable variance in funding administrative operations exists even within State averages. At public universities, 4-year colleges, and 2-year colleges in 1966–67 administration and general expenses averaged 25 to 30 percent of instructional costs. The low-high range at universities was 12 to 56 percent; at 4-year colleges, 11 to 53 percent; and at 2-year junior and community colleges, 15 to 58 percent. On a per student basis, the average (in parentheses) and range for universities was ($249), $152 to $882; for 4-year colleges ($217), $94 to $477; and for 2-year institutions ($138), $72 to $410. Similar comparisons on an institutional basis reveal an even greater differential.

Doubtless some of the variation in administration and general expenditures is due to differences in operational efficiency at various institutions. Overstaffing, unduly high salaries, an oversupply of clerical personnel, unproductive office routines, and poor management practices may cause inefficiencies that lead to excessive administrative costs. Yet none of the foregoing is the principal cause of the variability cited. The more likely reasons for the wide range of funding levels are (1) the great diversity in the type of expenditures included within the administration and general expense category that prevents meaningful comparisons of composite totals, even on a unit basis, and (2) the uncertain relationship that enrollment and

---

[34] Of the three measurements, the ratio of administrative expenditures to total educational and general expenditures is deemed the least acceptable for comparison studies. Total educational and general expenditures include expenditures for such activities as organized research, hospitals, agriculture stations, etc.—areas in which emphasis varies greatly among institutions. These expenditures may be so sizable as to distort the total, thereby precluding its use as a meaningful base for comparison. Because instructional expenditures and student enrollments are more stable bases and represent the general magnitude of the *principal* functions of an institution, they serve well in providing relevancy to secondary functions.

instructional costs exert on administrative funding practice—a relationship that precludes either factor from serving as a valid basis for establishing a unit or a relative measurement.

It should be clear that combining expenditures so diverse as the salary of the president's secretary, student counseling expenses, and the cost of commencement exercises leads to highly variable totals. Obviously the first step in designing an objective method of budgeting administrative costs is to specify the major components involved and define each as narrowly as possible. The classification of educational and general expenditures, initially proposed in 1962 by 'the National Committee on the Preparation of a Manual on College and University Business Administration and used since then by most colleges and universities in their accounting procedures, provides the necessary division by function required in formula budgeting. As outlined in the 1968 revised edition of *College and University Business Administration*,[35] three of the four expenditure accounts traditionally considered "administrative" expenses (general administration, student services, and general institutional expenses) represent suitable categories for *separate* formula budgeting. The fourth account within this classification—staff benefits, including expenditures for the welfare of the faculty and staff—is usually budgeted as part of instructional costs.

The *general administration* category, as defined in the manual, includes all expenditures—salaries, office equipment and supplies, and travel—by the general executive and administrative officers serving the institution as a whole. Excluded are expenditures for the library and for the operation and maintenance of the physical plant; also, administrative expenditures directly chargeable to "auxiliary enterprises" and to "organized activities relating to instructional departments." Examples of administrative officers concerned with the institution as a whole are members of the governing board, the president, vice presidents, dean of the faculty, business manager, treasurer, and legal counsel.

Included in the *student services* category are expenditures that benefit the student body as a whole; namely, health services, guidance programs, counseling, the placement bureau, student activities financed from institutional funds, the student employment office, registrar, dean of students, dean of women, and dean of men.

General institutional expenses include all other expenditures for operating the institution as a whole (exclusive of libraries and physical plant operation and maintenance). These include funds allocated to the alumni office, auditing, catalogs and other campus-sponsored publications, commencement exercises, convocations, the college or university press, financial campaigns, general insurance, inauguration ceremonies, the information

---

[35] Van Dyke, ed., op. cit., pp. 232–34.

Table XIV-4.—Selected current fund expenditures by function as a percentage of expenditures for instruction and departmental research, by type of public institution: Fiscal year 1967

	Universities					4-year institutions			2-year institutions		
	Extension & public service	Libraries	Plant maintenance	General administration	Organized research	Libraries	Plant maintenance	General administration	Libraries	Plant maintenance	General administration
	(1)	(2)	(3)	(4)	(5)	(6)	(7)	(8)	(9)	(10)	(11)
States and the District of Columbia	24%	9%	21%	24%	77%	10%	22%	30%	7%	19%	25%
New England											
Connecticut	14%	10%	23%	24%	23%	8%	16%	19%	11%	14%	27%
Maine	34	10	29	50	45	11	23	46	—	—	—
Massachusetts	9	10	45	20	26	8	16	22	11	12	38
New Hampshire	27	11	21	44	56	16	21	35	2	19	31
Rhode Island	6	6	31	25	65	5	13	19	10	23	25
Vermont	19	9	13	18	46	13	24	42	13	25	36
Mideast											
Delaware	26	9%	22%	41%	31%	11%	37%	53%	—%	—%	—%
District of Columbia	—	—	—	—	—	11	18	11	—	—	—
Maryland	15	6	23	13	52	12	28	29	12	17	36
New Jersey	21	8	23	33	58	7	16	22	17	23	46
New York	5	13	22	25	45	10	18	29	7	20	45
Pennsylvania	40	10	21	31	103	15	24	25	10	24	35
Great Lakes											
Illinois	20%	9%	32%	29%	45%	9%	24%	30%	9%	15%	26%
Indiana	21	8	22	28	37	—	—	—	6	15	41

Michigan	15	8	20	19	58	9	22	34	8	22	31
Ohio	32	6	17	23	24	10	28	38	7	22	43
Wisconsin	30	10	21	21	99	7	15	17	5	26	24
Plains											
Iowa	24%	7%	15%	14%	66%	9%	22%	22%	7%	14%	17%
Kansas	20	10	18	18	55	9	21	24	7	19	22
Minnesota	40	8	26	32	99	10	18	20	10	23	20
Missouri	27	8	28	42	50	8	22	30	13	20	54
Nebraska	46	9	21	20	79	10	22	34	5	31	29
North Dakota	21	6	32	19	34	8	32	17	5	26	15
South Dakota	28	7	16	22	38	7	21	31	—	—	—
Southeast											
Alabama	30%	8%	16%	26%	62%	12%	26%	27%	12%	15%	32%
Arkansas	56	6	23	33	94	11	26	40	11	20	23
Florida	16	12	20	26	62	17	27	26	14	17	25
Georgia	24	8	17	36	106	8	16	24	12	19	39
Kentucky	23	8	17	36	53	10	24	32	11	24	56
Louisiana	42	9	28	35	65	9	23	33	—	—	—
Mississippi	59	7	19	30	84	10	19	36	5	30	23
North Carolina	27	6	12	12	62	11	24	21	7	15	25
South Carolina	45	9	28	19	44	6	38	32	6	20	27
Tennessee	36	9	27	30	74	10	14	24	13	14	58
Virginia	34	11	19	20	71	7	19	26	8	21	27
West Virginia	26	6	24	29	48	9	18	31	10	29	34
Southwest											
Arizona	8%	8%	16%	20%	51%	8%	38%	22%	9%	27%	17%
New Mexico	18	9	19	17	109	10	28	28	11	36	49
Oklahoma	21	7	20	22	58	8	21	21	8	22	22
Texas	16	9	19	17	62	10	17	15	8	18	26

Table XIV-4.—Selected current fund expenditures by function as a percentage of expenditures for instruction and departmental research, by type of public institution: Fiscal year 1967—Continued

	Universities					4-year institutions			2-year institutions		
	Extension & public service	Libraries	Plant mainte-nance	General adminis-tration	Organized research	Libraries	Plant mainte-nance	General adminis-tration	Libraries	Plant mainte-nance	General adminis-tration
	(1)	(2)	(3)	(4)	(5)	(6)	(7)	(8)	(9)	(10)	(11)
Rocky Mountain											
Colorado	20%	9%	15%	24%	83%	9%	22%	24%	12%	18%	38%
Idaho	39	9	24	36	72	9	33	37	9	19	29
Montana	18	9	21	19	57	8	30	30	11	30	29
Utah	11	8	25	22	78	7	20	22	9	23	24
Wyoming	20	8	23	33	58	—	—	—	9	19	23
Far West											
Alaska	82%	13%	73%	56%	243%	—%	—%	—%	—%	—%	—%
California	26	13	16	28	253	11	17	20	5	18	16
Hawaii	14	8	12	18	59	—	—	—	—	—	—
Nevada	33	13	38	40	42	—	—	—	—	—	—
Oregon	23	7	11	19	75	10	12	28	8	12	28
Washington	11	9	15	28	71	11	15	31	7	15	18

NOTE.—Substantial errors in these data may have occurred because of inconsistencies in the reporting of related finances and enrollments.

Source: Computed from U.S. Department of Health, Education, and Welfare, Office of Education, *Financial Statistics of Institutions of Higher Education—Current Fund Revenues and Expenditures, 1966-67*, U.S. Government Printing Office, Washington, D.C., 1968.

office, interest on debts incurred, legal fees, receptions, telephone and telegraph, and travel.

The institutional expenses category is in effect a catch-all for any expenditure that cannot appropriately be classified elsewhere. Because of the diversity of these expenditures, it is impossible to establish a common workload measure. When the types of expenditures included within a single category are dissimilar, the appropriate budgeting approach is to appraise funding requests by comparison with actual expenditures in previous years, adjusting for increases in workload, salaries, and price levels. While not strictly a "formula" approach, it can lead to objectivity if user-unit cost or other relative measures are used to establish comparability among institutions. For example, selected student group enrollments and alumni are reasonable measures of user units for such expenditures as convocations, commencement exercises, catalogs, the alumni office, and so on.

As a suitable means for budgeting general administration and student services expenses, the traditional procedure of allocating administrative funds by a given amount per student or as a percentage of instructional costs should be questioned. The great variability among these factors in State averages demonstrates the tenuous relationship that enrollment and instruction costs bear to administration funding. In point of fact, because the relationship between instruction costs and administrative workload is at best spurious, the amount spent for instruction should not be allowed to dictate the budgeting of any aspect of the administrative function, however great may be the temptation to do so. Student enrollment fares little better as a measure of total administrative workload, although for certain types of expenditures (notably salaries) supplemental requirements beyond a basic complement can often be appropriately prorated according to enrollment. The difficulty of establishing the credibility of a given rate for either measure in the face of the mass of conflicting normative data should be sufficient to give any budgeting office pause for thought before adopting such an approach.

Some officials take the position that, since the administrative function is uniquely determined by special circumstances at each institution, its funding can be justified only on an individual case basis. This position is usually advanced by institutions defending their funding requests on the basis of previous expenditure requirements. The basic premise of formula budgeting—to relate accurately relevant costs to realistic load measurements—argues against accepting the expediency of assessing each case on its own merits.

For a number of reasons, a strong argument can be made for using a staffing formula to budget general administration and student services expenses. In both categories, the major share of expenditures is for salaries for services performed. Total salary requirements can most accurately be estimated by applying projected salary rates to a prepared staffing schedule

Table XIV-5.—Selected current fund expenditures per FTE student, by type of public institution: Fiscal year 1967

	Universities						4-year institutions				2-year institutions			
	Instruction and dept. research	Extension and public service	Libraries	Plant maintenance	General administration	Organized research	Instruction and dept. research	Libraries	Plant maintenance	General administration	Instruction and dept. research	Libraries	Plant maintenance	General administration
	(1)	(2)	(3)	(4)	(5)	(6)	(7)	(8)	(9)	(10)	(11)	(12)	(13)	(14)
States and D.C.	$1037	248	93	218	249	798	725	72	159	217	522	37	99	130
New England														
Connecticut	1041	146	104	239	250	239	529	42	85	101	418	46	59	113
Maine	605	206	60	175	302	272	667	73	107	127	—	—	—	—
Massachusetts	1193	107	119	537	239	310	558	45	89	123	326	36	39	124
New Hampshire	776	210	85	163	341	435	480	77	101	168	—	—	—	—
Rhode Island	800	248	48	248	200	520	1180	59	153	224	483	63	121	174
Vermont	1581	300	142	206	285	727	611	79	146	257	—	—	—	—
Mideast														
Delaware	857	223	77	189	351	266	900	99	333	477	—	—	—	—
Dist. of Col.	0	—	—	—	—	—	1019	102	183	112	—	—	—	—
Maryland	1145	172	69	263	378	664	785	94	220	228	516	88	119	237
New Jersey	1154	242	92	265	381	669	780	55	125	172	483	82	111	222
New York	1486	74	178	327	371	669	1060	11	191	307	670	47	134	301
Pennsylvania	1076	430	108	226	334	1108	607	91	146	152	689	69	165	241
Great Lakes														
Illinois	1217	243	110	389	340	548	822	74	197	247	459	41	69	119
Indiana	1037	218	83	228	290	384	—	—	—	—	504	30	76	131
Michigan	1237	186	99	247	235	717	700	63	154	238	517	41	114	160

Ohio	894	286	54	152	206	215	824	82	190	264	507	35	112	218
Wisconsin	1112	334	111	234	234	1101	785	55	118	133	551	28	143	132
Plains														
Iowa	1203	289	34	180	168	794	816	73	180	180	484	34	68	82
Kansas	845	169	84	152	152	465	638	57	134	153	402	28	76	88
Minnesota	697	279	56	181	223	690	345	54	98	109	429	43	99	86
Missouri	817	221	65	229	343	408	545	44	120	163	429	56	86	232
Nebraska	780	358	70	164	156	616	540	54	119	184	490	24	152	142
North Dakota	907	825	54	290	172	308	596	48	191	101	745	37	194	216
South Dakota	840	235	59	134	185	319	652	46	137	202	—	—	—	—
Southeast														
Alabama	1044	313	84	167	271	647	302	60	131	136	432	52	65	138
Arkansas	781	437	47	180	203	484	400	44	104	160	—	—	—	—
Florida	1105	177	133	221	232	685	800	136	216	208	489	68	83	122
Georgia	757	181	61	129	273	802	914	73	146	219	394	47	75	154
Kentucky	1651	380	132	280	594	875	457	46	110	146	303	33	73	170
Louisiana	2520	1058	227	706	882	1638	596	54	137	197	—	—	—	—
Mississippi	782	461	55	149	235	657	524	52	100	173	463	23	139	181
North Carolina	1689	456	101	203	203	1047	624	69	150	206	562	39	84	140
South Carolina	728	328	66	204	138	320	1228	74	467	393	481	29	96	130
Tennessee	838	302	75	226	251	620	550	55	77	132	737	96	103	427
Virginia	951	323	105	181	190	675	750	52	142	195	773	62	162	209
West Virginia	1072	279	64	257	311	515	504	45	91	156	480	48	139	163
Southwest														
Arizona	764	61	61	122	153	390	602	48	229	132	423	38	114	72
New Mexico	870	157	78	165	148	948	637	64	178	178	837	92	301	410
Oklahoma	747	157	52	149	164	433	449	36	94	94	380	30	84	84
Texas	934	149	84	177	159	579	531	53	90	80	451	36	81	117

Table XIV-5.—Selected current fund expenditures per FTE student, by type of public institution: Fiscal year 1967—Continued

	Universities						4-year institutions				2-year institutions			
	Instruction and dept. research	Extension and public service	Libraries	Plant maintenance	General administration	Organized research	Instruction and dept. research	Libraries	Plant maintenance	General administration	Instruction and dept. research	Libraries	Plant maintenance	General administration
	(1)	(2)	(3)	(4)	(5)	(6)	(7)	(8)	(9)	(10)	(11)	(12)	(13)	(14)
Rocky Mountain														
Colorado	813	163	73	122	236	675	589	53	130	159	460	55	83	175
Idaho	755	294	68	181	272	544	525	47	173	194	462	42	88	134
Montana	807	105	73	169	153	460	540	43	162	162	416	46	125	121
Utah	811	89	65	203	178	584	396	28	79	87	528	48	121	127
Wyoming	931	186	74	214	307	540	—	—	—	—	540	49	103	124
Far West														
Alaska	999	819	130	729	559	2428	—	—	—	—	—	—	—	—
California	1272	331	165	204	356	322	913	100	155	183	543	27	98	87
Hawaii	1133	159	91	136	204	668	—	—	—	—	—	—	—	—
Nevada	828	273	108	315	331	348	—	—	—	—	—	—	—	—
Oregon	1242	286	87	137	236	931	698	70	84	195	652	52	78	183
Washington	1490	164	134	223	417	1058	711	78	107	220	500	35	75	90

NOTE.—Substantial errors in these data may have occurred because of inconsistencies in the reporting of related finances and enrollments.

Source: Computed from U.S. Department of Health, Education, and Welfare, Office of Education, *Financial Statistics of Institutions of Higher Education—Current Fund Revenues and Expenditures, 1966–67*, U.S. Government Printing Office, Washington, D.C., 1968.

or to a manning table that identifies the number of positions for each type of job within the administrative organization. Operating expenditures for other than salaries (for travel, office expenses, supplies, etc.) can be added as justified by previous experience. The advantage of using a standard staffing schedule in formula budgeting is that, in the absence of any quantitative means to measure the administrative workload directly, such a schedule accomplishes the same purpose by providing a realistic and defensible projection of salary requirements.

In an effort to achieve economy and efficiency of operation, colleges and universities have over the years sought to refine their internal administrative organization and more clearly delineate the responsibilities of various line and staff members.[36] Because every organization is an expression of underlying philosophical assumptions and viewpoints of management, no organizational pattern equally suitable to all institutions can be established. For the purposes of State budgeting, however, typical designs of internal organization can be developed which, in most cases, will provide a suitable basis for funding. Unusual or exceptional requirements can always be met by honoring special requests without modifying the basic formula.

Some excerpts (table XIV-6) from the staffing standards developed by the California State College system illustrate the general degree of detail required for formula budgeting. Note that in many instances the number of positions is governed by an indirect workload measurement, typically FTE enrollment.

FORMULATING LIBRARY
BUDGETARY REQUIREMENTS

Comparing library operations among colleges and universities reveals little consistency or pattern that might serve as a basis for formula budgeting. Collections number as few as 100 volumes per faculty member to 10 times that number. Expenditures, which commonly range from 4 to 8 percent of the educational and general budget, range from a low of $400

---

[36] See for example: Archie R. Ayers and John H. Russel, *Internal Structure: Organization and Administration of Institutions of Higher Education*, U.S. Department of Health, Education and Welfare, Office of Education, U.S. Government Printing Office, Washington, D.C., 1962; Archie R. Ayers, Philip A. Tripp, and John H. Russel, *Student Services Administration in Higher Education*, U.S. Department of Health, Education and Welfare, Office of Education, U.S. Government Printing Office, Washington, D.C., 1966; and Paul K. Nance, *Business Management in Selected Colleges and Universities*, U.S. Department of Health, Education and Welfare, Office of Education, U.S. Government Printing Office, Washington, D.C., 1966.

Table XIV-6.—California State college system staffing standards

GENERAL ADMINISTRATION—Executive

Classification	Formula, standard, or workload measure
President	1 per college
Vice President, Academic Affairs	1 per college over 850 FTE
Dean of College[1]	1 per college below 850 FTE
Vice President, Business Affairs or General Administration	1 per college over 5,000 FTE
Executive Dean	1 per college
Vocational Instructor (12 months) (Building Program)	Based on individual justification
Publications Manager (academic year or 12 months)	1 per college
Administrative Assistant II (Assistant to President)	1 per college
Administrative Assistant I (Assistants to Vice Presidents)	1 per Vice President (or Dean of College)
Clerical	2 per President (1 secretary and 1 receptionist) 1 per other professional position except Admin. Assist. ⅓ per Admin. Assist.

GENERAL ADMINISTRATION—Business management

Classification	Formula, standard, or workload measure
Business Manager	1 per college
Secretary	1 ″ ″
Accounting Officer	1 ″ ″
Secretary	1 ″ ″
Cashier	1 ″ ″
Personnel Officer	1 ″ ″
Secretary	1 ″ ″
Purchasing Officer	1 ″ ″
Secretary	1 ″ ″
Duplicating services	1 ″ ″
Mail services	1 ″ ″

In addition to this basic complement of positions requiring specialized skills, marginal position requirements can be added in proportion to student enrollment.

See footnotes at end of table.

Table XIV-6.—California State college system staffing standards—Continued

STUDENT SERVICES—Dean's Office

Classification	Formula, standard or workload measure
Dean of Students	1 per college
Counselor (12 months) (Ombudsman)	1 per college
Administrative Assistant	1 per college over 5,000 regular FTE
Secretarial	1 per Dean
Other clerical	1 per Counselor and ⅓ per Admin. Asst.

STUDENT SERVICES—Admissions and Records

Classification	Formula, standard, or workload measure
Associate Dean	1 per college
Registrar	1 per college
Admissions Officer	1 per college over 5,000 regular FTE
Evaluation Tech. I or II	1 per college
Clerical and Technical (including additional Evaluation Technicians)	1 per 400 total individuals[2] 1 per 1,000 limited individuals[2] 1 for each professional position[3]
Clerical for New Admissions Policies	Semester System: .18 positions per 1,000 applications Quarter System: .23 positions per 1,000 applications

STUDENT SERVICES—Counseling and Testing

Classification	Formula, standard, or workload measure	
Associate Dean	1 per college	
Counselor	1 per 1,000 regular individual students over 1,000 (e.g. 1.0 position at 2,000 students)	
	Positions per college	Regular individual students
Test Officer (Class and Rank)	0.5	0– 5,000
	1.0	5,000–10,000
	1.5	10,000–15,000
	2.0	15,000–22,500

See footnotes at end of table.

Table XIV-6.—California State college system staffing standards—Continued

STUDENT SERVICES—Counseling and Testing—Continued

Psychometrist	1 per testing program
Clerical	1 per Dean, and 1 for Test Officers
Other Clerical	⅓ per Counselor

STUDENT SERVICES—Activities and Housing

Classification	Formula, standard, or workload measure
Associate Dean	1 per college

	Positions per college	Regular individual students
Activities Advisor	1.0	0– 5,000
	2.0	5,000–10,000
	3.0	10,000–15,000
	4.0	15,000–20,000

Housing Coordinator (12 months)	0.5–1.0 based on housing program
Secretarial for Associate Dean	1 position
Other Clerical	⅓ per Activities Advisors and Coordinator of Housing positions

STUDENT SERVICES—Placement

Classification	Formula, standard, or workload measure
Placement Officer (12 months)	1 per placement program

	Positions per college	Regular individual students
Placement Interviewer and Supervisor	1	1000 to 3000
	2	3000 to 5000
	3	5000 to 7500
	4	7500 to 10,000
	5	10,000 to 12,500
	6	12,500 to 16,500
	7	16,500 to 20,500

Secretarial for Placement Officer	1 position
Other Clerical	1 per 3500 FTE

See footnotes at end of table.

Table XIV-6.—California State college system staffing standards—Continued

STUDENT SERVICES—Foreign Student Program

Classification	Formula, standard or workload measure
	Positions per individual foreign student
Counselor (12 months)	0.5 less than 100 1.0 100 and above
Counselor	1.0 200 to 399 2.0 400 and above
Intermediate Stenographer	⅓ per Counselor

STUDENT SERVICES—Health Services

Classification	Formula, standard, or workload measure
Medical Officer II or III 1st two positions on 12-month basis	1 per 1,800 regular individual students
Nurse 1st two positions on 12-month basis	1 per 1,800 regular individual students
Technician 1st position on 12-month basis	1 per 4,000 regular individual students
Supervising Clerk	1 per college over 5,000 regular individual students without infirmary 1 per college over 4,000 regular individual students with infirmary
Clerical	1 for first 1,500 regular individual students, 1 additional for next 1,500, and 1 for each additional 2,000 regular individuals beyond 3,000 students
Student Assistant	$.50 for salaries per regular individual

FTE=full-time-equivalent (student enrollment).
1 Can be changed to Vice President, Academic Affairs, after 850 FTE student enrollment is reached, as indicated on line above.
2 Minus positions to be used in data processing.
3 Associate Dean, Registrar, and Admissions Officer.

Source: California State College System, "Budget Notes" (mimeographed), 1969.

to over $1,800 per year per faculty member. Although salaries and wages average 55 percent of total library operating costs, they may be as high as 80 percent. Expenditures for books and other library materials average 37 percent of the library budget but may be half this percentage.

This lack of uniformity stems partly from the fact that the many variables involved in library operations differ widely from institution to institution, not only in their relative importance but also in their susceptibility to measurement; partly from the several different ways in which library needs are determined; and partly from the varying institutional policies that determine the appropriate size and growth rate of the library.

Under these circumstances, to develop a systematic funding approach would require that the intangible components of library operation be identified and treated separately as matters of institutional policy. Once these actions have been taken, standards may be more precisely set in quantitative terms for those library operations closely related to measurable workloads. Because of collection deficiencies and competition for funds, allocations for the acquisition of books and other library materials appear to be predominantly a *policy* decision, irrespective of recommended collection goals and growth rates. On the other hand, library staffing and related administrative expenses can be and are funded by *formula* on the basis of detailed information related to workload, or, less precisely, in proportion to the number of students enrolled.

Separate funding for acquisitions and for staffing is recommended because the normative data can be clearly related to policy (for acquisitions) or to workload (for staffing) and are, therefore, useful for comparative study. Funding *total* library operations according to a fixed percentage of instructional costs or a fixed dollar amount per full-time-equivalent student is discouraged because the high degree of variability of the resulting data precludes any useful comparative analysis. The reason for the variability is that library needs are *not* indicated by the size of the "educational and general" budget, nor does the size of this budget necessarily indicate the institution's ability or intention to pay for library operations. Within institutional type and control groupings, library operational needs are governed principally by the size of the collection and its deficiencies with regard to program commitment, plus the number of faculty and graduate students served. These factors are at best only marginally reflected by the size of the "educational and general" budget. Even when library expenditures are related to the more stable "instructional" budget, the resulting range of ratios among institutions is substantial. State averages by type of public institution are presented in table XIV-4. The data illustrate the variability present and suggest the difficulty of justifying any given percentage.

The one intangible component of library operations that clearly requires funding on the basis of carefully established *policy* is the acquisition of books, periodicals, microfilm, and like materials. The need for judgment stems partly from the multiplicity of controlling factors that cannot be expressed by formula. It has been pointed out by numerous authorities that the adequate size of an academic library depends on the combined effect of a number of variables, the most important being the following: the size, composition, resident status, and intellect of the student body; the size, quality, and research orientation of the faculty; the nature of the curriculum, including the number of fields by degree level; the number and type of professional schools; the methods of instruction related to library use; and the proximity of the campus to other libraries.

Ideally, colleges should establish a basic initial collection and add volumes as the institution grows and changes. (See chapter IX for a discussion of desired collection size.) Unfortunately, most colleges fail to meet even minimum standards. For example, the American Library Association at one time suggested a minimum collection of 50,000 volumes for 4-year institutions with an enrollment of less than 600 full-time-equivalent students and recommended that 10,000 more volumes be added for every additional 200 students. For 2-year institutions, a collection of 20,000 carefully selected volumes was considered minimal for an enrollment up to 1,000 students; for each additional 500 students, 5,000 volumes should be added.[37] In 1962–63, 73 percent of 4-year institutions and 91 percent of 2-year institutions did not meet these standards.[38] Consequently, library funding at most colleges is not simply the task of maintaining an adequate collection proportionate to student enrollment, but rather a problem of determining how quickly the collection can be increased in order to meet minimum operating requirements.

Since most libraries could, with justification, spend much more money for new acquisitions than financial resources allow, the amount spent is a matter of judgment often gauged by the degree to which current holdings are considered deficient in comparison with the practices of competing or comparable institutions. Normative data that may be useful to budget policymakers in judging how much to spend for current acquisitions are presented in figures XIV-4 through XIV-7. While it is impossible to qualify certain important determinants, three measurable criteria have been selected to establish comparability: (1) the type and control of institution, including the importance of graduate programs, (2) the number of full-time-equivalent faculty, and (3) the current size of the collection.

Because of the distinct educational philosophy, purpose, and orientation of each segment of higher education—university, 4-year college, and 2-year college—separate statistical treatment for each segment is essential if comparability is to be obtained. While the size of the undergraduate student body is frequently cited as a primary consideration when the question of library size is raised, evidence suggests that this relationship is a

---

[37] American Library Association, *National Inventory of Library Needs*, Washington, D.C., 1965, p. 50.
[38] Ibid., p. 47.

spurious one. Through a multivariate analysis, Reichard and Orsagh[39] have concluded that the overwhelmingly important variable associated with both the size of the collection and the level of expenditures for college and university libraries is the size of the faculty. Their study also indicated that institutions with expanding graduate programs tend to increase their collections substantially. On the other hand, changes in undergraduate enrollment, without concomitant changes in either faculty or graduate programs, were found to exert little influence.[40] This evidence suggests that faculty size rather than student enrollment should be used as the second criterion for establishing institutional comparability, and, further, that the 4-year institution classification be divided into two categories: institutions with graduate programs and those without such programs. A third variable influencing library acquisition rate is the number of holdings. Through multiple regression analysis, a California survey revealed that of all tested factors related to the annual library growth rate, the most important was the number of volumes held.[41] Correlation coefficients for graduate and undergraduate enrollment were .74 and .73, respectively, compared with .88 for number of volumes held.

Figures XIV-4 through XIV-7, developed from U. S. Office of Education data, represent performance data that permit identification of levels of expenditure for current acquisitions at comparable public institutions with a similar number of faculty members and size of library. By tracing horizontally to the right the number of volumes held and vertically upward the number of FTE faculty members, an area can be identified (at the intersection) that includes comparable expenditure levels. For example, in figure XIV-4 a hypothetical public university with a collection of 700,000 volumes and 1,000 FTE faculty members might identify as possible realistic guidelines, expenditures (in 1968–69) of $402,000, $468,000, $541,000, and $584,000 per year for current acquisitions.

It is evident from the variability of these plottings that appropriate library expenditures are not highly predictable if based on such factors as

---

[39] Edwin W. Reichard and Thomas J. Orsagh, "Holdings and Expenditures of U.S. Academic Libraries: An Evaluative Technique," *College and Research Libraries*, November 1966, pp. 478–87. This article includes a predictive equation that may be useful to budget policy-makers—a process by which a library's response (expenditures for current acquisitions) to changing enrollment and faculty size may be compared to the response of other similar libraries over the course of time. The equation also permits a decision-maker to determine the size of the book collection that would be required if a given library were to attain a particular desired rank among libraries in its own class.

[40] A California State college study, through regression analysis, discovered that the enrollment factor exerts little influence on the number of volumes held by libraries except at private liberal arts colleges. See Committee on Library Development, *Recommendations for the Support of California State College Libraries* (Second Report to the Chancellor), April 1966, p. 5.

[41] Ibid., p. 8.

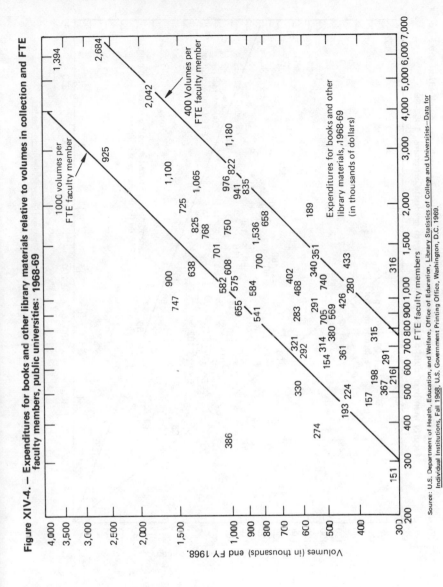

Figure XIV-4. — Expenditures for books and other library materials relative to volumes in collection and FTE faculty members, public universities: 1968-69

Source: U.S. Department of Health, Education, and Welfare, Office of Education, Library Statistics of College and Universities—Data for Individual Institutions, Fall 1968, U.S. Government Printing Office, Washington, D.C. 1969.

Figure XIV-5. — Expenditures for books and other library materials relative to volumes in collection and FTE faculty members, public 4-year institutions with graduate programs: 1968-69

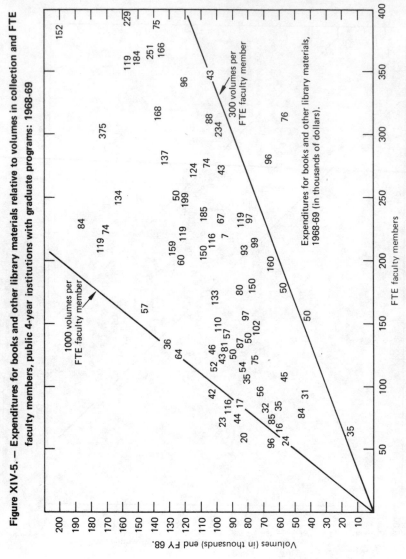

Source: U.S. Department of Health, Education and Welfare, Office of Education, Library Statistics of Colleges and Universities--Data for Individual Institutions, Fall 1968, U.S. Government Printing Office, Washington, D.C., 1969.

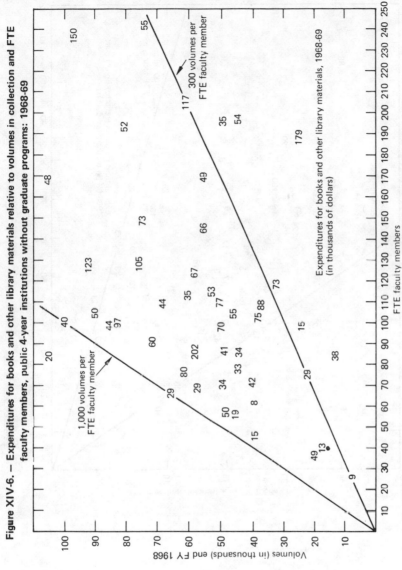

Figure XIV-6. – Expenditures for books and other library materials relative to volumes in collection and FTE faculty members, public 4-year institutions without graduate programs: 1968-69

Volumes (in thousands) end FY 1968

Expenditures for books and other library materials, 1968-69 (in thousands of dollars)

FTE faculty members

1,000 volumes per FTE faculty member

300 volumes per FTE faculty member

Source: U.S. Department of Health, Education, and Welfare, Office of Education, Library Statistics of Colleges and Universities–Data for Individual Institutions, Fall 1968, U.S. Government Printing Office, Washington, D.C., 1969.

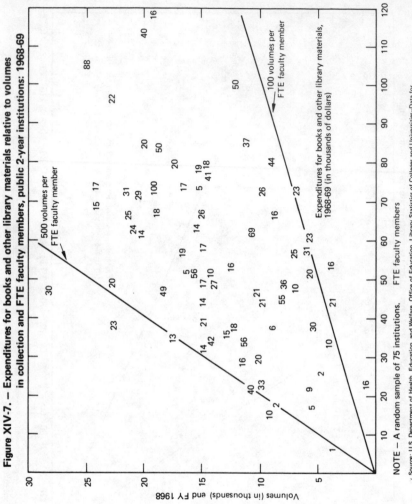

Figure XIV-7. — Expenditures for books and other library materials relative to volumes in collection and FTE faculty members, public 2-year institutions: 1968-69

Volumes (in thousands) end FY 1968

Expenditures for books and other library materials, 1968-69 (in thousands of dollars)

FTE faculty members

500 volumes per FTE faculty member

100 volumes per FTE faculty member

NOTE — A random sample of 75 institutions.

Source: U.S. Department of Health, Education, and Welfare, Office of Education, Library Statistics of Colleges and Universities—Data for Individual Institutions, Fall 1968. U.S. Government Printing Office, Washington, D.C., 1969.

collection size; faculty size; and institutional control, type, and graduate program. The interrelationships are unlikely to be other than complex and elusive. Better predictive means may possibly be developed by further study and by the introduction of new variables. However, for the purpose of providing a quantitative, unambiguous means of comparing the performance at one institution with that at other similar institutions, these figures provide normative data that currently involve the most significant variables. It is recommended that institutions or States searching for relevant normative data of this type prepare similar but up-to-date charts, identifying by name the institutions whose performance appears to offer reasonable guides to realistic library growth rates.

The second major component of library operation, staffing, may be more easily budgeted on a formula basis than can acquisition because workload factors accurately delineating staffing requirements are readily available. By multiple linear regression testing, studies reveal that workload factors have the following correlation coefficients with staff size: graduate students, .84; undergraduate students, .80; number of volumes added, .93; number of volumes held, .91; and number of periodicals received, .89.[42] It is apparent that each of these five factors, if considered separately, is significantly related to staff size. The coefficient of multiple correlation for all five factors (.94) indicates that they account for virtually all workload factors at the *mean* level of staffing. In the case of the *individual* library, the following additional factors influence staff size: the type of organization within the library, the character of the collection, the prevailing teaching methods, the number of hours the library is open, and the physical location within a building. Because there are so many variables, the librarian should be entrusted with the details of organizing and staffing and not be required to follow any set pattern.

While it is unreasonable to expect that all libraries adhere to a uniform staffing pattern, for budgeting purposes there are standard staffing formulas that can ensure funding levels within which most institutions can reasonably develop individualized library programs.[43] Most such formulas are based on the number of volumes acquired each year and the number of students and faculty served. With regard to the latter measurement of load, there is conflicting evidence as to the relative rate of book borrowing by student class levels. In 1940, Harvie Branscomb found that the average number of withdrawals per student progressed evenly from 1.79 among

---

[42] Ibid., p. 12.

[43] The State University of New York, for example, has prepared a library manpower budget formula for its several campuses by developing weighted standard working times for accomplishing library activities in various kinds of institutions and library conditions. See Gilbert W. Fairholm, "Essentials of Library Manpower Budgeting," *College and Research Libraries*, vol. 31, no. 5, September 1970, pp. 332–40.

freshmen to 4.97 among seniors.[44] But in 1962, Patrick Barkey's study revealed almost the reverse: More freshmen were using the library than were students in any other academic level, including graduate students.[45] Needless to say, any weighting of library use by academic level should be based on local studies.

The Committee on Library Development for the California State Colleges makes these recommendations: Staffing should be provided for three basic library functions (technical processing, public service, and administration) at the rate of 1 technical services position per 800 annual acquisitions; 1 public services position per 3,000 FTE students served; and 3 administrative positions for colleges up to 5,000 FTE students, 4 for 5,000–10,000 FTE students, and a maximum of 5 for more than 10,000 FTE students.[46] The results achieved through this staffing formula, while somewhat meager, compare favorably with actual practices. Other operating costs can be computed as a percentage of the combined total of salaries and volumes purchased.

FORMULATING PHYSICAL PLANT OPERATION AND MAINTENANCE BUDGETARY REQUIREMENTS

Campus buildings and grounds are operated and maintained to support the principal campus functions: instruction, research, and community service. Since plant operation and maintenance is a secondary activity involving a relatively small budget, there is a tendency to employ less than rigorous procedures in estimating its funding. This is unfortunate because the mechanical nature of plant operation and maintenance is particularly susceptible to quantitative analysis and comparative study. It is not difficult to determine, with reasonable accuracy, load factors and unit costs for plant operations and derive appropriate cost-estimating formulas by using standards established from time studies and normative data. Such an approach serves as a more accurate basis for estimating maintenance and operation costs than does a formula that estimates the cost of physical plant operations and maintenance simply as a percentage of instructional costs based on precedence.

---

[44] Harvie Branscomb, *Teaching With Books: A Study of College Libraries*, Association of American Colleges, Chicago, 1940, p. 35.

[45] Patrick Barkey, "Patterns of Student Use of a College Library," *College and Research Libraries*, vol. 26, no. 2, March 1965, pp. 115–18.

[46] Committee on Library Development, *Recommendations for the Support of California State College Libraries*, op. cit., p. 11.

This is not to dispute the fact that in a general way all institutional functions are related to enrollment and to the size of the instructional budget. But the specific workload factors that affect plant operations and maintenance are not affected by enrollments in the same way as are, for example, instructional costs. The relationship of instructional costs to enrollment is dependent on faculty salaries and class size, two variables quite unrelated to plant operation and maintenance costs. The latter costs depend strictly on the size of the physical plant and grounds, irrespective of the number of students enrolled.[47] Thus the absurdity of automatically increasing the budget for plant operations and maintenance whenever instructional costs are increased can be easily appreciated. Careful formula budgeting avoids such an oversimplified and erroneous approach.

To obtain precision in estimating expenditure requirements for physical plant operations and maintenance, it is advisable first to identify those component parts that require separate treatment either because of distinctive load factors or special associated costs. Three subdivisions are necessary: (a) custodial services and building maintenance, (b) maintenance of grounds, and (c) utilities. Custodial care is designed to maintain buildings in a clean and comfortable condition; building maintenance includes preventive maintenance, alterations, and emergency repairs and replacements, and also property insurance. The second division, grounds keeping, preserves and upgrades the beauty and functionalism of the campus—the roads and walks, landscaping, snow removal, trash collection, and the like. Utilities include the costs for heat, light, power, and water.

In developing a formula for estimating the cost of custodial services and building maintenance, the basic load factor is the total gross square feet (outside measurement) of all educational, general, and service buildings,[48] with allowances for all factors that determine the amount of service required: age of the buildings; type of construction; and the condition of floors, windows, stairways, equipment and fixtures, roofs, gutters, plumbing, heating systems, etc. Campus buildings may be classified in three or four categories, with a specified cost per square foot based on demonstrated effective staffing patterns and salary and equipment unit costs previously determined and projected. By conducting time studies and load-factor analyses, the number of man-hours required for custodial functions and maintenance of the various types of buildings can be accurately computed.

While there is general agreement that building area most accurately reflects the workload for custodial service, there is less agreement that this

---

[47] Exceptions to this rule are trash collection and security operations, both components of plant operation that are materially affected by total student enrollment.

[48] Inasmuch as auxiliary enterprises should be self-supporting, operation and maintenance of these facilities is usually financed by operating revenues rather than by formula budgeting.

same measure is an equally accurate indicator of workload for building maintenance and repair. Some States estimate the cost of building maintenance by classifying buildings by type of construction, then applying a percentage factor to the estimated building replacement *cost*. This procedure is not only more cumbersome than the one that uses building area, but provides no apparent improvement in validity. Generally, the maintenance task is proportional to the number of existing pipes, faucets, elevators, lights, doors, and other mechanical and electrical equipment and hardware. Items requiring maintenance are usually more closely related to building size than to building cost, since the latter may be greatly dependent on esthetic and architectural factors unrelated to maintenance. It is recommended, therefore, that maintenance cost requirements be estimated simply by multiplying the total number of square feet of building area by a per-square-foot-cost figure derived from past expenditures on buildings of the age and type involved.

There is little to recommend estimating ground maintenance costs as a percentage of building maintenance costs other than the fact that it is a simple procedure. The great variation in ground-to-building area ratios among urban and rural campuses clearly demonstrates the unsuitability of a fixed ratio for all campuses. A preferred method is to estimate ground maintenance requirements by applying previous unit costs, adjusted to compensate for salary increases and rising prices, to the overall size of the campus grounds, measured in square feet or acres.

The bulk of utility costs are expenditures for heat, air-conditioning, and light. Since all are proportional to building area, total utility costs may be estimated on this basis even though expenditures for power (usually electrical) and water are more closely related to the number of users— viz., students and faculty. Heat and air-conditioning consumption will vary greatly, depending on geographical location and type of building construction, although similarities in unit costs can be expected among institutions located in similar climate zones. It is important that the additional utilities required by schools of engineering, medicine, and the like are not overlooked when budgets are formulated.

BIBLIOGRAPHY

Farmer, James, *Why Planning, Programming, Budgeting Systems for Higher Education?* Western Interstate Commission for Higher Education, Boulder, Colo., 1970, 24. pp.

This brief volume is concerned with the kind of results that can be expected from the use of PPBS in higher education. The conceptual difficulties involved in applying the PPBS techniques—when outputs cannot always be identified and are the product of different joint inputs—are recognized. Knowing the limitations of the system adds strength to the author's several examples of the effective uses of PPBS: to provide additional insight into program changes by identifying resource requirements and to develop program costs to improve understanding of objectives and outputs. Three methods of implementing PPBS are listed: through planning studies, evolutionary development, and the "turn-key" changeover.

Green, John L., *Budgeting in Higher Education*, University of Georgia Business and Finance Office, Athens, 1971, 240 pp.

An overview of budgeting in higher education as seen through the eyes of a chief business officer, this book gives primary attention to an institution's operating budget. The various budgeting concepts described include performance, program, decision-making, zero-base, and formula. Other topics are budgeting cycles, budgetary planning and analysis, budgetary requests, allocation of funds and development of the operating budget, budget execution, costing for educational institutions, types of expenditure analyses, and computation of unit costs.

International Committee of Business Officers, *A Model Budget Analysis System for Program 05 Libraries*, Office of Interinstitutional Business Studies, Evergreen State College, Olympia, Wash., 1970, 16 pp., appendixes.

The authors present formulas and rationale for determining minimum quantitative adequacy of holdings, minimum number and unit cost of acquisitions, man-years of staffing, binding expenditures, and other operational costs. The resource formula is based on an approach designed to measure "threshold" adequacy; the staffing formulas relate to actual operation of libraries in the University of California system.

Kraft, Richard H. P., ed., *Strategies of Educational Planning*, Educational Systems Development Center, Florida State University, Tallahassee, 1969, 303 pp.

Eight papers deal with the directions that have been and might be taken in a systems approach to educational planning. A number of topics relate to program budgeting: performance relationships that exist between an educational system and its environment; use of operations research methods to aid in the setting of goals and objectives; utilities; criteria for evaluating educational programs; selected situations in educational project planning that involve consideration of the cost or dollar factor as well as time and performance variables; factors of obsolescence critical to the economic planning of buildings; and an economic analysis of educational demand.

Miller, James L., Jr., *State Budgeting for Higher Education: The Use of Formulas and Cost Analysis*, Institute of Public Administration, University of Michigan, Ann Arbor, 1964, 228 pp.

This comprehensive account and analysis of the growth, theory, and procedures of budget formulas and cost analysis is considered the principal reference in its field. The first three chapters describe the historical antecedents of formulas, patterns, and problems pertaining to relationships between State governments and higher education. This is followed by a State-by-State description of the formulas and cost analysis procedures currently in use, and delineates some generalized conclusions concerning them.

Millett, John D., *Planning, Programming, Budgeting for Ohio's Public Institutions of Higher Education*, Ohio Board of Regents, Columbus, 1970, 216 pp.

In setting forth certain common factors or aspects of planning-programing-budgeting for Ohio's public institutions of higher education, the author emphasizes that the Ohio Board of Regent's position is not to prescribe a standard pattern of purpose, organization, and output for any individual institution. The Board urges only that patterns of purpose, organization, and output be consciously determined and clearly delineated by individual institutions. The first chapters describe the general purposes of higher education and its inherent organization to utilize resources and establish objectives. Some rather straightforward quantitative measures of the outputs of a higher educational enterprise are described, together with associated programing procedures. For the purposes intended, the key chapters on budgeting inputs for current operations and the planning and programing of capital improvements are adequate. A more rigorous defense of suggested standards would, however, be welcome.

Novick, David, ed., *Program Budgeting: Program Analysis and the Federal Budget*, Harvard University Press, Cambridge, Mass., 1965, 382 pp.

The 11 authors who contribute chapters to this book direct their attention primarily to the principles of program budgeting and its practical application. The three-part organization of the book is as follows: Part I discusses the government decisionmaking process, the role of budgeting, and past efforts by the Federal Government to improve the planning-programing-budgeting process. The use of cost-utility analysis and other analytical techniques is considered, and the conceptual framework for program budgeting is systematically developed. In part II the evolution of program budgeting in the Department of Defense is described and examples given of ways in which this budgeting concept might be adapted to other activities of the Federal Government, including the space program, transportation, education, health, and natural resources. Part III, which deals with implementing the program budget, considers some potential problems and limitations and suggests ways with which to cope with them.

Public Administration Review, "Planning-Programing-Budgeting Symposium," vol. 26, no. 4, December 1966, and "Symposium on PPBS Reexamined," vol. 29, no. 2, March/April 1969.

The December 1966 *Review* and the March/April 1969 issue contain a total of 14 papers concerned with the development and application of planning-programing-budgeting. Since coverage of the topic is extensive, some papers are more relevant to use of PPBS in higher education than others. The two papers by Aaron Wildavsky, in this reviewer's opinion, are "must" reading for every would-be practitioner. In the first, Wildavsky describes with clarity the three methods of achieving efficiency—cost-benefit analysis, systems analysis, and program budgeting—then proceeds, in a most enlightening way, to show how much more than mere economizing is involved. The same theme permeates his second paper, "Rescuing Policy Analysis from PPBS," which includes the startling statement that "no one knows how to do program budgeting." Careful reading leaves little room for doubt.

Some of the other articles relevant to PPBS in higher education include Allen Schick's "The Road to PPB: The Stages of Budget Reform" and "Systems Politics and Systems Budgeting," and Bertram Gross's discussion on "The New Systems Budgeting." Papers on PPBS and State and city budgeting by William M. Capron, Frederick C. Mosher, and Selma J. Mushkin are also informative and relevant.

Rourke, Francis E., and Glenn E. Brooks, *The Managerial Revolution in Higher Education*, Johns Hopkins University Press, Baltimore, Md., 1966, 182 pp.

This study of recent changes in the administration of colleges and universities is based on responses from over 300 colleges and universities to four questionnaires and on 209 personal interviews conducted by the authors at 33 colleges, universities, and central governing boards in 16 States. Chapter four, which deals with allocating academic resources, provides an excellent overall view of the new philosophy and methodology employed by colleges in budgeting and space management. The comprehensive yet surprisingly detailed coverage provides so much perspective and direction that this chapter should be mandatory reading for all resource managers. Other areas of college and university operations employing new management techniques are treated equally effectively in the five other chapters of this exceptionally valuable book.

Russell, John Dale, and James I. Doi, "Analysis of Institutional Expenditures" (a series of 12 articles), *College and University Business*, vol. 19. nos. 3–6, September–December 1955; vol. 20, nos. 1–6, January–June 1956; and vol. 21, nos. 1 and 2, July–August, 1956.

Although 17 years have elapsed since this series of articles was published, their content represents the best available study of the techniques and problems of analyzing expenditures by institutions of higher education. The first two articles deal with general considerations underlying the analysis of expenditures. Of historical interest are the authors' examination of the need for suitable normative data. The original criticism of the data presented remain valid today; namely, gross totals rather than individual institution data are supplied and what is reported is frequently out of date. Subsequent articles deal with the analysis of the four basic expenditure categories: instruction, library, administrative and general purpose, and plant operation and maintenance. Expenditure data collected from six New Mexico institutions are used for illustrative purposes. The understanding of expenditure analysis that can be gained from these articles should prove invaluable as an orientation for planners intending to begin formula budgeting, and useful as a refresher for current practitioners.

Scheuerman, J. C., *Instructional Practices and Related Faculty Staffing in California Public Higher Education*, Staff Report 67–15, Coordinating Council for Higher Education (California), Sacramento, 1967, 85 pp., appendixes.

This comprehensive study covers numerous facets of faculty staffing formulas and guidelines, teaching loads, the effect of class sizes on staffing requirements, and unit costs. The primary focus is on examining instructional practices to ascertain how faculty personnel and other instructional resources can be utilized more effectively.

Prevailing instructional patterns and faculty workloads are examined, faculty workload is defined, and the problem of measuring teaching load is analyzed. Current instructional practices are related to student differences, to the relationship between knowledge and the curriculum, to methods of instruction, to class size, and to the multiple tasks of faculty.

The last section considers the bases for budgeting instructional resources and for reporting their use and effectiveness. Faculty staffing standards and other bases for budgeting instructional resources in California are reviewed, and criteria are posed by which the budgeting and reporting systems are evaluated.

Schultze, Charles L., *The Politics and Economics of Public Spending*, Brookings Institution, Washington, D.C., 1968, 143 pp.

Since 1961 the Federal Government has employed a system for planning, programming, and budgeting (PPB) to provide policymakers with an analytical evaluation of existing and proposed programs, buttressed wherever possible with quantitative measures of performance. In this book the author examines the relationship between the analytical approach to PPB and the political bargaining that necessarily characterizes program and budgetary decisions in a free society. After reviewing briefly the evolution of the Federal budget and the objectives of PPB, Schultze considers the strengths and weaknesses of both the analytical and the bargaining approach to program decisions and suggests ways in which the two can complement each other. In subsequent chapters the author discusses future applications of systematic analysis, and he concludes by offering suggestions for political and administrative improvements.

Stumph, Wayne J., "A Comparative Study of Statewide Operating Budget Formulas Administered by Statewide Coordinating Agencies for Higher Education in Selected States" (dissertation), University Microfilms, Ann Arbor, Mich., 1970.

This dissertation compares formula budgeting methods used by statewide coordinating boards in 10 selected States to determine the financial needs of State-supported institutions. Budgeting practices in six additional States, whose coordinating boards do not employ budget formulas, are included for comparison. Relevant data were collected and organized into a format that permits interstate comparisons and analysis. Two different basic approaches are identified. The first reestablishes each year's budget anew through a process based on standardized calculation of funding requirements for the various functions. The second approach extends the previous year's budget to the new year by adding or subtracting formula-derived amounts to account for various changes in programs, production rates, and costs.

The author analyzes various formula procedures and elements by using such evaluation criteria as the validity of a formula to measure actual financial requirements, simplicity, equitability, flexibility, and potential for improving efficiency and economy. The plan presented for the development of formula budgeting procedures consists of (1) a method for formula building, (2) a comprehensive framework, and (3) a set of recommendations for construction of formula elements. The author concludes that reconstructing each year's budget anew is superior to modifying the previous year's budget to meet the needs of the current year.

A detailed bibliography is included.

Uhl, Norman P., "Identifying College Goals the Delphi Way," *Administration and Organization*, Topical Papers and Reprints No. 2, National Laboratory for Higher Education, Durham, N.C., 7 pp.

This brief paper explains how the Delphi technique can be used to ascertain the manner in which constituent groups view the goals of a given institution, both as they *are* and as they *should be*, and to move diverse groups toward consensus. The Delphi technique, as utilized by the author, consisted of repeated samplings of the opinions of administrators, faculty, students, trustees, alumni, and community leaders regarding an institution's present and preferred goals. The participants did not meet face-to-face; rather, they completed opinionnaires (the Institutional Goals Inventory, IGI) and mailed them to the project staff. A second and a third opinionnaire, which were duplicates of the first except that the model responses were circled in red and a summary of minority views was presented, were later sent to each participant. A significant value of this Delphi technique is that it preserves independent thought and also permits the participant to tap the opinions of others through presentation of response data. Testing at five institutions with quite different characteristics demonstrated the adaptability and effectiveness of both the IGI opinionnaire and Delphi technique as a means of measuring constituent opinions concerning present and preferred goals.

Western Interstate Commission for Higher Education, *Outputs of Higher Education: Their Identification, Measurement, and Evaluation*, Boulder, Colo., 1970, 130 pp.

An outstanding collection of papers, this publication is concerned with the difficult task of measuring higher education outputs. The preface states: "We are looking for insight and understanding of just how the contributions, activities, and benefits of higher education may be shaped, modified, directed, and improved through intelligent decision-making and informed allocation of resources." The papers and their authors are as follows: "Thinking About the Outputs of Higher Education," F. E. Balderston; "The Outputs of Higher Education: Their Proxies, Measurement, and Evaluation," John Vaizey; "A Scheme for Measuring the Output of Higher Education," David G. Brown;

"R² on E: Some Suggestions for Research on the Role of Research in Higher Education," E. West Churchman; "Measures of the Outputs of Higher Education: Some Practical Suggestions for Their Development and Use," Alain C. Enthoven; "Higher Education and the Public Sector," Kenneth S. Tollett; "Measuring Student Outputs in Higher Education," Alexander W. Astin; "Public Service Outputs of Higher Education, An Exploratory Essay," John E. Brandl; "The Outputs of Undergraduate Education," Robbin R. Hought; and "Outputs of Higher Education: Graduate Education," John P. Miller.

Williams, Harry, *Planning for Effective Resource Allocation in Universities*, American Council on Education, Washington, D.C., 1966, 78 pp.

This report sets forth essential concepts and ground rules for establishing more program-oriented budgetary practices in colleges and universities. Of special value to those unfamiliar with the economic approach to resource allocation are the author's lucid explanation of the theory of constrained choice and the iterative analytical process by which equal marginal value for resource expenditures is obtained. That decision-making can be improved by shifting from budgets based solely on accounting data to program-derived, resource-oriented budgets is repeatedly demonstrated. Examples are limited to those applications in which program elements and relationships can be explicitly identified. Perhaps nothing more should be expected, but administrators familiar with the harsh realities of having to make decisions under uncertain conditions and intangible influences would argue that program budgeting can fulfill a greater promise.

The annual budget documents and study reports from a number of States offer transient sources of information concerning current formula budgeting practices, detailed cost data, and research findings. The documents reviewed that appear to have special value include those from California, Florida, Illinois, New Mexico, New York, Ohio, and Texas.

A continuing source of articles dealing with the more practical aspects of program and formula budgeting is the monthly McGraw-Hill publication, *College and University Business*. In the March 1969 issue, for example, Robert G. Cope argues that because formulas fail to stimulate the total instructional process, they should be replaced by models that demonstrate how the total effort depends on faculty workloads, supporting services, and number of students served, as well as on costs related to these factors. Other articles deal with a wide range of budgeting topics, including "Custodial Services Work Standards" and "Budgetary Accounting Procedures for the Small College."

Appendix A

METHODOLOGY FOR PROJECTING LARGE ENROLLMENTS

Among the references listed in the bibliography are a number which describe in detail the latest techniques for developing the best possible estimates of future college and university enrollment levels. The ensuing presentation of projection methodology summarizes those treatments of the topic most applicable to large enrollment projections, i.e., to total State enrollments or the total enrollment of a number of institutions. (The methodology for projecting the enrollment potential of *individual* institutions based on geographical analysis of attendance rates is presented in chapter VII.)

The simplest projection technique is a time-series analysis that graphically depicts the movement of data across time. Once enrollment data are plotted and the plotted points connected, the resultant curve hopefully will form the basis for projection. The data must cover a number of years and be comparable. Moreover, a continuation of the status quo must be anticipated for the major factors affecting the data. The accuracy of such projections depends almost entirely upon (1) the average amount of deviation of the plotted data from a smoothly drawn curve and (2) the complexity of the curve itself. If the variations are minor and the plotted points deviate only slightly from a smooth curve, or better, if they generally follow a straight line, very good enrollment projections can be made.

Enrollments may also be projected, or, more accurately, predicted by correlation techniques. Through multiple correlation and regression analysis, the relative influence that each of a large number of factors exerts on enrollment may be measured. Such measurements may in turn be used to predict enrollments based on related yet more stable socioeconomic characteristics. (The statistical complexities and involved analysis of correlation techniques preclude discussion in this summary.)

The two most reliable methods of forecasting large enrollments are the "ratio" method and the "cohort-survival" method or a variation of the latter. Briefly, the ratio method consists of deriving future estimates of college enrollments on the basis of predetermined projected ratios applied to one or more larger "predictor" populations. The ratios are generally total State college enrollment to State population ages 18 through 21.

719

The cohort survival method, although more complicated, usually yields more reliable results. Forecasts of enrollment are made on the basis of the "survival" of pupils from one grade to the next higher grade. "Mortality" in the school population is defined as those students who drop out, for whatever reason, in each school grade. The number of students in each grade likely to "survive" in the future is determined by means of projected survival rates based on past enrollment in each of the grades involved. When grade-by-grade enrollment figures are not available, a broader student category or so-called "modified" cohort survival method must be employed—a method in which survival rates are limited to those between high school graduates, first-time college entrants, and total college enrollment.

In the case of both the ratio and cohort methods, the derived forecasts are based on a single basic assumption, namely, that enrollment will be a proportion of some other quantity. As projections, they indicate what the general or mean trend of enrollment will be in light of past trends, modified in the forecast period by certain secondary assumptions regarding future social, economic, and political factors affecting education. Important as projection methodology and basic assumptions are to projection accuracy, it is vitally important that forecasts be based on reliable, comparable, and comprehensive data. Enrollment forecasts can never be any more reliable than the data on which they are based.

ENROLLMENT-RATIO METHOD

Four steps for projecting college and university enrollments by the enrollment-ratio method are outlined on the following pages. An example of this procedure (used to project undergraduate college and university degree-credit enrollment on a national level) appears in tables A-1 and A-2 and in figure A-1.

STEP 1: Obtain past, present, and future estimated college-age population data for the geographical area (usually a State[1]) from which the majority of the college enrollment is drawn. A principal source of these data is the Bureau of the Census. The population age group that best represents a majority of college students should be determined by local analysis. The widespread use of ages 18 through 21 is based on the fact that 74.2 percent

---

[1] It should be recognized that in those States in which college enrollments consist primarily of nonresident students, the State's population *does not* represent a suitable base for the ratio method.

Table A-1.—Example data and calculations for ratio method of projecting college and university enrollments

Year (fall)	Population 18–21 yrs. of age	Undergraduate degree credit enrollment	Percentage of population enrolled (Y)	t	Y=26.56+0.94t
1	8,491,000	2,303,000	27.12	1	27.50
2	8,666,000	2,530,000	29.19	2	
3	8,790,000	2,629,000	29.91	3	
4	8,979,000	2,785,000	31.02	4	
5	9,280,000	2,901,000	31.26	5	
6	9,724,000	3,073,000	31.60	6	
7	10,379,000	3,309,000	31.88	7	
8	10,857,000	3,574,000	32.92	8	
9	11,195,000	3,839,000	34.29	9	
10	11,519,000	4,222,000	36.65	10	
11	12,290,000	4,710,000	38.32	11	36.90

PROJECTED

Year (fall)	Population 18–21 yrs. of age	Undergraduate degree credit enrollment	Percentage of population enrolled (Y)	t	Y=26.56+0.94t
12	13,067,000	5,109,000		12	
13	13,809,000	5,510,000		13	
14	14,331,000	5,833,000		14	
15	14,280,000	5,926,000		15	
16	14,492,000	6,130,000		16	
17	14,835,000	6,394,000		17	
18	15,253,000	6,696,000		18	
19	15,655,000	6,998,000		19	
20	15,996,000	7,278,000		20	
21	16,300,000	7,547,000		21	46.30

of all entering freshmen are 18 years of age.[2] Separate projections for males and females are recommended.

STEP 2: Secure past enrollment data from institutions of higher education for which projections are to be made. Data covering the 10 most recent years usually suffice; earlier statistics will have little relevance to present and future trends.

STEP 3: Study the relationship between college enrollment and college-age population in an attempt to determine a reasonably definitive and precise trend between the two. To determine such trends, (1) divide annual enrollments by the college-age population in corresponding years; (2) plot

---

[2] American Council on Education, *The American Freshman: National Norms for Fall 1972*, Research Reports, vol. 7, no. 5, Washington, D.C., 1972, p. 33.

Table A-2.—Application of linear regression (least squares) formula

Formula: $Y = a + bt$ where Y = percent of population age group enrolled in college (data taken from table A-1)

$$a = \frac{(4n+2)S - 6S'}{n(n-1)} \qquad b = \frac{12S' - 6S(n+1)}{n(n^2-1)}$$

n = total number of successive past years on which trend is based.

S = summation of Y values for n successive past years.

S' = summation of cumulative values of Y for n successive past years.

Successive past years	Y values	Cumulative Y values	
1 (yr 1)	27.12	354.16	
2	29.19	327.04	for $n = 11$
3	29.91	297.85	
4	31.02	267.94	$a = \dfrac{46 \times 354.16 - 6 \times 2228.36}{11 \times 10} = 26.56$
5	31.26	236.92	
6	31.60	205.66	
7	31.88	174.06	
8	32.92	142.18	$b = \dfrac{12 \times 2228.36 - 72 \times 354.16}{11(121-1)} = 0.94$
9	34.29	109.26	
10	36.65	74.97	therefore $Y = 26.56 + 0.94t$
$n = 11$ (yr 11)	38.32	38.32	where t equals the number of years beginning with the base year (yr 1) equal to 1.
	$S = \Sigma = 354.16$	$S' = \Sigma = 2228.36$	

the data using the ratio of enrollment to population as the dependent variable and time in years as the independent variable; (3) study the plotted ratios to ensure that they are *stable over time* (this methodology is justified only if a consistent and stable ratio exists between enrollment and the predicted population); and (4) draw a trend line or regression line, either by "freehand" or by employing a widely used mathematical technique called the "least-squares fit."

A regression line produces a least-squares fit when the sum of the deviations of the plotted values from the calculated trend line equals zero. The sum of the squares of these deviations will be less than the sum of the squared deviations for any other trend line. A variety of formulas are available that will provide least-squares fit regression lines. The resulting lines may be mathematically described as linear, exponential, asymptotic, logarithmic, polynomic, first-degree curve, second-degree curve, etc. The formula that produces a line that best fits the data trend is said to have the highest index of determination. This index may be calculated mathematically and the best formula chosen accordingly.

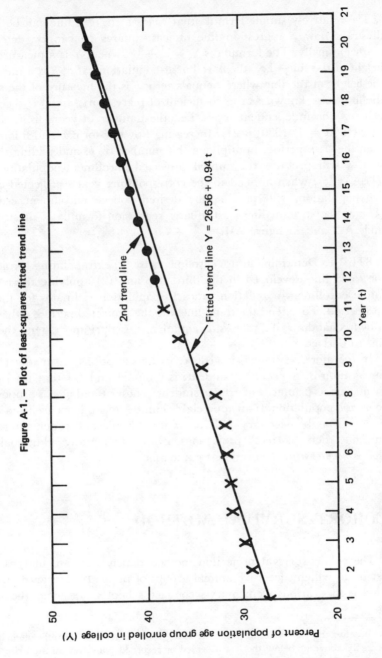

Figure A-1. — Plot of least-squares fitted trend line

2nd trend line

Fitted trend line Y = 26.56 + 0.94 t

Year (t)

Percent of population age group enrolled in college (Y)

NOTE.— See tables A-1 and A-2 for data and calculations.

The relatively simple formula that yields a straight line can be used to illustrate how a regression line of least-squares fit can be determined mathematically. The formula is $Y = a + bt$, where Y is a measure of the height of the line—i.e., the enrollment-population ratio; a is a measure of the height of the line where t equals zero; b is the measure of the slope of the line (also known as the coefficient of regression); and t is the known value of the independent series, i.e., the number of years from the base year (1960 = 1, 1980 = 21). Increasing t by one for each additional year from the base period, multiplying this number by b, and adding the constant a will produce the annual projected enrollment-population ratio. These ratios, when applied to the corresponding year's projected college-age population, will provide the desired college enrollment estimates. (Use of the straight line least-squares regression formula is illustrated in table A-2 and in figure A-1.)

STEP 4: Determine future enrollments by (1) extrapolating (projecting) the trend line developed in the third step and (2) applying the resulting future enrollment-population ratios to population estimates for the forecast period. To extend the trend line into the projected period, either draw it by freehand, or, if a regression equation is used, simply extend the trend line so derived.[3]

In the aforementioned procedure, two assumptions are made: (1) that inmigration of nonresident students is minimal and (2) that total enrollment consists primarily of *resident* students whose attendance is proportional to *resident* population. If an appreciable number of students are from out-of-State, it may be necessary to derive ratios of inmigrant students to resident students, then "correct" projections to account for any additional input that is *nonproportional* to resident population.

COHORT-SURVIVAL METHOD

The cohort-survival projection method depends on an analysis of the extent to which successive annual groups of pupils (called grade cohorts) survive the various elementary-secondary school grades and the various

---

[3] Because the line resulting from the straight-line regression formula often lies considerably above or below the last observed or recorded point, an unusual rise or drop will occur between the last actual observation and the first projected point. To avoid such an aberration and give validity to the projection, a second trend line can be drawn from the last observed point to the last projected point determined by the first trend line; annual readings of the projected data are then made from the second trend line (see figure A-1).

college class levels. While more laborious than the ratio method, the cohort method is the superior of the two because it relates college enrollments to known supporting enrollments—a more relevant and refined base than college-age population. Furthermore, since the cohort-survival method takes into account a considerably greater number of enrollment relationships, it adds precision and (hopefully) greater validity to the projection. (Example data and calculations using the cohort-survival method are shown in tables A-3 and A-4.)

STEP 1: For a reasonably stable population (the survey should be at least statewide), obtain actual enrollment statistics on a grade-to-grade basis from the 1st grade through the 4th year of college. Separate projections by sex should be made if possible. (Example enrollments on a national level are shown in table A-3.) It should be noted that this methodology is suitable only for *large* populations. (Techniques appropriate for projecting enrollments of small municipalities and individual institutions are discussed in chapter VII.)

STEP 2: Compute grade-to-grade survival rates by dividing the enrollment in a given grade by the enrollment in the next lower grade for the previous year. Using the example data in table A-3, the 1st-to-2d grade survival rate for year 10 to year 11 equals the year 11 enrollment in the 2d grade (3,708,000) divided by the year 10 enrollment in the 1st grade (3,928,000), or 94.4 percent. This value is recorded in table A-4 as the survival rate for grade levels 1 to 2 for years 10 to 11.

STEP 3: Project the survival rates for each grade into the future, either by drawing a freehand trend line or by utilizing a regression equation. (Projected survival rates based on linear "least-squares fit" regression equations are shown in table A-4.)

STEP 4: Compute future enrollment estimates. Such estimates for each grade for the 1st future year are computed by applying the 1st future year's projected survival rate to the actual enrollment for the last year for which figures are available. The enrollment estimates for the 2d year are then computed by applying the 2d future year's projected survival rate to the calculated estimated enrollment for the 1st year, and so on, until all cohorts are extrapolated through the projected years. Using the example data in tables A-3 and A-4, the projected fall (year 12) 2d-grade enrollment of 3,718,000 students is obtained by multiplying the previous year's (year 11) 1st-grade enrollment of 3,977,000 by the year-11-to-year-12, 1st-to-2d grade projected survival rate of 93.5 percent.

In the case of State projections, if an appreciable number of students are from out of State, a migration analysis must be made.

Table A-3.—Example enrollment and projected enrollment of public school and undergraduate degree-credit students, by year and by grade

(in thousands)

Year (fall)	Grade												Class				Total college enrollment
	1	2	3	4	5	6	7	8	9	10	11	12	Fresh	Soph.	Junior	Senior	
1	3441	3193	3240	2804	2443	2432	2503	2321	2109	1819	1518	1317	871	629	444	359	2303
2	3425	3179	3123	3176	2755	2396	2429	2414	2322	1936	1584	1336	933	682	513	402	2530
3	3525	3159	3121	3075	3127	2712	2416	2354	2436	2155	1705	1424	941	713	530	445	2629
4	3599	3273	3110	3074	3032	3068	2725	2329	2360	2267	1912	1538	1008	730	560	487	2785
5	3639	3350	3220	3067	3040	2993	3093	2634	2352	2201	2011	1707	1068	766	572	495	2901
6	3721	3410	3316	3192	3049	3014	3041	3002	2678	2194	1945	1772	1200	792	581	500	3073
7	3775	3491	3355	3271	3149	2999	3055	2956	3093	2543	1978	1755	1324	882	595	508	3309
8	3829	3539	3430	3306	3248	3110	3061	3006	3094	2908	2290	1820	1334	996	705	539	3574
9	3938	3627	3484	3393	3294	3228	3172	3011	3127	2947	2692	2117	1360	1017	805	657	3839
10	3928	3719	3583	3447	3391	3290	3291	3143	3134	3024	2723	2510	1592	1064	831	735	4222
11	3977	3708	3655	3534	3426	3347	3348	3242	3270	3040	2778	2530	1874	1239	857	740	4710
							PROJECTED										
12	3996	3718	3664	3615	3527	3412	3424	3308	3388	3165	2818	2592	1910	1428	991	773	5102
13	4053	3743	3672	3627	3608	3516	3494	3390	3460	3290	2947	2638	1978	1455	1142	894	5469
14	3952	3807	3702	3635	3620	3597	3604	3463	3549	3370	3073	2770	2034	1507	1164	1030	5735
15	3871	3724	3765	3665	3631	3613	3687	3575	3629	3464	3161	2898	2158	1550	1206	1050	5964
16	3775	3660	3687	3731	3661	3624	3707	3661	3747	3549	3260	2990	2281	1644	1240	1088	6253
17	3578	3581	3623	3654	3727	3654	3718	3681	3840	3672	3350	3094	2377	1738	1315	1118	6548
18	3557	3406	3549	3594	3650	3720	3753	3696	3861	3771	3477	3189	2484	1811	1390	1186	6871
19	3663	3397	3375	3521	3590	3646	3820	3734	3877	3799	3582	3317	2586	1893	1449	1254	7182
20	3771	3500	3370	3348	3521	3586	3748	3801	3917	3819	3620	3428	2717	1971	1514	1307	7509
21	3889	3625	3472	3346	3348	3517	3686	3733	3987	3866	3647	3472	2835	2070	1577	1366	7848

Table A-4.—Example survival rates and projected survival rates for public school grades and undergraduate degree-credit classes

(Percent)

Year-to-year	Grade-to-grade level												Fresh. to soph.	Soph. to junior	Junior to senior
	1 to 2	2 to 3	3 to 4	4 to 5	5 to 6	6 to 7	7 to 8	8 to 9	9 to 10	10 to 11	11 to 12	12–fresh.			
−1	92.2	97.1	98.4	97.9	97.9	98.4	97.0	93.4	95.1	87.7	88.4	68.8	76.0	80.0	90.1
1–2	92.4	97.8	98.0	98.3	98.1	99.9	96.9	100.0	91.8	87.1	88.0	70.4	78.3	81.6	90.5
2–3	92.2	98.2	98.5	98.5	98.4	100.8	96.9	100.9	92.8	88.1	89.9	70.4	76.4	79.7	86.7
3–4	92.9	98.4	98.5	98.6	98.1	100.5	96.4	100.3	93.1	88.7	90.2	70.8	77.6	78.5	91.9
4–5	93.1	98.4	98.6	98.9	98.7	100.8	96.7	101.0	93.3	88.7	89.3	69.4	76.0	78.4	88.4
5–6	93.7	99.0	99.1	99.4	99.1	101.6	97.1	101.7	93.3	88.4	88.1	70.3	74.2	75.8	87.4
6–7	93.8	98.4	98.6	98.7	98.4	101.4	97.2	103.0	95.0	90.2	90.2	74.7	73.5	75.1	86.7
7–8	93.7	98.3	98.5	99.3	98.8	102.1	94.8	104.7	94.0	90.1	92.0	76.0	75.2	79.9	90.6
8–9	94.7	98.4	98.9	99.6	99.4	102.0	98.4	104.0	95.2	92.6	92.4	74.7	76.2	82.9	93.2
9–10	94.4	98.8	98.9	99.9	99.9	102.0	99.1	104.1	96.7	92.4	93.2	75.2	78.2	81.7	91.3
10–11	94.4	98.3	98.7	99.4	98.7	101.8	98.5	104.0	97.0	91.9	92.9	74.7	77.8	80.5	89.0
PROJECTED															
11–12	93.5	98.8	98.9	99.8	99.6	102.3	98.8	104.5	98.6	92.7	93.3	75.5	76.2	80.0	90.2
12–13	93.7	98.8	99.0	99.8	99.7	102.4	99.0	104.6	97.1	93.1	93.6	76.3	76.2	80.0	90.2
13–14	93.9	98.9	99.0	99.8	99.7	102.5	99.1	104.7	97.4	93.4	94.0	77.1	76.2	80.0	90.2
14–15	94.2	98.9	99.0	99.9	99.8	102.5	99.2	104.8	97.6	93.8	94.3	77.9	76.2	80.0	90.2
15–16	94.5	99.0	99.1	99.9	99.8	102.6	99.3	104.8	97.8	94.1	94.6	78.7	76.2	80.0	90.2
16–17	94.9	99.0	99.1	99.9	99.8	102.6	99.3	104.9	98.0	94.4	94.9	79.5	76.2	80.0	90.2
17–18	95.2	99.1	99.2	99.9	99.8	102.7	99.4	104.9	98.2	94.7	95.2	80.3	76.2	80.0	90.2
18–19	95.5	99.1	99.2	99.9	99.9	102.7	99.5	104.9	98.4	95.0	95.4	81.1	76.2	80.0	90.2
19–20	95.8	99.2	99.2	100.0	99.9	102.8	99.5	104.9	98.5	95.3	95.7	81.9	76.2	80.0	90.2
20–21	96.1	99.2	99.3	100.0	99.9	102.8	99.6	104.9	98.7	95.5	95.9	82.7	76.2	80.0	90.2

MODIFIED COHORT-SURVIVAL METHOD

The modified cohort-survival method, an expedient means for projecting college enrollments, requires only the survival rate between high school graduates and entering college freshmen plus a "conversion" factor.

STEP 1: For the population, usually a State total, collect the following data for past years: (1) number of high school graduates, (2) freshman class enrollment, and (3) total undergraduate enrollment. (Examples of these data are shown in table A-5, columns (1), (2), and (5), respectively.)

STEP 2: Compute the high school graduate-entering freshman survival rate (table A-5, col. 3); also compute the annual ratio of actual under-

Table A-5.—Example data and calculations for projecting college enrollments by the modified cohort-survival method

(Enrollment in thousands)

Year	High school graduates (spring)	First-time degree-credit enrollment (fall)	Survival rate Col. (2) ÷ Col. (1)	First-time students in 4 successive years	Undergraduate degree-credit enrollment	Conversion factor Col. (5) ÷ Col. (4)
	(1)	(2)	(3)	(4)	(5)	(6)
1	1,202	670	.557			
2	1,263	718	.568			
3	1,282	724	.565			
4	1,344	775	.577	2,867	2,785	.965
5	1,447	822	.568	3,038	2,901	.955
6	1,633	923	.565	3,244	3,073	.947
7	1,728	1,018	.589	3,538	3,309	.935
8	1,681	1,031	.613	3,794	3,574	.942
9	1,717	1,046	.609	4,018	3,839	.955
10	2,015	1,225	.608	4,320	4,222	.977
11	2,369	1,442	.609	4,744	4,710	.993
			PROJECTED			
12	2,374	1,462	.616	5,175	5,046	.975
13	2,389	1,488	.623	5,617	5,477	.975
14	2,424	1,525	.629	5,917	5,769	.975
15	2,515	1,597	.635	6,072	5,920	.975
16	2,620	1,679	.641	6,289	6,132	.975
17	2,716	1,757	.647	6,558	6,394	.975
18	2,797	1,826	.653	6,859	6,688	.975
19	2,868	1,890	.659	7,152	6,973	.975
20	2,941	1,956	.665	7,429	7,243	.975
21	3,000	2,020	.672	7,692	7,500	.975

graduate enrollment to the total freshman class enrollment for that year and the 3 prior years. This "conversion" factor (table A-5, col. 6) is used to convert projected freshman class enrollments into total undergraduate enrollments.

STEP 3: Project the number of high school graduates, their survival rate, and the conversion factor, using one of the methods previously described.

STEP 4: Compute projected freshman class enrollments by applying the projected survival rates to the corresponding year's projected number of high school graduates. Add 4 successive years of per annum freshman class enrollments, then, using the projected conversion factor, calculate the estimated projected total undergraduate enrollment for each year.

SUGGESTED GUIDELINES FOR ENROLLMENT FORECASTING

By way of summary, the following are reemphasized as guidelines important to forecasting college and university enrollments:

1 Every effort must be made to minimize the possibility of altering the basic assumptions on which the forecast is based. The validity of the forecast depends on reliable reporting of academic and administrative policies, especially those pertaining to entrance requirements and tuition charges.

2. When the assumptions on which a given projection method is based are clearly fallacious, the method should not be used. No amount of ingenuity can compensate for inherent errors in the basic statistics from which the projections are to be made.[4]

3. Data must be reliable; if they include significant "errors," "omissions," and "guesses," the forecast will be invalid. In this connection, it is important that such terms as "full-time student," "undergraduate," "academic year," etc., be consistently and unambiguously defined.

4. The key to projection accuracy is to discern real trends, not short-term and random variations and fluctuations due to accidental or temporary influences. The more years for which *comparable* data are available, the better. However, true direction can be ascertained only on the basis

---

[4] David G. Hunt, "Methods and Procedures in Projecting Enrollment," in *Proceedings Conference of State Directors of Junior Colleges and Coordinators of State Systems of 2-year Colleges* (Dallas, Tex.), U.S. Department of Health, Education, and Welfare, Office of Education, Washington, D.C., 1962, p. 3.

of the strictest interpretation of comparability; i.e., unless all accountable variations in data due to known exceptional circumstances are discounted, data for the periods involved must be ignored.

5. Large populations can be more reliably forecast than small ones. At the State level, therefore, primary attention should be directed to projecting enrollments of many institutions grouped into meaningful categories. Trends from these totals can, in turn, be used by individual institutions to interpret their respective enrollment forecasts.

6. If more than one projection methodology is used and the resultant differences reconciled, the accuracy of the forecast will be greater.

BIBLIOGRAPHY

Folger, J. K., *Some Methods for Projecting School and College Enrollments*, Southern Regional Education Board, Atlanta, Ga., 1954.

Jaffe, A. J., *Handbook of Statistical Procedures for Long-Range Projections of Public School Enrollment*, U.S. Department of Health, Education, and Welfare, Office of Education, U.S. Government Printing Office, Washington, D.C., 1969, 118 pp.

Lins, L. J., *Methodology of Enrollment Projections for Colleges and Universities*, American Association of Collegiate Registrars and Admissions Officers, Washington, D.C., 1960, 67 pp.

Office of Program Planning and Fiscal Management for the State of Washington, *Higher Education Enrollment Projections: A Model*, Olympia, 1970, 72 pp.

Schmid, Calvin, F., and others, *Enrollment Forecasts State of Washington 1965 to 1985*, Washington State Census Board, Seattle, 1966, 78 pp.

Schmid, Calvin F., and F. J. Shanley, "Techniques of Forecasting University Enrollment," *Journal of Higher Education*, vol. XXIII, no. 9, December 1952.

Simon, Kenneth A., and Martin M. Frankel, *Projections of Educational Statistics to 1980–81* (1971 ed.), U.S. Department of Health, Education and Welfare, Office of Education, U.S. Government Printing Office, Washington, D.C., 1972, 176 pp.

Thompson, Ronald B., *Projections of Enrollment: Public and Private Colleges and Universities, 1970–1987*, American Association of Collegiate Registrars and Admissions Officers, Washington, D.C., 1971, 56 pp.

Appendix B

HIGHER EDUCATION PRICE INDEXES

An *index* number measures change in prices, wages, employment, etc., by showing the percentage variation from an arbitrary standard, usually 100, representing the status at some earlier time. One of the best-known and most useful indexes is the *price index*, which measures the average change in price of goods and services purchased by a particular group. The amount and quality of the selected commodities that comprise the market basket being indexed must remain constant so that only the effects of price changes are reflected. Under these restrictive conditions, the index (in actuality its reciprocal) is a measure of the purchasing value of money.

PROBLEMS OF INDEX CONSTRUCTION[1]

A higher education price index should answer the question: What is the relative price of a market basket of commodities purchased annually by colleges and universities if the amount and quality of the selected goods and services remain constant? In education, however, as in commercial enterprises, both the quantity and the quality of items purchased, as well as the amount spent on each, tend to change. For example, goods once included in the budget may no longer be needed; conversely, items not previously in existence may have been added to the purchase list. Changes of this kind must have no effect on price index values. Products are also continually redesigned to improve their quality. A price index must exclude those *measurable* changes in price which are the result of variances in product quality; improvements in quality that cannot be measured in dollars and cents are ignored.

---

[1] An explanation of the theory and procedures concerning the compiling of price indexes and the major problems pertaining to education indexes are presented in a basic text on this subject. See William Wasserman, *Education Price and Quantity Indexes*, Syracuse University Press, Syracuse, N.Y., 1963.

There is an index, called a *cost index*, which does attempt, in theory at least, to account for those quality changes that increase the productivity of an item or the satisfaction derived from ownership. The distinction between a price index and a cost index should be absolutely clear. A cost index measures much more than price changes. It takes into account the utility of the goods and services purchased, i.e., the satisfaction, benefits, or productivity derived therefrom. More specifically, a cost index measures changes in total expenditures over time to maintain a fixed level of welfare or satisfaction.[2]

In most fields cost indexes cannot be established because the utility or value derived from expenditures cannot be precisely measured. In education some outputs such as the number of college graduates or the number of research projects can, of course, be accurately ascertained, but their total value or worth cannot. Without a means of measuring the value of education returns, it is difficult to estimate, for pricing, what constitute equivalent outputs over time. Until the benefits of education can be measured, a true cost index remains only a theoretical concept.

It is important to understand that the introduction into a price index of intangible quality improvements and utility considerations would inject a wide element of subjective judgment that would tend to destroy the useful economic analysis the index now provides. Other than by opinionated estimates there is no statistically reliable way at the present time to measure in index form a person's needs or the degree to which these needs are satisfied by particular goods and services. Economic welfare as a measurable idea must currently be restricted to reporting the amount of goods and services purchased with the inference that the more purchased the better off the individual.[3] For this reason, price indexes normally account for quality and utility improvements only in that they exclude possible related changes in prices.

To avoid introducing intangible quality considerations in the structuring of a higher education price index, a practical assumption is made with

---

[2] One of the distinguishing factors between the two types of indexes is that a cost index is normally lower in value than a related price index. A buyer, for example, can substitute lower priced items for higher priced ones without experiencing any change in satisfaction from his purchases. He may therefore prevent his total budget (for maintaining a fixed level of utility) from rising as rapidly as the price of a given basket of market items.

[3] An example of a subjectively estimated index is the poverty index prepared by the Bureau of the Census. This index, which focuses on the Department of Agriculture's Economy Food Plan, reflects the different consumption requirements of families based on their size and composition, sex and age of the family head, and farm-nonfarm residence. See U.S. Department of Commerce, Bureau of the Census, "Revision in Poverty Statistics, 1959 to 1968," *Current Population Reports*, Special Studies, Series T-23, no. 28, Washington, D.C., August 12, 1969.

regard to the quality of teaching and other services rendered. For any given year, it is assumed that the faculty is *the best quality available for hire at that point in time*. This assumption permits faculty quality to be interpreted as constant from year to year in the *relative* sense that it is consistently the best available. Since in every instance the salary level reflects the price of a constant best-available service, justification can be made for unadjusted use of faculty salary data in price index construction.

METHOD OF INDEX CONSTRUCTION

Many current index numbers are constructed as a "weighted average of relatives" technically known as the Laspeyres method of combining prices representing each major group of items purchased. The steps used in constructing a Laspeyres[4] price index may be summarized as follows: (1) Current prices of representative commodities in each major item group are recorded at regular intervals; (2) the current price total for each group is expressed as a relative or percentage of that group's total price during a selected base period; (3) the relatives thus determined are weighted according to the proportion of budget expenditures allocated to each group during the base period; and (4) the weighted relatives are added to provide the current index number.

Step (3) requires further explanation. Price index formulas require the summation, for all items purchased, of price times quantity. In step (3) prices are weighted according to the corresponding *proportion* of total expenditures allocated to each item or group of items rather than according to the actual amount or *quantity* of goods and services purchased. The budget percentage spent for each item represents the relative "importance" dollar-wise that the consumer attaches to each item purchased. It is permissible, therefore, to replace the market basket concept with the idea of a budget and to substitute proportionate expenditures for physical quantities as item-weighting factors.

The proportion method of weighting is preferred to weighting by actual quantities because it is more feasible to determine spending patterns reported by institutions than it is to collect purchase-quantity data. The index weights are derived by determining stable relationships for selected goods and service items among average institutional expenditures. The assignment of weights in this manner makes it impossible to identify the physical quantities attached to each index item; quantity weights therefore are only implicit in the index structure.

---

[4] See "Technical Notes" for an explanation of the Laspeyres-type formula.

INDEX PARAMETERS

In constructing a price index, certain initial design features must be determined. It is important, for example, to decide who will use the index and to designate the particular group of consumers whose purchases are to be priced. The indexes discussed in this appendix are designed to measure the average change in prices of goods and services bought by a typical college or university. In this sense they are national indexes, representing all colleges and universities but not necessarily any one college or any special group of colleges.

Among the different U. S. higher education institutions there is considerable variation in the quantities and types of items purchased. In addition, price *changes* (the absolute price level has no effect on the Laspeyres formula) vary throughout the country. Such variances suggest the possible need to construct separate price indexes for certain categories of institutions and for specific geographical regions. It is unlikely, however, that indexes designed to reflect these variances would be sufficiently differentiated to warrant the time and effort required for their construction.

Most colleges and universities spend approximately 60 to 65 percent of their general and educational budgets (excluding sponsored research) on salaries of faculty, administrators, and other professional personnel. Consequently, the price trend for these salaries (a wage rate subindex) dominates overall price index values. There would be little difference in price index values between an index using the proportionate amounts spent for items (other than salaries) based on national averages and one using somewhat different proportionate amounts for a given institution. Furthermore, the high mobility of faculty—establishing what amounts to a near-national hiring market—supports the premise that over a period of years most colleges and universities experience similar growth rates in salary levels.[5]

It can be assumed, therefore, that most institutions face similar inflationary trends in the prices they pay to support current operations and consequently may use with confidence a common price index. Even if separate indexes were developed for certain categories of institutions or for specific

---

[5] Due to a number of changes in institutional classification categories, the American Association of University Professors salary data, organized by type and control of institution, are not strictly comparable over time. However, comparisons of AAUP salary data for associate professors over the 4-year period 1968–72 indicate a fairly equal average rate of increase at public and private universities and at liberal arts colleges. Associate professor salaries at 2-year colleges in both sectors rose at a slightly faster average rate during this period. Regional differences in salary growth rates appear small. For example, during the 10-year period 1961–71, the rate of increase in comparable faculty salaries ranged by region from 5 percent annually to 5.6 percent.

Table B-1.—Organization of college and university expenditures: 1970–71

	Amounts in millions of dollars		
Current funds expenditures	$23,505		
Educational and general		$17,729	
[1] General administration			$3,007
[1] Instruction and departmental research			7,849
[1] Extension and public service			595
[1] Libraries			720
[1] Plant maintenance and operation			1,740
[1] Organized activities of education depts.			695
Sponsored research			2,223
[1] Sponsored programs primarily for students			900
Student aid		1,110	
Major public service programs (hospitals, federally funded R. & D. centers)		1,672	
Auxiliary enterprises		2,994	
Expenditures for physical plant assets	$ 4,181		
Land		172	
Buildings		3,142	
Equipment		867	

[1] Expenditure function categories included in the current operations price index (HEPI).

Source: Paul F. Mertins and Norman J. Brandt, *Financial Statistics of Institutions of Higher Education: Current Funds Revenue and Expenditures 1970–71*, U.S. Department of Health, Education, and Welfare, Office of Education U.S. Government Printing Office, Washington, D.C., 1973.

geographical regions, they would only show how much prices have *changed* over time in one institutional category or region compared with another. They would *not* show whether prices were higher or lower in one institutional category or region than in another. For these reasons, only national indexes appear in this appendix.

A second design factor concerns the selection of an appropriate grouping of goods and services for pricing purposes. The organization of college and university expenditures shown in table B-1 indicates that at least two separate indexes are necessary: one dealing with current operations and another with plant assets. For current operations, the price index has been designed to measure price changes for goods and services purchased by current fund educational and general expenditures, excluding sponsored research. Since this index prices educational goods and services purchased by the student aid dollar, it may also be used for student aid expenditures. Because auxiliary enterprises (student residence halls, cafeterias, bookstores, student unions, infirmaries, etc.) are generally self-supporting, there is little need for a price index in these areas. The price index for plant assets reports price changes in expenditures for buildings and equipment. A detailed description of both the current operations price index and the physical plant price index follows.

EDUCATIONAL EXPENDITURES PRICE INDEX

The complete title of the index discussed in this section is: Index of Change in Prices of Goods and Services Purchased by Colleges and Universities Through Current Funds, Educational and General Expenditures, Excluding Sponsored Research.[6] For the sake of brevity, it is referred to as the Higher Education Price Index (HEPI). This index is concerned with price changes involving the salaries of faculty, administrators, and other professional personnel, nonprofessional salaries and wages, supplies and materials, equipment, utilities, books and periodicals, communications, and travel, all of which represent goods and services purchased by colleges and universities making current funds expenditures for educational and general purposes, excluding sponsored research. The index measures percentage price change from a 1967 reference date (expressed as 100) to an earlier or later date. (The index and its component subindexes appear in table B-2.[7])

Educational and general expenditures include those in the functional categories of general administration and expense, instruction and departmental research, extension and public service, libraries, plant operation and maintenance, sponsored research, and a number of other secondary expenditure category groupings.[8] Sponsored research is excluded from the index since it is a function performed almost exclusively by universities.

---

[6] Guidelines for this index were initially proposed by the author in an unpublished U.S. Office of Education paper, "An Introduction to the Technique of Developing a Higher Education Price Index," May 20, 1963.

[7] A similar price index for Instructional Operating Expenditures was developed in 1971 by June O'Neill (see bibliography). The O'Neill Index is based on three component subindexes: nonfaculty salaries, 28 percent; faculty salaries (a weighted average of separate indexes for salaries in each academic rank), 43 percent; and supplies and services, 29 percent. With 1958 as the base year, 1968 values for the O'Neill Index and the HEPI presented here are 151.4 and 153.0, respectively. The HEPI is technically superior to the O'Neill Index because it contains a more detailed breakdown of purchased items. However, greater detail does not necessarily add significantly to index validity because only a small proportion of the total goods and services is involved.

[8] For a detailed description of functional expenditure categories, see *College and University Business Administration* (rev. ed.), American Council on Education, Washington, D.C., 1968, pp. 195–98.

Table B-2.—Price index for educational and general expenditures, excluding sponsored research, for colleges and universities, and component subindexes: 1957–58 through 1971–72

1967 =100

Calendar year or academic year ending	Faculty salaries and staff benefits	Administrative officers and other professional salaries	Nonprofessional salaries and wages	Supplies and material	Equipment	Utilities	Books and periodicals, printing and binding	Communications	Travel	Other	Higher Education Price Index[1]
1958	61.3	59.8	75.0 est.	91.8	93.8	93.7	63.8	93.0	76.1	86.6	68.9
1959	64.9	63.8	77.5 est.	91.9	94.9	95.8	64.7	95.9	78.3	87.3	71.8
1960	68.6	67.9	80.1	93.0	95.5	99.5	65.7	97.7	81.0	88.7	75.0
1961	72.4	71.8	82.7	93.6	96.0	101.6	72.4	98.1	84.6	89.6	78.1
1962	76.2	75.8	85.4	93.8	96.2	101.7	73.8	98.2	87.4	90.6	81.1
1963	79.9	79.8	87.8	94.7	97.0	101.0	81.6	100.6	88.5	91.7	84.2
1964	83.6	83.8	90.3	94.9	97.1	100.1	86.2	101.2	90.1	92.9	87.1
1965	88.2	88.9	92.9	95.8	97.4	100.2	94.6	100.0	91.9	94.5	90.8
1966	93.8	94.0	95.9	98.6	98.1	99.9	98.6	98.4	95.2	97.2	95.1
1967	100.0	100.0	100.0	100.0	100.0	100.0	100.0	100.0	100.0	100.0	100.0
1968	106.8	106.0	104.9	100.9	100.7	100.4	106.2	102.5	104.6	104.2	105.4
1969	114.7	113.6	111.0	100.3	101.0	101.0	117.2	103.7	112.7	109.8	111.9
1970	122.4	121.2	118.0	103.5	103.9	107.0	142.2	105.3	128.5	116.3	119.3
1971	130.3	127.9	125.5	104.6	105.4	118.8	161.3	113.0	137.7	121.3	127.6
1972	136.2	134.6	133.3 est.	105.9	106.5	124.7	160.9	119.5	143.4	125.3	132.3

[1] Weighted average of all columns. The weights used are as follows: faculty salaries and staff benefits, 47.6 percent; administrative officers and other professional salaries, 14.3 percent; nonprofessional salaries and wages, 17.8 percent; supplies and material, 6.7 percent; equipment, 2.5 percent; utilities, 3.0 percent; books and periodicals, printing and binding, 2.0 percent; communications, 1.6 percent; travel, 1.4 percent, and other, 3.1 percent (see table B-4).

Sources: See "Prices Used" in this appendix.

Table B-3.—Percent distribution of educational and general expenditures, excluding sponsored research, by functional category and by type and control of institution: 1965-66

Educational and general expenditures functional category	All institutions			Universities		4-year colleges		2-year colleges	
	Total	Public	Private	Public	Private	Public	Private	Public	Private
General administration and expense	16.7	13.2	22.2	11.4	17.1	16.3	26.2	15.9	30.9
Instruction and departmental research	50.1	51.2	48.3	47.2	49.6	55.9	47.6	61.2	44.4
Extension and public service	5.9	8.5	1.6	12.6	1.8	1.5	1.4	3.4	1.2
Libraries	4.6	4.3	5.0	4.0	5.2	5.2	5.0	4.0	4.2
Plant operation and maintenance	11.2	10.6	12.3	9.6	11.1	12.6	13.1	11.2	14.9
All other educational and general expenditures, excluding sponsored research	11.5	12.2	10.6	15.3	15.2	8.5	6.8	4.3	4.4
Total	100.0	100.0	100.0	100.0	100.0	100.0	100.0	100.0	100.0

Source: Ernst Becker, "The Financing of Higher Education: A Review of Historical Trends and Projections for 1975–76," in *Trends in Postsecondary Education,* U. S. Government Printing Office, Washington, D. C., 1970, pp. 147–55.

(The percent distribution of educational and general expenditures, excluding sponsored research, by expenditure function category and by type and control of institution is shown in table B-3.) The goods and services priced by this index represent those that would be purchased through educational and general expenditures proportioned by functional category according to the weighted national average for all institutions.

The Index Market Basket

The HEPI measures the effect of price changes on the cost of goods and services in the college and university market basket purchased through expenditures for educational and general purposes, excluding sponsored research. Although colleges and universities purchase literally thousands of different items annually, only 10 item groups have been selected to represent, from a price standpoint, all the goods and services in the so-called education market basket. Each constitutes a significant component of the total, and for each there is a price series reasonably free from quality and quantity changes. The 10 items and the relative weights attached to each are shown in table B-4.

The assignment of index weights involves two steps: (1) identifying expenditure data by item or object classification and (2) adjusting the data to provide a nationally weighted average. Apparently the only published data in the United States that present expenditures classified by object items are those from the Oklahoma Board of Regents.[9] Such limited data mean that the basis for developing national averages is restricted to 18 public institutions, an extremely small sample. However, it is acceptable since most colleges face similar pricing trends when making the *major* purchases governed by price index values—viz., salaries of faculty, administrators, and other professional personnel. Furthermore, modest differences in the weights attached to budget items have little effect on overall index values. Index validity depends more on the weights being *constant* than on their values being absolutely accurate.[10] It can be assumed then, that if the national weights for items based on the Oklahoma sample are

---

[9] See Edward J. Coyle, *Current Operating Income and Expenditures, Oklahoma State Colleges and Universities*, Oklahoma State Regents for Higher Education, Oklahoma City, fiscal year 1965–66 and subsequent annual issues.

[10] This point may be illustrated as follows: If the weights attached to the two index items subject to the greatest inflationary trend—salaries of faculty, administrators, and other professional personnel—are reduced by 10 percent (i.e., reduced from 61.9 percent to 55.7 percent) and that weight transferred to a category priced by the Consumer Price Index, which represents an inflationary trend one-third as great, the resulting difference in HEPI values for the 10-year period 1958–68 is 3.7. With 1958 representing the base year (equal to 100), the HEPI value in 1968 would be 153.0 and after the aforementioned adjustment it would be 149.3.

Table B-4.—Percent distribution of educational and general expenditures, excluding sponsored research, by 10 object classifications and by type of institution: 1965–66

Institution	Total	Faculty salaries and staff benefits	Administrative and other professional salaries	Non-professional salaries and wages	Supplies and materials	Equipment	Utilities	Books and periodicals, printing and binding	Communications	Travel	Other[1]
Universities	100.00	43.0	17.0	18.0	8.5	2.0	3.0	2.0	2.0	1.5	3.0
4-year colleges	100.00	54.0	11.0	17.5	4.0	3.0	3.0	2.0	1.0	1.5	3.0
2-year colleges	100.00	50.0	11.0	18.0	6.5	3.5	3.0	2.0	1.0	1.0	4.0
Weighted national average[2]	100.00	47.6	14.3	17.8	6.7	2.5	3.0	2.0	1.6	1.4	3.1

[1] Includes expenditures for such other items as insurance, interest on debts, legal fees, and special services (trucking, etc.) performed by agencies outside the institution; also, livestock.
[2] Weights used represent the proportion of national total educational and general expenditures, excluding sponsored research, for each type of institution during the academic year 1965–66; universities, 55 percent; 4-year colleges, 36 percent; and 2-year colleges, 9 percent.

Source: For the three categories of institutions, estimates are based on normative data for 18 public institutions in the State of Oklahoma for the period 1965–66 through 1969–70 (see Edward J. Coyle, *Current Operating Income and Expenditures, Oklahoma State Colleges and Universities,* State Regents for Higher Education, Oklahoma City, fiscal year 1965–66 and subsequent annual issues).

reasonably representative, any deviation from unknown actual values will not significantly affect index validity.

Prices Used

The HEPI prices 10 item groups to represent the average price changes for all goods and services purchased by colleges and universities through expenditures for educational and general purposes. An explanation of the price series for each of the 10 item groups follows.

1. *Faculty salaries.* The faculty salary subindex consists of a weighted average of individual indexes of the salaries of professors, associate professors, assistant professors, and instructors (see table B-5). The weights are based on the proportion of each rank of full-time faculty in all institutions of higher education, spring 1963: professors, 26.4 percent; associate professors, 24.3 percent; assistant professors, 31.6 percent; and instructors, 17.7 percent.[11] From 1957–58 through 1963–64, the median 9-month salaries for full-time faculty at all institutions are those reported by the National Education Association. Starting in 1963–64 and linked[12] to the previous series, mean compensation for 9-month, full-time faculty at all institutions is that reported by the American Association of University Professors.

2. *Salaries of administrators and other professional personnel.* This subindex, based on a survey by the National Education Association, reports the average of the median annual salaries of administrative officers based on 11 or 12 months of service (see tables B-5 and B-6).

At 4-year and 2-year colleges, salary payments for the 14 administrative positions account for a large portion of total expenditures for this subindex item. Even though universities have more nonacademic positions—because of larger staffs in institutional development, research, student services, and library service—it is assumed that the price changes for these additional positions parallel those in the price series for the 14 administrative officers. It should be noted that the price series trend for faculty and that for administrative personnel is nearly the same (see table B-5, columns 9 and 11); therefore, any error in weighting between the two items is of almost no consequence to overall HEPI values.

---

[11] Ralph E. Dunham, Patricia S. Wright, and Majorie O. Chandler, *Teaching Faculty in Universities and Four-Year Colleges*, U.S. Department of Health, Education, and Welfare, Office of Education, U.S. Government Printing Office, Washington, D.C., 1966. (Data adjusted to include 2-year institutions.)

[12] For the linking procedure, see "Technical Notes."

Table B-5.—Indexes and dollar amounts of salaries of faculty, by rank, and administrative officers in colleges and universities: 1957–58 through 1971–72

1967 = 100

Academic year	Professors		Associate professors		Assistant professors		Instructors		Total faculty index[1]	Administrative officers[2]	
	Amount	Index	Amount	Index	Amount	Index	Amount	Index		Amount	Index
	(1)	(2)	(3)	(4)	(5)	(6)	(7)	(8)	(9)	(10)	(11)
1957–58	8,072	58.9	6,563	61.0	5,595	62.2	4,562	63.6	61.3	7,621	59.8
1958–59	8,589[3]	62.6	6,947[3]	64.5	5,913[3]	65.8	4,828[3]	67.3	64.9	8,134[3]	63.8
1959–60	9,107	66.4	7,332	68.1	6,231	69.3	5,095	71.1	68.6	8,647	67.9
1960–61	9,681[3]	70.6	7,749[3]	72.0	6,565[3]	73.0	5,338[3]	74.4	72.4	9,150[3]	71.8
1961–62	10,256	74.8	8,167	75.9	6,900	76.7	5,582	77.8	76.2	9,654	75.8
1962–63	10,784[3]	78.6	8,568[3]	79.6	7,219[3]	80.3	5,848[3]	81.6	79.9	10,164[3]	79.8
1963–64	11,312		8,969		7,539		6,114				
1964–65	12,980	82.5	9,800	83.3	8,140	83.8	6,540	85.3	83.6	10,674	83.8
1965–66	13,770	87.5	10,360	88.1	8,560	88.2	6,850	89.3	88.2	11,325[3]	88.9
1966–67	14,700	93.5	11,030	93.8	9,110	93.8	7,220	94.1	93.8	11,977	94.0
1967–68	15,730	100.0	11,760	100.0	9,710	100.0	7,670	100.0	100.0	12,741[3]	100.0
1968–69	16,807	106.8	12,573	106.9	10,371	106.8	8,160	106.4	106.8	13,505	106.0
1969–70	18,001	114.4	13,537	115.1	11,156	114.9	8,769	114.3	114.7	14,472[3]	113.6
1970–71	19,269	122.5	14,443	122.8	12,154	125.2	9,409	122.7	122.4	15,440	121.2
1971–72	20,398	129.7	15,330	130.4	12,647	130.2	10,086	131.5	130.3	16,297[3]	127.9
1972–73	21,227	134.9	15,969	135.9	13,205	136.0	10,669	139.1	136.2	17,153	134.6

[1] Weighted average of columns (2), (4), (6), and (8). The weights used represent the proportion of each category of faculty working full time in all institutions of higher education, spring 1963: professors, 26.4 percent; associate professors, 24.3 percent; assistant professors, 31.6 percent; and instructors, 17.7 percent.

Source: Ralph E. Dunham, Patricia S. Wright, and Marjorie O. Chandler, *Teaching Faculty in Universities and Four-Year Colleges*, U. S. Department of Health, Education, and Welfare, Office of Education, U. S. Government Printing Office, Washington, D. C., 1966. (Data adjusted to include 2-year institutions.)

[2] Average of the median annual salaries of administrative officers based on 11 or 12 months' service (see table B-6).

[3] Interpolated (data not available).

Sources: Faculty, for 1957–58 through 1963–64, median salaries for 9 months full-time faculty in all institutions from National Education Association; starting in 1963–64, mean compensation for 9-months full-time faculty in all institutions from American Association of University Professors; administrative officers, from National Education Association (see table B-6).

Table B-6.—Median annual salaries of administrative officers in 4-year colleges and universities: 1957–58 through 1971–72

Position	1957–58	1959–60	1961–62	1963–64	1965–66	1967–68	1969–70	1971–72
Mean for all positions	7,621	8,647	9,654	10,674	11,977	13,505	15,440	17,153
President	12,407	13,827	15,375	17,330	19,638	22,303	25,979	29,750
Vice president	12,013	14,154	16,000	17,130	19,012	21,458	23,250	26,313
Dean of the college	8,411	10,723	12,230	13,644	15,703	16,141	19,125	19,975
Dean of students	7,610	8,796	9,592	10,694	12,027	14,086	16,050	17,830
Dean of men	6,658	7,280	8,202	9,144	9,783	10,983	12,319	13,490
Dean of women	6,006	6,638	7,399	8,216	9,209	10,289	11,406	12,448
Dean of admissions	6,738	7,680	8,636	9,572	10,364	11,446	12,983	14,280
Registrar	6,032	6,340	7,312	8,142	9,123	10,366	11,743	13,108
Business manager	7,518	8,536	9,405	10,512	11,780	14,914	17,615	19,419
Chief librarian	6,134	7,078	8,163	8,883	10,225	11,817	13,439	14,891
Director of public relations	6,420	7,194	7,659	8,440	9,596	10,823	12,764	14,652
Director of athletics	7,292	8,104	8,930	9,871	11,125	12,470	14,311	15,821
Head football coach	7,077	7,824	8,554	9,321	10,716	11,488	13,395	14,591
Head basketball coach	6,382	6,888	7,700	8,542	9,383	10,485	11,779	13,208

NOTE.—Salaries of instructional staff are for 9 months of full-time teaching; salaries of administrative officers are usually for 11 or 12 months of service.

Source: National Education Association, Research Division, Research Report 1970-R3, Economic Status of the Teaching Profession, 1969–70; Research Report 1972-R5, Salaries Paid and Salary-Related Practices in Higher Education, 1971–72, Washington, D.C. (Copyright 1970 and 1972 by the National Education Association. All rights reserved.)

3. *Nonprofessional salaries and wages.* Price changes for this subindex are based on the Bureau of Labor Statistics salary series for office clerical personnel (see *Handbook of Labor Statistics 1970*, BLS Bulletin 1666, p. 217). It should be pointed out that the salary series for skilled maintenance and unskilled plant workers parallels almost exactly that for clerical workers. Consequently both types of positions are represented in this subindex.

4. *Supplies and materials.* This subindex is a composite of the wholesale price series for office supplies and accessories (BLS code no. 0915-06), e.g., carbon paper, typewriter ribbons, file folders, index cards, etc., and for writing paper (BLS code no. 0913-0141). The two series are weighted 80 percent and 20 percent, respectively, based on wholesale price index weights. In the absence of any college- and university-related weighting data, BLS weights are used.

5. *Equipment.* The wholesale price series for office and store machines and equipment (BLS code no. 1193) has been used for this subindex. This series prices adding machines, calculators, cash registers, typewriters, etc.

6. *Utilities.* This subindex is a composite of the wholesale price series for natural gas (BLS code no. 0531-0101), commercial electric power (BLS code no. 0542), and residual fuels (BLS code no. 0574). The weightings— gas, 33 percent; power, 54 percent; and fuels, 13 percent—are based on wholesale price index weights. Since related weighting data for colleges and universities are not available, BLS weights have been used.

7. *Books and periodicals, printing and binding.* This subindex (see table B-7) is a weighted average of the price series for selected hardcover trade and technical books (published in *The Bowker Annual of Library and Book Trade Information*) and the U. S. periodicals price series (published annually in the July issue of the *Library Journal*). The weights of 88 percent for hard-cover books and 12 percent for periodicals are based on an informal survey of expert opinion.

8. *Communications.* This subindex is a weighted average of the consumer price series for telephone rates (82 percent) and postal charges (18 percent).

9. *Travel.* This subindex, the consumer price series for public transporta-tion, represents fares for local transit, taxicab, railroad (coach), airplane (chiefly coach), and bus (intercity).

10. *Other.* This category includes such miscellaneous items as insurance, interest on debts, legal fees, special services (trucking, for example) per-formed by outside agencies, and livestock. This subindex is based on the Consumer Price Index.

Table B-7.—Average prices and indexes for hardcover books and U.S. periodicals: 1957 through 1972

1967 = 100

Year	Hardcover books		U. S. periodicals		Overall index[2]
	Average price	Index[1]	Average price	Index[1]	
1957	$ 4.86 est.	60.8	$ 4.74 est.	59.1	60.6
1958	5.12	64.1	4.92	61.3	63.8
1959	5.18 est.	64.8	5.12 est.	63.8	64.7
1960	5.24	65.6	5.32	66.3	65.7
1961	5.81	72.7	5.63	70.2	72.4
1962	5.90	73.8	5.92	73.8	73.8
1963	6.55	82.0	6.31	78.7	81.6
1964	6.93	86.7	6.64	82.8	86.2
1965	7.65	95.7	6.95	86.7	94.6
1966	7.94	99.4	7.44	92.8	98.6
1967	7.99	100.0	8.02	100.0	100.0
1968	8.47	106.0	8.65	107.9	106.2
1969	9.37[3]	117.3	9.31	116.1	117.2
	9.50				
1970	11.66	143.9	10.41	129.8	142.2
1971	13.25	163.5	11.66	145.4	161.3
1972	12.99	160.3	13.23	165.0	160.9

[1] Indexes are not fixed-weight indexes and reflect changes in the type and mix of books and periodicals from year to year.

[2] Weighted average of book index and periodical index. The weights used—hardcover books, 88 percent; U. S. periodicals, 12 percent—are based on an informal survey of expert opinion.

[3] Since the new category of travel was added, prices were linked in 1969.

Source: Prices of hardcover books are based on tabulations recorded in the "Weekly Record" section of *Publishers Weekly* for the years indicated. Not included are mass-market paperbacks, government documents, and certain multivolume encyclopedias. Published in *The Bowker Annual of Library and Book Trade Information*, R. R. Bowker, New York, 1972.

U. S. periodical prices are based on a total group of 2,372 titles published in the July issues of the *Library Journal* since 1964.

Limitations

The HEPI represents all colleges and universities but not necessarily any one college or any special group of colleges. The reason is that individual institutions or groups of colleges spend their income differently and are therefore differently affected by price changes. An institution may, of course, design its own index by using the price series in table B-2 and weighting the various items according to its own expenditures. Yet because faculty salaries account for the largest item in the budget and salary trends tend to be uniform throughout the country, a specially designed index will not as a rule vary substantially from the HEPI based on national average weightings.

Nearly every price index suffers some loss in validity as the result of the almost unavoidable inclusion of price changes due to improvement in the quality of items being observed. When measuring price changes, the Bureau of Labor Statistics makes every effort to exclude the effects of quality changes by insisting that detailed specifications be used to describe the items priced and by examining all merchandise to see that it consistently meets these specifications. No such safeguards exist, however, for pricing personal services. Factors that may alter the quality of personal services include (1) the level and quality of training received by the worker, (2) the worker's job experience, and (3) length of the work week. The few workers for whom these factors may be relatively constant from year to year are quite likely to be unrepresentative of the occupation in which they are employed. For example, the salary trend of newly hired instructors who hold similar degrees from a given type of institution and have had the same teaching experience does not necessarily represent the national trend in instructor salaries for the profession as a whole.

In recent years the quality of education acquired by faculty members has undoubtedly improved,[13] with commensurate increases in salaries. Changes in the age and experience level of college faculty have also affected salaries. These types of quality changes are not taken into account by the HEPI nor are the changes in pricing brought about by modification of the faculty work schedule. Although the amount of time faculty members spend in the classroom may have declined slightly in the past decade, any reduction in the number of teaching hours may have been more than offset by the additional time faculty have devoted to preparation and research. Actually, the extent of quality and quantity changes in faculty and administrative services and the influence of these changes on salaries is not known. Those who feel that the HEPI has a built-in upward price trend bias due to failure to exclude price increases resulting from improvements in the quality of services and goods purchased may wish to modify downward the trend in index values, or at least to exercise restraint in using the inflationary trend as reported by the index.

---

[13] The continuous increase in knowledge suggests that the more recently an individual has undertaken his training the more advanced his knowledge. Today's faculty are therefore more likely to be up to date in their professional knowledge than their predecessors. It is also true that the higher the level of training the more comprehensive the preparation. However, data for the long-run trend in the proportion of Ph.D's among college faculty are conflicting and inconclusive. The trend, whether up or down, is therefore probably slight and would have little influence on the faculty quality and hence on salary levels.

PHYSICAL PLANT EXPENDITURES PRICE INDEX

The price index for physical plant expenditures is entitled Index of Change in Prices of Building Construction and Equipment Purchased by Colleges and Universities (see table B-8). Expenditures for physical plant assets consist primarily of the investment in buildings and equipment. As shown in table B-1, land represents a relatively small annual investment, less than 1 percent of the total. Because geographical location plays a critical role in land values, a land price series based on national averages would have no relevancy either to a particular plot of land or to a single institution or group of institutions. Land as an item of expenditure is, therefore, excluded from the index calculations.

Table B-8.—Price index for building construction and equipment purchased by colleges and universities, and component indexes: 1957–58 through 1971–72

1967 =100

Calendar year or academic year ending	Building construction and improvements	Equipment	Overall index[1]
1958	75.2	90.5	78.1
1959	77.4	91.9	80.2
1960	79.7	92.6	82.2
1961	81.2	92.4	83.3
1962	83.5	92.8	85.3
1963	85.7	93.2	87.1
1964	88.0	93.6	89.1
1965	91.0	94.1	91.6
1966	95.5	96.4	95.7
1967	100.0	100.0	100.0
1968	106.8	102.9	106.1
1969	115.8	105.8	113.9
1970	124.8	111.4	122.3
1971	138	115.1	133.6
1972	151	117.3	144.6

[1] Weighted average. Weights used: building construction and improvements, 81 percent; equipment, 19 percent. Weights are based on the proportionate expenditures for these two items for all colleges and universities during the academic years 1966, 1967, and 1968.

Source: For building construction, the American Appraisal Company Index reported in *Construction Review* published monthly by the U. S. Department of Commerce.

For equipment, a weighted average of the following items from the Wholesale Price Index network: commercial furniture, 40 percent; office and store machines and equipment, 25 percent; general purpose machinery and equipment, 30 percent; and machinery and equipment, 5 percent.

The relative weights attached to building construction (81 percent) and equipment (19 percent) are based on proportionate expenditures by all colleges and universities for the academic years 1965–66, 1966–67, and 1967–68.

The source for the price series for building construction, the American Appraisal Company Index, is officially described as follows:

> This index is compiled on the basis of a detailed bill of quantities of material and labor required for typical frame, brick-wood frame, brick-steel frame, and reinforced concrete buildings, with allowances for contractor's overhead and profit, in various cities throughout the United States. Workmen's compensation and liability insurance, unemployment insurance, and old-age pension factors are included. The index covers the structural portion of the buildings but does not include such fixtures as plumbing, heating, lighting, and elevators. The material and labor costs are re-computed monthly in accordance with average prices and wages supplemented by personal investigation of appraisers and information from clients and others as to actual costs. These computations automatically result in weighted averages for the individual buildings. Arithmetic averages are computed for the individual buildings and cities to obtain city and national averages. The latter cover 30 cities. The index reflects changes in average price levels but does not reflect costs resulting from over-time wages and bonuses during boom periods or sacrifice prices and omissiont of overhead costs and profits during depression periods.

In collecting price data to be used in price indexes, the need has already been discussed for holding constant the quality or utility-determining specifications of all items. With regard to much equipment, such a practice is especially difficult and perhaps impossible. The utility of most products is continuously being improved and the improved product sold at a higher price to the consumer. This type of price increase, due to quality improve-ment, must be eliminated from any price series by a procedure called "linking" (see "Technical Notes"). Another problem in developing a price index for equipment is that colleges and universities purchase a wide variety of different products. If these were to be priced individually, the procedure would be time consuming.

The task of pricing many different product items while attempting to account for the effects on price of product innovation and redesign is performed by the Bureau of Labor Statistics in preparing a wholesale price index. To avoid incorporating price changes influenced by quality or quantity changes, the Bureau of Labor Statistics defines each commodity in the wholesale price index by precise specifications. These specifications not only include the principal price-determining characteristics of com-modities but the terms of sale between specified types of sellers and speci-fied types of purchasers. Many of the more sizable equipment expenditures by colleges and universities are represented in this wholesale price index.

Consequently, the BLS price series can be used to price the following four major groups of equipment purchased by colleges and universities:

Equipment	Relative weight*	Wholesale price index item used
Office and classroom furniture	40%	Commercial furniture (BLS code no. 12–2)
Office machines and equipment	25%	Office and store machines and equipment (BLS code no. 11–93)
Laboratory equipment	30%	General purpose machinery and equipment (BLS code no. 11–4)
Other	5%	Machinery and equipment (BLS code no. 11)

* The relative weight of each equipment component is based on data obtained from college purchasing officers.

TECHNICAL NOTES: ADJUSTMENTS FOR QUANTITY AND QUALITY CHANGES

Because items in any market basket are subject to change, index number comparisons over extended periods of time may be unreliable or even inaccurate. To account for changes in the composition of a market basket, the Laspeyres formula may be employed. A Laspeyres index number based on formula 1 below measures the price of fixed quantities of given commodities in the base year and in each succeeding year. Formula 2 measures the price of given commodities in each year weighted according to their fixed relative importance, i.e., to their proportionate share of the total budget in the base year. (By substituting $w_o = p_o q_o / \Sigma p_o q_o$ in formula 2 it can be shown that formulas 1 and 2 are equal.) By holding quantity or budget proportions constant, the Laspeyres formula makes possible reliable comparison of index values on a year-to-year basis. Moreover, after the basket composition of goods and services has been determined for the base year, it will seldom need to be revised. The formula for a weighted aggregate price index of the Laspeyres type is as follows:

(1) When prices are weighted by the *quantity* of each purchased item:
$$\frac{\Sigma\, p_i q_o}{\Sigma\, p_o q_o}$$

(2) When prices are weighted by the *proportion* of the total budget alloted for each purchased item:
$$\frac{\Sigma\, p_i w_o}{\Sigma\, p_o w_o}$$

where, for an individual commodity,

p_o = price in the base period, e.g., 1967,

p_i = price in the current period, e.g., 1973,

q_o = quantity in the base period, and

w_o = proportion of total budget in the base period.

While the simplicity of this formula eliminates the need for determining the yearly market basket composition, it does have one disadvantage. The Laspeyres index does not price the actual amounts and kinds of goods and services purchased in any given year; rather, it prices only those items identified as constituting the market basket during the base year. If there has been considerable change in the composition of the market basket over time, adjustments must be made. For example, colleges and universities now spend substantial sums for computer hardware, equipment not in existence until fairly recently. For index purposes, a process called linking is used to adjust for the purchase of goods that have undergone changes in either quantity or quality.

Adjusting for Quality Changes by Linking

Quality changes, as they relate to price index construction, are the result of (1) changes in the physical characteristics of products due to scientific and technological progress and (2) changes resulting from the purchase of larger quantities of one item as a substitute or replacement for another. The effect on prices of both types of changes can be reduced, within limits, by periodically substituting new items for old items and recording any accompanying change in quality as an increase in output, not a price change. The use of price relatives to make this type of adjustment can best be explained by use of the following tabulation.

Tabulation of Price-Change Computational Methods

	Base period	Period of substitution	Later period
1. Direct comparison:			
Reported price	$1.63	$1.94	$1.70
Price relative	—	$\frac{\$1.94}{\$1.63} \times 100 = 119.0$	$\frac{\$1.70}{\$1.94} \times 100 = 87.6$
Price index	100.0	119.0	$\frac{119.0 \times 87.6}{100} = 104.2$
2. Linking: (full difference in price between new item substituted for old item due to quality change)			
Reported price:			
Old item	$5.00	$5.50	—
New item	—	$6.00	$6.25
Price relative	—	$\frac{\$5.50}{\$5.00} \times 100 = 110.0$	$\frac{\$6.25}{\$6.00} \times 100 = 104.2$
Price index	100.0	110.0	$\frac{110.0 \times 104.2}{100} = 114.6$
3. Linking: (difference in price between new item substituted for old item due to changes in both quality and price)			
Reported price:			
Old item	$3.00	$4.00	—
New item	—	—	$4.50
Value of quality difference between old and new items	—	+$0.35	—
Price relative	—	$\frac{(\$4.00-\$0.35)}{\$3.00} \times 100 = 121.7$	$\frac{\$4.50}{\$4.00} \times 100 = 112.5$
Price index	100.0	121.7	$\frac{121.7 \times 112.5}{100} = 136.9$

When the quality of an item remains relatively constant over time, price changes from one period to the next may be calculated by direct comparison (example 1): dividing the price for an item in the current period by the price in the preceding period. A simple procedure, it has been used for all subindexes of the higher education price index.

Linking is the process whereby the price of a new item is tied to the price of an old item by factoring out the price difference due to the change in quality involved. In example 2 the full difference in price between the two items purchased during the period of substitution is assumed to be due to a quality change. This price difference is ignored. The price of the new item during a later period divided by its price during the period of substitution is called a link relative. The price index for the later period is calculated by multiplying the price index for the period of substitution by the link relative.

When the price difference between the two items is due to changes in both quality and in price, the procedure in example 3 applies. It involves reducing the price of the new item during the period of substitution by the estimated price value of the quality difference involved, then comparing the adjusted price of the new item with the price of the old item during the previous period.

Estimating the price value of quality changes requires considerable information about both quantities purchased and product specifications. The amount of effort required to secure these data and the amount of improvement that will accrue to index validity are primary factors to consider in determining the extent to which the linking methodology should be employed.

It should be kept in mind that, in a strict sense, index numbers are comparable only over relatively short periods of time. Repeated linking operations increase the combined effect that new products, market basket composition changes, and, to some extent, quality variations exert on index numbers. The longer the time span, the less comparability there will be in the series.

BIBLIOGRAPHY

Gavett, Thomas W., "Quantity and a Pure Price Index," *Monthly Labor Review*, vol. 90, no. 3, March 1967, pp. 15–20.

Gilbert, Milton, "The Problem of Quality Changes and Index Numbers," *Monthly Labor Review*, vol. 84, no. 9, September 1961, pp. 992–97.

Gordon, R. J., "Measurement Bias in Price Indexes for Capital Goods," *Review of Income and Wealth*, Series 17, no. 2, June 1971, pp. 121–74.

Griliches, Zvi, "Notes on the Measurement of Price and Quality Changes," in *Models of Income Detention, Studies of Income and Wealth*, vol. 28, National Bureau of Economic Research, Princeton, N.J., 1964, pp. 301–04; *Price Indexes and Quality Change*, Harvard University Press, Cambridge, Mass., 1971, 287 pp.; "Quality Change and Index Numbers: A Critique," *Monthly Labor Review*, vol. 85, no. 5, May 1962, pp. 542–45.

Hoover, Ethel D. "The CPI and Problems of Quality Change," *Monthly Labor Review*, vol. 84, no. 11, November 1961, pp. 1175–85.

Joint Economic Committee, Congress of the United States, *Government Price Statistics, Hearings . . . January 24, 1961*, U.S. Government Printing Office, Washington, D.C., 1961, 526 pp.

O'Neill, June, *Resource Use in Higher Education*, Carnegie Commission on Higher Education, Berkeley, Calif., 1971, Appendix B: "Price Indexes for Instructional Operating Expenditures."

Triplett, Jack E., *The Theory of Hedonic Quality Measurement and Its Use in Price Indexes*, U.S. Department of Labor, Bureau of Labor Statistics, U.S. Government Printing Office, Washington, D.C., 1971, 53 pp.

U.S. Department of Labor, Bureau of Labor Statistics, *Techniques of Preparing Major BLS Statistical Series*, Bulletin No. 1168, U.S. Government Printing Office, Washington, D.C., 1954, 126 pp.

Wasserman, William, *Education Price and Quality Indexes*, Syracuse University Press, Syracuse, N.Y., 1963, 166 pp.

Appendix C

COLLEGE AND UNIVERSITY FINANCIAL DATA

Table C-1.—Unrestricted educational and general revenues and student education expenditures, by control and type of institution, amount, percent of total, and amount per FTE student, in current and constant dollars: 1965–66 through 1971–72

PUBLIC UNIVERSITIES

	1965–66		1966–67		1967–68	
Number of institutions	90		92		92	
FTE enrollment[1]	1,372,558		1,476,669		1,592,487	

1st column—amount in thousands; 2nd column—percentage distribution

	1965–66		1966–67		1967–68	
Unrestricted educational and general revenues	$2,386,905	100.0	$2,731,708	100.0	$3,285,456	100.0
Student tuition and fees	506,606	21.2	581,226	21.3	710,192	21.7
Federal Government appropriations	203,983	8.5	144,536	5.3	144,340	4.4
State and local government appropriations	1,597,543	66.9	1,920,360	70.3	2,350,741	71.5
Endowment income	20,619	.9	27,890	1.0	31,283	.9
Private gifts	58,154	2.4	57,696	2.1	48,900	1.5
Student education expenditures	$2,406,666	100.0	$2,722,339	100.0	$3,287,173	100.0
Instruction & departmental research	1,338,660	55.5	1,532,787	56.3	1,853,550	56.4
Extension and public service	358,084	14.9	369,036	13.6	431,282	13.1
Libraries	113,739	4.7	133,373	4.9	169,454	5.2
Physical plant maintenance & operation	272,383	11.3	311,598	11.4	374,033	11.4
General administration & student services	323,800	13.4	375,545	13.8	458,854	14.0

1st column—amount per FTE student in current dollars [1]
2nd column—amount per FTE student in constant dollars[2] (1967 prices)

	Current	Constant	Current	Constant	Current	Constant
Unrestricted educational and general revenues	$1,739	$1,829	$1,850	$1,850	$2,063	$1,957
Student tuition and fees	369	388	394	394	448	425
Federal Government appropriations	148	156	98	98	91	86
State and local government appropriations	1,163	1,223	1,301	1,301	1,475	1,399
Endowment income	16	17	19	19	19	18
Private gifts	42	44	39	39	31	29
Student education expenditures	$1,753	$1,843	$1,844	$1,844	$2,064	$1,958
Instruction & departmental research	975		1,038		1,164	
Extension and public service	261		251		270	
Libraries	82		90		107	
Physical plant maintenance & operation	198		210		235	
General administration & student services	235		254		289	

See footnotes at end of table.

Table C-1.—Unrestricted educational and general revenues and student education expenditures, by control and type of institution, amount, percent of total, and amount per FTE student, in current and constant dollars: 1965-66 through 1971-72 —Continued

1st column—amount in thousands; 2nd column—percentage distribution

PUBLIC UNIVERSITIES	1968-69		1969-70		1970-71		1971-72	
Number of institutions	94		94		94		94	
FTE enrollment[1]	1,746,960		1,860,890		1,943,735		1,990,512	
Unrestricted educational and general revenues	$3,698,568	100.0	4,325,449	100.0	$4,797,542	100.0	$5,189,432	100.0
Student tuition and fees	798,748	21.6	982,269	22.7	1,132,779	23.6	1,285,005	24.8
Federal Government appropriations	140,615	3.8	187,483	4.3	185,800	3.8	181,039	3.5
State and local government appropriations	2,670,920	72.2	3,059,107	70.7	3,374,628	70.3	3,596,396	69.3
Endowment income	42,767	1.2	50,125	1.2	50,740	1.1	50,444	1.0
Private gifts	45,518	1.2	46,465	1.1	53,595	1.1	76,548	1.5
Student education expenditures	$3,669,716	100.0	4,223,787	100.0	$4,775,513	100.0	$5,070,812	100.0
Instruction & departmental research	2,071,158	56.4	2,370,928	56.1	2,663,359	55.8	2,844,796	56.1
Extension and public service	358,471	9.8	410,835	9.7	466,869	9.8	469,009	9.2
Libraries	190,387	5.2	216,385	5.1	235,583	4.9	244,734	4.8
Physical plant maintenance & operation	439,800	12.0	510,262	12.1	568,533	11.9	622,444	12.3
General administration & student services	609,900	16.6	715,377	16.9	841,169	17.6	889,829	17.5

1st column—amount per FTE student in current dollars
2nd column—amount per FTE student in constant dollars[2] (1967 prices)

	1st	2nd	1st	2nd	1st	2nd	1st	2nd
Unrestricted educational and general revenues	$2,117	$1,892	$2,324	$1,948	$2,468	$1,934	$2,607	$1,971
Student tuition and fees	457	408	528	443	583	457	646	488
Federal Government appropriations	80	71	100	89	96	75	90	68
State and local government appropriations	1,528	1,366	1,643	1,377	1,736	1,361	1,806	1,365
Endowment income	25	22	28	23	26	20	26	20
Private gifts	25	22	26	22	28	22	39	30
Student education expenditures	$2,101	$1,878	$2,270	$1,903	$2,457	$1,926	$2,547	$1,925
Instruction & departmental research	1,185		1,273		1,370		1,430	
Extension and public service	206		220		240		234	
Libraries	109		116		121		122	
Physical plant maintenance & operation	252		275		292		314	
General administration & student services	349		384		433		497	

See footnotes at end of table.

Table C-1.—Unrestricted educational and general revenues and student education expenditures, by control and type of institution, amount, percent of total, and amount per FTE student, in current and constant dollars: 1965–66 through 1971–72 —Continued

PUBLIC 4-YEAR COLLEGES

1st column—amount in thousands: 2nd column—percentage distribution

	1965–66		1966–67		1967–68	
Number of institutions	313		313		322	
FTE enrollment[1]	1,060,472		1,149,198		1,283,204	
Unrestricted educational and general revenues	$1,218,566	100.0	$1,485,013	100.0	$1,859,664	100.0
Student tuition and fees	247,843	20.3	299,883	20.2	347,236	18.7
Federal Government appropriations	111,566	9.2	114,259	7.7	179,929	9.7
State and local government appropriations	851,379	69.9	1,057,282	71.1	1,321,041	71.0
Endowment income	1,637	.1	2,356	.2	2,990	.2
Private gifts	6,141	.5	11,233	.8	8,468	.5
Student education expenditures	1,139,798	100.0	1,421,623	100.0	1,737,559	100.0
Instruction & departmental research	696,324	61.1	860,844	60.6	1,040,654	59.9
Extension and public service	19,307	1.7	31,065	2.2	39,988	2.3
Libraries	65,063	5.7	82,026	5.8	99,553	5.7
Physical plant maintenance & operation	157,379	13.8	192,970	13.6	222,497	12.8
General administration & student services	201,725	17.7	254,718	17.9	334,867	19.3

1st column—amount per FTE student in current dollars
2nd column—amount per FTE student in constant dollars[2] (1967 prices)

	1st	2nd	1st	2nd	1st	2nd
Unrestricted educational and general revenues	$1,150	$1,209	$1,292	$1,292	$1,449	$1,375
Student tuition and fees	233	245	261	261	271	257
Federal Government appropriations	106	111	99	99	141	134
State and local government appropriations	804	845	919	919	1,029	976
Endowment income	1	1	3	3	3	3
Private gifts	6	6	10	10	7	7
Student education expenditures	$1,075	$1,130	$1,237	$1,237	$1,354	$1,285
Instruction & departmental research	657		750		811	
Extension and public service	18		27		31	
Libraries	61		72		77	
Physical plant maintenance & operation	148		168		173	
General administration & student services	190		221		261	

See footnotes at end of table.

Table C-1.—Unrestricted educational and general revenues and student education expenditures, by control and type of institution, amount, percent of total, and amount per FTE student, in current and constant dollars: 1965–66 through 1971–72
—Continued

PUBLIC 4-YEAR COLLEGES	1968–69		1969–70		1970–71		1971–72	
Number of institutions	323		332		341		346	
FTE enrollment[1]	1,411,472		1,499,616		1,631,097		1,711,132	

1st column—amount in thousands; 2nd column—percentage distribution

	1968–69		1969–70		1970–71		1971–72	
Unrestricted educational and general revenues	$2,110,768	100.0	$2,617,820	100.0	$2,967,261	100.0	$3,332,990	100.0
Student tuition and fees	406,318	19.2	512,014	19.6	611,365	20.6	703,638	21.1
Federal Government appropriations	181,652	8.6	183,111	7.0	202,698	6.8	262,632	7.9
State and local government appropriations	1,512,807	71.7	1,907,632	72.9	2,138,395	72.1	2,351,722	70.6
Endowment income	3,845	.2	4,430	.2	3,289	.1	3,175	.1
Private gifts	6,146	.3	10,633	.4	11,514	.4	11,823	.4
Student education expenditures	$2,070,681	100.0	$2,474,762	100.0	$2,869,177	100.0	$3,188,939	100.0
Instruction & departmental research	1,211,368	58.5	1,472,478	59.5	1,719,851	60.0	1,859,565	58.3
Extension and public service	33,824	1.6	42,755	1.7	44,604	1.6	52,825	1.7
Libraries	119,664	5.8	138,595	5.6	156,628	5.5	170,935	5.4
Physical plant maintenance & operation	268,588	13.1	323,010	13.1	377,775	13.2	420,106	13.2
General administration & student services	437,237	21.1	497,924	20.1	570,319	19.9	685,508	21.5

1st column—amount per FTE student in current dollars
2nd column—amount per FTE student in constant dollars[2] (1967 prices)

Unrestricted educational and general revenues	$1,495	$1,336	$1,746	$1,464	$1,819	$1,426	$1,948	$1,472
Student tuition and fees	287	256	342	287	375	294	410	310
Federal Government appropriations	129	115	122	102	124	97	154	116
State and local government appropriations	1,072	958	1,273	1,067	1,311	1,027	1,374	1,038
Endowment income	3	3	3	3	2	2	2	2
Private gifts	4	4	7	6	7	6	8	6
Student education expenditures	$1,467	$1,311	$1,650	$1,474	$1,759	$1,379	$1,864	$1,409
Instruction & departmental research	858		982		1,054		1,086	
Extension and public service	23		28		27		32	
Libraries	85		92		96		101	
Physical plant maintenance & operation	192		216		232		245	
General administration & student services	310		332		350		400	

See footnotes at end of table.

Table C-1.—Unrestricted educational and general revenues and student education expenditures, by control and type of institution, amount, percent of total, and amount per FTE student, in current and constant dollars: 1965–66 through 1971–72 —Continued

PUBLIC 2-YEAR COLLEGES

	1965–66		1966–67		1967–68	
Number of institutions	422		479		520	
FTE enrollment[1]	722,497		812,667		928,573	

1st column—amount in thousands; 2nd column—percentage distribution

	1965–66		1966–67		1967–68	
Unrestricted educational and general revenues	$593,651	100.0	$741,540	100.0	$1,015,035	100.0
Student tuition and fees	91,662	15.4	116,310	15.7	151,901	15.1
Federal Government appropriations	25,608	4.3	24,205	3.3	41,475	4.1
State and local government appropriations	474,056	79.9	597,740	80.6	818,861	80.7
Endowment income	1,138	.2	999	.1	1,569	.2
Private gifts	1,187	.2	2,286	.3	1,229	.1
Student education expenditures	$534,035	100.0	$665,293	100.0	$888,665	100.0
Instruction & departmental research	341,507	63.9	426,452	64.1	563,062	63.4
Extension and public service	19,070	3.6	19,120	2.9	21,339	2.4
Libraries	22,451	4.2	30,623	4.6	38,612	4.3
Physical plant maintenance & operation	62,093	11.6	80,167	12.0	105,721	11.9
General administration & student services	88,914	16.6	108,931	16.4	159,931	18.1

1st column—amount per FTE student in current dollars
2nd column—amount per FTE student in constant dollars[2] (1967 prices)

	1st	2nd	1st	2nd	1st	2nd
Unrestricted educational and general revenues	$822	$864	$912	$912	$1,093	$1,037
Student tuition and fees	127	134	143	143	165	157
Federal Government appropriations	35	37	30	30	45	43
State and local government appropriations	657	691	735	735	882	837
Endowment income	2	2	1	1	2	2
Private gifts	2	2	3	3	1	1
Student education expenditures	$739	$777	$819	$819	$957	$908
Instruction & departmental research	472		525		607	
Extension and public service	27		24		23	
Libraries	31		38		41	
Physical plant maintenance & operation	86		98		114	
General administration & student services	123		134		173	

See footnotes at end of table.

Table C-1.—Unrestricted educational and general revenues and student education expenditures, by control and type of institution, amount, percent of total, and amount per FTE student, in current and constant dollars: 1965–66 through 1971–72 —Continued

PUBLIC 2-YEAR COLLEGES

	1968–69		1969–70		1970–71		1971–72	
Number of institutions	594		634		654		697	
FTE enrollment[1]	1,120,740		1,255,429		1,413,741		1,585,553	

1st column—amount in thousands; 2nd column—percentage distribution

	1968–69		1969–70		1970–71		1971–72	
Unrestricted educational and general revenues	$1,288,379	100.0	$1,624,985	100.0	$1,976,448	100.0	$2,278,570	100.0
Student tuition and fees	193,947	15.1	246,541	15.2	294,754	15.0	352,380	15.5
Federal Government appropriations	53,761	4.2	52,172	3.2	77,017	3.9	105,968	4.7
State and local government appropriations	1,036,324	80.4	1,322,501	81.4	1,596,902	80.8	1,816,048	79.7
Endowment income	1,901	.1	2,529	.1	1,465	.1	1,616	.1
Private gifts	2,446	.2	1,242	.1	6,310	.3	2,558	.1
Student education expenditures	$1,249,544	100.0	$1,528,898	100.0	$1,829,038	100.0	$2,171,259	100.0
Instruction & departmental research	757,121	60.6	920,335	60.2	1,130,575	61.8	1,313,684	60.5
Extension and public service	28,948	2.3	31,719	2.1	37,395	2.0	45,481	2.1
Libraries	50,515	4.0	62,966	4.1	74,646	4.1	86,595	4.0
Physical plant maintenance & operation	138,198	11.1	172,407	11.3	198,124	10.8	249,352	11.5
General administration & student services	274,762	22.1	341,471	22.3	388,298	21.2	476,147	21.9

1st column—amount per FTE student in current dollars
2nd column—amount per FTE student in constant dollars[2] (1967 prices)

Unrestricted educational and general revenues	$1,150	$1,028	$1,294	$1,085	$1,398	$1,096	$1,437	$1,086
Student tuition and fees	174	155	197	165	208	163	223	169
Federal Government appropriations	48	43	41	34	54	42	68	51
State and local government appropriations	925	827	1,053	883	1,130	886	1,144	864
Endowment income	1	1	1	1	1	1	1	1
Private gifts	2	2	1	1	4	3	1	1
Student education expenditures	$1,115	$996	$1,218	$1,021	$1,294	$1,014	$1,369	$1,035
Instruction & departmental research	676		733		800		828	
Extension and public service	26		26		26		29	
Libraries	45		50		53		55	
Physical plant maintenance & operation	124		138		140		157	
General administration & student services	246		272		275		300	

See footnotes at end of table.

Table C-1.—Unrestricted educational and general revenues and student education expenditures, by control and type of institution, amount, percent of total, and amount per FTE student, in current and constant dollars: 1965-66 through 1971-72 —Continued

PRIVATE UNIVERSITIES

1st column—amount in thousands; 2nd column—percentage distribution

	1965-66		1966-67		1967-68	
Number of institutions	65		65		64	
FTE enrollment[1]	513,490		543,351		550,997	
Unrestricted educational and general revenues	$1,069,440	100.0	$1,185,408	100.0	$1,283,039	100.0
Student tuition and fees	676,527	63.2	742,663	62.7	824,901	64.3
Federal Government appropriations	74,672	7.1	39,787	3.4	51,531	4.0
State and local government appropriations	50,699	4.7	79,555	6.7	52,122	4.1
Endowment income	132,239	12.4	163,458	13.8	184,357	14.4
Private gifts	135,303	12.7	159,945	13.5	170,128	13.3
Student education expenditures	$1,125,748	100.0	$1,251,861	100.0	$1,394,097	100.0
Instruction & departmental research	658,670	58.5	736,219	58.8	806,123	57.8
Extension and public service	23,918	2.1	29,246	2.3	55,666	4.1
Libraries	68,564	6.1	80,506	6.4	87,050	6.2
Physical plant maintenance & operation	147,212	13.1	160,332	12.8	179,107	12.8
General administration & student services	227,384	20.2	245,558	19.6	266,151	19.1

1st column—amount per FTE student in current dollars
2nd column—amount per FTE student in constant dollars² (1967 prices)

	current	constant	current	constant	current	constant
Unrestricted educational and general revenues	$2,083	$2,190	$2,182	$2,182	$2,329	$2,210
Student tuition and fees	1,316	1,384	1,368	1,368	1,498	1,421
Federal Government appropriations	148	156	74	74	93	88
State and local government appropriations	98	103	146	146	95	90
Endowment income	258	271	301	301	335	318
Private gifts	265	279	295	295	310	294
Student education expenditures	$2,192	$2,305	$2,304	$2,304	$2,530	$2,400
Instruction & departmental research	1,282		1,355		1,462	
Extension and public service	46		53		104	
Libraries	134		147		157	
Physical plant maintenance & operation	287		295		324	
General administration & student services	443		452		483	

See footnotes at end of table.

Table C-1.—Unrestricted educational and general revenues and student education expenditures, by control and type of institution, amount, percent of total, and amount per FTE student, in current and constant dollars: 1965–66 through 1971–72 —Continued

1st column—amount in thousands; 2nd column—percentage distribution

PRIVATE UNIVERSITIES	1968–69		1969–70		1970–71		1971–72	
Number of institutions	65		65		65		65	
FTE enrollment[1]	554,866		561,597		574,296		567,232	
Unrestricted educational and general revenues	$1,415,994	100.0	$1,540,999	100.0	$1,680,851	100.0	$1,837,605	100.0
Student tuition and fees	918,893	64.9	1,006,560	65.3	1,109,149	66.0	1,205,525	65.6
Federal Government appropriations	47,572	3.4	55,739	3.6	58,719	3.5	69,126	3.8
State and local government appropriations	50,167	3.5	79,348	5.1	68,826	4.1	81,887	4.5
Endowment income	202,593	14.3	215,199	14.0	238,184	14.2	241,754	13.2
Private gifts	196,769	13.9	184,153	12.0	205,973	12.3	239,313	13.0
Student education expenditures	$1,558,535	100.0	$1,713,795	100.0	$1,867,349	100.0	$2,000,329	100.0
Instruction & departmental research	914,657	58.7	1,004,256	58.6	1,086,541	58.2	1,142,801	57.1
Extension and public service	21,333	1.4	22,946	1.3	24,750	1.3	32,482	1.6
Libraries	99,354	6.4	109,371	6.4	116,993	6.3	121,786	6.1
Physical plant maintenance & operation	206,179	13.2	221,072	12.9	241,077	12.9	264,811	13.2
General administration & student services	317,012	20.3	356,150	20.8	397,988	21.3	438,449	21.9

1st column—amount per FTE student in current dollars
2nd column—amount per FTE student in constant dollars[2] (1967 prices)

Unrestricted educational and general revenues	$2,552	$2,281	$2,744	$2,300	$2,926	$2,293	$3,240	$2,449
Student tuition and fees	1,656	1,480	1,792	1,502	1,931	1,513	2,124	1,605
Federal Government appropriations	87	78	99	83	102	80	123	94
State and local government appropriations	89	80	140	117	120	94	146	110
Endowment income	365	326	384	322	415	325	427	323
Private gifts	355	317	329	276	359	281	420	317
Student education expenditures	$2,809	$2,510	$3,052	$2,558	$3,252	$2,549	$3,526	$2,665
Instruction & departmental research	1,649		1,788		1,892		2,014	
Extension and public service	69		40		43		57	
Libraries	180		195		204		216	
Physical plant maintenance & operation	371		394		420		466	
General administration & student services	570		635		693		773	

See footnotes at end of table

Table C-1.—Unrestricted educational and general revenues and student education expenditures, by control and type of institution, amount, percent of total, and amount per FTE student, in current and constant dollars: 1965–66 through 1971–72 —Continued

1st column—amount in thousands; 2nd column—percentage distribution

PRIVATE 4-YEAR COLLEGES

	1965–66		1966–67		1967–68	
Number of institutions	1088		1112		1110	
FTE enrollment[1]	968,996		1,019,915		1,057,601	
Unrestricted educational and general revenues	$1,426,464	100.0	$1,569,289	100.0	$1,722,539	100.0
Student tuition and fees	1,033,811	72.5	1,136,547	72.4	1,242,260	72.1
Federal Government appropriations	20,406	1.4	16,078	1.0	24,411	1.4
State and local government appropriations	11,975	.8	12,496	.8	15,077	.9
Endowment income	117,115	8.2	129,984	8.3	140,393	8.2
Private gifts	243,157	17.0	274,184	17.5	300,398	17.4
Student education expenditures	$1,362,826	100.0	$1,528,018	100.0	$1,698,546	100.0
Instruction & departmental research	694,605	51.1	771,673	50.5	842,738	49.6
Extension and public service	20,936	1.5	35,480	2.3	52,274	3.1
Libraries	72,996	5.4	85,168	5.6	94,440	5.6
Physical plant maintenance & operation	191,604	14.1	208,335	13.6	229,045	13.5
General administration & student services	382,685	28.1	427,362	28.1	480,049	28.3

1st column—amount per FTE student in current dollars
2nd column—amount per FTE student in constant dollars[2] (1967 prices)

	1st	2nd	1st	2nd	1st	2nd
Unrestricted educational and general revenues	$1,472	$1,548	$1,539	$1,539	$1,629	$1,546
Student tuition and fees	1,067	1,122	1,114	1,114	1,175	1,115
Federal Government appropriations	21	22	15	15	23	22
State and local government appropriations	12	13	12	12	15	15
Endowment income	121	126	128	128	134	127
Private gifts	250	263	269	269	283	269
Student education expenditures	$1,406	$1,478	$1,498	$1,498	$1,606	$1,524
Instruction & departmental research	718		756		797	
Extension and public service	21		34		50	
Libraries	76		84		90	
Physical plant maintenance & operation	198		204		217	
General administration & student services	395		421		454	

See footnotes at end of table.

Table C-1.—Unrestricted educational and general revenues and student education expenditures, by control and type of institution, amount, percent of total, and amount per FTE student, in current and constant dollars: 1965-66 through 1971-72 —Continued

1st column—amount in thousands; 2nd column—percentage distribution

PRIVATE 4-YEAR COLLEGES	1968-69		1969-70		1970-71		1971-72	
Number of institutions	1137		1148		1165		1,167	
FTE enrollment[1]	1,059,695		1,089,467		1,118,558		1,133,600	
Unrestricted educational and general revenues	$1,917,803	100.0	$2,154,320	100.0	$2,393,052	100.0	$2,674,462	100.0
Student tuition and fees	1,386,998	72.3	1,574,383	73.1	1,774,650	74.2	1,953,000	73.0
Federal Government appropriations	27,145	1.4	34,527	1.6	39,114	1.6	46,926	1.8
State and local government appropriations	16,759	.9	26,690	1.2	28,285	1.2	88,296	3.3
Endowment income	158,493	8.3	171,297	8.0	173,397	7.2	180,076	6.7
Private gifts	328,408	17.1	347,423	16.1	377,606	15.8	406,164	15.2
Student education expenditures	$1,946,680	100.0	$2,210,946	100.0	$2,406,335	100.0	$2,599,315	100.0
Instruction & departmental research	948,340	48.7	1,085,007	49.1	1,178,619	49.0	1,260,105	48.5
Extension and public service	29,315	1.5	21,254	1.0	20,028	.8	22,793	.9
Libraries	107,088	5.5	122,035	5.5	129,569	5.4	137,855	5.3
Physical plant maintenance & operation	264,044	13.6	296,773	13.4	327,858	13.6	354,072	13.6
General administration & student services	597,893	30.7	685,877	31.0	750,261	31.2	824,490	31.7

1st column—amount per FTE student in current dollars
2nd column—amount per FTE student in constant dollars[2] (1967 prices)

	1st	2nd	1st	2nd	1st	2nd	1st	2nd
Unrestricted educational and general revenues	$1,810	$1,618	$1,977	$1,657	$2,139	$1,676	$2,359	$1,783
Student tuition and fees	1,309	1,170	1,445	1,211	1,587	1,243	1,722	1,302
Federal Government appropriations	25	22	32	27	35	27	42	32
State and local government appropriations	16	14	24	20	25	20	78	59
Endowment income	150	134	158	132	155	121	158	119
Private gifts	310	277	318	267	338	265	359	271
Student education expenditures	$1,837	$1,642	$2,029	$1,701	$2,151	$1,686	$2,293	$1,733
Instruction & departmental research	895		996		1,054		1,111	
Extension and public service	28		20		18		21	
Libraries	101		112		116		122	
Physical plant maintenance & operation	250		272		293		312	
General administration & student services	564		629		671		727	

See footnotes at end of table.

Table C-1.—Unrestricted educational and general revenues and student education expenditures, by control and type of institution, amount, percent of total, and amount per FTE student, in current and constant dollars: 1965-66 through 1971-72 —Continued

PRIVATE 2-YEAR COLLEGES

	1965-66		1966-67		1967-68	
Number of institutions	260		276		266	
FTE enrollment[1]	115,859		124,205		126,360	

1st column—amount in thousands; 2nd column—percentage distribution

	1965-66		1966-67		1967-68	
Unrestricted educational and general revenues	$114,939	100.0	$134,806	100.0	$149,507	100.0
Student tuition and fees	92,232	80.2	105,840	78.5	117,114	78.3
Federal Government appropriations	103	.1	1,583	1.2	4,063	2.7
State and local government appropriations	457	.4	951	.7	648	.4
Endowment income	3,336	3.0	3,429	2.5	3,454	2.3
Private gifts	18,811	16.3	23,003	17.1	24,228	16.2
Student education expenditures	$109,751	100.0	$128,182	100.0	$140,450	100.0
Instruction & departmental research	50,944	46.4	57,168	44.6	60,410	43.0
Extension and public service	1,402	1.3	1,373	1.1	1,903	1.4
Libraries	4,832	4.4	5,969	4.7	6,620	4.7
Physical plant maintenance & operation	17,144	15.6	20,001	15.6	21,734	15.5
General administration & student services	35,429	32.3	43,671	34.1	49,783	35.4

1st column—amount per FTE student in current dollars
2nd column—amount per FTE student in constant dollars[2] (1967 prices)

Unrestricted educational and general revenues	$992	$1,041	$1,085	$1,085	$1,183	$1,122
Student tuition and fees	796	837	852	852	926	879
Federal Government appropriations	1	1	13	13	32	30
State and local government appropriations	4	4	8	8	5	5
Endowment income	30	32	27	27	27	26
Private gifts	162	170	186	186	192	182
Student education expenditures	$947	$996	$1,032	$1,032	$1,112	$1,055
Instruction & departmental research	439		460		478	
Extension and public service	12		11		16	
Libraries	42		49		52	
Physical plant maintenance & operation	148		161		172	
General administration & student services	306		352		394	

See footnotes at end of table.

Table C-1.—Unrestricted educational and general revenues and student education expenditures, by control and type of institution, amount, percent of total, and amount per FTE student, in current and constant dollars: 1965–66 through 1971–72 —Continued

PRIVATE 2-YEAR COLLEGES

	1968–69		1969–70		1970–71		1971–72	
Number of institutions	270		252		237		237	
FTE enrollment[1]	130,466		115,619		109,082		108,415	

1st column—amount in thousands; 2nd column—percentage distribution

	1968–69		1969–70		1970–71		1971–72	
Unrestricted educational and general revenues	$159,151	100.0	$153,093	100.0	$157,884	100.0	$166,291	100.0
Student tuition and fees	124,921	78.5	116,710	76.2	120,280	76.2	124,624	74.9
Federal Government appropriations	2,678	1.7	3,729	2.4	4,049	2.6	5,071	3.0
State and local government appropriations	895	.6	1,955	1.3	2,247	1.4	3,598	2.2
Endowment income	3,735	2.3	3,748	2.4	3,633	2.3	3,855	2.3
Private gifts	26,922	16.9	26,951	17.6	27,675	17.5	29,143	17.5
Student education expenditures	$162,876	100.0	$157,021	100.0	$163,481	100.0	$171,111	100.0
Instruction & departmental research	70,849	43.5	69,558	44.3	69,919	42.8	73,365	42.9
Extension and public service	1,272	.8	1,022	.7	1,070	.7	1,074	.6
Libraries	7,469	4.6	7,085	4.5	7,051	4.3	7,502	4.4
Physical plant maintenance & operation	26,613	16.3	25,508	16.2	26,539	16.2	26,879	15.7
General administration & student services	56,673	34.8	53,848	34.3	58,902	36.0	62,291	36.4

1st column—amount per FTE student in current dollars
2nd column—amount per FTE student in constant dollars² (1967 prices)

Unrestricted educational and general revenues							
Student tuition and fees	$1,220	$1,090	$1,324	$1,110	$1,447	$1,134	$1,537	$1,162
	958	856	1,009	846	1,103	864	1,152	871
Federal Government appropriations	21	19	32	27	37	29	46	35
State and local government appropriations	7	6	17	14	21	16	34	26
Endowment income	28	25	32	27	33	26	35	26
Private gifts	206	184	233	195	254	199	270	204
Student education expenditures	$1,248	$1,115	$1,358	$1,138	$1,499	$1,175	$1,578	$1,193
Instruction & departmental research	543		602		641		678	
Extension and public service	10		10		10		9	
Libraries	57		61		65		69	
Physical plant maintenance & operation	203		220		243		248	
General administration & student services	434		466		540		574	

NOTE.—For definitions of unrestricted revenues and student education expenditures see text chapter XII.

1 Full-time-equivalent enrollment from table C-2.

2 Amounts in current dollars were deflated with the Higher Education Price Index (appendix B) to obtain constant dollar values.

Source: U.S. Department of Health, Education, and Welfare, Office of Education, *Financial Statistics of Institutions of Higher Education: Current Funds Revenues and Expenditures; Physical Plant Assets,* relevant issues.

Table C-2.—Opening fall enrollment, by attendance status and institutional type and control: 1965–71

	PUBLIC			PRIVATE		
	Full-time	Part-time and extension	Full-time equivalent	Full-time	Part-time and extension	Full-time equivalent
UNIVERSITIES						
1965	1,230,114	427,333	1,372,558	437,892	241,796	513,490
1966	1,325,684	452,956	1,476,669	463,329	240,067	543,351
1967	1,437,048	466,317	1,592,487	468,630	247,102	55,0997
1968	1,578,626	505,002	1,746,960	480,272	223,782	554,866
1969	1,674,452	559,314	1,860,890	488,933	217,992	561,597
1970	1,740,500	609,704	1,943,735	498,075	228,662	574,296
1971	1,799,493	573,058	1,990,512	496,985	210,740	567,232
4-YEAR COLLEGES						
1965	941,151	357,964	1,060,472	873,839	285,470	968,996
1966	1,018,466	392,198	1,149,198	922,412	292,509	1,019,915
1967	1,138,658	433,637	1,283,204	959,294	294,922	1,057,601
1968	1,248,118	490,062	1,411,472	964,868	284,480	1,059,695
1969	1,320,506	537,331	1,499,616	990,923	295,632	1,089,467
1970	1,440,829	570,803	1,631,097	1,017,171	304,160	1,118,558
1971	1,508,937	606,585	1,711,132	1,031,493	306,320	1,133,600

2-YEAR COLLEGES

1965	562,057	481,321	722,497	107,051	26,423	115,859
1966	623,109	568,673	812,667	116,771	22,303	124,205
1967	705,525	669,145	928,573	117,836	25,573	126,360
1968	857,278	790,386	1,120,740	121,318	27,444	130,466
1969	959,188	888,722	1,255,429	106,808	26,432	115,619
1970	1,069,050	1,034,073	1,413,741	101,001	24,243	109,082
1971	1,195,023	1,171,589	1,585,553	100,218	24,590	108,415

NOTE.—Enrollment includes resident and extension degree and non-degree-credit. Full-time-equivalent (FTE) enrollment equals full-time enrollment plus one-third part-time and extension enrollment.

Source: U.S. Department of Health, Education, and Welfare, Office of Education, *Opening (Fall) Enrollment in Higher Education*, relevant issues.

Appendix D

COLLEGE AND UNIVERSITY STUDENT MIGRATION DATA

Table D-1.—Residence and migration of college students, by level of attendance: Fall 1963

	First-time undergraduate students			
	Public institutions in State			Residents attending college anywhere (A)
	State residents remaining (B)	Nonresident inmigration (F)	Total (B+F)	
	(1)	(2)	(3)	(4)
AGGREGATE U.S.	600,875	64,904	665,779	1,007,838
50 STATES and D.C.	596,195	64,706	660,901	999,347
Alabama	6,034	760	6,794	10,856
Alaska	220	47	267	764
Arizona	8,079	2,370	10,449	9,413
Arkansas	5,779	677	6,456	9,321
California	133,933	5,803	139,736	151,954
Colorado	7,965	2,272	10,237	10,675
Connecticut	4,051	352	4,403	16,121
Delaware	942	472	1,414	2,168
Dist. of Col.	389	312	701	3,199
Florida	19,191	1,262	20,453	28,668
Georgia	7,207	1,258	8,465	13,439
Hawaii	2,523	391	2,914	4,590
Idaho	3,219	455	3,674	5,515
Illinois	34,254	835	35,089	64,043
Indiana	14,031	2,181	16,212	22,515
Iowa	7,234	1,166	8,400	16,179
Kansas	10,722	1,678	12,400	14,879
Kentucky	7,715	2,100	9,815	13,017
Louisiana	12,600	615	13,215	15,662
Maine	1,733	373	2,106	3,381
Maryland	8,890	906	9,796	17,035

782

Table D-1.—Residence and migration of college students, by level of attendance: Fall 1963—Continued

	First-time undergraduate students			
	Public institutions in State			Residents attending college anywhere (A)
	State residents remaining (B)	Nonresident inmigration (F)	Total (B+F)	
	(1)	(2)	(3)	(4)
Massachusetts	8,439	293	8,732	30,767
Michigan	29,745	3,056	32,801	40,024
Minnesota	13,307	713	14,020	19,861
Mississippi	8,637	1,090	9,727	11,290
Missouri	14,468	1,899	16,367	22,897
Montana	3,290	338	3,628	4,816
Nebraska	6,237	1,122	7,359	9,073
Nevada	1,458	102	1,560	2,092
New Hampshire	1,121	493	1,614	2,499
New Jersey	9,866	419	10,285	34,529
New Mexico	3,140	1,042	4,182	4,628
New York	26,536	362	26,898	80,167
North Carolina	9,390	1,769	11,159	17,824
North Dakota	3,588	567	4,155	4,534
Ohio	23,697	3,245	26,942	45,337
Oklahoma	10,944	1,520	12,464	14,525
Oregon	7,757	1,162	8,919	12,102
Pennsylvania	12,251	902	13,153	47,858
Rhode Island	1,409	295	1,704	3,836
South Carolina	3,526	1,224	4,750	8,577
South Dakota	2,896	569	3,465	4,472
Tennessee	8,338	1,589	9,927	15,310
Texas	38,617	3,146	41,763	52,315
Utah	5,119	1,032	6,151	6,812
Vermont	880	578	1,458	1,641
Virginia	7,876	1,656	9,532	17,292
Washington	15,015	1,147	16,162	20,215
West Virginia	5,250	965	6,215	7,639
Wisconsin	14,960	2,416	17,376	20,624
Wyoming	1,727	443	2,170	2,397
U.S. Service Schools	NA	3,267	3,267	NA
Outlying areas of the U.S.	4,680	198	4,878	8,491

Table D-1.—Residence and migration of college students, by level of attendance: Fall 1963—Continued

	Undergraduate students			
	Public institutions in State			Residents attending college anywhere (A)
	State residents remaining (B)	Nonresident inmigration (F)	Total (B+F)	
	(5)	(6)	(7)	(8)
AGGREGATE U.S.	2,082,987	237,509	2,320,496	3,593,680
50 STATES and D.C.	2,062,592	236,689	2,299,281	3,562,721
Alabama	25,068	3,741	28,809	41,803
Alaska	940	196	1,136	2,760
Arizona	30,832	7,109	37,941	35,147
Arkansas	18,153	2,288	20,441	29,279
California	414,120	18,264	432,384	486,415
Colorado	24,956	8,447	33,403	34,970
Connecticut	18,391	1,053	19,444	60,475
Delaware	3,071	1,457	4,528	7,074
Dist. of Col.	2,737	2,002	4,739	13,239
Florida	62,233	4,033	66,266	99,912
Georgia	28,498	5,282	33,780	48,404
Hawaii	9,107	1,779	10,886	15,505
Idaho	8,476	1,516	9,992	15,322
Illinois	102,334	4,276	106,610	220,653
Indiana	47,857	8,372	56,229	79,712
Iowa	23,359	4,488	27,847	52,951
Kansas	37,483	6,290	43,773	51,760
Kentucky	26,760	6,624	33,384	45,225
Louisiana	45,679	2,599	48,278	58,680
Maine	6,305	1,228	7,533	11,645
Maryland	28,238	3,533	31,771	61,654
Massachusetts	24,286	718	25,004	105,129
Michigan	107,476	13,014	120,490	148,922
Minnesota	45,787	3,114	48,901	67,841
Mississippi	27,763	4,174	31,937	36,625
Missouri	39,823	7,109	46,932	69,657
Montana	10,692	1,840	12,532	15,559
Nebraska	20,016	3,971	23,987	29,710
Nevada	4,692	554	5,246	6,561
New Hampshire	3,901	1,840	5,741	8,753

Table D-1.—Residence and migration of college students, by level of attendance: Fall 1963—Continued

	Undergraduate students			
	Public institutions in State			Residents attending college anywhere (A)
	State residents remaining (B)	Nonresident inmigration (F)	Total (B+F)	
	(5)	(6)	(7)	(8)
New Jersey	43,341	1,646	44,987	135,301
New Mexico	12,513	3,678	16,191	17,140
New York	127,658	1,550	129,208	344,900
North Carolina	33,555	6,215	39,770	61,529
North Dakota	11,436	2,138	13,574	14,773
Ohio	93,197	12,013	105,210	173,193
Oklahoma	39,880	5,443	45,323	53,264
Oregon	24,845	4,522	29,367	36,942
Pennsylvania	47,981	3,866	51,847	187,346
Rhode Island	4,922	940	5,862	12,592
South Carolina	12,270	3,878	16,148	28,134
South Dakota	8,743	1,881	10,624	14,236
Tennessee	32,170	6,367	38,537	55,003
Texas	146,679	9,310	155,989	196,678
Utah	19,007	3,804	22,811	24,927
Vermont	2,755	1,974	4,729	5,579
Virginia	31,135	5,793	36,928	63,553
Washington	46,896	4,024	51,100	66,416
West Virginia	19,073	4,110	23,183	27,844
Wisconsin	50,498	7,649	58,147	74,869
Wyoming	5,005	1,452	6,457	7,161
U. S. Service Schools	NA	13,345	13,345	NA
Outlying areas of the U. S.	20,395	820	21,215	30,959

Table D-1.—Residence and migration of college students, by level of attendance: Fall 1963—Continued

	Graduate students			
	Public institutions in State			Residents attending college anywhere (A)
	State residents remaining (B)	Nonresident inmigration (F)	Total (B+F)	
	(9)	(10)	(11)	(12)
AGGREGATE U.S.	210,153	68,651	278,804	450,790
50 STATES and D.C.	209,979	68,645	278,624	450,286
Alabama	1,508	721	2,229	2,648
Alaska	62	28	90	244
Arizona	5,057	1,423	6,480	5,617
Arkansas	1,070	326	1,396	1,889
California	40,118	7,639	47,757	59,506
Colorado	2,164	1,848	4,012	4,312
Connecticut	2,931	387	3,318	10,450
Delaware	813	613	1,426	1,341
Dist. of Col.	0	0	0	3,542
Florida	2,132	1,750	3,882	6,205
Georgia	1,597	863	2,460	3,675
Hawaii	1,175	872	2,047	1,659
Idaho	341	136	477	1,029
Illinois	10,746	3,914	14,660	24,405
Indiana	8,634	5,660	14,294	13,381
Iowa	1,938	3,118	5,056	4,582
Kansas	3,882	1,911	5,793	5,623
Kentucky	2,387	581	2,968	4,029
Louisiana	3,093	678	3,771	5,283
Maine	184	63	247	742
Maryland	2,100	1,521	3,621	8,041
Massachusetts	4,932	489	5,421	19,472
Michigan	17,109	4,108	21,217	21,175
Minnesota	3,891	3,052	6,943	6,171
Missippi	1,083	350	1,433	2,006
Missouri	2,626	1,299	3,925	7,525
Montana	513	213	725	1,048
Nebraska	1,835	717	2,552	3,058
Nevada	243	110	353	440
New Hampshire	337	192	529	1,205

Table D-1.—Residence and migration of college students, by level of attendance: Fall 1963—Continued

	Graduate students			
	Public institutions in State			Residents attending college anywhere (A)
	State residents remaining (B)	Nonresident inmigration (F)	Total (B+F)	
	(9)	(10)	(11)	(12)
New Jersey	7,754	812	8,566	21,961
New Mexico	2,053	1,042	3,095	2,664
New York	22,874	732	23,606	80,029
North Carolina	3,012	2,082	5,094	4,668
North Dakota	542	317	859	1,060
Ohio	9,341	2,886	12,227	18,738
Oklahoma	4,404	1,741	6,145	6,179
Oregon	2,302	1,111	3,413	3,750
Pennsylvania	3,688	821	4,509	26,249
Rhode Island	579	183	762	2,267
South Carolina	1,171	356	1,527	2,123
South Dakota	413	281	694	1,085
Tennessee	3,006	1,107	4,113	4,904
Texas	12,347	1,522	13,869	19,226
Utah	1,923	828	2,751	2,989
Vermont	139	80	219	467
Virginia	1,552	840	2,392	6,332
Washington	2,831	2,241	5,072	5,422
West Virginia	1,323	628	1,951	2,163
Wisconsin	3,929	3,010	6,939	7,088
Wyoming	295	337	632	619
U. S. Service Schools	NA	1,106	1,106	NA
Outlying areas of the U.S.	174	6	180	504

Table D-1.—Residence and migration of college students, by level of attendance: Fall 1963—Continued

	First-professional students			
	Public institutions in State			Residents attending college anywhere (A)
	State residents remaining (B)	Nonresident inmigration (F)	Total (B+F)	
	(13)	(14)	(15)	(16)
AGGREGATE U.S.	47,034	9,742	56,776	148,019
50 STATES and D.C.	45,708	9,732	55,440	146,068
Alabama	728	214	942	1,532
Alaska	0	0	0	73
Arizona	294	42	336	805
Arkansas	827	13	840	1,330
California	3,975	570	4,545	11,586
Colorado	475	316	791	1,332
Connecticut	608	87	695	2,344
Delaware	0	0	0	323
Dist. of Col.	0	0	0	1,243
Florida	688	113	801	3,141
Georgia	1,226	268	1,494	2,665
Hawaii	13	8	21	213
Idaho	801	180	981	1,127
Illinois	2,236	79	2,315	10,125
Indiana	2,183	206	2,389	3,517
Iowa	1,151	368	1,519	2,202
Kansas	991	289	1,280	1,907
Kentucky	1,051	343	1,394	1,919
Louisiana	878	45	923	2,193
Maine	25	2	27	324
Maryland	1,105	378	1,483	3,511
Massachusetts	0	0	0	4,591
Michigan	3,245	1,113	4,358	6,093
Minnesota	1,321	263	1,584	2,851
Mississippi	217	35	252	846
Missouri	1,974	776	2,750	4,162
Montana	93	11	104	462
Nebraska	759	127	886	1,483
Nevada	0	0	0	157
New Hampshire	0	0	0	291

Table D-1.—Residence and migration of college students, by level of attendance: Fall 1963—Continued

	First-professional students			
	Public institutions in State			Residents attending college anywhere (A)
	State residents remaining (B)	Nonresident inmigration (F)	Total (B+F)	
	(13)	(14)	(15)	(16)
New Jersey	2,761	303	3,064	7,698
New Mexico	81	12	93	435
New York	1,795	106	1,901	18,411
North Carolina	763	113	876	2,418
North Dakota	189	44	233	459
Ohio	2,368	247	2,615	7,466
Oklahoma	951	187	1,138	2,296
Oregon	865	287	1,152	1,527
Pennsylvania	0	0	0	9,796
Rhode Island	0	0	0	514
South Carolina	549	26	575	1,360
South Dakota	142	80	222	492
Tennessee	1,708	569	2,277	2,866
Texas	3,317	192	3,509	6,645
Utah	345	124	469	750
Vermont	57	127	184	199
Virginia	849	915	1,764	2,636
Washington	786	273	1,059	1,872
West Virginia	510	147	657	992
Wisconsin	763	104	867	2,578
Wyoming	45	30	75	211
U. S. Service Schools	NA	NA	0	—
Outlying areas of the U. S.	1,326	10	1,336	1,951

Table D-1.—Residence and migration of college students, by level of attendance: Fall 1963—Continued

	High school graduates 1962–63	First-time undergraduate residents of State remaining to attend private institutions in home State (C)
	(17)	(18)
AGGREGATE U.S.	1,963,275	220,530
50 STATES and D.C.	1,943,603	217,198
Alabama	33,739	2,469
Alaska	1,638	116
Arizona	15,519	77
Arkansas	19,634	2,180
California	189,451	10,436
Colorado	19,359	635
Connecticut	28,825	4,812
Delaware	4,832	185
Dist. of Columbia	5,208	1,253
Florida	47,145	3,858
Georgia	37,892	3,430
Hawaii	9,494	518
Idaho	8,870	967
Illinois	101,347	15,336
Indiana	50,889	4,770
Iowa	34,083	5,118
Kansas	27,377	2,051
Kentucky	27,406	3,240
Louisiana	33,768	1,709
Maine	10,800	514
Maryland	33,178	3,386
Massachusetts	55,294	15,185
Michigan	89,883	6,128
Minnesota	43,838	3,627
Mississippi	21,671	1,698
Missouri	46,097	4,330
Montana	8,165	578
Nebraska	16,879	1,456
Nevada	3,001	0
New Hampshire	6,408	276

Table D-1.—Residence and migration of college students, by level of attendance: Fall 1963—Continued

	High school graduates 1962–63	First-time undergraduate residents of State remaining to attend private institutions in home State (C)
	(17)	(18)
New Jersey	65,631	7,615
New Mexico	9,830	201
New York	169,359	30,721
North Carolina	49,385	6,473
North Dakota	8,956	165
Ohio	101,469	13,381
Oklahoma	26,906	1,942
Oregon	22,349	2,378
Pennsylvania	122,862	23,399
Rhode Island	8,420	1,165
South Carolina	24,964	3,175
South Dakota	8,756	812
Tennessee	36,579	3,817
Texas	92,423	9,792
Utah	12,194	1,313
Vermont	4,654	160
Virginia	37,349	3,647
Washington	35,524	2,818
West Virginia	20,114	1,265
Wisconsin	50,450	2,621
Wyoming	3,799	0
U. S. Service Schools	NA	NA
Outlying areas of the U. S.	19,672	3,332

Source: Mabel C. Rice and Paul L. Mason, *Residence and Migration of College Students, Fall 1963*, U.S. Department of Health, Education, and Welfare, Office of Education, U.S. Government Printing Office, Washington, D.C., 1965.

Table D-2.—Residence and migration of college students, by level of attendance: Fall 1968

	First-time undergraduate students			
	Public institutions in State			Residents attending college anywhere (A)
	State residents remaining (B)	Nonresident inmigration (F)	Total (B+F)	
	(1)	(2)	(3)	(4)
AGGREGATE U.S.	1,065,678	94,243	1,159,921	1,569,496
50 STATES and D.C.	1,058,355	93,738	1,152,093	1,555,403
Alabama	16,058	1,401	17,459	21,475
Alaska	496	72	568	1,334
Arizona	16,600	3,247	19,847	18,465
Arkansas	9,723	937	10,660	13,762
California	169,760	5,655	175,415	192,129
Colorado	15,024	3,494	18,518	18,357
Connecticut	10,222	917	11,319	26,190
Delaware	1,607	661	2,268	3,453
District of Columbia	2,605	33	2,638	5,526
Florida	32,671	2,677	35,348	43,804
Georgia	15,230	2,232	17,462	22,471
Hawaii	4,561	464	5,025	7,196
Idaho	4,430	539	4,969	7,264
Illinois	59,933	1,478	61,411	94,191
Indiana	22,446	2,790	25,236	32,531
Iowa	13,611	1,443	15,054	24,123
Kansas	16,463	1,697	18,160	21,522
Kentucky	13,916	2,141	16,057	19,948
Louisiana	20,324	1,235	21,559	23,663
Maine	2,783	567	3,350	5,157
Maryland	15,852	1,915	17,767	25,468
Massachusetts	18,521	699	19,220	50,380
Michigan	51,821	3,424	55,245	64,349
Minnesota	23,836	1,216	25,052	32,352
Mississippi	15,257	1,403	16,660	18,668
Missouri	24,567	3,392	27,959	33,782
Montana	5,072	606	5,678	6,763
Nebraska	9,564	1,083	10,647	12,777
Nevada	1,946	369	2,315	2,717
New Hampshire	2,069	585	2,654	4,527

Table D-2.—Residence and migration of college students, by level of attendance: Fall 1968

	First-time undergraduate students			
	Public institutions in State			Residents attending college anywhere (A)
	State residents remaining (B)	Nonresident inmigration (F)	Total (B+F)	
	(1)	(2)	(3)	(4)
New Jersey	19,200	1,487	20,687	56,027
New Mexico	5,815	1,098	6,913	7,766
New York	87,407	1,792	89,199	157,537
North Carolina	16,004	2,693	18,697	26,427
North Dakota	5,610	741	6,351	6,725
Ohio	51,359	5,227	56,586	74,892
Oklahoma	17,225	1,953	19,178	22,098
Oregon	15,628	1,590	17,218	19,709
Pennsylvania	35,368	1,701	37,069	74,198
Rhode Island	3,399	584	3,983	7,471
South Carolina	6,152	1,623	7,775	13,252
South Dakota	4,898	638	5,536	6,935
Tennessee	15,235	2,444	17,679	22,469
Texas	65,171	4,028	69,199	81,033
Utah	7,594	1,145	8,739	9,668
Vermont	1,183	799	1,982	2,734
Virginia	14,909	3,367	18,276	27,280
Washington	30,692	1,959	32,651	35,828
West Virginia	8,383	1,747	10,130	11,283
Wisconsin	27,233	4,118	31,351	34,043
Wyoming	2,922	722	3,644	3,684
U.S. Service Schools	0	3,910	3,910	0
Outlying areas	7,323	505	7,828	14,093

Table D-2.—Residence and migration of college students, by level of attendance: Fall 1968—Continued

	Undergraduate students			
	Public institutions in State			Residents attending college anywhere (A)
	State residents remaining (B)	Nonresident inmigration (F)	Total (B+F)	
	(5)	(6)	(7)	(8)
AGGREGATE U.S.	3,734,461	365,048	4,099,509	5,683,300
50 STATES and D.C.	3,703,184	363,218	4,066,402	5,632,266
Alabama	60,765	6,641	67,406	80,648
Alaska	1,637	447	2,084	4,207
Arizona	53,303	10,717	64,020	59,898
Arkansas	30,894	3,574	34,468	44,682
California	611,329	22,385	633,714	704,728
Colorado	52,196	14,909	67,105	64,229
Connecticut	36,263	3,299	39,562	97,416
Delaware	5,808	2,324	8,132	11,709
District of Columbia	5,197	129	5,326	17,937
Florida	114,020	8,241	122,261	160,444
Georgia	61,031	9,727	70,758	86,835
Hawaii	13,802	3,067	16,869	22,068
Idaho	15,627	2,245	17,872	25,089
Illinois	187,135	5,203	192,338	332,353
Indiana	82,059	12,079	94,138	121,682
Iowa	42,065	5,644	47,709	81,036
Kansas	56,893	8,418	65,311	74,218
Kentucky	48,225	10,905	59,130	71,834
Louisiana	78,733	5,175	83,908	94,331
Maine	10,108	1,832	11,940	18,421
Maryland	55,699	7,177	62,876	99,404
Massachusetts	58,049	2,580	60,629	170,968
Michigan	188,072	15,926	203,998	236,564
Minnesota	79,043	5,562	84,605	108,397
Mississippi	45,118	5,082	50,200	56,435
Missouri	83,581	12,725	96,306	120,211
Montana	17,453	2,361	19,814	23,362
Nebraska	33,805	4,381	38,186	46,025
Nevada	6,728	1,379	8,107	9,461
New Hampshire	7,320	2,494	9,814	16,322

Table D-2.—Residence and migration of college students, by level of attendance: Fall 1968—Continued

	Undergraduate students			
	Public institutions in State			Residents attending college anywhere (A)
	State residents remaining (B)	Nonresident inmigration (F)	Total (B+F)	
	(5)	(6)	(7)	(8)
New Jersey	66,202	3,227	69,429	207,584
New Mexico	25,049	4,226	29,275	31,843
New York	310,382	5,556	315,938	600,626
North Carolina	56,789	10,575	67,364	90,529
North Dakota	18,518	2,840	21,358	22,815
Ohio	179,984	21,427	201,411	271,004
Oklahoma	61,399	7,532	68,931	79,095
Oregon	53,238	5,795	59,033	66,459
Pennsylvania	139,899	7,647	147,546	294,698
Rhode Island	9,940	1,815	11,755	24,704
South Carolina	20,022	5,454	25,476	41,993
South Dakota	15,756	2,494	18,250	22,765
Tennessee	59,440	10,746	70,186	86,045
Texas	236,510	14,420	250,930	302,136
Utah	32,046	4,502	36,548	41,103
Vermont	4,805	2,388	7,193	9,384
Virginia	53,057	10,049	63,106	97,698
Washington	86,668	7,440	94,108	107,227
West Virginia	29,656	8,047	37,703	39,615
Wisconsin	92,933	15,041	107,973	122,230
Wyoming	8,933	1,966	10,899	11,799
U.S. Service Schools	0	13,403	13,403	0
Outlying areas	31,277	1,830	33,107	51,034

Table D-2.—Residence and migration of college students, by level of attendance: Fall 1968—Continued

	Graduate students			
	Public institutions in State			Residents attending college anywhere (A)
	State residents remaining (B)	Nonresident inmigration (F)	Total (B+F)	
	(9)	(10)	(11)	(12)
AGGREGATE U.S.	402,594	128,396	530,990	763,695
50 STATES and D.C.	401,182	128,140	529,322	760,442
Alabama	3,957	1,103	5,060	6,210
Alaska	70	86	156	431
Arizona	7,451	2,788	10,239	8,599
Arkansas	1,388	625	2,013	2,890
California	59,573	11,299	70,872	91,544
Colorado	6,276	3,965	10,241	9,384
Connecticut	8,644	1,407	10,051	19,011
Delaware	1,155	1,055	2,210	2,079
District of Columbia	20	0	20	5,035
Florida	8,820	2,496	11,316	16,915
Georgia	4,508	2,009	6,517	7,964
Hawaii	4,345	1,631	5,976	5,254
Idaho	664	422	1,086	1,948
Illinois	18,608	7,204	25,812	42,090
Indiana	13,201	8,409	21,610	20,192
Iowa	4,381	4,054	8,435	8,569
Kansas	5,499	2,989	8,488	8,309
Kentucky	4,525	1,339	5,864	7,374
Louisiana	6,784	1,320	8,104	9,967
Maine	1,004	183	1,187	1,866
Maryland	6,692	2,967	9,659	17,759
Massachusetts	5,725	1,642	7,367	27,006
Michigan	27,095	7,545	34,640	32,851
Minnesota	6,430	4,203	10,633	10,174
Mississippi	2,529	980	3,509	4,129
Missouri	6,462	3,605	10,067	14,496
Montana	1,063	568	1,631	1,898
Nebraska	3,391	1,135	4,526	5,098
Nevada	952	296	1,248	1,358
New Hampshire	362	338	700	1,719

Table D-2.—Residence and migration of college students, by level of attendance: Fall 1968—Continued

	Graduate students			
	Public institutions in State			Residents attending college anywhere (A)
	State residents remaining (B)	Nonresident inmigration (F)	Total (B+F)	
	(9)	(10)	(11)	(12)
New Jersey	13,180	1,806	14,986	34,401
New Mexico	3,107	1,377	4,484	4,117
New York	40,959	3,200	44,149	123,133
North Carolina	5,846	3,795	9,641	8,609
North Dakota	805	686	1,491	1,555
Ohio	17,570	5,683	23,253	30,056
Oklahoma	5,606	2,209	7,815	8,807
Oregon	9,103	2,304	11,407	11,647
Pennsylvania	23,157	4,393	27,550	46,857
Rhode Island	3,180	394	3,574	4,848
South Carolina	1,989	970	2,959	3,613
South Dakota	945	624	1,569	1,821
Tennessee	6,265	1,925	8,190	9,191
Texas	21,475	4,684	26,159	31,580
Utah	3,317	1,302	4,619	5,091
Vermont	387	231	618	1,114
Virginia	6,151	2,000	8,151	14,415
Washington	4,715	4,118	8,833	9,131
West Virginia	2,102	1,180	3,282	3,243
Wisconsin	9,347	5,236	14,583	14,226
Wyoming	402	536	938	868
U.S. Service Schools	0	1,824	1,824	0
Outlying areas	1,412	256	1,668	3,253

Table D-2.—Residence and migration of college students, by level of attendance: Fall 1968—Continued

	First-professional students			
	Public institutions in State			Residents attending college anywhere (A)
	State residents remaining (B)	Nonresident inmigration (F)	Total (B+F)	
	(13)	(14)	(15)	(16)
AGGREGATE U.S.	53,197	11,851	65,048	153,900
50 STATES and D.C.	52,374	11,791	64,165	152,655
Alabama	1,089	351	1,440	2,047
Alaska	0	0	0	71
Arizona	522	88	610	1,002
Arkansas	621	71	692	1,041
California	5,298	747	6,045	13,936
Colorado	513	236	749	1,420
Connecticut	530	63	593	2,379
Delaware	0	0	0	299
District of Columbia	0	0	0	941
Florida	1,202	71	1,273	3,748
Georgia	751	100	851	2,152
Hawaii	0	0	0	314
Idaho	71	35	106	399
Illinois	2,752	153	2,905	10,778
Indiana	2,486	270	2,756	3,721
Iowa	1,306	413	1,719	2,330
Kansas	730	129	859	1,517
Kentucky	1,432	605	2,037	2,104
Louisiana	1,208	67	1,275	3,180
Maine	82	38	120	402
Maryland	1,170	314	1,484	3,823
Massachusetts	0	0	0	5,238
Michigan	4,769	1,410	6,179	7,720
Minnesota	1,524	276	1,800	3,276
Mississippi	571	64	635	1,182
Missouri	1,147	497	1,644	2,901
Montana	98	34	132	398
Nebraska	919	160	1,079	1,608
Nevada	0	0	0	234
New Hampshire	0	0	0	315

Table D-2.—Residence and migration of college students, by level of attendance: Fall 1968—Continued

	First-professional students			
	Public institutions in State			Residents attending college anywhere (A)
	State residents remaining (B)	Nonresident inmigration (F)	Total (B+F)	
	(13)	(14)	(15)	(16)
New Jersey	809	228	1,037	6,231
New Mexico	217	61	278	517
New York	2,210	146	2,356	18,423
North Carolina	859	217	1,076	2,381
North Dakota	155	73	228	489
Ohio	3,308	611	3,919	9,561
Oklahoma	713	264	977	2,047
Oregon	676	243	919	1,542
Pennsylvania	2,227	630	2,857	8,732
Rhode Island	0	0	0	496
South Carolina	775	97	872	1,385
South Dakota	148	83	231	504
Tennessee	1,026	493	1,519	1,991
Texas	3,786	475	4,261	7,067
Utah	449	144	593	857
Vermont	60	171	231	213
Virginia	1,193	793	1,986	2,853
Washington	881	304	1,185	2,300
West Virginia	622	195	817	1,004
Wisconsin	1,176	215	1,391	3,172
Wyoming	293	156	449	413
U.S. Service Schools	0	0	0	0
Outlying areas	823	60	883	1,245

Table D-2.—Residence and migration of college students, by level of attendance: Fall 1968—Continued

	High school graduates 1967–68	First-time undergraduate residents of State remaining to attend private institutions in home State (C)
	(17)	(18)
AGGREGATE U.S.	2,722,631	252,572
50 STATES and D.C.	2,694,535	246,862
Alabama	45,799	2,922
Alaska	2,905	174
Arizona	21,054	170
Arkansas	25,274	2,122
California	256,235	13,062
Colorado	29,989	704
Connecticut	38,974	5,017
Delaware	7,121	573
District of Columbia	6,822	682
Florida	67,214	4,053
Georgia	55,470	3,337
Hawaii	11,230	719
Idaho	11,750	1,448
Illinois	139,253	15,616
Indiana	70,033	5,370
Iowa	45,871	5,527
Kansas	33,693	2,821
Kentucky	40,326	3,421
Louisiana	47,897	1,538
Maine	15,014	803
Maryland	48,937	2,531
Massachusetts	76,530	21,516
Michigan	126,558	8,114
Minnesota	61,686	4,483
Mississippi	29,225	2,110
Missouri	59,851	4,388
Montana	11,642	496
Nebraska	22,871	1,512
Nevada	5,053	0
New Hampshire	10,086	786

Table D-2.—Residence and migration of college students, by level of attendance: Fall 1968—Continued

	High school graduates 1967–68	First-time undergraduate residents of State remaining to attend private institutions in home State (C)
	(17)	(18)
New Jersey	95,082	8,575
New Mexico	15,676	320
New York	223,000	38,979
North Carolina	64,994	7,694
North Dakota	10,768	161
Ohio	147,530	11,937
Oklahoma	35,445	2,975
Oregon	31,022	1,743
Pennsylvania	171,275	21,516
Rhode Island	11,189	2,114
South Carolina	34,367	4,387
South Dakota	12,497	1,062
Tennessee	48,522	4,316
Texas	133,192	11,313
Utah	16,999	1,534
Vermont	7,968	584
Virginia	57,790	4,287
Washington	49,190	2,464
West Virginia	26,899	1,564
Wisconsin	71,473	3,322
Wyoming	5,293	0
U.S. Service Schools	NA	0
Outlying Areas of the U.S.	28,096	5,710

Source: George H. Wade, *Residence and Migration of College Students, Fall 1968, Analytic Report*, U.S. Department of Health, Education, and Welfare, Office of Education, U.S. Government Printing Office, Washington, D.C., 1970.

INDEX

☆ U.S. GOVERNMENT PRINTING OFFICE: 1974 O—507–550